Without Guarantees

Without Guarantees

In Honour of Stuart Hall

Edited by
**Paul Gilroy, Lawrence Grossberg
and Angela McRobbie**

VERSO

London • New York

First published by Verso 2000
© in the collection Verso 2000
© in individual contributions the contributors 2000
All rights reserved

The moral rights of the authors and editors have been asserted

Verso
UK: 6 Meard Street, London, W1V 3HR
US: 180 Varick Street, New York, NY 10014–4606

Verso is the imprint of New Left Books

ISBN 1–85984–762–5
ISBN 1–85984–287–9 (pbk)

British Library Cataloguing in Publication Data
A catalogue record for this book is available from the British Library

Library of Congress Cataloging-in-Publication Data
Without guarantees : in honour of Stuart Hall / edited by Paul Gilroy, Lawrence
Grossberg, and Angela McRobbie.
    p. cm
  ISBN 1–85984–762–5 (cloth)—ISBN 1–85984–287–9 (pbk.)
  1. Society—Great Britain. 2. Great Britain—Race relations. 3. Great Britain—Politics
and government. 4. Hall, Stuart. I. Hall, Stuart. II. Gilroy, Paul. III. Grossberg,
Lawrence. IV. McRobbie, Angela.

HM479.G7 W57 2000
301′.0941—dc21
                                                                                    00–028986

Typeset in 10/12½pt ITC New Baskerville by
SetSystems Ltd, Saffron Walden, Essex
Printed by Biddles Ltd, Guildford and King's Lynn

All royalties earned on this book will be donated
to the Stephen Lawrence Trust

Contents

Preface

These writings are firstly and most importantly a gift. Their testimony to Stuart Hall's influence, and the esteem in which he is held by the contributors, affirm our profound appreciation for his work, our respect for his wisdom, his creativity, his language and, above all, his lengthy record of serious scholarly intervention in various inter-connected fields. Though it may be indiscreet to admit it, the pieces collected here demonstrate how his imaginative pursuit of political ends by other than obviously political means has inspired and moti-vated us. Everywhere, universities are beleaguered institutions and their definitions of what counts as acceptable scholarly activity are becoming more narrow and restrictive. Stuart's own record suggests that intellec-tuals – even academics – can still find important parts to play in cultural climates where the life of the mind is scorned.

Apart from that, these pieces are intended to show how the practical examples manifested in Stuart's life as an educator, thinker and writer have been registered in institutions of teaching and learning all over the world. The pedagogic resources that he has contributed have been received, debated, re-thought and then set to work again. These essays provide an opportunity to observe some of the results.

It is appropriate given the spirit of Stuart's own commitments that this volume has a second, subsidiary purpose. Cultural studies has been subjected to much abuse lately and the fragile institutional initiatives with which those words are entangled are now under great and growing pressure. In these circumstances, it seemed right to try to make this public gift a modest interventionist act in its own right. Here then are some implicit and explicit reflections on what cultural studies can be and what it might become.

1

Identity Blues

Ien Ang

There is something distinctly idealistic, if not utopian, in the statement that identities are a matter of becoming rather than being, a question, as Stuart Hall puts it, not 'of "who we are" or "where we came from", so much as what we might become'.[1] This idealism is tinged with a deep sense of historical and political urgency. In foregrounding the connection of 'identity' with the future, with what we might become, Hall's reflections on the meaning of cultural identity in contemporary life seek to provide a counter to the rampant tendency to use 'identity' as unfailingly chained to our real or imaginary past. Identity, says Hall, belongs to the future as much as to the past. 'Cultural identities come from somewhere, have histories. But, like everything which is historical, they undergo constant transformation. Far from being eternally fixed in some essentialised past, they are subject to the continuous "play" of history, culture and power.'[2] Consequently, the implication is, cultural identities may be the very subjective instruments, or discursive conduits, through which we may shape and construct our futures: they provide the 'stuff' that enables us to become political agents. Our role in the making of history depends on how we conceive of ourselves as active, changing subjects, in ways that generate meaningful links between 'how we have been represented and how that bears on how we might represent ourselves'.[3] By emphasizing the notion of becoming as central to our identities, Hall rescues the possibility for 'identity' – that is, the way we represent and narrativize ourselves to ourselves and to others – to be a resource of hope, to be the site of agency and attachment that energizes us to participate in the making of our own ongoing histories, the construction of our continuously unfolding worlds, now and in the future. It is in this implicit faith in the future that we can discern the idealism – in the non-philosophical, existential meaning of that word – of Hall's politics of identity. But how sustainable is this faith in these cynical times, when pessimism abounds and the future is envisaged by millions across the globe more with fear and dread than with hope and anticipation?

   Against the background of a worldwide proliferation of particularist, exclusionary, and determinist modes of identity politics – both on the right and on the left, in the developed as well as in the developing world, in the West and the 'Rest' alike – Hall has been at pains to fore-ground a double focus in his theoretical approach, one that highlights the inadequacy of conventional conceptions of 'identity', but simul-taneously affirms its irreducible political and cultural significance. We do not have to repeat here the well-known chorus of anti-essentialist, deconstructive and postmodern critiques which have stripped 'identity', as a concept, from its elevated status as the fundamental inner core of 'me' or 'us', representing the true, inalienable self of the subject, individual or collective. However, no matter how convinced we are, theoretically, that identities are constructed not 'natural', invented not given, always in process and not fixed, at the level of experience and common sense identities are generally expressed (and mobilized polit-ically) precisely because they *feel* natural and essential. Indeed, as Craig Calhoun has remarked, the constant emphasis on identity as *construction* in contemporary theoretical discourse (and, by implication, as some-how not 'real' and therefore not worth fighting for) 'fails to grapple with the real, present-day political and other reasons why essentialist identities continue to be invoked and often deeply felt'.[4] 'For better *and* worse,' James Clifford has recently observed, 'claims to identity – articulations of ethnic, cultural, gender, and sexual distinction – have emerged as things people, across the globe and the social spectrum, care about.'[5] The persistent gap between the imaginaries of everyday experience and the orthodoxies of contemporary theory points to the irreducibility of identity as an operative concept; in Hall's words, it is 'an idea which cannot be thought in the old way, but without which certain key questions cannot be thought at all'.[6] To put it differently, while we may have discarded 'identity' in theory, we cannot do away with cultural identities as real, social and symbolic forces in history and politics. In this context, according to Hall, we have fully and unambig-uously to acknowledge 'both the necessity and the "impossibility" of identities'.[7]
   It is in the face of this double bind between necessity and impossibil-ity that the idealistic move to highlight the possibility of future-oriented, open-ended identities acquires its understandable urgency. If we cannot do without identities, so the reasoning seems to go, then we'd better make sure that they are vehicles for progressive change! Indeed, the so-called new social movements that have emerged since the 1960s – feminism, gay and lesbian movements, anti-racist, ethnic and multicultural movements, various environmentalist, youth and counter-cultural movements, and so on – are often cited as forms of

identity politics that have contributed to democratization and progressive change in many arenas of social life, especially in the rich Western world. However, Calhoun rightly observes that this idea of new social movements is problematic because it 'groups together what seem to the researchers relatively "attractive" movements, vaguely on the left, but leaves out other contemporary movements such as the new religious right and fundamentalism, the resistance of white ethnic communities against people of color, various versions of nationalism, and so forth'.[8] Yet, Calhoun pointedly adds, these are equally manifestations of identity politics. Indeed, there is a streak of romanticism in critical intellectuals' identification of and with 'new social movements' as agents of left radicalism – a gesture all too rampant within cultural studies. It is clear that modes of identity politics are proliferating across the globe with which most cultural studies intellectuals would not be able or willing to identify, based on the articulation of identities we generally dismiss as conservative, right-wing, or simply *other*. How then can the pull of reactionary conservatism so manifest in so many assertions of collective identities in the late twentieth century be reconciled with the more hopeful association of identities with becoming, with an investment in a 'better future', however defined?

The conservative rhetoric of identity has permeated the cultural and political landscape everywhere in a time when old certainties – of place, of belonging, of economic and social security – are rapidly being eroded by the accelerating pace of globalization: the processes by which intensifying global flows of goods, money, people, technologies and information work to dissolve the real and imagined (relative) autonomy and 'authenticity' of local traditions and communities. The current salience of the discourse of identity signifies the level of resistance against the forces of globalization as they are experienced and perceived 'on the ground'. Indeed, Manuel Castells, author of *The Power of Identity*, volume two of his three-volume analysis of the contemporary world economy, society and culture, opens his book with the dramatic statement that 'Our world, and our lives, are being shaped by the conflicting trends of globalization and identity'.[9] As Castells observes, 'we have experienced, in the last quarter of the century, the widespread surge of powerful expressions of collective identity that challenge globalization and cosmopolitanism on behalf of cultural singularity and people's control over their lives and environment'.[10] In this scenario, globalization is constructed as an overpowering source of destruction, while identity is being launched not only as that which must be protected, but also, more defiantly, as that which will *provide* protection against the threat of dangerous global forces. In this sense, identity – together with its equally ubiquitous companion terms

'culture' and 'community' – becomes a key site for people's righteous
sense of self-worth and integrity, worth defending, perhaps even dying
for, against the onslaught of 'globalization'. In this light, struggles for
or on behalf of identity tend to be conservative, even reactionary
movements, aimed at restoring or conserving established orders of
things and existing ways of life, and keeping at bay the unsettling
changes that a globalizing world brings about.

This is not the place to provide a substantial assessment of the
complex, contradictory and multidimensional processes and forces that
have come to be subsumed under the shorthand term 'globalization'.
It is beyond doubt that the economic and cultural effects of diverse
globalizing forces such as the creation of a more or less borderless
world market, the virtual annihilation of time and space by the internet,
and the intensification of transnational migrations of people, are being
increasingly felt everywhere, though unevenly and unequally. It is clear,
too, that the world being remade by these forces is a deeply unjust and
inequitable one, dominated by the economic might of transnational
corporations, the elusive power of mobile finance capital, and the
ruthless logic of the market. Resistance, in this light, is completely
legitimate and politically necessary. However, as this resistance is
framed increasingly frequently through a downright oppositional
stance against 'globalization' *per se*, as if it were the cause of almost all
of the world's economic, social, political, cultural and ecological problems, identities are being (re)asserted that achieve imaginary closure
through an absolutization of a strictly localized, exclusionary 'us', and
the symbolic warding off of everything and everyone that is associated
with the invading 'outside'. The resurgence of ethnic nationalisms and
absolutisms in many parts of the world is one of the most frequently
cited examples of the increasing appeal of such fortress identities. It
seems clear, however, that such embattled identities, in their quest for
certainty, refuge and protection, can only represent a defensive resistance against the global disorder so relentlessly produced by the volatile
forces of capitalist postmodernity. They are driven not by a positive
hope for the future, or by a project to actively shape that future, but by
what Meaghan Morris calls 'future fear':[11] a sense that things can only
get worse. Ironically, perhaps it is precisely the presumed truth that the
battle against the monster of 'globalization' is a virtually hopeless one
that explains both the intensity and the tenacity of the defensive
identities forged against it.

Here in Australia, the turbulences and uncertainties arising from
the government's sustained and relentless pursuit of neo-liberal economic policies in the 1980s and 1990s – arguably to restructure the
nation so that it can take advantage with more gusto of the promise

of wealth delivered by a rapidly globalizing economy – have been all too palpable in recent years. It is important to note that the process of restructuring is not only an economic project, but also a cultural one, designed to rework and redefine the nation's representation of itself, its national identity – all with the ultimate economic motive of improving the national marketing image. As Morris puts it, the aim is 'make Australia "look better" to its trading partners'.[12] Thus it was only a few years ago that Australian official culture could present this nation proudly, and rather superciliously, as a progressive, world-class 'multicultural nation' which has successfully discarded and left behind its shameful racist past, embodied by the infamous White Australia Policy.[13] Under the flamboyant leadership of former prime minister Paul Keating (1992–96), Australians were interpellated to see themselves as an outward-looking, cosmopolitan and worldly nation, fully integrated and thriving in the global village and the new world order. But the failure of this globalist nationalist desire was rudely illuminated in the years after 1996, when it became clear that neither multiculturalism nor cosmopolitanism was universally embraced by the population at large.

Under the leadership of a woman called Pauline Hanson, who draws her charisma from an aggressively lower-middle-class, anti-intellectual and anti-cosmopolitan populism, a vigorous grassroots political movement emerged of disenchanted, mostly white, rural and working-class people who revolted against what they saw as the disempowerment of their identities as 'ordinary Australians'. Hanson's popularity has given the lie to the progressive national image preferred by the major political leaders, the corporate world and the intellectual class. For Hanson, divorced mother of four, small-businesswoman and anti-political politician, the future can only be secure if a certain, old-fashioned kind of Australian identity is upheld; notionally white, homogeneous, naturally parochial. 'Unless Australia rallies', she warned, 'all our fears will be realised, and we will lose our country forever, and be strangers in our own land.'[14] Hanson's apocalyptic future-fear, disguised under a thick dose of bad-tempered anger and aggression, made her turn against those she believes will rob her of her country: Aboriginal people and Asians, and their supporters in the intellectual and political elites. Not surprisingly, critics have routinely accused her of racism for her attacks on what she ungenerously calls 'the Aboriginal industry' and her infamous statement that Australia is being 'swamped by Asians'. But the moral(istic) critique of racism doesn't take account of the deeper, more pervasive sense of identity panic that underlies Hanson's call for the nation to retreat back into its insulated, isolated condition as a parochial island–continent, culturally and psychologically distant from

the rest of the world, particularly 'Asia', the geographical region the
country reluctantly, but inescapably, finds itself in.[15]

As the process of globalization in the past few decades has drawn
Australia irrevocably into the global network, particularly with 'Asia' –
through trade, travel and migration – many Australians, especially those
who lack the social, cultural and educational capital to adjust to and
survive in this brave new world, find themselves decentred, devalued
and marginalized from a national culture in which 'Australian identity'
can no longer be securely anchored in a safely secluded, British-
derived, white homogeneity but has become thoroughly unsettled and
opened up by the everyday impact of social, cultural and racial heterogeneity, difference, flexibility, and hybridity. Against this background,
Pauline Hanson's politics is exemplary of the kind of reactionary
identity politics I have outlined above, the tragedy of which is that it
contributes to its own continued self-disempowerment. The identity
asserted here, as Phil Cohen has remarked about the different but
similar case of the old, white working class in east London, is 'by and
large immobilised in a culture of nativist complaint'.[16] In other words,
the very terms in which they stake their claims to cultural entitlement
exclude them from the central sites of contemporary cultural *and*
economic power (where cosmopolitan sophistication and ease with
rapid change and multiple realities are the preferred, even necessary,
assets).

While Hanson's movement represents only a small minority of disaf-
fected Australians,[17] it would be a mistake to underestimate its cultural
significance as symptomatic of a much wider tendency, not only in
Australia but across the globe, for peoples who feel hard done by to
mobilize essentialized, backward-looking conceptions of identity in an
effort to find a magical solution to life in a world in which uncertainty
is the name of the global game. Indeed, it may not be an exaggeration
to say, sociologically speaking, that whenever the discourse of identity
is articulated today, the desire expressed in it has more to do with a
nostalgic harking back to an imagined golden past – embodied in the
selective memory of 'tradition' and 'heritage' – than with the visionary
articulation of a new future. This use of 'identity' is clearly in sharp
contradistinction to Hall's buoyant association of cultural identities
with becoming rather than being, with the confident embrace of the
open-endedness of history and destiny. On the contrary, here 'identity'
is firmly conjoined with the very antithesis of change, with some core,
immutable essence that needs to be cherished and protected, precisely
because recourse to the discourse of identity has become a key mechanism to alleviate the fear of the terrifying future associated with
'globalization'. Absent, in this perspective, is a sense of identities as the

dynamic repositories or channels of historical agency: clinging to (an imagined) past inheritance and to the idea of conservation, identity here is a sign not of the active making of history, but of being the passive prisoner of it.

I have invoked the Australian situation in order to expose the partiality of my own theoretical predilections. As a relatively recent immigrant into Australian and a person of 'Asian' background, I had (and have) a personal cultural stake in the redefinition of 'Australian identity' as an open space of diverse influences, traditions and trajectories and as the intersection of a multiplicity of global cultural flows; I have a personal stake in the redefinition of Australia as a 'transnation',[18] if you like, more rather than less prepared than others in the world to feel comfortable in the globalized world of the twenty-first century – in other words, as a future-oriented nation which is not just capable of change but actively desires change, turning necessity into opportunity in times of altered economic and geopolitical circumstances.[19] Indeed, as a migrant who was eager to find my place in this society I was excited to notice, in the early 1990s, that a new Australian nationalism could so elegantly, and with such apparent ease, shift its identificatory allegiance from being a racially and culturally exclusionary 'White Australia' to an inclusive and cosmopolitan 'multicultural Australia in Asia'. There was no lack of rationale for this triumphant national self-understanding. After all, Australia is a relatively new, settler nation mostly populated by waves of immigrants, and as such, so the theory goes, much less weighed down by historical establishment; it has an identity based much more on invention, improvisation and borrowing than on an entrenched sense of primordial givenness. Indeed, what seemed at stake in the new Australian nationalism was identity construction rather than identity expression, the sense that 'what we might become' is more important than 'who we are'. In this sense, Australian national identity could arguably be imagined as the perfect embodiment of Hall's preferred association of identity with becoming rather than with being, with the future as much as the past.

A quiet euphoria took hold of me when I found that my status as a well-educated Asian migrant added significantly to my cultural capital in early nineties Australia. I witnessed with rising excitement that 'Asia' had become, however ambiguously and not without harsh controversy, the sign of success, of Australia's becoming, Australia's fantasmatic passport to a prosperous and affluent future in a globalized world. This sense of euphoria was not unlike Stuart Hall's exhilarated realization, as a West Indian migrant in England, that he was 'centred at last' in the postmodern culture of multiracial London in the late twentieth century, precisely when many (white) British themselves, in Hall's

observation, had started to 'feel just marginally "marginal"'.[20] On the
other side of the world, I could similarly indulge in the feeling of being
on the right side of history, as it were, on the side of the future not the
past, of change rather than stasis, of becoming rather than being. I had
never previously thought I could ever experience my migrant identity
as an asset rather than a liability, but this was made possible in the
cultural ideological configuration of 1990s Australia – a configuration
that, in global terms, is part of 'that immense process of historical
relativization' that has seen the 'Rest' creeping into the 'West'.[21] My
euphoria was reassuringly validated by the popular assertion in much
recent cultural and postcolonial theorizing, from Iain Chambers to
Salman Rushdie, from Trinh Minh-ha to Julia Kristeva, from John
Berger to Paul Carter, that 'the migrant' embodies *par excellence* the
values and practices of cosmospolitanism, worldliness and multiple
identifications. These were the values that the new, multicultural and
globalizing Australia was supposed to have embraced: a postmodern
and postcolonial, transnational Australia in which my own subject
position would be, well, perhaps not quite socially centred, but certainly
symbolically central – central to some desired imaginary future of
Australia as 'part of Asia', not separate and aloof from it.[22]

Of course, my self-interested euphoria, always easily disrupted and
marred by distrust anyway, turned out to be premature and short-lived,
as the eruption of Pauline Hanson's movement made all too painfully
clear. People like Hanson had obviously started to feel more than just
marginally marginal, and resisted virulently that felt marginalization.
Worse, Hanson has pointed the finger at those who, from her point of
view, are the progenitors of her marginalization and decentralization:
all those who are the representatives and promoters of the forces of
'globalization'. As Peter Cochrane has noted, 'Hanson represents the
grief that goes with the loss of cultural centrality and the loss of identity
that happens when a cosmopolished (Anglo) elite lines up with the
new ethnic forces on the block.'[23] This means, logically and emotion-
ally, that I represent all that Hanson is fighting against! Yet it is far too
facile, in this context, to play the anti-racism card. As Meaghan Morris
remarks, 'When the overwhelming majority of poor, economically
"redundant", and culturally "uncompetitive" people in a nation are
white, [Pauline Hanson's voice] is very easily redeemed as that of the
oppressed – white victims of history silenced by the new, cosmopolitan,
multicultural elites.'[24] Against this background, how should the well-
educated Asian migrant and critical intellectual, presumably a card-
carrying member of the 'new, cosmopolitan, multicultural elites',
respond?

In the framework of my own analysis so far, what we have here is a confrontation of the past and the future, a tug of war between 'identity' as essential being, locked in (an image of) the past, and 'identity' as open-ended becoming, invested in a future that remains to be struggled over. But it is clear that the confrontation has to be negotiated, worked over: the very prominence and appeal of reactionary identity politics amongst those who feel left out and disempowered as we enter the twenty-first century betoken that we cannot simply dismiss their fears, anxieties and grievances as irrational, senseless or illegitimate. To put it differently, what is called for now is active negotiation within the *present*, a present in which, for better and worse, conflicting cultural identities share the same (national) space and cannot but relate to one another: as long as democracy prevails, these differences will have to be sorted out in some way, whether we like it or not. In this respect, the very relegation of 'the Hanson phenomenon' (as it is called in Australia) to 'the past' by the self-declared guardians of 'the future' is part of the problem rather than the solution – unless we declare that those often denigrated as 'white trash' have no place in the present world and simply write them off for the future.[25] I, for one, do not believe such a politics of exclusion is an option.

Meaghan Morris asks the hard, awkward questions this way: 'What sort of unity can be projected for a free-trading nation at the mercy of world economic forces that no government can control? for a society unable effectively to legitimize its norms with reference to a common culture, yet with large numbers of citizens yearning to do so?'[26] For Morris, these are political questions that require pragmatic answers, not principled ones: the national, in this light, is not to be defined in terms of 'identity' at all, but as a problematic *process*; the national is to be defined not in terms of the formulation of a positive 'common culture' or 'cohesive community' but as the unending, day-to-day hard work of managing and negotiating differences, the practical working out of shared procedures and codes for coexistence, conciliation and mutual recognition. As an Asian migrant and a member of the cosmopolitan, multicultural elites, I have nothing in common with the white, underprivileged, xenophobic Hanson supporter living in rural or suburban Australia. Yet as we share the physical and symbolic space of the nation, there is an involuntary relationship between us which I cannot simply extract myself from. What matters, I would argue, is the struggle over the ways in which this relationship is made to mean: either in terms of an absolute antagonism, as has been the dominant tendency on both sides (for example, global versus local, privileged versus marginalized, progressive versus reactionary), or in more negotiated, conciliatory, exploratory terms, terms in which no singular antagonism is allowed to saturate the entire significance of the relationship. How this relationship is made to mean is not predetermined, but is open to active intervention at diverse levels of political practice, including the often overlooked micropolitics of everyday life, where the concrete, practical implications of globalization are most keenly and intimately felt.

In this respect, we should take seriously the Hansonites' fear that they might become 'strangers in their own land' – which is another way of saying that they fear that 'others' will 'take over' the country. Even if these fears may be motivated by 'irrational' xenophobic impulses, they are still real, and need to be addressed as such. I myself, as a representative of the 'others', of the threat of 'globalization', am often deeply aware of these fears as I participate in the mundanest social interactions. I am aware, for example, that many white locals in my neighbourhood feel very uneasy about the large influx of Chinese and Vietnamese in recent years, which has qualitatively changed the streetscape, the social mix, and the range of services available in the neighbourhood. For example, there was fierce local protest against the establishment of a Chinese temple in the neighbourhood, on the grounds that it ran against the area's 'heritage'. Thus, it is clear that more established inhabitants feel dislocated as they see the area changing beyond recognition and being 'appropriated' by newcomers: a reactionary sense of loss, a nostalgic longing for the old days, and a notion of progressive decline are all too common responses amongst those who do not possess the cultural (and other) capital to benefit from these changes.[27] As Doreen Massey remarks, 'There is a need to face up to – rather than simply deny – people's need for attachment of some sort, whether through place or anything else.'[28] At the same time, because there is no going back to the old days we need to find ways of working towards, in Massey's words, 'an adequately progressive sense of place, one which would fit in with the current global–local times and the feelings and relations they give rise to'.[29]

Precisely as a member of the cosmopolitan, multicultural elites, I take it as my responsibility to take seriously not just the pleasures, but also the difficulties associated with the construction of such a progressive sense of place, not only in my neighbourhood but nationally and internationally, what Massey calls a 'global sense of place'. Self-reflexivity requires me to be aware of my own relative cultural empowerment *vis-à-vis* those much more restricted in their mobility, both physical and cultural, than I am, even as my 'Asianness' remains an at best ambivalent signifier for my (lack of) ability to belong, to feel at home in Australia. Of course this involves a political project on many levels of organization and agency, the full scope of which cannot be addressed here.[30] Let me therefore limit myself here to just a few levels in one person's individual life. As a critical intellectual, I can write essays such as this one, which attempts to understand the fears of cultural loss and exclusion rather than simply dismiss them as irrelevant or illegimate. But in daily life I can also try to help alleviate these fears in more practical, modest ways, by establishing cross-cultural rapport and a sense of social sharing on an everyday basis, however fleeting, in shops, at the train station, and so on. I make a point, for example, of using my cultural capital to act as a translator between different regimes of culture and knowledge in order to facilitate the creation of a sense of commonality, a togetherness in difference; I make a point, that is, of working to be a *part* of the 'local community' as much as I lead the globalized existence of a cosmopolitan and multicultural diasporic intellectual, simply by talking to people and sharing our experiences (about which fish to buy or the quality and the origins of the fruit in the fruit market, figuring out how to translate certain words, the state of the real estate market in the neighbourhood, and so on).

What such mundane local interactions can contribute to, I believe, is the incremental and dialogic construction of lived identities which slowly dissolve the boundaries between the past and the future, between 'where we come from' and 'what we might become', between being and becoming: being is enhanced by becoming, and becoming is never possible without a solid grounding in being. As subjects from multiple backgrounds negotiate their coexistence and mutual interconnection, the contradictory necessity and impossibility of identities is played out in the messiness of everyday life, as the global and the local interpenetrate each other. This gradual hacking away at the absolutist antagonism between 'identity' and 'globalization' in practice, while never guaranteed and bound to have its ups and downs in its own right, is a form of micro-politics of everyday life informed by pragmatic faith in the capacity for cultural identities to change, not through the imposition of some grandiose vision for the future, but slowly and unsensationally, by elaborating 'the practical means . . . that enable deep and lasting social change'.[31]

Notes

1. Stuart Hall, 'Introduction: Who Needs "Identity"?', in S. Hall and P. du Gay, eds, *Questions of Cultural Identity*. London: Sage, 1996: 4.

2. Stuart Hall, 'Cultural Identity and Diaspora', in J. Rutherford, ed., *Identity: Community, Culture, Difference*. London: Lawrence & Wishart, 1990: 225.

3. Hall, 'Introduction: Who Needs "Identity"?', p. 4.

4. Craig Calhoun, 'Social Theory and Politics of Identity', in C. Calhoun, ed., *Social Theory and the Politics of Identity*. Oxford: Blackwell, 1994: 14.

5. James Clifford, 'Mixed Feelings', in Pheng Cheah and Bruce Robbins, eds, *Cosmopolitics: Thinking and Feeling Beyond the Nation*. Minneapolis: University of Minnesota Press, 1998: 369.

6. Hall, 'Introduction: Who Needs "Identity"?', p. 2.

7. Ibid., p. 16.

8. Calhoun, 'Social Theory', p. 22.

9. Manuel Castells, *The Power of Identity*. Vol II of *The Information Age: Economy, Society and Culture*. Oxford: Blackwell, 1997: 1.

10. Ibid, p. 2.

11. Meaghan Morris, *Too Soon Too Late: History in Popular Culture*. Bloomington and Indianapolis: Indiana University Press, 1998: Epilogue.

12. Ibid., p. 217.

13. See my essay 'The Curse of the Smile: Ambivalence and the "Asian" Woman in Australian Multiculturalism', *Feminist Review*, No 52, Spring 1996: 36–49, and Ien Ang and Jon Stratton, 'Multiculturalism in Crisis: The New Politics of Race and National Identity in Australia', *Topia: Canadian Journal of Cultural Studies*, No 2, Spring 1998: 22–41.

14. Pauline Hanson, speech, quoted in Marian Wilkinson, 'Who's Afraid of Pauline Hanson?' *Sydney Morning Herald*, 12 September 1998, p. 43.

15. For some analyses that put the 'Hanson phenomenon' in Australia in historical, political and social context, see, for example, Geoffrey Gray and Christine Winter (eds), *The Resurgence of Racism: Howard, Hanson and the Race Debate*, Clayton, Vic: Monash Publications in History, 1997; Robert Manne (ed.), *Two Nations*, Melbourne: Bookman Press, 1998; Jon Stratton, *Race Daze: Australia in Identity Crisis*, Sydney: Pluto Press, 1998; Ghassan Hage, *White Nation*, Sydney: Pluto Press, 1998.

16. Phil Cohen, 'In Visible Cities', *Communal/Plural: Journal for Transnational and Crosscultural Studies*, 7 (1) 1999.

17. During the October 1998 elections, Pauline Hanson's One Nation Party failed to gain a single seat in the Federal House of Representatives. However, the party still managed to attract about 9 per cent of the electorate's vote nationwide, not an insignificant result.

18. Arjun Appadurai, 'Patriotism and Its Futures', in his *Modernity at Large*. Minneapolis: University of Minnesota Press, 1996.

19. Graeme Turner, 'Two Faces of Australian Nationalism', *Sydney Morning Herald*, 25 January 1997.

20. Stuart Hall, 'Minimal Selves', in Ann Gray and Jim McGuigan, eds, *Studying Culture*. London: Edward Arnold, 1993: 134–8.

21. Ibid.

22. The notion that Australia should become more integrated with its geographical region is one of the master narratives of Australian economic and political discourse. The necessity of this move is generally played out in the context of the globalizing world economy, and the creation of regional trading blocs. For the politics of the 'Asianization' of Australia, see, for example, Ien Ang and Jon Stratton, 'Asianing Australia: Notes Towards a Critical Transnationalism in Cultural Studies', *Cultural Studies*, 10 (1) 1996: 16–36. A good recent example of affirmative Asianization discourse is Stephen FitzGerald, *Is Australia an Asian Country?* St Leonards: Allen & Unwin, 1997.

23. Peter Cochrane, 'Race Memory', *Australian Review of Books*, November 1996, p. 9.

24. Morris, *Too Soon Too Late*, p. 221.

25. Pauline Hanson was reportedly very hurt, and cried, when she was called white trash by anti-racist protesters. For a look at the cultural politics of 'white trash' in the US, see Matt Wray and Annalee Newitz, eds, *White Trash: Race and Class in America*. New York: Routledge, 1997.

26. Morris, *Too Soon Too Late*, p. 208.

27. Such responses are empirically manifest internationally. See, for example, Jon May, 'Globalization and the Politics of Place: Place and Identity in an Inner London Neighbourhood', *Transactions of the Institute of British Geographers*, Vol 27, No 2, 1996: 194–215.

28. Doreen Massey, *Space, Place and Gender*. Cambridge: Polity Press, 1994: 151.

29. Massey, *Space, Place and Gender*, pp. 151–2.

30. For an important political treatise on this, see Mark Latham, *Civilizing Global Capital*. St Leonards: Allen & Unwin, 1998.

31. Morris, *Too Soon Too Late*, p. 209.

Sociology and the Metaphorical Tiger

Michèle Barrett

This chapter looks at the contribution of Stuart Hall's work to the rethinking of sociology that is now going on. It is a written version of a talk given at his retirement conference. The talk began with a clip from an unusual archive television programme. Made in 1967, by a team from the BBC's *Omnibus*, it was described as 'an enquiry into the power of a familiar poem'. The programme interviewed a young Stuart Hall, as well as Richard Hoggart and many others, including schoolchildren studying William Blake's poem 'The Tyger'. Stuart's contribution characteristically recalls how he was taught the poem himself as a child in Jamaica, where it was read as a little illustration of God's grace and power. He suggests that every time he has read it since then, its meaning has changed for him; 'I don't understand it at all,' he says. He goes on to describe the tiger in the poem as representing the physical, sensory, human world as opposed to the divine. Most interesting is the last section of the interview, in which Hall suggests that the tiger becomes something that its creator cannot control – it is as if the heart has started beating of its own accord. The poem is ambiguous in its ending. The tiger is 'much more terrible', 'much more other' than its creator had imagined. In the course of the poem we watch the creator move from a point where he can control the tiger to the point where 'he has to recognise it and salute it at the end as something separate from him'.

The tiger can stand in for the imaginative, the sensual, the emotional, the other, for that which we cannot control. Can sociology salute this tiger? Stuart Hall's work, as reflected in the consideration of 'race' and difference, cultural studies, and politics, obviously indicates a loosening up of what is regarded as 'sociology'. Nevertheless, there is still considerable tension between what he represents and those who support a more mainstream definition of the subject. Sociology has come to an accommodation of sorts with the 'cultural turn', but for many sociologists the screw is turning a bit too far and they don't want it to go all the way round. There is a fightback currently under way which takes the form of an urging 'let's go back' – let's go back to political economy, let's go back to the founding fathers, let's go back to epistemological realism. But 'going back' is not usually the best option. The cultural turn is better thought of as a cultural revolution.

I want to identify three types of problem in sociology: empirical problems, theoretical problems, and the problem of the metaphorical tiger. The easiest to deal with is the first. Sociology was set up in the late nineteenth century and its substantive concerns simply do not meet the social world that we now inhabit. These arguments have been well rehearsed, and indeed a lot has been done about the problems. Sociology traditionally overstressed the nation-state at the expense of the more detailed and local, as well as at the expense of understanding the supra-national, or global. Second, it overemphasized the determining effects of social structure, at the expense of an understanding of human agency and identity. Third, it viewed inequality in terms of social class, whose operations we now understand in the context of multiple forms of social advantage and power.

I put this description in the past tense, as I think a new sociology is being developed, which is decisively overcoming these problems. The discipline has been brought up to date and a new paradigm has emerged. Attention is now focused on the global context of social activity, a reconceptualization of politics, an awareness of risk and uncertainty, the inclusion of affect, the importance of self and identity, and the power of the media. All these are welcome, and are invigorating the discipline. In short, sociology is a sufficiently flexible rubric to be adaptable – though not without internal controversy of course – to the new social conditions we find ourselves in. Less tractable, perhaps unsurprisingly, are our current theoretical disputes. I want here to take up two issues on which sociology is in my view mistakenly taking to the intellectual barricades: postmodernism and post-structuralism.

'Postmodernism' is a term that has become the scapegoat of a hostile sociological response to the cultural turn. It has become a powerful signifier, of a very negative kind. Keith Tester has written a book in which he deliberately doesn't use the word (even though the book is about postmodernity) because, he says:

> The word is like a red rag to a bull for some people. As soon as they see the word they dismiss an argument without a second thought and dismiss it as incoherent, insubstantial and of quite questionable propriety. The word post-modernity has become an obstacle to principled debate.[1]

One interesting response to the spread of interest in postmodernism falls into the psychoanalytic category of denial. Perhaps my favourite example is the conference held at Essex in 1998 under the title 'After Postmodernism: Critical Realism?' For wishful thinking in a public place this takes some beating.

Those who used to object to postmodernism are now very busy telling us that it has passed over – they don't have to argue about it any more, they just announce (contrary to all the evidence) that it has Gone Away. Oddly, given the theoretical position from which many critics of postmodernism speak, they seem to believe that this little performative speech act will actually bring about what they would like. I was stopped (unfortunately on the first page of the preface) in my reading of what Perry Anderson on the jacket describes as W.G. Runciman's 'deeply impressive' and 'dazzling display of erudition' – his new book *The Social Animal*. Runciman declares that 'post-modernism has come, and largely gone, taking with it those aspects of the study of human social behaviour which properly belong with literature rather than science'.[2]

As well as claiming that postmodernism has come and gone, its critics also argue that we don't know what it is (or was, presumably). Actually, we do know what it is. At the simplest, empirically irrefutable level, postmodernism – like modernism before it – is a cultural movement, with characteristic aesthetic strategies, and it can be described and dated. Modernism was a movement in Western art in the early twentieth century, whose distinctive feature was a rejection of representational conventions such as realist narrative (in fiction), perspective and figuration (in painting), tonality and resolution (in music) and ornamentation (in architecture). Whatever you think about the more general use of the term 'modernism' that has subsequently come into play, there is little to be gained by denying that this specific artistic movement existed or claiming that we don't know what it is. Similarly postmodernism is an identifiable cultural movement of the late twentieth century, characterized by aesthetic strategies of intertextuality, a self-referential reversion to pre-'modernist' artistic forms, and a radical foregrounding of the means and conventions of representation. Although postmodernism in the arts has been most debated in relation to architecture, its characteristic features are clear to see in a number of contemporary art forms, and increasingly evident in popular culture.

The reason why these specific cultural movements are clouded in obfuscation is that lurking behind the relatively uncontroversial identification of an aesthetic project is a far more contentious debate about 'modernity' and 'postmodernity'. This is where the real conflict lies. Modernity as a category of analysis competes with industrial society for sociology, or capitalism for Marxism. (This is far more serious to sociologists than artistic and cultural trends.) Modernity is a more reflexive and 'aware' category than these. In one sense it can be described as a social order whose characteristics are (to take the Open University model) an industrial division of labour, a secular democratic nation-state, rationalism and the market. But it is also (as Hall and Gieben's *The West and the Rest in Formations of Modernity* makes clear) not simply a socio-economic order: the 'constitutive outside' of Western modernity involves a philosophy and self-identity constructed through its relation to the colonial other.[3]

The category of 'postmodernity' represents the disintegration of this philosophy and self-identity, as well as identifying a number of more specific social developments (displacement of the national by the global and local; the production of hybridization through migration and diasporic movement; the compression of time and space; the displacing of production by consumption and so on). The category of 'postmodernity', far more than that of 'postmodernism', is a troubling one for sociology and not least because of sociology's formation as a discipline in the period of modernity. These troubling questions are not resolved, however, by pronouncements that we are 'still in' modernity ... that postmodernity either hasn't arrived or never will. Sociology will have to do better than that if it is to come to terms with the legacy of its 'modern' ideas in a social world whose cultural forms – in the arts and the popular media – are increasingly postmodernist.

Here I want to point up the sharp difference between someone like Stuart Hall, whose recent work is couched within a vocabulary drawn from post-structuralism (Derrida, Lacan, Foucault), and most sociologists, of both the old and the new variants, who are generally hostile to these ideas. Post-structuralist ideas, nevertheless, are making a considerable impression in sociology. Before considering one particular aspect of the debate about post-structuralism I draw your attention to the following statement made by Anthony Giddens in 1987:

> Structuralism, and post-structuralism also, are dead traditions of thought. Notwithstanding the promise they held in the fresh bloom of youth, they have ultimately failed to generate the revolution in philosophical understanding and social theory which was once their pledge.[4]

This argument was wrong when it was made and even more wrong now. Post-structuralism has generated more of a revolution than he suggests. One of the difficulties that sociology has at present is that although many sociologists of a certain generation are keen to fight off post-structuralism as an enemy, these are the ideas that students and younger sociologists are interested in. (Sometimes I get the impression that my students are interested in more or less anything so long as it isn't mainstream sociology.)

I want to take up only one of the implications of post-structuralism for sociology. It concerns the relationship of social analysis to politics. Sociology has had, I think, a particularly engrained history on this question. Although it might seem that a necessary link between social analysis and politics is found only in the more strongly 'scientific socialist' strand of Marx's thought, the connection is a much more pervasive one in sociology generally. Sociologists classically produce evidence and arguments that support a particular political conclusion – it is second nature to them. You may ask what is wrong with that? What is wrong is that it hides political choices behind a veil of apparent objectivity. The theorists who have done most to expose the assumptions behind this specious connection are those influenced by post-structuralist ideas.

One way of posing this desire to couch a political choice as the inevitable outcome of sociological fact would be to think of it in terms of Foucault's artful dissection of a 'will to truth'. The judgement lies hidden behind a panoply of expertise that justifies and legitimates it. Sociology's 'will to truth' is perhaps less apparent to us than it might otherwise be, for the reason that the choices being legitimated in these moves are traditionally progressive ones – choices that could not be articulated without a barrage of empirical proof.

Another way of looking at this would be to consider more critically, as Zygmunt Bauman has done, the effects of attaching sociology to a rational scientism so firmly that we have buried any possibility of considering the issues with which it deals as ethical issues.

> So sociology promoted, as its own criteria of propriety, the same principles of rational action it visualized as constitutive of its object. It also promoted, as binding rules of its own discourse, the inadmissability of ethical problematics in any other form but that of a communally-sustained ideology and thus heterogenous to sociological (scientific, rational) discourse.[5]

This means that sociology can only relate to ethics as the ideologies of groups being studied. As Bauman points out, moral judgements are as out of place in a sociology seminar as they are in bureaucracy.

A third approach to this question would be Stuart Hall's conception of 'without guarantees'. I want to make a double point about all this. Post-structuralism has made an enormous contribution, indeed a revolution, in exposing the processes that help us to understand how sociology has allied itself to a modern rationalism, and has hidden its judgements behind a rhetoric of scientificity and objectivity. We cannot move on from that position without accepting the validity of these arguments. Post-structuralism, therefore, poses the issue of a more open, more explicit statement of choices and priorities, not defensible in another register. Political choice becomes a matter of ethical choice, a matter of personal responsibility. Yet post-structuralism's belligerent anti-humanism (I tend to repeat this second point every time I make the first one) has made it difficult to take this forward – a problem that a number of writers are now addressing.[6]

To take this forward, as Keith Tester does in an argument against the complicity of orthodox sociology with dehumanization, is to confront head on the problem of science raised in the passage by Runciman quoted above: postmodernism equals literature, sociology equals science. Stuart Hall does not give us a sociology with much of the apparatus of social science. There are no tables to be found in his work, though there may often be pictures. His insights are imaginative, sensual even, in that they speak to experience, which includes the senses, rather than simply cognition. We have here a sociologist (if he is one) whose sociology is based on perception.

For Runciman, sociology is a social science; for others it is much more naturally located in the humanities. It is, indeed, a strength of the pluralist British tradition that sociology here does include those whose work would not be regarded as sociology in the USA. I do not propose now to go into the debate about how historically the line between social science and the arts as academic disciplines was drawn (though Stephen Horigan has an interesting argument about its discursive function).[7] I would suggest, however, that sociology has at least as much to learn from the arts as from the sciences (whose scientificity is usually misunderstood).

In that context I want to make one, final point about the prospects for rethinking sociology now. I refer you back back to the tiger. Sociology is conspicuously inadequate in the tiger department. Physicality, humanity, imagination, the other, fear, the limits of control; all are missing in their own terms, in their own dynamic, as Stuart put it. This is the single most serious difficulty of contemporary sociology – far more intractable even than the troubling theoretical issues I have been discussing.

Virginia Woolf has told us that the first duty of a lecturer is to hand you 'a nugget of pure truth to wrap up between the pages of your notebooks and keep on the mantelpiece for ever'.[8] The nugget of truth that I suggest now is a simple one; it is that *sociology has become boring.* Some might formulate this as sociology *is* boring, but I don't agree with that – it's a more recent development. I can illustrate this point about boredom with just one example. Looking through a recent publisher's catalogue (that of Sage) I found a very strange book endorsement. The book is *Contested Natures*, by Phil Macnaughton and John Urry; the endorsement is from Ulrich Beck, and he says: 'Quite astonishing; sociology of the environment becomes exciting.' The environment is an intrinsically interesting topic. Sociologists started working on it fairly recently. What can they possibly have done in a few short years to make it so boring that this endorsement makes any sense?

Sociology is not likely to be rethought in such a way as to grip the imagination of a new generation if it cannot make itself interesting again. Since writing this, I have come across a book review that begins, 'If sociology could talk, it would say, I am tired.'[9] If it is to wake up, it needs more humanity, it needs more imagination, it needs more perception, it needs more appeal to experience beyond cognition. It needs more respect for other ideas on their own terms, not translated into its own. It is time to take a cue from Stuart Hall, and bring out the tigers.

Notes

1. Keith Tester, *The Inhuman Condition*, Routledge 1995, p. xiii.
2. W. G. Runciman, *The Social Animal*, HarperCollins 1998, p. vii.
3. Stuart Hall and B. Gieben, eds., 'The West and the Rest', in *Formations of Modernity*, Polity Press 1992, pp. 275–333.
4. Anthony Giddens, 'Structuralism, Post-structuralism and the Production of Culture', in his *Social Theory and Modern Sociology*, Polity Press 1987, p. 73.
5. Zygmunt Bauman, *Modernity and the Holocaust*, Polity Press 1989, p. 29.
6. See, for example, Tester, *The Inhuman Condition*.
7. Stephen Horigan, *Nature and Culture in Western Discourses*, Routledge 1988.
8. Virginia Woolf, *A Room of One's Own*, Penguin 1993, p. 5.
9. Peter Beilharz, 'Calhoun's Critical Theory', in *Thesis Eleven*, No. 55, November 1998.

3

Resisting Left Melancholia

Wendy Brown

> In every era the attempt must be made anew to wrest tradition
> away from a conformism that is about to overpower it. . . . only
> that historian will have the gift of fanning the spark of hope in
> the past who is firmly convinced that even the dead will not be
> safe from the enemy if he wins.[1]
>
> Walter Benjamin

It has become commonplace to lament the current beleaguered and
disoriented condition of the Left. Stuart Hall is among the few who
have tried to diagnose the sources and dynamics of this condition.
From the earliest days of the rise of the Thatcher–Reagan–Gingrich
Right in Europe and North America, Hall insisted that the 'crisis of the
Left' in the late twentieth century was due neither to internal divisions
in the activist or academic Left nor to the clever rhetoric or funding
schemes of the Right. Rather, he charged, this ascendency was consequent to the Left's own failure to apprehend the character of the age,
and to develop a political critique and a moral–political vision appropriate to this character. For Hall, the rise of the Right was a symptom
rather than a cause of this failure, just as the Left's dismissive or
suspicious attitude toward cultural politics is for Hall not a sign of its
unwavering principles but of its anachronistic habits of thought, and its
fears and anxieties about revising those habits. In short, the Left's
disintegration and disarray must be pinned not on external events or
developments in the late twentieth century, but on the way the Left
positions itself in relation to those events and developments.

In his reflections on two decades of Left troubles, Hall often teeters
on the brink of psychological speculation – he speaks in terms of
fears, anxieties, and rigidities – but despite his extensive use of psychoanalytic insight in his work on identity and subjectivity, here he never
takes the plunge. Undoubtedly this hesitation pertains to Hall's abiding generosity and concern for coalition building, his sensitivity to the
potentially chilling sectarian effects of psychologizing those with whom

one disagrees. So in what follows I shall briefly go where our angel appropriately fears to tread. I want to think about Hall's account of Left travails in terms of 'Left melancholia', a term coined by Walter Benjamin in the 1930s.

Benjamin was neither categorically nor characterologically opposed to the value and valence of sadness as such, nor to the potential insights gleaned from brooding over one's losses. Indeed, he had a well-developed appreciation of the productive value of *acedia*, sadness, and mourning for political and cultural work. Moreover, in his study of Baudelaire, Benjamin treated melancholia itself as something of a creative wellspring. But 'Left melancholia' is Benjamin's unambiva-lent epithet for the revolutionary hack who is, finally, not serious about political change, who is more attached to a particular political analysis or ideal – even to the failure of that ideal – than to seiz-ing possibilities for radical change in the present. In the context of Benjamin's enigmatic insistence on the political value of a dialectical historical grasp of 'the time of the Now', Left melancholia represents not only a refusal to come to terms with the particular character of the present, that is, a failure to understand history in terms other than 'empty time' or 'progress'. It signifies as well a certain narcissism with regard to one's past political attachments and identity that exceeds any contemporary investment in political mobilization, alliance, or transformation.[2]

The irony of melancholia, of course, is that attachment to the object of one's sorrowful loss supersedes any desire to recover from this loss, to live free of it in the present, to be unburdened by it. This is what renders melancholia a persistent condition, a state, indeed, a structure of desire, rather than a transient response to death or loss. In Freud's 1917 meditation on melancholia, he reminds us of a second singular feature of melancholy: it entails 'a loss of a more ideal kind [than mourning]. The object has not perhaps actually died, but has been lost as an object of love.'[3] Moreover, Freud suggests, the melancholic will often not know precisely what about the object has been loved and lost – 'this would suggest that melancholia is in some way related to an object-loss which is withdrawn from consciousness, in contradistinction to mourning, in which there is nothing about the loss that is uncon-scious'.[4] The loss precipitating melancholy is more often than not unavowed and unavowable. Finally, Freud suggests that the melancholic subject – who is low in self-regard, despairing, even suicidal – suffers this way because it has displaced a potential reproach of its once-loved object onto itself. The reproach of the loved object pertains to its failure to live up to the idealization by the beloved, and the displace-ment of this reproach results in the melancholic's misery. In other words, the love or idealization of the object is preserved, even as the loss of love occasioned by the shattered idealization is converted to the terrible suffering of the melancholic, a suffering resulting from a withdrawal of love but a withdrawal now turned against the self rather than the other.

Now why would Benjamin use the term 'melancholia', and the emotional economy it represents, to talk about a particular formation on and of the Left? Benjamin never offers a precise formulation of Left melancholy. Rather, he deploys it as a term of opprobrium for those beholden more to certain long-held sentiments and objects than to the possibilities of political transformation in the present. Benjamin is particularly attuned to the melancholic's investment in 'things'. In *The Origin of German Tragic Drama*, he argues that 'melancholy betrays the world for the sake of knowledge', here suggesting that the loyalty of the melancholic converts its truth ('every loyal vow or memory') about its beloved into a thing, indeed, imbues knowledge itself with a thing-like quality.[5] Benjamin provides another version of this formulation: 'in its tenacious self-absorption [melancholy] embraces dead objects in its contemplation'.[6] More simply, melancholia is loyal 'to the world of things',[7] a formulation that suggests a certain logic of fetishism – with all the conservatism and withdrawal from human relations that fetishistic desire implies – contained within the melancholic logic. In the critique of Kastner's poems in which Benjamin first coins 'Left melancholia', he suggests that sentiments themselves become things for the Left melancholic who 'takes as much pride in the traces of former spiritual goods as the bourgeois do in their material goods'.[8] We come to love our Left passions and reasons, our Left analyses and convictions, more than we love the existing world that we presumably seek to alter with these terms or the future that would be aligned with them. Left melancholy, in short, is Benjamin's name for a mournful, conservative, backward-looking attachment to a feeling, analysis, or relationship that has been rendered thing-like and frozen in the heart of the putative Leftist. If Freud is helpful here, then this condition presumably issues from some unaccountable loss, some unavowably crushed ideal, con-temporarily signified by the terms 'Left', 'socialism', 'Marx', or 'movement'.

Certainly the losses, accountable and unaccountable, of the Left are many in our own time. The literal disintegration of socialist regimes and of the legitimacy of Marxism may well be the least of it. We are awash in the loss of a unified analysis and unified movement, in the loss of labour and class as inviolable predicates of political analysis and mobilization, in the loss of an inexorable and scientific forward move-ment of history, and in the loss of a viable alternative to the political economy of capitalism. And on the backs of these losses are still others: we are without a sense of international, and often even local, Left community; we are without conviction about the Truth of the social order; we are without a rich moral–political vision to guide and sustain political work. Thus we suffer with the sense not only of a lost movement but of a lost historical moment; we suffer with the sense not only of a lost theoretical and empirical coherence, but of a lost way of life and a lost course of pursuits.

This much many on the Left can forthrightly admit, even if we do not know what to do about it. But in the hollow core of all these losses, perhaps in the place of our political unconscious, is there also an unavowed loss – the promise that Left analysis and Left commitment would supply its adherents with a clear and certain path towards the good, the right, and the true? Is it not this promise that formed the basis for much of our pleasure in being on the Left, indeed, for our self-love as Leftists and for our fellow feeling towards other Leftists? And if this love cannot be given up without demanding a radical transformation in the very foundation of our love, in our very capacity for political love or attachment, are we not doomed to Left melancholia, a melancholia that is certain to have effects that are not only sorrowful but self-destructive? Freud again:

> If the love for the object – a love which cannot be given up though the object itself is given up – takes refuge in narcissistic identification, then the hate comes into operation on this substitutive object, abusing it, debasing it, making it suffer and deriving sadistic satisfaction from its suffering.[9]

Now our challenge would be to figure out who or what is this substitutive object. What do we hate that we might preserve the idealization of that romantic Left promise? What do we punish that we might save the old guarantees of the Left from our wrathful disappointment?

Two familiar answers emerge from recent quarrels and reproaches on the Left. The first is a set of social and political formations variously known as 'cultural politics' or 'identity politics'. Here the conventional charge from one portion of the Left is that political movements rooted in cultural identity – racial, sexual, ethnic, or gendered – not only elide the fundamental structure of modernity – capitalism – and its fundamental formation – class – but fragment Left political energies such that socialist coalition building is impossible. The second culprit also has various names – post-structuralism', 'discourse analysis', 'postmodernism', 'trendy literary theory got up as political analysis'. The murder charges here are also familiar: post-foundational theories of the subject, truth, and social processes undermine the verifiable empirical objectivity necessary to sustain a theoretically coherent and factually true account of the world, and also challenge the putatively objective grounds of Left norms. Together or separately, these two phenomena are held responsible for the weak, fragmented, and disoriented character of the contemporary Left. This much is old news. But if read through the prism of Left melancholy, the element of displacement in both sets of charges may appear more starkly since we would be forced to ask: what aspects of Left analysis or orthodoxy have wilted on the vine for its adherents, but are safeguarded from this recognition through the scornful attention heaped on identity politics and post-structuralism? Indeed, what narcissistic identification with that orthodoxy is preserved in the lament over the loss of its hold on young Leftists and the loss of its potency in the political field? What love for the promises and guarantees that a Left analysis once held is preserved, as responsibility for the tattered condition of those promises and guarantees is distributed onto debased others? And do we here also see a certain thingness of the Left take shape, its reification as something that 'is', the fantastical memory that it once 'was', at the very moment that it so clearly is not/one?

For all his political and intellectual generosity, it is what I have termed Left melancholics for whom Stuart Hall has least forbearance. If Hall understands our failure as a Left in the last quarter-century as a failure within the Left to apprehend this time, this is a failure that is only reiterated and not redressed by our complaints against those who are succeeding (liberal centrists, neo-conservatives, the Right), or by our complaints against one another (anti-racists, feminists, queer activists, and 'postmodernists'). In Hall's understanding, this failure is not simply the consequence of adherence to a particular analytic orthodoxy – the determinism of capital, the primacy of class – although it is certainly that. Rather, this failure results as well from a particular intellectual straitjacket – an insistence on a materialism that refuses the importance of the subject and the subjective, the question of style, the problematic of language. And it is the combination of these two causes of failure that is deadly: 'Our sectarianism', he argues in the conclusion of *The Hard Road to Renewal*, consists not only of a defensiveness towards the agendas fixed by now-anachronistic political–economic formations (those of the 1930s and 1945), but 'is also due to a certain notion of politics, inhabited not so much as a theory, more as a habit of mind'.

> We go on thinking a unilinear and irreversible political logic, driven by some abstract entity we call 'the economic' or 'capital', unfolding to its preor-dained end. Whereas, as Thatcherism clearly shows, politics actually works

more like the logic of language: you can always put it another way if you try hard enough.[10]

Certainly the course of capital shapes the conditions of possibility in politics, but politics itself 'is either conducted ideologically or not at all'.[11] Or, in another of Hall's pithy formulas, 'politics does not reflect majorities, it constructs them'.[12]

It is important to be clear here. Hall never claims that ideology determines the course of globalization, but that it harnesses it for one political purpose or another, and when it is successful, the political and economic strategies represented by a particular ideology will also themselves bring into being certain political–economic formations within global capitalist developments.

> Now we are beginning . . . to move into a 'post-Fordist' society – what some theorists call disorganized capitalism, the era of 'flexible specialization'. One way of reading present developments is that 'privatization' is Thatcherism's way of harnessing and appropriating this underlying movement within a specific economic and political strategy and constructing it within the terms of a specific philosophy. It has succeeded, to some degree, in aligning its historical, political, cultural and sexual 'logics' with some of the most powerful tendencies in the contemporary logics of capitalist development. And this, in part, is what gives it its supreme confidence, its air of ideological complacency: what makes it appear to 'have history on its side', to be coterminous with the inevitable course of the future. The left, however, instead of rethinking *its* economic, political, and cultural strategies in the light of this deeper, underlying 'logic' of dispersal and diversification (which after all, need not necessarily be an enemy of greater democratization) simply resists it. If Thatcherism can lay claim to it, then we must have nothing to do with it. Is there any more certain way of rendering yourself historically anachronistic?[13]

If the contemporary Left often clings to the formations and formulations of another epoch, one in which the notions of unified movements, social totalities, and class-based politics were viable categories of political and theoretical analysis, this means that it literally renders itself a conservative force in history – one that not only misreads the present but instils traditionalism in the very heart of its praxis, in the place where commitment to risk and upheaval belongs. Walter Benjamin sketches this phenomenon in his attack on Erich Kästner, the popular Left-wing poet in the Weimar Republic who is the subject of his 'Left melancholy' essay: 'This poet is dissatisfied, indeed heavy-hearted. But this heaviness of heart derives from routine. For to be in a routine means to have sacrificed one's idiosyncracies, to have forfeited the gift of distaste. And

that makes one heavy-hearted.'[14] In a different tonality, Stuart Hall
sketches this problem in the Left's response to Thatcherism:

> I remember the moment in the 1979 election when Mr Callaghan, on his
> last political legs, so to speak, said with real astonishment about the offensive
> of Mrs Thatcher that 'She means to tear society up by the roots.' This was an
> unthinkable idea in the social-democratic vocabulary: a radical attack on the
> status quo. The truth is that traditionalist ideas, the ideas of social and moral
> *respectability*, have penetrated so deep inside socialist consciousness that it is
> quite common to find people committed to a radical political programme
> underpinned by wholly traditional feelings and sentiments.[15]

Traditionalism is hardly new in Left politics, but it has become
especially pronounced and pernicious in recent years as a consequence
of (1) its righteous formulation as a defence against the Thatcher–
Reagan 'revolutions' (epitomized in the dismantling of the welfare
state and the privatization of a number of public functions and services), (2) the development of cultural politics, and especially sexual
politics, (3) the disintegration of socialist regimes and the severe
discrediting of Left political–economic aims this disintegration occasioned. The combination of these three phenomena yields Left formulations that tend to have as their primary content the defence of liberal
New Deal politics and especially the welfare state on one hand, and the
defence of civil liberties on the other. In short, the Left has come to
represent a politics that seeks to protect a set of freedoms and entitlements that confront neither the dominations contained in both, nor
the limited value of those freedoms and entitlements in contemporary
configurations of capitalism. And when this traditionalism is conjoined
with a loss of faith in the egalitarian vision so fundamental to the
socialist challenge to the capitalist mode of distribution, and a loss of
faith in the emancipatory vision fundamental to the socialist challenge
to the capitalist mode of production, the problem of Left conservatism
becomes very serious indeed. What emerges is a Left that operates
without either a substantive critique of the status quo or a substantive
alternative to it. But perhaps even more troubling, it is a Left that has
become more attached to its impossibility than to its potential fruitful-
ness, a Left that is most at home dwelling not in hopefulness but in its
own marginality and failure, a Left that is thus caught in a structure of
melancholic attachment to a certain strain of its own dead past, whose
spirit is deathly, whose structure of desire is backward-looking and
punishing.

What is entailed in throwing off the melancholic and conservative
habits of the Left to invigorate it with a radical (from the Latin *radix*,

meaning 'root'), critical and visionary spirit again? This would be a spirit that embraces the notion of a deep and indeed unsettling transformation of society rather than recoiling at this prospect, even as we must be wisened to the fact that neither total revolution nor the automatic progress of history would carry us towards whatever reformulated vision we might develop. What political hope can we nurture that does not falsely ground itself in the notion that 'history is on our side' or that there is some inevitability of popular attachment to whatever values we might develop as those of a new Left vision? What kind of socialism can we imagine that is neither state-run nor utopian, neither repressive nor libertarian, neither economically impoverished nor culturally grey? My emphasis on the melancholic logic of certain contemporary Left tendencies is not meant to recommend therapy as the route to answering these questions. It does, however, suggest that the feelings and sentiments – including those of sorrow, rage, and anxiety about broken promises and lost compasses – that sustain our attachments to Left analyses and Left projects ought to be examined for what they create in the way of potentially conservative and even self-destructive undersides of putatively progressive political aims.

Notes

1. 'Theses on the Philosophy of History', in Walter Benjamin, *Illuminations: Walter Benjamin, Essays and Reflections*, edited by H. Arendt (New York: Schocken Books, 1969), p. 255.

2. For Benjamin's bewitching formulation of the 'Then' and the 'Now' as political terms unapproachable by 'Past' and 'Present', see his notes on method for *The Arcades Project*, published as 'N [Re the Theory of Knowledge, Theory of Progress]' in *Benjamin: Philosophy, Aesthetics, History*, edited by G. Smith (Chicago: University of Chicago Press, 1989), especially pp. 49, 51–2, and 80.

3. 'Mourning and Melancholia', *The Standard Edition of the Complete Psychological Works of Sigmund Freud*, translated by J. Strachey, (London: Hogarth Press, 1957), Volume XIV, p. 245.

4. Ibid.

5. Walter Benjamin, *The Origin of German Tragic Drama*, translated by J. Osborne (London: Verso, 1977), pp. 156–7.

6. Ibid., p. 157.

7. Ibid.

8. Walter Benjamin, 'Left-Wing Melancholy', republished in *The Weimar Republic Sourcebook*, edited A. Kaes, M. Jay, and E. Dimendberg (UC Press, 1994), p. 305.

9. Benjamin, 'Mourning and Melancholia', p. 251.

10. Stuart Hall, *The Hard Road to Renewal: Thatcherism and the Crisis of the Left* (London: Verso, 1988), p. 273.

11. Ibid., p. 274.
12. Ibid., p. 266.
13. Ibid., p. 276.
14. Benjamin, 'Left-Wing Melancholy', p. 305.
15. Hall, *The Hard Road to Renewal*, p. 194. One might recall, in another context, James Miller's scandalized response to a remark by Foucault that he 'wanted to destroy the whole of society', a remark Miller not only excised from the context of Foucault's critique of totalization represented by the very notion of social wholes, but also treated as a signature of decadent nihilism rather than as an utterance compatible with a radical Left tradition aspiring to uproot all existing social practices. See James Miller, *The Passion of Michel Foucault* (New York: Simon & Schuster), 1993.

4

Agencies of Style for a Liminal Subject

Judith Butler

The location of agency is not easy to determine, for if we are no longer talking about agency as a robust force lodged in the subject, indeed, if we are no longer talking about agency as a property or an attribute that an agent possesses, it is difficult to know what we are talking about. When I write that 'we are no longer talking about agency as a property of the subject', I do not mean to suggest that grammatical formulations such as 'I do' and 'I will' have come under some form of theoretical censure. Hardly. We do speak that way and will continue to do so. Indeed, I cannot even confirm the grammatical necessity of such speech without, as it were, speaking in the grammar that I claim to be apparently inevitable. The question, however, pertains to the philosophical implications of grammar, whether the grammar does not shore up an ordinary sense of a metaphysical ruse. In the mode of the early Wittgenstein, one might respond that any and all metaphysical implications we draw about the subject and its agency are derived from the grammar of its use. Only by ignoring the shift from the earlier to the later Wittgenstein could one derive from the claim that grammar sets the stage for the analysis of the subject and its agency the erroneous conclusion that a metaphysics of agency is mimetically reflected in the grammar of agency. It would, moreover, constitute a form of linguistic quietism to conclude that however grammar is currently used is the way that it must be used, as if the forms of life encoded there are not problematically restrictive, as if new forms of life have not challenged grammar to permit something other than what already firmly exists within its terms.

It seems to me that simple assertions of agency have emerged from at least two different sources in recent decades. The one is the theory of power as it takes place in the vicissitudes of culture. The other is psychoanalysis as it insists upon the unconscious as that which decentres claims to self-transparency. In Stuart Hall's introduction to *Questions of Cultural Identity*, he traces the various ways in which psychoanalysis, as a theory of the psyche, is brought into contact first with Althusser's theory of the interpellated subject and then with Foucault's theory of subjection and subjectivation.[1] Hall points out that agency takes a more pronounced position in Foucault's writing as he turns to consider the practices of freedom. And although Hall warns that 'there is certainly no single switch to "agency", to intention and volition', Foucault's emphasis on 'practices of freedom prevent(s) this subject from ever being simply a docile sexualized body'(p. 13). The discourse on subjectivation produces 'for the first time in Foucault's major work the existence of some interior landscape of the subject, some interior mechanisms of assent to the rule', which makes clear that the decentring of the subject is not its destruction (p. 13).

But what is left of the subject once it is decentred, and where are we then to find its agency? Hall refers us to Foucault's notion of 'the deliberate stylization of daily life' which becomes the reiterated condition of the subject's self-production. This turn to an aesthetic category to describe the constitution of the subject is, as usual, open to ethical critique. Notice in the following characterization offered by Slavoj Žižek how quickly the notion of the stylized self-production of the subject slides into the production of the fascinating sexual spectacle:

> With Foucault, we have a turn against that universalist ethics: each subject must, without any support from universal rules, build his own mode of self-mastery; he must harmonize the antagonism of the powers within himself – invent himself, so to speak, produce himself as a subject, find his own particular art of living. This is why Foucault was so fascinated by marginal lifestyles constructing their own particular mode of subjectivity (the sadomasochistic homosexual universe, for example: see Foucault 1984).[2]

Žižek recasts gay sadomasochism as a 'homosexual . . . universe', global and monolithic in character, and figures Foucault as its fascinated observer, and thus misses the sense in which sadomasochistic sexual practice is a *practice* (not a 'universe'), stylized not merely by a self who 'invents' him- or herself, but one for whom sexual norms are constitutive without, therefore, becoming deterministic. This sexual subject receives, appropriates, and revises norms of sexual exchange, domination, and constraint in a social context in which legal, ethical and political denunciation, exposure, internment, pathologization, and criminalization are ever possible. Whereas Hall points to the practices of self-production in Foucault as the signs of a new region for agency in a post-Althusserian scene, Žižek proceeds to invoke Althusser as the 'solution' to the impasse he envisages between a universalistic Habermas and a particularistic Foucault.

Indeed, Foucault's effort to establish the subject in its self-production as a ritual affair does not, however, dissociate from the Althusserian project. Remember the place of ritual, the temporal reiteration of social structure, in Althusser's very definition of ideology, as well as his insistence that ritual links the ideational dimension of a practice with its material status: 'practices are governed by rituals in which these practices are inscribed, within the material existence of an ideological apparatus', and 'ideas are . . . material actions inserted into material practices governed by material rituals which are themselves defined by the material ideological apparatus from which derive the ideas of the subject'.[3]

If we were to consider sexual practice as one such ritual, or consider, in Žižek's parlance, the bathhouse 'universe' in terms of its enduring practices, as Gayle Rubin's recent ethnography has done, we are engaged with bodies that negotiate a series of tense, erotic relations with one another in spaces that are governed by zoning laws, in states and cities with various legal strictures against public sex and/or sodomy.[4] The acts performed are not radically sequestered from the larger economic and legal context in which they are performed, and there is also a way, significantly, that that context is *also* performed precisely through the sexual acts themselves. Hence, the self is not produced *ex nihilo*, and the 'stylization' of the subject under such conditions is not itself radically voluntaristic self-invention, but a negotiation of patrolled urban space, of the public circumscription of sexuality, of the place and meaning of consent, freedom of association, and the pursuit of pleasure not over and against its constituting limits, but a pursuit for which limits become the condition of eroticization itself. In other words, it is not as if the ready-made subject meets its limits in the law, but that the limits that the law sets decide in advance what will and will not become a subject. Sadomasochistic practice might then illustrate the way in which erotic constraints operate as the condition of possibility for sexual agency. This 'limit' is not a static foreclosure, a boundary that is in place and known once and for all, but precisely that which is worked (made to resignify and reverse its usual meanings, parody itself, display its own impossibility) and in being worked, becomes the occasion for eroticization.

Of course, some biographers such as James Miller in recent years have offered tired dismissals of Foucault's theory of power as the projection of a sadomasochistic point of view, reducing his reflections on the constitution of the subject to the psychological reductionism of biography. These views tend not to ask what, however, the theoretical consequences of sadomasochism might be, how it operates, in its specificity, as a sexual practice, its relation to its conditioning contexts, its place and meaning within the emergence of marginalized sexual communities at risk of public censure and repression. In the place of such an inquiry, sadomasochism is offered as the trope of fascinating perversion, part of an accessible visual culture of commodified sexuality.

Although it would doubtless be a mistake to uphold sadomasochism as the paradigmatic allegory for the production of the subject – a move that would generalize in an unwarranted way from a sexual practice to a non-sexual mode of self-constitution – it would be mistaken as well, I believe, to consider sadomasochistic practice as if it had no relation whatsoever to typically modern or late-modern modes of self-constitution. In other words, it may be that this apparent 'aberration' lays open something central to the operation of the norm.

If sadomasochism involves the 'working of a limit', then to what extent does it offer an example of a relation to the norm which is neither that of simple acceptance or refusal. It exposes a vexed relation to a set of norms, ones that not only call into question the fixity of the norm, but underscore the difficulty of working it, rendering it malleable, and working it through, turning it into something else. The limit becomes material to be worked, but it is also there, insistent, as *the* material to be worked, obdurate, but not for that reason unyielding. The action on the limit, we might say, produces a new possibility for a subject, one who was supposed to be bound by the limit, one who moves past the norms of civility that bound the 'human' – control its morphology, its orifices, its positionality, its appearance of freedom – to a deformation and contestation of those very norms. On one level, the question may be posed in this way: how does a human come to perform this or that act, acts that may well put certain civilizing norms into question (barriers against defecation, for instance, which seem central to most notions of 'civilization', but also acts that put gender itself into crisis or that refigure forms of dominant social power through fantasy which puts the mimetic status of fantasmatic enactment into crisis).

The question, however, cannot be restricted to that of how a subject comes to accept or refuse or even 'work through' – in the sense of 'overcome' – certain social positions, cultural norms, or political identifications, since certain kinds of acts put the status of the subject into crisis. As Hall insists, the question of the subject must also include an inquiry into the mechanisms of its self-constitution. Power does not exist over and against the subject or, perhaps better said, it does not exist *only* in such an exterior relation. The subject is itself constituted through the embodiment of certain norms that establish in advance and with considerable social force what will and will not be a recogniz-

able subject. Indeed, this is the abiding limit of the Hegelian struggle
for recognition. A subject does not simply come upon a scene in which
it recognizes another as itself and then worries the line of non-
differentiation that besets that encounter. For the subject to 'come
upon a scene' and to be capable of recognizing something as similar to
itself implies that its self and its other already conform to some pre-
established norms of recognizability. Such subjects have been entered
into the norm of the human prior to any recognition, and recognition
consists precisely in the reflective awareness that each has already been
constituted as 'human'. Accordingly, the failure of recognition in such
a scene indicts the norms of intelligibility that govern the constitution
and exclusion of subjects from the variable sphere of the human.

A socially instituted act that puts the subject into crisis thus brings us
to psychoanalysis, and to the possibility of a mutually productive
relation between Foucault and psychoanalysis. Hall thinks that this
relation is possible, and asks us, indeed, indirectly asks me to think
further about this subject.[5] It is clear that both Foucault and psychoanalysis (of the non-egological sort) produce post-foundationalist views
of the subject, views that maintain that the subject is not its own
foundation, cannot ground itself, cannot come to know and grasp its
'ground' and, thereby, gain conceptual mastery of its own conditions
of emergence. The kinds of differentiation that individuals undergo, as
they attain the status of subject, involve the individuals' insertion into
grammars of bodily action and speech, grammars that regulate the
bodily performance of speech ('rituals' in the Althusserian sense). The
differentiation of human from animal takes place precisely through
this accession to speech – an accession that involves what we might call
the grammatical control of the body. When we ask what, in these
instances, 'differentiation' means and whether such differentiations
work (what it might mean to say that they work), psychoanalysis enters
precisely as an analytic perspective that allows us to understand how
that from which we are differentiated continues to condition us essentially, how differentiation is not abolition, and how the 'not-me',
although not finally fully recoverable by us or, indeed, produced by
our acts of repudiation, is never fully sequestered as a psychic elsewhere. It enters *as an absence* into the scene of the present as its
interruption, its compulsion, its necessity.

If we accept, then, the formative status of exclusion, differentiation,
and repudiation (without collapsing them too easily into one another),
what happens when we return to this very field of differences through
a theory of power? Will psychoanalysis be the generalized theory that
provides the account of the genesis of the subject through differentiating – and binding – relations (relations, in other words, founded in

ambivalence), or will it be subject to a redescription on the basis of a political critique of the norms of intelligibility that orchestrate the genesis of the subject? In one sense, no political regulation of the subject's genesis can take place without identification and differentiation, and these later processes or, rather, *fantasies* never quite work in the way they are supposed to. That from which I am differentiated returns to me at the heart of what I am. By virtue of the repression that cuts and grips and forms me, I am perhaps least capable of expressing what is repressed within the grammatical modes that the differentiating process has made available to me.

But the 'I' who is in this bind does not rest easily there, for I also understand something of the problem that the prevailing grammar imposes upon me, and rail against it. And though the political temptation is to insist that all that remains unspeakable become speakable now and in the future, the fulfilment of that demand would entail the unravelling of the subject and the demise of political agency itself. And yet, the fact that subjects are variably excluded from the sphere of the human, the intelligible, the speakable, means precisely that we do struggle against those confining and life-denying norms. We struggle against them, seek to establish new norms of intelligibility, and yet cannot fully transform all that is unspeakable in our genesis into what is speakable.

Those who would insist on the priority of a structuralist psychoanalysis to any consideration of social power will dismiss the 'railing' against the limits of speakability as a doomed and defeated enterprise, and will refer the politicization of the problem back, as it were, to the stark reality principle of psychoanalytic law. And those who fear that psychoanalysis will emerge as a foundationalism debasing and reducing the political sphere will be tempted to dismiss psychoanalysis altogether, charging it with a failure to politicize adequately the scenes of founding and formative exclusion. I can feel the allure of each position as I write them, knowing I am in grip of both discourses, wondering what or who this 'I' might be who finds itself articulated precisely as this particular vexation.

When a psychoanalytic foundationalism mocks the claims of political agency as the 'pathos' of a necessary failed resistance, and when a political response asserts a limitless agency as a counter to that pathos, we see the bind of agency eluded from two different directions. For it is one thing to struggle, politically, to extend the claims that might be made in the name of the human, to overcome the exclusions that have formed the human in violently restrictive ways, and quite another to claim that a full overcoming of all the exclusions that form the human might be made. A full reversal of every formative exclusion into an 'inclusive feature' would undo the condition of the subject itself, leading to a bloated form of Hegelian aggrandizement or, equivalently, a psychotic unravelling that would, paradoxically, signal the end of all deliberate agency. So one struggles to overcome certain exclusions without the possibility of overcoming every one. And what makes this problem more difficult is that these exclusions are not clearly separable by kind. For what are the social and political exclusions that return us to the primary structures of subject formation, that call into question the possibility of being a subject at all, a subject of the predicate 'human'? That we are all formed by certain exclusions means simply that we are all vulnerable to those pervasively social occasions in which the tenuous status of the subject is brought into stark relief, the occasions in which we are not sure we are among those interpellated as the enfranchised, the survivable, the intelligible. That psychic fragility of the subject is precisely what gives a particular meaning to the dissolution of the subject wrought through political means, through the circumscription of norms by which recognition is conferred and received: it is our psychic vulnerability to exploitation, what threatens us with a loss of the sense of survivability.

If the subject is produced in ritualized and stylistic ways, as a practice that takes shape and changes through time, it is also that which is at risk of not being produced or, indeed, of being undone or destroyed.[6] There is no fervent *conatus* that guarantees the survivability of every subject. The occasions in which the norms that govern the recognizability of the human operate to exclude a potential member from the fold are ones that exploit the demand for an enduring life, a sustaining ritual, only to thwart its satisfaction. Living – if one can call it 'living' – on this hard edge is irreducibly psychological and political at once, and it is, we might say, precisely the socially regulated psychic condition for the emergence of the humanizing norm. We have doubtless failed to reconcile the political and the psychoanalytic on the question of agency, but perhaps we have cleared the way to ask another sort of question, one that brings the question of style together with the urgency of survival: how do we read the agency of the subject when its demand for cultural and psychic and political survival makes itself known as style? What sorts of style signal the crisis of survival? What sort of hermeneutics do we need to read the subject in its tenuous relation to cultural emergence, a hermeneutics that does not take the self-constituting subject for granted, but reads its life-and-death struggle with its conditioning norms in the agrammatical styles of its emergence?

Notes

1. Stuart Hall, 'Introduction: Who Needs "Identity"?', in Stuart Hall and Paul du Gay, eds., *Questions of Cultural Identity* (London: Sage Publications, 1996).

2. Slavoj Žižek, *The Sublime Object of Ideology* (London: Verso, 1989), p. 2.

3. Louis Althusser, *Lenin and Philosophy and Other Essays,* translated by Ben Brewster (New York: Monthly Review Press, 1971), pp. 168–9.

4. See Gayle Rubin's anthropology dissertation at the University of Michigan: 'The Valley of the Kings: Leathermen in San Francisco, 1960–1990'.

5. I did this to some degree in *The Psychic Life of Power* (Stanford, CA: Stanford University Press, 1997) just after the publication of *Questions of Cultural Identity* (1996), but see that more is to be done on the question of norms, identification, and desire, as he suggests. See Hall, 'Introduction', p. 15.

6. See Stuart Hall and Tony Jefferson, eds., *Resistance through Rituals: Youth Sub-cultures in Post-war Britain* (London: Routledge, 1975).

5

The State of War and the
State of Hybridization

Néstor García Canclini

What will we take with us from the twentieth century into the twenty-first century? This is one way to phrase the question about what we understand today by the patrimony of humanity. This question has been prompting varying answers in recent decades. At first, we compiled lists of goods that made different cultures proud. Then, debates arose because the goods recognized as the patrimony of humanity were associated with colonialism and imperialism. In addition questions were raised about the tendency to overvalue tangible, monumental goods to the detriment of intangible ones, such as language and music which, because of their key role in the maintenance and cohesion of societies, deserved to be preserved as patrimony.

As the twentieth century came to an end we found that a good part of the assumptions that nourished those definitions of patrimony have been modified. We live in a globalized world where imperialist and national structures, differences between the tangible and the intangible, the monumental and the everyday, and even the very notion of humanity are no longer the same as our characterizations of them twenty years ago. What we consider valuable or representative of all humanity and necessary for its reproduction has also changed.

Today we value transnational resources which are not, or should not be, controlled only by one government as goods of humanity. Biodiversity is one of those. Another example is found in the messages produced by the culture industry: thus, supranational agreements are made to encourage audiovisual co-production and international regulation of those messages keeping in mind public interests. If the decision about patrimony, about what will be conserved from the twentieth century for the next, is to a great extent a matter that exceeds each nation, it becomes key to understanding how interactions between societies are being reformulated.

Globalization, or the West versus the Rest of the World?

If we adopt this more ample vision of what one epoch hands over to another, cultural heritage does not comprise simply a list of monuments and goods but also certain ways of distinguishing them and interrelating them. The second half of the twentieth century bequeathed to the future a new mode of interconnection between cultures that has come to be called globalization. There is no agreement concerning whether the growing interdependence among nations is leading towards the integration of markets and communications, homogenizing ways of life and modes of thinking, or if it generates new forms of diversity and makes confrontations between distant cultures more complex.

There are two narratives that attempt to account for these tensions between globalization and interculturality. The first is that which recounts globalization as a process of world integration, in which ethnic and national differences would dissolve. A brief way of explaining this is through the metaphor proposed by Yukinory Yanagi at the Venice Biennial of 1993, at the multinational showing of urban art *In site*, held in 1994 in Tijuana and San Diego, and at the Biennial of San Paulo in 1996. The experience consisted of placing some one hundred flags of various countries of the world on top of a wall, all made with small acrylic boxes filled with coloured sand. The flags were interconnected by plastic tubes through which travelled ants that went along corroding and mixing up each one of those flags. After two or three months all of them had become unrecognizable. Yanagi's work can be interpreted as a metaphor of workers who, as they migrate through the world, go about breaking down nationalisms and imperialisms. But not all receivers paid attention to that. When the artist presented this work at the Venice Biennial, the Society for the Protection of Animals managed to close it for a few days so that Yanagi would not continue the 'exploitation of the ants'. Other reactions arose from the fact that the spectators could not accept seeing the differences between nations destabilized. The artist, on the other hand, was trying to take his experience all the way to the dissolution of identity marks: the species of ant found in Brazil seemed too slow to Yanagi, and he expressed fear at the beginning of the exhibition that it would not be able to disrupt the national flags sufficiently.

Yanagi's transformational game coincides with the accounts that present globalization as a system of flows and interactivity that positions all peoples in a situation of co-presence. Nevertheless, various anthropologists call attention to the fact that 'flows have directions' and preponderant settings. Those principal settings are almost all found in the United States and Japan, some still in Europe and almost none in Latin America or Africa. Some of these marginal regions produce counterflows, for example exhibitions of African artists in London and therapeutic groups in Oslo that base their work on Malayan techniques of dream interpretation (Hannerz 1996, 1997), but these and other recognitions of crafts, literature and peripheral knowledges do not allow us to forget the asymmetry of the fluxes, manifested in the unequal dissemination of fundamental abilities and modern institutional forms, of Western types of basic and advanced education. Nothing allows us to expect that at the beginning of the new century globalization will eliminate the distances between centres and peripheries.

The other narrative, circulated principally in the political field, discerns a certain complexity within globalization, but reduces it to wars between cultures. The impetuous advance of the market economy that has taken hold of almost the entire planet, including the countries of the former Soviet region, has led some to declare the end of the period of economic and ideological conflict. Authors such as Francis Fukuyama and Samuel Huntington claim that the confrontations on which we must now focus are wars between cultures: Western, Confucian, Japanese, Islamic, Hindu, Slav Orthodox, Latin American and African. As the world shrinks there is an intensification of exchanges between diverse conceptions in matters as basic as that which is individual and that which is communal, the rights of men and women, equality and hierarchy. It is foreseeable, then, that ethnic and religious conflicts will worsen, conflicts in which negotiation is more difficult than it is in either economic or political conflicts. According to Huntington (1998), this confrontation can be summarized as encounters between the West and the East.

There was no lack of examples in the 1990s to support these premonitions. The Gulf War – interpreted by many Arabs as 'the West against Islam' – and the confrontations between Catholics and Muslims in former Yugoslavia and other zones are alarming pieces of evidence that could multiply. But there is also much information about another type of interaction in which the hybridization of diverse cultures is possible. Not all religions are dominated by fundamentalists, nor do all modes of giving continuity to one's own culture allow each patrimony to be conceived as a compact totality, closed to changes and mixings. The coexistence of cultural systems in one country does not always lead to its division, nor does a high number of foreign migrants always end fatally in racist fights.

The narratives of global homogenization and of the conflict between cultures correspond to processes that are taking place, but they leave out a large number of facts. How can we explain that in societies with half a century of accelerated industrial development, like Brazil and Mexico, ethnic crafts continue to be produced, and that modern sectors – in the same countries and in others even more developed – buy them and use them on their bodies and in their homes? Why do folk musics from Africa, Asia and Latin America, whose disappearance was announced by the expansion of modern education and of culture industries, continue not only to be strong but also to take advantage of communication technologies (radio, television, compact discs) to gain distribution beyond the original territories? The millions of Latin Americans who live in the United States make it possible to conclude that Los Angeles is the third-largest Mexican city and that Miami is the second-largest Cuban city. These and other intercultural interlacings, which do not dissolve under homogenization and do not imply only conflicts, have encouraged a growing use of the term 'hybridization'.

The Current Debate over Hybridization

Strictly speaking, hybridization is not a question of a new process. Many modern nations were formed, on all continents, by mixing cultures. Often, national integration was articulated around the symbolic patrimony of the elite, of European origin, and without recognizing socio-cultural heterogeneity. But this heterogeneity is emerging, and more and more is asserting its demands in political cultures. In many societies, *mestizaje* and syncretism attain recognition both in the law and in everyday practices (Kymlicka 1996). Nevertheless, the elaboration of the concept of 'hybridization' effected in recent years seeks to confront a different problematic to that the previously cited notions embrace. *Diversity* and *heterogeneity* are terms that serve to establish catalogues of differences, but they do not account for intersections and mixings between cultures. The term *mestizaje* tends to be limited to what happens to races, to the biological aspect of the crossings, while *syncretism* almost always refers to fusions of religions or of traditional symbolic movements.

Hybridization can embrace these 'classical' mixings and also include interlacings of the traditional and the modern, of elite, popular and mass cultures. One characteristic of the second half of the twentieth century that makes a more inclusive concept necessary is that all these types of intercultural fusion intermixed and reinforced each other during that period.

This *descriptive* contribution to the notion of hybridization can acquire *explanatory* power if we situate it within structural relationships of causality or correlation, and it can also operate as a *hermeneutic* resource when it alludes to relationships of meaning. In order to fulfil these last two functions, it is necessary to articulate hybridization with other concepts, such as modernity/modernization/modernism, social integration/segregation, difference/inequality and reconversion. I am going to synthesize here a few recent analyses that justify the use of the expression 'hybridization' epistemologically, and that permit us to show its utility for the development of democratic cultural politics.

1. *Hybridization, as a social process, has not been in the past nor has any reason to be in the future a natural or infertile integration.*

Those to whom we speak about hybridization sometimes question the use of this notion which comes from the biological sciences. Isn't the hybrid something infertile, like a mule? Doesn't 'cultural vitality' reside in 'the capacity for the reproduction and renovation of culture' (Schmilchuk 1995)?

We know that examples of productive, enriching hybridizations exist in biology which generate expansion and diversification. Karpeah-enko's experiments which crossed radishes with cabbages succeeded in making use of cells originating from different plants in order to improve the growth, resistance and quality of the product. The majority of corn developed commercially in the United States is the result of processes of hybridization undertaken by geneticists to improve its strength. We also see the hybridization of human DNA in order to produce proteins, a process that has become the principal method of generating insulin.

In any case, I don't see why one should remain trapped in the biological dynamic from which the concept is taken. The social sciences have imported many notions from other disciplines without having them invalidated by the conditions in which they are used in the originating science. Biological concepts such as that of reproduction were re-elaborated to talk about social, economic and cultural repro-duction: the debate carried out from Marx until today over such reproduction is founded on the relationship of the theoretical consist-ency and the explanatory power of this term; it does not derive from any fatal dependence on the use that another science assigned to it. Similarly, the polemics over the metaphorical use of economic concepts to explain symbolic processes – for example by Pierre Bourdieu in his reference to cultural capital and linguistic markets – should be centred not on the migration of these terms from one discipline to another but on the epistemological operations that situate the explanatory productivity of any new concept and its limits in the interior of cultural discourses: does it permit a better understanding of something that hithterto had remained unexplained, or not (Bourdieu 1979)?

The linguistic (Bakhtin, Bhabha) and social (Friedman, Garciá Canclini, Hall, Papastergiadis) constructions of the concept of hybridization have collaborated in moving beyond biologistic and essentialist discourses of identity authenticity and cultural purity. They help to identify and explain multiple productive alliances: for example, between cultured and popular languages (Bakhtin); between the pre-Colombian imaginary and that of the New Spanish colonizers, and later that of the culture industries (Bernard 1993; Gruzinski 1988); between the popular aesthetic and that of tourists (de Grandis 1997); between national ethnic cultures and those of the metropolis (Bhabha 1994); and among global institutions (Harvey 1996). The few written fragments of a history of hybridization have demonstrated the productivity and innovative power of many intercultural mixings.

Frequently hybridization transcends the simple fusion of discrete social structures or practices that existed separately: by combining, they generate new structures and new practices. At times this occurs in an unplanned fashion, or is the unforeseen result of the practices of migration, tourism, or economic or communicational exchange. But often hybridization arises from individual and collective creativity – not only in the arts, but also in everyday life and in technological development. We seek to reconvert one patrimony (a factory, professional qualifications, a set of knowledges and techniques) in order to reinsert it into new conditions of production and market. Reconversion: this term is used to explain the strategies through which a painter becomes a designer, or the national bourgeoisies acquire the languages and other skills necessary to reconvert their economic and symbolic capital within transnational circuits (Bourdieu 1979: 155, 175, 354). Strategies of economic and symbolic conversion are also found in popular sectors: migrant farm workers who adapt their knowledges in order to work and consume in the city, or to fit their crafts to modern uses in order to interest urban shoppers; the workers who reformulate their culture of labour given the new productive technologies; the indigenous movements that reinsert their demands into transnational politics or into ecological discourse, and learn to communicate them through radio and television. For such reasons, I maintain that the object of study is not hybridity, but instead the processes of hybridization. The empirical analysis of these processes, articulated to strategies of reconversion, shows that hybridization is of interest both to hegemonic sectors and to popular sectors which desire to make the benefits of modernity their own.

2. *While there are many linguistic and social examples of productive
hybridization, these are multidirectional and do not favour a single
programme or meaning of the exchange and fusion. They may contribute to
the dissolution of weak cultures located in a situation of inequality, they
may promote multicultural integration or emancipation, and they are also
capable of stirring up intercultural contradictions.*

Cultures do not coexist with the serenity with which we experience
them as we pass from one room to the next in a museum, but neither
can their interaction be reduced to wars. In order to understand
cultural interactions, it is necessary to construct through investigation
a typology that will recognize the diverse contexts and experiences of
hybridization as part of the conflicts of modernity. Without claiming to
be exhaustive, I am going to differentiate three types of hybridization:
those that occur in the processes of migration; those that result from
hegemonic cultural politics; those that are constructed in markets of
communication.

(a) *Hybridization in processes of migration.* The social sciences have constructed the theory of modernity as a theory of nations organized by
states (Beck 1998). By imagining nations as homogeneous communities
(with a history, a language, a market), the question of intercultural
differences was reduced during the nineteenth century and the first
half of the twentieth to differences between nations. Thus the tremen-
dous migratory movements that occurred during that period remained
hidden, as well as the complex processes of multiculturality and hybridization that they generated.

The massive migrations to which we are so sensitive today were not
lesser during the nineteenth century or the early twentieth century. It
is calculated that between 1846 and 1930 some 52 million people left
Europe, of whom 72 per cent travelled to the United States, 21 per
cent travelled to Latin America and 1 per cent travelled to Australia.
Those who most contributed to these movements were from the British
Isles (18,020,000 immigrants). Of the Europeans who arrived in Latin
America in this period, 38 per cent were Italians, 28 per cent were
Spanish and 11 per cent were Portuguese. The majority of these
migrants chose Argentina as their destination, followed by Brazil, Cuba
and the Antilles, Uruguay and Mexico. At the beginning of the twentieth century the total population of Europe was 200 million people;
thus one quarter of them left. With respect to the Americas, the arrival
of migrants during the period 1840–1940 raised the population of
Argentina by 40 per cent, that of the United States by 30 per cent and
those of Canada and Brazil by approximately 15 per cent.

These migrations generated, as we know, interethnic syntheses, important hybrid products such as jazz, tango, and a large part of what today is known as Afro-Caribbean and Afro-Brazilian music, and novel mixings in architecture and the visual arts. Nevertheless, the formation of transnational hybrid circuits remained submerged – until a few years ago – under national homogenizing politics laid out according to a uniform conception of modernity.

(b) *The hybridization of cultural politics.* Although states tended to subsume migratory multiculturality in national identities, there were different ways of doing this, with more or less possibility of acknowledging the 'impure' processes of hybridization. In Argentina a compact economic, political and military system formed a nation in which the Indians were exterminated and millions of Spaniards, Italians, Russians, Jews, Syrians and Lebanese were ethnically 'refashioned' through mass education (Tedesco 1986). In Mexico, on the other hand, the indigenous population was subordinated to the national white *criollo* project of Western modernization, permitting a *mestizaje* in which indigenous social relationships and cultural products survived with limited possibilities of reproduction; nevertheless, Mexico may be the Latin American country where Spanish integration with the natives was the most successful from the point of view of the hegemonic sectors and of the now-questioned stability of the national political system.

The case of the United States was very different. Although the expression 'melting pot' may be compared to notions like '*crisol de razas*' or 'cultural pluralism' used in Latin America, in the United States the separate identification of the migratory contingents was preserved: the originating opposition between 'whites' and 'blacks' continued to diversify with the arrival of diverse European, Latin American and Asian nationalities. While in almost all of Latin America cultural politics sought integration under one white, hegemonic pole, in the US a segregated model was established in which identities are affirmed in a more essentialist way: 'multiculturalism means separatism' (Hughes 1993). In more democratic conceptions the diverse ethnic and cultural traditions are legitimated, and, through affirmative action, the mixing is limited. Michel Walzer states that the acute conflict today in North American life does not oppose multiculturalism to a particular hegemony or singularity, to 'a vigorous and independent North American identity', but instead 'a multitude of groups to a multitude of individuals' (Walzer 1995: 109).

In contrast to the previous cases, Brazil presents a national society more available for hybridization. Without denying its enormous inequalities, class and regional fractures, various anthropologists highlight the 'multiple interpenetrations' that exist between the migratory contingents that formed it. Frequently political leaders, for example the president, Fernando Enrique Cardoso, speak about their African or indigenous ancestors, and view ethnic affiliations as voluntary and able to be mixed. The African culture especially permeates the society as a whole in a 'diffuse and enveloping' way: this is demonstrated not only by the transethnic and transclassist convocation of carnival (da Matta 1978; Segato 1997), but also by the ubiquity, in all segments of society, of the idea of possession by spirits, which originated in Afro-Caribbean tradition and was reinforced by syncretism with European spiritism. Many ethnic components, through playful practices and rituals, and also through cultural politics, are introduced into the patrimony of other groups and come to form part of their horizon. Without losing their distinctiveness, the identities are less monolithic. The centrality of possession by spirits, as a 'founding and common experience of Brazilian society, could be considered a metaphor' of 'allowing oneself to be inhabited by the other', while still recognizing it as other (Segato 1997: 15–16).

Movements of hybridization occur in each of the three states discussed above. Therefore, it is not consistent to talk about pure or authentic identities, even in the countries where cultural politics seek to constitute these as such, not in Argentina, not in Mexico, not in the United States, not with respect to White, or Anglo, or Chicana or Black identities. Hybridization proceeds in different ways according to how the migratory movements succeeded in expressing themselves in either a homogenizing institutionality (Argentina), one that favours heterogeneity (US) or one more prone to fusion (Brazil). It also depends on the interactions that have occurred in each country, and in each epoch, between hegemony politics and social movements.

(c) *Hybridization as an operation of markets of communication.* Current population movements are distinguished not so much by their size as by other characteristics. The migrations of the nineteenth century and the first half of the twentieth, which were also massive, were almost always definitive, and disconnected those who left from those who remained, while current displacements include permanent, temporary and tourist transfers as well as brief business trips. Another difference is that nowadays a large proportion of migrants or travellers maintain easy communication with their places of origin: we are able to buy newspapers from our country of origin in many other countries, and cable television in hotels and homes in European and some Latin American countries allows access to channels from the United States. Electronic mail and networks of families and friends have turned what used to take weeks or months into uninterrupted intercontinental contacts. To come ashore is not the same thing as to touch down, nor is a physical voyage the same as electronic navigation. Today interculturality is produced more through mediating communications than through migratory movements.

In recent years, hybridization has been realized through the transfer of populations and – even more – through mass communications and the integration of markets. The capital, goods and media messages pass from one country to another more freely than people. It is easier to send messages and even to make investments in a foreign country than to become a citizen. As mass displacements are facilitated – not so much of migrants as of tourists, commercial operators, academics and students – these movements accentuate the deterritorialization of practices and the heteroclite appropriation of diverse repertories. But above all it is audiovisual and electronic communications, subject to the rules of market expansion, that activate hybridization within each country and in a transnational form.

Given that markets are ruled by competition, and that globalization intensifies competition, hybridization tends to be presented in trade circuits as *reconciliation and intercultural equalization.* Races living together on Benetton's publicity posters; flamenco, Italian, English and even non-European melodies that overcome their local differences in concert tours by the Three Tenors; global exhibitions, Olympic spectacles and sports festivals that 'join all peoples as brothers' and offer everyone simple versions of the diverse and the multiple; the zapping that permits us to link up in a few minutes with channels from fifteen or thirty countries: these are some of the experiences that create the illusion that the cultural repertory of the world is at our disposal in a pacified and comprehensible interconnection.

When hybridization is the mixing of elements from many diverse societies whose peoples are seen as sets of potential consumers of a global product, the process that in music is called equalization tends to be applied to the differences between cultures. Thus, in the same way that through electronic tricks in recording and reproduction variations in timbre and melodic styles lose their specificity, incompatible cultural forms can much too easily become commensurable.

The search for an aesthetic of resonant equilibrium that saw its first manifestations in airports, restaurants, malls and other places that sought to 'climatize' the atmosphere is now spread through industrial recording techniques that eliminate 'discord'. Carvalho (1995) has studied some of the principal procedures used: (1) the intensities of distinct musical genres and instruments, pianissimos and fortissimos, are balanced out so that they are heard as part of an orchestral homogeneity or subordinated to the line of the voice; (2) the abuse of the effect of interference or reverberation of sound in shows and bars, which diminishes the capacity of the listener to catch the most subtle passages, is extended to the habits of groups of young people, and even individuals with Walkmans, for whom the best way of listening to music is with the highest amplification and volume of the sonic mass; (c) the compact disc establishes the standardizing paradigms of listening by offering 'purified' versions that are presented as if they were produced in acoustically balanced rooms, with the perfect orchestra, and with the spectator in the ideal position for listening – the equalized recording, with the impartial listening subject always in the centre (de Carvalho 1995).

Forged as a device of Western taste, equalization becomes a procedure of tranquillizing hybridization, a reduction of points of resistance from other musical aesthetics, and a reduction of the challenges that diverse cultures bring. Under the appearance of amiable reconciliation between cultures hides the pretence that we are able to be near others without worrying about trying to understand them. Like hurried tourism, like so many transnational filmic superproductions, equalization is often an attempt at monologic climatization, the forgetting of differences that do not allow themselves to hybridize.

It is a question not only of a process of abolition of differences, but also of a covering up of the inequalities of access to the production, circulation and consumption of culture. An analysis of the strategies of commercial hybridization should situate them in what Ulf Hannerz calls the 'political economy of the culture inherent to the mestizo continuum', that is to say, the distribution of centres and peripheries, and even the 'coexistence of various continuums instead of one unique and inclusive continuum' (Hannerz 1997: 115–16). The fact that the centre sometimes hybridizes in the peripheries and with elements of those peripheries, and that migrants and peripheral messages sometimes hybridize in the centre (discs of ethnic music recorded in New York; Miami, Mexico City and Buenos Aires converted by MTV, all at the same time, into the capitals of Latin American rock) does not mean that the centre and the periphery disappear.

Cultural Politics Based on Hybridization?

We thus see that hybridization is not synonymous with reconciliation among ethnicities or nations, nor does it guarantee democratic interactions. It is a point of departure from which to break from fundamentalist tendencies and from the fatalism of the doctrines of civilizing wars. It serves to make us capable of recognizing the productivity of exchanges and crossings, it enables us to participate in a variety of cultural repertories, to become multicultural gourmets, to travel between patrimonies and savour the differences (Werbner and Modood 1997; 11). Historical patrimonies, understood in this open and changing way, can be enriched and act as bridges of understanding between different societies. But hybridization can also be the place in which cultures lose their defining characteristics or are thwarted, as is demonstrated by the migrants who are forced to renounce their language or who watch it disappear in their children.

It is true, as Nikos Papastergiadis affirms, that hybridization – such that it conceives of identity as 'constructed through a negotiation of difference' – has served as 'principal organizer for international cultural initiatives' (Papastergiadis 1997: 257–8). But hybridization does not by itself guarantee democratic multicultural politics. By being not only the sum of the contributions that converge in it but 'the third space that makes the emergence of other positions possible' (Bhabha 1994: 211), hybridization is more than a simple overcoming that denies and conserves, that synthesizes opposites, like the Hegelian *Aufheben* (Beverley 1996); it is a field of energy and sociocultural innovation. It can be exhausted as a scene of equalized World Music, but it is capable, at the same time, of promoting unforeseen unplugged improvisations. It can be a pretext for commercial manoeuvres or a support for conversations that inaugurate unexpected visions. It is not just cultural meanings that circulate in the processes of hybridization; in addition the relatively arbitrary and contingent character of all culture is experienced, one of the bases of the recognition of difference that is necessary in the democratic game.

As tends to happen in other topics of cultural studies, Stuart Hall particularly has progressed in the political analysis of hybridization. Here I want to evoke the incisive clarity with which he responded to a text in which I was presenting a few of these questions at the University of Stirling in October 1996. He said that one of the merits of hybridization is that it 'undermines the binary way of thinking difference'. Nevertheless, he explained, we must rediscover a way to talk about difference not 'as a radical alterity, but as *difference*'. While one difference, a radical alterity, opposes one system of difference to another, we are negotiating the processing of a difference that slips permanently within another. It is not possible to say where the British end and where their colonies begin, where the Spanish end and where Latin Americans begin, where Latin Americans begin and where the indigenous do. None of these groups still remains within their original limits. What is happening is a kind of Derridean expression about the erasure of all these terms. That is to say that boundaries, borders, instead of detaining people, are places that people cross in a continuous manner, illegally (see Hall in Morley and Chen 1996).

'Seeing through' is not achieved in the same way in the three modalities of hybridization discussed above. The analytical distinction between them seems to me to be useful for analysing limits, but in order to overcome them it is necessary to place in relationship critically the possibilities of hybridizing that these distinct processes offer. A hybridization initiated as a sociocultural movement, for example certain successful Mexican crafts, certain tropical types of music or music of protest, can be converted into products that enact the recognition of the exotic or the reconciliation between cultures in a transnational market. Innovative aesthetic constructions can become market operations: magical realism, which in Alejo Carpentier and in García Márquez's first novels placed a value on hybridizing synthesis and played with the surprise of non-routine intercultural associations, became a marketing device in the literary and filmic *macondismo* of the eighties and nineties. And vice versa: a homogeneous fusion of cultures under the trade rules of globalization can be deglobalized when we reconstruct its original environments, the sociocultural meaning that caused it to arise. I'm thinking of some of Wim Wenders's films and of the adaptations of media slogans in order to express local political demands.

One of the necessary political tasks today is to rework the difference and the inequality in hybridizations of the global and the local, to discover how the old patrimonies of humanity and the new patrimonies of globalization are at the same time specific modes through which local cultures found themselves and had to decide if they would enter into war or into hybridization. Borges wrote that perhaps the aesthetic element is the 'imminence of a revelation' in 'the faces worked over by time, a certain twilight and certain places' or music that 'wants to tell us something', 'or something that they said we should not have lost, or they are about to say something' (Borges 1994: 13). Perhaps the patrimonies that are worth keeping are formed not only of works in which a self-sufficient history (official or popular) is sedimented or of products well tailored by the market so that everyone is able to digest them, but also with those works in which beats the imminence of uncertain encounters, when a collection of men and women feels challenged by another culture and has to choose between hybridization and confrontation.

Translated by Kristin Pesola

References

Appadurai, Arjun (1996) *Modernity at Large: Cultural Dimensions of Globalization*, Minneapolis, University of Minnesota Press.

Beck, Ulrich (1998) *Qué es la globalización?*, Barcelona, Paidós.

Bernand, Carmen (1993) 'Altérités et métissages hispano-américains', in Christian Descamps, ed., *Amériques latines: une altérité*, Paris, Editions du Centre Pompidou.

Beverley, John (1996) 'Estudios culturales y vocación política', *Revista de crítica cultural*, Chile, No. 12, July.

Bhabha, Homi K. (1994) *The Location of Culture*, London and New York, Routledge.

Borges, Jorge Luis (1994) 'Ostras inquisiciones', in his *Obras completas*, Vol. II, Buenos Aires, Emecé Editores.

Bourdieu, Pierre (1979) *La Distinction*, Paris, Minuit.

da Matta, Roberto (1978) *Carnavais, Malandros e Heróis*, Rio de Janeiro, Zahar.

de Carvalho, José Jorge (1995) 'Hacia una etnografía de la sensibilidad musical contemporánea', *Serie Antropología*, Brasilia, Department of Anthropology, University of Brasilia.

de Grandis, Rita (1997) 'Incursiones en torno a la hibridación: una propuesta para discusión de la mediación lingüística de Bajtin a la mediación simbólica de García Canclini', *Revista de crítica literaria latinoamericana*, Lima–Berkeley, Vol. 46, No. 2.

Friedman, Jonathan (1997) 'The global struggle for cultural identity and intellectual porkbarrelling: cosmopolitans versus locals, ethnics and nationals in an era of de-hegemonisation', in Pnina Werbner and Tariq Modood, *Debating Cultural Hybridity*, London and New Jersey, Zed Books.

García Canclini, Néstor (1990) *Culturas híbridas*, Mexico, Grijalbo (translated into English as *Hybrid Cultures*, Minneapolis, University of Minnesota Press, 1995).

——(1997) 'Hybrid cultures and communicative strategies', *Media Development*, Vol. XLIV, No. 1.

González Martinez, Elda E. (1997) 'Españoles en América e iberoamericanos en España: cara y cruz de un fenómeno', *Arbor*, Madrid, CLIV, 607 (July).

Gruzinski, Serge (1988) *La Colonisation de l'imaginaire*, Paris, Gallimard.

Hannerz Ulf (1996) *Transnational Connections*, London, Routledge.

——(1997) 'Fluxos, fronteiras, híbridos: palavras-chave da antropología transnacional', *Maná*, 3(1): 7–39.

Harvey, Penelope (1996) *Hybrids of Modernity*, London, Routledge.

Hughes, Robert (1993) *Culture of Complaint: The Fraying of America*, New York, Oxford University Press.

Huntington, Samuel P. (1998) *El choque de civilizaciones*, Mexico, Paidós.

Kymlicka, Will (1996) *Ciudadanía multicultural*, Barcelona, Paidós.

Lommnitz, Claudio (1995) *Las salidas del laberinto*, Mexico, Joaquín Mortiz.

McLaren Peter (1994) 'White Terror and Oppositional Agency: Toward a Critical Multiculturalism', in David Theo Goldberg, ed., *Multiculturalism: A Critical Reader*, Cambridge, Blackwell.

Morley, David, and Chen, Kuan-Hsing (1996) *Stuart Hall: Critical Dialogues in Cultural Studies*, London, Routledge.

Papastergiadis, Nikos (1997) 'Tracing Hybridity in Theory', in Pnina Werbner and Tariq Modood, *Debating Cultural Hybridity*, London and New Jersey, Zed Books.

Schmilchuk, Graciela (1995) 'La fabrica de identidades', paper presented to the symposium 'Beyond Identity, Latin American Art in the 21st Century', Austin, Texas, 21–22 April.

Segato, Rita Laura (1997) 'Alteridades históricas/identidades políticas: una crítica a las certezas del pluralismo global', work presented to the Simposio Central del VIII Congreso de Antropología in Bogota.

Tedesco, J. C. (1986) *Educación y sociedad en Argentina (1990–1945)*, Buenos Aires, Solar.

Velho, Gilberto (1992) 'Unidade e fragmentacao em sociedades complexas', in Velho, Gilberto and Otávio, *Duas conferencias*, Rio de Janeiro, forum de Ciencia e Cultura.

Wallach, Lori M. (1998) 'Golpe de estado contra el Estado' *Le Monde diplomatique*, Mexico, No. 10, March–April.

Walzer, Michel (1995) 'Individus et communautés, les deux pluralismes', *Esprit*, Paris, June, pp. 103–13.

Werbner, Pnina, and Modood, Tariq (1997) *Debating Cultural Hybridity*, London and New Jersey, Zed Books.

6

Critical Dialogues on Chicana/o Cultural Studies

Angie Chabram-Dernersesian

1. By Way of an Introduction

Chicana/o cultural studies? A multiply positioned critical practice where . . . new social, political and theoretical alliances and publics are made possible; (critical) languages are strategically 'interrupted' by the markings[1] of emergent social identities and productions; the border zones between different forms of 'critical' intellectual work are continuously negotiated; 'American' cultural studies gets unpacked, pluralized, and relocated; cultural studies meets area studies; and we re-encounter 'the ones who came before us'. However partial, this abbreviated description captures some of the elements that have surfaced within a little-examined Chicana/o *and* cultural studies legacy that imagines a cultural studies movement with 'different histories', 'different conjunctures and moments in the past' (Hall 1992). In the pages that follow I record a series of critical dialogues with cultural practitioners who reflect on the encounter between cultural studies and Chicana/o studies; the new formations of cultural studies; the nature of some of our travels to cultural studies; and the importance of Stuart Hall in generating new cultural studies agendas.

Together these dialogues form part of an ongoing study which was initially inspired by the probative question. '[J]ust what is it that we (those of us who make some claims to be doing "cultural studies") do?' (Gray 1996: 203). In my particular context, grappling with this question meant not only recovering – and coming to terms with – important shifts and decisive ruptures in Chicana/o critical epistemologies. This endeavour also meant generating a discussion about some of the 'movements of the past' with cultural practitioners who claimed a cultural studies affiliation. In short, it meant engaging in a critical retrospective around a contemporary practice of cultural studies which was visibly 'different' – and providing another 'public' forum where we could voice some of 'the intellectual conditions, frustrations, retreats, desires', and figures that led us to form either personal or professional 'connections' to cultural studies.[2]

Clearly these dialogues are 'partial' representations; not only do they have to be edited and reassembled but also they do not examine all the pressing issues that have inspired some to affiliate with cultural studies formations and others to disaffiliate. However, they do capture important positionalities that continue to matter within an emerging cultural studies legacy that values the importance of criticism and self-criticism, and that is not exhausted by any single intervention. In Sections 2 and 3 I drive home this point by punctuating a conversation with a thematic collage of critical interventions, which provide a sampling of a greater collective as well as counter points.

I initiate this representation of dialogues in Chicana/o cultural studies with an excerpt from a conversation I had with Rosa Linda Fregoso in December 1997. Years ago we co-edited a special issue of *Cultural Studies* (October 1990) which engaged Stuart Hall's work on cultural representations. Here we address some of the developments that have contributed to the formation of a conjunctural relationship with cultural studies. We began our conversation with a discussion of her book *The Bronze Screen* (1993).

2. Reframing Alternative and Critical Discourses: A Conversation with Rosa Linda Fregoso, Professor, Davis, California

ACD: Rosa Linda, I thought that we could begin our discussion by reflecting on a statement that you made in your introduction to Chicana/o film cultures, where you talk about how you got into cultural studies. There you outline how you initially came to know Chicano films through a nationalist formation in south Texas; your theoretical formation in San Diego; and your confrontation with the 'return of the repressed' (your early nationalist formation) in the workforce as an academic. You also highlight the importance of the writings of US Third World feminists and the studies (on race–gender–sexuality) undertaken by the cultural studies group in Birmingham in terms of how they allowed you to re-view Chicana/o films with 'fresh eyes'.

What was very interesting in this autoethnography was the way in which the cultural studies perspectives got filtered through a kind of re-routing and partnering of critical discourses and cultural studies legacies. I wanted you just to elaborate on this re-routing and partnering of critical discourses, which speaks to a different kind of connection with cultural studies. . . . Clearly, it sidesteps the widely circulated idea that cultural studies is an imperial model, which in this case has been transplanted from Europe into Aztlan for 'native consumption'. This is disturbing to me; here we have no agency, and within this mind-set, cultural studies is singularized and unaffected by its travels. . . .

RLF: And the model is completely inappropriate. I think that cultural studies participates in paradigm shifts in scientific thought. . . . Cultural studies allows one to see social reality in terms of networks and interrelationships as opposed to seeing reality in terms of objects and in terms of objectivity. Cultural studies acknowledges the fact that any theoretical approximation is always partial, never absolute. So this idea of a model that you just impose on an object is a very kind of Cartesian idea. . . . And cultural studies is about problematizing those views of reality, opposing the idea that you can just apply those paradigms from the outside of the objects that you are analysing. Cultural studies suggests that the way you look at the object is affected by the object itself.

ACD: I would like to turn for a moment to a discussion of how people are framing the discussion of cultural studies legacies around the issue of 'origins'. Some people argue that we've always already done cultural studies in ethnic studies or Chicana/o studies, so what's the fuss? Clearly, this is intended to end the conversation! I think that this idea stands in sharp contrast to the spirit of our initial contact with cultural studies . . . to the whole idea of double positioning that we tried to relay in that introduction to the cultural studies volume. Looking back, we were very conscious of the fact that we were doing something very *different* there, both within the native legacy of Chicana/o studies, and the broader cultural studies legacy. . . . We were aware of the fact that this work was not the old-style Chicano studies, and that it was also different from what people understood as cultural studies *per se.* Here I'm referring to widely popularized representations that often engage in certain types of erasures of hybrid cultural studies legacies. You know, the ones that mention a black cultural studies (in the US and Britain), or a generic ethnic studies or feminism or women's studies. Those of us who are contextualizing cultural studies in particular ways – or operating in a variety of fields simultaneously or nuancing important connections, well this model just completely negates us.

Now that people are just disclaiming or claiming this emergent space of cultural studies, I think it's important to ask why there has been an interest in cultural studies. What has the cultural studies network provided this generation with?

RLF: One of the things that I feel kind of gelled and came together for us is that our previous formations had not allowed us to see the complexity of objects that we were looking at, because we were being confined by a disciplinary framework. So if you were going to do a Marxist literary criticism, it had to be a particular way. If you brought in gender or race, that wasn't Marxist criticism. . . . The foundation of Marxist literary theory was about class, so that everything else was either superstructural or ideological – or peripheral to the analysis of class.

What did cultural studies contribute? I think that what cultural studies allowed one to do was not to privilege any one axis. What was privileged here was intersectionality, multiplicity, the interplay of all of these things. . . . Ultimately that's the only way that your analysis becomes more refined. That's why I like to talk about the field of cultural studies as a network. I find it very useful because it's almost like the object is within the network, and the network is pluralized. I don't mean to say it's pluralized in a pluralistic way, but pluralized in terms of multiplicity. And I think cultural studies enabled one to see that. And let me say that while there's been a kind of co-operation of cultural studies, for me cultural studies is not just about studying culture; it's about studying culture in a particular historical context that is itself constituted in terms of power relations. In the USA, those power relations are racialized, those power relations are classed; they are gendered; and they are sexualized in particular ways. So if you are going to deal with culture in this country, you've got to deal with those contradictions.

For me cultural studies has a political agenda, which is to usher in a more egalitarian society. If you want to talk about its socialist under-pinnings – its anti-capitalist, anti-racist, and anti-imperialist underpin-nings . . . They are there . . . I don't think that you can deny that in the work of Raymond Williams – he was anti-capitalist; the work of Stuart Hall, who refined cultural studies to add a kind of anti-racist critique; and the feminist critique of McRobbie . . . Cultural studies is always about transforming social relations of exploitation and oppres-sion, and that's the only way I can talk about it. To talk about cultural studies as pluralism – that's not cultural studies, it's an apolitical project.

ACD: How do you see this kind of cultural studies network interacting with US Third World feminism?

RLF: US Third World feminism allowed me to contextualize and specify cultural studies in a US context. (It grounded cultural studies for me.) I think I make the point when I talked about the various intellectual and cultural traditions that influence my work. I embrace these traditions through the rebel spirits of US Third World feminists who reside 'between and among different subject positions and critical cultural discourses'. . . . My cultural studies approach is a *mestizaje*, a bricolage.

I'd also like to emphasize that this, the US, is the context that I study, and that this context has impacted my approach. . . . And I think that's what the articulation (of cultural studies) is about: locating cultural studies socially and historically, and engaging the context in which you're working.

ACD: Would you like to add anything to what you've said about the objection that has been raised – that 'we were already doing cultural studies'?

RLF: The idea that 'we were here first'? This is the flip side of the imperial model. There's a kind of hierarchy of oppressions behind that idea that 'we were always already doing it' that makes me mad. There's a mantra there that makes me very uncomfortable because it's colonialist. Who cares if you didn't call it cultural studies (before) and now we call it cultural studies? Let's go from here, let's trace the genealogy (in the Americas), but let's not say, 'We were here first.'

I think that perhaps the new social formation of Chicana/o studies intersects with cultural studies in a much more productive way than the old Chicano paradigms, which were very vertical. They assumed that we were all working-class in origin, instead of saying we were working-class in solidarity: this was supposed to guarantee our politics.

ACD: I also think that there were certain presuppositions lurking behind the idea that 'we've always done cultural studies' that dictated how far you could manoeuvre theoretically and put limits on who you could speak to.

RLF: But you know what? Initially I was reflecting on the paradigms of the older generation, but I see these problematic trends with the younger people too in ethnic studies who are claiming a modified version of the vertical Chicano studies model. This model looks at race in a very essentialist way. So now, they've got all the people of colour grouped together, because here you don't look at gender, you don't look at sexuality. This is a race theory, and the paradigm is still very

vertical. . . . When you really get down to it, this is very antithetical to
the cultural studies project. Because cultural studies is about all kinds
of oppressions and all kinds of social transformations. . . . That's our
world and that's our work!

The more contradictions you find, the more you've got to struggle
around. I mean, I'm not tired of it: . . . *Dále más.* [Go for it/Step on it.]
There are more things to think about now, and *si te aburres de uno* [if
you get bored of one], you go on to another one.'

ACD: I think the idea that 'we've always already done cultural studies'
is a way to suppress these contradictions. There's a nationalist subtext
there.

RLF: But that's not true, we haven't been doing it all the time. Chicano
studies was about examining racial oppression, so they (the ones who
claim that) haven't been doing cultural studies all the time. . . . That's a
myth, no they were doing race, then class. . . . Among the initial pieces
that theorized culture, such as in Juan Gómez's work, class was the
foundation, and then he added race (*lo mexicano*). Race was like a
superstructural representation. . . . Race was class and race was ideology,
and that's how they studied culture. . . . They didn't look at it in terms
of gender, and they didn't deal with sexuality or other axes of oppression
and exploitation. All those things were considered to be superstructural.

ACD: I'd like to move along to the nineties. There's a way in which our
introduction moved away from earlier paradigms in that it speaks to a
kind of recognition of what Stuart Hall calls 'the end of innocence'.
There's a recognition there of the fact that even when you are working
in the alternative sector with the best of intentions, there aren't any
guarantees. . . . Clearly just quoting a Chicano doesn't offer any guarantees. (We learned this early on in San Diego, right?) What matters is
how you are going to change or enlighten the critical project. . . . If a
multicultural studies formation does it, well, that's OK. That's a Chi-
cana/o cultural studies too.

RLF: Well, in reference to citation, I also want to add that I think it's
important to be strategic. Chicanas/os have had such a hard time
coming into theoretical discourse. So if I can find a Chicana/o that says
the same thing as Stuart Hall, I like to quote her or him. I also think
it's important to muddle the discourse up, to dirty it up, you know. . . .
Meter a las rasquachis [the irreverent improvisational aesthetic of the
poor or downtrodden] there *también* – put us, the *rasquachis*, in there
too. You know what I mean?

ACD: I think a late-nineties style of *rasquachismo* is a way to go. I base a lot of my work on recovering the sayings of public intellectuals who are not recognized as such. But I also get a kick out of having them 'talk' to Stuart Hall. I like to create dialogic spaces where cultural studies discourses are 'worlded'.

RLF: For me it's the same thing about film. I like to write about films that nobody would write about, except people in the independent community. But this is not about any kind of essentialist belief that the Chicana/o perspective is better, or that it is more lucid. It's about the fact that I'm committed to muddling up the canon, to complicating it. . . . There are people who don't have any institutional clout, but have similar perspectives to influential critics. . . . If I can quote my mother – if my mother's saying something very similar to Kristeva – well then I'll quote my mother . . . It's all very strategic. . . .

As far as the end of innocence . . . I think I finally got it through to my Chicano film students when speaking about post-Chicano Movement film. We are in a stage where we don't have to be perfect for white people. We can talk about our contradictions, talk about what's wrong with Chicanas/os, and talk about it *publicly*. It's like airing dirty laundry, and this is a discussion among ourselves. If white people are listening in, who cares? When you keep all the dirty laundry inside, you're never gonna talk about the shit. I think maybe that's what you are relating to in terms of the end of innocence of the Chicano subject. And I think Chicana feminists broke the ground on this because they began to air the dirty laundry in the 1970s and the 1980s.

(In Section 3 I interject other reflections on Chicana/o cultural studies and cultural studies, which engage these and other issues concerning overlapping concerns. Constraints of space prevent a more inclusive representation of my dialogues with these and other practitioners.)

3. Broadening the Discussion: Other Exchanges, Other Positions

Always already Chicana/o cultural studies?

Rafael Perez-Torres, Professor of English, Los Angeles, California:
I think Chicana/o cultural studies is a different space. Here there's a calling into question of earlier categories within Chicano studies (notions of race, for example), especially when the issues of hybridity, hybridization and *mestizaje* are raised. Then there's a questioning of

sexual and gender categories. So that even the nature of what opposi-
tionality is in Chicana/o studies comes into question.

What's enabling this space of cultural studies is what Chicana femi-
nist/womanist and *mestizaje* consciousness have brought to the table.
That is to say, an awareness of the fact that difference is itself different.
That there's difference *within*. (November 1997)

Michelle Habell-Pallan, Professor of Ethnic Studies, Seattle, Washington:

To say that we've always done cultural studies, well in a sense that's
true. We've always studied culture and how Chicano culture is suppressed by dominant culture, but I think that the conversation changes.
We're trying to create an oppositional culture, but the conditions of
the world have changed. Chicano studies can only get richer by
engaging theories that address the way different marginalized peoples
in different locations are talking back to the dominant culture and
transforming the dominant culture. (April 1998)

Raymond Rocco, Professor of Political Science, Los Angeles, California:

I absolutely don't agree with the idea that we've always been doing
cultural studies, even though we didn't know it. I think that the majority
of us from the seventies and eighties were trained in rather strict
disciplinary terms. . . . I didn't see much in terms of real transdisciplinary work there, so I don't think Chicano studies was really into it
[cultural studies]. What I think you had was a gathering of people
together into Chicano studies from History, Spanish, English. . . . I
don't think that was interdisciplinary – I think it was an amalgam of
groups. . . .

That issue of *Cultural Studies* that I participated in . . . I think it was a
very propitious time for that type of intervention. The fact that it was
well received was a verification – an affirmation – of the fact that the
old ways were really not paying off, and that we needed to bring
together the interdisciplinary . . . or actually the transdisciplinary. What
I saw in that issue was a real attempt – given the limitations of our
training – a trying to engage across our disciplinary lines, which is what
I think cultural studies is urging. (February 1998)

Richard Chabrán, Director of the Center for Virtual Research, Riverside, California:

Well, in some ways, Chicano/a studies prefigured many of the debates
which would later take place in cultural studies, and this is seldom
acknowledged. In the early period in Chicano studies, there was a

rebellion or a speaking-out against traditional works and disciplines. But ironically, at the same time, many Chicano graduate students were being trained in traditional methods within the academy, especially within an empirical method. This method (number-crunching, certain types of archival work, even literary criticism) gained strength during the late seventies and early eighties in the social sciences and the humanities. It was really at the height of that trend that some of us realized that those approaches could not suffice to answer some of the questions that underlay Chicana/o studies. That's when I started to read outside. I need to mention the importance of Raymond Williams here; clearly he was against the kind of mechanical Marxism that was also prevalent during his time, so he tried to open spaces for the cultural moment. This really corresponded to how I felt about Chicano studies at that point because that's when political economy was also very strong in Chicano intellectual circles and its application was very mechanical. This didn't allow us to take into account the way people lived questions of race, class or gender. Culture was seen more as institutional mechanisms rather than phenomena that people lived. . . . So Raymond Williams really helped us to see that the moment of culture was very important within emerging societies.

Rosaura Sánchez, Professor of Literature, San Diego, California:
For me, of course, cultural studies and Marxism go together – I can't do cultural studies without doing it from a Marxist perspective. For example, I've written on the *testimonios* [dictated recollections of the original Spanish-speaking settlers of California] (in *Telling Identities*, 1995), which would be considered by some as historical texts, but to me they are *testimonios*,[3] popular texts, which had not been published because they were not seen as 'literary'. Looking at these non-canonical texts required that I do a historical analysis of the period, of the texts, and of the individuals involved. And this required that I also do an analysis of those who like Hubert Howe Bancroft [a rich San Francisco book dealer and publisher] would profit from the words of those people who wrote for them. In some cases these people would only be given a footnote or not even be credited for their recollections in the writings of others. So, for me the whole cultural production was as important as the text itself. . . . Even Bancroft saw this production as a cultural enterprise, or, as he called it, 'cultural industries'. He paid people to write, so he took credit as the author.

That's one example of how I do cultural studies. . . . Cultural studies is not only about looking at the present. You can do cultural studies work on the past. . . . And cultural studies is determined not simply by the object of study but also by the type of analysis. How you look at the object (under analysis) is important. And so in that sense, you could be looking at popular music, such as rap or *conjunto* for instance, and not be looking at the practice of the text as a social and political product and as a commodity or commodified practice. One also needs to study the relations of the object (rap or *conjunto*) to other texts and consider as well the place of music within this period of late capitalism.... For me, these elements have to come into play for the analysis to be cultural studies.... And no, we've not always done this kind of work, even when we've done work on popular culture. (July 1998)

On the relationship between Chicana/o studies and cultural studies

Michelle Habell-Pallan:
You know that sometimes there's no relationship [between them]. Sometimes cultural studies doesn't want to see Chicana/o studies and vice versa.... If there's a general thing called cultural studies, well this formation sometimes overlooks Chicana/o voices. At least in Chicana/o studies you are going from the assumption that Chicanas/os are speaking subjects and intellectual subjects! This is something you might have to fight for in the larger cultural studies that might tend to see race as black and white. (April 1998)

Alejandra Elenes, Professor of Women's Studies, Tempe, Arizona:
One of the fears that people have now is that scholars have gravitated to cultural studies, and redefined cultural studies from the inside (of Chicana/o studies). So that a lot of the major works in the field of Chicana/o studies are very cultural-studies-focused. I'm very much into cultural studies – and I want to push it – because it has really good things to offer, but I am also in favour of a [Chicana/o studies] discipline that can be multifaceted.... I am aware that whenever you focus too much in one area (cultural studies), other areas might fall. (February 1998)

Richard Chabrán:
A clear difference between Chicana/o studies and cultural studies is cultural studies' refusal to be contained with a discipline or to view itself in this institutional form, while Chicana/o studies has always fought to be viewed as a discipline and as a separate institutional space. (December 1997)

Rafael Perez-Torres:
Chicano studies brings different ways of thinking about the intersections between high culture and popular culture.... In the articulation

of Chicano studies, high culture is always the unspoken other, the unspoken evil. High culture doesn't exist for us . . . right? So there's an uncoupling of the high culture/low culture paradigm that's significant. . . . Another difference is the highlighting of racial categories that are not strictly in terms of black or white. I guess what I'm saying is that in cultural studies there's this idea that culture develops out of hybrid moments. Within Chicano studies that hybridity is always connected to some type of racial or historical connection. So hybridity is never innocent, it's always engaged in a kind of power dynamic that's related to colonialism, to the local history. (November 1997)

Staking the claim: a Chicana/o Latina/o cultural studies

Rafael Perez-Torres:
Yes, yes, yes, and I think we should stake a claim, but I don't think that claim should be the ultimate claim, like 'This is . . . alterity's statement on cultural studies!' I think that that's a danger that's already been articulated in certain formations of Chicano studies, OK? This is what I think Chicana/o cultural studies should avoid. It should avoid becoming the-voice-of-the-colonized cultural studies. (November 1997)

Michelle Habell-Pallan:
While I write about transnationalism, feminism, and the violence that women have to endure, the artists are providing the inspiration on where to go. They are talking about families living on both sides, about aunts working in the US but living in Mexico; and immigrant women coming to work in the sweatshops of LA. That's why I find Chicana feminism so useful, but that's not to say that I'm not engaged in the writings by black British cultural studies. My readings of Stuart Hall have been very helpful for me in understanding issues of popular culture and issues of race. (April 1998)

Rosaura Sánchez:
The importance of Stuart Hall? He generates a lot of ideas in terms of the work I'm doing on Chicanos. About ten years ago, I became aware of his work on ideology (the more Althusserian work). At the time I was interested in looking at the text as discursive construction. This of course requires a social and historical analysis, an ideological analysis of discourse. . . . Stuart Hall helped in that sense. . . . And, as I told [Carlos] Blanco at the time, 'This man is saying what I want to say.' So, after that, I began looking for more of his work in the library, and found absolutely nothing. But from Hall's bibliography, I found out about the group in Birmingham. So I started looking at what they were

doing, and I was especially impressed, not only by the theory on ideology and popular culture but also by the way that they worked. They produced several articles that included work by professors and students. After I read their work, I started to talk to my graduate students, and I suggested that maybe we could produce this type of collaborative theoretical work. . . . I decided to do a seminar in English, and I did a course on cultural studies. . . . I tried to introduce the students to what was going on. And then we started talking about cultural studies in the department. . . . Later (at UCSD), we created a cultural studies section and began attracting graduate students, and I was the head of the section for several years . . . (July 1998)

Frances Aparicio, Professor of Spanish and American Culture, Ann Arbor, Michigan:
My interest (in Puerto Rican and Latino popular music) was pretty much inspired by the postmodern narratives that were coming out in the seventies in Puerto Rico. That's how the critical project (for *Listening to Salsa*, 1998) began. Then I realized that this approach was very limited, largely because of all of the theory coming out in cultural studies and the work that was being done on popular culture. This work helped me to realize that I had more options in terms of approaching the subject. . . . I wanted literature to be another voice, another cultural text that was addressing larger issues about gender, race, and cultural identity. So, both literature and music became complementary voices in the study of these larger issues. (September 1998)

José David Saldívar, Professor of English/Ethnic Studies, Berkeley, California:
'What Chicana/o cultural studies offers the loose group of tendencies, issues and questions in the larger cultural studies orbit . . . is the theorization of the US–Mexico borderlands – literal, figurative, material, and militarized – and the deconstruction of the discourse of boundaries. . . . If the international cultural studies movement . . . is an ongoing discursive formation, with no simple origin, cultural theory in the US–Mexico borderlands has charted itself in the multiple discourses of ethnography, feminist theories of subjectivity and oral history . . . ethno-racial and historical becoming, and the politics of postmodernism and postcolonialism.' (from *Border Matters*, 1997, pp. 25 and 29)

Notes

1. Slashes, hyphens, x's, and unexpected vocalizations, to name a few.

2. I am building on Herman Gray's observation here. He asks: 'And what is the nature of our travel to cultural studies – that is, what are the intellectual conditions, frustrations, retreats, desires that lead us to cultural studies?' (Gray 1996: 203). My reading of Chicana/o cultural studies epistemological shifts is influenced by Stuart Hall's essay 'Cultural Studies and Its Theoretical Legacies', and in particular, his framing of the 'positions that matter'. My representation of Chicana/o cultural studies through 'critical dialogues' is an effort to reckon with the under-representation of Chicana/o voices in general representations of cultural studies. Finally, my take on *rasquachismo* is affected by the writings of Yolanda Broyles and Tomás Ybarra on the subject. I would like to thank all the critics who have granted me these interviews. Many of these critics are listed in the text as Professors, and this is intended as a reference to occupation, not professional rank.

3. Rosaura Sánchez explains that testimonials are 'narratives of identification'. She elaborates: 'In all testimonials, the subaltern seizes the liminal space of mediated representation to "write" or narrate identity. In view of the subaltern's separation from hegemonic means of production, the testimonial is the subaltern's site for constructing collective identity or identities, be it in terms of class, gender, culture, or nation, within hegemonic spaces' (p. 12). See 'Testimonials as Dependent Production' in her *Telling Identities* (pp. 1–49). This discussion sets the stage for her discussion of the testimonials of the Californios, a conquered and dominated population, who were approached by agents of Bancroft to narrate their past as part of a research project on California history.

References

Aparicio, Frances (1998) *Listening to Salsa: Gender, Latin Popular Music, and Puerto Rican Cultures*, Hanover, NH: University Press of New England.

Chabram, Angie, and Fregoso, Rosa Linda, eds. (1990) *Chicana/o Cultural Representations*, special issue of *Cultural Studies*, Vol 4, No. 3, October.

Chabram-Dernersesian, Angie, ed. (1999) *Chicana/o Latina/o Studies: Transnational and Transdisciplinary Movements*, special issue of *Cultural Studies*, Vol. 13, No. 2, April.

Fregoso, Rosa Linda (1993) *The Bronze Screen: Chicana and Chicano Film Culture*, Minneapolis: University of Minnesota Press.

Gray, Herman (1996) 'Is Cultural Studies Inflated? The Cultural Economy of Cultural Studies in the United States', in Cary Nelson and Dilip Parameshwar Gaonkar, eds., *Disciplinarity and Dissent in Cultural Studies*, London, Routledge, pp. 203–16.

Hall, Stuart (1996) 'Cultural Identity and Cinematic Representation', in Houston A. Baker Jr, Manthia Diawara and Ruth H. Lindeborg, eds., *Black British Cultural Studies: A Reader*, Chicago: University of Chicago Press.

Hall, Stuart (1992) 'Cultural Studies and Its Theoretical Legacies', in Larry Grossberg, Cary Nelson and Paula Treichler, eds., *Cultural Studies*, New York: Routledge, pp. 277–94.

Saldívar, José (1997) *Border Matters: Remapping American Cultural Studies*, Berkeley: University of California Press.

Sánchez, Rosaura (1995) *Telling Identities*, Minneapolis: University of Minnesota.

7

At the End of This Sentence a Sail Will Unfurl . . . Modernities, Musics and the Journey of Identity

Iain Chambers

The particular form of 'globalization' which is undermining and transforming modernity today (the internationalization of production, consumption, markets, and investments), is only the latest phase in a very long story; it is not a new phenomenon.[1]

The result is: the tendentially and potentially general development of the forces of production – of wealth as such – as a basis; likewise, the universality of intercourse, hence the world market as a basis. The basis as a possibility of the universal development of the individual, and the real development of the individual from this basis as a constant suspension of its barrier, which is recognized as a barrier, not taken for a sacred limit.[2]

. . . the horizon spins slowly and Authority's argument diminishes in power . . .[3]

In a string of words, a handful of images, a temporary organization of thought, I wish to propose neither commentary nor critique, but rather a tentative discussion that begins in the space provided by Stuart Hall's 1996 essay 'The Question of Cultural Identity'.[4] Here, called upon to consider the question of identity in the context of global modernity, I am invited to take up a critical journey that reveals a necessary questioning of the political and cultural premises of my world. What I propose to add to this invitation is to follow a series of tracks that I feel Stuart himself would appreciate: those of the historical traces and cultural testimony disseminated by music. These are tracks destined to cross critical terrain and historical itineraries – pertaining to political economy, cultural agency, conjunctural analyses, that is, to the composite historical delineation of cultural studies –

that Stuart's work over the past three decades has done so much to establish and illuminate.

Perhaps identities have always been in process, in question, open-ended and in the making. What, today, has seemingly become more acute with the 'crisis of identity', located in a critique of certain existing forms of ethnic, linguistic, national, sexual and gendered individuality, is the impossibility of ignoring that perpetual sense of process by appealing to a stable or fixed state. Rendered vulnerable by proximity and the intersection of my world by the worlds of others, my identity is both contested and reconfigured in the reply to such 'intrusions'. The countervailing excursion of other identities into 'my' world, induced by the breaking open and scattering of a previous locality, is invariably explained in terms of the radical configuration of late modernity; a late modernity that has been irreversibly invested by the interactive econ-omical, social, cultural and political procedures of 'globalization'. And yet, as Stuart insists, if this specific drama is also accompanied by 'that slow and uneven but continuing story of the decentring of the West', then identity formation also invokes deeper historical currents.[5] I am carried back at least to that instance in which the West and the 'world' are recognized and institutionalized as stable conceptual frames of reference in a particular period, place and population.

The instance the West identifies itself and simultaneously establishes the world in its image is clearly the historical moment when a certain intellectual and cultural formation confidently brings all within and under a single point of view, subject to a unique and unilateral perspective. Fears and desires are objectified, a sense of 'home' and 'abroad', of the domestic and 'otherness', is firmly established. What today is experienced as a 'loss' is surely the security of such premises? And if this 'world picture' (Heidegger) is an integral part of the initial disposition of Occidental modernity, of its powers and the subsequent mapping of itself on the rest of the globe, then its contemporary interrogation, displacement, dislocation, perhaps alerts us to a poten-tial epochal shift? It is this particular narrative of coherence and spatial reasoning, this individual story and collective his-story, that, Stuart justly reminds us, is increasingly being interrupted, truncated, brought to a self-conscious stutter in the presence of other narratives with their claims on the world.

When the 'outside' of the European subject constitutes an 'inside' of egocentric design and desire then all the world becomes its stage. Notwithstanding the later sociological understanding of symbolic inter-actionism and its notion of identity emerging in the relationship between self and society, here we encounter an already more complex historical, cultural and psychic configuration in which there emerges a historically elaborated self rather than a stable essence who is subsequently stitched or 'sutured' into external political and cultural structures. The 'out there' is also 'in here': 'no man is an island, each is a part of the main', John Donne famously reminds us. This is to propose not merely a commonwealth of identification, but also an uncomfortable understanding of identity, including its deepest psychic recesses, being formed, articulated, extended and explored as a 'way in the world' (V. S. Naipaul) that has precise historical, political and philosophical contours and configurations. Such is the space, and the limits, of modern, Occidental identity.

This is a prospect that shifts our gaze back in time, even beyond the usual critique of the Enlightenment as representing the triumph of a unilateral and imperious rationality, to heed an earlier epoch and set of circumstances in which the world was for the first time considered as a single entity, however unknown and unexplained, subject to uniform conceptualization, trade, industry, mapping, exploration and exploitation.[6] For prior to the summation of knowledge in the *Encyclopédie* there had already emerged in altogether less systematic manner the powerful structures of modern science and modern racism, just to render disturbingly proximate two crucial dimensions of Western modernity. If not here, in an epoch of scientific revolution, European conquest, plantation slavery and global trade and colonialism, where does modernity commence? This may be to modify Foucault's deeply instructive reading of the eighteenth-century systemization of the 'order of things' by stretching backwards through the altogether less ordered figurations of the Baroque into the late Renaissance. Alongside the elegant edifice of Foucault's crucial *oeuvre* it offers an altogether more ragged account as a complement, not a confutation.

This suggests that the much-quoted process of 'globalization' is not simply a contemporary phenomenon but is integral to the making of Occidental modernity from the beginning. It was inaugurated with the possibility of reducing the world to a single map or 'world picture', to a single point of view representing the interests and desires of the Occidental observer. The black diaspora out of Africa into slavery, the systematic exploitation and genocide of the Americas, were central, not peripheral, to the global making of the modern Western world. Within this modernity the specific geopolitical location of the observer assumes a universal relevance; subjectivity and objectivity become one. This, of course, is Occidental humanism, and it helps us to understand the political significance of 'post-humanism' as the reinscription of locality and limits into the point of view, the voice, the knowledge, that now finds itself speaking in the vicinity of a heterogeneous, rather than homogeneous, world; a world, as Paul Gilroy consistently reminds us, that was historically constructed in terror as well as in reason.[7] In this sense, we are all postcolonial: it is not merely a question for the other, a minority culture or subaltern history. We in the West are all postcolonial in the moment we respond to the invitation to return and relocate our histories in a worldly response and responsibility.[8]

In all the present-day discussion on 'time–space' compression, the vector of velocity, and the unprecedented scale of technological innovation and social transformation, there is the danger of overlooking, underplaying or simply ignoring this deeper historical structuration of modernity and the radically violent alignment of the globe from a European point of view. Speed, space and time, in their varying velocities, extensions and precision, remain inherently universal categories. To talk of the present world as a compressed reality living in overdrive is perhaps to accept too hastily the teleology (and theology) of a linear temporality in which modernity, however geopolitically diverse and historically uneven the pace, results homogeneous, unilateral and inevitable in its 'progress'. The inequitable, the irruptive, the regressive, the deviant and the heterodox, what remains out of joint and whereby modernity is brought to account in specific historical places and cultural locations, where it is translated and transformed into something more (or less) than its proponents foresee, tends to be banished from the breathless prose of many present-day critics and social scientists (Jameson, Harvey, Giddens, Virilio). No going back, no return, no revisiting, no memory that is not historically transparent, is contemplated ... the accounting of time and identity, of being and possibility, however diverse and irregular the pace, moves in only one direction: towards the teleological tyranny of the future. While apparently critiquing the omniverous powers and presence of capitalism, the *telos* of technology and the propaganda of 'progress', this style of criticism inadvertently celebrates and succumbs to their potency. Confidently responding to the history of modernity in the self-fulfilling explanation of a rationalized condition, such analyses conveniently avoid the ambiguity, uncertainty and opaqueness of a disquieting historical respons-ability that might also augment critical sensibility.[9]

For modernity is not only about *trans*national flows, velocities of change, the dispersal of tradition and the omnipotence of 'progress'; it is also about *trans*mutation, traces, survivals and living on. Violence is deeply embedded in the equation. Teleology is confronted, and sometimes confuted, by translation.[10] Modernity is also a home for metamorphoses, for the multiple and the unacknowledged. Even a concept such as hybridity, apparently so attuned to the idea of a disrupted and reworked modernity, is not immune to the criticism of overemphasizing the planetary power of the modern in unilaterally determining local sense. For hybridity itself does not involve a single, homogeneous effect or set of semantics. The recent use of industrial materials in the making of decorated shields in Papua New Guinea, for instance, does not necessarily or automatically imply a globalization of the local, or vice versa. In fact:

> a preoccupation with hybridity may exaggerate the extent to which particular cultural expressions relate to the Western origins of the materials, objects, forms or images that are employed. The meanings things possess are defined in the context of their use. They are not prescribed by their producers. Hybridity may be an appearance salient to an outside viewer rather than a condition that is in any way significant to local people engaging in a particular practice or producing a particular form.[11]

As a minimum this suggests a doubling and dislocation of the semantic axis, resulting in a multidimensional historical configuration irreducible to a single 'reason' or point of view. This is to recognize, *not to relativize*, the historical and political potential of the incalculable. To the horizontal connections of globalizing modernity there is always to be added the vertical location of the historical act that intercedes to translate, transform and transfigure such connections. Every connection is sumultaneously shadowed, doubled, and potentially travestied, by a disconnection.

Surely a certain tradition in British cultural studies could be recalled at this point in order to sustain and extend this critical perspective? I am thinking in particular of the reworking of Antonio Gramsci's crucial understanding of the making of modernity. It is the constitution of modern historical formations and their flexible exercise of hegemony that seek to contain the incalculable in a consensual coherence. Both the later reflections of Raymond Williams and, above all, Stuart Hall's work at Birmingham in the analysis of male subcultures, the racialization of crime in the 'mugging crisis', and his subsequent exposition of 'Thatcherism' remain deeply pertinent in both introducing to the Anglophone world, and effectively illustrating, the importance of the Italian thinker's work for a critical understanding of modernity.[12] Gramsci's careful attention to the political, cultural and economic dynamics involved in the realization of the powers of modern social formations contested not only the economism of so much Marxism, but also the teleology that Marx himself seemed to ascribe to the forces of capitalist production in the refashioning of the world. Above all, Gramsci's work set the terms, and still does in my opinion, for all affirmative political projects that refuse to discard the cultural and historical complexities of modernity for the sake of instrumental, that is, merely 'political', affirmation.

I promised neither commentary nor critique; so, equipped with these
dimensions and suggestions drawn from Stuart Hall's work, I wish to
consider identity and modernity in the tension, both historical and
immediate, that unfolds between the poles of popular musics and
postcolonial identities. This is a journey that does not seek a settlement
or point of arrival. As a critical itinerary it is a venture into crisis, not
offering the illusory shelter of analytical conclusion but evoking the
open, questioning region in which we dwell.[13] Although Hall might not
immediately recognize himself in such metaphors, and would, I think,
strive harder than me to reach for the conclusive shore, it is personally
this historical sense of opening, rendered susceptible to the winds of
the world, caught on the coast but desirous of the open sea, that
represents the greatest gift of his critical work and continuing intellectual example.

To seek a passage of understanding that passes from popular musics
in an urban, Occidental and youth culture context, to the perspective
of music as providing a language for sounding out the possibilities of
the world – from local questions of male, white, subcultural inscriptions
in urban postwar British culture to the worldly interrogation posed by
subaltern histories and marginalized identities – can music do this?
Can it provide a sense for these diverse socio-historical configurations?
Perhaps the sense I am referring to here is not one of fixed or stable
meaning, but rather sense as *sens*, as a direction, a way, a mobile act of
transformation, of ontological transit, that permits diverse inscriptions
of being in the world: traces of historical passages, song lines, sonorial
tracks.[14] If music is a language its semantics are particularly ambiguous;
it is the truth of that ambiguity, the ambiguity of truth, that encourages
me to pursue a line of thinking attentive to sounds in the belief that
they announce more than merely a musical or instrumental logic.

In the case of both the popular and the postcolonial I could propose
a set of definitions that talk of economic, political, historical and
cultural subalternity. Both the popular and the postcolonial are elaborated in terms of contesting the powers of a hegemonic formation
that seeks to establish and maintain their subalternity not only in
economic and political terms but also in cultural and aesthetic ones.
So, beginning some thirty years ago, there occurred, under the influence of Stuart's own work and his intellectual leadership at the Centre
for Contemporary Cultural Studies at Birmingham, a sustained intellectual struggle, which was intrinsically political, to open up the academic
world to the study of contemporary urban popular cultures and to
establish critical perspectives that challenged not only the narrow
confines of academic study but also the wider currency of everyday
convictions – namely, that popular culture not only was without signifi-

cant intellectual or aesthetic content, but also lacked historical, social and critical significance. Emerging from this prospect, previous distinctions such as those between the economical and the cultural, between the political and the poetical, became increasingly difficult to sustain. The noted work on male subcultures, moral panics, mugging and popular conservatism is part of that history.

Until recently, European critical traditions have tended, with the notable German exception of the urban thinking of Simmel, Kracauer, Benjamin and the Frankfurt School, to treat the economical and the cultural, the commercial and the aesthetical, as separate spheres, just as the 'popular' was separated off from 'culture'. So, the overwhelming tendency has been to separate the aesthetic from the merely commercial, the genuine and the spontaneous from the artificial and the manufactured. Here lie the origins of those debates against 'Americanization', seen as the epitomy of a crass, commercial challenge to the authenticity of local, presumably noncommercial, cultures. And yet, if we return to Antonio Gramsci's noted comments on Americanism and Fordism ('Americanismo e fordismo', 1934), for example, we discover something far more radical than the mere denunciation of a foreign, commercial threat and imported modalities of production. Gramsci speaks of 'americanismo' as the drastic reconfiguration of modern Occidental societies that leads to an irreversible change in political and cultural conditions. 'Americanism' at this point becomes the allegory of not only economic, but also political and cultural innovation: a 'new order' that threatens to sweep away the resistance of certain traditional social strata.[15] Here, rather than a defence of the 'local', the 'traditional' and the 'national', we encounter a sense of culture as process in which inherited historical configurations are both interrogated and reconfigured in response to change.

At this point I am encouraged to challenge the separation of the economic from the cultural, the 'natural' from the manufactured, not only bearing in mind the Gramscian understanding of 'hegemony' as a complex socio-political, cultural and economic formation, but also in response to the anthropological insistence on culture 'as a whole way of life' (Raymond Williams), and Michel de Certeau's more recent insistence, which echoes Gramsci's verdict on Americanism and Fordism, that there is no 'outside' to this commercial, historical, social and political economy that we call modernity. Naturally, all of this has major implications for how we might understand both the 'political' and the 'poetical' today.

To return to the question of language, to music as a language and historical configuration. Where, for example, does the song end and the social begin? Or, in another lexicon, where does the commercial

commence and the æsthetic conclude? The impossibility of defining
such boundaries draws me beyond the narrow distinctions that seek to
maintain such mediums, such languages and technologies, at a distance, whether critical or social. We cannot withdraw from them, they
are always at hand. We are forced to recognize their ontological
centrality to who we are, and to what we might desire to become.
Perhaps this lack of distance, resulting in a propensity to be enveloped
and made over in the multiple languages of modernity, so that, beyond
the obvious instrumental reach of economic and political profit, they
also come to resonate deeply with the ambiguous journeying of our
identity in the world, is most acutely signalled, though rarely considered, in the dominion of sound. The journey of sound and the
sobering thought of the inconclusive betrays all pretensions to grasp
and reduce our surroundings to a common measure, a transparent
economic and cultural logic.

   Hall himself talks at some length of the conditions of language and
history as productive cultural forces, as constitutive elements in the
making of identity. He draws attention to the Marxian displacement of
the sovereign subject by the conditions of historical production, whereby
we make history under conditions not of our own choosing, and the
forcible reminder of this prospect enacted in the Althusserian critique of
empiricist and idealist humanism. This is also linked to the Swiss linguist
Ferdinand de Saussure's establishment of structural linguistics and the
concomitant implications of our subjection to the already existing rules
and logic of language. Significantly, both critical currents were brought
into contact in Louis Althusser's psychoanalytically inflected analysis of
the interpellation of ideology (itself indebted to Lacan). While recognizing the historical importance of these theoretical 'signals' for the Anglo-
American world in the 1970s, I think that today we can historically
stretch, extend and relocate this discussion. Not only is the displacement
of the sovereign subject announced with the Freudian 'discovery' of the
unconscious introducing a perpetual instability into identity, it was also
anticipated in Nietzsche's critique of the accepted belief that the world
emanates from the grammatical 'I'. Further, Althusser's anti-humanism
was surely anticipated at least twenty years previously by Heidegger in
the noted 'Letter on Humanism' (1946).[16] Yet, if both thinkers were
clearly united against Sartre, Heidegger would certainly have considered
Althusser's deployment of 'scientific' protocols not separate but actually
central to the rational sovereignty claimed by humanism. It was above
all from Heidegger's thought, rather than with *Pour Marx* (1966), that
the influential post-1945 French intellectual renaissance, including such
voices as Jacques Derrida and Michel Foucault, drew its subsequent
critique of the humanist subject.

Such supplementary details do not detract from the direction of Stuart's account, but they may help us to map more richly the difficult terrain we are crossing. And the direction itself? The overall combination of this disposition of displacement is that 'reason' is no longer transparent to itself, and the subject, whatever she or he thinks, is no longer the master and origin of language, discourse, sexuality, gender, history. The subject can no longer be critically conceived as sovereign, even if common sense and psychic survival continue to insist that it is. We are inducted into a subjunctive condition: we act 'as if' we have a coherent identity and control our thoughts, language and being, even if we know that the narrative is critically suspect.

Of course, the refusal of Gramsci and observers like Simmel and Benjamin to separate the economic from the cultural was fundamentally stimulated by the emergence of the modern city and the radical configuration of social and economic space in the industrialization and urbanization of time, perception, production and consumption on an unprecedented and variegated scale. It is this urban constellation that not only frames modern musical and cultural sense, but also interrogates such inherited concepts as tradition and authenticity and establishes the city as the hubris of potential cultural contaminations and historical hybridities. For it is here that the global tendencies of economic, historical and social forces combine in the formation of an ongoing cultural configuration that dislocates and relocates the histories and cultures, the collective and individual lives, of those who find accommodation, establish their homes, there. Here cultural traditions, both local and imported, are translated and mutually interrogated by the tempi of metropolitan modernity. Both – and I emphasize *both* – the 'native' and the 'foreign' are subject to being translated into the syntax most appropriate to the continual transit of urban becoming. There occurs a simultaneous and *mutual translation* (Rey Chow) of both centre and periphery, of Europe and the rest. Roots becomes routes.

When Sud Sound System, a contemporary hip-hop collective from Lecce in southern Italy, rap in local dialect over rhythmic inspirations initially registered in Los Angeles and London, there occurs an act of translation in which both tradition and the transnational, the local and the global, are repeated to release something more. This, as Salman Rushdie reminds us, is how 'newness enters the world'. In the same period in London, for example, a descendant of the Indian diaspora – Nitin Sawhney – is busily editing the mix of 'In the Mind' in which both Indian classical vocals and present-day British soul music are combined to affirm what for Walter Benjamin was the only authentic tradition, that of discontinuity. Here the structural dynamics – economic, cultural and political – whereby the local is articulated through

the global, and the global through the local, creating new configurations and identifications in both sites, becomes palpable, immediate. It
is where the 'local' results in being simultaneously beneath *and* beyond
the nation.

The upshot is not merely a weakening in an earlier sense of domestic
or national identity, but rather, and more significantly, the underlining
of the historical, hence open, question of the making of 'home' in
modernity. The active identification with an earlier sense of 'homeland', with what many of us have been taught to recognize as the stable
representation of our historical and cultural 'selves' in the narration of
a national culture, comes now to be distilled into the fluid questioning
of what it means to be 'English', 'European', 'American', 'heterosexual', 'white', 'male'. What apparently grows and unfolds without substantial disturbance down through the passage of time – natural,
organic . . . inevitable, just like the English rose reminding us of a
peculiar national alliance with the garden and the nationalized specificity of an idealized feminity – now becomes specific, located, limited,
mutable.

For, despite the metaphors of organicity, national identification
develops within educational and disciplinary structures, ranging from
schools and medicine to prisons, the armed forces and the legislative
and punitive organs of the state. These are structures, processes, that
while seeking to transform the heterogeneous into a homogeneous
identity are continually subject to challenge and change. They are
structures forged in the global relations of production of the modern
nation-state; they were proposed and prospered in the colonial and
imperial relationships that established European nations, in all their
internal diversity, at the centre of a global economy for whom the rest
was always the peripheral object of that specific history. Internally
diversified, and formed in response and relation to an other, 'modern
nations are all cultural hybrids'.[17] In Stuart Hall's timely reminder,
hybridity is thus not the final stage of modernity, but rather its
repressed basis.

All of this implies that the city, and its languages, its modernities, is
no one's individual property. No one, not even the most powerful
transnational corporation, is able to control it. As a historical, economic, political and cultural space it is open to transformation into
different understandings of place, accommodation and home. Of
course, some versions of the city, of modernity and its languages, are
far more powerful, more hegemonic, than others, and their subsequent
realization in political, cultural and economic projects is altogether
more firmly guaranteed. But – and this perhaps is the point – there is,
however belated, dreaded and disdained, the unavoidable contact and

confirmation that the modern metropolis is not unique and homogeneous, that it is not simply 'yours' or 'mine': that it is a home for other
histories, a home for others. This renders a previous authority vulnerable, susceptible to claims increasingly made on it in the languages it
once presumed to own.

As the music of the subaltern, popular musics, blues, rock, reggae,
rap and the multiple urban variants that have subsequently emerged
are invariably considered to be the sounds of social, cultural and ethnic
resistance. The music of the subaltern is what, implicitly or explicitly,
challenges the existing cultural economy and the social relations (of
production) that sustain it: capitalism. Implicit in this judgement is the
idea that such music precedes and remains exterior to the economy in
which it circulates. Subsequent history becomes the narrative of charting its resistance and/or incorporation in the logic of commodification.

This, for me, raises two problems; one concerns the particular
historical, cultural, and, I would say, ontological, importance I would
want to ascribe to music; the other is tied to a critical understanding of
the cultural (and political) implications of the capitalist mode of
production.

First, I will consider the question of musical production as cultural
inscription and temporal witness – as an event, a product and a process
that occurs within historically formed social relations (of production).
The sound is not separate from this historical sociability, even if it is
played or heard in isolation. But neither is it reducible, except in the
crudest and most reductive fashion, to that economy. If music speaks
of its being in a particular time, place and set of social relations, it also
supplements and surges through and beyond the logic of such categories – it is never fully absorbed in the immediate cycle of production–
distribution–exchange and consumption. As a language that is more
than merely instrumental, music transforms the given into the unexpected, the prosaic into the poetic.

So, to speak of post-Bhangra Asian dance music or the legacy of Bob
Marley in terms of political economy and their subsequent absorption
into the commercial mainstream, for example, is not wrong or misguided, but to remain at that point is also, perhaps, to miss the point
and the incalculable politics that might follow.[18] Apparently rendering
transparent the structural logic in which sounds are produced, distributed and consumed, a further critical question cannot be ignored: does
such an analysis represent a conclusion, the last word on the sound,
and is the music merely the direct echo of the mode of production, or
is such an analysis a necessary, but not sufficient, point of departure
for responding to the interrogation that such sounds sow?

A possible critical exit surely lies in lending attention to the idea of sound as a historical configuration that continually confutes a merely causal or transparent representation of its production and consumption. To consider sound as a historical configuration, as a process and not merely a prisoner of its conditions of existence, is also to consider it as always and already existing within the economy that exhibits it. Music does not move from a state of innocence to decadence, from firm authenticity to commercial manipulation; it neither pre-exists nor steps outside the cycle that produces it. That does not automatically imply, however, that it blindly reproduces the logic in which it occurs. As sound it also sounds out those conditions and their limits. The commodity does not simply satisfy the requirements of capital, it also involves the decomposition of the product and its appropriation on the part of an 'active subject'.[19] The reproduction of capital encounters more than it can control or programme. In consumption, music returns to production the completion of a cycle, but not necessarily acritically or smoothly; further, and this is perhaps the critical lever of my whole argument, the disturbance, the dissent, the disavowal, occurs within the structure, within the possibilities and potential, of that historical configuration. Today this 'within' is not merely worldly, in the sense of being part of a specific social life and cultural experience, part of a national and historical formation; it is also recognizably inserted into a global frame.

But if there is no music that exists outside the planetary relations of production, there is a poetics that while always historically configured sounds within, through and beyond instrumental, economic and ideological inscription. For if the West has become the world, in the process its languages are also destined to be displaced and rendered homeless with respect to their 'origins'. If the political economy, technology and accompanying legal and political structures of the West have achieved a planetary dominion over the rest, the 'West' itself is increasingly destined to experience the unguaranteed passage of translation, transit, rerouting and deviancy in which specific, local cultures prove stronger than the abstract law of profit and the calculation of investments, where custom locates the commodity not in the abstract space of the market but in a precise and complex historical utterance of place.

This is not merely to register the frontiers of hybridity in which the West is forced to accommodate itself to other histories, other cultures, within its own cities and languages; it is also to argue that the very concepts the West has employed in identifiying itself and its others – the 'progress' of the 'centre' as opposed to the 'archaism' of the 'periphery' – represent a conceptual organization open to interrogation, interruption, rearticulation elsewhere, in 'other worlds'. Perhaps here there is a further critical temporality to be considered: the initial planetary logic of Occidental modernity that seemingly reduced all to a common commercial circuit subsequently, and inadvertently, provides the basis for 'expanded intercourse on the part of individuals'.[20] This universalizing tendency simultaneously evokes connections and disconnections in the perpetual negotiation of a place in modernity. It also transforms the very sense of modernity. For in the process of such universalization there emerge places that world the world following diverse histories, rhythms, rhymes and reason.

I would like to draw this discussion to a temporary halt by listening to the case of reggae music in Lee Tamahori's film on modern Maori culture, *Once Were Warriors* (1994). In the urban ghettos of New Zealand this music simultaneously stands for both modernity and tradition. It evokes not only the globalization of Occidental culture and capital but also the simultaneous elaboration of a specific sense of place within the space provided by international rock music. In this space there emerges a sense of 'home': the scene of memory, the scene of re-membering, of putting back together past fragments, in which the sound of the Caribbean dispossessed is repeated and re-elaborated by another sea in another hemisphere to release a further promise.

This is a cultural practice and historical redemption elaborated within the languages at hand that is also visibly commemorated in the Maori tradition of tattooing. Here both local tradition and modern globality are displayed and doubled in the same language, physically in-corporated in the same signs. Here both tradition and modernity are simultaneously translated and transformed as the signs are connected to and disconnected from both Occidental metropolitan subcultures and the traditional tattoo cultures of the Pacific (from where the Occidental metropolis first acquired them). Both are translated into a 'third space' (Homi Bhabha) that cannot be explained in terms of its 'origins' in either the culture of tradition or that of modernity, but rather must be understood in terms of cultural and political survival in the contagious processes of worldly hybridization.

This is to introduce a final argument about the performative nature of culture. If culture is a process and not a state, it perhaps requires consideration not so much as a stable condition of being but rather as one of perpetual becoming. Here, to borrow a further analogy from the paradigm of language, this idea perhaps suggests that we look more to the instance of cultural speech, to the dialects, idiolects and variants of cultural saying, rather than to the structural rules of its grammar. It is to displace the prescribed with the inscription, the articulation, the historical instance. Speech, dialogue, the call – the excess of language that spills over the edges of formal enclosure – propose the opening of the event, rather than the institutional closure of logic and rules. (This recalls Walter Benjamin's insistence on the *Jetz*, the historical instance that resonates in a temporal combination or performative mix – what today also resounds in Homi Bhabha's comprehension of postcolonial cultures and Judith Butler's interpretation of gender identities.) Such an uncertain and unstable constellation is what Edouard Glissant, speaking out of the Caribbean, out of Martinique, proposes as an 'exploded discourse'; it draws us to 'an exemplary phenomenon, serving as an example, in the modern drama of creolization'.[21] Perhaps such a relationship to more than ourselves, to more than we can contain or explain, to his felt incommensurability, is what Bob Marley once called 'the lost truth of the earth'.[22]

The political and the poetical are here conjoined, the aesthetical flows into the ethical. The divisions and abstract management of the categories – politics, art, economics, government, justice – that have sustained a certain Occidental calculus, what Edouard Glissant calls 'the functional fantasy of the West', are exposed to a vulnerability – exposed to the opening of a historical imperative that refuses to allow the world to be locked up in the prison of logical categories. The absolutism of this style of thought is forced to confront its terrestrial location. There is no intellectual synthesis or conceptual conciliation. No rationalist ordering can guarantee the truth of our being, no formal intellectual device is capable of holding the world in its analytical vice. The interminable working with, working through, working at, the limits of the materials, forces and inheritance at hand is, as Stuart Hall pointed out many years ago, what constitutes critique.[23] And before this difficult sea of critical endeavour that Hall's work has so consistently navigated I am brought to another shore. From here I have to look again, to draw up another map, or, altogether more difficult to contemplate, to lower my eyes, abandon the map, and listen to the narration that comes from elsewhere; to seek, in a reply historically framed by terms that exceed my understanding, my world, a more fitting, a more timely, response. At the end of this sentence, a sail will unfurl . . .[24]

Notes

1. Stuart Hall, 'Introduction', in Stuart Hall, David Held, Don Hubert and Kenneth Thompson, eds., *Modernity: An Introduction to Modern Societies*, Oxford, Blackwell, 1996, pp. 6–7.

2. Karl Marx, *Grundrisse*, Harmondsworth, Penguin, 1973, p. 542.

3. Derek Walcott, *The Bounty*, London, Faber and Faber, 1997, pp. 9–10.

4. Stuart Hall, 'The Question of Cultural Identity', in Hall, *et al.*, eds., *Modernity*.

5. Ibid., p. 632.

6. Cf. Stuart Hall, 'The West and the Rest: Discourse and Power', in Hall, *et al.*, eds., *Modernity*.

7. Paul Gilroy, *The Black Atlantic*, London, Verso, 1993.

8. In this short phrase lies the crux of a raging polemic that can be summarized in the demand 'Postcolonial for whom?' I personally consider the 'postcolonial' as an invitation to world the world differently, a concept that while conceptually investing all people in their respective differences, is a precise critique of the hegemony of Occidental ontology. Not all agree. See, for example, the recent exchange in *Postcolonial Studies* between Simon During and Bart Moore-Gilbert: Simon During, 'Postcolonialism and Globalisation: A Dialectical Relation after All?', Bart Moore-Gilbert, 'Postcolonialism: Between Nationalism and Globalisation? A Response to Simon During', *Postcolonial Studies*, Vol. 1, No. 1, April 1998. Hall himself has offered an important overview of the question; see Stuart Hall, 'When Was "The Post-Colonial"? Thinking At The Limit', in Iain Chambers and Lidia Curti, eds., *The Post-colonial Question: Common Skies, Divided Horizons*, London and New York, Routledge, 1996.

9. The texts invoked here are: David Harvey, *The Condition of Postmodernity*, Oxford, Blackwell, 1989; Fredric Jameson, *Postmodernism or the Cultural Logic of Late Capitalism*, London, Verso, 1991; Anthony Giddens, *The Consequences of Modernity*, Cambridge, Polity, 1990.

10. Stuart Hall, 'The Question of Cultural Identity', pp. 629–30.

11. Nicholas Thomas, 'Hybrid Histories: Gordon Bennett's Critique of Purity', *Communal/Plural*, Vol. 6, No. 1, April 1998.

12. Cf. Stuart Hall and Tony Jefferson, eds., *Resistance through Rituals: Youth Sub-cultures in Post-war Britain*, London, Hutchinson, 1976; Stuart Hall, Chas Critcher, Tony Jefferson, John Clarke and Brian Roberts, *Policing the Crisis: 'Mugging', the State, and Law and Order*, London, Macmillan, 1978; Stuart Hall, *The Hard Road to Renewal: Thatcherism and the Crisis of the Left*, London, Verso, 1988.

13. The proximity of Hall to Heidegger ('the open region in which man dwells'), but also to Fanon's final prayer ('On my body, make of me always a man who questions!') is, of course, my responsibility.

14. Reiner Schürmann's comments on Heidegger's understanding of 'sense', understood as direction rather than meaning, are instructive here: 'Only then does it become apparent how time can be "der Sinn des Seins": not the "meaning" of being, but its directionality; the "sense" as the direction in which something, e.g., motion, takes place (the acceptance of both the English "sense" and the French sens – "sense" of a river, or of traffic – stems, not from Latin, but from an Indo-European verb that means to travel, to follow a path).' Reiner Schürmann, *Heidegger. On Being and Acting: From Principles to Anarchy*, Blooming-ton, Indiana University Press, 1990, p. 13.

15. Antonio Gramsci, *Quadernidelcarcere*, Vol. 3, Turin, Einaudi, 1975, p. 2179.

16. Althusser himself came explicitly to acknowledge such a connection in his later elaboration of historical contingency in such writings as 'The Subterranean Current of the Materialism of the Encounter' (1982). Here an 'aleatory

materialism' is contrasted with 'dialectical materialism' which, 'like every materialism in the rationalist tradition, is a materialism of necessity and teleology, that is to say, a transformed and disguised form of idealism'. See Gregory Elliott, 'Ghostlier Demarcations: On the Posthumous Edition of Althusser's Writings', *Radical Philosophy*, 90, July/August 1998.

17. Stuart Hall, 'The Question of Cultural Identity', p. 617.

18. Aswani Sharma, 'Sounds Oriental: The (Im)possibility of Theorizing Asian Musical Cultures', in Sanjay Sharma, John Hutnyk and Aswani Sharma, eds., *Dis-Orienting Rhythms: The Politics of the New Asian Dance Music*, London, Zed Books, 1996; Michelle A. Stephens, 'Babylon's "Natural Mystic": The North American Music Industry, the Legend of Bob Marley, and the Incorporation of Transnationalism', *Cultural Studies*, Vol. 12, No. 2, April 1998.

19. Marx, *Grundisse*, p. 91.

20. Ibid, p. 540.

21. Edouard Glissant, *Caribbean Discourse: Selected Essays*, Charlottesville, University Press of Virginia, 1989, p. 159.

22. S. Davis and P. Simon, *Reggae Bloodlines*, London, Thames & Hudson, 1983, p. 66.

23. Stuart Hall, 'Marx's Notes on Method: A "Reading" of the "1857 Introduction"', *Working Papers in Cultural Studies* 6, Autumn 1974, pp. 165–7.

24. With apologies to Derek Walcott: 'At the end of this sentence, rain will begin. / At the rain's edge, a sail.' (From 'Map of the New World', in Derek Walcott, *Collected Poems 1948–1984*, New York, Farrar, Straus & Giroux, 1986).

8

Unfinished Business?
Struggles over the Social in Social Welfare
John Clarke

Conflicts around social welfare have exposed the unstable and contradictory relationships between citizenship, social divisions and the state.
These tensions are significant because not only the terms – citizenship,
social divisions and the state – but also the forms of relationship
between them are contested (Hughes 1998). The 'crisis of welfare' is
conventionally equated with the break-up of the political–economic
settlements that sustained welfare states in Western capitalist societies,
settlements that were often associated with corporatist approaches to
economic and social management (for example, by Mishra 1990;
Pierson 1993). Some of these changes have been explored in more
'cultural' terms, for example through Foucauldian studies of governmentality and the rise of neo-liberalism (for example, Rose 1996;
Fitzpatrick 1998). Both of these emphases seem to me to underestimate
the contradictory and contested character of the 'social' in social
welfare.

I want to argue that the crisis of welfare also had important roots in
the struggles intended to expand and transform, rather than retrench
or reduce, state welfare. Although they differed in significant ways,
many of these struggles shared some important tendencies. Perhaps
the most striking is their insistence on the *social* character of patterns
of difference, division and inequality. Welfare politics around gender,
'race', sexuality and disability may well have been particularistic in
organizational forms and the demands expressed, but they were linked
by a commitment to reveal the socially produced or constructed
character of difference. They shared a systematic refusal to accept the
dominant *non-social* constructions of their positions in social welfare.
Such constructions were, of course, predominantly biological, identifying difference as naturally constituted. Thus, prevailing gender divisions were treated as the optimal evolutionary outcome. Embedded in

the nuclear family form, they also represented the happy coincidence of God and Nature in the reproduction of individuals and society. Such biological constructions defined the place, character and significance of sexualities, both in their normative heterosexual forms and in their pathologized 'deviant' forms (Saraga 1998). The racialization of difference entangled the biological categorization (and hierarchization) of 'race' with imperial geographies which distributed those categories to places still coded as 'countries of origin' in official discourses (Lewis 1998a and b). Meanwhile, disability was inscribed as biological misfortune, requiring the attentions of medical power (for example, Campbell and Oliver 1996; Hughes 1998).

The significance of these constructions lay not only in their ideological or discursive dominance, and their naturalization across a whole society, but especially in the way that they were enacted or instantiated in and through the policies and practices of state welfare provision. Welfare institutions produced and reproduced such divisions and the positions resulting from them. Such institutions formed one of the most potent fields of articulation between state power, discursive formations and the fabric of everyday lives. Welfare institutions and their practices can be viewed as producing a field of social differentiation with immediate (and often severe) consequences for those positioned by and within it. This field cannot be read simply as a structure of inclusions and exclusions, although there continue to be formalized exclusions, particularly at the intersection of 'race' and geographical mobility (see Morris 1998). Rather, this field of welfare was formed out of interlocking processes of differentiation, marginalization, pathologization and subordination, as well as exclusion. For example, 'children' were constituted as different (from mature, independent adults), as subordinate to familial and public authority (because of their dependence), and as needing both familial and public 'care' (to produce them as independent adults). Within this differentiated biological category, however, there were specific groups of children who were constituted as the objects of special concern (children with special needs; children in need of care, protection or control; delinquent children; and so on). Each of these was differentially positioned in the field of welfare and was practised upon in specific ways. Of course, the 'occupancy' of different categories intersected with a range of (apparently) non-social markers, particularly those of gender and 'race'.

This field of naturalized and normalized positions in relation to social welfare was the focus of a range of attacks from what are usually identified as the 'new social movements' (Pierson 1993; see also Williams 1996 and 1998). The insistence on the 'social' character of differences produced and reproduced through welfare institutions formed a point of connection between different struggles. They share a critique of the non- or extra-social ideologies of difference and instead assert the plastic or malleable character of socially constructed differences, identifying them as historically and culturally contingent. This insistence on the 'social' produces a view of difference, division and inequality as remediable or capable of being redressed. This view also makes explicit – as a target of political attention – the ways in which constructions of difference are implicated in forms of power, ranging from the juridical authority and boundaries of the nation-state to the micro-politics of professional power enacted in face-to-face work with welfare 'clients' (Newman and Williams 1995; Williams 1996).

Fiona Williams has recently drawn out a series of guiding principles from this range of struggles around the 'old' welfare state that might guide future transformations of welfare (1998). Her arguments challenge the temptation to create simplifying categorizations of contemporary politics which distinguish 'redistributive' from 'recognition' politics, or even 'real politics' from 'identity' or 'cultural politics' (see, for example, the arguments in and between Butler 1998, Fraser 1997 and 1998, and Ross 1998). The struggles around social welfare seem to me to sit oddly with such categorizations. Their demands have not been simply 'redistributive', at least in the social policy sense of economic transfers. There have been arguments for transforming access to welfare (and indeed access to all domains of social, economic and political life). These struggles have been about the 'redistribution' of citizenship – contesting the limits of who counts as a citizen, as well as what social citizenship might mean in practice. They might even be seen as demanding the redistribution of independence (or autonomy) as well as the resources to make independence come true in practice, while other struggles have claimed the right to have (recognized or legitimated) dependants and the right to those dependant-supporting services and resources provided by the state. In some senses, these were demands for recognition: the claim to 'legitimate membership of the welfare community' (Morris 1998) through expanding and transforming the juridical categories of citizen, welfare user, and so on. But such recognition has redistributive implications. These struggles aimed to redistribute access, resources and power through the transformation of the juridical categories, the subject positions of welfare policy, and the daily reproductions of subordination in welfare practice. This complexity seems to me to outrun the distinction between redistribution and recognition, understood either as the defining tendency of a specific struggle or as its foundation in the ordering of social division. For me, such politics may be more productively understood as *relational struggles*, a term that focuses on their efforts to transform the 'old' social relations of welfare and to construct new social settlements (see also Hunter 1995). In their engagement with social welfare, these struggles either demanded or implied a range of different patterns and levels of social relations. Most expansively, they have challenged the formation and categories of the nation-state and citizenship. They have laid siege to established forms of power, position and equity within welfare institutions and policies. And they have contested the practical orchestration of power and identity within such institutions, for example, refusing the normative evaluation of needs, risk or desert at the point of access to welfare (Langan 1998).

Such attempts to transform the conditions of 'second-class citizenship' destabilized the field of welfare positions and the wider framework of constructions of nation, state and welfare. They contributed to the 'crises of the welfare state' through their questioning of what belonging to a (national) welfare state could mean (Clarke and Newman 1997; Hughes 1998). Starting from these struggles gives a rather different inflection to contemporary debates about 'welfare reform' (Williams 1998). It reminds us that the welfare state already had a complex trajectory *before* the arrival of retrenchment, reconstruction and residualization. It was never a simple – or static – monolithic entity. Emphasising these struggles also draws attention to the way that the welfare state has remained contested throughout its reconstruction by the New Right. It might be worth putting this point more strongly. What the New Right attacked was not only the 'old' welfare state but also what it might have become as a result of the socialising claims and demands articulated around the field of differences and inequalities. The New Right assault was directed at both the dominant political formation of social-democratic corporatism that was institutionalized in the construction of the post-1945 welfare state, and the expansionist and transformative demands of those struggling to challenge and enlarge this social democratic welfarism.

While such struggles made an impact on aspects of social welfare, they have been fiercely contested from a range of positions that have attempted to *desocialize* social welfare. In this context, I want to focus on three overlapping discourses that are at play in this desocializing political work: neo-liberalism, managerialism and neo-conservatism. There are others: for example, the revitalization of biologism through the sign of the gene or what Gail Lewis has called the 'dis-placement' of racialized divisions through geographical localization (Lewis 1998b). However, I want to concentrate on the three discourses mentioned above because their coincidence and interconnection has been the source of some difficult analytical and political problems. At the heart of these is the risk of reducing the New Right (as a political formation and project) to neo-liberalism (as a discourse and strategy). Here I want to begin from neo-liberalism and then move to exploring its relationship with the other two strands. In relation to social welfare, neo-liberalism has deployed at least three desocializing tactics. The first – and most blatant – is simply the Thatcherite claim that 'there is no such thing as society', only individuals (properly construed as 'economic men') and their families. This reductionism foregrounds enterprise, exchange, and the pursuit of individual interests. State-provided welfare is viewed as disrupting the free play of individual choice (and thus the workings of the market). As a result, welfare provision should become a matter of individual responsibility. The second – and related – tactic has involved the attempt to dismantle 'social' explanations of inequality, substituting a combination of economic inevitability and natural differentiation. The third tactic has been the sustained attempt to 'de-differentiate' public sector provision, insisting that the combination of a consumerized public, marketized co-ordination of services, and a managerialized or corporate form of organization will transform welfare (Clarke and Newman 1997). In this way, neo-liberalism has rhetorically combined the *desocialization* of difference, inequality and need with the *privatization* of welfare provision. In neo-liberalism, 'privatization' has always carried a double implication, identifying both the 'private sector' of the economy and the 'private realm' of the family. There are ways in which it may be helpful to separate out two distinctions in this field (between social and non-social and public and private) and I will return to them later.

Managerialism has often appeared as simply the organizational proxy or agent of neo-liberalism, installing its truths within organizations and providing the appropriate forms of co-ordination and discipline. In New Right reconstructions of social welfare, managerialism indeed played a central role, transforming the internal order of organizations and the relations between them (Clarke and Newman 1997). But it is worth thinking about managerialism as a distinctive force, in alliance with neo-liberalism, rather than a subordinate agent. Such a view enables us to see what managerialism brought to the alliance: the 'business voice' (rather than economics); the 'real world' (rather than government); and a vocabulary of dynamic transformation. Such a view also allows us to see that managerialism is not inevitably tied to New Right politics. On the contrary, its practitioners pride themselves on being able to 'do business with anyone', including, of course, New Labour and its managerialized view of politics as well as public services. Whilst managerialism is formally antithetical towards politics and political control ('dogma reduces efficiency'), it is ambiguous about the social. In part, this concerns the relation between managerialism and the internal order of organizations. As a number of writers have suggested, contemporary forms of managerialism seek to make the social – or cultural – world of the organization, including the identities, motives and affiliations of its 'members', both visible and manageable (for example, du Gay 1996). Managerialism's ambiguity about the social also relates to the world beyond the organization. The search to make that world knowable, through market research, focus groups and so on, acknowledges the existence of (at least some forms of) the social while trying to make the social world manageable, productive and profitable. The 'customer' orientation of managerialism is a richer and denser conception of transactional relationships than the rationalist view of the calculating consumer in neo-liberalism.

In this sense, managerialism involves a rather different 'settlement' with socializing demands around social welfare. Difference becomes a matter of 'customization', expressing the corporate capacity for flexibility and responsiveness (Williams 1996). As a result of such ambiguities, managerialism occupied a rather different place in the reconstruction of social welfare from neo-liberalism. It operated in a sort of 'arm's length relationship' and, in some respects, proved more engaging to workers in, and users of, public services than the impoverished economism of neo-liberalism (Clarke and Newman 1997). None the less, it too has desocializing effects. The social is only valued to the extent that it is corporately manageable and productive: unruly elements and disruptive problems that threaten organizational efficiency are always likely to be 'someone else's business'. The combined processes of dispersal and managerial co-ordination in welfare reconstruction have both diminished the social and fragmented 'the public' – understood as a people, a sector and an interest.

As a political project, the New Right was always an uneasy alliance between neo-liberalism and neo-conservatism. In relation to social welfare, the two strands have rather divergent emphases: the individualist, privatizing, anti-statism of neo-liberalism sometimes sits uncomfortably with the authoritarian, familialist traditionalism of neo-conservatism (Clarke 1991). This complex cocktail of different political projects was registered in Stuart Hall's paradoxical designation of Thatcherism as 'regressive modernization' (Hall 1988, p. 164; see also Hay 1996, pp. 170–3; Clarke and Newman 1997, pp. 142–59). Neo-conservative concerns with the reproduction of authority, the restoration of the patriarchal family form, and the revitalization of conceptions of duty, descent, obligation and responsibility have been potent, if unpredictable, elements in the politics of welfare in Britain and the USA. Neo-conservatism's desocializing project is a distinctive one. It refuses the abstract individualism of neo-liberalism, insisting that there is – and indeed ought to be – such a thing as society. But neo-conservatism views the 'socializing' challenges as having dislocated the normal and natural order of things – the state where (human) nature and social institutions were appropriately united. Tampering with any of the elements of this order – encouraging people not to 'know their place' – threatens to unlock everything, unleashing the forces of disorder. Neo-conservatism works across this border of the natural and the social. Nature needs both to be recognized (no social constructionism here) and to be disciplined and contained by social institutions. From the standpoint of neo-conservatism, the socializing demands of the marginalized, subordinated and excluded challenge both Nature and Social Order. They promote 'un-natural' attitudes and behaviour, sponsor dis-orderly conduct and refuse authority (see also Cooper 1998). Since the early 1980s, neo-conservatism has forged more or less unstable *political* accommodations with neo-liberalism within the New Right. To some extent, those accommodations have been enabled by the attractions of authoritarianism and the question of order (understood in the neo-liberal perspective as a 'good business climate'). They have also been made possible by the methodological familialism that neo-conservatism and neo-liberalism share. The rhetorical dominance of the individual and individual choice in neo-liberalism tends to disguise the extent to which the family is a core (and naturalized) unit of analysis. The family is the privileged site of consumption, reproduction and the generation of desire, need and motivation.

What is striking about these anti-social discourses is their mobility and adaptability. Although intimately related to the rise of the New Right, they have also become articulated into the political (re)formation of Democratic and Labour repertoires in the USA and Britain. Much emphasis has been placed on the continuities between Thatcherism and New Labour (and between Reaganite Republicanism and the Clinton administrations). Within the formation of New Labour, neo-liberalism has occupied a significant place, in particular providing a dominant conception of work, the economy and its place in a new global system. This has shaped policies towards financial and labour markets and is at the heart of the mission to save Europe from itself by 'liberalizing' (or even Americanizing) economic institutions (see also Marquand 1998). Neo-liberalism (especially in the form of the discourse of globalization) has thus framed issues of the nation's 'mission' and the direction of modernization (Massey forthcoming).

Managerialism, too, has proved predictably resilient. New Labour has drawn from it a technocratic and evaluative view of modernizing public services. In part, this was organized around a commitment to improving standards and procuring still greater efficiency, in serving what the Green Paper on Welfare Reform (Secretary of State 1998) described as the 'sceptical citizen-consumer'. Managerialism was also implicated in what we have described as New Labour's 'dogmatic pragmatism', expressed in the insistent claim that 'what counts is what works' (Clarke and Newman 1998; Newman 1998). Such managerialist approaches to public services underpin the rhetorical imagery of New Labour's Third Way(s), in which past failures are attributed to ideologically motivated commitments to either the state or the market. In such ways, New Labour tried to position itself against (the excesses of) neo-liberalism, whilst embedding neo-liberal views of the economy, and the state's relation to it, as a taken-for-granted part of the 'modern' condition.

This hint of distance between New Labour and neo-liberalism becomes more visible, and more uncomfortable, around issues of the 'social'. New Labour may have emerged into a 'post-Thatcher settlement', as Hay (1996) has argued, but its place has been marked by the need to negotiate the unfinished business of the 'social'. Despite their ferocious efforts, the New Right failed to close off the socializing struggles around welfare. Both organized resistance and a more inchoate popular scepticism refused the claim that 'there is no such thing as society'. New Labour was the beneficiary of such active and passive dissent and, indeed, laid claim to it, albeit in rather muted tones. But New Labour also brought with it a set of recognitions, accommodations and unresolved contradictions around the social, social policies and the role of public services in a field of relational struggles. Such elements were visible in the party's membership, in its policies and, perhaps most significantly, in its practices in large swathes of local government. Let me be clear: this is not a claim that either 'new' or 'old' Labour were converts to these relational struggles, but such struggles formed significant features of the political terrain that had to be negotiated, both within and beyond the party. The partial and contingent accommodations of equal opportunities policies, multiculturalism, anti-racism, anti-discrimination and anti-oppressive practice form markers that indicate the continued existence and salience of struggles over the social.

In its first wave of welfare reform plans, New Labour attempted to reconcile its mission to lead institutional and economic modernization with its commitment to what Blair once described as 'social-ism': an attenuated acknowledgement that individuals are socially connected. This reconciliation was constructed in two very different ways. The modernizing commitment to reform welfare to make it fit a changed world was articulated as an 'equal opportunities' view of waged work.

Anybody could (and should) support themselves and their family. Acknowledging both past discriminations and the impact of social changes that made the model of the white, male, able-bodied breadwinner anachronistic and untenable, New Labour committed itself to the proposition that *anyone* could be a white, male, able-bodied breadwinner. Work would deliver the income, the self-respect, the social inclusion and the independence that any individual needed. Social security was then rhetorically residualized: the provision of security for those who *cannot* work (Lister 1998).

However, even this attenuated view of the social contradicted New Labour's neo-conservative inheritances. New Labour condensed a variety of socially and morally conservative strands: for example, long-standing labourist puritanism about welfare and 'cultural' issues; a 'workerist' suspicion of new social movements; and, above all, a revitalized 'Christian socialism'. This neo-conservatism was articulated in a range of policies and initiatives addressed to the restoration of civility and authority (parental responsibility, child curfews, 'bad neighbour' policies, et cetera). These tendencies interrupt the modernizing discourse of New Labour in potent ways. While welfare reform proposals addressed the need for change in a changing world, the family was imagined as being under 'strain', which prevented it from successfully performing its role as the 'bedrock of a decent and *stable* society' (Secretary of State for Social Security and Minister for Welfare Reform 1998, p. 13). This contradictory assemblage of economic modernization, social dynamics and traditionalist restoration registers both the continuities from the New Right and the differences in the formation of New Labour. In the end, the recognition of a complex and dynamic social realm was (at least rhetorically) subordinated to both economic modernization and neo-conservative authoritarianism. The twin figures of work and the family provided the points of articulation – linking individual enterprise with social responsibility, and connecting social responsibility with family, community and nation in the imagining of a 'modern British people'.

But – and this is the final but – rhetorical subordination is not the same as subordination in practice. To identify the attempts at ideological or discursive closure is not the same as exposing their effective accomplishment. The dominance of neo-liberal, managerialist and neo-conservative ideologies may, to borrow Meaghan Morris's metaphor, make the spaces of political and cultural practice more 'cramped', but those spaces and the struggles within and from them persist (Morris 1998, p. xviii). The 'social' still disrupts the attempts to reproduce subordinations, even though it may only be visible in contingent and even contradictory fragments. New Labour may offer one

more version of 'regressive modernization', but the 'social' still refuses
to go quietly.

References

Butler, J. (1998) 'Merely Cultural', *New Left Review*, No. 227, pp. 33–44.
Campbell, J. and Oliver, M. (1996) *Disability Politics: Understanding Our Past, Changing Our Future*, London, Routledge.
Clarke, J. (1991) *New Times and Old Enemies: Essays on Cultural Studies and America*, London, HarperCollins.
Clarke, J. (1997) 'Capturing the Customer: Consumerism and Social Welfare', *Self, Agency and Society*, Vol. 1(1), pp. 55–73.
Clarke, J. and Newman, J. (1997) *The Managerial State: Power, Politics and Ideology in the Remaking of Social Welfare*, London, Sage.
Clarke, J. and Newman, J. (1998) 'A Modern British People? New Labour and the Reconstruction of Social Welfare.' Paper presented to the Discourse Analysis and Social Research conference, Ringsted, Denmark, September.
Cooper, D. (1998) *Governing out of Order: Space, Law and the Politics of Belonging*, London and New York, Rivers Oram Press.
du Gay, P. (1996) *Consumption and Identity at Work*, London, Sage.
Fitzpatrick, T. (1998) 'The Rise of Market Collectivism', in E. Brunsdon, H. Dean and R. Woods, eds., *Social Policy Review 10*, London, Social Policy Association.
Fraser, N. (1997) *Justice Interruptus: Critical Reflections of the 'Postsocialist' Condition*, New York, Routledge.
Fraser, N. (1998) 'Heterosexism, Misrecognition and Capitalism: A Response to Judith Butler', *New Left Review*, No. 228, pp. 140–9.
Hall, S. (1988) *The Hard Road to Renewal: Thatcherism and the Crisis of the Left*, London, Verso.
Hay, C. (1996) *ReStating Social and Political Change*, Buckingham, Open University Press.
Hughes, G. (1998) 'A Suitable Case for Treatment? Constructions of Disability', in E. Saraga, ed. *Embodying the Social: Constructions of Difference*, London, Routledge.
Hughes, G., ed. (1998) *Imagining Welfare Futures*, London, Routledge.
Hunter. A. (1995) 'Rethinking Revolution in Light of New Social Movements', in M. Dranovsky, B. Epstein and R. Flacks, eds., *Cultural Politics and Social Movements*, Philadelphia, Temple University Press.
Langan, M., ed. (1998) *Welfare: Needs, Rights and Risks*, London, Routledge.
Lewis, G. (1998a) 'Welfare and the Social Construction of "Race"', in E. Saraga, ed., *Embodying the Social: Constructions of Difference*, London, Routledge.
Lewis, G. (1998b) 'Same Place, Different Cultures? Thinking Welfare through the Postcolonial'. Paper presented to the Social Policy Association conference 'Social Policy in Time and Space', Lincoln, July.
Lister, R. (1998) 'From Equality to Social Inclusion: New Labour and the Welfare State', *Critical Social Policy*, Vol. 18(2), pp. 215–25.

Marquand, D. (1998) 'The Blair Paradox', *Prospect*, No. 30, pp. 19–24.

Massey, D. (forthcoming) 'Imagining Globalisation: Power-Geometries of Time–Space', in A. Brah, M.J. Hickman, M. MacanGhaill, eds., *Future Worlds: Migration, Environment and Globalization*, Basingstoke, Macmillan.

Mishra. R. (1990) *The Welfare State in Capitalist Society*, Hemel Hempstead, Harvester Wheatsheaf.

Morris, L. (1998) 'Legitimate Membership of the Welfare Community', in M. Langan, ed., *Welfare: Needs, Rights and Risks*, London, Routledge.

Morris, M. (1998) *Too Soon, Too Late: History in Popular Culture*, Bloomington, Indiana University Press.

Newman, J. (1998) 'What Counts is What Works: The Evaluation of Markets in Public Services'. Paper presented to Employment Research Unit conference 'Markets or Bureaucracies? Public Services under Labour', Cardiff, April.

Newman, J. and Williams, F. (1995) 'Diversity and Change: Gender, Welfare and Organisational Relations', in C. Itzin and J. Newman, eds., *Gender, Culture and Organisational Change: Putting Theory into Practice*, London, Routledge.

Pierson, C. (1993) *Beyond the Welfare State?* Cambridge, Polity Press.

Rose, N. (1996) 'The Death of the Social? Re-figuring the Territory of Government', *Economy and Society*, Vol. 25(3), pp. 327–56.

Ross, A. (1998) *Real Love: In Pursuit of Cultural Justice*, London and New York, Routledge.

Saraga, E. (1998) 'Abnormal, Unnatural and Immoral? The Social Construction of Sexualities', in E. Saraga, ed., *Embodying the Social: Constructions of Difference*, London, Routledge.

Saraga, E., ed. (1998) *Embodying the Social: Constructions of Difference*, London, Routledge.

Secretary of State for Social Security and Minister for Welfare Reform (1998) *New Ambitions for our Country: A New Contract for Welfare*, London, HMSO (Cm 3805).

Williams, F. (1996) 'Postmodernism, Feminism and the Question of Difference', in N. Parton, ed., *Social Theory, Social Change and Social Work*, London, Routledge.

Williams, F. (1998) 'New Principles for a Good-enough Welfare Society in the Millennium'. Paper presented to the World Congress of Sociology, Montreal, July.

9

Taking Identity Politics Seriously:
'The Contradictory, Stony Ground . . .'

James Clifford

Gramsci said: 'Turn your face violently towards things as they exist
now.' Not as you'd like them to be, not as you think they were
ten years ago, not as they're written about in the sacred texts, but
as they really are: the contradictory, stony ground of the present
conjuncture.

Stuart Hall (1989: 151)

Pour moi, ce qui est authentique, c'est ce qui donne de la saveur
à ce que chacun vit. Ce que mon père, mon grand-père, mon
arrière-grand-père ont vécu, toutes leurs expériences des rites, de
la tradition, de l'environnement sont différentes. Ils en ont été
imprégnés sociologiquement et psychologiquement. Mais pas
moi, qui ait ma propre expérience du monde. Je serai peut-être
un jour authentique dans un musée de l'an 2000 ou de l'an 3000.
En attendant, c'est moi qui invente.

Jean-Marie Tjibaou (1996: 306)

We can build upon the contributions of cultural studies to dispose
of the idea that identity is an absolute and to find the courage
necessary to argue that identity formation – even body-coded
ethnic and gender identity – is a chaotic process that can have no
end. In this way, we may be able to make cultural identity a
premise of political action rather than a substitute for it.

Paul Gilroy (1996: 238)

'Identity politics' is under attack from all sides these days. The political
right sees only a divisive assault on civilizational (read national) traditions, while a chorus on the Left laments the twilight of common
dreams, the fragmentation of any cumulative politics of resistance.
Meanwhile intellectuals of a post-structuralist bent, when confronted
with movements based on tribal, ethnic, gender, racial or sexual
attachments, are quick on the anti-essentialism trigger. Now there is no

doubt that group identity narrowly defined and aggressively sustained can be a serious obstacle to wider, more inclusive solidarities; and the ideological work of clearly defining a sense of community or people-hood often violently erases historical experiences of entanglement, border crossing, and coexistence. The tragedy in the former Yugoslavia stands as a brutal, inescapable warning. But however justified our revulsion in particular instances of exclusivism or separatism, if the criticism hardens into a general position against identity politics as such, or leads to arguments for getting 'beyond' such claims, the effect may be disabling. We risk being left with a narrowly foreshortened view of contemporary social movements around culture and identity, miss-ing their complex volatility, ambivalent potential, and historical necessity.

In a recent collection, *Social Theory and the Politics of Identity*, Craig Calhoun (1994a) challenges a widespread perception that the identity-based politics of racial/ethnic groups, the women's movement, the gay movement, and other self-assertions by excluded peoples represent something new. Social theory, he argues, has tended to repress the centrality of such mobilizations in heterogeneous, more-or-less demo-cratic, public spheres. Identity has been seen as preceding political participation, rather than as made and unmade, connected and discon-nected, in the interactive arenas of democratic, national, and transna-tional social life.

> Identity formation on most models – including for example Habermas's famous theory of the public sphere – prepares one for entrance into the public arena. It gives one individual strength and individual opinions. Conversely, the public sphere calls on one to put to the side the differences of class, ethnicity, and gender in order to speak as equals. And it thereby makes it all but impossible to thematize those very differences as the objects of politics instead of as obstacles to be overcome before rational political formation of the collective will. (Calhoun 1994b: 3)

Since the project of identity, whether individual or collective, is rooted in desires and aspirations that cannot be fulfilled, identity movements are open-ended, productive, and fraught with ambivalence. Calhoun argues that this generative 'tension' is 'the source of identity politics that aim not simply at the legitimation of falsely essential categorical identities but at living up to deeper social and moral values'(1994c: 29). Collective self-assertions may thus be traced simul-taneously to the manipulations of leaders such as Slobodan Milošević and to noble community aspirations and self-sacrificing moralities. Indeed, modern national projects – identity politics writ large – have always articulated noble goals of freedom, equality and solidarity with chauvinistic projects of exclusion and sometimes genocide. Such inclusive 'communities' can never be finished or whole: to differing degrees they are unstable, complicated and undermined by other identifications. It follows that national and transnational orders are domains not of teleological progress, but of continual struggle and negotiation, formation and breakup.

One suspects that 'identity politics' needs to be contained, even scapegoated at times, because it is a figure for chaotic cultural and political articulations that exceed systemic, progressive determination. Collective agency, for better and worse, has long been exercised at discrepant scales: particular colonial and neo-colonial contact zones; regional, religious, ethnic mobilizations and resistances, specific transnational and diasporic circuits. It is on this uneven terrain, grasped with ethnographic complexity, that we can begin to track less heroic, more contradictory and multivalent processes of historical transformation. History without guarantees.

Stuart Hall has worked to keep this more complex field of identifications in view. From his crucial linkage of Gramscian politics with racial and ethnic formations (1986), to his recent attempts to reclaim 'ethnicity' from exclusivist nationalisms (1988), Hall recognizes the constitutive role of cultural, ethnic, and racial identifications in contemporary politics. Human beings become agents, capable of effective action, only when they are actively sustained 'in place' through social and historical connections and disconnections. For Hall, this relational positioning is the work of culture, ensuring that 'as subjects [social actors] function by taking up the discourses of the present and the past'.

> It is that taking up of positions that I call 'identities'. You see the consequence of turning the paradigm around that way, the political question (for there is always a political question, at any rate, in the way I pose the issue) is not 'How do we effectively mobilize those identities which are already formed?' so that we could put them on the train and get them onto the stage at the right moment, in the right spot – an act the left has historically been trying to do for about four hundred years – but something really quite different and much deeper. (Hall 1998: 291)

Throughout the world, people are caught up in, and excluded by, the powerful currents of capitalist markets, religious movements, and national projects. Embracing and resisting these forces they struggle to position themselves, to establish home bases, sites of collective support and action. Communities need to make 'room' for themselves (Turner 1992: 14) in a crowded world. If in the late twentieth century they have done this through cultural processes of ethnic, regional, tribal, class, racial, gender, and sexual identification (in tactical combination) this is not something we have the luxury, or the privilege, to lament. As George Lipsitz (1998) trenchantly argues, opposition to the special claims of racial or ethnic minorities often masks another, unmarked, 'identity politics', an actively sustained historical positioning and possessive investment in Whiteness. This defensive response, most aggressively mobilized by the Right, in fact spans the political spectrum. It thus behoves those of us on the Left to be especially wary of any absolute, self-righteous opposition to identity claims. The lesson Gramsci learned from the devastating victory of national over class identifications in 1914 remains inescapable. Cultural politics is not secondary to more 'material' political/economic agencies. Effective democratic mobilizations begin where people are (not where they 'should be'): they work through the cultural discourses that situate groups, that provide them with roots (always spliced), with narrative connections between past and present (traditions), with distinctive social habits and bodies.

This hooking-up and unhooking, remembering and forgetting, gathering and excluding of cultural elements – processes crucial to the maintenance of an 'identity' – must be seen as both materially constrained and inventive. Of course it is difficult, analytically and politically, to sustain this double vision, just as it is hard to work with the ambivalence inherent in processes of identification: the practical inseparability of empowerment and chauvinism, of community and exclusion, of performance and commodification, of positioning and governmentality. And yet it is precisely in this uncomfortable site of cultural process and politics that we begin, and begin again. Moreover, it is here that we can cultivate a kind of historical 'negative capability', aware of our own partial access to other historical experiences, tracking interference patterns and sites of emergence, piecing together more-than-local patterns, big-enough stories of the 'global', of intersecting 'historical' trajectories.

In what follows I begin thinking in this comparative, historicizing spirit about contemporary claims for 'tradition', claims that are central to the deeper and more differentiated politics of identitifications Stuart Hall helps us keep in view. For if, as he reminds us, a discursive linking of pasts and futures is integral to the positioning of collective actors, then some gathering up and performance of 'traditions' must inform all political subjecthood. To imagine a coherent future, people selectively mobilize past resources. Articulations of tradition, never simply backward-looking, are thus generative components of peoplehood, ways of belonging to some discrete social time and place in an interconnected world.

To take these complex, historically specific processes seriously we need to keep in view an uneven, broadly distributed, always unfinished range of phenomena. The task requires representational tact, a patient, self-reflexive 'listening' across cultures and histories. Towards the end of my remarks I will urge the importance of a reconstituted cultural anthropology for this project. The anthropology I have in mind is no longer part of a unified 'science of man', a science which sorted out the world's cultures, synchronically and diachronically, from a privileged standpoint at the end, or cutting edge, of history. Rather I want to affirm another strand of anthropology which points towards more tentative, dialogical but still realist, ethnographic histories: a work of translation which focuses not so much on cultures as on conjunctures, on complex mediations of old and new, of local and global.

More explicitly than the term 'culture', the word 'tradition' (along with its many near-equivalents: *costumbre, coutume, kastom,* et cetera) highlights a historical break, a relinking of past and future in a collective dynamism. Tradition becomes problematic, and thus politicized, in situations of rapid 'modernization'. Three canonical cultural-studies works, grappling with changes in Britain after World War Two, may be said to have introduced a contemporary, critical approach to the topic: Richard Hoggart's (1957) evocation of a threatened working-class way of life, Raymond Williams's (1958) critique of elitist appeals to 'cultural' value and continuity, and E.P. Thompson's (1963) history of artisanal traditions and the rights of 'freeborn Englishmen' in the popular politics of early industrialism.[1] These seminal works responded to a society struggling with industrial and imperial decline, with the emergence of mass politics and consumerism, and with a new international order increasingly dominated by US economic, military, and cultural power. Hoggart, Williams, and Thompson, in their different ways, were concerned to salvage and revitalize British, indeed rather narrowly English, currents of democratic community and contestation in a rapidly changing global context not yet fully visible when they wrote in the late 1950s (Gilroy 1996: 234–8). All three saw democratic politics as crucially a clash and negotiation of 'traditions'.

Twenty years later, two influential works would cast this critical approach to tradition in a wider frame: *The Invention of Tradition* (1983) by Hobsbawm and Ranger, and Benedict Anderson's *Imagined Communities* (1983). Together they epitomized a paradigm in which the authenticity claimed for any tradition, culture, or identity would be interpreted as a historical and political process involving the selective and creative manipulation of symbols, stories, spaces and times. While the two books focused on national projects, their general approach extended to a wider, more disorderly range of creations. Since the early eighties countless works have been written on the 'invention' of almost everything, from the Gaucho and George Washington, to Appalachia and the Shtetl. The 'invention paradigm' spilled out of the constraints Hobsbawm and Ranger placed on it. Their distinction between 'custom' which was (authentically) lived and 'tradition' which, under modernizing pressures, was (inauthentically) invented, quickly came under pressure. Indeed, Roy Wagner, in *The Invention of Culture* (1975), had already shown in a Melanesian context that cultural process is always invention, all the way down. He argued that the notion of 'culture' was a relatively new way of objectifying collective meanings – emerging from the distinct but connected modern projects of natives and anthropologists. But the basic symbolic production at work, the marking off of value and the social processing of novelty, was not qualitatively new in Melanesian inventions of tradition – cargo cults or a range of '*kastom*' movements.

In the 1980s the invention paradigm often fused with poststructuralist theories, underwriting a deeply sceptical stance toward all identity claims, and often a prescriptive anti-essentialism. In its more pragmatic forms, this disposition opened important new ways of imagining political agencies and alliances: the coming together of complex, multiply identified subjects in particular conjunctures around specific struggles (for example, Radhakrishnan 1989; Grossberg 1996). But given the well-established propensity of people to locate themselves in more enduring (if dynamic) traditions, this paradoxical 'politics of singularity' (Grossberg 1996: 102–5) retains a theoretical, utopian cast. Moreover, when post-structuralist critiques of identity have hardened into theoretical dogma they may dismiss historically adaptive forms of cultural *integrity* in the same breath as essentialist assumptions of *authenticity*. It is not surprising, then, that the invention paradigm itself quickly became a violently contested set of propositions wherever identity-based social movements need to make cultural claims against hegemonic systems. Seen from the standpoint of resistance movements, critiques of authenticity articulated from a dominant position appeared as disempowering, and sometimes, when matters ended up in court, as actively hostile.[2] The resulting battles over cultural authority and colonial legacies, intellectual and material turf, have helped to focus attention on newly intractable, comparative questions.

How, in practice, is the gathering, locating, narrating power that the term 'tradition' implies mobilized and challenged? How do a range of peoples (nations, ethnicities, tribes, and other mobilized communities) distinguish relatively invariant, 'past'-oriented, dimensions of their collective life from changing, creative ('future'-oriented) dimensions? And to what extent are the very temporal markers 'past' and 'future' skewed by a particular history of modernization? The culture wars of seventeenth- and eighteenth-century Europe opposed ancients and moderns, religious orthodoxy and scientific enlightenment. This Western historical transition may be sedimented in the term 'tradition' whenever it is defined in implicit or explicit opposition to 'modernity'. But much is obscured by this prefiguration when we consider Melanesian invocations of '*kastom*', or other local, regional, and national claims integral to the process of patching together new nation-states. Is 'tradition' an adequate translation for pan-Mayan *costumbre* articulated in current struggles for a multi-ethnic Guatemalan polity? Indigenous traditionalisms, Marshall Sahlins (1994: 381) has proposed, might better be compared with a different European transition, one that returned to a classical past to innovate a dynamic future: 'the Renaissance'.

Tradition, in this view, is less about preservation than about transformative practice and the selective symbolization of continuity. But how much interaction and hybridity – mix and match – can a given set of conventions and filiations accommodate without losing the ability to assert the integrity of a discrete tradition? Apparently quite a lot. For the practical limits on 'invention' are primarily political (What does it take to *convince* ourselves and others?) rather than empirical (How *much*, exactly, is new?) or moral (Is this the *real* tradition?). Articulations of tradition can take many forms in a range of historical conjunctures, from early contact histories in the Pacific analysed by authors such as Greg Dening (1980) and Sahlins (1985), where more or less intact local cultures can still process novelty on indigenous terms, to the Caribbean of scholars such as Sidney Mintz (1966), Richard Price (1998), and Daniel Miller (1994), where cultural roots have long been radically cut and remixed. Differently hybrid versions of continuity and peoplehood need to be distinguished across a spectrum of post- and neo-colonial histories, a range of indigenous, local, national, and diasporic cultural projects.

As the twenty-first century begins, we confront a spectacular (I use the word advisedly) proliferation of claims to culture and identity. Can these be accounted for in a systematic way? An influential and important argument proposes that the prolific invention and reinvention of identities is integral to a late-capitalist, or 'postmodern', world system of cultures. In this view, globalization, at a cultural level at least, permits and even encourages ethnic, racial, gender and sexual differences – so long as they do not fundamentally threaten the dominant political–economic order. Traditions are thus constantly salvaged, created, and marketed in a productive game of identities. In the work of Fredric

Jameson (1984) and especially David Harvey (1990) the commodification of identities and traditions is linked to a historical moment, a
global change that brings with it newly flexible and decisive restructur-
ings of local worlds. While accounts vary as to where, when, and how
unevenly the change occurs – the global economic crisis of the 1970s is
often seen as a turning point – the outcome is a significantly new form
of cultural production: postmodernity.

In the globalizing condition of postmodernity, local communities
are reconstituted within a superficial shopping mall of identities.
Where 'culture' and 'place' are reasserted politically in the new system, it is increasingly in nostalgic, commodified forms. Thus the
before/after structure of 'authentic custom'/'invented tradition'
assumed by Hobsbawm and Ranger is given a postmodern reworking.
Traditional heritage persists as simulacrum, folklore as fakelore. We
increasingly confront what Dean MacCannell (1992: 158) calls 'reconstructed ethnicity . . . new and more highly deterministic ethnic forms
. . . ethnicity-for-tourism in which exotic cultures figure as key attractions'. I wish to argue, however, that this growing tendency to objec-
tify, commodify, and perform identities is only part, albeit a crucial
part, of the story.

In *The Condition of Postmodernity*, Harvey significantly identifies a
crucial 'paradox' (1990: 295). Homogenization breeds difference. As
geographic barriers and distances are erased by mobile commodity,
labour and capital flows, as a global postmodern 'space' is created,
simultaneously an increasingly explicit, performative differentiation of
'places' becomes apparent. What accounts for the contradiction? 'If
capitalists', Harvey writes, 'become increasingly sensitive to the spatially
differentiated qualities of which the world's geography is composed,
then it is possible for the peoples and powers that command those
spaces to alter them in such a way as to be more rather than less
attractive to highly mobile capital.' Local elites 'package' their place so
as to attract investment; and in a competitive environment, this leads
to 'the active production of places with special qualities'. Cities, for
example, need 'to forge a distinctive image and to create an atmosphere of place and tradition that will act as a lure to both capital and
people "of the right sort"'. 'Heightened inter-place competition should
lead to the production of more variegated spaces *within* [my emphasis]
the increasing homogeneity of international exchange' (Harvey 1990:
295).

The paradox is thus functionally explained. Within the expanding
'space' of capital, 'places' exist as consumable commodities. Cultural
differences produced by the postmodernist marketing of local aura and
distinction tend, Harvey argues, towards the replication of nearly

identical patterns from city to city. To clinch his argument, he cites New York's South Street Seaport, Boston's Quincey Market, Baltimore's Harbor Place (Harvey 1990: 295). This is, however, a very specific list of sites – all certifiably 'postmodern'. When we expand the range of performative sites for culture, locale, and tradition, the 'systematic' determination of heritage and identity is crosscut by other contributions. Indeed, an *unresolved* paradox is presented by the florescence of claims to difference (by people of both the right and the wrong sort) in contexts of political–economic globalization – a paradox Harvey clearly names but perhaps too quickly explains away. Ethnographic realism requires that we inhabit the paradox, if I may put it thus, more actively and attentively.[3]

Different versions of a global-systemic approach – for example, the work of Jonathan Friedman (1994), of Aiwah Ong and Donald Nonini (1997), or of Alan Pred and Michael Watts (1992) – leave more room for the transformative continuity of older elements in new situations, a politics of articulation rather than of functionalist containment. In these ethnographically based analyses, the old/new cultural claims and emergent identities cannot be ultimately determined by an expansive capitalism. Global-systemic forces do play a profound structuring role, but they do so *in relation to* local agency and prior traditions – structures negotiated in specific contact histories, which retain their own transformative momentum. A growing number of historically minded anthropologists have clearly shown the dynamism and transformative capacity of indigenous social structures and cosmologies. Overall, this work tends to shift the emphasis from inventions of tradition to traditions of invention. But *both* processes are at work in most contemporary conjunctures, and it is often hard to say definitively which plays the dominant role. The distinction between a transformed older structure and novel hybrid forms will necessarily be debatable.[4]

Ethnographic/historical research makes clear, in any case, that the relative dynamism and power of interacting local and global forces, and the ultimate question of determination – who consumes whom in a spectrum of culture-contact situations – cannot be read off in advance. While we can, and must, track the constitutive force of a world-system of cultures and identities, this cannot be the only, or the final, moment in our analysis. All global-systemic approaches run the risk of reductionism, where difference becomes merely derivative of, or contained by, structural power. But when a systemic approach is kept in serious tension with historical-ethnographic specificity, it can yield textured, realistic (which is not to say objective or uncontested) understandings of contemporary cultural processes. The challenge is to recognize overlapping but discrepant histories that struggle for position, for room to manoeuvre, in a paradoxically systematic and chaotic modernity.

I have suggested that the perspective of a historically informed ethnography is indispensable to a comparative understanding of the politics of identities. In conclusion I would like to urge the point more strongly, particularly since cultural/historical anthropology does not appear to be required reading for a broad range of cultural studies scholars. Too often anthropology is stereotyped and misunderstood – seen as confined to 'pre-modern' societies, irreparably tainted by colonialism, or fatally hemmed in by its own forms of textual and institutional authority. The discipline has, of course, been going through an epistemological and political crisis, and it has been significantly transformed by the intense questioning (James *et al.* 1997). Indeed, one wonders how many academic fields could survive this kind of very public scrutiny, both of its methods and of its global positioning. The result in many departments today is a series of intense debates and turf battles – as a disarticulated anthropology debates its central heritage and essential methods. In this context (and as someone whose work is sometimes cited as having contributed to anthropology's disarray) I hasten to affirm some traditions worth reinventing.[5]

Cultural anthropology has characteristically made two irritating but crucial interventions, calling everyone up short: 'What else is there?' 'Not so fast!' The discipline pays serious attention to people at the margins: relatively powerless, non-literate or differently literate communities whose particular stories are left out of national or global histories. Of course this professional brief for diversity carries evident risks: nostalgia (the belief that distinctive traditions are vanishing, or must always be defended) and wishful thinking (an uncritical tendency to celebrate difference as 'resistance', either in traditional survivals or in a new world of hybrid forms). But a disposition to perceive and value difference can also be understood not as a reification of otherness but as an awareness of excess, of the unwoven and the discrepant in every dominant system, the 'constitutive outside' of even the most hegemonic social or ideological formations. In times of presumed globalization, 'brushing history against the grain', as Walter Benjamin (1969) put it, is more critical than ever. It is in the emergent sites, the things that don't quite fit, the remembered or revived alternatives, that we look for utopian, transformative visions and practices.

'What else is there?' Perhaps this question is all that can be reclaimed from anthropology's exoticist heritage, a systematic interest in what does not match familiar patterns. Ethnographic exoticism no longer presumes cultural isolates. It tracks, instead, 'out-of-the-way places' intimately engaged with national and transnational powers (Tsing 1993) or populations that occupy, in Kathleen Stewart's (1996) title, 'a space on the side of the road'. Nor is this a matter of 'speaking for' the others – primitives or subalterns. What is at issue is more like listening than speaking. 'What else is there?' persistently reminds us not to skip over the marginal, the 'small', sites when thinking historically at global, national, or regional scales. In California, for example, one hears a great deal about the 'Asia-Pacific Region' or 'the Pacific Rim' – discussions in which the Island Pacific, Oceania, regularly drops from view. Yet places like Vanuatu or Papua New Guinea are extraordinary laboratories for 'postmodern' nation-making, and the latter is home to one-seventh of the world's languages. Melanesia is anything but small, in that register! Such places seem, always, to be left behind, playing historical catch-up. What changes of perspective, asks the Tongan anthropologist and novelist Epeli Hau'ofa (1993), would be needed to recast isolated dots scattered in a distant sea (as viewed from Europe) into a historically interconnected, culturally dynamic 'sea of islands'?

Or consider contemporary Mayans. I am often struck by the surprise many people evince when told that there are thirty living Mayan languages – not 'native dialects'. (The conversation reverts quickly to the ancient ruins.) Surviving Mayan societies are relatively small, to be sure; but their old/new traditions loom large in post-1992 reimaginings of the history of the Americas. One of several major pre-Columbian 'civilizations', Mayans are a past-becoming-future – active in a culturally complex present. Seen in global perspective, they shrink in importance; but within Guatemala, Mayans form a majority of the population. As they mobilize politically and culturally in the current conjuncture, they become a force to be reckoned with (Warren 1992, 1996, 1999; Fischer and Brown 1996). There are, of course, differences between the various local and pan-Mayan articulations of *costumbre*, tensions present, to varying degrees, in all contemporary indigenous movements: regional, linguistic, and class factions; urban and rural, traditionalist and mod-ernizing agendas. The movement standardizes languages and customs, producing a newly objectified culture, and folklore. But its roots in local places and politics remain strong. Clearly the work of linguistic and cultural advocacy pursued by Mayan intellectuals and activists is a far cry from the state-sponsored nostalgia decried by First World critics of the 'heritage industry'. Nor is it very much like MacCannell's (1992) 'reconstructed ethnicity', a production for the White-dominated cul-ture market – though tourism, these days, will always be somewhere in the picture.

Comparative ethnography – sensitive to historical patterns of domi-nance, accommodation and resistance, to gendered and regional formations – helps us appreciate the uneven landscape, Hall's 'contradictory, stony ground', of contemporary identity claims. Are we concerned with colonial Williamsburg (Handler and Gable 1997), with English country houses (Hewison 1987), with newly 'traditional' Japanese sites of mourning (Ivy 1995), or with pan-Indian movements in North America – their powwows, art markets, and long histories of cultural performance across generations, for other Indians, and for tourists? Is our focus the mobilization by Melanesians of '*kastom*' in response to Christian missions, labour recruitment, and Western political institutions, a mobilization with different stakes for men and women (Jolly 1994)? Are we considering the cultural politics of Hawaiian sovereignty, including the quite recent and booming hula competitions (Buck 1993), or the extraordinary, transnational 'revival' of klezmer, described by its historian, Mark Slobin, as 'a reasonably rootless but deeply rooted music that has no geographic center, no living community it's attached to by continuous practice, a capricious and shifting audience, and no fixed body of music that defines its contours' (1998: 5)? Are we talking about Kayapo Indians from the Amazon, regaled in feather crowns and body paint to demonstrate in Brasília or at the World Bank against land encroachments, while recording these demonstrations on video for internal and external use (Turner 1991, 1992)? What is the ambivalent mix of local empowerment, self-stereotyping, alliance and chauvinism in such mobilizations of 'authentic' tradition (Conklin 1997)? How do differently positioned audiences (insiders, outsiders, border crossers) consume cultural performances for tourists – for example, mobilizations by the 'primitive' Ainu in Japan (Friedman 1990) or by the 'savage' Small Nambas of Malekula, Vanuatu (Tilley 1997)? What is the 'second life of heritage' (Kirshenblatt-Gimblett 1998) in these experiences: the intricate mix of backward- and forward-looking agendas enacted in the myriad museums, villages, monuments and landscapes where 'tradition' is currently preserved and displayed?

'Not so fast.' The survival (and renaissance) of 'doomed' tribal peoples, or the variety of African Christianities and Islams, makes it clear that 'Westernization' has not been a linear progress. The local outcomes of 'acculturation' or religious 'conversion' can be surprising. It thus behoves us to hesitate when assessing the effects of cultural contact, staying alert for unexpected consequences and mixtures. Most histories of global development have had few second thoughts about people on the margins: 'pre-modern' societies are destined either to assimilate or to vanish in a relentless homogenizing process. As we have seen, visions of globalization tend to smooth over the constant (re)articulation of cultural identities and differences: in nationalist

visions, large- and small-scale (Gladney 1996); in supporting and sub-
verting established states (Comaroff 1996); in proliferating ethnic
claims, creative and virulent (Roosens 1989); in diverging local practices of consumption (Miller 1995c); in the politics of neo-tribal and
'Fourth World' movements (Sharp 1996).

It is all too obvious when identity turns ugly, when self-assertion
requires scapegoating, when people kill and expel their neighbours
(Ignatieff 1993; Ryan 1996). Rwanda, Sarajevo (now Kosovo), Belfast,
Cyprus, Indonesia . . . the list is depressingly long. Given the constitutive tension of positive and negative impulses in claims to peoplehood,
all assertive identity movements, including those that empower the
dispossessed, can seem to be symptoms of a general disease. But only
when looked at abstractly. A more conjunctural understanding will
grapple with a shifting mix of political relations (hostility, tolerance,
indifference, alliance) and with the specific historical conditions of
social crisis and material insecurity that are conducive to chauvinism.
The range and outcome of identity politics can never be guaranteed.
In relatively secure times, movements of self-assertion by the less
powerful will include a combination of tactics, affirmations and negotiations around separation *and* interaction. Effective group action in
complex civil societies means recognizing that there are times for
gathering in and times for reaching out, for the 'barred room' and for
'coalition politics' (Reagon 1983). Identity can be a basis for connection as well as disconnection. Let me end with two brief evocations,
offered in the spirit of ethnographic attention and historical open-
endedness I have been urging.

New Caledonia, a 'small' Oceanic place, has undergone a particularly
disruptive, at times deadly, colonization over the past century and a
half. Important white settler and diasporic Pacific populations are well
established there. The Kanak independence movement which emerged
in the 1960s has championed an island-wide politics of Melanesian
identity, organizing important heritage festivals and cultural centres
with the aim of repositioning dispersed 'tribal' groups as 'Kanaks'.
(The new name is a critical appropriation of the generic French
colonial label 'Canaque'.) This articulation (in Stuart Hall's terms, a
political cobbling-together) of a new ethnicity has been crucial for a
movement working, simultaneously, on cultural, economic, and political fronts. And here, unlike the more diasporic experiences central to
much postcolonial and cultural studies work, a traditional attachment
to land, to particular sites and valleys, is a structuring element of the
old/new mix.

The Kanak movement's goal of rooted independence does not
presuppose, however, an absolute separation from France with its

ongoing cultural and economic contributions, or from the world system of markets, media, and cultures. Rather, the movement works to achieve a real measure of political autonomy and control over the processes of import and export that inescapably connect places in the world. Thus the struggle for sovereignty is not to opt out but to find new – engaged and embattled – ways to be Kanak in a cosmopolitan Pacific of the twenty-first century. The tactical politics of de-linking and re-linking are inseparable. I derive this pragmatic vision from the writings of the movement's late leader, Jean-Marie Tjibaou (1996). The vision is not uncontested. Tjibaou was seen by some as too accommo-dationist, and he was assassinated by a member of his movement's radical fringe. His views have, however, generally prevailed. Given the picture of local/global entanglement I have been sketching, Tjibaou's understanding of independence as an interactive autonomy, and of *la coutume* as a way of reaching back in order to be differently modern, appears as something like realism.

What else is there? Not so fast! At the conclusion of a recently published book, I quoted the long historical vision of Barbara Shangin, an Alutiq (Koniag) elder from Alaska. I still can't quite assimilate her statement. I don't think we should assimilate it too easily. 'Our people have made it through lots of storms and disasters for thousands of years. All the troubles since the Russians [arrived] are like one long stretch of bad weather. Like everything else, this storm will pass over some day' (Clifford 1997: 343). What will it take for this invocation tradition – a temporality cast in the cyclical rhythms of weather – to be widely accepted as realizable history, a differently modern past-becom-ing-future?

Notes

1. In Thompson's *The Making of the English Working Class* the centrality of 'cultural' politics to 'class' politics is inescapable. There is nothing universal about the emerging consciousness Thompson traces: it is a historically contin-gent articulation of local traditions. Indeed his most engaged critics have shown the 'making' he traces to be strongly determined by populist movements of local self-defence (Calhoun 1982) and by a gendered artisanal subjectivity (Clark 1995) – the very limitations often laid at the door of 'identity politics' by advocates of wider class mobilizations. Class that is 'for itself', that mobilizes self-consciousness and agency, is always an articulated cultural formation. For a recent example, see Ortner's (1998) ethnographic account of the fusion of class with race and ethnicity in US social practices.

2. See Jolly (1992) and Briggs (1996) for sensitive accounts of the ongoing disputes over 'invented' traditions and for the repositioning of anthropology

that follows from taking the challenges seriously. Indigenous perspectives are articulated by Jaimes and Noriega (1988), Trask (1991), and Hau'ofa (forthcoming).

3. See *Worlds Apart: Modernity through the Prism of the Local* (Miller 1995a) for a sampling of ethnographic work in a less determinist vein. The editor, Daniel Miller, argues for a bifocal historical attention to both 'apriori' and 'aposteriori' differences. The former are transformed, or syncretic versions of pre-modern cultures. The latter, 'rarely acknowledged or theorized', reflect the 'quite unprecedented diversity created by the differential consumption of what had once been thought to be global and homogenizing institutions' (Miller 1995b: 2–3). Miller's distinction, though no doubt heuristic, helps us keep a very wide range of local/global articulations in view. Another exemplary recent collection is Gupta and Ferguson (1997).

4. One might note, for example, the difference of *emphasis* underlying the disagreement between Nicholas Thomas (1992, 1993) and Marshall Sahlins (1993) over the Fijian custom of *kerekere* – dynamic local tradition and/or colonial invention. A sampling of recent work in historical ethnography/ ethnographic history might include, along with the well-known scholarship of Sahlins, Thomas, and Greg Dening, the work of John and Jean Comaroff (1992), James Carrier (1992), Paul Sullivan (1989), and Carolyn Hamilton (1998), among many others. Sahlins (1994) provides a brilliantly argued manifesto for the general approach, diminished, however, by slapdash polemics and an unmotivated, almost Hegelian, vision of an emerging 'world culture of cultures'.

5. They are not, of course, the only ones. See also Clifford 1997, Chapter 3. Whilst I cite, for the most part, works by academic scholars based in the United States, Australia, and Europe, it is important to recognize that professional anthropology today includes Western, non-Western and in-between perspectives. Moreover, academic anthropology is not the only place one can go for a textured sense of local/global histories. As ongoing debates around the 'invention' of tradition show, no professional or geo-political standpoint enjoys a monopoly of authority, either scientific or indigenous. Indeed, many Western-based scholars now present their accounts in dialogue and tension with indigenous authorities. The work of Kay Warren, cited below, is exemplary.

References

Anderson, Benedict (1983) *Imagined Communities: Reflections on the Origin and Spread of Nationalism.* London: Verso.
Benjamin, Walter (1969) 'Theses on the Philosophy of History', *Illuminations: Walter Benjamin, Essays and Reflections.* edited by Hannah Arendt. New York: Schocken, 253–65.
Briggs, Charles (1996) 'The Politics of Discursive Authority in Research on the "Invention of Tradition" ', *Cultural Anthropology* 11 (4): 435–69.
Buck, Elizabeth (1993) *Paradise Remade: The Politics of Culture and History in Hawai'i.* Philadelphia: Temple University Press.
Calhoun, Craig (1982) *The Question of Class Struggle.* Oxford: Blackwell.
——ed. (1994a) *Social Theory and the Politics of Identity.* Oxford: Blackwell.

——(1994b) 'Preface', in Craig Calhoun, ed., *Social Theory and the Politics of Identity*. Oxford: Blackwell, 1–7.

——(1994c) 'Social Theory and the Politics of Identity', in Craig Calhoun, ed., *Social Theory and the Politics of Identity*. Oxford: Blackwell, 9–36.

Carrier, James, ed. (1992) *History and Tradition in Melanesian Anthropology*. Berkeley: University of California Press.

Clark, Anna (1995) *The Battle of the Breeches: Gender and the Making of the British Working Class*. Berkeley: University of California Press.

Clifford, James (1997) *Routes: Travel and Translation in the Late Twentieth Century*. Cambridge, MA: Harvard University Press.

Comaroff, John (1996) 'Ethnicity, Nationalism, and the Politics of Difference in an Age of Revolution', in Edwin Wilmsen and Patrick McAllister, eds., *The Politics of Difference: Ethnic Premises in a World of Power*. Chicago: University of Chicago Press, 162–84.

Comaroff, John, and Jean Comaroff (1992) *Ethnography and the Historical Imagination*. Boulder, CO: Westview.

Conklin, Beth (1997) 'Body Paint, Feathers, and VCRs: Aesthetics and Authenticity in Amazonian Activism', *American Ethnologist*, 24 (4): 711–37.

Dening, Greg (1980) *Islands and Beaches: Discourse on a Silent Land, Marquesas, 1774–1880*. Honolulu: University Press of Hawaii.

Fischer, Edward, and R. McKenna Brown, eds. (1996) *Maya Cultural Activism in Guatemala*. Austin: University of Texas Press.

Friedman, Jonathan (1990) 'Being in the World: Globalization and Localization', in Mike Featherstone, ed., *Global Culture: Nationalism, Globalization and Modernity*. London: Sage, 311–28.

——(1994) *Cultural Identity and Global Process*. London: Sage.

Gilroy, Paul (1996) 'British Cultural Studies and the Pitfalls of Identity', in Houston Baker, Manthia Diawara, and Ruth Lindeborg, eds., *Black British Cultural Studies: A Reader*. Chicago: University of Chicago Press, 223–39.

Gladney, Drew (1996) 'Relational Alterity: Constructing Dungan (Hui), Uygur, and Kazakh Identities Across China, Central Asia and Turkey', *History and Anthropology*, 9 (4): 445–77.

Grossberg, Lawrence (1996) 'Identity and Cultural Studies – Is That All There Is?', in Stuart Hall and Paul du Gay, eds., *Questions of Cultural Identity*. London: Sage, 87–107.

Gupta, Akhil, and James Ferguson, eds. (1997) *Culture, Power, Place: Explorations in Critical Anthropology*. Durham, NC: Duke University Press.

Hall, Stuart (1986) 'Gramsci's Relevance for the Study of Race and Ethnicity', *Journal of Communication Inquiry*, 10 (2): 5–27.

——(1988) 'New Ethnicities', in Kobena Mercer, ed., *Black Film, British Cinema*. BFI/ICA Documents 7: 27–31.

——(1989) 'Then and Now: A Re-evaluation of the New Left' (discussion), in Oxford University Socialist Group, ed., *Out of Apathy: Voices of the New Left Thirty Years On*. London: Verso, 143–70.

——(1998) 'Subjects in History: Making Diasporic Identities', in Wahneema Lubiano, ed., *The House that Race Built*. New York: Vintage, 289–300.

Hamilton, Carolyn (1998) *Terrific Majesty: The Powers of Shaka Zulu and the Limits of Historical Invention*. Cambridge, MA: Harvard University Press.

Handler, Richard, and Eric Gable (1997) *The New History in an Old Museum: Creating the Past at Colonial Williamsburg*. Durham, NC: Duke University Press.

Harvey, David, (1990) *The Condition of Postmodernity*. Oxford: Blackwell.

Hau'ofa, Epeli (1993) 'Our Sea of Islands', in Eric Waddell, Vijay Naidu, and Epeli Hau'ofa, eds., *A New Oceania: Rediscovering Our Sea of Islands*. Suva: School of Social and Economic Development, University of the South Pacific, 2–19.

——(forthcoming) 'Pasts to Remember', in Robert Borofsky, ed., *Exploring Pacific Pasts: An Invitation*. Honolulu: University of Hawai'i Press.

Hewison, Robert (1987) *The Heritage Industry*. London.

Hobsbawm, Eric, and Terence Ranger, eds. (1983) *The Invention of Tradition*. Cambridge: Cambridge University Press.

Hoggart, Richard (1957) *The Uses of Literacy: Changing Patterns in English Mass Culture*. Fair Lawn, NJ: Essential Books.

Ignatieff, Michael (1993) *Blood and Belonging: Journeys into the New Nationalism*. New York: Farrar, Straus and Giroux.

Ivy, Marilyn (1995) *Discourses of the Vanishing: Modernity, Phantasm, Japan*. Chicago: University of Chicago Press.

Jaimes, M. Annette, and George Noriega (1988) 'History in the Making: How Academia Manufactures the "Truth" about Native American Traditions', *Bloomsbury Review*, 4(5): 24–6.

James, Allison, Jenny Hockey and Andrew Dawson, eds. (1997) *After Writing Culture: Epistemology and Praxis in Contemporary Anthropology*. London: Routledge.

Jameson, Fredric (1984) 'Postmodernism, or the Cultural Logic of Late Capitalism', *New Left Review*, 146: 53–97.

Jolly, Margaret (1992) 'Specters of Inauthenticity', *The Contemporary Pacific*, 4(1) 49–72.

——(1994) *Women of the Place: Kastom, Colonialism and Gender in Vanuatu*. Chur, Switzerland: Harwood.

Jolly, Margaret, and Nicholas Thomas, eds. (1992) *The Politics of Tradition in the Pacific*. Special issue of *Oceania*, Vol. 62, No. 4.

Keesing, Roger (1996) 'Class, Culture, Custom', in Jonathan Friedman and James Carrier, eds., *Melanesian Modernities*. Lund Monographs in Social Anthropology 3. Lund, Sweden: Lund University Press, 162–82.

Keesing, Roger, and Robert Tonkinson, eds. (1982) *Reinventing Traditional Culture: The Politics of Kastom in Island Melanesia*. Special issue of *Mankind*, Vol. 13, No 4.

Kirshenblatt-Gimblett, Barbara (1998) *Destination Culture: Tourism, Museums, and Heritage*. Berkeley: University of California Press.

Linnekin, Jocelyn, and L. Poyer, eds. (1990) *Cultural Identity and Ethnicity in the Pacific*. Honolulu, University of Hawai'i Press.

Lipsitz, George (1998) *The Possessive Investment in Whiteness: How White People Profit from Identity Politics*. Philadelphia: Temple University Press.

MacCannell, Dean (1992) *Empty Meeting Grounds: The Tourist Papers*. New York: Routledge.

Miller, Daniel (1994) *Modernity: An Ethnographic Approach*. Oxford: Berg.

Miller, Daniel, ed. (1995a) *Worlds Apart: Modernity through the Prism of the Local.* London: Routledge.

——(1995b) 'Introduction: Anthropology, Modernity and Consumption', in Daniel Miller, ed., *Worlds Apart: Modernity through the Prism of the Local.* London: Routledge, 1–23.

——(1995c) 'Consumption and Commodities', *Annual Review of Anthropology,* 24: 141–61.

Mintz, Sidney (1966) 'The Caribbean as a Socio-Cultural Area'. *Cahiers d'histoire mondiale,* 9: 912–37.

Ong, Aiwah, and Donald Nonini, eds. (1997) *Ungrounded Empires: The Cultural Politics of Modern Chinese Transnationalism.* New York: Routledge.

Ortner, Sherry (1998) 'Identities: The Hidden Life of Class', *Journal of Anthropological Research,* 54(1): 1–17.

Pred, Alan, and Michael Watts (1992) *Reworking Modernity: Capitalisms and Symbolic Discontent.* New Brunswick: Rutgers University Press.

Price, Richard (1998) *The Convict and the Colonel.* Boston: Beacon Press.

Radhakrishnan, R. (1989) 'Poststructuralist Politics: Towards a Theory of Coalition', in Douglas Kellner, ed., *Postmodernism/Jameson/Critique.* Maisonneuve Press, 301–32.

Reagon, Bernice Johnson (1983) 'Coalition Politics: Turning the Century', in Barbara Smith, ed., *Homegirls: A Black Feminist Anthology.* New York: Kitchen Table Press, 356–68.

Roosens, Eugeen (1989) *Creating Ethnicity: The Process of Ethnogenesis.* London: Sage.

Ryan, Stephen (1996) '"The Voice of Sanity Getting Hoarse"'? Destructive Processes in Violent Ethnic Conflict', in Edwin Wilmsen and Patrick McAllister, eds., *The Politics of Difference: Ethnic Premises in a World of Power.* Chicago: University of Chicago Press, 144–61.

Sahlins, Marshall (1985) *Islands of History.* Chicago: University of Chicago Press.

——(1993) 'Cery Cery Fuckabede', *American Ethnologist,* 20: 848–67.

——(1994) 'Goodbye to Tristes Tropes: Ethnography in the Context of Modern World History', in Rob Borofsky, ed., *Assessing Cultural Anthropology.* New York: McGraw-Hill, 377–94.

Sharp, John (1996) 'Ethnogenesis and Ethnic Mobilization: A Comparative Perspective on a South African Dilemma', in Edwin Wilmsen and Patrick McAllister, eds., *The Politics of Difference: Ethnic Premises in a World of Power.* Chicago: University of Chicago Press, 85–103.

Slobin, Mark (1998) 'Scanning a Subculture: Introduction to Klezmerology', in Slobin, Mark, *et al.,* 'Klezmer: History and Culture: Papers from a Conference', special section of *Judaism,* 47(1): 3–5.

Stewart, Kathleen (1996) *A Space on the Side of the Road: Cultural Politics in an 'Other' America.* Princeton: Princeton University Press.

Sullivan, Paul (1989) *Unfinished Conversations: Mayas and Foreigners Between Two Wars.* New York: Knopf.

Thomas, Nicholas (1992) 'Substantivization and Anthropological Discourse: The Transformation of Practices and Institutions in Neotraditional Pacific Societies', in James Carrier, ed., *History and Tradition in Melanesian Anthropology.* Berkeley, University of California Press, 64–85.

——(1993) 'Beggars Can Be Choosers', *American Ethnologist*, 20(4): 868–76.

Thompson, E. P. (1963) *The Making of the English Working Class*. London: Victor Gollancz.

Tilley, Christopher (1997) 'Performing Culture in the Global Village', *Critique of Anthropology*, 17(1): 67–89.

Tjibaou, Jean-Marie (1996) *La Présence Kanak*. Edited by Alban Bensa and Eric Wittersheim. Paris: Editions Odile Jacob.

Trask, Haunani-Kay (1991) 'Natives and Anthropologists: The Colonial Struggle', *The Contemporary Pacific*, 3: 159–77.

Tsing, Anna Lowenhaupt (1993) *In the Realm of the Diamond Queen: Marginality in an Out-of-the-Way Place*. Princeton: Princeton University Press.

Turner, Terence (1991) 'Representing, Resisting, Rethinking: Historical Transformations of Kayapo Culture and Anthropological Consciousness', in *History of Anthropology* 7. Edited by George Stocking, Madison: University of Wisconsin Press, 285–313.

——(1992) 'Defiant Images: The Kayapo Appropriation of Video', *Anthropology Today*, 8(6): 5–16.

Wagner, Roy (1975) *The Invention of Culture*. Chicago: University of Chicago Press.

Warren, Kay (1992) 'Transforming Memories and Histories: The Meanings of Ethnic Resurgence for Mayan Indians', in Alfred Stepan, ed., *Americas: New Interpretive Essays*, Oxford: Oxford University Press, 189–219.

——(1996) 'Reading History as Resistance: Maya Public Intellectuals in Guatemala', in Edward Fischer and R. Mckenna Brown, eds., *Maya Cultural Activism in Guatemala*. Austin: University of Texas Press, 98–106.

——(1999) *Indigenous Movements and their Critics: Pan-Maya Activism in Guatemala*. Princeton: Princeton University Press.

Williams, Raymond (1958) *Culture and Society: 1780–1950*. London: Chatto and Windus.

10

Representing 'Globalization': Notes on the Discursive Orderings of Economic Life

Paul du Gay

In the early days of her first government Margaret Thatcher spelled out the evangelical ambition of her political programme. 'Economics is the method,' she said. 'The aim is to change the soul.' In *The Hard Road to Renewal* (1988), Stuart Hall traced the imbrication of these economic and moral strands that produced the 'enterprise culture' as the symbol and goal of Thatcherism. In so doing, he indicated how the discursive, or meaning, dimension is one of the constitutive conditions for the operation of economic strategies. That the 'economic', so to speak, could not operate or have 'real' effects without 'culture' or outside of meaning or discourse.

Despite Stuart's (1996) insistence – and the example provided by his own work – that the (positive) rejection of 'economism' attendant on taking the 'cultural' or 'discursive' turn does not need to and, indeed, must not result in a flight from the 'economic' (or, by the same token, presage a return to a thoroughly acultural 'political economy'), something akin to such a flight does appear to have taken place in recent years. At one level, this is not too surprising. The move towards a greater engagement with 'the cultural turn' within the social and human sciences was obviously bound to possess its own logics of inclusion and exclusion, just as economism had. However, in an era in which economics has been heralded as offering an approach capable in principle of addressing the totality of human behaviour and in which more and more domains of existence have found themselves reimagined as forms of the economic, the costs of such marginalization seem increasingly difficult to bear.

And, what's more, there are no good reasons why they should be borne. As Stuart (1997a) has consistently argued, if the 'cultural turn' teaches us anything it is that culture is involved in all those practices and processes that carry meaning for us, that need to be meaningfully interpreted by others, or that depend upon meaning for their effective operation.

So does this exclude the 'economic'? Of course it does not. For 'economic' processes and practices, in all their plurality, whether we refer to management techniques for restructuring the conduct of business, contemporary strategies for advertising goods and services, or everyday interactions between service employees and their customers, depend upon meaning for their effects and have particular cultural conditions of existence (Hall 1997a; du Gay *et al.* 1996; du Gay 1996, 1997). Meaning is produced at 'economic' sites (at work, in shops) and circulated through economic processes and practices (through economists' models of how economies or organizations work, through adverts, marketing materials and the very design of products) no less than in other domains of existence in contemporary societies.

Let us think for a moment about that object we refer to as 'the economy'. How do we actually go about managing that entity? Obviously, one of the first things we need to do is to build a clear(ish) picture of what an economy looks like. We need to ask ourselves what are its main components and how do these work? In other words, before one can seek to manage something called an 'economy', it is first necessary to conceptualize or represent a set of processes as an 'economy' that are amenable to management. We need, therefore, a discourse of the economy and this discourse, like any other, will depend upon a particular mode of representation: the elaboration of a language for conceiving of and hence constructing an object in a certain way so that that object can then be deliberated about and acted upon. Discourses of the economy, like any other sort, carry meaning.

In this piece, I want briefly to try to 'do' the sort of 'cultural economy' that Stuart Hall has undertaken to such effect. I take as my object a particular discourse of economic globalization and seek to explore, in a suitably ramified manner, how this discourse problematizes the ways in which economic security is to be obtained under conditions of extreme uncertainty. In particular, I focus on the ways in which this discourse of economic globalization simultaneously defines the circumstances in which states, organizations and persons find themselves and advocates particular mechanisms through which their economic security might conceivably be obtained under those circumstances.

Imagining 'Economic Globalization'

'Globalization' has become possibly the most fashionable concept in the social sciences, a core axiom in the prescriptions of management consultants, and a central element of contemporary political debate. As Paul Hirst and Grahame Thompson (1996: 1) have indicated, it is widely asserted that we live in an era in which the greater part of social life is determined by global processes, in which national cultures, national economies and national borders are dissolving. Central to this assertion is the notion of a truly globalized economy. The emergence of such an entity, it is claimed, makes distinct national economies and, therefore, domestic strategies of national economic management irrelevant. The world economy is increasingly globalized in its basic dynamics, it is dominated by uncontrollable market forces, and it has as its principal economic actors and strategic agents of change truly transnational corporations, which owe allegiance to no nation-state and locate wherever in the world that market advantage dictates (Angell 1995; Ohmae 1990, 1993; Osborne and Gaebler 1992; Reich 1990, 1992). This representation of 'globalization' connects with the most diverse outlooks and social interests. It covers the political spectrum from left to right, and it is endorsed in several, diverse academic disciplines – from international relations to management science, and from sociology to cultural studies.[1]

Indeed, the concept of 'globalization' has achieved such widespread exposure and has become such a powerful explanatory device and guide to action that it sometimes appears almost unquestionable. Certainly its effects have been pronounced. As Hirst and Thompson (1996) have also suggested, one effect of the dominance of this representation of contemporary economic life has been the effective paralysis of racial reforming national strategies, which have been seemingly unviable in the face of the judgement and sanction of global markets.

Although there continues to be considerable academic debate about precisely how far and in what respects economic and other activities are actually 'globalizing' (as opposed to 'internationalizing', for example) (Boyer and Drache 1996; Hirst and Thompson 1996; Lane 1995) there can be no doubt that this dominant conception of the problem of globalization has played a crucial role in transforming the character of Western governments' perceptions of the ways in which their own national economies should be managed, with consequent changes in these governments' understandings of the relations between economic activity and other aspects of the life of a national community.

In other words, regardless of what one might think of this 'globaliza-tion' hypothesis, an awful lot of things are being done in its name.

In the rest of this chapter I want briefly to delineate some of the ways in which this particular discourse of 'globalization' comes to problematize conduct in a diverse range of sites, and to indicate some of the mechanisms through which authorities of various sorts seek to shape, normalize and instrumentalize the conduct of institutions and persons in the name of making 'globalization' manageable.[2]

Globalization and National Economic Security

If the widespread consensus of the 1950s and 1960s was that the future belonged to a capitalism without losers, securely managed by national governments acting in concert, then the late 1980s and 1990s have been dominated by a consensus based on the opposite set of assump-tions: namely, that global markets are basically uncontrollable and that 'the only way to avoid becoming a loser – whether as a nation, an organization, or an individual – is to be as competitive as possible' (Hirst and Thompson 1996: 6; see also Krugman 1996).

This zero-sum conception has serious implications for the ways in which states are encouraged to view their own security, for example. Of course, security, and security of economic activity in particular, is a primary concern for any state. What the discourse of 'globalization' problematizes is the ways in which security is to be obtained under conditions of extreme uncertainty. Indeed, the discourse of globaliza-tion both defines the circumstances in which states find themselves and advocates particular mechanisms through which security might conceiv-ably be obtained under those circumstances.

Simply stated, nation-states embedded in (what is represented as) an increasingly competitive global market and hence exposed to (what are represented as) supranationally ungovernable economic forces are encouraged to guarantee their survival through devolving responsibility for the 'economy' to 'the market' – using what remains of their public powers of intervention to limit, as it were constitutionally, the claims that politics can make on the economy, and citizens on the polity. Wolfgang Streeck (1996a: 307), for example, testifies to the power of the discourse of globalization when he writes that 'in many countries today, disengagement of politics from the economy is defended with reference to constraints of economic internationalization that would frustrate any other economic strategy'.

In place of a representation of the national economy as a resource, and therefore as contributing to the well-being of the national com-

munity in other respects – and, of course, in place of specific mechanisms designed to make this practicable – we now find an inversion of
that perception, with other aspects of the life of the national community increasingly perceived in terms of their contributions to economic efficiency. In this new light, security can only be obtained, it
would appear, through allowing economic problems to rebound back
on society, so that society is implicated in resolving them, where
previously the economy was expected to provide for society's needs.

So what are the implications of this new image of the national
economy for governmental perceptions of relations between national
economic activity and other aspects of the life of the national community? Under the old regime, the national economy could be seen
both as a largely self-regulating 'system' and as a resource for other
component parts or domains of a larger national unity. Since pruden-
tial government would secure the conditions of economic growth, its
output, net of depreciation and replacement costs, could be deployed
for investment on the one hand and for other crucial national purposes, such as defence and social welfare, on the other. These latter
expenditures might or might not be seen as 'economic costs' but their
net effect would only be to reduce the rate of growth to rather less
than it might otherwise have been (Hindess 1997).

Within the discourse of globalization the pursuit of national economic efficiency is the *sine qua non* of national security and well-being.
This incessant hunt for economic efficiency appears as a foundation
not only of economic growth but also of all those other activities that
must be financed from growth. As I indicated above, this strategy of
economic governance undermines existing divisions between the economy and other spheres of existence within the nation-state. The image
of the well-ordered national economy providing resources for the
national state and society is now replaced by the image of the extrava-
gant 'big government' state and society undermining efficient national
economic performance. This shift helps account for the seemingly
paradoxical situation in which governmental discourse in the wealthi-
est nations on earth contains an assumption that social welfare
regimes are no longer affordable in the forms we have come to knew
them. Anything that might seem to have a bearing on economic life
(and this includes education, defence and health as well as social
welfare) is assessed not only in terms of the availability of resources
and the alternative uses to which those resources might be put, but
primarily in terms of its consequences for promoting or inhibiting the
pursuit of national economic efficiency. The aim here is not simply to
save money in the short term but also to induce efficiency-enhancing
'cultural change' in organizational and personal conduct through the

introduction of market-type relationships into ever more spheres of existence.

The notion of 'enterprise' occupies an absolutely crucial position in this endeavour. It both provides a critique of 'big government' and offers a solution to the problems posed by 'globalization' through delineating a new set of ideals and principles for conceiving of and acting upon organizational and personal conduct.

Enterprising up Organizations and Individuals

This emphasis on enterprise should come as no surprise, given the foundational place accorded to market forces in the discourse of economic globalization (Ohmae 1990). If the winners and losers in the global economy are to be determined largely, if not exclusively, by their competitiveness, then obviously enterprise is a quality no player in the global market game can afford to be without, whether nation, firm or individual.

Accordingly, the foremost consideration for national governmental players is the necessity of constructing the legal, institutional and cultural conditions that will enable the game of entrepreneurial and competitive conduct to be played to best effect. For these anti-political liberals or neo-liberals, it is a question of extending a model of rational economic conduct beyond the economy itself, of generalizing it as a principle both limiting and rationalizing government activity. National government must work for the game of market competition and as a kind of enterprise itself, and new quasi-entrepreneurial market models of action or practical systems must be invented for the conduct of individuals, groups and institutions within those areas of life hitherto seen as being either outside or even antagonistic to the economic.

Looking briefly at developments in the UK, for example, we can see that, while the concrete ways in which this model of rational economic conduct has been operationalized in the public sector have varied considerably, the forms of action that have been made possible for different institutions and different types of person – schools, general practitioners, housing estates, prisons and so forth – do seem to share a general consistency and style.

One characteristic feature has been the crucial role allocated to 'contract' in redefining organizational relationships. The changes affecting schools, hospitals, government departments and so on, in the United Kingdom, have often involved the reconstituting of institutional roles in terms of *contracts strictly defined*, and even more frequently have

involved a *contract-like* way of representing relationships between institutions, and between individuals and institutions.

An example of the former occurred when fund-holding medical
practices contracted with hospital trusts for the provision of health care
to particular patients, whereas previously that provision was made
directly by the National Health Service. Examples of the latter include
the relationships between central government departments and the
new executive agencies – where no technical contract as such exists but
where the relationship between the two is governed by a contract-like
'framework document' which defines the functions and goals of the
agency, and the procedures whereby the department will set and
monitor performance targets for the agency.

This process, which Jacques Donzelot (1991) has termed one of
'contractual implication', typically consists in assigning the performance of a function or an activity to a distinct unit of management –
individual or collective – which is regarded as being accountable for
the efficient (that is, 'economic') performance of that function or
conduct of that activity.

By assuming active responsibility for these activities and functions –
both for carrying them out and for their outcomes – these units of
management are in effect affirming a certain type of identity. This
identity is basically entrepreneurial in character because 'contractualization' requires these units of management to adopt a certain entrepreneurial form of relationship to themselves 'as a condition of their
effectiveness and of the effectiveness of this type of government'
(Burchell 1991: 276). To put it another way, contractualization makes
these units of management function like little businesses or 'enterprise
forms'.

According to Colin Gordon (1991), entrepreneurial forms of governance such as contractualization involve the reimagination of the social
as a form of the economic. 'This operation works', he argues, 'by the
progressive enlargement of the territory of economic theory by a series
of re-definitions of its object.' He continues, '[E]conomics thus
becomes an "approach" capable in principle of addressing the totality
of human behaviour, and, consequently, of envisaging a coherent,
purely economic method of programming the totality of governmental
action' (Gordon 1991: 43).

It would be a mistake, however, to view these developments as simply
expressing the latest and purest manifestation of the rise of *homo
oeconomicus*. For the subject of entrepreneurial rationality is both
'a reactivation and a radical inversion' of traditional representations
of 'economic man'. The reactivation consists 'in positing a fundamental human faculty of choice, a principle which empowers economic

calculation effectively to sweep aside the anthropological categories
and frameworks of the human and social sciences'. The great innovation occurs in the conception of the economic agent as an inherently
manipulable or 'flexible' creation (Gordon 1991: 43; du Gay 1996:
Chapter 2)

Gordon argues that whereas *homo economicus* was originally conceived
of as a subject, the wellsprings of whose activity were ultimately
'untouchable by government', the subject of enterprise is imagined as
an agent 'who is perpetually responsive to modifications in its environment'. As he suggests, 'economic government here joins hands with
behaviourism' (Gordon 1991: 43). The resultant subject is in a novel
sense not simply an 'enterprise' but rather 'the entrepreneur of himself
or herself'. In other words, entrepreneurial rationality makes up the
individual as a particular sort of person – as 'an entrepreneur of the
self' (Gordon 1987: 300).

So what does it mean to conceptualize a human being as an 'entrepreneur of the self'? This idea of an individual human life as an
'enterprise' suggests that, no matter what hand circumstance may have
dealt a person, he or she remains always continuously engaged (even if
technically 'unemployed') in that one enterprise, and that it is 'part of
the continuous business of living to make adequate provision for the
preservation, reproduction and reconstruction of one's own human
capital' (Gordon 1991, p. 44).

Once a human life is conceived of primarily in entrepreneurial
terms, the 'owner' of that life becomes individually responsible for
their own self-advancement and care; within the ideals of enterprise,
individuals are charged with managing the conduct of the business
of their own lives. The vocabulary of enterprise reimagines activities
and agents and their relationship to one another according to its
own ideals. Thus, the entrepreneurial language of responsible self-
advancement and care, for example, is linked to a new perception of
those who are 'outside civility' – those who are excluded or marginalized because they cannot or will not conduct themselves in an appropriately 'entrepreneurial' and hence 'responsible' manner. In the UK,
for example, pathologies that were until recently represented and
acted upon 'socially' – homelessness, unemployment and so forth –
have become reindividualized through their positioning within entrepreneurial discourse and hence subject to new, often more intense,
forms of surveillance and control. Because they are now represented
as responsible individuals with a moral duty to take care of themselves,
pathological subjects can blame no one but themselves for the problems they face. This individualization of social problems is evidenced
in the UK as elsewhere by the introduction of a new terminology to

describe the unemployed person – 'job seeker' – and the homeless person – 'rough sleeper'.

Because a human being is considered to be continuously engaged in a project to shape his or her life as an autonomous, choosing individual driven by the desire to optimize the worth of his or her own existence, life for that person is represented as a single, basically undifferentiated, arena for the pursuit of that endeavour. As previously distinct forms of life are now classified as 'enterprise forms', the conceptions and practices of personhood – or forms of identity – they give rise to are remarkably consistent. Thus, as schools, prisons, charities, and government departments, in the UK for example, are re-presented as 'enterprises' they all accord an increased priority, in terms of judging their own success, to the development of the 'enterprising subject'.

Concluding Comments

The main tenets of the globalization hypothesis have been subject to extensive and largely convincing critique. As Hirst and Thompson (1996:199), for example, have argued, even if classical national economic management is now represented as having only limited scope, this does not mean that economic relations at both international and national levels are beyond governance, that is, means of regulation and control. Much, they argue, depends on political will and co-operation between the major economic powers.

In the absence of such will and co-operation, socio-economic analysis indicates that persisting unemployment, recurring financial crises, rising inequalities, underinvestment in productive activities such as education and research, and cumulative asymmetries of information and power are ever more likely outcomes of continuing reliance on 'pure' market functioning (Boyer 1996, p. 108).

So what signs are there that such co-operation and will are emerging? Not many, according to Wolfgang Streeck (1996a), who points to two divergent political responses taking place at the national level. On the one hand, he identifies those nation-states, such as the UK and the USA, that see their principal contribution to competitiveness in handing responsibility for it to 'market forces'. Such an approach has involved large-scale privatization, retrenchment of social protection, market-driven industrial restructuring, restoration of managerial authority, downwardly flexible wages and working conditions, the disablement of organized interests, particularly trade unions, and the promotion of a low-wage, low-skill sector to absorb some of the unemployed. The alternative response, what might remain in a era of 'over-

diminished expectations' of social democracy, neo-corporatism and
social partnership, is the construction at the national level of what
Streeck (1996, p. 311) terms 'coalitions to modernize' the national
economy, with all other political objectives subordinate to that of
increasing national competitiveness.

> Post-social democratic coalition building can draw on the institutionalism
> and economic nationalism of labour movements prevented from acting at
> the supranational level by lack of state capacity and employer interlocutors.
> It may also count on the employers, whose main interest is to forestall
> supranational state formation and economic intervention; who therefore
> benefit from labour being contained in national political circuits; and who
> can be certain that, in the face of external competitive pressures and because
> of their capacity to exit, they will be the alliance's senior partners. Finally,
> national governments can hope to increase their support from both business
> and labour for defending joint national interests in the international arena,
> thereby defending their own legitimacy as well as and further reinforcing the
> national organization of politics and the intergovernmental character of
> international economic governance. (Streeck 1996a: 311)

Despite their obvious differences, these two governmental responses
are by no means mutually exclusive. For one thing, it is still the case
that the globalization hypothesis provides a discursive framework in
relation to which both sets of policies are pursued. As Streeck has
argued in another context, the globalization hypothesis 'discriminates
against modes of economic governance that require public intervention
. . . it favours national systems like those in the United States and
Britain that historically relied less on public–political and more on
private–contractual economic governance' (quoted in Milner 1996).
To this extent, it comes as no surprise to learn that the competitive
coalition-building model is in many respects as dependent on the
voluntarism of the marketplace as the neo-liberal deregulation model.

Under both, national governments refrain from imposing obligations
on market participants, especially business, as much as possible, either
because they believe that market intervention is by its very nature
dysfunctional, or because they are legally obliged by international treaty
to restrict such public intervention to the creation of incentives and
the removal of deterrents for mobile investors. At the same time,
nationally based democracy in both models is constrained by a presumed need not only to respond to competitive pressures before
responding to citizen's democratic demands – or to interpret the latter
in terms of a technically correct response to the former – but also to
make sure that it stays within the boundaries of the rules and regulations imposed on national economic decision-making by intergovern-

mental agreement. As constraints on national economic intervention become more severe, 'national governments . . . become dependent on *the voluntarism of the market-place*, having lost recourse to the "hard law" that used to be the main tool of state interventionism in the past' (Streeck 1996b, p. 311).

While the main tenets of this discourse of economic globalization have been subject to extensive and largely convincing critique, important economic and political decisions continue to be taken in their name. The effect of this is to make the system of international economic governance that is developing – one dominated, in Streeck's terms, by 'the voluntarism of the marketplace' – increasingly difficult to buck. Far from increasing the likelihood of an alternative system of governance emerging, one capable of civilizing and domesticating rampant market forces, current developments seem to be effectively negating this possibility. The danger, as Stuart Hall (1997b) has indicated on a number of occasions, is that what we've got is what we may be stuck with for the foreseeable future and that this is far less than is needed to ensure that contemporary economies are viable social as well as economic entities.

Notes

1. In sociology and cultural studies, as Doreen Massey (1996: 8) has argued, the most characteristic presence of this discourse is as an iconic summary of 'economic globalization' in the opening paragraphs of a treatise on something more 'social' or 'cultural'. At its worst it becomes something of a mantra: CNN, McDonald's, Sony, time/space compression, local/global, information flows, the internet, all these characteristic names, words and phrases make an obligatory appearance.

What is puzzling and disturbing about this is the ease with which scholars otherwise committed to various forms of contractionist analaysis grant a particular vision of globalization the status of 'fact'. As Massey (1996: 9) points out, it is almost as if the 'economic' has once again become the essential, if now largely unacknowledged, backdrop to other stories. There is, we assume, before going on to recount the complex results of our own researches, this sort of economic globalization. This is a dodgy move. Not only because it involves the reintroduction, by omission, of a sort of economism, but also because the acceptance by omission of a particlar version of economic globalization brings other effects in its wake. Most notably, it bestows authority and validity upon a vision of globalization that is not so much a description of the way things are as an image in which the world is being remade.

2. The texts I draw upon and refer to here are largely Anglo-American in origin. However, the discourses they articulate can be observed to have structured policy initiatives in national contexts from Canada to Australia and to

have been advocated by political regimes on the left and right of the political spectrum. That said, however, I do not want to overexaggerate the convergence in the forms of organizational and personal conduct they have engendered in different social contexts.

References

Angell, I. (1995) 'Winners and Losers in the Information Age', *LSE Magazine*, 7(1).

Boyer, R., (1996) 'State and Market: A New Engagement for the Twenty-first Century?', in R. Boyer and D. Drache (eds.) *State against Markets*, London: Routledge, pp. 84–114.

Boyer, R., and Drache, D. (eds.) (1996) *State against Markets*, London, Routledge.

Burchell, G. (1993) 'Liberal Government and Techniques of the Self', *Economy and Society*, 22(3), 266–82.

Donzelot, J. (1991) 'The Mobilization of Society', in G. Burchell *et al.* (eds.) *The Foucault Effect*, Brighton: Harvester Wheatsheaf, pp. 169–79.

du Gay, P. (1996) *Consumption and Identity at Work*, London: Sage.

du Gay, P. (ed.) (1997) *Production of Culture/Cultures of Production*, London: Sage.

du Gay, P., Hall, S., *et al.* (1996) *Doing Cultural Studies: The Story of the Sony Walkman*, London: Sage.

Gordon, C. (1987) 'The Soul of the Citizen: Max Weber and Michel Foucault on Rationality and Government', in S. Whimster and S. Lash (eds.) *Max Weber: Rationality and Modernity*, London: Allen & Unwin, pp. 293–316.

Gordon, C. (1991) 'Governmental Rationality: An Introduction', in G. Burchell *et al.* (eds.) *The Foucault Effect*, Brighton: Harvester Wheatsheaf, pp. 1–51.

Hall, S. (1988) *The Hard Road to Renewal*, London: Verso.

Hall, S. (1996) 'When Was the "Post Colonial"? Thinking at the Limit', in I. Chambers and L. Curti (eds.) *The Post Colonial Question*, London: Routledge, pp. 242–60.

Hall, S. (1997a) 'The Centrality of Culture: Notes on the Cultural Revolutions of Our Time', in K. Thompson (ed.) *Media and Cultural Regulation*, London: Sage, pp. 207–38.

Hall, S. (1997b) 'Les Enfants de Marx et Coca-Cola', *New Statesman and Society*, 5 December 1997, pp. 34–6.

Hindess, B. (1997) 'Neo-liberalism and the National Economy', in B. Hindess and M. Dean (eds.) *Governing Australia*, Sydney: Cambridge University Press.

Hirst, P., and Thompson, G. (1996) *Globalization in Question*, Cambridge: Polity Press.

Krugman, P. (1996) *Pop Internationalism*, Cambridge, MA: MIT Press.

Lane, C. (1995) *Industry and Society in Europe*, Aldershot: Edward Elgar.

Massey, D. (1996) 'Imagining Globalization: Power-Geometries of Time–Space'. Keynote address to the British Sociological Association Annual Conference, University of Reading.

Milner, M. (1996) 'A Timely Global Warning', *Guardian*, 7 September, p. 23.

Ohmae, K. (1990) *The Borderless World*, London: Collins.

Ohmae, K. (1993) 'The Rise of the Region State', *Foreign Affairs*, 72(2), 78–87.

Osborne, D. and Gaebler, T. (1992) *Re-inventing Government*, Reading, MA: Addison-Wesley.

Reich, R. (1990) 'Who Is Us?', *Harvard Business Review*, January–February, 53–64.

Reich, R. (1992) *The Work of Nations*, New York: Vintage

Sabel, C. (1992) 'Moebius Strip Organizations and Open Labour Markets: Some Consequences of the Reintegration of Conception and Execution in a Volatile Economy', in P. Bourdieu and J.S. Coleman (eds.) *Social Theory for a Changing Society*, Boulder, CO: Westview Press, pp. 23–54.

Streeck, W. (1996a) 'Public Power beyond the Nation State: The Case of the European Community', in R. Boyer and D. Drache (eds.) *States against Markets*, London: Routledge, pp. 299–315.

Streeck, W. (1996b) *German Capitalism: Does it Exist? Can It Survive?*, Cologne: Max Planck Institute.

11

The Sugar You Stir . . .

Paul Gilroy

Stuart Hall's work has helped us to appreciate that we have been living through a profound transformation in the way that 'race' is understood and acted upon. This short chapter is premised upon the idea that we must try to take possession of that change and somehow set it to work against the tainted logic that produced it. In other words, the argument here proceeds from the utopian prospect that the current crisis of 'race' and representation, of politics and ethics, offers a welcome cue to free ourselves from the bonds of all raciology in what might be an ambitious new 'abolitionist' project. Among other things, this crisis has changed the status of blackness. The old American-centred specifications of black life as abjection, though tied to the immiseration of so many people, are incompatible with the new currency of black culture as commodity and cipher of vitality, fitness and health in a weightless global market that relies more than ever on blacks to supply some of its most alluring 'software'. We must also note that – to oversimplify somewhat – the period of decolonizing struggles is basically over. These conflicts, even when they are played out in the courtrooms of South Africa, no longer supply the primary moral and political referents for black aspirations towards freedom and justice in other parts of the world. How then are we to define our pursuit of freedom? What are the versions of justice towards which we orient ourselves?

These questions have to be understood through local political imperatives. I must emphasize that point because it underlines the enduring relevance of national 'ecologies of belonging'. Though we suffer the multiple pathologies of nationalism, Britain has been judged to be a relatively successful multicultural society. Our problems with the ultra-right are fewer than those in many other places, and we are obliged to intervene in discussions of what Europe will be in the future in a different, more urgent, postcolonial spirit. Through the lens provided by our emergent multiculture, it appears that the politics of race in its

Manichean black/white configurations will be increasingly confined in future to the deindustrializing, but still overdeveloped, world.

Important opportunities arise from the great transformations that have created this crisis. We ought, for example, to be able to use these historical changes to update our theories of culture and its technological and communicative mediations, and if we become committed to working against the reification of identity and the trivialization of its complex mechanisms – too readily reduced, these days, to the iconic associations that characterize authoritarian and fundamentalist politics – we will be able to build upon the precedents of double consciousness without fear and create something more fluid: a future-oriented political mentality that is more comfortable with the idea of multiplicity, less prone to the fatal lure of simplistic solutions and short cuts to the political solidarity that is both demanded and contradicted by the tenor of these difficult times.

Perhaps we can remember and adapt Marx's insight: we make our identities, but with inherited resources and not under circumstances of our own choosing. That old 'ecological' theme of imaginative identity-work, always materially constrained and culturally specified, has some enduring uses. It might, for example, be employed loosely to bond the subaltern histories of blacks in Europe with the larger narrative of blacks in a catastrophic, colonial modernity that extended beyond Europe's imperially expanded geo-body. This counter-history encompasses strange and absorbing stories that stretch back into the times before Europe was Europe. At the very least, it demands a comprehensive rethinking of the impact of the brutal market activity in human beings which culminated in coffee, sugar, chocolate and tea, not to mention new forms of banking, insurance and governmental administration, becoming familiar – even essential – elements in the common European habitus.

There is insufficient space here to summon up adequately that still underexplored history which gets assigned far too frequently to a separate distant, colonial space or to pay adequate homage to the forgotten figures – real and imagined – who might serve as ideal ancestors or prototypes for today's black would-be Europeans. As an absolute minimum we should acknowledge the itinerant presence of exotic entertainers, strange sojourners, servants, workers and fugitives whose eruptive appearance in the European metropolis became an irresistible symptom of the crisis of aesthetic modernism identified so precisely by Edward Said. Woven into a revised account of that crisis, we can locate the lives of articulate figures with open philosophical and critical aspirations who proudly exemplified what the black American exile Richard Wright called a negative loyalty to modernity's embattled traditions.

Because I recognize that the historic force of fascism and its overt
raciological ambitions are central to defining the integrity and moral
constituency of Europe, and because I know that the seductive powers
of what Primo Levi called 'the silent nazi diaspora' neither defer to
skin colour nor respect the formal boundaries erected against them in
vain by liberal and socialist political ideology, I want to direct our
attention precisely towards the thoughts of the black intellectuals who
lived through the period of fascist governments and their immediate
aftermath.

This was not a unified group for whom the catastrophe represented
by the Nazi genocide was a simple revelation. Their diverse colonial
histories and attenuated memories of slavery meant that they already
inhabited a world that had acknowledged these possibilities. The most
insightful of them connected their understanding of the fascist period
into the frameworks with which they made sense both of the immediate
Cold War future and of the long-term prospects for building a political
culture in which democracy would not be qualified by divisions based
on colour, phenotype or 'race'. They could not fail to consider the
ways in which colonial power had corrupted and brutalized its supposed
beneficiaries as well as those it enslaved and exterminated. That was
the inventory created by the obligation to subject scientific and culturalist versions of raciology to a relentless political and moral onslaught.

Their theories of intermixture, hybridity, universality and indivisible
justice, plurality and complex identity were tempered by their proximity
to Europe's most profound modern catastrophe: the industrialized
murder of millions in pursuit of racial purity and homogeneity. The
memory of that offence no longer supplies the intellectual constellation
under which we strive to do critical work on 'race' and its pathologies.
Recognition of its loss provides an additional inducement to recover
and restore an ethical dimension to action against racial injustice and
its hierarchies.

Our transitional situation demands a more extended consideration
of this group's lives and their dissident work. They were among the
first thinkers to identify the seemingly intractable problems arising
from the racialization of democracy, capitalism and industrialization,
phenomena that had preceded their arrival in Europe but which had
endured and assumed new permutations since then. They recorded
the catechism of promises fulfilled and broken where blacks in vain
sought recognition of their humanity and their moral personality. They
argued that European modernity's finest philosophical currency had
been debased by these oversights and showed, in turn, that the same
cognitive and perceptual habits fostered and accentuated patterns of
power, violence and authority which produced catastrophic conse-

quences. The story of their dissonant relationship to Europe's political culture should become an essential part of contemporary inquiries into an ethical, less market-driven multiculturalism and into the political and historical resources necessary if 'non-white' Europeans are to dwell peacefully in Europe in the twenty-first century

The lucid, bitter words with which Césaire, Senghor and others less well known, indicted the race-specific, anthropological humanism that they identified as a powerful link between genocidal events inside and outside Europe do not always span the gulf between languages. Nevertheless, we should recall their contribution here. I must emphasize that the small act of recovery and translation proposed here would not primarily be a means to rethink the embattled black political cultures of the new and neo-colonial worlds. It ought now to be recognized as an aspect of Europe's internal conflicts: one more event in a chaotic pattern of ongoing struggles which aim at nothing short of making Europeans more comfortable with their continent's irreversibly heterocultural character and at breaking the vicious circles of their phobic responses to alterity.

This involves more than the admittedly difficult task of reacquainting wilfully uninterested and complacent academic orthodoxy with the colonial dynamics and relations that have conditioned the development of the academic humanities as well as the material life of the overdeveloped countries even when the arrival of particular nation-states at imperial status was late, uneven or ambivalent. Whatever value this reflection may still have in nurturing the self-consciousness of 'ethnic minorities', I want to argue that the critique of racialized identity it promotes cannot be a matter for them alone. The growth of ultranationalist and neo-fascist movements suggests that agonized reflections on the limits of being European have acquired a signal importance in the considerations of identity that are taking place among the dominant groups. Their initial difficulties with the idea of admitting 'aliens' into the primordial sylvan belonging that connects authentic Euros created forms of racism in which the idea of cultural and ethnic difference qualified earlier and simpler notions of biological hierarchy. It is worth repeating that there are important signs that this culturalism has given way to a bio-technological determinism that thrives outside the fading shadows cast by the living memory of the Nazis' industrialization of killing.

Responding to this new circumstance can only proceed via a renewed critique of the idea of race itself – and, it is to be hoped, view its death as a principle of moral and political calculation – but it cannot end with that. There have to be further confrontations, on one side with the human body represented as the fundamental repository of the order of racial truth, and on the other, as I have already hinted, with the idea of culture itself as it is pluralized, multiplied and deterritorialized. The latter task asks us to identify again the distinctive rationalities, logics, metaphysics, pathologies and oppositional possibilities of a more complex cultural ecology: one that sees species life as the outcome of interplay between communicative systems and the environments they incorporate but also modify and transcend.

It would be wrong to overlook the possibility that, while racisms endure, a distinctive understanding of identity does emerge from serious consideration of these dense, hybrid formations of postcolonial culture in which translation is simultaneously both unremarkably routine and burdened with a particular ethical significance. In its simplest form, this understanding of solidarity, selfhood and subjectivity might be congruent with a problem the radical humanist Jean Améry enumerated when he spoke long ago of the exilic, transcultural condition he identified as the simultaneous necessity and impossibility of his being a Jew. Though he was unaware of it, a comparable state of being but not belonging had already been named by black thinkers often as well-versed as he in the esteemed traditions of philosophical thought from which they were sometimes excluded by the non-negotiable force of racial typology. They had different names for this state of being (double consciousness)

The work of the Négritude writers provides one of many possible entry points into this translocal and intercultural history of ideas and movements. This is not because they transcoded the Hegelian speculations of African Americans like DuBois into a different moment, a different idiom but because, as Sandra Adell has so brilliantly shown, the black identities they argued with and argued over were partly created with strange conceptual tools furnished by the anthropology of Leo Frobenius and the existential outlook of Heidegger.

Like a great many New World blacks, this group pondered Hitler's fragmentary pronouncements in *Mein Kampf* on the Negro and the perils of intermixture. During the 1930s, they followed the beleaguered position of European Jews very attentively and considered the relationship between the familiar patterns of pre-genocidal terror and discrimination against the German Jews and the different but certainly comparable situation to be found both in America's Southern states and their less formal Northern approximations. Having savoured his victories at the 1936 Olympics, they recoiled when, at a Republican Party rally, Jesse Owens pronounced upon the greatness of Hitler while comparing him to perfidious Roosevelt. They cheered loudly when noble, heroic black American manhood in the form of Joe Louis defeated the Nazi-nudger Max Schmeling and the idea of Aryan supremacy in that fateful second fight. These important examples point forwards out of their time, towards a transformation in the meaning and status of the black male body and some unprecedented patterns of identification and desire which have become routine in the logo-emblazoned age of Michael Jordan's planetary stardom.

More than any other figure, it is of course Fanon who carried the anxieties and insights of this group into subsequent political gener-ations. Transformed now into an anti-colonial activist, he spoke for a far larger dissenting formation – from a position inside and against the structures that had shaped him – when, as both beneficiary and victim of European progress in its blood-spattered colonial mode, he demanded national liberation for colonial peoples but tied that project of revolutionary reconstruction to the deliberate production of a new conception of humanity:

> It is a question of the Third World starting a new history of Man, a history which will have regard to the sometimes prodigious theses which Europe has put forward, but which will also not forget Europe's crimes, of which the most horrible was committed in the heart of man, and consisted of the pathological tearing away of his functions *and the crumbling away of his unity*. . . . For Europe, for ourselves and for humanity, comrades, we must turn over a new leaf, we must work out new concepts, and try to set afoot a new man. [emphasis added][1]

There is more to this powerful exhortation than Fanon's attempt to transcode Jacobin aspirations into the distinctive tones of colonial conflict. You will note that he objects not merely that European imperial powers have wrongfully deprived colonial subjects of their humanity, but that Europe has perpetrated an even greater crime: that of despoiling humanity of its elemental unity as a species. Fanon's call for the institution of a decidedly anti-racist – that is, post-anthropologi-cal – universalism is a significant gesture. It reveals his debts to the political imaginary of the Western world even in his greatest gestures of disavowal. What is most important about this stance is his insistence that the lost grail of universalism can be recovered only at the price of a reckoning with the ambivalences of the colonial modernity that travellers like him brought back to Europe with them when they arrived to claim their elite educations. The argument became even stronger when they were followed by itinerant workers and settlers who claimed their citizenship. These groups have laid the cornerstones of our legacy today.

We should not have to recall the Enlightenment pretensions that were compromised from the moment of their conception in the womb of the colonial space; the foundations destabilized by that initial

configuration, by the intermittent endorsement of 'race' as a central
political and historical concept and by the violence done to the central
image of man by the exigencies of colour-coded power which offered
an ascending path towards the prison of exotic status as the only escape
route from worldly terror.

In this festive setting it is probably wise to remain agnostic about
whether the equilibrium of the Western political imaginary is recoverable or whether the confidence and authority of epistemological and
moral claims staked in that tradition can be restored. Instead, I would
suggest that their rehabilitation can proceed only if the real depths of
the Western political imaginary's persistent difficulties with difference
are fully appreciated. I would also suggest that a survey of these
problems would have to acknowledge the recurrence of terror and
barbarity as more than mere lapses from more exalted standards of
rational conduct. You can perhaps see how *this* version of multiculturalism ceases to be about the problems of administering the lives of
'immigrants'.

Many contemporary questions about the integrity and continuity of
race thinking and raciology, the limits of purely national cultures, the
ethics of anti-racist struggles and the political character of ethnic
absolutisms have a significant presence in the work of the next cohort
of black thinkers, that which succeeded the war veterans. We can call
this group the Stuart Hall generation. They had to apply the insights
derived from the earlier group consistently in the difficult climate of
Cold War struggles for independence, citizenship, rights and recognition. They watched the West begin to disappear and a new version of
Europe begin to take its place. All of them had things to say about the
character of Western culture and civilization from which we must learn.

They were not exposed to Nazism on the battlefield or, more
characteristically, in the camp, and they arrived in Europe after formal
hostilities were concluded, as part of the process of cleaning up after
the war. My basic point here is that we postcolonial Europeans can
claim their Cold War experiences and set them to work as part of our
speculations as to what Europe might be and become.

These examples demand more from us than just better accounts of
itinerant, travelling culture and an active scepticism with regard to the
consistency of the race concept, the claims of nationality, and the
coherence of raciological thinking. They underline the fact that modern racial typology and hierarchy have demanded the interconnection
of Enlightenment and myth. What do we say when we recognize that it
is the contested idea of integral and exclusive culture that has supplied
the very principle of the articulation of myth and Enlightenment? We
can respond that theories about culture are unholy parts of the broken

world they strive to explain. We can show that we know there are still too many fortified zones bounded by deference to the authoritarian claims that origins and territorial cultures can make, where purity is prized and mutability arouses only fear, resentment and distrust. More happily, we can observe that there are also precious moments when concern with the mechanisms of cultural transmission and translation must become a priority, when the promiscuous anti-discipline associated with complex cultural dynamics rewrites the rules of criticism, appreciation and, yes, politics in emphatically post-anthropological codes.

We have a cue to explore the movement from culture to multiculture and the other openings created by culture's routine and irreverent translocation: something that is all the more precious now not only because it repudiates the claims of raciology but also because it is incompatible with the arcane desires of the butterfly collectors of alterity who prefer their cultures integral and like their differences to remain absolute. Their power is growing as people cast about seeking antidotes to the perils of globalization. For that reason alone, our arguments need to invent an assertive, cosmo-political mode that concedes nothing to either the primordialization or the reification of culture.

Note

1. Frantz Fanon, *The Wretched of the Earth*, translated by Constance Farrington, Penguin, 1967, pp. 254–5.

12

Public Pedagogy as Cultural Politics: Stuart Hall and the 'Crisis' of Culture

Henry A. Giroux

> What does it mean to take seriously, in our present conjuncture, the thought that cultural politics and questions of culture, of discourse, and of metaphor are absolutely deadly political questions? . . . I want to persuade you that that is so. And we ought to sort of preach on this occasion, no, not only to give up the bad habits of smoking and drinking and whoring and gambling, but to give up certain forms of political essentialism and the way in which it makes you sleep well at night.
>
> Stuart Hall, 'Subjects in History'[1]

Within the last forty years, Stuart Hall has produced an impressive body of work on the relationship between culture and power, and culture's constitutive role as a political and pedagogical practice produced and mediated within different social contexts, spatial relations, and historical conjunctures.[2] Refusing to confine culture to narrow epistemological categories or to matters of taste, Hall argues that cultural power is what distinguishes cultural studies from other disciplines and academic areas. Cultural politics in this discourse proposes 'combining the study of symbolic forms and meanings with the study of power', or more specifically what he calls the 'insertion of symbolic processes into societal contexts and their imbrication with power'.[3] According to Hall, culture is central to understanding struggles over meaning, identity, and power, and he has written repeatedly on the importance of the relationship between culture and politics, power and subjectivity as it is reconfigured at all points along the circuit of cultural production.[4]

Hall's work provides an important theoretical framework for making pedagogy central to the politics and practice of cultural production, and for understanding pedagogy as a mode of cultural criticism that is essential for questioning the conditions under which knowledge and identifications are produced and subject positions are taken up or refused. Hall also offers a critical and strategic challenge to the backlash against the pedagogy and politics of culture that has emerged in the United States by proponents as different as Harold Bloom, Richard Rorty, and Todd Gitlin.[5] Essential to this debate is not simply the issue of how we think politics, how we understand the dynamics of culture within the shifting discursive practices and material relations of power, but also how we can, as Larry Grossberg suggests, 'inquire into the conditions of the possibility of agency'.[6] For theorists such as Hall, Grossberg, and others, culture is a strategic pedagogical and political terrain whose force as a 'crucial site and weapon of power in the modern world'[7] can, in part, be understood in its contextual specificity, but a specificity that can only be engaged in relation to its articulation with other sites, practices, and public discourses.

In what follows, I argue that Hall's attention to the relationship between culture and politics provides a valuable theoretical service to educators by contributing to a notion of public pedagogy that makes the pedagogical a defining principle of cultural politics. Moreover, Hall's work amplifies the role that educators might play as public intellectuals working in diverse sites and projects to expand the possibilities for democratic struggles. For Hall, such struggles are not predefined but rest on the ethical and political imperative to find and use 'the intellectual resources in order to understand [and transform] what keeps making the lives we live, and the societies we live in, profoundly and deeply antihumane in the capacity to live with difference'.[8]

But before I take up some of Hall's contributions to a politics of public pedagogy, I want to interrogate the recent attack on education and cultural politics, which has cut across ideological lines, and examine how such arguments undermine the possibility of making the political more pedagogical as part of a broader democratic project for radical change. Hall's work will be taken up in opposition to these discourses. I will conclude by exploring the implications of Hall's writings for those of us who believe that pedagogy is central to any notion of a radical cultural politics, and that cultural politics is a crucial precondition for understanding the struggle over meaning, power, and identities in public spheres such as public and higher education.

Schooling without Politics

These are hard times for educators and advocates of democratic schooling. Besieged by the growing forces of vocationalism and the neo-conservative cultural warriors, prospective and existing classroom teachers are caught in an ideological crossfire regarding the civic and political responsibilities they assume as engaged critics and cultural theorists. Asked to define themselves either through the language of the marketplace or through a discourse of liberal objectivity and neutrality that abstracts the political from the realm of the cultural or social, educators are increasingly being pressured to become either servants of corporate power or disengaged specialists wedded to the imperatives of a resurgent and debasing academic professionalism.

What is surprising about the current attack on education, especially the growing corporatization at all levels of schooling, is the refusal on the part of many theorists to rethink the role academics might play in engaging the university as a crucial public sphere, one that warrants a reinvigorated cultural politics that addresses what it means to make the pedagogical more political in a time of growing conservatism, racism, and corporatism. Even more surprising is the common ground shared by a growing number of progressive theorists who narrowly define politics and pedagogy within a dichotomy that pits the alleged 'real' material issues of class and labour against a fragmenting and marginalizing concern with the politics of culture, textuality, and difference.

The attack on culture as a terrain of politics is evident in the works of a number of renegades from the New Left, the most notable of whom are Todd Gitlin, Michael Tomasky, and Jim Sleeper.[9] Unlike conservative theorists such as Harold Bloom and liberals such as Richard Rorty, Gitlin and his ideological cohorts speak from the vantage point of Left politics, but display a similar contempt for cultural politics, popular culture, cultural pedagogy, and differences based on race, ethnicity, gender, and sexual orientation. In what follows, I want to highlight some of the more repeated arguments made by this group. I will focus on the work of Todd Gitlin, one of its most prolific and public representatives.

For Gitlin, contemporary cultural struggles, especially those taken up by social movements organized around sexuality, gender, race, the politics of representation, and, more broadly, multiculturalism, are nothing more than a weak substitute for 'real world' politics, notably one that focuses on class, labour, and economic inequality.[10] According to Gitlin, social movements that refuse the primacy of class give politics a bad name; they serve primarily to splinter the Left into identity sects, fail 'to address questions of economic equity and redistribution',[11] and offer no unifying vision of the common good capable of challenging corporate power and right-wing ideologues.

Gitlin's critique of social movements rests on a number of erasures and evasions. First, in presupposing that class is a transcendent and universal category that can unite the Left, Gitlin fails to acknowledge a history in which class politics was used to demean and domesticate the modalities of race, gender, and sexual orientation. Convinced that race and gender considerations could not contribute to a general notion of emancipation, the past practitoners of class-based politics left as their legacy a history of subordination and exclusion toward marginalized social movements. Moreover, it was precisely because of the subordination and smothering of difference that social groups, in part, organized to articulate their respective goals, histories, and interests outside of the orthodoxy of class politics. Judith Butler is right is arguing, 'How quickly we forget that new social movements based on democratic principles became articulated against a hegemonic Left as well as a complicitous liberal center and a truly threatening right wing[.]'[12] Moreover, not only does Gitlin limit social agency to the pristine category of class, he can imagine class only as a unified, pre-given subject position, rather than a shifting, negotiated space marked by historical, symbolic and social mediations, including the complex negotiations of race and gender. Within this discourse, the history of class-based sectarianism is forgotten, the category of class is essentialized, and politics is so narrowly defined as to freeze the open-ended and shifting relationship between culture and power.[13]

Second, by reducing all social movements to the most essentialistic and rigid forms of identity politics, Gitlin cannot understand how class is actually lived through what Stuart Hall has called the modalities of race and gender. In Gitlin's discourse, social movements are nothing but particularistic; hence, it is impossible for him to 'conceive of social movements as essential to a class-based politics'.[14] For instance, Robin Kelly points out the failure of Gitlin and others to recognize how the pressure group Act UP made AIDS visible as a deadly disease that is now taking its greatest toll among poor black women.[15] Nor is there any recognition of how the feminist movement made visible the dynamics of sexual abuse, particularly as it raged through the communities of poor black and white households. Nor is there any understanding of how a whole generation of young people might be educated to recognize the racist ideologies that permeate representations in advertising, films, and other aspects of media culture that flood daily life.

Third, Gitlin's appeal to majoritarian principles slips easily into the reactionary tactic of blaming minorities for the white backlash that characterizes the present moment, going so far as to argue that because the followers of identity politics abandoned a concern for materialist issues, they opened up the door for an all-out attack on labour and the poor by the Right. At the same time, identity politics bears the burden in Gitlin's discourse for allowing the Right to attack 'racialized rhetoric as a way of diverting attention from the economic restructuring that has been hurting most Americans'.[16] Thoughtlessly aligning himself with the Right, Gitlin seems unwilling to acknowledge how the historical legacy of slavery, imperialism, urban ghettoization, segregation, the extermination of native Americans, the war against immigrants, and the discrimination against Jews as it has been rewritten back into the discourse of United States history may upset a majoritarian population that finds it more convenient to blame subordinate groups for their problems rather than have to engage their own complicity.

Against this form of historical amnesia, the call to patriotism, majoritarian values, and unity shares an ignoble relationship to a past in which such principles were rooted in the ideology of white supremacy, the presumption that the public sphere was white, and the prioritizing of a 'racially cleansed notion of class'.[17] If identity politics poses a threat to the endearing (because transcendent and universal) category that class represents to some critics, as the historian Robin Kelly argues, it may be because such critics fail to understand how class is lived through race, sexual orientation, and gender. Or it may be that the return to a form of class warfare against corporate power represents simply another form of identity politics, that is, an identity-based campaign that stems from the anxiety and revulsion of white males who cannot imagine participating in movements led by African Americans, women, Latinos, or gays and lesbians speaking for the whole or even embracing radical humanism.[18]

Finally, Gitlin's materialism finds its antithesis in a version of cultural studies that is pure caricature. If Gitlin is to be believed, cultural studies is a form of populism intent on finding resistance in the most mundane of cultural practices, ignoring the ever-deepening economic inequities, and dispensing entirely with material relations of power. Banal in its refusal to discriminate between a culture of excellence and consumer culture, cultural studies becomes a symbol of bad faith and political irresponsibility. For theorists in cultural studies, Gitlin argues, it is irrelevant that African Americans suffer gross material injustice, since what really matters is that 'they have rap'.[19] It seems that for Gitlin, cultural studies should 'free itself of the burden of imagining itself to be a political practice'[20] since the locus of much of its work comes out of the university – a thoroughly delegitimatized site for intellectuals to address the most pressing questions of our age and take responsibility for what Stuart Hall calls 'translating knowledge into the practice of culture'.[21]

Gitlin's model of politics is characteristic of a resurgent economism rooted in a totalizing concept of class in which it is argued that 'we can do class or culture, but not both'.[22] Within this discourse, social movements are dismissed as merely cultural, and how we might think the political is removed from considering the cultural sphere as a serious terrain of struggle. Unfortunately, this critique not only fails to recognize how issues of race, gender, age, sexual orientation and class are intertwined, it also refuses to acknowledge the pedagogical function of culture as the site where identities are constructed, desires are mobilized, and moral values are shaped. Ellen Willis rightly argues in opposition to positions such as Gitlin's that if people 'are not ready to defend their right to freedom and equality in their personal relations, they will not fight consistently for their economic interests, either'.[23] Questions of agency or resistance in Gitlin's version of cultural studies are dismissed as retrograde forms of populism, while cultural pedagogy is traded for an anti-intellectual and anti-theoretical incitement to organizing and pamphleteering.

What is disturbing about this discourse is that it not only separates culture from politics, but also leaves no room for capturing the contradictions and spaces within dominant forms that open up political and social possibilities for contesting domination, doing critical work within the schools and other public spheres, or furthering the capacities for students and others to question dominant authority and the operations of power. For instance, when theorists such as Francis Mulhern suggest that cultural studies seeks to subordinate or subsume the meaning of the political into popular culture, he does more than misrepresent cultural studies, he unwittingly argues that where culture is merely educative it is not deliberate and therefore not political.[24] This is a reckless theoretical move, one that fails to grasp what Stanley Aronowitz has called the transformation of information as a new mode of production in the post-Fordist era and what Hall refers to as the centrality of culture in the formation of subjective and social identities.[25] Mulhern has no discourse for examining how the educational force of the culture works to disrupt dominant forms of common sense and provide alternative identifications and subject positions that become crucial pedagogically for providing the categories, maps of meaning, and contours of possibility through which people choose to imagine, define, or write themselves as political agents and social actors.[26]

In short, this totalizing model of class, power, and politics functions largely to cancel out how culture as a terrain of struggle shapes our sense of political agency and mediates the relations between materially based protests and structures of power and the contexts of daily struggles.

It is against the current onslaught on cultural politics and its attempt to discredit the role that educators might play as public intellectuals working in a diverse range of public spheres that Stuart Hall's work provides an important theoretical and political service. In what follows, I want to focus on some important elements in Hall's work that constitute what I loosely call a theory of critical public pedagogy.

Struggling over Culture

For Hall, culture provides the constitutive framework for making the pedagogical political – recognizing that how we come to learn and what we learn is imminently tied to strategies of understanding, representation, and disruption that offer the possibilities and opportunities for individuals to engage and transform when necessary the ideological and material circumstances that shape their lives. One of Hall's lasting contributions has been also to make the political more pedagogical. By repeatedly pointing to the diverse ways in which culture is related to power and how and where it functions both symbolically and institutionally as an educational, political, and economic force, Hall provocatively argues that cultural pedagogy is the outcome of particular struggles over specific representations, identifications and forms of agency. Both the urgency and relevance of such struggles become more clear in defining questions of identities and identifications as, in Hall's words,

> questions of using the resources of history, language and culture in the process of becoming rather than being: not 'who we are' or 'where we came from' so much as what we might become, how we have been represented and how that bears on how we might represent ourselves.[27]

In this discourse, public pedagogy as a struggle over identifications is crucial to raising broader questions about how notions of difference, civic responsibility, community, and belonging are produced 'in specific historical and institutional sites within specific discursive formations and practices, by specific enunciative strategies'.[28]

Such strategies are organized around not only the theorization of meaning, but also the struggle implied in what Hall has recently called the 'governing of culture'.[29] The term 'governing of culture' refers to the struggle over the control, regulation, and distribution of resources that mediate the range of capacities and possibilities that enable individuals and social groups to choose, inhabit, and transform particular identifications, subject positions, and history itself. Cultural politics, for Hall, is in part about the regulation and distribution of resources.

But our capacity to think politics is also mediated by the ways in which culture actually governs, the ways in which it actually shapes 'our conduct, social action, human practices and thus the way people act within institutions and in society at large' as well as the ways it establishes the terrain 'through which boundaries mark differences as potential sites of contestation over meaning, a politics of identity'.[30] In short, culture is constitutive of agency(ies) and politics because it provides the resources through which individuals learn how to relate to themselves, others, and the world around them.

For Hall, culture is neither free-floating nor does it stand still. Amplifying the relationship between learning and social change, Hall does more than acknowledge that culture is a terrain of struggle, he insists that cultural workers deepen the meaning of the political by producing pedagogical practices that engage and challenge those representational strategies, material machineries and technologies of power that condition and are conditioned by the indeterminate play of power, conflict, and oppression within society. Culture is the social field where power repeatedly mutates; identities are constantly in transit; and agency is often located where it is least acknowledged. Agency in this discourse is neither prefigured nor always in place but subject to negotiation and struggle and open for creating new demo-cratic possibilities, configurations and transformations. How one 'deals with the place of cultural politics' remains essential to any viable notion of politics concerned with how subjects are situated within historical, social, economic, and cultural relations.[31]

For Hall, the educational force of culture resides in its attentiveness to representations and ethical discourses as the very condition for learning, agency, the functioning of social practices, and politics itself. As a pedagogical force, culture is saturated with politics and offers in the broadest sense the context and content for the negotiation of knowledge and skills that enable a kind of critical reading of the world from a position of agency and possibility, within unequal relations of power. The changing nature of the representations, space, and insti-tutions of culture in modern times is central to an understanding of its pedagogical function. On the one hand, culture is substantive in that, as a complex of institutions, new technologies, practices, and products, it has vastly expanded 'the scope, volume, and variety of meanings, messages, and images that can be transmitted' through time and space.[32] On the other hand, the explosion of information produced within the cultural realm registers the shift in thinking about know-ledge as a primary form of production, if not the key productive force. Culture in these terms is more than 'either a text or a commodity': it is the site 'of the production and struggle over power'.[33] The primacy of culture as a substantive and epistemological force highlights the educational nature of culture as a site where identities are being continually transformed and power is being constantly enacted. Within this context, learning itself becomes the means not only for the acquisition of agency but for the imaginary of social change itself.

Culture as Public Pedagogy

According to Hall, the educational force of culture redefines the politics of power, the political nature of representation, and the centrality of pedagogy as a defining principle of social change; it also expands our understanding of the public reach of pedagogy as an educational practice that 'operates both inside and outside the academy',[34] expanding its reach across multiple sites and spheres. As a performative practice, pedagogy inhabits all of those public spaces where culture works to secure identities, does the bridging work for negotiating the relationship between knowledge, pleasure, and values, and renders authority both crucial and problematic in legitimating particular social practices, communities, and forms of power. It is precisely this legacy of both politicizing culture and insisting on the pedagogical nature of the political that makes Hall's work so important at the present time. If agency is negotiated, made and remade within the symbolic and material relations of power and enacted within diverse and changing historical and relational contexts, agency cannot be abstracted from the self-reflexive possibilities of pedagogy, nor can it be removed from the dynamics of cultural politics.

Of considerable importance to critical educators is Hall's theory of articulation for analysing how authority and power actually work in linking texts to contexts, ideology to specific relations of power, and political projects to existing social formations.[35] For educators this is an important insight and points to the centrality of context in shaping cultural pedagogy as a form of practical politics. Not only do political projects emerge out of particular contexts, but because contexts change as the relations between culture and power shift, such projects become practical only if they remain open, partial, and incomplete. Central to Hall's work is the insight that public pedagogy is defined through its performative functions, its ongoing work of mediation and its attentiveness to the interconnections and struggles that take place over knowledge, language, spatial relations, and history. Public pedagogy for Hall represents a moral and political practice rather than merely a technical procedure. At stake here is the call not only to link public pedagogy to practices that are interdisciplinary, transgressive, and oppositional, but also to connect such practices to broader projects designed to further racial, economic, and political democracy, to strike a new balance and expand what Stuart Hall and David Held have called the 'individual and social dimensions of citizenship rights'.[36]

The concept of articulation does more than provide a theoretical rationale for 'the making of a relationship out of a nonrelationship or, more often, the making of one relationship out of another one';[37] it also reaffirms the political nature of cultural work that gives meaning to the resources that students bring with them to various sites of learning, while simultaneously subjecting the specificities of such meanings to broader interrogations and public dialogue. This is a crucial concept for any notion of public pedagogy. Central to such a project is the need to begin at those intersections where people actually live their lives and where meaning is produced, assumed, and contested in the unequal relations of power that construct the mundane acts of everyday relations. Public pedagogy in this context becomes part of a critical practice designed to understand the social context of everyday life as lived relations of power.

At the same time, Hall has consistently insisted that cultural workers examine critically how meanings work intertextually to resonate with ideologies produced in other sites and how they work to legitimate and produce particular practices, policies, and social relations. Educators cannot treat cultural texts as if they were hermetic or pure; such approaches often ignore how representations are linked to wider social forms, power, and public struggles. Engaging cultural texts as part of a critical public pedagogy means refusing to limit our analysis of popular texts by focusing on either the polyphonic meanings at work in such texts or formalist strategies to decipher what is perceived as a text's preferred meanings. On the contrary, a critical public pedagogy should ascertain how certain meanings under particular historical conditions become more legitimate as representations of reality and take on the force of commonsense assumptions shaping a broader set of discourses and social configurations at work in the dominant social order. Hall's work has continually reinforced the necessity for educators to focus on representations as a mode of public exchange in order to explore, as Herman Gray attests, the ways 'these images, especially the historical and contemporary meanings they carry and understandings they express, are aligned and realigned with broader discourses'.[38] As public discourses, representations can be understood for the ways in which they shape and bear witness to the ethical dilemmas that animate broader debates within the dominant culture. This suggests a cultural politics that investigates how popular texts are articulated within structures of affect and meaning mediated by networks of power and domination bound to the specific historical, social and economic conditions of their production.

Public Pedagogy as Politics

I have argued that Hall's work supports a notion of public pedagogy that is interdisciplinary and continually involved in border crossings, transgressive in its challenge to authority and power, and intertextual in its attempt to link the specific with the national and transnational. The project underlying such a pedagogy may take many forms, but its deepest impulse is rooted in issues of compassion and social responsibility aimed at deepening and expanding the possibilities for critical agency, racial justice, and economic and political democracy.

Stuart Hall's work is refreshingly interdisciplinary, theoretical, contextual, and rigorous; it is accessible but refuses easy answers. But most important, Hall attempts to make hope practical and social justice the foundation of his cultural politics and pedagogy. Hall's work both instructs and disrupts, opens a dialogue, and refuses to close down deliberation and reflection. In doing so, his work takes risks, opens the possibility for a shared investigation, and reproduces, both in the structure of his arguments and the representation of his politics, a political discourse and practice that are passionately committed but offer no guarantees.

Finally, Hall's writing has always refused to limit the sites of pedagogy and politics to those 'privileged' by the advocates of 'genuine' politics. Organizing labour unions, demonstrating in the streets for legislation to curb corporate crimes, and organizing workers to promote radical forms of social policy are important forms of political practice, but working in the schools, the television industry, law firms, museums, or in a vast number of other public spheres does not constitute for Hall a less reputable or less important form of political work. In fact, Hall has continually called for intellectuals to 'address the central, urgent, and most disturbing question of a society and a culture in the most rigorous intellectual way we have available'.[39] He has urged cultural workers to take up this challenge in a variety of pedagogical sites, and in doing so has opened the possibility for working within dominant institutions, while challenging their authority and cultural practices. For Hall, the context of such work demands confronting a major paradox in capitalist societies – that of using the very authority vested in institutions such as schools in order to work against the grain of such authority. Such action is not a retreat from politics, as Gitlin and others believe, but an expansion of the possibility of politics and critical agency to the very institutions that work to shut down notions of critical pedagogy, politics, and social agency. Authority in this context pushes against the tendency to be complicitous and opens up the possibility of being resistant, transformative, and contestatory. Within this discourse, public pedagogy and cultural politics are located 'on the dividing lines where the relation between domination and subordination continues to be produced, lines that extend into the academy itself'.[40] Hall's call for a cultural politics implies a public pedagogy in which learning becomes indispensable to the very process of social change, and social change becomes the precondition for a politics that moves in the direction of a less hierarchical, more radical democratic social order.

Notes

1. Stuart Hall, 'Subjects in History: Making Diasporic Identities', in Wahneema Lubiano, ed., *The House that Race Built* (New York: Pantheon, 1997), p. 290.

2. An excellent bibliography of Stuart Hall's work can be found in a collection of his writings compiled by David Morley and Kuan-Hsing Chen. See David Morley and Kuan-Hsing Chen, eds., *Stuart Hall: Critical Dialogues in Cultural Studies* (New York: Routledge, 1996).

3. Peter Osborne and Lynne Segal, 'Culture and Power: Interview with Stuart Hall', *Radical Philosophy*, No. 86 (November/December 1997), p. 24.

4. Hall elaborates his theory of culture best in a series of books designed for the Culture, Media, and Identities Series at the Open University and published by Sage. See, for example, Stuart Hall, Paul du Gay, Linda Janes, Hugh Mackay, and Keith Negus, *Doing Cultural Studies: The Story of the Sony Walkman* (London and Thousand Oaks, CA: Sage, 1997); Stuart Hall, *Representation: Cultural Representations and Signifying Practices* (Thousand Oaks, CA: Sage, 1997); Stuart Hall, 'The Centrality of Culture: Notes on the Cultural Revolutions of Our Time', in Kenneth Thompson, ed., *Media and Cultural Regulation* (London and Thousand Oaks, CA: Sage, 1997).

5. Harold Bloom, *The Western Canon* (New York: Riverhead Books, 1994); Richard Rorty, *Achieving Our Country: Leftist Thought in Twentieth Century America* (Cambridge: Harvard University Press, 1998); Richard Rorty, 'The Inspirational Value of Great Works of Literature', *Raritan* 16:1 (1996), pp. 8–17; Todd Gitlin, *Twilight of Our Common Dreams* (New York: Metropolitan Books, 1995).

6. Lawrence Grossberg, 'Identity and Cultural Studies: Is That All There Is?', in Stuart Hall and Paul du Gay, eds., *Questions of Cultural Identity* (London and Thousand Oaks, CA.: Sage, 1996), p. 102.

7. Lawrence Grossberg, 'Toward a Genealogy of the State of Cultural Studies', in Gary Nelson and Dilip Parameshwar Gaonkar, eds., *Disciplinarity and Dissent in Cultural Studies* (New York: Routledge, 1996), p. 142.

8. Stuart Hall, 'Race, Culture, and Communications: Looking Backward and Forward at Cultural Studies', *Rethinking Marxism*, 5:1 (Spring 1992), pp. 17–18.

9. See Gitlin, *Twilight of Our Common Dreams*; Michael Tomasky, *Left for Dead: The Life, Death and Possible Resurrection of Progressive Politics in America* (New York: Free Press, 1996); Jim Sleeper, *The Closest of Strangers* (New York: W. W. Norton, 1990).

10. Gitlin's most sustained development of this argument can be found in *Twilight of Our Common Dreams*.

11. Judith Butler, 'Merely Cultural', *Social Text*, 15:52–3 (Fall/Winter 1997), p. 266.

12. Butler, 'Merely Cultural', p. 268.

13. For an insightful analysis of this position, see Lawrence Grossberg, 'Cultural Studies: What's in a Name?', in *Bringing It All Back Home: Essays on Cultural Studies* (Durham, NC: Duke University Press, 1997), pp. 245–71.

14. Robin Kelley, *Yo' Mama's Disfunktional!* (Boston: Beacon Press, 1997), pp. 113–14.

15. Ibid.

16. Iris Marion Young, 'The Complexities of Coalition', *Dissent* (Winter 1997), p. 67.

17. Butler, 'Merely Cultural', p. 268.

18. Kelley, *Yo' Mama's Disfunktional!*.

19. Todd Gitlin, 'The Anti-political Populism of Cultural Studies', *Dissent* (Spring 1997), p. 81.

20. Ibid., p. 82.

21. Stuart Hall, 'The Emergence of Cultural Studies and the Crisis of the Humanities', *October*, No. 53 (Summer 1990), p. 18.

22. Ellen Willis, 'We Need a Radical Left', *Nation* (29 June 1998), p. 19.

23. Ibid.

24. Francis Mulhern, 'The Politics of Cultural Studies', *Monthly Review*, 47:3 (July 1995), pp. 31–40.

25. See Stanley Aronowitz, *The Politics of Identity*, especially the chapter 'On Intellectuals' (New York: Routledge, 1992), pp. 125–74; Stuart Hall, 'Centrality of Culture', pp. 207–38.

26. The abstraction of the pedagogical from the politics of culture is also evident in the work of Ian Hunter, who in dismissing pedagogy as simply another form of governmentality rejects any possibility for fashioning forms of pedagogical practice that actually call attention to the ways in which authority might work to undermine forms of social and cultural reproduction in public spheres such as schools. Reducing all pedagogy to the imposition of authority and all pedagogical practices to the rule of law, Hunter can only imagine pedagogical authority working in the interest of moral regulation and social reproduction. Self-reflexive dialogue drops out of this discourse, as well as the possibility of teachers and students becoming critical of the very institutional forms, academic relations, and disciplinary knowledge regulations that consti- tute the complex and varied spaces of schooling. Within this narrow under- standing of the relationship between culture and politics, there is no possibility for imagining schools as a place to resist dominant authority, to unsettle the complacency of strategies of domination, or to re-elaborate institutional author- ity from a position of auto-critique and critical agency. That the legacy of such cultural regulation can be challenged, pedagogically turned in on itself, or used

as a resource to refigure the basis of teaching as a deliberative practice in the service of a progressive cultural politics seems impossible within this discourse. See Ian Hunter, *Rethinking the School* (New York: St Martin's Press, 1994). This position is also argued for in Tony Bennett, 'Out in the Open: Reflections on the History and Practice of Cultural Studies', *Cultural Studies*, 10:1 (1996), pp. 133–53. An interesting critique of the work of Tony Bennett and Ian Hunter and the limits of governmentality as they apply it can be found in Toby Miller, *Technologies of Truth* (Minneapolis: University of Minnesota Press, 1998).

27. Stuart Hall, 'Introduction: Who Needs "Identity"?', in Stuart Hall and Paul du Gay, eds., *Questions of Cultural Identity* (London and Thousand Oaks, CA: Sage, 1996), p. 3.

28. Ibid., p. 4.

29. Stuart Hall, 'Centrality of Culture', p. 237.

30. Ibid., p. 232.

31. Stuart Hall, 'Subjects in History', p. 289.

32. Hall *et al.*, *Doing Cultural Studies*, p. 23.

33. Grossberg, 'Cultural Studies: What's in a Name?', p. 248.

34. Stuart Hall, 'Race, Culture, and Communications', p. 11.

35. One of the most incisive commentaries on the meaning and importance of Hall's theory of articulation can be found in Lawrence Grossberg, 'On Postmodernism and Articulation: An Interview With Stuart Hall', *Journal of Communication Inquiry*, 10:2 (Summer 1986), pp. 45–60.

36. Stuart Hall and David Held, 'Citizens and Citizenship', in Stuart Hall and Martin Jacques, eds., *New Times: The Changing Face of Politics in the 1990s* (London: Verso, 1990), pp. 173–88.

37. Grossberg, 'Cultural Studies: What's in a Name?', p. 259.

38. Herman Gray, *Watching Race* (Minneapolis: University of Minnesota Press, 1995), p. 132.

39. Hall, 'Race, Culture and Communications', p. 11.

40. John Beverly, 'Pedagogy and Subalternity: Mapping the Limits of Academic Knowledge', in Rolland G. Paulston, ed., *Social Cartography* (New York: Garland, 1996), p. 352.

History, Imagination
and the Politics of Belonging:
Between the Death and the Fear of History

Lawrence Grossberg

I. In the Beginning

This chapter is about time, perhaps humankind's biggest problem, since we can't seem to escape it. In fact, it is always overtaking us and, not to sound too Heideggerian, projecting us into a future which is, increasingly, not of our own making. In fact, it is projecting us in ways that seem to call forth apocalyptic – yet utterly believable – scenarios and discourses. This is also a chapter about history – the fear of history and the death of history – and about belonging to and in time.

The notion of belonging comes to me through Heidegger and Foucault/Deleuze on the one hand, and (especially) Stuart Hall and Paul Gilroy on the other.[1] In my reading of Hall's work, 'belonging' opens up the possibility of an*other* theory of identity and *other*ness, of identification and affiliation. For a geography of belonging is not, at least in the first instance, mappable onto an economy of difference and signification. Instead it recognizes the spatial and affective organizations of social life. One is – 'placed'. Yet too often such theoretical geographies are only constructed along two dimensions – belonging among (and within) social formations, and belonging in space. Theorists continue to take it for granted, apparently assuming that it is obvious, that human beings are always and necessarily historical.

So this chapter takes another lesson from Stuart Hall: I remember him once saying that the more 'obvious' a statement, the more ideological it is. And his own recent turn into issues of colonialism and 'postcolonial theory' reinforces this lesson, for such work is teaching us much about the 'common sense' of the West and its relationship to colonialism. Drawing upon this turn, this chapter is finally about the transformation of time into history, and about imagining alternative ways humankind has belonged and can belong in and to time. In this attempt at a radical questioning (in its political, theoretical, and contextual sense), I hope I am continuing along the path Stuart Hall has illuminated for many of us.

First beginning

Ten years ago, I wrote: 'What do you do when every event is potentially evidence, potentially determining, and at the same time, changing too quickly to allow the comfortable leisure of academic criticism?'[2] I intended this sentence to be a statement about the problems of being a scholar of the contemporary, whether he or she is studying culture, economics, social relations or any other aspect of human existence.[3] Meaghan Morris, in 'Metamorphoses at Sydney Tower', describes herself in a concrete instance of this problem: '[T]here was a crazed culture critic staggering round the turret [of Sydney Tower] saying "What have you done with the evidence?"'[4] While challenging my description of the condition of scholarship as 'comfortable leisure', she echoed my dilemma when confronting the 'methodological problem . . . of stabilizing an object of analysis, in an economy of rapid turnover and accelerating obsolescence'.[5] Yet Morris also significantly turns my question around on itself, by asking why this kind of change is a problem. In a very different reading of my question, Dipesh Chakrabarty claimed that it constructed 'a place without history'. In fact, he argued, I seemed to be declaring 'the death of history'.[6]

Ironically, the occasion that led me to write this essay was built around a question that seemed to be the exact opposite of my own original question.[7] At least, this is how I took the import of the image: 'When the twentieth century is no longer contemporary' or, as it was later elaborated: when the contemporary becomes historical. This seems to express something like a fear of history, a desire to escape or avoid it, or at least to put it off as long as possible.

Second beginning

At the 'Cultural Studies Now and in the Future' conference (1990), the eminent British cultural and feminist historian Carolyn Steedman closed the conference by asking some rather obvious but nevertheless odd questions: 'Why does cultural studies want history? What good is it at all to you, anyway?'[8] There may be a certain disingenuousness here, however, since she had earlier quoted Carl Schorske: since the 1950s, 'one discipline after another in the human sciences [has] cut its ties to history, strengthened its autonomy with theory, and produced its meanings without that pervasive historical perspective that in the nineteenth century had permeated the self-understanding of almost every branch of learning'.[9] Faced with 'a general flight from the historical: in the abandonment of time in favor of the culture concept',[10] one might expect a historian to welcome almost any overtures, especially from cultural studies. Indeed Steedman is convinced that 'any rigorous theoretical form or mode of inquiry needs a historical perspective, a proper historicity'.[11] So one might think that the apparent turn of cultural studies to history is a return from the Fall. But having set up the dichotomy between history (or at least time) and the 'culture concept', Steedman is obviously hard pressed to accept any reconciliation of the two discourses.

At the same time, one might question Steedman's claim that there is a flight from history. After all, history is still a universally required subject and still functions as the *sine qua non* of the human sciences. It continues to provide the universally desired standard and condition of relevance and utility. Even cultural studies is constantly seeking 'historical specificity'. And history is still one of the two taken-for-granted 'essences' of human existence; along with language (or culture), it is our history – our historicality – that differentiates us from the animals. Thus, alongside Steedman's question, we need to add the following question posed by Dipesh Chakrabarty: 'What is the stake in doing History – its teaching, writing, methods, evaluative procedures, etc. – that has allowed it to become . . . such a universal technique of the self?'[12]

More to the point, how do we adjudicate between these questions? And how do we understand the conditions that enable and even require both to be asked at the same – this – moment?

Third beginning

What is modern time and modern history? Modernity – by which I mean North Atlantic modernity, to use Paul Gilroy's phrase[13] – is commonly said to embody a particular temporalizing logic. This logic not only separates time from space; it also privileges time over space.[14] And this modernity embodies a specific temporality: linear, one-dimensional ('the fourth dimension'), irreversible and unrepeatable. Modern time is comprised of a single vector (understood as a series of points in time) and a single plane of effectivity.

Modernity, it is often observed, is constituted only through its construction of a difference – between the modern and the traditional, and through its radical separation of secular time from sacred time.

Modernity comes into being when it declares itself to be different from and independent of its other. Similarly, the very notion of history as a modern experience/reality involves the construction of another difference: between the past and the present. This difference is the very being of history itself.

Further, history involves the affirmation of the continuity and coherence of a totality of time (which may yet be open at either end, as long as it is split in the middle). Progress is the most optimistic articulation of this totality (but modern forms of apocalyptic and millennial imagination are also among its possibilities). History is the realization of the conclusion that follows from the beginning. It is the logical and processual unfolding or self-realization of events in time. However distant the payoff, the lesson of history is that you (or someone) reap what you sow. As Takeuchi argues: 'History is not an empty form of time. It consists in an eternal instance at which one struggles to overcome difficulties in order thereby to be one's own self. . . . The idea of progress . . . would be unintelligible without reference to this continual search for the self, a ceaseless process of self-recentering.'[15]

Now we can perhaps see why the transformation of the contemporary into history (the twentieth – or the twenty-first – century) is a problem. Because in modern history, the present, the contemporary, is precisely not history (the past). It is the permanent present, that which escapes the past, that which cannot become a historical period. It is the phenomenologically available ever-passing presence of the present. The contemporary is that which in some way defines us as modern, as momentarily outside of history.

But what does it mean to recognize that history, the very structure of time that permeates the educational curriculum, the scholarly research practice and the popular common sense of our society, is an invention of modern Europe? Of course, it has become almost a cliché to say that the appearance of history was bound up with the emergence of capitalism, the nation-state and colonialism.[16]

For example, Chakrabarty argues that 'This sense of history was absolutely essential to the relations and structures of power the Europeans set up in India.'[17] For Chakrabarty, what is most crucial is that this sense of history was and is embedded in a particular 'meta-narrative . . . of the modern (nation-) state'.[18] The connection between nationalism and history becomes foundational, and creates a space of equivalence between citizenship (as the construction of a particular form of political individuality), identity and subjectivity.[19]

Of course, the fact that the emergence of this construction of time as history was articulated to specific social organizations and structures of power does not guarantee that it is always and necessarily articulated to the same organizations and structures, or that, if it is, it is articulated in just the same ways.

We can perhaps better understand Chakrabarty's argument if we recall Takeuchi's link between the modern historical construction of temporality and modern subjectivity. Modern subjectivity is a subjectivity always and already split. The modern subject is always both a public citizen and an 'interiorized private self incessantly' revealing itself. And moreover, the modern subject is always incomplete, lacking something (just as, by definition, the pre-modern is always lacking something), projected into an unknown and unknowable future. Thus, Chakrabarty says: 'this self-division of the (colonial) subject, the double movement of recognition by which it both knows its "present" as the site of disorder and yet moves away from this space in desiring a discipline that can only exist in an imagined but historical future. . . . This split is what is history.'[20]

II. Revising Time

Recently, this modern construction of history has been questioned from a variety of positions and directions. For example, Dick Hebdige has written that 'a growing skepticism concerning older explanatory and predictive models based in history has led to a renewed interest in the relatively neglected, "under-theorised" dimension of space. . . . [S]patial relations are seen to be no less complex and contradictory than historical processes, and space itself is refigured as inhabited and heterogeneous.'[21] Interestingly, even in attempting to critique history, Hebdige not only buys into the separation of time and space, but also assumes that history is the necessary form or construction of temporality. Similarly, Edward Soja laments the 'deep historicization of critical consciousness': 'Putting phenomena in a temporal sequence . . . somewhere came to be seen as more significant and critically revealing than putting them beside or next to each other in a spatial configuration. . . . Why is it that while time was treated as richly filled with life, with agency . . . space was treated as something fixed, lifeless, immobile? History was socially produced. Geography was naïvely given.'[22]

Such arguments are easily articulated to, if not intimately connected with, invocations of the end of history which have become so common.[23] Consider the following examples:

> Time has ceased to be anything other than velocity, instantaneousness and simultaneity. . . . [t]ime as history has vanished from the lives of all people.[24]

[The present age] is an epoch of space, simultaneity, juxtaposition, the near and the far, the side by side, the dispersed. . . . Time probably appears to us only as one of the various distributive operations that are possible for the elements that are spread out in space.[25]

History has been replaced by geography, stories by maps, memories by scenarios. We no longer perceive ourselves as continuity but as location, or rather dislocation.[26]

Prophecy now involves a geographical rather than a historical projection. It is space not time that hides consequences from us.[27]

In all these statements, temporality is constructed as either historical or random and ineffective. And ironically, in each statement, it is history itself that has determined its own disappearance. Temporality in the form of history is, finally, always opposed to space and, apparently, agency must belong to one or the other.

Even as astute a social scholar as Manuel Castells, who rejects the assumption that there is a singular organizational logic of temporality, falls back into a logic of reversal which temporarily (and epiphenomenally) privileges space over time. He talks about 'the historical revenge of space, structuring temporality in different, even contradictory logics according to spatial dynamics'.[28] It is space that is shaping time here, reversing what Castells calls a historical trend. But in the end, space is nothing but crystallized time, and 'We are embodied time, and so are our societies, made out of time'.[29] So, in the end, it is still time – and history – that is really determining.

I want to suggest that such simple attempts to reverse the binary of space and time, especially since they leave time in the form of history as determining in the last instance, are inadequate. They do not sufficiently take into account the radical implications of the recognition that history 'both as a form of knowledge and as a primary state of being of empirical phenomena . . . is itself a historical phenomenon . . . even if its problematic of temporality spills over into many others'.[30] This would require us to rethink what we call history and what we call time, opening up the possibility of transforming or imagining history into a totally different form of time and a different set of relations to time.[31]

This is not the same as what Philo calls 'a spatialized perspective on what history actually is'.[32] That is, it is not enough to see history as fractured and fragmented by space. It is not enough to assert – the truism – that things turn out differently in different places, that specificity always involves a place as well as a time. For example, Castells argues that time is specific to its context, that time is local, so that changes in the economic, political, cultural and social spheres transform time itself.[33] While I would not contest such statements, I would also want to argue that they are inadequate by themselves. They represent what Philo describes as 'a geographical way of looking at the world in which one sees *only* "spaces of dispersion": spaces where things proliferate in a jumbled-up manner on the same "level" '.[34] But such a view still leaves in place the assumption that 'one and the same form of historicity operates upon economic structures, social institutions and customs, the inertia of mental attitudes, technological practice, political behaviors and subjects them all to the same type of transformation'.[35]

How then do we deconstruct history and transform time to allow us the possibility of new imaginations, not only of our present but also of our collective future? Stuart Hall talks about 'the recreation, the reconstruction of imaginary, knowable places in the face of the global post-modern which has, as it were, destroyed the identities of specific places, absorbed them into this post-modern flux of diversity. So one understands the moment when people reach for those grounds, as it were, and the reach for those groundings is what I call ethnicity.'[36]

I want to read this image of reaching for grounds – a bit too intentional and individualistic for my taste – as a matter of belonging, as asking what it means to be or be anchored in a particular temporality or a particular milieu of time (or more accurately, time–space). Belonging is a matter less of identity than of identification, of involvement and investment, of the line connecting and binding different events together. The question of our present and our future is a matter of the different possibilities or modalities of belonging. It is a question of the ways people are attached to, and the ways people attach themselves to – what? A complexly structured set of practices and events, a milieu. But belonging is also a production. To belong – in a different mode – to and in a specific temporality – or a specific piece (milieu) of time–space – is also to belong to a different time–space.[37]

III. The Production of Evidence and the Representative Text

Let me return now to the question with which I began. Exactly how does the modern construction of time as history play out for scholars? In one sense, the answer is embodied in the notion of anachronism: the idea that things can be out of date (and therefore out of their proper time precisely because they properly belong in history). As Chakrabarty puts it:[38]

> Constructing 'evidence' . . . is a project of preservation, of making 'monuments' of certain objects that are actually contemporaneous with us. For them to acquire the status of 'historical evidence', however, we have to be able to deny them their contemporaneity by assigning them to a specified period in a calendrical past, an act by which we split the 'present' into the 'modern' and the 'traditional' or the 'historical' and thereby declare ourselves to be modern. This denial of the contemporaneity of certain objects is what constitutes the historical sense of anachronism. . . . History is therefore a practice of monumentalising 'objects' . . . of simultaneously acknowledging and denying their existence in our own time.

Chakrabarty's point is simple and profoundly disturbing: what is taken as evidence of the past belongs, in the first instance, in and to the present rather than the past. As objects existing in the present, they might serve many functions, produce many effects, mark, indicate or signal the existence or identity of many different things, in many different ways. Taking them as evidence – in the present – of the past implicates them in a synecdochic logic – a miniaturization – of the production of history. The production of the difference between the past and the present appears again in the distribution across time of contemporary objects or events, all of which belong to the present, according to a difference in how and where they 'properly' belong. But a question remains: how is this difference itself accomplished?

This miniaturization is, according to Chakrabarty, completed in a monumentalization, by locating the event or object within a narrative. After all, Walter Benjamin said that modernity was the addiction to the narrative form (that is, to history). The object becomes a sign with its proper place and role in the story of how the past has led to the present.[39]

What sort of thing then is this historical event or object, this evidence or monument? How can it exist, paradoxically as both timeless and in time?[40] How can it be both singular (particular) and universal (exemplary of some generality)? The key to understanding this monumentalization might lie in the link between the historicality of evidence (and human existence) and the second – other – most essential feature of human existence, at least according to the common sense of modernity: culture, language, narrative. The historical event or object – as evidence – becomes, as Morris has argued, a singular text to be interpreted or a symptom to be deciphered, of a certain state of or force behind history, which is always known in advance.[41] The result is that evidence is always inscribed into and reinscribes the inevitability of the movement from the past to the present.

Further, the monumentalization of historical evidence reproduces the modern construction of culture.[42] First, it extricates the text from its actual lived context and its various temporal existences (as if the evidence could and does stand apart from that of which it is evidence). Second, it locates agency outside the text itself. And, third, it reduces the 'effectivity' of the text to the mediating function of meaning. But this monumentalizing also has another dimension; it has to do with the problem of archives, and the basis on which one constructs events as valuable.[43] As the contemporary becomes historical (the twentieth – or the twenty-first – century), the problem of the archive is itself transformed into the more 'traditional' problem of the canon. Whilst there can be no canon of the present, history is always constructed by what Raymond Williams called 'the selective tradition'.[44] And in that way history always appears – and I think it is only appearance – to limit our choice of exemplary texts. It is here that the 'culture wars' are being fought, on a ground already structured by the very terms of modernity that those challenging the canon want to challenge.

What might an alternative critical practice look like? Instead of asking about how texts represent the active forces of the past, it would explore how cultural events construct and participate in the ways people live their lives – their conduct, the sites and modes of their belonging, their possibilities of agency and of what I want to call 'becoming'. In another context I have described this view of the agency of culture (or discourse) as the production of a lived geography – of enabled and enabling, prohibited and disabling practices. A lived geography describes – constructs – an economy of belongings. It describes daily life in terms of the ways people and practices move and the ways in which they are anchored (or at rest as it were). It constructs a map of mobilities and stabilities, spaces and places, vectors and powers. It describes – constructs – the transformations, the intersections, that define the ambiguous and open possibilities of changing directions, speeds, and homes.

But this lived geography, this economy, is also about temporality and temporal belongings; it is also a geography of becomings.[45] For different ways of belonging in and to time imply changes in the very meaning and possibility of change; every lived geography implicates its own modes of change.

IV. Musical Belongings

Let me briefly try to be a little more concrete by turning to music. On the surface, one might argue that music is the modality of expression that has been least theorized in traditions of modernity. And yet, it is also possible to argue that music has been completely saturated by the theorizations of modernity that have defined and constructed music as a formalization/structuring of time. Yet Deleuze and Guattari offer a very different take on music as producing the mode of belonging by which we are connected to and in a particular time–space milieu.[46]

> A child in the dark, gripped with fear, comforts himself by singing under his breath. He walks and halts to his song. Lost, he takes shelter, or orients himself with his little song as best he can. The song is like a rough sketch of a calming and stabilizing, calm and stable, center in the heart of chaos. . . . Now we are at home. But home does not preexist: it was necessary to draw a circle around that uncertain and fragile center, to organize a limited space. . . . A mistake in speed, rhythm, or harmony would be catastrophic because it would bring back the forces of chaos.

Or consider the following statement by Charles Stivale:[47]

> As Henri Lefebvre notes, music and dance rhythms 'embrace both [the] cyclical and [the] linear,' and it is 'through the mediation of rhythms . . . [that] an animated space comes into being which is an extension of the spaces of bodies.' . . . I maintain that these variable experiences of speed and affect circulating intensely between musicians and dancers/spectators contribute . . . to the incessant reconstitution of spaces of affect within specific performance arenas.

Such modes of belonging to time and space, or, more accurately, to the event of the music's presence, are defined not by the music alone although there are sonorial elements, but by a whole complex of determinations, producing what I have called elsewhere apparatuses or alliances. To put it simply, different alliances within musical culture (always including the performance of listening, taste and fandom) produce different temporalities and different modalities of belonging to time. In music, a mode of belonging is also a way of hearing, and relating to, the music itself. It defines how we empower the music and how the music both empowers and disempowers its fans and listeners. It defines as well how we hear and experience time and change within the music, as well as the nature of change within the musical style/ alliance. Compare: classic rock (which has neither a present nor a future); alternative rock (which has no future – it does not progress – but a canonical past always present but rarely invoked musically); dance (always a teleological sequence in which its past is constantly remade in the present).[48] These organizations offer us imaginations – and even embodiments – of different ways of belonging and different ways of becoming.[49]

V. Imagination and Time

The apparent fear of history is perhaps not a fear of history at all, for the academy has already historicized contemporaneity. Cultural criticism has already monumentalized the present, so that its promise of a different mode of belonging in time, its threat to constantly escape every narrative and every structure of power and control, has itself been transformed into another narrative, another structure of power and control.[50] This is, as Lefebvre acknowledged, the fate of everyday life (or, in our terms, the contemporary) in the modern world.

On the contrary, I think the fear of history is a fear of the present; at least it raises questions about the authority and politics of the present. It has to do with how one might imagine a different relationship between the past, the present and the future, with how one imagines one's way out of the historical structuring of temporality, with how one produces a temporality (and politics) in the present tense. Such a transfigured history would have to recognize a multiplicity of unevenly unfolding temporalities, a multiplicity of belongings.

In other words, I wonder if the real point of these questions, whether framed as the death of history or the fear of history, is a matter of rethinking the political function of the intellectual, once modernity itself has been called into question and become an object of critical scrutiny. Meaghan Morris, for example, proposes a re-vision of her function as a feminist intellectual: 'To act ... to bring about social change while at the same time contesting the very meaning of change.'[51] That is, to make change, including the kind of change that increasingly characterizes our data/evidence, into both an object of study and a potential goal. Or, to put it yet another way, to understand belonging itself as always implicating particular modes of change.

As scholars, I believe we need to recognize that the future, whether of our planet or of our research – and I believe that there is a relationship between these (that intellectual work does matter) – depends upon rejecting both the death of and the flight from history. Nor is it enough to simply embrace plural histories, multiple narrative lines, where each such line continues to move from a limited collective past, through a fleeting (but determined) present and into an unknown (but largely determined) future. We need to find new ways of imagining our relations to the multiple temporalities of objects, people and events, and of the worlds that they and we inhabit.

It might be objected that we don't need to imagine new histories; instead, we need to gather the facts to produce a more accurate history. Or that we need to acknowledge that history means different things to different people. Yet, once the facts are there – and, of course, the notion of facticity is a difficult one – they can still be assigned to someone else's life; I can still refuse to belong with them, as it were. Thus, while 'white' people might have to acknowledge that 'whites' were responsible in significant ways for slavery, they still have the option of refusing the burden of their ancestors. There are only two other responses possible: first, a politics of guilt in which children inherit the sins of their fathers; or, second, imagining a new mode of belonging to and in history, a new mode of relating what history divides into the past and the present. Or, to put it another way, it is not enough to simply break down the historical unities that modernity has constructed, to fragment people and history. Nor will it suffice to take account of the dis-unities and differences that modernity similarly constructs. We must also begin to listen to other ways of being temporal, of reconfiguring history. This is necessary if we are to begin to reconstitute new collectivities and new collective ways of belonging, not just to one past but to all of our pasts. I might mention here that, alongside imagining how people can belong to time, we also need to rethink and re-imagine how people belong to culture; after all, our understanding of culture – as/and communication – is also an inheritance of North Atlantic modernity.[52]

As Meaghan Morris suggested a number of years ago, 'things are too urgent now for [intellectuals] to be giving up [their] imagination. . . . The very last thing that's useful now is a return . . . to the notion of one "proper" critical style, one "realistic" approach, one "right" concern.'[53] Or, I might add in conclusion, one inevitable – to say nothing of 'proper' – mode of belonging to and in history. Nor do we need one 'proper' way of understanding the relationship of the contemporary to history, and of locating/analysing events within this space–time milieu.

Instead we must embrace temporality in the celebration of imagination, as the attempt to discover new ways of belonging to time, to the past as well as to the present and the future. In this way we might also begin to imagine new forms and formations of a political will, and political collectivities capable of imagining new futures. In this way we might be able to give up the assumed distance between the contemporary and the historical, and reject both the closure of history (around its constitutive difference) and the illusory escape of the contemporary.

Indirectly, I am arguing against the modern fragmentation of imagination, reason (cognition) and affect (emotion, desire, et cetera).[54] It is important that we begin to recognize that cognition is a mode of imagination and affect, that affect is a mode of cognition and imagination, and that imagination is a mode of cognition and affect. Thus, I want to argue that research/scholarship, teaching, and the various

creative arts all function within multiple economies of truth production, although each has its own modes (note the plural) of rigour –
which does not mean that each has some 'proper' mode of functioning.[55] As Foucault might say, we need to embrace the multiplicity of
ways in which we can and do live 'in the true' and the practices by
which we 'fiction the truth'.

And I think a good place to begin is to listen to the sounds of
belonging to time. Listen to the contemporary – or, better, listen to
the sounds around you! Listen in order to imagine a nonhistory of the
future. Learn to listen in new ways, ways that open us up to new
possibilities. Without the ability to stop the change, one listens to the
change itself. Without the ability to distinguish between the important
and the trivial, one listens to whatever, or, perhaps, to whatever it is
that matters. Sometimes such imaginations can be heard in the speed
of change itself, and in how easy it is for those living in its midst to live
with this as well. Sometimes it is heard in what Foucault calls 'the
general politics of truth', that is, within our own practices and concerns
as scholars in and of the present. And sometimes it can be heard in the
popular languages of the day. Let's imagine one small example: once
one might have heard, 'That is so old-fashioned or traditional.' But in
the past decades, one is more likely to have heard, 'That is so seventies.'
And now one can hear, 'That is so yesterday.' Does this represent a
different sense of time, perhaps even the collapse of time? Perhaps, but
I don't know how anyone could tell unless one assumes that the story
has already been written. But I do think – at least potentially – that it
can be part of a different geography, a different way of belonging to
time. Trivial! – you might say. But then, isn't that exactly where I
began?

Notes

1. Like so much of my work at the moment, this chapter is also a conversation with Meaghan Morris and Doreen Massey. I want to thank them both as
well as Stuart and Paul. See Morris 1998 and Massey (forthcoming a and b).

2. Grossberg 1997b, 229.

3. I was perhaps echoing the problems of ethnography, of anyone entering
into the world of everyday life or lived reality. However, I also intended the
question to point to the impossibility of identifying which events actually do –
or more important will – matter. Which events will have the most pertinence?
Which will have a significant or measurable – spatial and temporal – reach and
effects?

4. Morris 1990, 11.

5. Ibid., 5.

6. Chakrabarty 1992a, 49.

7. This chapter is an edited version of a paper written at the invitation of the Wayne State University College of Fine, Performing and Communication Arts as part of the inauguration of their new president. It was delivered as 'When the Twentieth Century is No Longer Contemporary' in September 1998. I want to thank the respondents for their valuable comments: Professors James Hartway, Christopher Schroll, Edward Smith and Erika Wolf. I would also like to thank Lezlie Hart Stivale for her help and support.

8. Steedman 1992, 621.

9. Ibid., 620.

10. Ibid.

11. Ibid.

12. Chakrabarty 1992a, 56.

13. Gilroy 1993, *passim.*

14. This is as true of Derrida as of any other modernist philosopher. As Stacey Langwick has explained to me, time permits the establishment of regularities and stable (statistically measurable) distributions.

15. Cited in Sakai 1997, 171

16. Notice the circularity of this logic of history – since even in our endeavour to delimit its power, we are forced into statements of historical specificity and origins. This is in fact a characteristic of the various logics of North Atlantic modernity. See Grossberg 1998.

17. Chakrabarty 1992a, 50.

18. Chakrabarty 1992a, 52.

19. This is the Hegelian logic of history.

20. Chakrabarty 1992b, 345. If Steedman sees culture as the other of history, for Chakrabarty it is capitalism and the consumer: 'History will die when this contradiction between the citizen and the consumer, between the nation-state and capitalism, is resolved . . . in favor of the consumer and capital' (1992a, 64). In the land of pure consumerism, there is (or will be) no use for the historical construction of temporality. This conclusion depends upon an understanding of capital as constantly attempting to erase differences, an understanding of capitalism I would strongly contest (although it is interesting and important to observe the neo-liberal reduction of citizenship to consumerism). See Grossberg 1999.

21. Hebdige 1990, vi–vii.

22. Soja 1996, 168.

23. Despite the media hype, and the fears of the Left, Fukuyama did not invent this, nor did he elaborate it as eloquently as others.

24. Heidegger, cited in Harvey 1989, 208.

25. Foucault 1986, 22.

26. Olalquiaga 1992, 93.

27. John Berger, cited in Soja 1996, 166.

28. Castells 1996, 467.

29. Ibid., 429.

30. Young 1990, 74.

31. More accurately, one would want to unthink the separation of space and time and begin to think of new possibilities of space–time. This would presum-

ably require us to recognize that continuity and sequentiality are themselves constructs that organize time as history.

32. Philo 1992, 139.

33. Castells 1996, 429.

34. Philo 1992, 139.

35. Foucault, cited in Philo 1992, 141.

36. Hall 1991, 35–6.

37. Consider, for example, Tony Swain's (1993) construction of the experience and thought of Australian Aborigines, 'prior to' the various colonizations they have lived through. Swain claims that the Aborigines had 'no notion of time as a determinate quality of being' and instead 'they affirmed place', and affirmed that all knowledge derives from place (rather than time). Yet, I prefer to read Swain's argument as contesting a particular construction of time (or, better, time–space), namely one in which the 'past, present and future' are 'worked into an ontology which concedes the sovereignty of time' (23).

38. Chakrabarty 1992a, 63.

39. Benjamin (1968, 223) also describes this process working in reverse – the historical dehistoricized and made contemporary – through the economy of mechanical reproduction: 'The technique of reproduction detaches the reproduced object from the domain of tradition.' To make the historical contemporary is to refuse the separation of art (evidence, the historical) and everyday life.

40. As a monumentalization, this production of historical evidence places the object or event in a paradoxical temporality, although its historical/narrative place – its time – becomes the source of its intelligibility and identity. Castells (1996, 464) argues that the temporality of cultural expressions exists as 'timeless time', as simultaneous, eternal and ephemeral. It is a nonsequential timelessness, which is nevertheless always narrativized. It is an undifferentiated time because as culture it is always the same. The object or event remains untouched by the temporal vector into which it is assigned and it remains uncontaminated by the context of its temporality; its 'faire' – what it does – cannot change. Like a monument, it is both in time and out of time.

41. See the 'Introduction' in Morris 1998.

42. See Grossberg 1998.

43. The question is how the value of the event is to be grounded. Presumably, the answer must lie in the event itself as a singularity, but is this singularity of the event opposed to or constitutive of its status as an exemplification or representative of something outside of itself, its status as a witness of reality?

44. Williams 1965, 67–76.

45. The notion of 'becomings' here is taken from Deleuze and Guattari (1987). Among other things, this concept assumes that change is more fundamental than stability. Importantly, change as becoming is bidirectional: as a is becoming b, b is becoming a. See 'Great Moments in Social Climbing' in Morris 1998.

46. Deleuze and Guattari 1987, 311.

47. Stivale 1997, 133.

48. Of course, I am invoking musical genres here, rather than actual apparatuses. See Grossberg (1997a); Straw (1991).

49. There are obvious allusions here to Heidegger's notion of dwelling,

which is importantly distinguished from ways of being-in-the-world (of which being-in-time is the most visible).

50. The question can be raised whether this sense of the promise and threat of the present is itself a construction within the logic of modern history.

51. Morris 1998, xv.

52. See Grossberg 1999. Consider the following example: does rap music belong to 'black people' or 'black kids'? It is by now common to point out that as rap music became more popular with white kids, black musicians often tried to make it sound more 'black', which only made it even more popular with white kids. Is this a problem of appropriation and authenticity? Or is it that we might want to begin to think about, to re-imagine, the nature of the relationships between white and black kids and how these have changed and continue to change in the US? In the 1950s, white kids dreamed of being black in order to avoid the boring future that stretched out before them. In the 1990s, white kids seemed to identify with black kids (their own sense of themselves is involved in an economy of identification with blacks) in a society in which youth has increasingly become 'the other'. Our failure to recognize this is partly the result of the fact that we universalize the meaning of youth and the way in which youth belongs to the world: as if youth always attempts to break with the past in a search for identity. Instead, I would argue that youth is about what matters and how one belongs. Rap music does not belong to 'blacks', nor is it even a representation of the black experience; it is rather youth seeking to find a new way of belonging.

53. Morris 1988, 186.

54. And thus I am arguing against Kant's philosophy as the most articulate and influential statement of this modern theory of the faculties.

55. Whilst I want to emphasize the imaginative function of scholarship, I also want to assert its rigour. There is a propensity to take the former without the latter, with the result that scholarship is too often reduced to fiction or autobiography, or overwhelmed by self-reflexivity.

References

Benjamin, Walter (1968) *Illuminations*. New York: Harcourt, Brace and World.

Castells, Manuel (1996) *The Rise of the Network Society*. Oxford: Blackwell.

Chakrabarty, Dipesh (1992a) 'The Death of History: Historical Consciousness and the Culture of Late Capitalism', *Public Culture*, 4–2.

——(1992b) 'Provincializing Europe: Postcoloniality and the Critique of History', *Cultural Studies*, 6–3.

Deleuze, Gilles, and Guattari, Felix (1987) *A Thousand Plateaus: Capitalism and Schizophrenia*. Translated Brian Massumi. Minneapolis: University of Minnesota Press.

Foucault, Michel (1986) 'Of Other Spaces', *Diacritics*, 16.

Gilroy, Paul (1993) *The Black Atlantic: Modernity and Double Consciousness*. Cambridge, MA: Harvard University Press.

Grossberg, Lawrence (1997a) *Bring It All Back Home: Essays on Cultural Studies*. Durham, NC: Duke University Press.

——(1997b) *Dancing in Spite of Myself: Essays on Popular Culture*. Durham, NC: Duke University Press.

——(1998) 'The Victory of Culture', *Angelaki*, 3–3, pp. 3–29.

——(1999) 'Some Speculations and Articulations of Globalization', *Polygraph*, No. 11, pp. 11–48.

Hall, Stuart (1991) 'The Local and the Global', in Anthony D. King (ed.), *Culture, Globalization and the World System*. London: Macmillan.

Harvey, David (1989) *The Condition of Postmodernity*. Oxford: Blackwell.

Hebdige, Dick (1990) 'Subjects in space', *New Formations*, 11.

Massey, Doreen (forthcoming a) 'Spaces of Politics'.

——(forthcoming b) 'Imagining Globalisation', in *Future Worlds*.

Morris, Meaghan (1988) *The Pirate's Fiancée: Feminism Reading Postmodernism*. London: Verso.

——(1990) 'Metamorphoses at Sydney Tower', *New Formations*, 11.

——(1998) *Too Soon Too Late: History in Popular Culture*. Indianapolis: Indiana University Press.

Olalquiaga, Celeste (1992) *Megalopolis: Contemporary Cultural Sensibilities*. Minneapolis: University of Minnesota Press.

Philo, C. (1992) 'Foucault's Geography', *Environment and Planning D: Society and Space*, 10.

Sakai, Naoki (1997) *Translation and Subjectivity: On 'Japan' and Cultural Nationalism*. Minneapolis: University of Minnesota Press.

Soja, Edward W. (1996) *Thirdspace*. Oxford: Blackwell.

Steedman, Carolyn (1992) 'Culture, Cultural Studies, and the Historians', in Lawrence Grossberg *et al.* (eds.), *Cultural Studies*. New York and London: Routledge.

Stivale, Charles J. (1997) 'Of *Hecceites* and *Ritournelles*: Movement and Affect in the Cajun Dance Arena', in Ann Cvetkovich and Douglas Kellner (eds.), *Articulating the Global and the Local*. Boulder, CO: Westview.

Straw, Will (1991) 'Systems of Articulation, Logics of Change', *Cultural Studies*, 5, pp. 368–88.

Swain, Tony (1993) *A Place for Strangers: Towards a History of Australian Aboriginal Being*. Cambridge: Cambridge University Press.

Young, Robert (1990) *White Mythologies: Writing History and the West*. London: Routledge.

Williams, Raymond (1965) *The Long Revolution*. Harmondsworth: Penguin.

14

When the Subalterns Speak, What Do They Say? Radical Cultural Politics in Cardiff Docklands

Glenn Jordan and Chris Weedon

I come back to the deadly seriousness of intellectual work. It is a deadly serious matter. I come back to the critical distinction between intellectual work and academic work: they overlap, they abut with one another, they feed off one another, the one provides you with the means to the other. But they are not the same thing. I come back to the difficulty of instituting a genuine cultural and critical practice, which is intended to produce some kind of organic intellectual political work, which does not try to inscribe itself in the overarching metanarrative of achieved knowledges, within the institutions. I come back to theory and politics, the politics of theory. Not theory as the will to truth, but theory as a set of contested, localized, conjunctural knowledges, which have to be debated in a dialogical way. But also as a practice which always thinks about its intervention in a world in which it would make some difference, in which it would have some effect. Finally, a practice which understands the need for intellectual modesty. I do think there is all the difference in the world between understanding the politics of intellectual work and substituting intellectual work for politics.

Stuart Hall 1992a: 286

[H]e is as much a teacher and an activist as a writer. . . . Anyone who has had the pleasure of hearing or meeting Hall knows the special quality of his presence, a presence that combines his political and intellectual passion with the commitment to human decency that pervades all his interactions.

Lawrence Grossberg 1986: 61–2

What should cultural studies be? What should cultural studies practitioners do? Does the discipline require its practitioners to assume the stance of committed critical intellectuals? Does it require engagement with the 'real world' outside the walls of the academy?

Stuart Hall is modest, and not very inclined to tell people what they should do. However, his own practice, and occasional comments he has made – for example, 'cultural studies isn't every damn thing' (Hall 1992a: 292) – provide us with some clues.[1] Throughout his career, in 'his practice as a writer, teacher, theoretician, cultural critic and political strategist' (Grossberg 1986: 62), Stuart Hall has been involved in radical, critical–intellectual projects which aim to transform the cultural and political landscape of Britain and beyond. His intellectual formation, like that of Raymond Williams, crucially included involvement both in the British/European New Left and in mainstream, avant-garde and radical cultural institutions.[2] Consider, for example, his involvement in *New Left Review* and subsequent left-wing journals such as *Marxism Today*, the *New Socialist* and *Soundings*; his work for nearly twenty years as a Professor of Sociology at the Open University, where he served as one of the UK's most public intellectuals – frequently appearing on television and radio, reaching thousands via this 'university without walls'; his numerous articles and talks which sought to make sense of Thatcherism and the crisis of the Left (see Hall 1988); and his role as mentor to black British photographers (see Bailey and Hall 1992), filmmakers, visual artists and art/cultural critics.[3] Stuart Hall's life and work, like those of the Welsh critic Raymond Williams, provide a model for what the committed intellectual in cultural studies might do.

For us, as for Stuart Hall and Raymond Williams, cultural studies is, or should be, a kind of radical intellectual practice intervening in the academy and in the cultural–political spaces of everyday life. This does not mean that it is characterized by a narrow, prescribed set of theories or questions. However, it does not follow that it has no boundaries, no shared concerns, no ethical–political stance. Hall argues against the idea that cultural studies should be whatever people want to do, so long as they, the publishing industry or the academy refer to it as such:

> It does matter whether cultural studies is this or that. It can't be just any old thing which chooses to march under a particular banner. It is a serious enterprise, or project. . . . Not that there's one politics already inscribed in it. But there is something at stake in cultural studies, in a way that I think, and hope, is not exactly true of many other very important intellectual and critical practices. (Hall 1992a: 278)

For Hall, among the most important features of cultural studies are its *seriousness* and *worldliness*, its rigour and its engagement (Hall 1992a).

At stake are questions of knowledge and power, meaning, subjectivity, identity and agency. Cultural studies, in this view, is more like women's studies and black studies – at their best – than like anthropology, English or history. It is a critical–radical practice that knows the difference between intellectual work and academic work (Hall 1992a). It is contextually and historically located.

The remainder of this chapter looks at a grounded, critical–intellectual intervention – Butetown History and Arts Centre – an initiative that, we think, offers some insights into the kind of engagements that a radical, 'worldly' cultural studies might seek to have. Based in the old Tiger Bay (docklands) area of Cardiff, Wales, Butetown History and Arts Centre began life as a people's history project in a local community centre. In the following, we focus on (1) how this initiative embodies a radical cultural–political practice, incorporating and echoing some of the ideas and practices of Stuart Hall (and Raymond Williams); and (2) how – when given the chance – the people of Tiger Bay – our local subalterns – represent themselves, their history and their community in the context of dominant media and fictional representations. We do not argue that locally based, radical cultural–political work is an easy matter, but we do suggest that it is important.

A Radical, Cultural–Political Intervention
(On a Complex Terrain)

> Indeed, it can hardly be stressed too strongly that Cultural Studies, in the sense we now understand it, for all its debts to its Cambridge predecessors, occurred in adult education: in the WEA [Workers' Educational Association], in the extramural Extension classes. . . .
>
> Raymond Williams 1989: 154

> Think of Raymond Williams's notion that cultural studies is a pedagogical project that we bring to people for whom these issues are real, personal, and immediate concerns. Cultural studies has not succeeded in doing that very well.
>
> Lawrence Grossberg 1997a: 268

Founded in 1988 by Glenn Jordan and a half-dozen or so local residents, Butetown History and Arts Centre (BHAC)[4] seeks to realize *cultural democracy* in one of Britain's oldest multi-ethnic, mixed-race, working-class communities, Butetown or 'Tiger Bay', Cardiff.[5] Dating from the mid-1800s, this mile-long dockland district linked the port of Cardiff (which was, during its heyday, the leading coal-exporting port in the world) with the city centre. From the 1840s to the 1950s, it was one of Britain's largest immigrant and minority communities. With a population usually varying between 5,000 and 10,000. Butetown was home to more than fifty nationalities from virtually all over the world.[6] It also included a thriving commercial sector and one of the UK's most notorious 'sailor towns' – with prostitution, gambling, and numerous legal and illegal drinking establishments. Its 'dens of vice' were the frequent target of Victorian moralists' campaigns; its alleged activities inspired a series of moral panics – over tuberculosis, venereal disease and mixed-race relationships. Throughout most of its history, the area was physically isolated – an 'island' bounded by (now filled-in) canals, railway tracks and the sea, whose geographical separateness helped to naturalize its otherness.[7] Today, Butetown sits in the middle of a massive docklands regeneration scheme, involving some 2,700 acres (virtually the whole southern end of Cardiff) and featuring a huge artificial lake, leisure complexes, luxury hotels, restaurants, galleries and other attractions catering primarily for tourists and the local middle classes. The scheme is billed as 'Europe's Most Exciting Water-front Development'.

Grounded in an ethos of *collective* work and *collective* responsibility, Butetown History and Arts Centre is an intervention on the terrain of culture and power. It began as a serious attempt to develop a group of locally based indigenous researchers – working-class, 'organic intellec-tuals'[8] – and to create a space for the production of alternative histories, identities and representations of life in this dockland com-munity. Here is Marcia Brahim Barry, a founder member of Butetown Community History Project (as BHAC was orginally called), describing our practice in the early years (1988–1990):

> We knew that we had a unique history but we hadn't realised how unique it was until someone [a black American anthropologist called Glenn Jordan] came in and said, 'You *are* history and if we don't do something about it, it will be lost.' So in a way, for me, because that's the way I am, it became a crusade. . . . I suddenly realised that everything around us was changing – we could actually see it – and that the elderly people were dying and lots of residents had moved away through the 'slum clearance' of the 1950s and 1960s, so the community had depleted and from I believe about 5,000 in the 1950s, we're now down to two and a half thousand. . . . We realised that we had to start to do something about it. . . . We didn't have any money so we had the Butetown Community Centre for nothing on Tuesday nights. . . . I used to bring the kettle from home. Molly and Rita or Olwen or any of us – we all pooled our money and we bought biscuits and tea and coffee. The first half of the sessions would be for us to learn interviewing techniques, and so we used a book by Paul Thompson namely, [*The Voice of the Past*] . . . .

Glenn got a stack of them. We were all supposed to pay him but I don't think anybody did. In the end he gave us all a book. So we used to talk about oral history and we used to think of questions and themes and we used to read passages out of the books, so that it helped. I don't think we realised what was happening to us, but we were actually developing skills. (Barry 1996)

BHAC's work concerns what Stuart Hall and his team at the Open University came to call *the circuit of culture* (see Hall 1997a and du Gay, Hall *et al.* 1997): grounding itself in issues of the production and consumption of cultural representations, it also explores the role of culture in the constitution and reconstitution of subjects. Over the last dozen years BHAC has developed into a unique community-based education, history and arts organization aimed at developing an extensive local people's history archive – consisting of oral history, photographs and other documents – which it seeks to make accessible in interesting ways. We have collected several hundred hours of audiotaped oral histories, published a series of local history books (see Johnson 1993; Sinclair 1993; Chappell 1994; Cook 1995; Stradling 1996), run various community education courses, staged exhibitions, organized cultural activities for local school-age children, run workshops for teachers, hosted small performing arts events, and engaged in various other cultural–political activities (see Jordan and Weedon 1995: 134–73). Central emphases in our work have always been adult education, working-class culture, 'history from below' and the politics of representation[9] – in addition to struggling to secure financial viability. The centre currently occupies some 2,500 square feet of ground-floor space in the heart of Cardiff docklands and includes two galleries, a meeting space, office space and a small shop. Our budget for 1997–2000 – raised primarily from one- to three-year grants – is about £80,000 ($130,000) per year. Our staff consists of three full-time workers, two part-time workers, and a dozen or so volunteers. By 2003 or so, we intend to have purchased the building in which we reside and developed a people's history museum and arts centre – targeting not only the long-established local community, but also the new, middle-class incomers and tourists.

The authors have been involved in developing and running this project for ten and eight years respectively and we both work as volunteers and officers on the board of BHAC. We would like to emphasize that it is not simply a question of *sharing* our knowledge – that model would seem to presuppose all-knowing intellectuals teaching 'the people'. Nor is it a matter of purist radical politics. Our practice, which must negotiate the *real world* of local knowledge, local politics and local interests, is far more dialogic, far less certain than that.[10] To echo Stuart Hall, ours is a radical cultural–political practice 'living with tension' and 'without guarantees'. It is also, we hope, 'a practice which understands the need for intellectual modesty' (Hall 1992a: 286).

'The Spectacle of the Other':
Hegemonic Representation and Real Effects

Why is 'difference' so compelling a theme, so contested an area of representation? What is the secret fascination of 'otherness' and why is popular representation so frequently drawn to it?

Stuart Hall 1997c: 225

Racism, of course, operates by constructing impassable symbolic boundaries between racially constituted categories, and its typically binary system of representation constantly marks and attempts to fix and naturalize the difference between belonging-ness and otherness.

Stuart Hall 1992b: 255

A key issue for the local residents who founded the Butetown Community History Project in 1988 was the question of representation: how their lives and community figured in mainstream accounts of the area. The poetics and politics of representation (Hall 1997b) are of fundamental importance in defining, reproducing and contesting social meanings and values and in the formation of individual subjectivity and group identities. Residents and former residents of Butetown/Tiger Bay found little of their history or sense of identity in outsider accounts of the community. Before Butetown Community History Project, this history found little expression beyond the medium of orally transmitted popular memory.

The power to create recognized versions of history and culture – to give authoritative accounts – is largely a property of political, cultural and educational institutions, but it affects all areas of individual and social life. It includes, for example, government statements and surveys, police and media reports, as well as academic narratives of history and ethnography. In the case of Tiger Bay, this official literature is voluminous and is further complemented by a substantial number of novels, plays, songs, poems and short stories.[11] The images and narratives of Butetown/Tiger Bay that these texts have produced and reproduced over 150 years are often negative: the area has been constructed as dirty, violent, diseased and immoral. Others are romantic: the area is portrayed as exotic and a Mecca of racial harmony.[12] For many decades social researchers, journalists, photographers and others have come to study, to observe, to gaze at, to re-present this community. Local people tend to find this practice offensive.

The history of negative representation has had observable *material* effects on the community – shaping the attitudes of outsiders to Butetown, directly affecting policing policy and social policy such as the local 'slum' clearance of the 1960s. It also affects the employment prospects of the people who live there. Sometimes the material effects of this *regime of representation* (Hall 1997c) are insidious. Consider the workings of the criminal justice system in the notorious case of the so-called 'Cardiff Three', who were wrongly convicted of murdering a mixed-race prostitute, Lynette White, in Butetown in February 1988. As John Williams shows in his book on the case, *Bloody Valentine* (1993), the police set out to convict five local black and mixed-race men on no conclusive evidence and succeeded in convicting three of them, at a trial held some forty miles away in Swansea. Williams recounts the serious effects of the long history of hegemonic negative representations of Butetown on the all-white Swansea jury:

> In the key speech of the epic 115-day trial the prosecutor for the crown, Mr David Elfer, made ample use of those innate South Walean prejudices. 'Butetown', he said, 'it is an upside-down society.' It is a place, he said, where people carry knives as a matter of routine, where terrible acts of violence, he implied, are no more than commonplace.[13] The effect of this speech was simple and deadly. Suddenly it was not simply these five men who were on trial for this particular murder, it was Butetown that was on trial for having an evil reputation. (Williams 1993: 104)

Prejudices about Butetown and Tiger Bay are far from 'innate'; they have been repeatedly manufactured and reinforced by literature, the media, social science and a range of other influential social institutions and practices. Moreover, as suggested above, hegemonic representations of Tiger Bay over the last century and a half have been consistently far more romantic than negative. Literature and the press, in particular, have reproduced representations that betray a strong element of romantic and voyeuristic desire to see, experience, almost become the Other (see Jordan 1988).[14]

Cultural Democracy and Counter-narratives

> [W]hat happens when an academic and theoretical enterprise tries to engage in pedagogies which enlist the active engagement

of individuals and groups, tries to make a difference in the
institutional world in which it is located?

Stuart Hall 1992a: 284

Access to the means of cultural production is crucial to the counteract-
ing of hegemonic narratives. It enables individuals and groups to
represent themselves and their interests; to have their work published,
displayed and distributed; to define, for example, what it means to be
a person of colour, a woman or working-class; and to shape social
values. Each of these objectives is integrally related to broader questions
of power and empowerment. In an interview about her involvement in
the Butetown people's history project, local mixed-race woman Marcia
Barry reflected thus:[15]

> But it was also quite thrilling just for the people to be together and to be
> talking about our history and also I think we jelled as a group and it was just
> nice. I think it made us feel . . . well we always knew that we were special and
> that we came from a special area but nobody actually ever said, you know,
> this is something you should be proud of. . . . I believe that most of us . . .
> felt that we were lucky to be born in Tiger Bay and the Docks. And that
> people who lived outside the area were not so lucky. . . . All right, we knew
> that there were other issues going on around racism etc., but that didn't
> actually – how shall I say? – disadvantage us because we actually had a sort of
> armour around us that told us that we were okay. Because there were all
> sorts of other people around us who looked like us. So you know, there were
> people of mixed race, or there were people who might be African, you know,
> who might come from Africa, but then you could have an African married to
> a Jew. I mean you know that was the mix. . . . I've always called the area a
> cosmopolitan community. (Barry 1996)

Hegemonic narratives of Tiger Bay over150 years created a commonsense perception of the area which promotes racism and class discrimination. Crucial in this process has been the rhetorical strategy of
marking off the people of Tiger Bay from *us*, presenting *them* as
essentially different from the rest of Cardiff and Britain. Against this
history of negative representation local people have attempted to keep
alive a counter-narrative which can function as the basis for positive
forms of identity and subjectivity. These resistant subjectivities are
important since the forms of subjectivity that we inhabit play a crucial
part in determining whether we accept or contest existing power
relations. Moreover, for marginalized and oppressed groups, the construction of new and resistant identities is a key dimension of a wider
political struggle to transform society.

Experience has taught us that developing a community-based organization committed to cultural democracy and to democratizing the

means of representation is no easy process. Most people tend to view culture as a set of products to be more or less passively consumed; they view the active production of culture as something done by others with special skills and talents. Questions of education and skills lie at the heart of cultural democracy and are linked directly to the project of empowerment through participation. Successful ventures in cultural democracy also require the creation of new modes of distribution and access to pre-existing channels. In BHAC, members of the local community have been involved in oral history interviewing, archive work, publications, exhibitions and educational work.

Oral testimony is particularly important in Butetown. As a working-class community, it had no written history of its own and no museum to show social life from below. The recently closed Welsh Industrial and Maritime Museum had numerous documents and photographs about shipping and ship owners, but little on the men who manned the ships or their families and communities. It is here that oral history interviews and written life histories, collected and published by BHAC, have begun to redress the balance. In what follows we look at some of the key features of these oral and written testimonies, and how they relate to hegemonic narratives of Tiger Bay.[16]

The Subalterns Speak, But What Do They Say?

> [C]ultural studies is still often identified with the speaking position of the marginal. Many cultural theories, including cultural studies, have privileged the position of the outside, the marginal, the émigré; they have often argued that such a position enables a uniquely insightful understanding. . . . But, as Tony Bennett (1993) has argued, this 'logic of charismatic closure' too easily reduces knowledge to biography and fetishizes marginality.
>
> Lawrence Grossberg 1997: 250

> Representation is a complex business.
>
> Stuart Hall 1997c: 226

In the preface to *The Tiger Bay Story* (1993), the first book in the series 'Life Stories from Tiger Bay', Neil Sinclair, born and bred in Butetown, stresses the importance of the oral tradition in the community, recounting the 'moments spent at many a kitchen table or by a fireside or nowadays in a pub or community centre, imbibing the many tales passionately and humorously told of Old Tiger Bay from the people who knew them best' (Sinclair 1993: 1). Sinclair tells of growing up in the Bay 'from the inside out', explicitly aiming to counteract the

hegemonic 'negative mythology' (1993: 3) which characterized the
Lynette White trial. Against this negative image, Sinclair's text – like
the taped oral histories – stresses Tiger Bay's strong sense of community
and its rich racial and ethnic mix, an emphasis that lies at the heart of
insider representations. This perspective reverses the dominant rhetorical strategies found in outsider discourses which work with a binary
opposition between 'them' and 'us', defining them – the people of
Tiger Bay – as negatively different from us. It also challenges many
hegemonic assumptions about racial difference and identity including
the idea, imposed from without by both white and black outsiders, that
Butetown is a 'black' community.

In interviews and written texts, Butetown residents claim identities
that are both mixed-race and Welsh, challenging hegemonic versions
of Welshness which define it as intrinsically white. Sinclair, for example,
dedicates his *Tiger Bay Story* to Butetown's mothers, adapting a line
from the Welsh national anthem and replacing the word 'fathers' with
'mothers': 'Mae hen 'wlad fy mamau yn annwyl i fi' (The old country
of my mothers is dear to me). The mothers in question are those
hundreds of white Welsh women, mostly from the South Wales Valleys,
who married seamen of colour from all over the world and fought for
their families' right to exist:

> Tiger Bay was the safest haven in Britain for men of colour. The people of
> Tiger Bay fought well for this tiny piece of land, for their community's right
> to be. Our Celtic mothers fought in this battle too and preserved a harmoni-
> ous multi-racial way of life which forms one of the most endearing aspects of
> community life in the history of South Wales. (Sinclair 1993: 34)

The insider reversal of the hegemonic opposition between *them* and
us presents the community as *threatened by* rather than a threat to those
outside it. Moreover, the threat from outside is represented as provok-
ing heroic resistance. This is in stark contrast to the versions found in
outsider histories and historical novels. Sinclair emphasizes unified
resistance and the haven that the Bay offered to people of colour. He
recounts the terror directed at a mixed-race couple (his grandparents)
in the adjoining Cardiff district of Grangetown and continues:

> In Tiger Bay things were different. The 'Bayites' were armed to the teeth.
> Chinese restaurateurs provided 'plenty pepper' to the housewives, pepper
> that was hurled into the faces of the horses on which the white rioters rode
> down into Bute Street. As the horses reared up and the white men fell, Tiger
> Bay men, women, boys and girls of every race and nationality you can think
> of pounced upon them and gave them the hiding they never forgot. (Sinclair
> 1993: 34)

At issue here is a rewriting of the history of Tiger Bay that can serve as the basis for community pride and a positive sense of identity.

In their constructions of alternative representations (see Hall 1997c), insider accounts often tend to romanticize the past as a better place than the present. Racism is depicted as something foreign to Tiger Bay but fundamental to the wider Cardiff. It is identified as a chief motivation behind local authority policies such as the redevelopment in the 1960s. This is seen as a wanton and unwanted external intervention by outsiders bereft of respect for difference. This perspective is linked to the widely held insider belief in the importance of urban space and its effects on community. Whereas fiction, press and official local government descriptions saw the physical layout of old Tiger Bay as conducive to ghettoization and criminality, insiders saw and still see it as crucial to community.

Counter-hegemonic narratives of the history of Tiger Bay present it as a unique community, offering a model of racial and ethnic tolerance from which the rest of Britain could learn. Refusing binary categories such as *white* and *black*, the community promotes an image of itself as quintessentially *mixed* – racially, ethnically and culturally. While insider oral and written life histories take up some of the more romantic and primitivist images found in mainstream representations, they radically distance themselves from hegemonic images of poverty, crime, immorality and racial conflict. The exotic others of outsider texts become the normal; faceless, nameless people become named individuals with families and recognizable everyday lives. Much stress is laid on intermarriage and on a nonconflictual multiculturalism in which people participate in the different rituals and festivals of ethnic groups other than their own. Insider texts are characterized not only by positive images of racial and ethnic difference but also by affirmative images of working-class family life and community.

Yet insider narratives of Tiger Bay remain trapped within that binary *them* and *us* logic that has long governed mainstream representations, recyling some of the more attractive racial stereotypes. Of course this logic reflects a reality in which there is too little respect for difference and too great a willingness in society at large to cling to those hierarchical binary oppositions that people in Tiger Bay sought on the ground to move beyond. The versions of history, community and identity produced by local people in the context of a project committed to the democratization of the means of representation are contradictory and complex (and often disappointing). They reinforce the fact, which we have learned and relearned in the course of our own critical–political engagements with 'the people', their voices and experience: 'experience itself is a product of power' (Grossberg 1997: 250), as is the 'voice of the people'. This complexity does not, however, detract from the empowering effects for marginalized individuals of involvement in the politics of representation. This can, in Stuart Hall's words, 'make a difference'.

Notes

Part of this chapter was facilitated by a grant from the Regional Research Programme, School of Humanities, University of Glamorgan. The chapter's title is inspired by Gayatri Chakravorty Spivak's famous (1988) question, 'Can the Subaltern Speak?'

1. An extended argument for a radical, engaged cultural studies – one profoundly influenced by Stuart Hall's writings and practice – is provided in Grossberg 1997.

2. For an excellent discussion of the relation between New Left politics and the development of cultural studies in Britain, see Dworkin 1997.

3. Stuart Hall's interest in the arts and popular culture is long-standing: see, for example, Hall and Whannel 1964. Hall currently serves on the boards of both Autograph: the Association of Black Photographers and the International Institute of the Visual Arts. His son, Jess, is a talented young film artist.

4. The organization was initially known as Butetown Community History Project – which reflects its commitment to locally based people's history. Co-founders include Glenn Jordan, Marcia Brahim Barry, Olwen Blackman Watkins, Keith (Nino) Abdi, Rita Hinds Delpeche and Vera Roberts Johnson. Chris Weedon became involved in 1990 and has served as Chair for several years.

5. Known as Butetown (after the Marquis of Bute who financed the development of Cardiff docks), this central docklands area is a mile long and a quarter of a mile wide. Local residents refer to the top (northern) half or so of the area as 'The Bay' or 'Tiger Bay' and the bottom part as 'The Docks'. Outsiders often refer to the whole district as 'Tiger Bay' – a name whose origin is shrouded in mystery.

6. For a list of the various nationalities and ethnic groups that were represented in Butetown, see Jordan and Weedon 1995: 135.

7. On the naturalization of difference as a key strategy in racialized regimes of representation, see Hall 1997c: 245.

8. There is an interesting parallel here with what Stuart Hall and his colleagues were trying to accomplish at the Centre for Contemporary Cultural Studies: 'there is no doubt in my mind that we were trying to find an institutional practice in cultural studies that might produce an organic intellectual' (Hall 1992a: 281). The question of whether CCCS or BHAC succeeded in this is one that we might wish to pursue on another occasion.

9. Readers will note parallels with the cultural politics of three of the 'fathers' of British cultural studies, namely, E.P. Thompson, Raymond Williams and Stuart Hall. We are proud to continue key aspects of that legacy – including the commitment to adult and popular education.

10. Consider funding. The 'real world' with which BHAC must negotiate for

grants and other forms of financial support includes local government, the Arts Council of Wales, the Charities Lottery, the Heritage Lottery, the Arts Lottery, Cardiff Bay Development Corporation, private businesses and foundations. BHAC must also generate money through its own activities. One of the implications is that we have had to become 'experts' in cultural policy.

11. For a sampling of the social science and social history literature on Tiger Bay, see Sharpe 1932; Fletcher 1930; Little 1942a, 1942b, 1943 and 1948; Wilson 1950; Drake 1954 and 1955; Collins 1957a and 1957b; Bloom 1972; N. Evans 1980 and 1985; and Tweedale 1987. Also see Daunton 1977 and Jordan 1988 and 1991. A photo-history is provided in C. Evans *et al.* 1984.

12. There have been numerous feature articles in the regional and national press on 'life in Tiger Bay'. Local newspapers that have routinely featured articles on the area include the *Cardiff Times* and *South Wales Daily News* (in the nineteenth and early twentieth centuries) and the *Western Mail* and *South Wales Echo*. For early, and racist, constructions of 'Tiger Bay' in popular trade union papers, see the *Maritime Review* and the *Police Gazette*, including the editorials and cartoons. In the 1950s and 1960s, *Picture Post* and *Illustrated* published several high-quality photo-essays on 'Tiger Bay' – from a documentary-reformist perspective.

For novels and short stories set in Tiger Bay, see Walsh 1936, 1947 and 1952; Martin 1946; Jones 1979; Cordell 1986; Davies 1989; and Williams 1994. For an example of poetry, see Cooke 1993. BHAC publications include three life stories from the area: Neil M. C. Sinclair, *The Tiger Bay Story* (1993), Phyllis Grogan Chappell, *A Tiger Bay Childhood* (1994) and Harry Cooke, *How I Saw It* (1995). Other BHAC publications include Johnson (1993) and Stradling (1996).

13. This is pure myth. There is very little violent crime in Butetown today – much less than in many other parts of South Wales. Both the police and the insurance companies acknowledge as much.

14. Although this chapter puts most emphasis on the negative dimension of outsider representations of Tiger Bay, the actual fact is that *most* of these constructions are tinged with romantic imagery and voyeuristic desire. There is at least as much fascination with the Other as there is repulsion from it. (See the discussion of power, fantasy and fetishism in Hall's excellent essay 'The Spectacle of the Other' (Hall, 1997c).)

15. 'Mixed-race' can be a misleading term, as it tends to mask complexity. Consider, for example, the case of Marcia Brahim Barry: her father was a Muslim from Malaysia; her mother, a Catholic, was born in Cardiff of a Nepalese father and French and Welsh mother. As Stuart Hall has said, 'Identity is not as transparent or unproblematic as we think' (Hall 1990: 222).

16. For more indepth analysis of hegemonic representations of Tiger Bay, see Jordan 1988 and 1991.

References

Bailey, David A. and Stuart Hall, eds. (1992) *Critical Decade: Black British Photography in the 80s*. London: Ten 8.

Barry, Marcia Brahim (1996) 'Interview with Marcia Barry' (transcribed), Appendix 4 (22 pp.) in Gehrke 1996.

Bloom, Leonard (1972) 'Introduction', in Little 1972: 1–45.

Chappell, Phyllis Grogan (1994) *A Tiger Bay Childhood: Growing Up in the 1930s*. Cardiff: Butetown History and Arts Centre.

Collins, Sydney (1957a) 'A Negro Community in Wales', in his *Coloured Minorities in Britain*. London: Lutterworth Press.

——(1957b) 'An Arab Community in Wales', in his *Coloured Minorities in Britain*. London: Lutterworth Press.

Cooke, Harry 'Shipmate' (1993) *Bay Dreams: Poems of Cardiff Bay*. Cardiff: Making Waves Publications.

——(1995) *How I Saw It: A Stroll Thro' Old Cardiff Bay*. Cardiff: Butetown History and Arts Centre.

Cordell, Alexander (1986) *Tales from Tiger Bay*. Abergavenny, Wales: Blorenge Books.

Daunton, Maurice J. (1977) *Coal Metropolis: Cardiff, 1870–1914*. Leicester: Leicester University Press.

Davies, Tom (1989) *Fire in the Bay*. London: Collins.

Drake, St Clair (1954) 'Value Systems, Social Structure and Race Relations in the British Isles'. PhD thesis, Dept. of Anthropology, University of Chicago.

——(1955) 'The "Colour Problem" in Britain: A Study in Social Definitions', *Sociological Review* (new series), 3: 197–217.

Dworkin, Dennis (1997) *Cultural Marxism in Postwar Britain: History, the New Left, and the Origins of Cultural Studies*. Durham, NC, and London: Duke University Press.

Evans, Catherine, Steve Dodsworth and Julie Barnett (1984) *Below the Bridge: A Photo-Historical Survey of Cardiff's Docklands to 1983*. Cardiff: National Museum of Wales.

Evans, Neil (1980) 'The South Wales Race Riots of 1919', *Llafur: Journal of Welsh Labour History*, 3(1): 5–29.

——(1985) 'Regulating the Reserve Army: Arabs, Blacks and the Local State in Cardiff, 1919–1945', *Immigrants and Minorities*, 4(2): 68–115.

Fletcher, Muriel (1930) *Report on an Investigation into the Colour Problem in Liverpool and Other Ports*. Liverpool: Association for the Welfare of Half-caste Children.

Gehrke, Karen (1996) 'Struggling For Cultural Democracy: A Case Study of Butetown History & Arts Centre'. Dissertation for BA degree in Communication Studies, University of Glamorgan.

Grossberg, Lawrence (1986) 'History, Politics and Postmodernism: Stuart Hall and Cultural Studies', *Journal of Communication Inquiry* (special issue on Stuart Hall), 10(2): 61–77. Reprinted in Morley and Chen (1996).

——(1997) 'Cultural Studies: What's in a Name? (One More Time)', in L. Grossberg, *Bringing It All Back Home: Essays on Cultural Studies*. Durham, NC, and London: Duke University Press, pp. 245–71.

Hall, Stuart (1988) *The Hard Road to Renewal: Thatcherism and the Crisis of the Left*. London and New York: Verso.

——(1990) 'Cultural Identity and Diaspora', in Jonathan Rutherford, ed.,

Identity: Community, Culture, Difference. London: Lawrence & Wishart, pp. 222–37.

——(1992a) 'Cultural Studies and Its Theoretical Legacies', in Lawrence Grossberg, Cary Nelson and Paula Treichler, eds., *Cultural Studies*, NY and London: Routledge, pp. 277–94.

——(1992b) 'New Ethnicities', in James Donald and Ali Rattansi, eds., *'Race', Culture and Difference.* London: Sage, pp. 252–9.

——(1997a) 'Introduction', in S. Hall, ed., *Representation: Cultural Representations and Signifying Practices.* London: Open University Press and Sage, pp. 1–12.

——(1997b) 'The Work of Representation', in S. Hall, ed., *Representation.* London: Open University and Sage, pp. 13–72.

——(1997c) 'The Spectacle of the "Other"', in S. Hall, ed., *Representation.* London: Open University and Sage, pp. 223–90.

Hall, Stuart and Paddy Whannel (1964) *The Popular Arts*, London: Hutchinson and Boston, MA: Beacon Press.

Johnson, Mike (1993) *Old Cardiff Winds: Songs from Tiger Bay and Far Beyond.* Cardiff: Butetown History and Arts Centre.

Jones, Jack (1979) *Rivers out of Eden.* London: Pan Books. Originally published 1951.

Jordan, Glenn (1988) 'Images of Tiger Bay: Did Howard Spring Tell the Truth?', *Llafur: Journal of Welsh Labour History*, 5(1): 53–9.

——(1991) 'On Ethnography in an Intertextual Situation: Reading Narratives or Deconstructing Discourse?', in Faye V. Harrison, ed., *Decolonizing Anthropology.* Washington, DC: American Anthropological Association, pp. 42–66.

Jordan, Glenn and Chris Weedon (1995) *Cultural Politics: Class, Gender, Race and the Postmodern World.* Oxford: Blackwell.

Little, Kenneth (1942a) 'Loudoun Square: A Community Survey I', *Sociological Review*, 34: 12–33.

——(1942b) 'Loudoun Square: A Community Survey II', *Sociological Review*, 34: 119–46.

——(1943) 'The Psychological Background of White–Coloured Contacts in Britain', *Sociological Review*, 35: 12–28.

——(1948) *Negroes in Britain: A Study of Racial Relation in English* [sic] *Society.* London: Routledge and Kegan Paul.

——(1972) *Negroes in Britain.* 2nd edn. London: Routledge and Kegan Paul.

Martin, David (1946) *Tiger Bay.* London: Martin and Reid.

Morley, David and Kuan-Hsing Chen, eds. (1996) *Stuart Hall: Critical Dialogues in Cultural Studies.* London and New York: Routledge.

'Scrutator' (pseudonym), *Darker Cardiff: Seamy Side of the Great Seaport.* Series of fourteen feature articles from the *South Wales Daily News*, 22 November 1893–5 January 1894.

Sharpe, Nancie (1932) *Report on the Negro Population of London and Cardiff.* London: League of Coloured Peoples.

Sinclair, Neil M.C. (1993) *The Tiger Bay Story.* Cardiff: Butetown History and Arts Centre.

Spivak, Gayatri Chakravorty (1988). 'Can the Subaltern Speak?', in Cary Nelson and Lawrence Grossberg, eds., *Marxism and the Interpretation of Culture.* London: Macmillan Education, pp. 271–313.

Stradling, Rob (1996) *Cardiff and the Spanish Civil War*. Cardiff: Butetown History and Arts Centre.

Thompson, Paul (1978) *The Voice of the Past: Oral History*. Oxford: Oxford University Press.

Tweedale, Iain (1987) 'From Tiger Bay to the Inner City: One Hundred Years of Black Settlement in Cardiff', *Radical Wales*, Spring Issue, pp. 5–7.

Walsh, J.M. (1936) *Once in Tiger Bay*. London: Collins.

——(1947) *Return to Tiger Bay*. London: Collins.

——(1952) *King of Tiger Bay*. London: Collins.

Williams, Herbert (1970) *The Legend of Tiger Bay*. Series of nine feature articles (plus letters to the editor and a final assessment), from the *South Wales Echo*, 18 September 1970–2 October 1970.

Williams, John (1993) *Bloody Valentine: A Killing in Cardiff*. London: Harper-Collins.

Williams, Raymond (1989) 'The Future of Cultural Studies', in his *The Politics of Modernism: Against the New Conformists*. London and New York: Verso, pp. 151–62.

Wilson, Harriett (1950) 'A Housing Survey of the Dock Area of Cardiff', *Sociological Review* 42(2): 201–213.

15

The Second Modernization Failed:
Discourse Politics from
'New Korea' to 'Globalization'

Myung Koo Kang

In all political systems, political symbols and discourses develop as means to connect individuals to a larger political order (Elder and Cobb 1983). Politics is a huge system of discourse and, as such, it is hard to find any political action that does not carry with it political symbols and discourses. Political symbols and discourses should not be understood, of course, as a simple rhetoric that wraps a political action; reaching far beyond mere rhetoric, political symbol and discourse play an essential role of mediation in conferring authority on a particular political system, as well as in justifying the existing power structure.

Since the mid-1980s, the authoritarian political system of Korea has been challenged by a strong social movement for democratization which eventually developed into the civil uprising of June 1987. Such a process, however, could not dissolve the collective challenges by the people, since the change they demanded was not related simply to matters of political procedure. Rather, they demanded a restructuring of the entire Korean economy and political system formulated in the process of modernization: territorial division and ensuing civil war, which fostered a strong regime of anti-communism; long reign by an authoritarian power; and a rapid process of capitalistic industrialization.

After thirty years, the whole process finally resulted in the appearance of a civilian government. With the establishment of a civilian presidency, the military regime that had been in power for thirty years disappeared from the political scene; thereafter, Korean politics became equipped with basic procedures requisite for democracy. Furthermore, when the new civilian government, led by Kim Young-Sam, proposed reform without reserve and reform without stopping, the process of democratization in Korea seemed to reach a turning point.

But even though there has been strong popular demand for democracy and economic justice, the dominant political and economic system has been kept intact without much change. The economic system that favours monopolization and plutocracy still has not been reorganized, and the huge system of bureaucracy that affects every aspect of civil society is being reproduced in the political–economic domain beyond civil control. Repressive state apparatuses such as police and secret agencies have restricted human rights, yet the laws and institutions that support them remain unchanged. The threshold of representative politics, which accepts only the narrow political interests of civil society, still remains as high as before. Nevertheless, the strong popular resistance that developed in 1987 has not been witnessed again, and in consequence the minimum requirements for democratic procedure exist side by side with the politico-economical structure built by the authoritarian regime of the past.

How can we explain the remarkable discrepancy between today's politico-economic reality and people's expectation of change and reform together with the will-to-reform as proposed by civilian government in its earlier period? Why is it that the alternative forces could not organize an effective resistance? To answer these questions, this study analyses discourse politics during the Kim Young-Sam government – focusing on the hegemonic articulation of discourse and political powers that can be conceptualized as the second modernization: this produced discourses such as 'New Korea' (in 1993), 'Internationalization' (in 1994), and 'Globalization' (in 1995).

This essay basically depends on Hall's theory of articulation (1983a; 1985). As Hall has pointed out, 'there are different regimes of truth in the social formation . . . which have certain effects for the maintenance of power' (quoted in Grossberg, 1996: 136). In line with this claim, this study first defines the politics of discourse as a process by which the ruling bloc – or those controlling the political symbol and value systems – can promote their interests, justify them to the people, and ensure the people's support. Second, as Hall has clarified, the whole dynamic process in the politics of discourse includes the response of the people as well as the opponents of their discourse. Through analysis of the hegemonic process of political discourse, this study tries to clarify the unwarranted relationship between governing structure and discursive practice during the period of civilian government as well as the articulation of political discourse with politico-economic power relations.

True, the Kim Young-Sam regime produced much discourse, most of which has proved to be rhetorical gestures designed to influence the general public's values and ideology. This discourse also brought about legal and institutional changes that were to redistribute political and economic power. When a particular discourse reaches beyond the rhetorical level and shows its effect, it causes complicated conflicts both inside and outside the ruling bloc. That explains the appearance of feverish conflicts among the various discourse agents concerning reform and competitiveness, two of the discourse constituents of the 'New Korea' in 1993. The analysis of discourse politics, therefore, should integrate not only the content of a discourse, but also the social context in which discourse-producing agents compete among each other. Accordingly, this study tries to ask such questions as who (which discourse-producing agents) at what point (that is, in what social context) says what (that is, raises what issues and which agenda) in which composition and style (the thematic structure of discourse). This study also asks how these discourses are related to non-discursive practices of institutions and organizations. As O'Donnell (1979) has pointed out, the dominant character of a state as an organizer of social relations of governing can be confirmed 'only through analysis' because such a hypothetical work can only guarantee an elucidation of the connection between discourse and governing, two seemingly unrelated areas.

Methodological Notes: A Theory of Hegemonic Articulation

The discourse-producing agents chosen as objects of analysis here represent government, market, and civil society. (1) The *National Affairs Weekly*, issued by the Ministry of Information, delivers various governmental statements and policies. (2) *Weekly Trend* of the Nationwide Business Association (NBA) represents the big corporations. (3) As for oppositional voices produced by alternative forces[1] such as the National Federation of Labor Unions, the study checked the various organizational documents and small media affiliated to labour unions and civil groups. (4) Additionally, in order to examine the social distribution of political symbols and discourses in a particular period, the study did a content analysis of relevant news articles in nine national daily newspapers. The Korean Institute of Newspaper Databases (KINDs) provided a comprehensive search of them.

The purpose of the hegemonic theory of articulation which I use following Hall (1983b) is to understand and explain how ideological elements are integrated into discourse in a particular social context. As used here, articulation means 'a form of connection by which two different elements are united under a specific circumstance' (Hall 1983b; Grossberg 1996). The reason I use the word 'articulation' instead of 'connection' (rather a plain term), is to express the multidimensionality of structure that unites various elements, and also to express the process in which structures are composed, destroyed and reconstructed (Grossberg 1992).

I introduce here the hegemonic theory of articulation as a methodological strategy in order to explain the articulation of discourse and competition among those agents and social organizations that try to obtain support for their interpretation of their discourse. We cannot elucidate the ideological effect of the ruling discourse during the Kim regime simply by interpreting the discursive practices of such social organizations as the state, business, the media and the social movement. The ruling bloc and state have been employing diverse discursive strategies in order to ensure their political justification and to maintain the ruling order; these discourses, however, cannot necessarily guarantee their effect simply by being expressed. As Hall says, discursive practices and ideological practices continually compromise, change and are redefined in the ruling structure. We call this an unwarranted and incomplete relationship between practices and structures. By 'unwarranted' I mean that no stratum or structure can take a superior or prior position in the causal or combinational relationship of articulation. Because of this, the hegemonic ruling structure combines, in order to retain its leadership, the common sense of the people with the economic, political and ideological institutions of the society. Within and through such an articulation, the governing bloc tries to get the agreement of the people regarding both its position and its ways of resolving the crises that continually come up. By analysing such a process from the perspective of the hegemonic theory of articulation, I intend to clarify the formation and change of the ruling relation in Korean society during the Kim Young-Sam regime.

Three Periods of Discourse Politics

This section briefly examines the formation and change of discourse politics in the civilian government. The summary of statements and symbolic terms employed in each of the periods by discourse-producing agents is shown in Table 1. We can identify several characteristics from it. First, the thematic areas in which discourse-producing agents struggle against one another are made up of 'reform', 'economic jump-starting' and 'national security crisis'. The thematic area of 'reform' brought about discourse tension between 'reform that should

Table 1 *Changes of Major Discourse Production*

	New Korea (February–November 1993)	Internationalization (December 1993–October 1994)	Globalization (November 1994–September 1997)
Government	Corruption-purge Project from Above / Recovery from the Korean Disease/ Sharing of Pain & New Economy / Establishment of National Principle	Internationalization is Reform / Period of Limitless Competition / National Competitiveness / No Allowance of Collective Egotism	Reform without Discouraging Investment / Central Nation in the World/A Superpower Nation / Sales Diplomacy/Productive Politics / Productive Welfare/Small but Strong Government
Mainstream Press	Short Reform, Long Business / Economic Recovery/Reinforcement of International Competitiveness / Nuclear Threat from the North	Reinforcement of National Competitiveness / Economy without Politics / Threatening the Enemy in the Period of Competition	New Global Strategy / No Burden to Economy / Continuation of Stabilization Basis
Big Capital	Reinforcement of Competitiveness / Efficiency of Government / No More Political Conflicts over Consumption	Competitiveness is the Only Way to Survive / The World of Limitless Competition / Recovery of Competitiveness	World First Industry/World Management / Globalization Initiated by Industry / No Burden to Economy
Alternative Groups	Radical, Structural Reform / An End to Mobocracy / Reform of the Authoritarian Labour Policy	Pro-Farmer, Pro-Worker Policy / New National Security/McCarthyite Witch-hunting / Democratic Dictatorship/ Developmental Dictatorship	Globalization of Labour Policy / Globalization of Welfare Standard / Globalization of Environmental Policy / Reform of Plutocracy

lead to structural transformation' and 'reform that encourages the market economy'. The thematic area of 'economic jump-starting' led to discourse tension between 'the supreme objective in the period of unlimited competition' and 'the reappearance of developmental dicta-torship'. And the thematic area of 'national security crisis' brought about tension between 'security stabilization against threats from within and without' and 'the new security logic of McCarthyism'. Second, while the thematic area of 'reform', which caused conflict and splits within the ruling bloc, underwent changes of meaning and a reduction of significance in government policy, the thematic area of 'economic jump-starting'continued to develop through statements about competi-tiveness, internationalization and globalization. Examined in the con-text of the whole period of the Kim Young-Sam regime, accordingly, the reform drive in the earlier part of 1993 was exceptional.

Third, the ruling discourse that penetrated the whole period of Kim's regime included crucial statements about 'management of national affairs that does not burden national economy' and 'no discouragement of the investment plans of industries' in order that Korea might leap towards becoming 'the central country in the man-agement of the whole world'. In the meanwhile, the agenda related to democratization as well as to reform of the politico-economic structure was, naturally, excluded. President Kim demonstrated this by saying, 'Until today, I only did my utmost to promote the democratization of this country. But now I believe that it is my historical mission to rebuild the economy of this country.'

Fourth, the agents of production of the ruling discourse appeared as an alliance of discourses that included not only the Blue House of the President and the Cabinet but the mainstream media, the National Business Association and professional scholars both in academia and business-support research institutes. Fifth, the discursive practice of Kim's regime could not possess any hegemonic ruling effect because it carried with it neither reform steps nor sacrifice and concession of short-term interests on the part of the ruling bloc. The regime's political foundation, as a consequence, gradually dwindled, and politi-cal instability repeatedly appeared. The discourse of 'security' was periodically employed in the meantime in order to prevent alternative groups from organizing a critical multitude – just as it had been employed by former regimes. Sixth, the discursive practices of alterna-tive groups could, nevertheless, neither compose an efficient discourse of resistance nor establish a wide range of discourse alliances because they did not ensure an institutional basis in the decision-making process as well as in civil society.

The Second Modernization Failed:
Toward a Neo-liberal Economy

As we have seen, during the Kim Young-Sam regime a discourse produced by 'the state as a prime organizer of ruling relations' was continually changed and recomposed according to strategic situations under a certain historical conjuncture. The ruling politico-economic relations of Korean society were connected with such a thematic structure of discourse. First of all, I would like to conceptualize the landscape of competing discourses as 'the second modernization failed'. Then I will argue that the alliance of the ruling bloc mobilized the doctrine of the 'second modernization' in order to unite their interests one-sidedly and to exclude the demand for more fundamental democratic reform of political and economic structures.

All political symbols and statements possess a conventionalized frame of interpretation that requires of individuals repeated use in their everyday lives. Such a frame of interpretation necessarily resorts to a 'mobilization of bias' that takes advantage of certain kinds of conflict while repressing other kinds, and possesses through this method a systematic mechanism that adopts specific sorts of topic and agenda while ruling others out of the political scene (Lukes 1974). In order to analyse the conventionalized frame of interpretation of the ruling discourse during Kim's regime and also to analyse it again compatively, first of all we need to conceptualize its meaning and structure.

Simply put, it can be summed up as: 'Let's reinforce national competitiveness and jump toward supreme economic power by harnessing all the national ability.' As soon as our situation was regarded as 'a period of limitless competition on which the survival of the nation desperately depended', the agenda of democratic reform was torn up. When the weakening of the work ethic was criticized as an abhorrent trend that aggravated the economic crisis of the nation, the demands of the workers were duly repressed as behaviour that took no account of the crisis. Whether or not Korea would emerge as 'a central nation in the management of the world' was seen by all of the Korean people as a matter of life and death, and 'excessive' demands for social welfare and redistribution of wealth were criticized as 'collective egotism'. To put creativeness and diligence to work for the improvement of productivity was set up as the supreme individual principle of behaviour in order to achieve the national aims. In so doing, that 'no action should be allowed that may create obstacles for the national economy' was underscored as the ultimate value of the period. Both productivity and efficiency were established as principles of the management of national

affairs, and people were expected to demand not the expansion of
social welfare provision or redistribution of wealth, but economic
growth. What is interesting is that statements were widely employed in
this period that were related to 'a return to morality', 'traditional values
and good manners' and 'family–community'. It was up to 'neighbours'
and family to take care of those who had fallen out of 'the market';
misguided family education and loss of morality were to blame for their
derailed behaviours. Government was not, by definition, to take any
responsibility for the cost of welfare, redistribution of wealth, or
maintenance of the community.[2]

We term 'neo-liberalism' that logic that takes efficiency as its behavioural principle, placing the ultimate value of national policy not on
welfare but on an increase in national wealth. Neo-liberalism subordi-
nates the political logic of social cohesion to the economic logic of
competition. Any positive response by the government on welfare issues
and redistribution of wealth is to be criticized as the source of inefficiency; voluntary solutions in private areas are recommended (Przeworski, 1990: 20–23). Accordingly, 'the obligation principle of the profited'
and 'the revival of the traditional family–community' are the representative doctrines of the 'new Right', which believes in neo-liberalism; we
usually call 'neo-conservatism' the logic that tries to combine, in this
manner, the strengthening of competitiveness with the traditional
ethics of the family. Viewed from this perspective, the ruling discourse
in the period of Kim's regime can possibly be labelled as typical neo-
conservatism.

What sort of political significance can be deduced from the wholesale
employment in the early 1990s of the neo-conservative discourse that
gives supreme priority to economic development, subordinating the
logic of politics to that of economics? A comparative examination from
the historical perspective of the principles of economic development
during Park Chung-Hee's regime (1961–79) can provide some clues. If
we can label as 'the first modernization' the economic-development
principle of Park's regime that can be summarized as 'the construction
of the collective system for the sake of national modernization', we can
conceptualize that of Kim Young Sam's regime as 'the second modernization doctrine'.

What is different is that the Park regime headed towards the negative
goal of 'getting rid of poverty', while the Kim regime suggests such
positive goals as 'a superpower nation' and 'a central nation of world
management'. The adoption of the principle of giving priority to
growth, the postponement of democratization and redistribution of
wealth, and the suggestion of productivity and efficiency as the key

principles for the management of national affairs by Kim's regime, however, connects it to Park's regime.

What we should notice here, however, is the different historical conditions that each of the doctrines of modernization is based on. In social terms, Park's regime was a period of general suffering because of the underdevelopment of capitalist industrialization. The doctrine of modernization during Park's regime, accordingly, can be seen as the product of a historical stage when the government tried, by its own guidance, to establish rapid industrialization as well as capitalist social relations. Even if Korea had to pay the political cost of an authoritarian regime, the improvement of material conditions that she got as a reward cannot altogether be evaluated in a negative way, considering that Korea's general condition was too low to combine economic development with political democratization.

On the contrary, Kim's regime was the first to reach the stage at which complete capitalist social relations were established, whose condition is that private areas independent of the government spontaneously reproduce discourses. The Park doctrine of modernization was to establish the capitalist development of the whole society rather than to support vested class interests, while Kim's doctrine of the second modernization had to relate itself directly to the relations of power of the classes. This is clear from the fact that vested powers such as big corporations welcomed Kim's doctrine of economic development, whilst alternative forces resisted it, complaining that it involved a 'dictatorial logic of development', that it was 'a logic that justified the special interest of the plutocracy', and that it was 'an ideology that aimed to hide class relations in a national government by appealing to chauvinistic feelings through the competition logic among national governments'. Second, the fact that the democratization movement in the mid-1980s got nationwide support, and also that the reform drive in 1993 was welcomed throughout the nation, does not mean that most of the public regarded political authoritarianism as the inevitable opportunity cost of economic development.[3]

Moreover, the continued large-scale organization and resistance of the workers since the mid-1980s shows that most of them are no longer tolerant of the socio-economic ruling system equipped with development-preference logic. The pressing task of Korean society should therefore be to increase the redistribution of wealth and welfare that was sacrificed in the industrialization process in the earlier period. Such a significance was embedded, I believe, in the macro process of democratization with its collective power as an organization since the 1980s. Seen from this perspective, Kim's doctrine of the second

modernization has proved to be a discourse project intended to combine procedural democracy, as was recovered by the democratization
struggle in June 1987, with the politico-economic ruling system of
Korean society as established in the industrialization process of the
authoritarian regime of the past. It truly was a discourse project that
tried to adapt the latter to the former. The discourse project of the
second modernization doctrine, to be sure, did not carry with it any
'hegemonic effect by organizing voluntary support and agreement of
the subordinated class'. The doctrine of the second modernization,
without any concessions to temporary and union interests, may well
have been recognized by the working class as being repressive in
character. A labour union activist said, 'There is no place in the media
that we cannot find the term globalization, and our thinking may be
suspected unless we use the term.' (*Newspaper of the Workers*, 21 February
1995.)

None the less, the doctrine of the second modernization proved to
be neither a political slogan nor 'false consciousness' without material
foundation. It sought, rather, a certain material foundation in the fact
that the material benefit of the people was subordinated to macro-
economic conditions, and its human foundation in the middle class
who are most perceptive to the economic situation. That the middle
class provides the political support for the second modernization
doctrine is due to the fact that they happen to be the least organized
class as well as being one of the classes that benefited most from rapid
capitalistic industrialization. When the middle class has believed that
a rapid change or degradation of their financial status was about
to occur, the modern history of Korea has shown that their individual
and collective choice has occasionally been to accept authoritarianism
by reserving support for democratization and reform (Choi Jang-Jip,
1985; 46–55). It is highly suggestive that in May 1994 the general
secretary of the Confederation of Practising Economic Justice, a civil
movement group based on the middle class, expressed the following
attitude:

> The confederation should advocate the reinforcement of national competi-
> tiveness. If national competitiveness fails, welfare also fails. If an industry is
> 100 per cent perfect, there is no need for civil activism. If most of the people
> recognize that the confederation stands in the way of strengthening national
> competitiveness, it should reflect on itself. (Cho Yu-Shik, 1994)

We can understand in the same context why 'improvement of the
international status of Korea' was 'first among the merits of the
contemporary government' according to a survey of public opinion

carried out by the Ministry of Information. On the basis of this, the government made haste to join the OECD.

The second modernization doctrine, briefly put, can be called a dominant discourse of a ruling bloc by which they wanted to unite their interests one-sidedly, without any concession and sacrifice. It has the character of a discourse project in that it tries, by excluding the agenda of reform and democratization, to adapt the politico-economic ruling system that had been established in the authoritarianism of past regimes to the new condition of recovered procedural democracy as well as open civil society. Resistance of the people against this was not, nevertheless, easily organized. When such discourses as 'economic crisis' and 'national security' were reverberating among and appealing to the people, especially to the common sense of the middle class, efforts by the alternative social movement to organize popular resistance against the ruling discourse did not succeed. The second modernization doctrine, by appealing to the conservative sentiments of the middle class, has been effectively blocking efforts to organize popular resistance to the politico-economic ruling system of Korean society.

Notes

1. By alternative forces here, I designate quite roughly various discourse-producing agents which challenge the establishments of political and economic power as well as political legitimization in a society. Trade unions and civil movement groups are included. After the Democratization Struggle in 1987, social movement has been divided into the labour movement and civil movement. Nevertheless, these movements can be understood as a unique collective category because the collective significance of their statements, individual or organized, clearly has an independent position in the social context.

2. In 1995, the president suggested such concepts as 'the quality of life' and 'productive welfare', though Suh Sang-Mok, the Minister for Health and Welfare at that point, explained in a radio interview that it was his intention to implement health and welfare policies 'as far as this did not burden the economic growth of the country'. He added that he would solve those demands out of reach of national welfare policy through a national movement geared to the revival of family–community ethics.

3. The Research Centre for Modern Society conducted research each year from 1981 to 1987, which showed that 73 per cent of people on average responded 'yes' when asked if democracy should be realized even if it blocked more economic development. (The Research Centre for Modern Society, 1981–87)

References

(*in Korean*)

Cho Yu-Shik (1993). 'How does the Progressive Respond to the Age of Internationalization?', *Language Monthly*, November.

Choi Jang-Jip (1985). 'State, Class Structure and Political Change for Forty Years after Liberation', *Modern Korean History*, Vol. 1. Seoul: Yuleum-sa.

Choi Jang-Jip (1989). *Structure and Change in Modern Korean Politics.* Seoul: Kachi.

Research Centre for Modern Society (1981–87). *Annual Survey of People's Values and Consciousness, 1981–1986.* Seoul: Research Centre for Modern Society.

(*in English*)

Elder, C. and Cobb, R. (1983). *The Political Use of Symbols.* New York: Longman.

Grossberg, L. (1992). *We Gotta Get out of This Place: Popular Conservatism and Postmodern Culture.* New York: Routledge.

Grossberg, L. (1996). 'On Postmodernism and Articulation: An Interview with Stuart Hall', in D. Morley and K.H. Chen (eds.), *Stuart Hall: Critical Dialogues in Cultural Studies.* London: Routledge.

Hall, S. and Jacques, M. (1983a) *The Politics of Thatcherism.* London: Lawrence & Wishart.

Hall, S. (1983b). 'The Problem of Ideology: Marxism without Guarantees', in B. Matthews (ed.), *Marx: 100 Years On.* London: Lawrence & Wishart, pp. 57–84.

Hall, S. (1985). 'Signification, Representation, Ideology: Althusser and the Poststructuralist Debates', *Critical Studies in Mass Communication*, 2(2), pp. 91–114.

Hall, S. (1988). *The Hard Road to Renewal.* London and New York: Verso.

Lukes, S. (1974). *Power: A Radical View.* New York: Macmillan.

O'Donnell, G.A. (1979). 'Tensions in the Bureaucratic-authoritarian State and the Question of Democracy', in D. Collier (ed.), *The New Authoritarianism in Latin America*, Princeton, NJ: Princeton University Press.

Petras, J. (1986). 'The Redemocratization process', *Contemporary Marxism*, 14 (Fall).

Przeworski, A. (1990). *The State and Economy under Capitalism.* Harwood Academic Publishers.

Stuart Hall and Social Policy:
An Encounter of Strangers?

Gail Lewis

In 1967 the Community Relations Commission published a short pamphlet by Stuart Hall called *The Young Englanders* in which he offered a brief but tightly packed description of the circumstances surrounding and mediating the contacts between racially differentiated adolescents – the young Englanders of the title. Running alongside these descriptions were a number of emergent analytical points – often felt or half-indicated, rather than fleshed-out and theorized – which we would come to recognize as central to his oeuvre: racial identities as relational; as formed at the intersection of subjectivity and culture; as articulated through and with diverse, intersecting fields of social relations understood as the social, the political, the economic, the ideological. The aim of the pamphlet was to identify the issues and 'problems' facing young (not yet) black teenagers, and to begin to elicit the sources of these 'problems'. Hall felt that this process was a necessary prelude to any attempt to try and find 'solutions'. The pamphlet was, then, a piece of writing positioned directly in the field of social policy if we understand social policy as being concerned with the ways in and mechanisms through which social integration and social order are achieved and maintained in ways which carry popular consent. In subsequent publications produced while he was at the Centre for Contemporary Cultural Studies at Birmingham and at the Open University, Stuart Hall was to show his connection to social policy, most obviously in the collectively produced *Policing the Crisis* (1978), but also in publications such as *Drifting into a Law and Order Society* (1979), 'Teaching Race in the School in the Multicultural Society' (1981), and *The Voluntary Sector Under Attack?* (1989).

Despite the apparently self-evident connection between Hall and social policy that these publications demonstrate, the relevance of his work to social policy is not one that is widely recognized by the majority of those working in the field of social policy as either academics or welfare professionals. In my view this lack of recognition is the result of four factors. First, it derives from social policy's roots in empiricism and its early practice as social *administration*. Second, it is a product of the fact that, until very recently, the discipline of social policy had remained untouched by what have come to be known as post-structuralist approaches, and even now the number of people working through these perspectives remains small. Third, Hall has tended to be understood as primarily a commentator/theoretician of 'race', with the result that where his work has been used in the analysis of social policy it has tended to be located in considerations of the relationship between social policies and the welfare needs and outcomes of 'ethnic minority' populations. As in many fields, 'race' here is understood as being commensurate with diverse groupings of black people. The fourth, closely connected but different, point is that as an *embodied* intellectual Hall has been ensnared (in social policy, at least) in his own blackness so that what he speaks – however eloquently – is understood as only being about blackness, about black peoples in Britain, only relevant when these peoples are explicitly there: visible. The implication of these four overlapping tendencies is that a potentially rich method of analysis is closed off to social policy academics at exactly the moment in New Labour Britain when we could most usefully deploy it. I want to try and indicate what I mean by taking two articles – one published in 1978, the other in 1987 – and thinking about what they might offer for an analysis of the changed and changing landscape of social policy and welfare practice – changes that began in the Thatcher years and continue, albeit with some differences of emphasis, under New Labour. The two articles are 'Racism and Reaction' (Hall 1978) and *Minimal Selves* (Hall 1987), exemplars, I believe, of the two analytic 'poles' around which Hall has crafted his particular intellectual project and called for a politics of articulation. But let me begin by returning to that early, 1967 piece.

Right at the beginning of *The Young Englanders* we are told that

> Race relations are not – as is commonly believed – simply the relations of the immigrant community to the host community. They are the mutual inter-relations of both groups – English-to-immigrant; immigrant-to-English. Race is a collective concept. Essentially, race relations are relations between groups of people rather than individuals; relationships in which the personal exchanges between individuals are mediated through and affected by the whole body of stereotyped attitudes and beliefs which lie between one group and another. (p. 3)

Toward the end we read:

The lived experience of the immigrant teenager is a little like that of the traveller whose routes in and out of home take him along extended bridges across deep and dangerous chasms. Already the young immigrant is trying to span the gap between Britain and 'home' ... There is the identity which belongs to the part of him that is West Indian, or Pakistani or Indian ... there is also the identity of 'the young Englander' towards which every new experience beckons ... school, friends, the street, work and England itself. (p. 10)

Somehow he must learn to reconcile his two identities and make them one. But many of the avenues into the wider society are closed to him. If he ventures into the clubs, he feels as though he is permanently on trial. This he finds especially difficult to bear because the relationship which the youth culture values most is the relaxed relationship in which people are not on trial, in which they simply belong and are accepted. . . . Yet he can't go 'home' again. The route back is closed. But so too is the route forward. (p. 12)

And so in this context

the young immigrants I have met in the last year or two are falling back on their own reserves. They are closing-in their lines of contact, re-discovering their own racial and national identities and stereotyping their white counter-parts. . . . There is a pride and independence among these youngsters which is a tribute to their resilience, their capacity to survive, their determination to respect and honour not only themselves but also their families, home countries, culture, prowess and achievements. This may be the only platform from which an 'assault' on the host community can be made. (p. 14)

I have quoted at length from this piece because I think we can already detect some of the lines of thinking that were to become characteristic of Hall's sociological and cultural analyses of contemporary life in Britain. Hall's theoretical approach developed, it seems to me, between two analytical poles, themselves the product of his attempt to work through a non-determinist Marxism and an appropriation of the insights of (post-)structuralism. Thus, on the one hand, Hall has insisted on the development of politically committed theoretical work which excavates the webs of social relations – political, economic, cultural – in which signs are embedded and through which their meanings are constructed and mediated. On the other hand, or perhaps it is better to say, from the other pole, he has wanted to discern and understand the processes by which identities are con-structed within fields of difference – not in the sense of an endless play of difference (Hall 1981) but rather as the ground upon which a politics of articulation might be constructed. He has, then, been concerned to think about and theorize the intersections – the consti-tutive force – of the conjunctural and the contingent. These two 'poles' are brought together on the terrain of culture which, for him, is the site of struggle over meaning – not just of the abstracted sign but also of the 'real' of lived experience. In this context, ideological practices become understood politically as the attempt to fix meanings, yoke together in particular ways diverse facets of social life and thus assume authority to determine, and indeed authorize, that which is understood as real.

I have already suggested that 'Racism and Reaction' and *Minimal Selves* exemplify the 'poles' of the conjunctural and the contingent in Hall's work and that they do so in ways which I think could be adopted by those of us working in the discipline of social policy. I will elaborate this point below. 'Racism and Reaction' was one of five articles published by the Commission for Racial Equality and broadcast on BBC Radio in 1978. In it Hall attempts to delineate the *faire* – or work – of 'race' and racism in a particular historical moment. Beginning by situating the unfolding, and potentially explosive, field of race relations in the interstices between, on the one hand, changing economic, political and urban landscapes and, on the other, the emergence of 'the teenager' and associated youth cultures, he argues that the sign of 'race' (and the practice of racism) came to occupy a specific place in the wider economy of signs and social practices that signalled the transition to a new conjuncture in the late 1960s and 1970s. Situated within a deepening and more visible 'organic crisis' (Hall 1983; CCCS 1982), 'Race . . . [became] the prism through which the British people . . . [were] called upon to live through, then to understand, and then to deal with the growing crisis' (Hall 1978: 30). 'Racism represents the attempt ideologically to construct those conditions, contradictions and problems in such a way that they can be dealt with and deflected in the same moment. That instead of confronting the conditions and problems which indeed do face white and black in the urban areas, in an economy in recession, they can be projected away through race' (Hall 1978: 35). And, whilst this 'is not a crisis of race' (Hall 1978: 31)) its position as ideological practice lies in its ability to speak to and express – (to connect) – in condensed form the lived realities of vast numbers of Britons. The conjunctural character of this moment of 'race' and racism lies in the way in which the organic crisis constituted the particularity of its shape and modes of expression and thus in the place it occupied in the shift into an authoritarian populism begun in Powellism and coming into full flourish in Thatcherism.

In *Minimal Selves* published nine years later, in 1987, we have, I think, a good example of Hall's thinking through the other 'pole' – through the other end of the theoretical terrains he is attempting to meld together in the spirit of political openness and strategic effectivity. His argument here centres on the question: what kind of politics is it necessary and possible to construct now that 'we' all 'know' that identity – 'the self' – is fictional? Given that identities are formed at the (unstable) intersections of subjectivity and history, culture, *and* that 'the politics of infinite dispersal is the politics of no action at all' (p. 45), Hall both poses a question and makes a political statement. The question is: how do we go about constructing a politics around 'unities-in-difference' (p. 45) – what we might call communities of identification and articulation? And the statement is: we have to do so. 'I think that is a new conception of politics, rooted in a new conception of the self, of identity. But I do think, theoretically and intellectually, it requires us to begin, not only to speak the language of dispersal, but also the language of, as it were, contingent closures of articulation' (p. 45). Now, in the social policy context, what interests me about this piece is that Hall gets to these 'universal' questions through the terrain of a given 'particular', namely the identity of 'black' – the processes of its constitution; and how the paradox had seemingly arisen that young black people had come to occupy simultaneously the positions of marginalization, disadvantage, displacement *and* 'a new kind of space at the centre' (p. 44). In social policy discourses and analyses this kind of contradictory positioning is rarely, if ever, recognized. Moreover, 'black' as signifier or embodied welfare subject (see Lewis 1998) is seldom used as the starting point through which to unfold an analysis of the conjunctural and contingent 'moments' that circumscribe and mediate the lived – in social policy's case the lived of the social relations of welfare. Finally, *Minimal Selves* raises questions about how we can understand the category and status of the margins/marginal. It is to these issues that I now turn my attention.

One effect that accompanied the rise of 'new social movements' was the emergence of a series of challenges to the settlement that had been at the core of the Beveridge welfare state. These challenges involved critiques of at least three aspects of the post-1945 welfare settlement: the social subject which had come to symbolize the welfare citizen; many of the criteria through which welfare services and benefits were accessed; and the diverse practices of a range of welfare agencies and professionals (Williams 1989; Hughes and Lewis 1998). In challenging the terms of the social democratic welfare settlement the 'new' social constituencies also revealed the normative aspects of social policy: how welfare policies and practices were constitutive of, and constituted by, a range of social relations, not just class – the social division with which social policy had been explicitly concerned between the 1940s and 1970s. In contrast to an analysis of social policy through the singular lens of class, feminist, anti-racist, disabled rights and gay and lesbian activists revealed that welfare policies and practices held in place dominant assumptions about gender, 'race', (dis)ability and sexuality and actively worked to reproduce the marginal or subordinated status of these, and a range of other social constituencies. On the basis of their analyses, collective claims were made for a widened welfare citizenship based on recognition of the autonomous rights of these groups.

This is by now a well-known story and does not need elaborating here. What I do want to suggest, however, is another dimension to these challenges which is often unrecognized and which centres on two points that are of direct relevance to the argument I am making here. The first point is that the construction of a series of new welfare subjects, with diverse and differentiated claims to welfare citizenship, was in part a claim from the margins which wanted both to legitimate and to hold on to specificity but in a form that disarticulated specificity from marginality. It was one form of expression of 'living with, living through difference', as Hall put it in *Minimal Selves* (p. 45). Directly connected to this is the second point: that in being an expression of collective claims from 'new' political constituencies, these challenges to welfare also necessarily involved points of 'arbitrary closure'. These closures represent the points of anchorage and articulation of the collective claims and the political strategies designed to achieve them. Now, it seems to me that it is possible to use Hall's analytical approach to unmask these aspects of the claims for an expanded and more differentiated welfare citizenship. Moreover, Hall's utility in this field points to the limitations of viewing his analytical relationship to social policy as only narrowly construed through the lens of 'race' if this is taken to signal the category 'black' and the lived experiences of those who inhabit this and/or other ethnic minority statuses and identities. In contrast to the tendency to consign his approach to the confines of a 'particular' forever closed off from a normative 'universal', I would argue that his approach enables those of us working in the discipline of social policy to interpret a number of moves within welfare politics. Specifically, his use of a Gramscian approach to analyse 'race', difference and politics offers social policy a methodological stance, by which I mean an analytic practice around three intersecting dimensions: (1) how welfare policies and practices signal a particular conjuncture through the ways in which they form a particular notion and image of 'the people' as welfare citizens around a series of relationships connecting economic, social, political, moral and administrative elements; (2) the ways in which welfare policies and practices are implicated in the processes through which difference, identity and identification are produced; (3) the ideological work that 'race' does in given conjunctural and contingent contexts.

Each of these dimensions figured in the Thatcherite reforms in welfare which began in the 1980s, gathered pace after 1988, and seem to be being held in place in their basic form under New Labour. At one level, we need do little more than understand the Thatcherite project on welfare reform within the conjunctural context suggested by Hall and Jacques (1983), who noted that what made it possible for Thatcherism to emerge as the dominant political force of the 1980s was the combination of national and international factors at ideological, economic and social levels. It was in this context that the social democratic consensus of the period following World War Two was finally eroded. However, using Hall's approach to cross-read the conjunctural and the contingent opens an analytic space through which to develop a richer, more finely textured and nuanced analysis of the radical restructuring of welfare in the UK. Thus, whilst the *decomposition* of the social democratic welfare settlement involved a project of radical transformation of the existing consensus, commitments and understandings about the relationship between the state, 'the people' and welfare, its *reconstitution* involved something more. That this 'more' comprised a change in the character of social welfare and the role of the state in providing it; that it involved a move to forms of marketized relationships within and between welfare agencies and their 'customers'; and that it involved new organizational structures of both delivery and accountability is well known. That the 'more' also involved a new common sense and set of knowledges about state welfare and the creation of a field of relationships deployed under the sign and practice of managerialism is both less well known and, within the field of social policy, less analysed (as opposed to described). As Janet Newman (1998) has noted in an exemplary and thought-provoking article, managerialism

> forms the nexus of a changing field of relationships within and beyond social welfare. This changing field of relationships includes those between the state and the business world; between employers and employees; between organizations in the public, private and voluntary sectors; and between organizations and their users, customers or clients. (p. 334)

In displacing a bureau-professional mode of co-ordinating relationships between and within welfare agencies, and between them and their clients, managerialism was aimed both at producing economies and efficiencies *and* at producing new forms of consciousness and identification.

In restructuring the field of relationships and identifications within the welfare nexus, the radical recomposition of state-regulated welfare was articulated through both conjunctural and contingent processes. This suggests that only tracking these changes through one or the other axis occludes significant transformations in the webs of social relations, images and identifications constituted by and constitutive of welfare in the contemporary UK. Hall's two-poled approach through the conjunctural and the contingent helps us to devise a methodological stance that can capture this complexity. Moreover, it can help us to do so in a way that enables us to think about the shifting significance and role of 'race' in the restructured welfare regime that characterizes social welfare today.

Questions of 'race', ethnicity and national identity have been at the core of the various forms of welfare regime that have developed in Britain at least since the onset of industrialization, as is evident in the development of widened and more inclusive forms of welfare citizenship (see, for example, Hickman 1995; Braidwood 1994). Since the 1960s the link between 'race', ethnicity and welfare has tended to be conceived in two ways. On the one hand, it has been seen as indicative of the existence of essentialized and particular welfare needs which derive from the racial and/or ethnic origins of racialized minorities (as in, for example, the widespread proscription, during the 1980s and early 1990s, of transracial adoption and fostering, in the interest of the assumed identity needs of the children involved. On the other hand, 'race' and/or ethnicity have been used as a way to map the social and geographical landscape in the process of identifying the specificity of need of particular places. In this case the distribution of central and local government grants to local areas followed a racial topography.

Certainly these two ways into the connections between 'race' and social policy can lead to fruitful investigations of the degree to which racialized minorities are faring in the process of distribution of welfare services and benefits. But we have seen from both 'Racism and Reaction' and *Minimal Selves* that 'race' works in much wider and deeper ways than simply signalling a set of essentialized and particular welfare needs. Rather, it intersects with other axes of differentiation such as gender, class, age, to articulate fields of power, and this within social policy as elsewhere, as Williams (1989) has so cogently shown. Given this, we can take our cue from Hall's insistence on an analytical stance that is as attentive to the ideological and cultural as it is to the economic, social and political, and think about the place 'race' occupies in constructing forms of national integration and belonging. To do this means taking account of the presences and absences of racial discourse and/or the sign of 'race' in discussions of social policy at national level. In this context, what we in the discipline of social policy should be looking for is the way in which welfare policies and practices inscribe racial and ethnic belongings and identities in the process of attempting to craft forms of social integration. Now, in 'Racism and Reaction', Hall noted three tendencies in British political debate: to construct 'the British people' (and especially the English) as without ethnicity; to treat the social practice of 'race' and racism as if it were external to the British social formation; and, therefore, to construct the problematic as if it were only 'a matter of policy . . . not a matter of politics' (p. 24). This suggests that a view through the Hall analytic would push us towards a discernment of the play of 'race' in social policy even when explicit reference to it is minimal.

In my view, this is exactly the kind of analytic work that social policy academics need to undertake in this age of New Labour. For it is clear from the reading of a number of social policy Green and White Papers (and from public statements from a number of ministries) that New Labour is treating the social divisions of 'race'/ethnicity and gender as if they are the markers of the age of 'immature', Left Labour councils of the 1970s and 1980s, as if they are the signs of Labour's consignment to the political wilderness, as if they are now settled concerns. In current national political debate the only social divisions and patterns that really matter are those of social exclusion, understood in European Union terms as exclusion from the labour market, and the proliferation of forms of family away from the normative nuclear family. In this context, questions of 'race' and ethnicity are again treated as if they are external features which are brought into the British welfare community by migration (see the White and Green Papers on Health); or as features of particular and pathologized places and groups (see the White Paper on Education). 'Race' is once again displaced into particular territories; it is disconnected from social, cultural and economic processes, divorced from the social formation.

To counter this ideological work, social policy needs to reinvigorate its imaginative power. It needs to seize the time and offer alternative visions of the relationship between the state and social welfare. It needs to be brave enough to suggest new and contestatory welfare identities. To do this we need to think social policy through both the conjunctural and the contingent, to think about the constitutive force of the dynamic between these fields. If we dare, the work of Stuart Hall might help us to do it.

References

Braidwood, S. (1994) *The Black Poor and White Philanthropy: The Sierra Leone Project*, Liverpool: Liverpool University Press.

CCCS (Centre for Contemporary Cultural Studies) (1982) *The Empire Strikes Back*, London: Hutchinson.

Hall, S. (1967) *The Young Englanders*, London: Community Relations Commission.

Hall, S. (1978) 'Racism and Reaction', in *Five Views of Multi-Racial Britain*, London: Commission for Racial Equality.

Hall, S., (1979) *Drifting into a Law and Order Society*, London: Cobden Trust.

Hall, S., (1981) 'Teaching Race in the School in the Multicultural Society', in James, A., and Jeffcoate, R. (eds.), *The School in the Multicultural Society*, London: Harper & Row/Open University Press.

Hall, S., (1983) 'The Great Moving Right Show', in Hall, S., and Jacques, M. (eds.) *The Politics of Thatcherism*, London: Lawrence & Wishart in association with *Marxism Today*.

Hall, S., (1987) *Minimal Selves*, ICA Documents 6, London.

Hall, S., (1989) *The Voluntary Sector Under Attack?*, London: Islington Voluntary Action Council.

Hall, S., and Jacques, N. (eds.) (1983) *The Politics of Thatcherism*, London: Lawrence & Wishart in association with *Marxism Today*.

Hall, S., Clarke, J., Critcher, C., Jefferson, T., and Roberts, B., (1978) *Policing the Crisis*, Basingstoke: Macmillan.

Hickman, M. J. (1995) *Religion, Class and Identity: The State, the Catholic Church and the Education of the Irish in Britain*, Aldershot: Avebury.

Hughes, G., and Lewis, G. (eds.) (1998) *Unsettling Welfare: The Reconstruction of Social Policy*, London: Routledge in association with the Open University.

Lewis, G., (1998) 'Coming Apart at the Seams: The Crises of the Welfare State', in Hughes, G., and Lewis, G. (eds.) *Unsettling Welfare: The Reconstruction of Social Policy*, London: Routledge in association with the Open University.

Newman, J., (1998) 'Managerialism and Social Welfare', in Hughes, G., and Lewis, G. (eds.) *Unsettling Welfare: The Reconstruction of Social Policy*, London: Routledge in association with the Open University.

Williams, F., (1989) *Social Policy: A Critical Introduction – Issues of Race, Gender and Class*, Cambridge: Polity.

17

Absolute Beginnings:
In Search of a Lost Time

Rolf Lindner

1

The title page of issue 7 of *Universities and Left Review* (autumn 1959) shows a photo of a young couple by Roger Mayne; it belongs to the same series as the cover photo of Colin MacInnes's cult novel *Absolute Beginners* (1965 [1959]). The posture of the couple, turning half away from, half towards, the observer/photographer, is like a visualization of the attitude that, in 1956, the French film director François Truffaut attributed to contemporary youth: 'the refusal to fit in and the simultaneous desire for community'. The clear message to anyone looking at the photograph is that this is a new generation, a sceptical generation (as the West German sociologist Helmut Schelsky called it in 1957), not easily roused, taking cover behind a cool attitude, yet at the same time extremely vulnerable. John Dos Passos was not the only one to see James Dean as its prototype.

'The refusal to fit in and the simultaneous desire for community' – the Secondary Modern generation, on which Stuart Hall reflects in a review essay in the same issue of *Universities and Left Review*, is also characterized by this ambivalent attitude. 'At the age of 13/14', writes Hall, the youngsters at the Secondary Modern, 'begin to pass out of the direct influence of home-and-school, and into the wider world of their own groups, the friendships and rivalries of their local gangs, the culture of the youth club and skiffle group, the heady atmosphere of the mass entertainments' (Hall 1959: 18).

Many observers, Hall continues, are of the opinion that the important changes in adolescent experience take place during the transition from school to working life. 'But I have little doubt that the most important formation point lies between junior and adolescent phases – roughly at a breaking-point between the second and third years of the

Secondary Modern career.' 'Work, of course, adds responsibilities, new skills, a new environment, a wider pattern of movement from the home and the surroundings. But basically, work modifies a pattern of feeling, responses and attitudes already established by the age of fourteen' (Hall 1959). At fourteen these youngsters are already adult in many ways and are without illusions regarding their future prospects. Convinced of the relative unimportance of school, which after all prepares then for nothing more than semi-skilled positions, they transfer their energies and aspirations to the informal group and to the future world of work, 'anxious to get out and get on with it' (Hall 1959). In this portrait of the 'Sec Mod Boys', who react to cultural deprivation with wilful noise, inattention and sudden explosions of violence towards authority and towards each other, it is not difficult to recognize, as if surfacing for the first time, the 'informal group with negative orientation towards school', the 'lads', whom Paul Willis made the heroes of his study *Learning to Labour.* Astonishingly, Stuart Hall prefigures here the cultural principle, which Willis opened out ethnographically in his Social Science Research Council (SSRC) project, 'The Transition from School to Work': 'the most profound transition these lads make is not the physical passage from school into work, it is their experiential entry into the distinctive non-conformist group and its culture within the school and this transition may occur anywhere between the second and fifth years' (Willis 1975: 69).

In retrospect, 'Absolute Beginnings', the title of Hall's review essay – borrowed from Colin MacInnes's novel *Absolute Beginners* – appears visionary. This modest article, which is not listed in the Morley and Chen (1996) catalogue of Hall's published work, is something like a blueprint for the research programme that the Centre for Contemporary Cultural Studies (CCCS) pursued under Stuart Hall as director, and that made it famous. This is perhaps even more evident in the second part of the essay. This addresses the so-called 'teenage revolution' by way of Mark Abrams's *The Teenage Consumer* and, above all, MacInnes's *Absolute Beginners*. 'Teenage revolution', first of all, means pop entertainment and youth culture as new economic and cultural phenomena, central themes of the media and subculture groups at the CCCS. But the centre had no monopoly on these subjects; on the contrary, the youth sociology of the late 1950s and early 1960s, with its critiques of consumption and ideology, was just as dependent on the figure of the teenager and served as a foil to research at the centre. What distinguishes Hall's reflections from other contemporary comments on this new 'superficial and hedonistic generation', is a view of the latter that is remarkably restrained and free of ideology, and, if it is not too overused and old-fashioned a word, *understanding.* He also sees teenagers, and this is truly visionary, as 'the first generation of the Common Market' (Hall 1959: 23). In its restraint, Hall's reflective stance corresponds exactly to the 'modern attitude', which an older generation can easily misinterpret as lack of commitment and morals. 'To be modern' in 1959 meant not letting anyone put one over on you, starting from zero, being without preconceptions; in a word: absolute beginners. What marks out the new type, which MacInnes introduced in the shape of his hero, is a combination of attitudes previously considered incompatible: that is, for all the ostentatious cool, to have strong moral views on certain subjects. Truffaut, referring to the James Dean generation, drew a similar picture of a 'moral purity', which has nothing to do with the bourgeois moral code. The conflicting attitudes find expression in an argument between MacInnes' hero and his half-brother Vernon, who 'is one of the last of the generations that grew up before teenagers existed' (MacInnes 1965 [1959]: 37). What Vernon has in mind is a world of class solidarity, the world of traditional popular culture, which has settled down with the dichotomy of 'them' and 'us'. What the hero has in mind is a world in which no one cares, 'what your class is, or what your race is, or what your income, or if you're a boy, or girl, or bent, or versatile, or what you are – so long as you dig the scene and can behave yourself, and have left all that crap behind you, too, when you come in the jazz club door' (MacInnes 1965 [1959]: 64). 'The Modern Jazz Quartet Generation', writes Stuart Hall, 'may also be the first generation that *could* lift its eyes above the slums of Paddington. Its horizons may be carefully manipulated by Fleet Street and ARTV: they are somehow broader, more comprehensive and basically more humane. Are they in any sense 'socially' more responsible? No. But they are socially more responsive. They have views which include people other than themselves' (Hall 1959: 24). Hall's sensitive analysis captures precisely the generational difference between responsibility, which is always also a duty, and understanding, which requires empathy, as individual codes of conduct.

This 'advance guard of the teenage revolution' (Hall 1959) is aware of itself, is able to catch the spirit of its time; its members are cosmopolitan working-class adolescents, critical consumers who know that the teenage thing is basically a racket and yet pity everyone who grew up before the teenage thing existed. It is this uniting of incompatibles, the multiplicity of perspectives, that characterizes the 'modern attitude' of the new generation, and that also demands a new attitude of analysis. The new generation is a media-aware advance guard, which, sensitive to change, plays with meanings, appears amoral because it has no principles, is not committed to any cause, and yet has pronounced moral views, is dedicated to pleasure, but will not stand any nonsense on certain social issues, demands a sophisticated reading, which does not follow a crude either...or/if...then logic but is familiar with semiotics, is able to decode contradictions and knows that the assumed rules of commerce may be negotiated, displaced, even broken: Resistance through Rituals.

> 'Those clothes you wear', he said at last, 'disgust me.' And I hope they did! I had on precisely my full teenage drag that would enrage him – the grey pointed alligator casuals, the pink neon pair of ankle crepe nylon-stretch, my Cambridge blue glove-fit jeans, a vertical-striped happy shirt revealing my lucky neck-charm on its chain, and the Roman-cut short-arse jacket just referred to ... not to mention my wrist identity jewel, and my Spartian warrior hair-do. (MacInnes 1965 [1959] 32)

Youth style as a dramaturgical statement about the self.

2

Only forty years ago, pop(ular) culture did not exist as a subject of research. Knowledge of pop(ular) culture, came, as Iain Chambers (1986) put it, from direct experience – 'watching commercial television, listening to pop music, sipping cappuccino in a newly opened coffee bar' – and not from book learning. That has to be remembered in order to understand even something of the immense changes that have taken place in this area since 'Absolute Beginnings'. The bearer of this transformation was the self-conscious, because self-reflexive, advance guard of pop culture marked out by Stuart Hall, an avant-garde that produced its own interpreters. From the start, pop culture, unlike mass culture, had a more or less self-conscious attitude to the media and its representatives. A figure embodying this attitude is the smart interpreter inside the scene who supplies journalists who want to know, 'what young people are thinking today', with 'first-hand reports', admittedly mystifying ones.[1] This participant observer in the original sense[2] – the scene insider who functions as informant – is the forerunner, the larva, of the 'fan with special skills' (Frith and Savage 1993), who makes academic capital by combining his experience and knowledge with a fashionable academic theory. It is not hard to imagine the hero of MacInnes's novel as a student of cultural studies. This is not only because MacInnes later was called the 'first Pop anthropologist, the first post war style sub-culture essayist' (Peter York, in MacInnes 1986), a kind of godfather of cultural studies,[3] not only because it was the 'modernists' (named after their taste for modern jazz), the generation that had grown up with pop culture, who provided the first generation of cultural studies students, but because the curriculum of cultural studies corresponds to the 'syllabus' of the jazz club, where one meets 'all kind of cats, on absolutely equal terms, who can clew you up in all kinds of directions – in social directions, in culture directions, in sexual directions, and in racial directions' (MacInnes 1965 [1959]: 64).

Translated into the terminology of cultural studies, the curriculum of the jazz club – race, class and gender – turns out to be astonishingly contemporary. If pop(ular) culture 'is a direct expression of the aspirations and dreams of society as it is, rather than an attempt to impose a "desirable" culture from above' (Melly 1989 [1970]: 8), then cultural studies is the form of analysis homologous to this cultural form. This provides both its strength and its limitations. In contrast to mass culture studies, which are conceived from the top down ('the manipulated consumer', 'teenage nihilism', 'the mindless hooligan') and in which the ideology/manipulation thesis is inherent, cultural studies proceeds from the bottom up and from within. Thanks to this change of perspective, the object of research gains a new dignity. Where previously the existence of an imposed delusion was asserted, now questions are asked as to meaning: what does it mean to be a mod, a *Dallas* fan, a hooligan? Instead of unhesitatingly assuming ideological incorporation by consumption, modes of consumption are investigated for resistant readings. That makes not only analysis more complicated, of course, but also the act that is being analysed. Nothing, or at least so it seems, can be done 'simply' any more; everything is a sign of something, has a deeper meaning. Stanley Cohen early on drew attention to this consequence of paradigm shift. Referring to the analysis of style, he concluded 'that the symbolic baggage the kids are being asked to carry is just too heavy' (Cohen 1980: xv). Through these readings, everyday practices are elevated beyond recognition. For example, the meaning of the Sony Walkman may thus be understood as 'the unobtrusive link in an urban strategy', which permits the possibility 'of imposing your soundscape on the surrounding aural environment and thereby domesticating the external world'. Or the graffii artist appears as the 'flaneur of the late twentieth century', who 'places his signs of life' (tags) 'in highly coded form'. Thus the desire to lend actors a voice comes true in a manner that amounts to self-fulfilling prophecy: the analysis provides them with an elaborated explanatory model of their own activity. This double-coded change of perspective has another consequence. A distinction is no longer made between 'actor' (or the object of the discourse: delinquent, consumer, recipient, et cetera) and judge (or subject of the discourse:

anthropologist, intellectual, savant, et cetera); on the contrary, the new
perspective not only legitimates one's own knowledge, but privileges it.
In the academy, therefore, cultural studies do not only constitute
something like absolute beginnings because they put pop(ular) culture
on the academic agenda, but also and above all because they do so
while drawing in the researcher him- or herself. The formula 'culture
as a whole way of life' also refers to the way of life of the researcher,
which is not restricted to academic life. For the first time in the history
of the social sciences the researcher's own inclusion in what is being
researched – as a fan, for example – no longer needs to be concealed
in the academy: 'I tried to understand all these existential cultural
practices, in whose repertoire of signs (music, fashion) I myself lived,'
reports Hebdige (1996: 162).

At first sight it is surprising that the Birmingham school, contrary to
the prevailing image, produced so few ethnographical studies in the
classic sense. Since, however, the latter are always descriptions of the
other, this can be explained by the involvement of the researcher – just
as the prevailing image can be explained by way of the ethnographic
touch the studies gain through preparation saturated in experience:
they simply *seem* ethnographic. The formula 'ethnography equals
anthropology' is a thin description. The fundamental difference
between cultural anthropology and cultural studies lies, I believe, in
the opportunity, in principle, which the latter offers of making the
researcher him- or herself the subject (see, on this debate, Nugent and
Shore 1997). Whereas in cultural anthropology what is at issue, epistemologically, is understanding the other (which is demonstrated, not
least, by the fact that in research 'at home' the familiar always has to
be made alien), cultural studies, as is evident above all from its
offshoots, is characterized by the insider perspective. *Auctoritas* in the
field of cultural studies is established, or so it appears, by the cultural
homology of form of life and form of knowledge. This development
adds a new dimension to Merton's (1972) question, in the sociology of
knowledge, as to the relative importance of Outsider vs. Insider knowledge. In cultural studies, which produces a hybrid synthesis of Insider
and Outsider perspectives, there is no longer a strict opposition. As
Hebdige puts it, 'I conceived my imaginary readership as being like
myself, ambivalent towards the university. Interested in the academy,
but with one foot always outside in another world' (Hebdige 1996:
162). Cultural studies is a discipline that gives this simultaneity of
inside out and *outside in*, 'the rare and enriched dual vision of a
thoroughly inside outsider', as MacInnes himself put it in *England, Half
English* – an institutional form. It is probably not by chance that in
Germany, where there is as yet no cultural studies degree course, non-

institutionalized research into pop culture (for example, around the music magazine *SPEX*) has assumed the task of creating something independent to counter the academic production of knowledge (though it is oriented to the US models of cultural studies and subaltern studies).[4]

3

'For better or worse', George Melly wrote in 1966, 'pop culture has changed everything, and nothing can be the same again. It has acted as a catalyst' (Melly 1989 [1970]). If one bears in mind the humanities and social science publishers' lists of recent years with their immense number of popular culture studies – from subculture to cyber culture – it becomes clear that the culture industry principle has also caught up with cultural analysis: every fad and fashion is immediately packaged, given an interpretation and therefore importance. It's a long way from the 'absolute beginnings', when it was a question of confronting academic ignorance and arrogance with respect to popular culture (and in no other field was it so evident that arrogance and ignorance go hand in hand). And yet it was a relatively short way, when one considers the period of time within which the changes have taken place. That is itself a consequence of the pop principle described by Melly, which consists of catalysis, of acceleration, and has not spared the analysis of pop cultural phenomena. It appears to me that for some time now, the real danger has no longer been the 'academicisation of pop discourse', the 'dead hand of the academic embalmer', as Melly could still put it, but the pop culturalization of academic discourse. Here too the in-and-out logic of pop culture has taken hold, here too it's a matter of trends, fads and fashion (names, themes, neologisms), which turn students into trendwatchers and dedicated followers of fashion.[5] It is inherent in the logic of a cultural analysis, that casts doubt on the omnipotence of ideologies and manipulators by emphasizing the cultural skills of consumers, that the traditional distinction between encoder and decoder has become largely obsolete. But this innovative approach also has a drawback, because it leads to a crisis of qualitative judgement (see McGuigan 1992: 79), Today cultural analysis, with its emphasis on symbolic creativity on the part of consumers/recipients has become part of the product, of product innovation and/or product marketing. Cultural studies has become CultStuds, a subject that not only investigates cults but has become a cult itself. To use Barthes, Baudrillard, Derrida for advertising or promotion has become a sign of semantic sophistication. What is in demand today is the encoding expert, who understands the art of deconstruction (as ironic game and to make space for the new) and is simultaneously enough of a discourse analyst to be able to code a message for a specific target group: 'These commentators, whether in print or in the lecture room, are fans, but with special consuming skills; they can read the codes, place the labels, identify the quotes' (Frith and Savage 1993: 113). In the course of the semioticization of society, to which the analysis of style as hermeneutics of decoding has *also* contributed, the art of making allusions and of understanding allusions has become one of the most important social skills.[6]

While this chapter was being completed, an advertisement co-sponsored by *Werben & Verkaufen* (W&V), the German trade paper for marketing communications, appeared in *Jetzt*, the youth magazine of the *Süddeutsche Zeitung* (a German daily newspaper). Under the headline 'Absolute Beginners' it promoted a 'trainees' fair in advertising, marketing, communications and journalism'. If one clicks the appropriate page on the internet, then one discovers that 'Absolute Beginners is a joint project created by W&V, Media Design Academy (a private educational institution for marketing communications and new media) and *Jetzt*. Absolute Beginners is the first internet trainees' fair directed specifically at students of marketing, advertising and communications' (http://www.wuv.de). Do you want to bet that knowledge of the allusion pays off?

Translated by Martin Chalmers

Notes

1. Remember, for example, 'The average week of the ideal London mod' originally published in the *Sunday Times* (April 1964), reprinted in Hebdige (1975).

2. Eduard C. Lindeman (1924), *Social Discovery*, New York. In his investigation of taxi-dance halls in Chicago, Paul G. Cressey relied on the principle of 'participant observers as informants'.

3. Eva von Schirach is completing a MA thesis on the imaginary relationship between Stuart Hall, Colin MacInnes and MacInnes's hero.

4. See the articles presented under the heading 'Gegen die Uni studieren' (Studying against the university), in *SPEX*, no. 5, 1996, pp. 44–55.

5. In August 1995, the periodical *Theory, Culture and Society* organized a major four-day conference in Berlin on 'Culture and Identity: City, Nation, World' with more than 300 speakers. 'It was a fashion show of the contemporary mind', wrote Jens Jenssen, who reviewed the conference for the *Frankfurter Allgemeine Zeitung*. He thereby inadvertently formulated the principle of the pop culturali-

zation of academic discourse: 'The researchers, every one of them a well-proportioned mannequin, displayed in exemplary manner what the great couturiers, Lacan and Foucault and Derrida and even the long démodé Nietzsche, had charged them with wearing. The well-fitting "other" was followed, in accordance with the dramatic principles of the catwalk, by the shorter and more flirtatiously tailored "desire" and after that, as climax, the "body", the evening dress, so to speak, of the cultural sciences.' After a digression on accessories, which included both the 'virtual' and the 'multi-cultural' as well as the rather colourless 'ecological', the reviewer concluded: 'Thus we learn that scholarship too is a design, which can be applied to every object .' (*Frankfurter Allegmeine Zeitung* 16 August 1995).

6. The author of this chapter has obviously also tried his hand at this art as have Lawrence Grossberg (*Bring It All Back Home*), Dick Hebdige ('Learning to Live on the Road to Nowhere') and other exponents of cultural studies before him.

References

Abrams, Mark (1959) *The Teenage Consumer*, London.

Chambers, Iain (1986) *Popular Culture: The Metropolitan Experience*, London/New York.

Cohen, Stanley (1980) 'Symbols of Trouble', introduction to the new edition of *Folk Devils and Moral Panics*, London.

Frith, Simon and John Savage (1993) 'Pearls and Swine: The Intellectuals and the Mass Media', *New Left Review*, 198, pp. 107–116.

Hall, Stuart (1959) 'Absolute Beginnings: Reflections on the Secondary Modern Generation', in *Universities and Left Review*, No. 7, pp. 17–25.

Hebdige, Dick (1975) 'The Meaning of Mod', *Working Papers in Cultural Studies*, No. 7/8, pp. 87–96.

Hebdige, Dick (1996) ' "Heute geht es um eine antiessentialistische Kulturproduktion vom DJ-Mischpult aus". Über Cultural Studies, die Autorität des Intellektuellen, Mode und über die Module des Theorie-Samplings. Gespräch von Christian Höller', *Kunstforum*, No. 135, pp. 160–4.

McGuigan, Jim (1992) *Cultural Populism*, London.

MacInnes, Colin (1965[1959]) *Absolute Beginners*, London.

MacInnes, Colin (1986[1961]) *England, Half English*, London.

Melly, George (1989[1970]) *Revolt into Style*, Oxford.

Merton, Robert K. (1972) 'Insiders and Outsiders: A Chapter in the Sociology of Knowledge', *American Journal of Sociology*, Vol. 78, pp. 9–47.

Morley, David and Kuan-Hsing Chen (eds.) (1996) *Stuart Hall: Critical Dialogues in Cultural Studies*, New York and London.

Nugent, Stephen and Chris Shore (eds.) (1997) *Anthropology and Cultural Studies*, London and Chicago.

Willis, Paul (1975) 'The Main Reality: Final Report on the SSRC project entitled "The Transition from School to Work" ', stencilled occasional paper, Birmingham, October.

18

Stuart Hall:
The Universities and the 'Hurly Burly'

Angela McRobbie

> In thrusting onto the attention of scholarly reflection the hurly
> burly of a rapidly changing discordant and disorderly world –
> where everyday social change exists out there – cultural studies
> tries in its small way to insist on what I want to call the vocation
> of intellectual life.
>
> S. Hall (1992) quoted by Grossberg 1994

'A More Popular Pedagogy'

Two things about Stuart Hall's career as a teacher as well as an
intellectual are particularly significant. First, his practice as a teacher
has at every point departed from the university tradition embodied in
the Oxbridge model. Second, in the British post-1945 context where
the agenda for public intellectual debate remains firmly set by the
standards and the concerns of Oxbridge, and symbolized in the role of
the BBC, Hall's field of influence is less in the establishment channels
of the quality press and the portals of government, and more in the
lecture theatres and seminar rooms of the redbrick and new universities, and, of course, in the late-night broadcasts of the Open University.
Stuart Hall has operated throughout his career very much as a teacher,
and indeed as a certain kind of teacher. As he himself has said in
interview, 'Open University courses are open to those who don't have
any academic background. If you are going to make cultural studies
ideas live with them, you have to translate the ideas, be willing to write
at that more popular and accessible level. I wanted cultural studies to
be open to that sort of challenge. I didn't see why it wouldn't "live", as
a more popular pedagogy' (Hall 1996, p. 501).

Stuart Hall has positioned himself over the years as somebody who neither wants to court the attention of the Labour Party establishment (ending up, as that pathway does, with a seat in the House of Lords), nor seeks out the celebrity status of the internationally acclaimed academic (although of course he is that). He has resisted the self-promotional ethos that the new managerialism in higher education has encouraged. It is impossible to imagine him aggressively promoting a new book. When giving a lecture based on his recent work he never says, 'If you read Chapter 4 of my new book . . .' Or indeed, 'If you buy my book you will find that . . .' He is not the sort of celebrity academic to do signings, to have an eager 'PR' to get him on all the right programmes, to have someone else do a press release on his latest work to be faxed round all the relevant radio and TV slots. Instead, when he appears on television or takes part in radio debates it is the issue that is at stake, not the personality or the celebrity which is on display. This is not to say that he is not effective in these situations: quite the opposite. The conviction with which he speaks and the power of his argument clearly surprise and impress the more cynical and media-weary of presenters used to the politics of the plug and the cult of the celebrity. For this reason on *Newsnight* (BBC2) and on *Start The Week* (Radio 4) Stuart Hall appears to take everybody by surprise. In addition to having a ferocious intelligence he is also funny, charming, courteous, politically uncompromising, and not concerned to ingratiate himself into the inner circles of the media elite. He is not hoping to be asked back, nor is he waiting for a phone call offering him his own slot. This puts his identity as an intellectual at odds with what is now the norm of academic life. As Debray writes:

> Hence the new conception of labour among advanced intellectuals: the practice came before the concept. The productive labour of the intellectual is no longer 'intellectual labour' – a naïve concept of olden days – but the extended reproduction of his social relations (priority being given to relations with the popular press). What strikes the observer most about the thinkers of the culture show is how little time they have left to think once you have subtracted the working breakfasts, radio breakfast shows, lunches, dinners, interviews, statements, travel, phone calls, press conferences, TV debates, and the rest. (Debray 1981, p. 219)

In describing the intellectual manner of Stuart Hall I have described a certain way of being, an identity forged out of, I would argue, a political conviction that puts ideas first, and personalities and personal advancement second, and also a historical formation based round being black and in Britain and having been at Oxford, and then after Oxford having opted for an academic career that did not follow the traditional pathway. Being a teacher, for example, in a secondary school, then taking part-time work lecturing in media studies (at the time virtually nonexistent as a subject) at Chelsea College, and then joining Richard Hoggart in Birmingham. Although Raymond Williams also spent a good deal of his working life teaching mature students through the Workers' Educational Association, and like Richard Hoggart was a scholarship boy uneasy in the common-room atmosphere of Oxford and Cambridge, it is not the case that Stuart Hall's career merely continues this kind of pathway. The convergence of the historical moment in Birmingham in the 1970s and the particular pedagogic values that Stuart Hall brought to bear on the enterprise of the Centre for Contemporary Cultural Studies set him even further apart from the UK academic and political establishment.

The 1970s in Birmingham and in the West Midlands provided a stimulating environment in which to confront issues around race, the local press and media, and rising youth unemployment. For the critics, however, the combination of detailed empirical analysis of local press coverage of race with a broader Gramscian account of the breaking up of the postwar consensus in *Policing the Crisis* proved too innovative and too outside the scholarly tradition (Hall *et al.* 1978). Even magazines usually sympathetic to covering social and cultural issues with some seriousness, such as *New Society* (now merged with the *New Statesman*), ridiculed the style of writing and the use of theory. Otherwise the book was more or less ignored, even though twenty years later it is still in print, on sociology reading lists up and down the country and, even more significantly, now acknowledged as having laid the theoretical groundwork for understanding the conditions that swept the Conservatives to power in 1979.

There was a not-insignificant degree of 'little Englandism' in the dismissive responses by the critics to this work. The charge of relying on continental theory is one that has since been repeatedly made against Stuart Hall's work. For British journalists and broadcasters, social observation and the Orwellian tradition of social reportage remain the favoured way of doing sociological work. Drawing on the work of Althusser and Gramsci and combining it with a forceful political history of the present was too adventurous, too ambitious, for Hall's contemporaries both inside the British universities and outside in the press and TV. Their antagonism was exacerbated when in 1979 the community access programme *Open Door* (BBC2) offered Stuart Hall and Maggie Stead the opportunity to confront television with its own racial stereotypes. 'It Aint Half Racist Mum' (named after the unfunny and offensive situation comedy of British squaddies facing the heat of the Asian subcontinent titled *It Aint Half Hot Mum*) provided a detailed and scathing critique of the way in which television comedies relied on racist stereotypes, while documentaries on race and migration fully subscribed to a pathologizing concern with 'numbers' and a desire to placate the assumed fears of the white population. All hell broke loose as key establishment figures including Sir Robin Day perceived themselves (rightly) to be under attack. It is not hard to imagine that memories of the impertinence of confronting the liberal intelligentsia in this way linger in Broadcasting House, even though some twenty years later no producer of comedies or editor of a news programme would consider using such material as Hall and Stead criticized.

The experimental character of Hall's pedagogy and his practice as an academic were also evident in books like *Resistance Through Rituals* and *Policing the Crisis* (Hall and Jefferson 1976; Hall *et al.* 1978). For a start the traditional hierarchies of the academy were overwhelmingly abandoned in the planning and the writing of these books. Contributors ranged from the director of the Centre for Contemporary Studies, Stuart himself, to students who like myself had arrived in Birmingham simply to do a master's degree. But likewise the question of what kind of degree was being pursued was subordinate to the real issue, which was that of doing research that could be combined with political work. Not surprisingly, the complications of multiple authorship and the inexperience of the student contributors frequently meant that the entire enterprise of writing a book ran aground. Or else the books and publications displayed some of this rough-and-ready spirit. It is also the case that although there was fierce argument at the centre, there was also a remarkable spirit of collectivity. For every book or chapter made up of sections written by different people in different styles all of which would then simply be put together, there were also just as many times when whole chapters would be written by one person and then completely redrafted by another.

Nor were the claims of authorship of any real concern at that time. Part of the style of that political moment meant that we were more likely to favour anonymity, as part of a 'red cell', than to seek self-advancement. A good deal of the work was written more in the spirit of pamphleteering than with a view to getting an academic job. However, this was neither bravado nor lofty disregard for earning a living. Quite the opposite; there was also, I think, a pervasive sense that we might never get proper jobs. We were a bit isolated up there in the Muirhead Tower. There were no women's studies jobs to apply for, and as women we were certainly aware that the kind of academic work we were engaged in was bound to appear illegitimate. So perhaps our lack of ambition was also a protective mechanism which masked a pervasive unconfidence on the basis that on a wide number of fronts we remained far removed from the traditional pathways of academia.

Despite this I think the 'hands off' conditions, where we all got on with the work, in whatever collective or group-based form seemed most appropriate, but over which no senior person exerted his or her ultimate authority, were the only conditions in which it was possible for women to find their feet in this new field of study.

Stuart Hall has encouraged a form of Marxist scholarship that conveys the extent to which the forces of power act to maintain and continuously reproduce social, cultural and economic hierarchies. Just as important, however, to his work are the complex dynamics of change and the opportunities for transformation. What has also been a hall-mark of Hall's thinking is the way in which by continually connecting with the 'hurly burly' he sets himself apart from that tradition of Marxists who resolutely commit themselves to revealing the power of capital, but do so leaving readers only with a sense of the inexorable and the seemingly inevitable. The scale of the enterprise of adapting a lifetime of Marxist thought to engage fully and directly with the present condition, and to extract a viable politics from it, is more often than not too great for Hall's contemporaries. Many Marxist scholars now find themselves either participating in a cynical exercise in 'postmod-ern bashing' or else curiously partaking in a longing for the bad old days when at least the model of class analysis held true.

There is an even greater silence about political practice, indeed about what it means to be a socialist, among Hall's critics from the 'political economy of the media' corner. Instead of openly admitting the difficulties of forging a new Left for the new century where that traditional terrain is increasingly fractured by issues around globaliza-tion and new nationalisms, as well as by the priorities of the social movements, and where the Right has won so much ground, they scornfully direct their anger towards cultural studies. Instead of asking why their students seem to be attracted by politics other than those of class, by queer politics, by eco-activism, these same academics dismiss cultural theory as 'merely fashionable' and misunderstand their stu-dents' activism as 'merely subcultural'. Instead of showing a willingness to debate the consequences for Marxist analysis where the politics of race and sexuality now occupy such a central place, these critics can only reply by advocating a return to 'real issues' such as poverty (as though these are not real for women and black people). In complete contrast to this mode is a brief but telling comment about the changing place of black people in urban Britain by Stuart Hall which encapsu-lates the double recognition of hardship and the refusal of subjugation. He says in this context that black people 'can possess their blackness in a society still ugly with the inscriptions of racism. This is a culture which signals a new axis along which the structures of racial difference

move, and which anticipates the possibilities for a genuinely multicultural Britain' (Hall 1998, p. 44).

The British Universities in the 1990s

How can we reproduce future generations of intellectuals who share
the commitment and enthusiasm that Stuart Hall has so manifestly
demonstrated throughout his years of being a teacher, writer and
intellectual? This seems to me an urgent question. I am fearful of two
things: first, that because feminism and women appear to have entered
the academy, in the curriculum and as undergraduates, there is a sense
that somehow, now, gender issues have been dealt with; and second,
that, in the competitive environment of the Research Assessment
Exercise (RAE) culture (the UK system of quality control involving the
measurement of research output), we overlook the apparently stagnant
if not declining number of young black and Asian people embarking
on academic careers. Three specific aspects of academic life are in
danger of being overshadowed by the climate of accountability, and
the new managerial language of league tables and performance vari-
ables. The first is the politics of higher education in the here and now
(which can be summed up in the phrase 'Yes, but does it count for the
RAE?'). Second are the intergenerational debates around feminism in
the academy and the impact they have on young women scholars. The
third aspect is the means by which a new generation of black and Asian
intellectuals can be recruited into the university system so as to contribute to and enlarge the fields of research so richly described by what
remains a small but committed band of scholars.

If I was to say the words *WPCS*; Open University course units; *Marxism
Today; Soundings*; and if I was to add to that list, giving talks to Sign of
the Times groups, chairing panels at *New Times* day conferences, or
doing interviews for Japanese journals, it would be perfectly appropriate to associate such activities with the work of Stuart Hall.[1] It would
also be possible to comment that none of the above counts for the
RAE. Of course, it could then be said that senior academics are
expected to juggle a diverse range of activities and that this kind of
work is exactly what constitutes the diary of the public intellectual.
These activities are carried out in conjunction with the publications
that do count. But it would be very unwise nowadays to encourage any
younger scholar to put his or her time into such activities. They would
have nothing to put down when the next RAE takes place. What I want
to suggest is that the new regime of accountability in higher education,
in the name of modernization and detraditionalization, can actually

have the opposite effect. It can in fact reinstate traditional hierarchies and reproduce in the academy the 'gentlemanly mode'. It can also reduce the public sphere of intellectual debate and de-democratize the academy. It can create a new divide between those who are concerned to widen the net of access and to talk as Ron Dearing did about setting up new universities in Drumchapel, or to talk about lifelong learning and bridges from further education to higher education, as Helena Kennedy did, and those for whom only research matters (Dearing 1996; Kennedy 1997).

In some respects the RAE culture is to be welcomed. It has rid the academy to some extent of the leisurely style which I am sure we can all remember stumbling across in senior common rooms, where a job for life meant a life in the pub. In a world where young women and people from a range of different ethnic backgrounds are and were completely unrepresented on the faculties, I personally am not going to shed a lot of tears when these privileges are withdrawn. Unfortunately the current changes stop short at truly modernizing and extending the university system. And consequently they end up producing new barriers to access. Indeed if we connect RAE culture with the introduction of tuition fees, and then with broader social changes in the world of work, welfare and family life, it could be argued that the long apprenticeship into a full-time academic job will become completely unfeasible for those without access to a private source of income. Or else there may be an almost unconscious return to the traditional means by which young male and white scholars invest in this pathway and at the same time maintain a family life through the support of a working wife. Indeed, it is slowly becoming apparent that the cost of women entering relatively well-paid and secure work might well be that they must forgo having a family. This is the point at which gender inequality hits home. There may well be equal opportunities in place and even nurseries on site. Universities may well be good employers, as many are. And in sociology, women's studies, and also in cultural studies, issues of gender and employment have been long established in the curriculum. And yet as an older generation begins to slow down, having fought so many battles, we fail to turn our attention to the changing conditions both inside and outside the universities which have repercussions for the academic career and the future for intellectual work.

Let me illustrate. A young women stays the course of doing a PhD but to make ends meet and because it is good for her CV combines this with part-time teaching. With the PhD turned into a book and a few other articles in respectable journals she is thirty-two before she eventually gets a proper job. The job carries three years' probation.

While the trade union would support her should she decide to have a baby during this period, it is hard to see how she could fulfil all the expectations of the job. And heaven help her should she decide to have two children, close to each other. What would it look like in RAE terms? But why should women like this be virtually forced to put off motherhood until well into their late thirties, when no such requirements are expected of their male counterparts? There is also the anomaly that while young women in the broader culture are now seen as full of determination to gain a good job and economic independence, at thirty-two years old in the academy they are still considered 'junior' members of staff (too junior to be put in charge of invigilation, for example). Meanwhile a whole stratum of 22- to 26-year-old young women occupy key positions as political advisers to New Labour, or are deputy editors of national newspapers. In the last three months, at least two young black British women (one of whom was a single parent) have said to me (as head of the PhD programme in my department) that they would love to do a PhD, but they 'have to earn a living'.

This suggests that conditions have not necessarily improved a great deal for women or for black people in higher education. Of course we all now live in a risk society, where individuation and flexibility are the name of the game. But the danger is that embarking on an academic career, for those who cannot afford it, will soon become a risk not worth taking. For young women and black people for whom earning a decent living is now a priority, the prospect of spending several years on low-paid, part-time or temporary contracts in the hope that eventually they will get a more secure post is increasingly unattractive. There are other consequences of RAE culture which need to be challenged more directly by those within the academy. If universities are to remain, albeit in conditions of adversity, what Edward Said has called 'utopian spaces', if they are to be able to function as places of dissent, then I would recommend some risky strategies. There is a good deal of RAE culture which is simply conservative, and the more this can be demonstrated the better. For example, last year I was in the audience at an academic media and communications conference where a whole array of editors were on the stage and asked to give an update on publishing in their RAE-rated journals. Not one flinched when they described their readerships as a paltry 300 or 400 internationally (and some were read by even smaller numbers).

Call me a populist, but for me the idea of speaking to a larger section of the population, including part-time and mature students, and even some who are not students at all, indeed those who may belong to the socially excluded, remains one means by which the traditional barriers between the elite universities and the outside world are broken down.

Setting the goal of being read by a few dozen fellow academics worldwide, indeed by an increasingly dwindling bunch, marks to me the end of an important conversation; it marks a return to tradition, a retreat into the safety of the senior common room, by sections of the academic Left, rather than the beginning of a new period of access and communication. My preference, then, would be to encourage a greater diversity of types of publication, where perhaps the rules of anonymous peer reviewing and all the paraphernalia involved in getting RAE-rated work into print might be suspended in favour of attention to the quality of the written work and the spirit of experiment and innovation. The system the RAE has put in place operates as a means of disciplining young scholars to conform to the rules of their seniors. In a nutshell, they have to go through the route of the established journals rather than start their own. This is also a constraint on critique and on healthy intellectual insubordination.

Mags, Ads and Soaps: 'Pedagogies of the Feminine'

Whom do we represent when we establish courses on gender and sexuality? On whose behalf are we speaking? What if the young women write good essays to get through the exams, but make no attempt to disguise their distance from (if not distaste for) feminism *per se*, as something attached in their minds with their teachers and perhaps also with their mothers. To paraphrase Charlotte Brunsdon, what happens when feminism becomes part of the academic canon (Brunsdon 1997)? Brunsdon has described the whole array of responses among students in her 'women's genres' classes where a feminist approach is what has constituted the field of study in the first place. Courses on mags, ads and soaps are popular. Feminist scholars including myself have also attempted to understand and explain the role of these cultural forms within the everyday lives of women across the boundaries of age, sexual identity, ethnicity and social class. We have even gone so far as to argue that these blatantly commercial forms can incorporate and address feminist issues. This claim has produced loud choruses of disapproval from what Butler might describe as the neo-conservative Left (Butler 1998). It has also in many ways accounted for the backlash against cultural studies, on the mistaken grounds that because some cultural forms can sometimes be said to tackle questions of sexual inequality and injustice, feminists like myself no longer see any need to challenge the capitalist social order.

In contrast I would suggest that failure to recognize small spaces for opposition in cultural forms, as well as those areas of everyday life to which people are attached, is a recipe for political and intellectual disaster. It leads to aloof isolationism and a carelessness about what the future holds for those students we teach who, as I have already argued, are not going necessarily to enter the academy, and who need to be able, as young women or as black people, to enter the labour market and do jobs where what they have learnt can be of value, where it is not just a matter of selling out. The problem is that the Left generation and some feminists in the academy have felt that good students should be like themselves, interested in the same things as themselves. When this doesn't happen, they merely wash their hands of their students by saying they are all Thatcher's children. If we imply that all magazines are a waste of time, mere vehicles for the perpetuating of capitalist ideology, and that getting a job in an advertising agency is sleeping with the enemy, then we can hardly expect the dialogue set up in the seminar room to continue in working life. It is a terrible missed opportunity if we cannot hope that what we present to students in the classroom for these three brief years is of value to themselves and to what they will do in the future. Recognizing and engaging in our academic work with the sheer complexity of growing up female in a culture where 'popular feminism' takes on the most unpredictable and sometimes downright unpleasant guises (I am thinking of TV programmes like *Friday Night Fever*, or *God's Gift*) and where suddenly young males are seen as the social losers, is simply one of our responsibilities as feminist academics.[2]

This strategy will also inevitably involve run-ins with RAE culture, and it will also on occasion mean breaking some of the rules of the academic game. For fear of weakening the currency of feminist scholarship I have recently become extraordinarily wary of ever using the first person in any academic publication I write. Despite the recognized place for subjects such as memory, autobiography and testimony in the academy, I have had my fingers burnt. Consequently, in a recent piece for *Feminist Review* on the fashion industry and on homeworking practices in the midst of consumer culture, and on how feminists should not overlook questions of poverty and low pay, almost no pay, I intended to omit a comment about how these practices were going on literally next door to where I lived (reprinted in McRobbie 1999). On both sides of my home in Holloway we could hear the whirring of sewing machines through the night and we could see the black plastic bags being delivered and then collected. One of the homeworkers was a Greek Cypriot woman and the other a Mauritian grandmother (who had a day job as a childminder). In the end I left the anecdote in as illustration. A young Asian student doing media studies immediately picked up on it. She said to me that her mother had worked all her life with 'bags' being delivered every day. Her mother sewed loops onto trousers so that the belt could go through. Her eyesight was failing and often she sewed them on in the wrong place and had to undo the work and start again. Every night the children would help her, watching TV soaps and sewing at the same time. This sewing and watching TV had given this girl the taste for media studies, and she wanted to produce an Asian soap. But the anecdote in the article (and the double anecdote as I now write it) enabled her to make the connection between her mother's hardship and the wider existence of sweated ethnic labour markets as part of the structure of social inequalities.

The final, and in my mind most pressing, issue is that of encouraging more young black and Asian students to train as academics. In Britain, even in universities where there are substantial numbers of nonwhite students, among staff this percentage remains tiny. What is it that puts off so many from becoming a university teacher? The answer to this must surely lie to some extent in the elite image and seemingly arbitrary and unpredictable structure of the traditional academic career. If you train for five years in medicine, or in law and then the Bar, the chances are that as long as you pass the examinations you will get a job. But even if you have a good first degree, a master's degree and a PhD, it may be that jobs in your field are suddenly frozen, because of changes in funding, or that none exist within commutable distance of family life. There is also inevitably a sense of professional uncertainty: 'Will I be able to keep on churning out publishable articles good enough for me to succeed in this field?' So there is also a question of confidence and the way in which traditionally (and to the 'outsider') academic life remains cloaked in mystery.

It is almost impossible to convey how much this was true for myself, a middle-class young woman going from school in Glasgow to the university less than a mile away. At that time, in the early 1970s, Glasgow University arts and social science faculties were staffed almost entirely by Oxbridge-educated English-accented males (and a sprinkling of women). In contrast the students were lower-middle-class and working-class Glaswegian and in addition had all been at school together. The Oxford types were a completely unknown quantity to us. 'We' felt keenly that 'they' looked down on us as untutored 'natives'. We did not speak properly, and we certainly were not familiar with the Oxbridge style of argument. We also picked up something of their discontent as though a posting in Glasgow or 'north of the border' was some unfortunate and disappointing outcome. Despite a high level of school education (in the sixth form I had read all the classics of literature in French, from Flaubert to Gide) we lacked the cultural capital to know how to make the most of this knowledge. In short there was the sense that none of us could possibly possess the right kind of attributes for 'postgraduate training'. We did not come from families where this was a recognized career pathway and so not one of my school friends, male or female, was ever encouraged in this way. At school we did not know that such an occupation existed; at university we were no wiser. It was luck that I struck up a friendship with another student, Ian Connell (who tragically died in summer 1998), who had found out about 'Birmingham'. I relate this not to suggest some sort of Scottish post-coloniality, but rather to remind readers of the subtle way in which opportunities are withheld and possibilites for participating in the public sphere of intellectual discourse and the world of ideas are confined to those who already possess the social and cultural capital.

Where I part company with Stuart Hall in his characterization of the 'vocation' of intellectual life is that this implies a sacrifice. It is hardly any gain for women that they should eventually win a place within the academy if they feel they have to forgo having children to be successful in their career. Nor should it be the case that in trying to complete a PhD part-time (in the absence of a reasonable provision of student-ships), young people like my own graduate students find themselves doing up to five different jobs at one time (in one case, teaching in three different institutions, doing the PhD, working freelance as a journalist). The present government now needs to look into postgrad-uate training and education, with a view to extending access here as well as elsewhere in the system. If it fails, the anti-elitist and 'open' tradition of scholarship established by Stuart Hall may find it even more difficult to survive.

Notes

1. Most of the early work carried out in Birmingham was published in-house as stencilled papers or else in the work-in-progress journal titled *Working Papers in Cultural Studies*. Open University Course Units are teaching materials avail-able only to students. The magazine *Marxism Today* was published throughout the 1980s; the final edition appeared in 1991. *Soundings* is a recent journal of politics and culture with a magazine format.

2. Both these programmes are broadcast late-night. They combine youthful hedonism and excess (in particular the consumption of alcohol) with the idea of 'turning the tables on men'. *Friday Night Fever* comprises live coverage from around the UK as rowdy, drunken young women (and men) take to the streets after the pubs close. *God's Gift* features an audience of young women putting a parade of men in their underwear on display as sex objects. The men are subjected to lewd comments and sexual banter.

References

Brunsdon, C. (1997) 'Pedagogies of the Feminine', in *Screen Tastes: Soap Opera to Satellite Dishes*, London: Routledge.

Butler, J. (1998) 'Merely Cultural', *New Left Review*, 227, pp. 33–44.

Dearing, R. (1996) *The Dearing Report*, London: HMSO.

Debray, R. (1981) *Teachers, Writers, Celebrities: The Intellectuals of Modern France*, London: New Left Books.

Grossberg, L. (1994) 'Introduction', in H. Giroux and P. McLaren (eds.), *Between Borders: Pedagogy and the Politics of Cultural Studies*, New York: Routledge.

Hall, S. (1996) 'The Formation of a Diasporic Intellectual: An Interview with Stuart Hall by Kuan-Hsing Chen', in D. Morley and K.H. Chen (eds.), *Stuart Hall: Critical Dialogues in Cultural Studies*, London: Routledge.

Hall, S. (1998) 'Aspiration and Attitude – Reflections on Black Britain in the Nineties', *New Formations*, No. 33, Spring, pp. 38–47.

Hall, S. and Jefferson, T. (eds.) (1976) *Resistance Through Rituals: Youth Subcultures in Post-war Britain*, London: Hutchinson.

Hall, S. *et al.* (1978) *Policing the Crisis: 'Mugging', the State and Law and Order*, Basingstoke: Macmillan.

Kennedy, H., QC (1997) *The Kennedy Report*, London: HMSO.

McRobbie, A. (1999) *In The Culture Society: Art, Fashion and Popular Music*, London: Routledge.

Travelling Thoughts

Doreen Massey

Let me begin by proposing the following:

Space is a configuration (a 'simultaneity' but I'll come back to that) of a multiplicity of trajectories.

The coexisting multiplicities and the necessary but incomplete (potential) interrelatedness which that entails give rise to time and space together.

We must think space and time together, time and space (I know we're always saying that these days, but bear with me a little).

If that is really so, we can no more go back in space, return to whence we came, than we are able to go back in time.

What we *can* do is meet up again; catch up with where another's history has got to 'now'; interlace again (on terms that must be the stuff of politics) with another of those multiple trajectories.

For many years, from 1982 until he so inconsiderately retired, Stuart used to give me a lift to work. From northwest London, up the motorway more or less fifty miles; out of the capital's basin, through the chalk hills and down into the flat clay midlands; to Milton Keynes. And back again at night. A journey: 'across space'? And 'back again'? In political terms, and in terms of our theories being means of getting by, of going on (Thrift, 1996), it may be adequate thus to conceptualize this quotidian commute. But some of the thoughts I want to develop here began on those car journeys, and they have continued to develop since, on the train which I now so much more often take. So let me stick with that journey for a moment.

If we take the opening proposals seriously, when you make that journey, from London to Milton Keynes, you are *not* just travelling across space.

First, of course, since as now seems to be widely recognized space is the co-constitutive product with relations/interactions you are also helping – although in this case in an unpretentious, fairly minor way –

to produce it. You are part of the constant process of the making and breaking of links that is an element in the constitution (1) of you yourself, (2) of London, which will not have the pleasure of your company for the day, (3) of Milton Keynes, which will (and whose existence as, say, an independent node of commuting is reinforced as a result) and thus (4) of space itself. You are not just travelling across space; you are altering it a little, moving it on, producing it. The relations that constitute it are being reproduced in an always slightly altered form.

Second, this journey of yours is anyway not just spatial. It is also temporal. It is a movement in/of (a production of) both space and time. The London you left just half an hour ago (as you speed through Cheddington, its clay-damp fields spreading away on either side) is not the London of now. It has already moved on (without you). And you are on your way to meet a Milton Keynes that is also moving on, and that has been doing so, in large measure without the slightest regard for, and with no relation to, your impending arrival. It has its own story, in which you once again, and in a pretty minor way, are about to participate. Movement and the making of relations also take/make time.

(Of course, you may well be objecting by now, and correctly, that Milton Keynes has more than one 'story' going on within it (and even more so is this the case for London) and that some of these stories have indeed been preparing for your arrival. Security guards and secretaries have already arrived at the university, doors have been unlocked, telephone messages have been taken; the cleaners overnight have emptied your wastepaper basket (thus are we academics served). Agreed. Indeed, the way one might conceptualize towns, and cities even more, is precisely as peculiarly intense, and probably heterogeneous, constellations of social trajectories (see Massey, Allen and Pile 1999).)

Third, however, if space and time are both dimensions of this journey, then what is at issue is not my crossing space to get to Milton Keynes but my constructing a trajectory that meets up with the trajectory that is Milton Keynes and, within the intense multiplicity of trajectories that is that city, seeking out just some of them with which to interact. In this space of fresh configurations new stories will emerge, new trajectories will be set in motion.

Other people and things indeed have been collected there, some precisely for this purpose. People and papers have gathered for a meeting, faxes have arrived from around the world, an e-mail from Larry reminding me that I am late with this piece; and I in turn will despatch a whole cartography of communications while I am 'there'. Meetings-up in, and dispersals out from, this focus of space–time.

And then, come the evening, weary, we set off again, making our way home to the big city. Yet that going home is not at all going back to the same place. London is not the same place we left this morning. It, too, has moved on; things have been happening while we've been gone. Once again, as in the morning meeting with Milton Keynes, this is not a matter of crossing space to a static place that has been somehow lying there, waiting for our arrival. You have to catch up with what's been happening, with how this place, too, has been moving. Emerging into the crush of Euston station I scan the headlines in the evening paper to see what's new; leaving the station I search the sky and pavements, feel the air, wondering what the weather's been like (will my garden be crying out for water?); finally arrived in my apartment I check the post, the telephone messages, find out 'what's been happening here' while I've been away. Bit by bit I reimmerse myself in the trajectories of London.

There was a point in my describing, earlier, the journey from London to Milton Keynes in terms of the landscape we were crossing. For it seems to me that we frequently understand space in this way, in terms of travelling across it. The very surface, of land or sea, becomes equated with space itself. We do it without thinking (and maybe will deny it when faced with the explicit proposition), but it has serious effects.

For one thing it makes space seem so very much more *material* than time. We seem to find it easier to think temporality in the abstract, as a dimension of and formed out of relations, than we do space/spatiality. Perhaps it's precisely to do with the fact that we think we can 'see' space, stretching out and around before us. Space so often (from at least Plato on) has been equated with 'extension' and through that with the material. It's an assumption we should abandon.

But the second effect of this imagining space in terms of the landscape is that it makes it seem like a *surface*; something with continuity, and given. This is reinforced by another common elision: that between space and maps. This, too, is unfortunate. In fact, it may indeed well be that our usual notion of maps has pacified, has taken the life out of, how most of us most commonly think about space. Of course, maps anyway are a particular form of representation: they are not 'space itself'. But that is not the point that is important to me here. What worries me here is another and less recognized aspect of this illicit elision: that maps, too, give the impression that space is a surface.

So why does it matter if we imagine space like that? Well, I would argue that it evokes the understanding of other places, peoples, cultures . . . as located *on* this surface. Immobilized, they await our arrival. They lie there, in place, without trajectories; we can no longer see in our minds' eyes the stories they, too, are telling, living out, producing. It is to render them, as Eric Wolf (1982) at the end of a rather different argument has put it, 'without history'.

There are many who have tried to puncture that smooth surface. The art events of Clive van den Berg (1997) aim to disrupt the complacent landscape of white South Africa with reminders of the history on which it is based. Iain Sinclair's (1997) *dérives* through eastern London evoke, through the surface, pasts (and presents) not usually noticed. Anne McClintock's (1995) provocative notion of 'anachronistic space' – a permanently anterior time within the space of the modern – is catching at something similar. Between London and Milton Keynes indeed, right by Berkhamsted station, there's a Norman motte and bailey, getting on for a thousand years old, which I always try to glimpse as we pass and which always sets me thinking. We know, then, that the present-ness of the horizontality of space is in fact a product of a multitude of histories whose resonances are still there, if we would but see them, and which sometimes catch us with full force unawares.

Yet it is also more than this that I am trying to get at here. These are all tales of the continued presence of 'the past' in the spatial surface of today. Yet surely the point is rather that the whole of the simultaneity that is 'the spatial surface of today' – even the mundane things, the modern things, the easily normally recognized things – consists of such moments, together, in their histories. This is no spatial surface; it is a contemporaneity of trajectories.

Some years ago, a geographer named H.C. Darby wrote an article entitled 'The Problem of Geographical Description' (1962). In it, he argued that while histories were relatively straightforward to tell, the problem of describing the spatial was how to represent, on the page in words and in a single story, its *simultaneity*. Now, many criticisms could be, and have been, made of Darby's piece. But one element of the significance of the argument has often been missed. Darby was, it seems to me, both making a fundamental mistake and grasping at something really important. The mistake was to assume that the temporal is easy to represent, and that one does so in a single narrative. His insight was the mirror of this: his recognition that the 'problem' of the spatial is its character of multiplicity. Darby is by no means the only person to have worked with that combination of ideas. Fredric Jameson (1991) in a very similar formulation finds the complexity of spatial multiplicity so utterly disconcerting that he calls not only for a cognitive 'map' but for the restoration of some notion of narrative (see Massey 1992). *That*

will restore order to things. The assumption is, of course, that 'narrative' is in the singular, and it is an assumption that may be wielded
precisely to tame the unnerving multiplicities of the spatial. Taking
space seriously, or thinking space–time, makes that manoeuvre
impossible.

What the simultaneity of space really consists in, then, is absolutely
not a surface, a continuous material landscape, but a momentary
coexistence of trajectories, a configuration of a multiplicity of histories
all in the process of being made. This is not a 'problem', unless of
course you long for the order of the singular story and the legibility of
the smoothness of a surface; rather, it is part of the delight, and the
potential, of space.

(I cannot resist here a parenthesis, just to unsettle things a little more.
First, to put our human movements into context, remember that this car
trundling so mundanely up the M1 (while we argue with Melvyn Bragg
on the radio) through the sunshine or the slush and spray is moving, so
minutely it seems once the perspective is changed, on an earth that is
itself spinning in a wobbly fashion upon its axis, and that is held in an
annual rotation about the sun, that is . . . And the landscape that
stretches away on either side across middle England (the chalk rocks
laid down, 70 million to 100 million years ago) is of course still moving
now as the southeast of this island tips downwards towards the sea, in
compensation for the north's recovery (and it must be quite a relief)
from being pressed down by the unimaginable tons of ice that lay there
only 10,000 years ago. All movement, as they say, is relative. And second,
of course, remember that in the midst of all of this we each stand (or,
better, travel) in a different place. There is perhaps, then, not even a
single simultaneity on which we would all agree; we each have access to
our own. Situated simultaneities we might call them.)

To imagine space in this way, of course, means thinking time and
space together (see also Grossberg 1996) and thinking both of them as
the product of interrelations. We don't perhaps then need to insist as
forcefully as we customarily do on the difference between them. Time
may be irreversible ('You can't go backwards in time') but so may be
space. Or, rather, it is better not to separate them in this way. You can't
go back in time–space. What you *can* do, as was stated in the proposals
that opened this chapter, is meet up again, catch up with where
another's history has got to 'now', but where that 'now' (or, more
rigorously, that 'here and now') is itself constituted by nothing more
than – precisely – our meeting up again.

It may not matter so much, in the end, how I imagine that journey
between London and Milton Keynes. But the thoughts that it evoked

do have, I would argue, a more general relevance. And their import is political.

To begin with, and most obviously, they mean that we can never go 'home', or at any rate we cannot do so if we imagine home as an enduring site from whence we came. You can't go back. It is a point that is often made. Neither Stuart nor I 'come from' this tract of southeastern England but we both know that neither Jamaica nor Manchester is the same as when we left. It is obvious yet it is often forgotten. England's 'Angry Young Men' who came south in the fifties both ridiculed and held in aspic the northern places they had left. That kind of longing for a place called home, that view of place in nostalgia, precisely robs it of a history. (And if nostalgias are not necessarily bad, as Wendy Wheeler (1994) has persuasively pointed out, we none the less do maybe need to rework them so that they are less immobilizing of others.) For this is an approach that operates, as is often recognized, in the same way as those great dualisms between Culture and Nature, and it resonates too with views of place as Woman, as Mother – as what has been left behind and is (supposedly) unchanging. It is a view found in songs of home, in novels, in academic writing. It is beautifully captured and critiqued (in the migrant's desire to cling to the supposed traditions of home while the visitor from this supposedly traditional place is all jazzed-up in thoroughly 'modern' gear) in *Bhaji on the Beach*. It is deep in Raymond Williams's *Border Country*. It is comforting, but it is to be rejected. Places change; they go on without you. Just as Mother has a life of her own.

So you can't go back. There is nothing for it but to keep trucking on. And that's OK.

But the real reason behind this point is that others have their stories too. When Hernán Cortés heaved to the top of the pass between the snow-covered volcanoes and looked down upon the incredible island city of pyramids and causeways, the immense central valley between the mountain ranges stretching away into the heat, he wasn't just 'conquering space'. What was about to happen, as he and his army, and the locals they had recruited along the way, marched down upon Tenochtitlán, was the meeting up of stories, each already with its own spaces and geographies, two imperial histories: the Aztec and the Spanish. We read so often of the conquest of space, but what was/is at issue is also the meeting up with others who are also journeying, also making histories.

What is fascinating is how the most frequent imagination of this process performs a double operation. Not only is space, lazily, conceived of as a surface, but crossing it in this context (the voyages of discovery, the explorations of anthropologists) is indeed imagined as temporal too. But this is time travel that goes *backwards* in time. Instead of producing space–time in its voyages forth, the West imagined itself going out and finding not contemporary stories but the past. This latter imagination is now commonly acknowledged and criticized (for example, Fabian 1983). But maybe there is, also, no simple 'conquering of space' at all. The ravages of imperialism and the conquerings and co-optations of colonialism were not horizontal movements across a space that is a surface. They were engagements of previously separate trajectories. And it is the terms of that meeting that are the stuff of politics. The shift in naming, from *la conquista* to *el encuentro*, speaks also of a more active imagination of the engagement between space and time.

And while, maybe, we think we know all this already (and maybe we do, for the events of centuries past) we nevertheless keep making the same mistake. And so current tales of 'globalization' evoke images of capital's virtually frictionless movement, across a 'space' which has been frozen, smoothed over and de-historicized: a passive surface before the unstoppable dynamism of modern capitalism. Again we rob others of a history, their stabilization providing the solid ground for our own story.

But finally. Once we drop the assumption of the mutual exclusivity of space and time, once we recognize the multiplicity of histories that is the spatial, then what could be more both ordered and chaotic than space, with all its happenstance juxtapositions and unintended emergent effects? Here, for certain, there can be no guarantees.

References

Darby, H.C. (1962) 'The Problem of Geographical Description', *Transactions of the Institute of British Geographers*, Vol. 30, pp. 1–14.

Fabian, J. (1983) *Time and the Other: How Anthropology Makes Its Object*, New York: Columbia University Press.

Grossberg, L. (1996) 'The Space of Culture, the Power of Space', in Chambers, I. and Curti, L. (eds.) *The Postcolonial Question*, London: Routledge, pp. 169–88.

Jameson, F. (1991) *Postmodernism; or, the Logic of Late Capitalism*, London: Verso.

Massey, D. (1992) 'Politics and space–time', *New Left Review*, No. 196, pp. 65–84 (reprinted in Massey, D. 1994 *Space, Place and Gender*, Oxford: Polity Press, pp. 249–272).

Massey, D., Allen, J. and Pile, S. (eds.) (1999) *City Worlds*, Routledge and the Open University.

McClintock, A. (1995) *Imperial Leather: Race, Gender and Sexuality in the Colonial Contest*, London: Routledge.

Sinclair, I. (1997) *Lights out for the Territory*, London: Granta Books.

Thrift, N. (1996) *Spatial Formations*, London: Sage.

van den Berg, C. (1997) 'Battle Sites, Mine Dumps, and Other Spaces of Perversity', in Golding, S. (ed.) *The Eight Technologies of Otherness*, London: Routledge, pp. 297–305.

Wheeler, W. (1994) 'Nostalgia Isn't Nasty: The Postmodernising of Parliamentary Democracy', in Perryman, M. (ed.) *Altered States: Postmodernism, Politics, Culture*, London: Lawrence & Wishart, pp. 94–109.

Wolf, E. (1982) *Europe and the People without History*, London: University of California Press.

A Sociography of Diaspora

Kobena Mercer

Stuart Hall's approach to the subject of diaspora is indirect or even circuitous, rather than programmatic or goal-oriented. Whereas such essays as 'New Ethnicities' (1988) and 'Cultural Identity and Diaspora' (1990) addressed the topic explicitly, the issue was implicit in Hall's early work on the sociology of immigration, such as *The Young Englanders* (1967). Key contributions to postcolonial theory, such as 'The Question of Cultural Identity' (1992), are of recent provenance, although Hall's long-standing interest in conceptualizing diaspora dates back to such publications as *Africa is Alive and Well and Living in the Diaspora* (1975). In other words, Stuart Hall's writings on diaspora are themselves scattered and dispersed within his *oeuvre* as a whole.[1]

This chapter will not attempt to synthesize a general theory of diaspora from these disparate texts and interventions. This is because it seems that what is distinctive about Hall's perspective is how his conjunctural approach touches upon all aspects of the cultural studies repertoire, while at the same time moving across or against the borders of various disciplines in such a way that the connective dots between them remain valuably open. Stuart Hall does not write about diaspora as a discrete sociological object so much as he writes *from* the social worlds of diaspora to produce knowledge as a situated practice of interruption. The twists and turns involved in the journey of the diaspora concept have opened up one of the most compelling stories in recent intellectual life. Hall's influence on this broad trajectory has been crucial and subtle. It seems timely, then, to trace its passage within his own work, as well as to ask whether the diaspora concept is now due for some interruption of its own.

'The career of sociology has been coterminous with the career of nation-state formation and nationalism,' observes Jan Nederveen Pieterse, who has taken the view that, in the context of late-twentieth-century globalization, this trajectory 'is in for retooling'. 'A global sociology is taking shape,' he argues, 'around notions such as social

networks (rather than "societies"), border zones, boundary crossing
and global society. In other words, a sociology conceived within the
framework of nations–societies is making place for a post-international
sociology of hybrid formations, times and places.'[2]

No one could overestimate Hall's contribution to such paradigm
shifts. The displacement of sociology's immigration narrative and its
transformation into the expanded field of postcolonial theory have
given rise to far-reaching changes. Moreover, insofar as such theoretical
developments have intertwined with cultural practices in the arts and
throughout the public sphere at large, there has been a significant
alteration in the commonsense terms available to liberal democracies
as they try to apprehend the social, cultural and political dynamics of
multiculturalism. But just as the analysis of Thatcherism was one of the
big success stories of British cultural studies in the eighties, could it
also be said that one of the ironies of the nineties was that the keywords
of postcolonial thinking perhaps became globalized as merely commonplace rather than critically interrogative?

To the extent that the postcolonial vocabulary, characterized by such
terms as 'diaspora', 'ethnicity' and 'hybridity', has displaced an earlier
discourse of assimilation, adaptation and integration, we have witnessed
a massive social transformation which has generated, in the Western
metropolis, what could now be called a condition of *multicultural
normalization*. Norms are slippery things. Not as formal as rules or laws,
they require social consent and psychic investment in order to regulate
structural contradictions and social antagonisms. But what happens
when hitherto contested notions of cultural difference become socially
normative?

When *Newsweek* described Tony Blair's New Britain as 'one of the
most comfortably multicultural nations in Europe',[3] and accompanied
its assertions with pictures of smiling black, brown and white faces
amongst a flurry of Union Jacks, should we be led to believe that the
story of racism and reaction has been happily resolved by such a
process of normalization? Or should we recall Hall's trenchant remarks,
from 1970, that although 'black immigrants . . . are certainly going to
be citizens of this society for a long time to come . . . this does not
mean that they are necessarily going to be *happy* Black Britons'?[4]

From the vantage point of the cultural practices that some of the
third-generation discontents went on to produce – in the visual art of
Keith Piper, Zarina Bhimji and Sonia Boyce, the films of Isaac Julien,
Gurinda Chadda or John Akomfrah, or the photography of Rotimi
Fani-Kayode – one can see the story of the intervening thirty years in
microcosm. In the transition from multiculturalism to globalization,
artists who were once domesticated by paternalist notions of 'ethnic

arts' have seen the reception and interpretation of their work taken up and translated into a wide range of transnational milieux. The close articulation of aesthetics and politics in earlier debates about representation and cultural difference has been reconfigured. Although norms are not the same as trends, it could be said that the subversive potential once invested in notions of hybridity has been subject to pre-millennial downsizing. Indeed, hybridity has spun through the fashion cycle so rapidly that it has come out the other end looking wet and soggy.

To the extent that hybridity theory has come in for a drubbing in the context of multicultural normalization, we need to take account of the critiques of artworld institutions put forward by Jean Fisher and Nikos Paperstergiadis. They perceive a major area of complicity between the demand for minority representation and the adaptation to diversity that the global marketplace seems happy to make.[5] In contrast to criticisms of hybridity that take aim at postcolonial theories *tout court*,[6] the challenge implicit in rethinking hybridization as socially and culturally normative can be met by refusing the seductive attraction of simplistic polarities and turning to a historically specific account of the more messy and ambivalent intermezzo worlds between the local and the global, which in my view is something that Hall's work already provides, albeit within a fragmented form.

Revisiting such early texts as *The Young Englanders* and 'Black Britons' provokes an eerie feeling. They speak in a sociological idiom from a world whose internal relations of race, class and culture have been utterly transformed by struggles over the past thirty years, even though the uncanny familiarity of the issues implies that some things have not changed that much. When Hall pinpointed a political agon between 'formal acceptance and informal segregation' in UK race relations,[7] as the period of *laissez-faire* accommodation in the fifties gave way to the sharply polarized frontier effects of the late sixties, it is hard not to see the same old story replayed in today's disjuncture between the pastiche patriotism of New Brit Art and the critical pluralism of the new internationalism. But the consistency of Hall's analytical attention to black Britain as a local site of diaspora formation demands that, rather than frame this strand of work through a general theory of postcoloniality, the question is how the story of the intervening period is broadly (and even globally) understood – the story of how England became Other than what it always imagined itself to be, and, in a twist to sociology's immigration narrative, how the third generation 'became black because they could not go back'. Revisiting Hall's diaspora-based writings casts a range of contemporary dilemmas in a critical light.

In 1967 Hall observed that 'the lived experience of the immigrant teenager is a little like that of the traveller whose routes in and out of the home take him along extended bridges across deep and dangerous chasms'.[8] It would be anachronistic, not to say merely academic, to note how the terms of Hall's account – voiced in the idiom of symbolic interactionism – anticipate key themes in postcolonial studies. Having said this, however, when he described the teenage 'natives' of the indigenous white working class (whom he taught in London schools and some of whom were active in the Notting Hill riots), and observed how they 'held two quite separate and contradictory ideas'[9] about West Indians, it is difficult not to infer the view of the racist stereotype as a representational fetish, complete with its ideational splitting of the other. Similarly, when black youth are described as 'the busiest travel-ler[s]' who have 'to "translate" between the groups,',[10] Hall's account of the familial and intersubjective ruptures involved in becoming black *and* British emphasized the ambivalent push and pull of loyalties involved in negotiating multiple identifications. With regard to the national agony involved in 'becoming a multicultural society', the recto/verso implications of this relational outlook led him to say that:

> it will be as hard for adult West Indians, Indians or Pakistanis to accept the fact that their children and grand-children will be progressively 'at-home' in a different country, as it will be for white people to accept that the presence . . . of second and third generation black people will irreversibly alter *their* culture and social patterns.[11]

'Can we tackle change or will we allow it to tackle us?' he asked. While the conjunctural character of the question foreshadows his more recent queries about the time of the double inscription – when was the postcolonial?[12] – the important point is that it remains unanswered insofar as Hall's culturally materialist view holds that the historical outcomes of struggles over social or cultural norms can never be guaranteed in advance.

However misleading it would be to say that these texts magically anticipated the way postcolonial theory conceptualizes diaspora today, it is none the less compelling to examine the crosscutting passageways that connect Stuart Hall's writings on how Britishness has changed as a result of the migrancy of Caribbean, African and South Asian peoples into post-1945 society, and his subsequent studies of post-independent Caribbean nations, which abut on to the question of diaspora from the other end of the transnational chain. In this regard we find that not only is Hall's conceptual movement back and forth across disparate national sites and cultural locations a vivid example of the sociological imagination thinking diasporically, but that also there is a kind of stereographic writing (in Barthes's phrase) in which ideas and issues from one problematic reverberate with others put forward in seemingly incommensurable contexts.

The strongest example of this dialogic interplay is the call-and-response relationship between 'Pluralism, Race and Class in Caribbean Society' (1978) and 'Racism and Reaction' (1978).[13] Both are centrally concerned with the articulation of race and class, but in two very different sorts of social formation. One addresses a postcolonial society, Jamaica, which only 'became black' at a relatively recent moment of its cultural history, and the other addresses Britain as a post-imperial nation-state, which found its social predicament mirrored and magnified in moral panics over 'mugging'. While the latter essay is widely known as a summary and introduction to the breadth of ground covered in *Policing the Crisis: 'Mugging', the State and Law and Order* (1978), the former, which was contributed to *Race and Class in Post-Colonial Society* (1978), was one of the earliest attempts to address the distinct structural features of the postcolonial moment.

It may seem odd to revisit the race-and-class problematic, but my interest lies in passages that connect the culturally materialist notion of 'the ethnic signifier', which Hall develops in accounting for the volatile mix of cultural elements in Caribbean social structure, with one of the conclusions of the cultural studies account of British neo-conservatism, namely that 'race is the modality in which class is lived'.[14] The vicissitudes of the ethnic signifier, which illuminate the ways in which 'race is the modality in which class is lived' in a formerly colonized setting, also shed light on the structural convulsions whereby Britain 'became a multicultural society'. Could the concept further help to clarify how these processes have given rise to a cultural mix that differs from, while overlapping with, situations of ethnic pluralism found elsewhere in Western Europe or in the United States?

The synchronic rapport between Hall's 1978 essays turns around a critique of the impasse created by economic determinism and cultural reductionism with regard to conceptualizing social relations of 'race' and ethnicity. Although often overlooked, 'Pluralism, Race and Class' was of pivotal importance because it mapped out the space subsequently addressed in the Althusserian vocabulary of 'Race, Articulation and Societies Structured in Dominance' (1980) and in 'Gramsci's Relevance for the Study of Race and Ethnicity' (1986).[15] These essays expanded the critique of Marxist ethnocentrism and Weberian pluralism in relation to the interdependence of units in a world-system. The formidable scholarship Hall brought to bear on these intellectual traditions turned attention to the history of Caribbean culture and society to test the minimum threshold of theoretical generality required to activate the question of hegemony. As he stated:

Once we grasp the two ends, so to speak, of this chain – differentiated specificity/complex unity – we see that we are required to account, not simply for the existence of culturally distinct institutions and patterns, but also for that which secures the unity, cohesion and stability of this social order in and through (not despite) its 'differences'.[16]

It is precisely the 'differentiated specificity/complex unity' couplet that underpins *Policing the Crisis* as a sustained analysis of the long-term crisis of hegemony in post-1945 Britain, in which the break-up of social-democratic consensus led to the neo-conservative vision of governing a wholly different sort of society. The irony is not simply that one of the most radically distinctive contributions to modern British social theory was authored by someone who was neither British nor a sociologist as such,[17] but that the mix of conceptual tools in the cultural studies account of the crisis of Britishness was honed and refined through Hall's dialogue with the hybrid matrix of Caribbean societies as the 'other scene' in which the postcolonial predicament was brought to light.

Another way of looking at the antiphony is to consider Hall's neo-Gramscian approach to the problem of structure and agency in the semiotic model of culture. Hall's notion of the ethnic signifier crosses over potentially unbridgeable spaces not by positing a comparative relationship in which the differences between Jamaican and British societies could be resolved in an anthropological conception of human culture, but by wielding a diacritical conception of antagonism in which relations of power and resistance enter representation and consciousness unevenly. A bald summary this may be, but it lies at the heart of the explanatory force of Hall's materialist conception of culture. 'Racism and Reaction' offered an account both of the 'differentiated specificity/complex unity' that articulated the populist and neo-nationalist unities sought by and secured for neo-conservative hegemony *and* of the cultural construction of those counter-hegemonic unities, found in symbolic and imagined practices of community, whereby black Britain articulated its response. It would be hard to overestimate the decisive impact of these conceptual linkages in providing the conditions of possibility for *The Empire Strikes Back* (1982) and subsequent black interventions in cultural politics.[18]

The interrogative conception of diaspora has since flourished. Propelled by a far-reaching critique of 'ethnic absolutism' and elaborating a conception of 'travelling culture' as a mobile network of affinities, Paul Gilroy's pathbreaking work on the Black Atlantic reveals a tradition of counter-modernity in relation to which Enlightenment ideals of democracy can be examined through the 'double consciousness' bequeathed by slavery.[19]

What is at stake in the currency of the diaspora concept today? In asking this question, James Clifford maps the expanded field with a discerning eye.[20] Alongside social science 'ideal type' approaches – which hold that diaspora formations involve the catastrophic separation of a people from their natal origin; that ethno-communal solidarity around myths of return to the homeland develops in the face of rejection by the host society; and that lateral connections among diasporic sites may generate metaphorical flows with other social groups around abstract ideals such as social justice – Clifford seeks to underline more nuanced contemporary views. From the US–Mexico borderlands of Chicano life in California, or the contact zones of Native American worlds, through the revisionist outlook on contemporary Jewish diasporas, his lucid account offers an indispensable overview of key insights and fault lines among potential candidates for the 'post-international sociology' that Pieterse has called for. But what seems to have disappeared in Clifford's account is the knotted density of the 'differentiated specificity/complex unity' of the social entanglements he describes, even though he has subsequently taken the view that 'Discrepant cosmopolitanisms guarantee nothing politically. They offer no release from mixed feelings, from utopic/dystopic tensions. They do, however, name and make more visible a complex range of inter-cultural experiences, sites of appropriation and exchange.'[21]

Would this persuade Jean Fisher? She argues that the language of cultural studies is now actually part of the problem in a global art-system in which 'cultural marginality [is] no longer a problem of invisibility but one of *excess* visibility in terms of a reading of cultural difference that is too easily marketable'.[22] To the extent that multiculturalism implicitly prescribes black artists to be ethnically representative, and thus visibly different, arts policy is reduced to a simplistic equation whereby retroactive inclusion supplements and compensates for past exclusion. This makes the art world's demand for difference an institutional fetish in a regime of visuality more or less continuous with the ethnocentric ideology it sought to modify. Fisher regards the eighties black visual arts sector as a 'limited success' because the actual artwork was absorbed and overwhelmed by identity politics. To what extent did diaspora-based artists get stuck in a critically modernist episteme of visual culture?

Multicultural normalization means that global popular culture has moved the goalposts around the rights and wrongs of black representation. In fact, the stakes have changed so rapidly that, as media sociologist Herman Gray observes, 'given the level of saturation of the media with representations of blackness, the mediascape can no longer be characterized accurately using terms such as invisibility. Rather, we might well describe ours as a moment of *hyperblackness*.'[23] If hip-hop capitalism is the only game in town, to what extent does the postmodern regime of hyperblackness associated with Nike advertising and Rupert Murdoch's Fox television channel conform to the McDonald's model of global standardization? Is this the background against which artists like Chris Ofili, Steve McQueen or Yinka Shonibare have pursued a new individualism as a nineties corollary to new internationalism?

As the 'post-' acquired a viral-like pervasiveness in the social body, there was a countervailing trend towards minimizing or downsizing difference. When the available forms of 'unity, cohesion and stability' constitutive of a society are said to belong to the past, would it be fair to say that the postmodern social – with multicultural normalization as a key feature – inscribes the decoupling of 'differentiated specificity/ complex unity' as we know it? 'Capitalism only advances, as it were, on contradictory terrain. It is the contradictions which it has to overcome that produce its own forms of expansion,' Hall has said on the subject of globalization and ethnicity.[24] For Gayatri Spivak, 'the concept of a diasporic multiculturalism is irrelevant', so far as women in the workplaces of the transnational world are concerned: 'large groups within this space of difference subsist in transnationality without escaping into diaspora'.[25] Does hybridity screen off the ugly side of the social?

While Fisher values the decentring of classificatory oppositions associated with Homi Bhabha's influence on the postcolonial turn, she echoes a criticism voiced by Sarat Maharaj that, 'in its popularity hybridity risks becoming an essentialist opposite to the now denigrated "cultural purity".'[26] The idea that, 'two discrete entities combine to produce a third which is capable of resolving its "parents'" contradictions' is something Fisher finds to be 'fraught with connotations of origin and redemption [which] do not extricate us from a self/other dualism'.[27] Counterposing syncretism to hybridity, however, evades historical differences among Anglophone, Hispanic and Francophone dispositions towards cultural mixing, all of which can be found in the Caribbean region.

Ethnographic terms such as *méstizaje* in Mexico, like *métissage* in Martinique, seemingly denote cultural interactions signified by *miscegenation* in English-speaking regions such as the British West Indies. But the tolerance of cross-cultural leakages as complementarities in Latin American syncretism contrasts markedly with Anglo-Protestant anxieties of the Manichean variety which Fanon theorized psychoanalytically. As a geographical site of many, overlapping, diasporas – African, Asian, European, American – the Caribbean is constituted as a composite cultural unity formed out of a great many differentiated specificities. Forms of *créolité* in Haiti or Cuba, whose influence on the paintings of

Wilfredo Lam is discussed by Gerardo Mosquera, are both intimately linked to, but sharply distinct from, the poetics of patois and other signifying practices of *creolization* in Jamaica examined by Kamau Brathwaite.[28]

The syncretism-versus-hybridity argument elides the issue of ethnicity in the construction of the social contexts of artistic reception and production. I would suggest that, in contrast to the deconstructive emphasis on *difference* as inherently subversive, the key concerns that Fisher highlights can be clarified by Pieterse's view that the flip side to hybridization as pluralization or multiplicity is the recognition and re-evaluation of 'transcultural correspondences' – where discrepant *sameness* disrupts social perceptions of symbolic categories and classificatory systems.[29] This view shares common ground with Hall's concept of 'new ethnicities' in taking the position that hybridization is a universalist, rather than minoritarian, process. Although the task has not been widely seized upon with much passion, this was the context in which Hall called for a rethinking of ethnicity:

> The term 'ethnicity' acknowledges the place of history, language and culture in the construction of subjectivity and identity, as well as the fact that all discourse is placed, positioned, situated, and all knowledge is contextual. Representation is possible only because enunciation is always produced within codes that have a history, a position within the discursive formations of a particular space and time.[30]

Taking 'the Caribbean' as the name of a habitus where hybridization is normal – where the encounter with difference is a regulating convention of social interaction – is not to say that everywhere else is like that now, but that the worlding of the ethnic signifier can take forms other than the prevailing trends of multicultural normalization. In fact, the normative presence of hybridization, as the articulation of sameness and difference together, may have already happened in the cultural studies story itself.

During the late sixties Stuart Hall was peripherally involved in the Caribbean Artists' Movement (CAM). This was a loose network of writers, artists, students and teachers convened by John La Rose, Andrew Salkey and Kamau Brathwaite at the West Indian Students' Centre in London between 1966 and 1972. In 1968 Hall took part in CAM's second large-scale conference at the University of Kent. CAM brought artists like Wilson Harris and Aubrey Williams together with key intellectuals of the post-independence generation – Orlando Patterson, Sylvia Wynter, Jan Carew – who either returned to the Caribbean or remigrated to the United States – as well as those who stayed on and undertook initiatives that laid the basis for the black arts sector in the seventies. But prior to Ann Walmsley's documentation of the CAM story, few had heard of it, even though CAM's transnational location in London made it a site of a specifically *British* critical modernism.[31]

To conceptualize hybridization as socially normative for Western liberal democracies is to open up a dialogue with the cultural study of the plural modernities of mixed times and places in which the process of cultural mixing is more or less repressed or acknowledged, more or less disavowed or incorporated, as a general feature of everyday life.

In contrast to the readerly mode of speech characteristic of the naturalistic strategy of authority in the social sciences, it could be said that Hall's voice errs on the side of the writerly text. His *oeuvre* reveals an individual attitude towards authorship that is neither possessive nor patriarchal, but which, rather, is collaborative, dialogic and often decentred. While I have sketched tentative pathways between his dispersed writings on diaspora, the texts have another common feature inasmuch as they are instances of Stuart Hall's practice as a public intellectual. Whether published by UNESCO in Paris, or the National Committee for Commonwealth Immigrants in London, they are texts that participate in a broad public sphere of democratic debate, of a piece with the diverse genres of writing that Hall has disseminated through magazines like *Marxism Today* and through television programmes of the Open University.

One could call this a practice of sociography in the sense that Hall's writing inscribes itself through such a wide variety of institutions and spaces in civil society. Although the UNESCO texts are often hard to track down (which makes one wonder how public the public sphere has to be), I have to say that in my own case, staying up watching BBC2 as a teenage insomniac in the seventies and coming across Stuart giving a lecture on Althusserian Marxism, the encounter with this sociography was a brilliant introduction to cultural studies, even though one discovers that it does not help you get to sleep any more easily.

Notes

1. Stuart Hall, 'New Ethnicities', in *Black Film/British Cinema*: ICA Documents 7, London: Institute of Contemporary Arts, 1988. Stuart Hall, 'Cultural Identity and Diaspora', in Jonathan Rutherford, ed., *Identity: Community, Culture, Difference*, London: Lawrence & Wishart, 1990. Stuart Hall, *The Young Englanders*, London: National Committee for Commonwealth Immigrants, 1967. Stuart Hall, 'The Question of Cultural Identity', in Stuart Hall, Bram Gibbens and A. McGrew, eds., *Formations of Modernity*, Cambridge: Polity, 1992. Stuart Hall, *Africa is Alive and Well and Living in the Diaspora*, Paris: UNESCO, 1975

2. Jan Nederveen Pieterse, 'Globalization and Hybridization', in Mike Featherstone, Scott Lash and Roland Robertson, eds., *Global Modernities*, London: Sage, 1995, p. 63.

3. *Newsweek*, 5 May 1997, p. 35.

4. Stuart Hall, 'Black Britons, Part 1: Some Problems of Adjustment', *Community*, Vol. 1, No. 2, 1970, London: Commission for Racial Equality, p. 3.

5. See Nikos Papastergiadis, *The Complicities of Culture: Hybridity and 'New Internationalism'*, Manchester: Cornerhouse Communique No. 4, 1995; and Jean Fisher, 'The Work Between Us', in Okwui Enwezor, ed., *Trade Routes: History and Geography* (exhibition catalogue), Johannesburg: Second Johannesburg Biennale, 1997.

6. See Robert Young, *Colonial Desire: Hybridity in Theory, Culture and Race*, London and New York: Routledge 1995; and Pheng Cheng, 'Given Culture: Rethinking Cosmopolitical Freedom in Transnationalism', in Bruce Robbins and Pheng Cheng, eds., *Cosmopolitics: Thinking and Feeling beyond the Nation*, Minneapolis: University of Minnesota Press, 1998.

7. Hall, 'Black Britons', p. 4.

8. Hall, *Young Englanders*, p. 10.

9. Ibid., p. 3.

10. Ibid., p. 10.

11. Hall, 'Black Britons', p. 3.

12. Stuart Hall, 'When Was "The Post-Colonial"? Thinking at the Limit', in Iain Chambers and Lidia Curti, eds., *The Post-colonial Question*, London and New York: Routledge, 1996.

13. Stuart Hall, 'Pluralism, Race and Class in Caribbean Society', in *Race and Class in Post-colonial Society*, Paris: UNESCO, 1978. Stuart Hall, 'Racism and Reaction', in *Five Views of Multi-racial Britain*, London: Commission for Racial Equality, 1978.

14. Stuart Hall, Chas Critcher, Tony Jefferson, John Clarke, and Brian Roberts, *Policing the Crisis: 'Mugging', the State and Law and Order*, Basingstoke: Macmillan, 1978, p. 394.

15. Stuart Hall, 'Race, Articulation and Societies Structured in Dominance', in *Sociological Theories: Race and Colonialism*, Paris: UNESCO 1980. Stuart Hall, 'Gramsci's Relevance for the Study of Race and Ethnicity', *Journal of Communication Inquiry*, No. 10, Iowa: University of Iowa, 1986.

16. Hall, 'Pluralism, Race and Class', p. 158.

17. A point made by Michèle Barrett at 'The Stuart Hall Conference', Open University, 15 May 1998.

18. Centre for Contemporary Cultural Studies, *The Empire Strikes Back: Race and Racism in 70s Britain*, London: Hutchinson, 1982.

19. See, among others, the following works by Paul Gilroy: *There Ain't No Black in the Union Jack: The Cultural Politics of Race and Nation*, London: Hutchinson, 1987; 'Cultural Studies and Ethnic Absolutism', in Lawrence Grossberg, Cary Nelson and Paula Treichler, eds., *Cultural Studies*, London and New York: Routledge, 1992; and *The Black Atlantic: Modernity and Double Consciousness*, Cambridge: Harvard University Press, 1993.

20. James Clifford, 'Diasporas', in his *Routes: Travel and Translation in Late Twentieth Century Culture*, Cambridge, MA: Harvard University Press, 1997.

21. James Clifford, 'Mixed Feelings', in Robbins and Cheng, *Cosmopolitics*, p. 369.

22. Jean Fisher, 'The Syncretic Turn: Cross-cultural Practices in an Age of Multiculturalism', in *New Histories* (exhibition catalogue), Boston, MA: Institute of Contemporary Arts, 1996, p. 35.

23. Herman Gray, *Watching 'Race': Television and the Struggle for Blackness*, Minneapolis: University of Minnesota Press, 1995, p. 230.

24. Stuart Hall, 'The Local and the Global Part 1: Globalization and Ethnicity', in Anthony King, ed., *Culture, Globalization and the World System*, Binghamton, NY: State University of New York, 1991, p. 29.

25. Gayatri Spivak, 'Diasporas Old and New: Women in the Transnational World', *Textual Practice*, Vol. 10, No. 2, 1996, London: Routledge, pp. 246 and 247.

26. Fisher, 'The Syncretic Turn', p. 36. See Sarat Maharaj, ' "Perfidious Fidelity": The Untranslatability of the Other', in Jean Fisher, ed., *Global Visions: Towards a New Internationalism in the Visual Arts*, London: Kala Press, 1994.

27. Fisher, 'The Syncretic Turn', p. 36.

28. See Gerado Mosquera, ed., *Beyond the Fantastic: Art Criticism from Latin America*, London and Cambridge, MA: Institute of International Visual Arts and MIT, 1996; and Edward Kamau Brathwaite, *The Development of Creole Society in Jamaica*, London and New York: Oxford University Press, 1974.

29. Pieterse, 'Globalization and Hybridization', pp. 60–3.

30. Hall, 'New Ethnicities', p. 29.

31. Ann Walmsley, *The Caribbean Artists Movement, 1966–1972: A Literary and Cultural History*, London and Port of Spain: New Beacon, 1992.

21

Cultural Studies and Common Sense:
Unresolved Questions

David Morley

A reviewer of a book on Stuart Hall's work that I co-edited with Kuan-Hsing Chen (Morley and Chen 1996) observed that, so far as he could see, when cultural studies argues for the importance of questions of culture and identity in contemporary politics and social life, this seems 'so obviously a move in the direction of common sense that it hardly deserves all this attention' (Rogers 1996). Alongside this comment, I'd just like to quote from Stuart's 1977 essay 'Culture, the Media and the Ideological Effect', where he argues that 'what passes for common sense feels as if it has always been there, the sedimented, bedrock wisdom of "the race". A form of "natural" wisdom, whose content has changed hardly at all with time' (Hall 1977a: 325). However, as Stuart argues, common sense does, indeed, have a content – and a history. My point is simply that if the arguments to which this reviewer refers are now no more than 'common sense', that is in some large part because work in cultural studies – and Stuart's work in particular – has made them so. This itself is no mean achievement.

However, contemporary 'common sense' in the UK, at least, is also pretty sceptical about the value of media and cultural studies as academic subjects. In the wake of popular and governmental attacks on these subjects, we do now seem to face a similar antagonism to cultural studies from more established disciplines within the academy. The chorus of external criticism of cultural studies is increasingly being met by a defensive response within some parts of academia, which would have us ditch the supposedly 'wilder' shores of cultural studies' interdisciplinary project, for the safe havens of the (nowadays) more 'respectable' disciplines of sociology (or anthropology) and their (apparently) tried and trusted analyses of culture. It is in the face of these tendencies that I feel the need to defend again, here, the interdisciplinary nature of the cultural studies project.

Media Studies, Cultural Studies and the Social Sciences

There are, evidently, a number of delicate balances to be struck here. If the interdisciplinary study of the media is important, and if the specificity of cultural and linguistic mechanisms of meaning require detailed attention, still one would not want to fall into the dangers of a media-centric perspective. Here I would simply note that, when I began work as External Assessor on the Open University course that Stuart and his colleagues have recently completed, the initial papers referred to it as a course in 'Media, Culture and Identity', whereas by the time it was opened to its public, it was described as a course in 'Culture, Media and Identity' (Open University Course D318). What's in a name, you might ask? Quite a lot, I'd reply. One of Stuart's major contributions in this field has always been, in my view, his insistence that work on the media must be set within a broad framework of cultural theory, rather than simply ploughing the established furrows of the 'sociology of mass communications' in the way that much of the work in this area, in the UK, has always done.

One of the most crucial 'balancing acts' in matters of interdisciplinarity is, of course, that which Stuart has endlessly juggled, between the 'textualizing' tendencies of literary versions of cultural studies and the deterministic or essentialist tendencies of the more social-science-based alternatives. All I want to do here is point to one continuous thread in Stuart's comments on these matters, a thread that stretches from his 1977 essay on 'The Hinterland of Science' (Hall 1977b), to his (closing) contribution to the new Open University course referred to above, where he addresses the recent 'Cultural Turn' in social science (Hall 1997). The issue is that of cultural studies' relationship with sociology.

In his 1977 essay Stuart observes that, when Levi-Strauss succeeded to the Chair of Social Anthropology at the Collège de France, and delivered the inaugural lecture which declared that the centrepiece of social anthropology should be the study of 'the life of signs at the heart of social life', he was able to defend this enterprise as nothing more or less than the resumption of the 'forgotten part of the Durkheim Mauss programme' (Hall 1977b: 23). In the 1997 version of this argument, Stuart explains that 'this programme . . . was defined for many years as "too idealist" for mainstream sociology . . . Durkheim's more positivistic work being preferred' and he goes on to argue that 'the (recent) much heralded "cultural turn" can more properly be read as (in fact) representing a "return" to certain neglected classical and traditional themes' (Hall 1997: 223). In this argument, cultural studies stands not against sociology *per se*, but rather as the 'rescuer' of a 'lost' tradition, the recovery of which has done much to reinvigorate contemporary sociology.

Stuart himself has always argued that a crucial part of what was going on in Birmingham in the 1970s was the 'posing of sociological questions against sociology' (Hall 1980: 21) as it then stood. Those 'questions' have clearly had an impact – I can also recall Stuart saying, when in 1980 he took the job at the Open University from which he has now retired, that he was happy to become a Professor of Sociology, now that the sociologists seemed less clear than they used to be about what that meant. In this connection, Greg McLennan has argued that 'If sociology is attractive today as . . . an increasingly eclectic forum, that is not least due to the impact of radical cultural studies and other . . . interdisciplinary currents' (McLennan 1994: 128). However, as he also notes, it does now seem to some commentators (who identify cultural studies exclusively with its relativist, postmodern variant) that if, once upon a time, cultural studies posed as the 'radical' alternative to a moribund sociology, nowadays, to some critics, such as Keith Tester, it seems that sociology is in a position to wreak its revenge, taking the theoretical and moral high ground – on account of its apparently 'greater seriousness of moral (and critical) purpose' (Tester 1994: 4).

There are also those who would claim that a reinvigorated sociology of culture, with sound and proper methodological protocols, is now in a position to move in on this field (which is, of course, recruiting students rather nicely) and 'clear up' a number of the 'unfortunate' confusions created by cultural studies' various inadequacies (see Alexander 1988). For some of us, and here I speak as one who has always defended sociological approaches in cultural studies, the price of that process of 'Clarification by Social Theory' might well be rather too high. It all depends on how much store you set by 'Theory' with a big T.

However, it is not only sociologists who are exercised about cultural studies. One of the other ghosts at this particular feast is, of course, the venerable discipline of anthropology. Not so long ago, the Group for Debates in Anthropological Theory organized a debate in the anthropology department of Manchester University on the motion that 'Cultural Studies will be the death of Anthropology' (see Wade 1996). In that debate, some participants argued that cultural studies was merely parasitic on anthropology's long tradition of expertise in matters of culture (quite apart from its 'misappropriation' of anthropological methods of study such as ethnography). However, what was clearly of much more concern to many there was the perceived problem that the 'superficial attractiveness' of cultural studies to students as compared

to the regrettable (but necessary) 'dullness' of 'good, serious anthropology' was driving anthropology out of business 'as bad money pushes
out good money' (Werbner, in Wade 1996: 52–3).

Happily, from my own perspective, there were also those (such as
Mark Hobart) who took a more sanguine view, declaring both that the
conventional anthropological project had 'run out of (epi)steme'
(Hobart, in Wade 1996: 12) and indeed that they were pleased to see
anthropology transformed into a transnational, comparative cultural
studies. Indeed, Paul Willis, who had argued earlier in that debate that
much cultural studies work still really lacked a fully developed ethnographic practice when compared with anthropology, nevertheless concluded his contribution to the debate with the rallying cry:
'Anthropology is dead: long live theoretically integrated ethnographic
study' (Willis, in Wade 1996)

Beyond Cultural Studies? Dead Ends and Reinvented Wheels

There have also recently been a series of very strongly worded critiques
of the overall project of cultural studies, which argue variously that it
has led us into a political 'dead end' (particularly in its emphasis on
the study of cultural consumption); that it has abandoned 'politics'
altogether (at least, in one definition of that term); that it has done
little more than reinvent (in ignorance) the old theoretical wheels of
an earlier sociological tradition; and that, in general, the 'excesses' of
its project have only confirmed the worst fears of those who were
opposed to it in the first place (for particularly vitriolic versions of this
attack on cultural studies, see Ferguson and Golding 1997, and Philo
and Miller 1997; for an earlier version, see also Curran 1990). In these
critiques it is argued that it is (somehow) both time to move 'beyond'
cultural studies altogether, and time to return to the more secure
disciplinary foundations and rigorous methodological procedures of
sociology (and/or political economy). The question would then be
whether this proposed return to 'the good old ways' is still possible,
even if it were desirable.

Let us take just a few samples of the critique of 'So-called British
Cultural Studies' (Frith 1990: 233). Ferguson and Golding tell us that
the biography of cultural studies is a story of 'patron saints, superstars,
hot gospellers and true believers', characterized by an 'inward looking
narcissism' (1997: xv), which has led those working in cultural studies
to be 'ignorant of significant developments elsewhere in academia' and
thus to end up, in their ignorance, merely 'reinventing the conceptual
wheel of cultural analysis' (Ferguson and Golding 1997: xix). Cultural

studies has apparently suffered a narrowing of vision exemplified by a drift into an uncritical populist mode of interpretation and 'a celebration of the ephemeral and superficial' (McGuigan 1992: 244).

Perhaps worst of all, from my personal point of view, media audience researchers, according to Philo and Miller, have been engaged in an examination of the social relations of media consumption, which could come down to asking people if they 'listened to the radio while they did the ironing' (Philo and Miller 1997: 13). Clearly, on this view, it has been a sad and mistaken journey from the (apparently now halcyon) days of 'Encoding/Decoding' to the days of treating 'Television as [if it were like a] Toaster' (ibid., 13). At the same time, some political economists (see Garnham 1995) have claimed that, of course, they have always recognised that there is more to life than class; that questions of culture and meaning have long been important to them; that questions of race, gender and sexuality have always been among their concerns; that, naturally, the analysis of low-status forms of fictional media production is important; and indeed, that they have never thought of audiences as passive dupes or zombies. Tell it to the marines, say I. All these things that now, it seems, these scholars have 'long recognized' had, as I remember it, to be fought for inch by inch, against the background of much wailing and gnashing of teeth (see Murdock and Golding 1977; Connell 1978 and 1983; Garnham 1983). I am sorry if here I seem to be, in James Carey's words, simply 'waking up the past in order to sing it back to sleep' (1995: 87), but perhaps it will sleep better, this time.

One issue is that of the teleological structure of the arguments of many of the critics of cultural studies. Certainly, in my own field of research, critics of the supposedly 'pointless populism' of 'active audience theory' have tended towards a structure of argument in which, having identified some particular case where consumer/audience 'activity' is uncritically celebrated by an author with cultural studies allegiances, they then retrospectively declare that this is the kind of (bad) thing to which cultural studies, in general, was bound to lead, and that therefore (conveniently reversing the terms of the argument) we can now see that the whole enterprise was, from the start, misconceived – as it has (in fact) led to whatever example of bad practice they have identified. So much for the wisdom of hindsight – which leaves these critics in the happy position of saying that they always knew it would end in tears.

The Gender of the Real

The supposed depoliticization of contemporary cultural studies work
has also been denounced as somehow being responsible for redirecting
attention away from the 'real' world of parliamentary politics, hard
facts, and economic truths (and their ideological misrepresentation),
towards the (supposedly) 'unimportant' realms of the domestic functioning of the media and of the consumption of fictional pleasures. It
is thus argued that 'media power as a political issue' has simply slipped
off our research agenda as this agenda has descended into 'a form of
sociological quietism . . . in which increasing emphasis on the micro-
processes of viewing relations displaces an engagement with the macro
structures of media and society' (Corner 1991: 4) – a formulation
which seems to me both to reify the macro and to equate it unproblem-
atically with the 'real'.

This critique also fails to address the articulation of the divisions
macro/micro, real/trivial and public/private with those of masculine
and feminine. Ann Gray (1999) has captured the gendered spirit of
this critique, in her comments on Dennis McQuail's striking use of the
words 'flighty and opinionated' (McQuail 1997: 55, quoted in Gray
1999) to characterize cultural studies work. As she notes, the supposed
loss of critical energy involved in attending to the role of the media in
the articulation of the public and private spheres, and the analysis of
the inscription of the media in the gendered realm of domesticity,
could only ever be understood as an 'abandonment' of politics within
an unhelpfully narrow and heavily gendered definition of what constitutes the real and/or the political. The sphere of political communication has, as its necessary foundation, the series of inclusions and
exclusions (in relation to questions of race and ethnicity, as well as
gender), on the basis of which only the private, domestic experiences
of some categories of people are connected (or mediated) to the
political realities of the sphere of citizenship.

In response to the continuing critique of work on consumption in
cultural studies, all I will say is that the origin of the model of the
'circuit of culture' (and of the articulation of its elements) outlined in
the Open University course referred to earlier can already be found in
Stuart's 1973 paper on Marx's Introduction to the *Grundrisse* (Hall
1973). As that paper explains, consumption is no secondary or dependent part of a linear narrative, in which 'in the Beginning was Production'. As the introduction to the Open University course has it, rather
than privileging one single phenomenon in its explanatory structure,
this model involves a 'circuit of culture' so that 'it does not much

matter where (on the circuit) you start, as you have to go the whole
way round before your study is complete' (du Gay 1997: 4). Quite so:
which also means attending to the cultural dimensions of production
and economic life, rather than treating them as some free-standing
foundation of the 'real'.

The Slippery Slope of Intellectual Progress: Stuart Hall's Intellectual Practice

Clearly, in conceptualizing the slippery slope of intellectual progress,
rather than thinking in terms of a linear succession of truths, paradigms
or models, each displacing the other in some triumphal progress, we
are better served by a multi-dimensional model, which builds new
insights on to the old, in a process of dialogue and transformation.
This has always been the primary modality of Stuart's own work. A
principled commitment to provisionality and open-endedness is of the
essence here. It is always necessary to appreciate the value of previous
analytical work in the context in which it was produced. One very good
example of this can be found in Stuart's retrospective comments (Hall
1994) on the 'Encoding/Decoding' model, now so much reified in the
field. When interviewed about it, a few years ago, Stuart was at pains to
stress the extent to which it had been developed, for specific polemical
purposes, in the context of a particular debate. Moreover, he insisted
that if the model still has any remaining 'purchase', that's only 'because
it suggests an approach; it opens up new questions. But [as he says] it's
a model which has to be worked with . . . developed and changed'
(Hall 1994: 255). If some part of that 'development' has involved
investigating the media in their domestic setting – the 'TV-as-Toaster'
analogy mentioned earlier – that is not to say that one is, somehow, no
longer interested in the 'old' questions of media power, but rather that
one is also interested in different versions and dimensions of those
questions.

Let me end with an analogy between Stuart's work and that of Bertolt
Brecht. Among other things, Brecht is famous for endlessly reworking
his texts, producing different versions for different occasions, so that it
becomes hard to say which is the 'definitive' version. I think one might
say something of this sort about Stuart's work. Just as he has declared
that he is not interested in 'Theory', but only in 'moving things on'
and 'going on theorizing', one might also say that he is perhaps
opposed in principle (if not allergic) to the very idea that our task is
the production of definitive Answers or Theories, as opposed to the
production of questions.

You may perhaps be familiar with Brecht's 'Anecdotes of Mr Keuner' (Brecht 1966). I will quote two of them. The first, I think, is very apposite to Stuart's intellectual approach; the second describes a worrying type of experience which I feel sure that he will never have to suffer. In the first of these little stories, Mr Keuner notices that 'a lot of people are put off by our teaching, because we seem to know the answer to everything' – and so he suggests that perhaps the best response would be to 'draw up a list of questions which appear to us quite unresolved' (Brecht 1966: 124). Thinking up good questions is, of course, always the heart of the matter, and it has always been Stuart's great gift to be able to formulate very good questions. In the second story, a man whom Mr Keuner hadn't seen for a long time met him again, in the street, and said to him, in a very reassuring tone, 'Mr Keuner – you haven't changed at all.' 'Oh!' said Mr Keuner, looking very troubled. Happily, this is not, as I say, an experience Stuart is ever likely to have.

References

Alexander, J. ed. (1988) *Durkheimian Sociology: Cultural Studies*, New York: Cambridge University Press.

Brecht, B. (1966) 'Anecdotes of Mr Keuner', in his *Tales from the Calendar*, London: Methuen.

Carey, J. (1995) 'Abolishing the Old Spirit World', *Critical Studies in Mass Communications*, No.12.

Connell, I. (1978) 'Monopoly Capitalism and the Media', in S. Hibbin, ed., *Politics, Ideology and the State*, London: Lawrence & Wishart.

Connell, I. (1983) 'Commercial Broadcasting and the British Left', *Screen*, Vol. 24, No. 6.

Corner, J. (1991) 'Meaning, Genre and Context: The Problematics of "Public Knowledge" in the New Audience Studies', in J. Curran and M. Gurevitch, eds., *Mass Media and Society*, London: Arnold.

Curran, J. (1990) 'The "New Revisionism" in Mass Communications Research', *European Journal of Communications*, Vol. 5, No. 2 and 3.

du Gay, P. ed. (1997) *Production of Culture/Cultures of Production*, London: Sage.

Ferguson, M. and Golding, P. (1997) 'Cultural Studies and Changing Times', Introduction to their co-edited volume *Cultural Studies in Question*, London: Sage.

Frith, S. (1990) Review article, *Screen*, Vol. 31, No. 2.

Garnham, N. (1983) 'Public Service Versus the Market', *Screen*, Vol. 24, No. 1.

Garnham, N. (1995) 'Political Economy and Cultural Studies: Reconciliation or Divorce?', University of Westminster; reprinted (1997) as 'Political Economy and the Practice of Cultural Studies', in M. Ferguson and P. Golding, eds., *Cultural Studies in Question*, London: Sage.

Gray, A. (1999) 'Audience and Reception Research in Retrospect: The Trouble with Audiences', in P. Alasuutari, ed., *The Inscribed Audience*, London: Sage.

Hall, S. (1973) 'A Reading of Marx's 1857 "Introduction" to the Grundrisse', Centre for Contemporary Cultural Studies, University of Birmingham.

Hall, S. (1977a) 'Culture, the Media and the Ideological Effect', in J. Curran, M. Gurevitch and J. Woollacot, eds., *Mass Communications and Society*, London: Arnold.

Hall, S. (1977b) 'The Hinterland of Science', in *Working Papers in Cultural Studies*, No. 10.

Hall, S. (1980) 'Cultural Studies and the Centre', in S. Hall, D. Hobson and A. Lowe eds., *Culture, Media, Language*, London: Hutchinson.

Hall, S. (1994) 'Reflections upon the Encoding/Decoding Model', in J. Cruz and J. Lewis eds., *Viewing, Reading, Listening*, Boulder, CO: Westview Press.

Hall, S. (1997) 'The Centrality of Culture', in K. Thompson, ed., *Media and Cultural Regulation*, London: Sage.

McGuigan, J. (1992) *Cultural Populism*, London: Routledge.

McLennan, G. (1994) 'Margins, Centres', in *Sites*, No. 28, Autumn.

McQuail, D. (1997) 'Policy Help Wanted: Willing and Able Media Culturalists Please Apply', in M. Ferguson and P. Golding, eds., *Cultural Studies in Question*, London: Sage.

Morley, D. and Chen, K.H. (1996) eds., *Stuart Hall: Critical Dialogues in Cultural Studies*, London: Routledge.

Murdock, G. and Golding, P. (1977) 'Capitalism, Communications and Class Relations', in J. Curran, M. Gurevitch and J. Woollacot, eds., *Mass Communications and Society*, London: Arnold.

Philo, G. and Miller, D. (1997) 'Cultural Compliance: Dead Ends of Media/ Cultural Studies and Social Science', Glasgow Media Group, University of Glasgow.

Rogers, B. (1996) 'Burchill's Daddies' (review of Morley and Chen 1996) *Independent on Sunday*, 18 February 1996.

Tester, K. (1994) *Media, Culture and Morality*, London: Routledge.

Wade, P. ed. (1996) *Cultural Studies Will Be the Death of Anthropology*, Group for Debates in Anthropology, University of Manchester.

22

Intervening in Popular Culture:
Cultural Politics and the Art of Translation

Sean Nixon

Cultural studies and the engaged cultural analysis with which it is associated has come in for some severe criticism from a number of quarters in recent years. One celebrated version of this critique has homed in on the apparent populism of cultural studies scholarship, particularly in that work focused upon popular cultural forms and practices. Most associated with Jim McGuigan's 1992 book *Cultural Populism*, this critique has proved to be an effective rallying point for a host of critics of cultural studies, offering an easy stick with which to beat it and sanctioning a very peculiar rereading of the terms and ambitions of the cultural studies project. Thus, for example, Simon Frith and Jon Savage, in an at times interesting but intemperate and often eccentric essay, take McGuigan's book as the starting point for a piece of cultural-studies-bashing (Frith and Savage 1993). Locating the rise of cultural studies within a broader drift to cultural populism also evidenced in serious journalism, they contend that 'for cultural populists of all sorts, the popular is to be applauded with new modern assumptions, assumptions about the power of market forces, assumptions about the creativity of consumers' (Frith and Savage 1993: 108).

In one sense, of course, this characterization does touch a nerve and reveal a tendency across work that has been produced under the banner of cultural studies. As a serious account of an intellectual field, however, it won't do, building up a skewed picture through alluding to those sinners at the court of populism (who most certainly do exist) as if that exhausted all there was to say about cultural studies scholarship. This sloppy analysis of an intellectual field notwithstanding, however, Frith and Savage do raise more serious and significant questions in their essay, questions that have been conflated with and obscured by the recent charges of populism against cultural studies. These concern the rather old, but still thorny issues of how we should think about popular culture, how we should study it, and how we should value it and weigh the authority of accredited reading of popular forms and practices (those of academics, but also of serious journalists) against popular knowledge.'[1]

Frith and Savage are a little disingenuous in implying that these questions have completely disappeared from the study of popular culture. On the contrary, it is clear that they are not unknown to those working on popular culture within cultural studies. In fact, the questions of what popular culture is as an object of study and the intellectual and political issues at stake in its analysis were central to the key theoretical essay that has shaped recent cultural analysis of popular culture: Stuart Hall's 'Notes on Deconstructing "the Popular"' (Hall 1981). In this short chapter, I want to reflect on 'Notes on Deconstructing "the Popular"' and the broader, generative impact it has had upon the study of popular culture. It seems a particularly opportune moment to do this. Not only has the cultural analysis of popular culture been roughed up in the course of the 'cultural populism' attacks, but it has also been subject to another vigorous critique in the work of one of its former advocates and devotees, Tony Bennett. At the root of Bennett's argument is a critique both of the very conception of the cultural field that underpins the cultural analysis of popular forms and practices set in motion by Hall's work and of the model of intellectual and political intervention that has flowed from it. These challenges do demand, I think, some serious engagement. They certainly warrant more attention than the dreary sniping sanctioned under the flag of the cultural populism debate. I want in this chapter, then, to set Bennett's critique next to my reflections on Hall's theoretical formulations on popular culture.

The Problem with Popular Culture

'Notes on Deconstructing "the Popular"', as Bill Schwarz reminds us, came out of 'the mind-bending, schismatic History Workshop Conference of 1979' (Schwarz 1989: 251). The context of the essay's publication partly accounts for the strong emphasis on periodizing cultural change which takes up much of its early pages, but more important, in relation to Hall's own work, the essay offers an elaboration on and crystallization of some of the themes that were central to his two previous, collaboratively authored books: *Resistance through Rituals* and *Policing the Crisis* (Hall *et al.* 1976 and 1978). Specifically, of course, the essay sets out to clarify the conceptual meaning of popular culture as an object of study. Drawing pre-eminently on Gramsci's writings, 'Notes

on Deconstructing "the Popular"' conceives of popular culture as a
domain constituted by an historically specific set of cultural relations
between subordinate and dominant cultures. More starkly, it expresses
this as a set of relations between 'the people' and the 'power bloc'. In
charting these relations, what is prioritized are the forms of cultural
authority or hegemony that are secured through them. Popular culture
is characterized then as a domain constituted by a set of institutions,
cultural forms and practices through which active consent by 'the
people' to a dominant culture is won and reproduced. In this conceptualization, however, the process of establishing cultural authority by
dominant groups is not a simple process of domination. It requires
that elements of the subordinate cultures are actively incorporated into
the representation of a legitimate way of life. Hegemony is necessarily,
then, in its Gramscian sense, a contingent and ongoing process.
Popular culture is one central arena of this translation and negotiation.

   This sense of the necessarily hybrid space of popular culture and the
contingent nature of hegemony is key. It shapes a conception of
popular culture that emphasizes not only that it is a domain through
which consent to a dominant culture is secured, but also that it is in
addition a site where the dominant culture or dominant forms of
cultural authority can be contested. It is the place where an alternative
way of life can be articulated and a new cultural authority can be
forged. This characteristic of popular culture – its structuring around,
in Hall's phrase, 'the double movement of containment and resistance'
– is the founding premise of engaged cultural criticism and cultural
politics in its Gramscian form.

   These remain powerful formulations, both concerning popular culture as an object of study and concerning the intellectual and political
imperatives bound up in its analysis. More than that, they have had an
enormously generative and enabling impact on the cultural analysis of
popular forms and practices. A plethora of concrete studies have
followed from them. Many of these have extended the emphasis on the
processes of negotiation and translation between class cultures and the
interest in forms of class resistance that are central to Hall's essay to
both the 'racial' and gendered dynamics of popular culture. Studies
like those pioneered by – inter alia – McRobbie, Winship, Mort, Mercer
and Julien have been orientated by an understanding of the negotiations and translations produced within popular culture between
(notably) competing formations of gender and sexual cultures (dominant, subordinate and oppositional). Such work, then, has been shaped
by a concern to identify the ways in which specific popular forms and
practices could be read as progressive – that is, as disruptive of
dominant forms of gender and sexual relations and sympathetic to a

new alignment of relations between men and women. For those cultural critics following this route, then, a politicized sense of intervention has been the corollary to critical readings of the progressive dimensions of popular culture. The aim of this cultural politics has been to articulate the progressive elements within popular culture to a vision of a new alignment of (for example) gender and sexual relations.

'Notes on Deconstructing "the Popular"', however, has not only continued to be a major point of reference for others working on popular culture. Hall himself has explicitly returned to its central concerns twice in recent years in order to amplify and extend its conceptual arguments (Hall 1992b and 1993). Much of the impetus for doing this has come from an engagement with the work of Stallybrass and White and a meditation on – as Hall has put it – the 'elective affinities' between his own work (including, prominently, 'Notes on Deconstructing "the Popular"') and the arguments set out in *The Politics and Poetics of Transgression* (Stallybrass and White 1986). The results of this meditation have been rich in their insights.

At their centre has been a concern to push further the implications of the relational definition of popular culture set out in 'Notes on Deconstructing "the Popular"'. This definition emphasized the way popular culture and high culture could not be identified by a fixed inventory of forms and practices that remained more or less stable over time; rather, it was by means of the active operation of culture power that the popular was defined in a subordinate relation to high or legitimate culture. For Hall – in the light of the work of Stallybrass and White – this relationship between popular culture and high culture is not best seen as a simple opposition governed by the logic of difference, but is better thought of as a process in which the popular – as integral to the constitution of the 'high' – continues to haunt it, to function as a constitutive trace. The emphasis for Hall, then, is now much more upon the interdependence of the 'high' and 'popular', rather than upon their opposition. This shift of conceptualization is important. It draws attention to the way – in the terminology of Stallybrass and White – the expulsion and splitting of the 'popular' (the low) from the 'high' has complex effects, producing, at the level of the 'political unconscious', a set of hybrid, heterogeneous forms (Stallybrass and White 1986: 193). The move to fix cultural hierarchies, then, through the classification of the 'high' and 'the popular' both produces a fascination with the low-Other (the expelled objects) and generates a realm of objects that transgress and blur its boundaries. For Hall, this points to the dialogical relation between high and popular culture. This insistence allows him to reaffirm not only that the regulation and structuring of the cultural field into its binary

opposites are fundamentally linked to the broader processes of cultural
hegemony, but also that the concern to fix cultural hierarchies also
produces new hybrid, mixed forms. This is a conceptualization of
popular culture, then, more fully conversant in a psychoanalytic vocabulary than the original formulations in 'Notes on Deconstructing "the
Popular"', and one that gives a more central role to the operation of
desire and fantasy in understanding the dynamics of popular culture.

From Cultural Politics to Cultural Policy

The ongoing influence and conceptual resonance of 'Notes on Deconstructing "the Popular"' have not, however, gone unchallenged. Working against the evolving thrust of Hall's work, in three challenging
essays Tony Bennett has taken to task the analysis of culture and the
form of cultural politics articulated in Hall's essay.[2] Bennett opens his
argument – and it is most fully developed in 'Putting Policy into
Cultural Studies' (Bennett 1992a) – by taking issue with the conception
of cultural politics promoted within Hall's essay. Bennett argues that
there are two major problems with this Gramscian conception of
cultural politics. First, he contends that the texts that stand at the
centre of the moves by cultural critics to challenge particular social
hegemonies are the artefacts of an academically authored interpretative
practice. The implication of this is that the readings of these texts
produced by cultural critics make most sense to those who have been
through a specific kind of academic training and that, further, these
readings circulate almost exclusively amongst a narrow group of academic readers and remain disconnected from the popular subjects at
whom they are supposedly directed. In this sense, for Bennett, politics
is largely rhetorical within these forms of engaged cultural analysis; a
critical reading is its beginning and end point.

There is a second, related problem for Bennett in the assumptions
of cultural politics. He argues that as an interventionist intellectual
practice it is flawed by its conception of culture as, primarily, a domain
of signifying practices. The consequence of this, he suggests, is that it
pays insufficient attention to the institutional conditions that regulate
different fields of culture (Bennett 1992a: 25). It is this provocation
that leads Bennett onto his major thesis: namely, that the conception
of culture that has underpinned cultural politics and cultural studies
more generally is in need of revision. Thus, he argues, culture is best
understood as a domain associated with the emergence in the late
eighteenth and nineteenth centuries of new fields of social manage-

ment in which it figured as both the object and the instrument of government:

> its object or target insofar as the term refers to the morals, manners, and ways of life of subordinate social strata; its instrument insofar as culture in its more restricted sense – the domain of artistic and intellectual activities – that is to supply the means of government intervention in and regulation of culture as the domain of morals, manners, codes of conduct etc. (Bennett 1992a: 26)

In advancing this case for a more historically specific understanding of culture, Bennett suggests that one of the major advantages of such an understanding is that it makes visible the 'programmatic, institutional and governmental calculations in which cultural practices are inscribed and which have a substantive priority over the semiotic properties of such practices' (Bennett 1992a: 28). Figuring prominently in this refocusing of the priorities of cultural analysis is the role played by cultural technologies in the organization of fields of culture and its associated categories of the person and conduct. In Bennett's own work, a study of public museums and related forms of public exhibition has constituted the cultural technologies through which he has explored particular fields of culture.

Conceiving of culture in this way opens up a new way of practising cultural politics and engaged cultural criticism, a shift Bennett formulates as a move from 'cultural politics' to 'cultural policy'. Thus,

> my contention is that the key questions to pose of any cultural politics are: how does it stand within a particular cultural technology? In which direction will it point it? And to say that is also to begin to think the possibility of a politics which might take the form of an administrative program, and so to think of a type of cultural studies that will aim to produce knowledges that can assist the development of such programmes rather than endlessly continuing to organise subjects which exist only as the phantom effects of its own rhetorics. (Bennett 1992a: 29)

The Limits of Cultural Policy

I think Bennett's interventions have added to our understanding of the historical complexity of the field of culture and he has performed a useful service in helping to open up the previously neglected relations between culture and government. The force of Bennett's critique of the purely rhetorical conception of politics sanctioned within cultural politics is also undeniable and usefully exposes the emptiness of certain

kinds of 'textual politics'. It seems to me entirely right to want to have
spelt out as a dimension of analysis the ends to which the analysis is
being made if a political impact is being claimed. Such an insistence –
and the practical, pragmatic understanding of intervention into fields
of culture that ought properly to follow from this – does force a
recasting of some of the more heroic metaphors that have guided
engaged cultural criticism and cultural politics. There is also more at
stake here than a shift of terminology. The notions of resistance and
counter-hegemony which have provided the terms through which a
critical reading of cultural forms and practices has often been orientated, remain locked into an ideational conception of social or cultural
practice in which struggles over culture are seen pre-eminently as
struggles over consciousness. The battle for 'hearts and minds', then, is
how cultural change is persistently cast.

In taking issue with this focus, Bennett makes good use of Foucault's
insights into the way the reforging of identities works not so much
through consciousness and individuals' self-perceptions as through the
'brute outcome' of practices.[3] In this sense, rethinking how we view
cultural change will mean learning from ninetenth-century social
reformers like Henry Cole, cited by Bennett in his work on museums,
who clearly understood the practice-driven dimension of cultural
change. During his questioning by a Parliamentary Select Committee,
quoted by Bennett, Cole could not be shifted from the belief that just
attending museums and galleries – simply experiencing the spatial and
technical dimensions of these exhibitionary forms – mattered more
than the content of the works and exhibits displayed (and their
imagined effects on consciousness). It was the 'brute outcome' of
'doing' museum attendance – including mixing with your 'social bet-
ters' – that inculcated new habits and ways of being. There is, of course,
a good dose of polemic in Cole's dogged insistence on this fact (and
Bennett's take on it), but it none the less offers some important
pointers for thinking about cultural transformation.

Henry Cole is an appropriate figure to dwell on because he also
points us towards those aspects of Bennett's argument where I think he
overplays its novelty and also, more significantly, exposes some of the
limits of his understanding of cultural policy. Bennett makes much in
his essays of the need for figures like Cole – cultural administrators –
to figure more prominently in the analysis of fields of culture. But an
awareness of such figures and the role they play in the social management of culture has been a feature of Gramsci-informed work on
popular culture. Such figures may have been less well foregrounded,
and more attention may have been given to the institutions they
inhabited within the state and civil society, but the whole thrust in

Gramscian work on the 'educative' role of the State assumes their presence. Thus, in 'Notes on Deconstructing "the Popular"', Hall is explicit, in those sections where he is reflecting on the periodization of popular culture, in drawing attention to the role of institutional figures like the magistrate and the 'evangelical police' in accounts of the transformations in popular culture. As he notes, such figures played a key role in both the banning and the proscription of cultural forms and practices, as well as in the more productive processes of 'reforming' popular recreations through the eighteenth and nineteenth centuries.

Bennett, in fact, does acknowledge that his own account of the moves to reshape the habits and ways of life of subordinate social groups through the public museums programme could have been told in very similar terms using Gramsci's work. This is a revealing moment in his argument. Thus, although his Foucauldian account does add something new to our understanding of the workings of cultural institutions such as the public museum, I am not convinced that it is necessary to counterpose so sharply the two kinds of accounts (the neo-Gramscian and neo-Foucauldian). I would certainly be interested – as Colin Mercer, one of Bennett's former colleagues at the Centre for Cultural Policy suggested some years ago – to consider the fruitful connections between Gramsci and Foucault (Mercer 1980).

Inasmuch as both writers are attentive to the more decentred forms of power that emerge in the modern period and the new problems of governance associated with the emergence of modern (especially, mass democratic) societies, there are substantive as well as conceptual grounds for creative dialogue between the two traditions. Let me give one instance, without labouring the point, of what might be gained from thinking creatively in this way. It concerns the question of politics and political forces.

Neo-Foucauldian accounts, like Bennett's, which draw imaginatively on Foucault's writings on governmentality, are very good at pulling out the way in which localized practices and techniques of government (and their related cultural technologies) connect with broader policy programmes and their associated political rationalities. The best of this work, then, effectively holds together in the same analysis these two dimensions of the dynamics of government: what O'Malley *et al.* call 'the nexus between political rationalities [the broad discourses of rule] and technologies of rule [the practices, materials, agents and techniques that are deployed to put abstract programmes into effect]' (O'Malley *et al.* 1997). However, despite the sophistication of this work, it does, in the end, operate with an attenuated conception of politics and political forces, one that is overwhelmingly defined around the formulation of government in its programmatic forms and the ongoing attempts to find new ways of governing occasioned by the failure of particular governmental programmes. O'Malley *et al.* call this an over-emphasis on the 'moment of the programme' and the restriction of politics to 'mentalities of rule' (O'Malley *et al.* 1997). It is here that neo-Gramscian work – exemplified by Hall's formulations in 'Notes on Deconstructing "the Popular"' – is useful and can help to flesh out this rather narrow conception of politics. Neo-Gramscian writings work with a broader notion of politics conceived of as relations of contest and struggle and involving, centrally, the construction of collective political identifications. There is also a strong sense in this work that the performance of politics necessarily requires the building of political alliances and the cementing of political formations – centrally con-nected in modern liberal democracies to social classes, but not restricted to them. There is, further, a strong insistence on attending to the conjunctural alignment of political forces. This understanding of politics, then – its conception as a 'war of position' between complexly constituted antagonists – foregrounds its embedding in social relations. In so doing, it presents us with a picture of a more diverse field of social identities and relations than that found in the governmentality literature. This is a vision of the political, however, that recognizes not only the plurality of political spaces and social antagonisms, but also the lines of connection and overdetermination that can exist between them (Laclau and Mouffe 1985).

How might such a conception of politics add to the neo-Foucauldian accounts? One implication of thinking of politics in this way is the requirement – to put it in a summary form – to draw up a broader balance sheet of the political forces and relations that operate both within and across the particular field of government. It might also include moves to situate socially and politically the cultural adminis-trators (like Cole) who wield influence within cultural technologies. This leads to a further point. It concerns the relationship between academic knowledges and the field of cultural policy as it is understood by Bennett. What I think his account misses out or short-circuits is the nature of the exchanges between critical intellectuals and the prac-titioners who populate specific cultural technologies. If we want to intervene in the uses to which culture is put by these technologies, we need to be aware of a number of preconditions to effective interven-tion. Pre-eminent in this is the process of translation required in reaching beyond a conventional academic audience. This means think-ing more broadly about the style and forms of writing and representa-tion we deploy in order to connect more effectively with practitioners' own world-views. To say this is in one sense to state the obvious. But, to take my own work on cultural intermediaries (specifically, advertising practitioners), such a process of engagement means negotiating some obstinate forms of institutional competence and expertise – competencies and expertise that have historically taken their cue from expert knowledges such as behavioural psychology rather than from sociology and cultural studies.

Understanding the world-views of this grouping of practitioners as a precondition for effective dialogue also means more than understanding the formalized knowledges they wield. It requires a broader understanding of their intellectual and cultural formation. Intervening in one set of institutions associated with cultural production – like the advertising industry – might mean exploring the gendered culture through which creativity is understood and practised within agencies. Intervening in the fields of representation linked to advertising, then, might involve producing policy initiatives regarding recruitment and selection in order to help shape a more culturally diverse (and representative) workplace, as well as engaging in a dialogue over the representations they are producing.

In making these points I am doing no more than reiterating what seem to me well-established features of the way cultural studies academics have in practice engaged with particular fields of culture. Stuart Hall has done more than most to insist on this combination of pragmatic intervention and critical, theoretical engagement with popular representation in a way that tries in addition to connect with audiences beyond the academy. He has recently articulated this as the necessarily 'worldly' vocation of cultural studies. That is, its need to both be rigorous and serious in its intellectual work and formulations, but also to take equally seriously the responsibility of 'transmitting those ideas, that knowledge . . . to those who do not belong, professionally, in the intellectual class' (Hall 1992b). In doing so, he has offered a passionate defence of the value of cultural analysis (including the study of popular forms) in relation to the crisis around AIDS. Thus, while he forcefully acknowledges that the urgency of the human tragedy represented by AIDS reveals the marginality of critical intellectuals and their limited ability to make a real difference in the world, he also insists that the crisis points to the importance of working on representation:

> AIDS is the site at which the advance of sexual politics is being rolled back. It's a site at which not only people will die, but desire and pleasure will also die if certain metaphors do not survive, or survive in the wrong way. Unless we operate in this tension, we don't know what cultural studies can do, can't, can never do; but also, what it has to do, what it alone has a privileged capacity to do. It has to analyse certain things about the constitutive and political nature of representation itself, about its complexity, about the effects

of language, about textuality as the site of life and death. Those are the things cultural studies can address. (Hall 1992b)

These are concerns already central to 'Notes on Deconstructing "the Popular"'. And, along with many other practical, pragmatic interventions into the field of popular politics and cultural representation that Hall has engaged in – such as the project that eventually appeared as the television programme *It Ain't Half Racist, Mum* – they continue to constitute a powerful model for cultural politics and the art of translation central to its success.[4]

Notes

1. A similar set of questions are raised by O'Shea and Schwarz 1987.

2. I have focused on three of Bennett's essays: 'Putting Policy into Cultural Studies' (Bennett 1992a); 'Useful Culture' (Bennett 1992b) and 'The Multiplication of Culture's Utility' (Bennett 1995). This chapter was written before the publication of *Culture, a Reformer's Science*, Sage, 1998.

3. The phrase is Ian Hunter's (Hunter 1993).

4. *It Ain't Half Racist, Mum* was broadcast on BBC2's *Open Door* programme in March 1979.

References

Bennett, Tony (1992a) 'Putting Policy into Cultural Studies', in Grossberg, L. *et al.*, *Cultural Studies*, London: Routledge.

Bennett, Tony, (1992b) 'Useful Culture', *Cultural Studies*, Vol. 6, No. 3.

Bennett, Tony (1995) 'The Multiplication of Culture's Utility', *Critical Inquiry*, 21 (Summer).

Bourdieu, P. (1984) *Distinction: A Social Critique of the Judgement of Taste*, London: Routledge.

Frith, Simon, and Savage, J. (1993) 'Pearls and Swine: The Intellectuals and the Mass Media', *New Left Review*, No. 198.

Hall, Stuart (1981) 'Notes on Deconstructing "the Popular"', in Samuel, R. (ed.) *People's History and Socialist Theory*, London: Routledge & Kegan Paul.

Hall, S. (1992a) 'Cultural Studies and Its Theoretical Legacies', in Grossberg, L., Nelson, C., and Treichler, P. (eds.) *Cultural Studies*, London: Routledge.

Hall, S (1992b) 'What Is This "Black" in Black Popular Culture?', in Dent, G. (ed.) *Black Popular Culture*, New York: Bay Press.

Hall, S. (1993) 'For Allon White, Metaphors of Transformation', in White, A. (ed.) *Carnival, Hysteria and Writing*, Oxford: Clarendon Press.

Hall, S., and Jefferson, T., eds. (1976) *Resistance through Rituals*, Birmingham: Hutchinson.

Hall, S., Crichter, C., Jefferson, T., Clarke, J., and Roberts, B. (1978) *Policing the Crisis*, London: Macmillan.

Hunter, I. (1993) 'Subjectivity and Government', *Economy and Society*, Vol. 22, No. 1.

Laclau, Ernesto, and Mouffe, Chantal (1985) *Hegemony and Socialist Strategy*, London: Verso.

McGuigan, J. (1992) *Cultural Populism*, London: Routledge.

Nixon, S. (forthcoming) *Creative Cultures: Gender and Creativity at Work in Advertising*, London: Sage.

O'Malley, Pat, Weir, Lorna, and Shearing, Clifford (1997) 'Governmentality, Criticism, Politics', *Economy and Society*, Vol. 26, No. 4.

O'Shea, Alan, and Schwarz, Bill (1987) 'Reconsidering Popular Culture', *Screen*, Vol. 28, No. 3.

Schwarz, B. (1989) 'Popular Culture: The Long March', *Cultural Studies*, Vol. 3, No. 2.

Stallybrass, P., and White, A. (1986) *The Politics and Poetics of Transgression*, London: Methuen.

23

Matters of Selfesteem

Flemming Røgilds

It's the diversity of
the material that makes it so
interesting to be human it's the
diversity of human interactions and
encounters that makes words as death destiny and disaster
so attractive when bodies as well as the emotions that bind us together matter
                                                                    so what constitutes
the field of ethnic and racial studies
the ethnic cleansing in the former Yugoslavia or the racial harassment
on the council estates in London where gangs of youth strive for a white utopia
using machetes and harpoon guns to protect their area against what they term aliens
there certainly is a need for the rehabilitation of politics there might even be a need of
letting the concept of race go demythologizing the history of raciology forcing our
minds to perceive the world in a complete new manner so that the trope trope
trope of race in the age of globalization is placed in jeopardy because
they know where you live and it takes two to tango and having said
that there are plenty of racisms plenty of anti-racisms around
in fact there's an overproduction of both (in fact also
a lack of production of humans) so let's take a
look at words like blackness positive black
identity black separatism and black
nationalism as well as blacks and
whites not being either black
or white enough but
helplessly in
search of
a more
open
        definition of what it means
to be on the other side of what used to be a border
fighting every kind of policing every kind of reference to authenticity & nationality
creating a new space for openended questions
not caring for the answer whether I am
black white or inbetween because
my heart tickles just the way

yours do my skin is layered
with the same pain and
anguish the same joy
and embarrassment
when love is just
about to fall
into
the
    lipservice of destined raciologies
that's what matters when the dark prince raises the necessary question which
way is home if you want to get beyond the trap of shortcomings
not being human enough or???

24

Becoming Postcolonial

Bill Schwarz

When the French were expelled from Indochina in 1954 Stuart Hall and his West Indian friends at Oxford cooked 'a massive celebration dinner'. Here indeed was a momentous defeat for the colonial order. And in those early days in England it was colonialism that touched Stuart Hall most deeply. 'Up until 1954, I was saturated in West Indian expatriate politics. Most of my friends were expatriates, and went back to play a role in Jamaica, Trinidad, Barbados, Guyana. We were passionate about the colonial question'.[1] West Indian federation and independence were in the air. The final dramas of British rule were being played out. Postcolonialism, in the idiom of our own times, was present in Stuart Hall's intellectual and political life from the start.

I like this idea of the anti-colonial celebration dinner. In my imagination it's a dinner that could rank with Mrs Ramsay's in *To the Lighthouse*, when (in the Oxford case) the larger arena of empire was becoming 'already the past'. But unfortunately this is too fanciful, for it obscures historical realities that need to be held clearly in sight. If the French were dispatched from Indochina in 1954, it was not long before the US moved in. The process of becoming postcolonial can boast its celebratory occasions. But its histories are necessarily more complex. Becoming postcolonial is not only a protracted, uneven transformation, pitting colony against metropolis; it also has its subjective dimensions, in which that which is 'already the past' and that which is the present never quite seem to stay in place.

We also need to recollect the specificity of the West Indian experience. This was the time when the black immigrants from the Caribbean, of whom Stuart Hall was one, came to Britain, and indeed when many came to stay. This dual process – decolonization and immigration – had a profound impact on domestic Britain, whose consequences we are only slowly beginning to see. It seems perfectly proper to highlight the peculiarities of West Indians at this moment, doubly positioned inside and out, simultaneously present in colony and metropolis, and agents of a history that required the dismantling of the given structures of actually existing colonial England. The proximity of the formal culture of the Caribbean – in language, religion, schooling, sport – to that of the metropolis, combined with a distinctively hybrid vernacular culture, ensured that the final moments of the relations between centre and colony were peculiarly overdetermined, not least in Britain itself. In becoming postcolonial (if this is indeed what has occurred) Britons owe much to the West Indian diaspora: not merely for effecting the formal transition in which political authority shifted from metropolis to former colonies, but also for creating the intellectual means by which this complex, far-reaching history – what happened, amongst other things, to the British themselves – can be understood.

The full dimensions of this postcolonial narrative have yet to be written. It is a story not only of talented individuals, but also of particular movements of people, and of corresponding movements of thought. As the memoirs and imaginative fiction testify, the moment of arrival in Britain for the West Indian immigrant was a moment of intense dislocation, when perceived realities turned in on themselves. This was a collective, social experience of subjective crisis – described most recently by Mary Chamberlain as a shared 'cognitive dissonance', in which inherited systems of thought simply could no longer map the new realities with which they were confronted.[2] But out of this crisis – at once psychic and political – new ways of being could be imagined, which ultimately were to serve white Britons as much as black West Indians.

Yet from the perspective of the metropolis it can sometimes seem as if West Indians arrived in Britain bearing *only* loyalty to the crown and fascination for all the flummery of imperial England. In reality, they came from societies that were already well advanced in the formal and informal prerequisites of breaking with colonialism. Stuart Hall describes his own formation as classically 'colonial', but demonstrates at the same time that his own intellectual and political world in Jamaica, and that of his friends, prefigured the formalities of postcolonialism. 'You can see that this formation – learning the whole destructive colonized experience – prepared me for England.'[3] How Stuart Hall reconstructs this 'destructive colonized experience' in his own life is through a succession of family tragedies and battles, which at first sight might appear to bear little relation to the larger narratives of decolonization. The subjective journeys of breaking free from inherited systems of thought could occur in many different locales, in many different registers, and in many displacements.

Stuart Hall is distinctive in thinking postcolonialism in its broadest ramifications. He is always careful to attend to its inner, subjective forms. Talking of the turmoil of his own family life in Kingston, he notes:

> From then on, I could never understand why people think these structural questions were not connected to the psychic, with emotions and identifications and feelings because, for me, those structures are things you live . . . they have real structural properties, they break you, they destroy you.[4]

He's distinctive too in thinking how the centring of vernacular or popular forms marks the moment when 'the world begins to be decolonized'.[5] In spirit, this is far removed from much of what passes today in the guise of postcolonial theory: it carries with it a profound, encompassing sense of *emancipation*.

My own interest in these matters lies in the various pressures, from both inside and outside the metropolis, that have decolonized the parochial world of the domestic British. The West Indian dimension plays a critical part in this larger history. This is a story that stretches back before the arrival of *Windrush* in 1948. I consider here C.L.R. James, and reflect upon one crisis in his own political and subjective life in which he struggled to resolve some of these larger issues. James remains a captivating figure. Irresistibly he was drawn to the world-historical and to theory in seven-league boots, an Odyssean figure always on the point of discovering a new universal in which the future of world history would be embodied. But at the same time he also anticipated a politics a deal more modest, everyday and deconstructive in inclination, in which the ambivalences of his own subjective life broke through. One can see, I think, the drama of this struggle taking place in the more intimate of his writings.

A little while ago I interviewed Stuart Hall for *History Workshop Journal* about C.L.R. James's *The Black Jacobins*. We talked in his kitchen, with all the usual domestic bustle of people coming and going, the phone ringing. There is no reason to think James happened to be prominent in Hall's mind on that particular day. News passed back and forth about mutual friends. The fate of the garden, clearly, was pressing, the object of a new-found passion. No doubt a dozen or more intellectual projects, far removed from James and the 1930s, were more active in his imagination. And yet, within the shortest time, he was talking with ever greater engagement about James: the timbre of Hall's voice – now playful and ironic, now pressing home a point – would rise in crescendo, filling the kitchen with his enthusiasm. It wasn't just that he seemed to know everything there was to know about James: he talked, from inside this history, of a shared predicament, and of shared privileges too. In elaborating his account of C.L.R. James, he was invoking memories of the West Indian moment of decolonization, his as well as James's, which – remote as they may seem from our present – still have the power to resonate.

James – didactic, finger wagging with all the imperturbable confidence of a Victorian upbringing – believed, as Stuart Hall put it, that the double consciousness of the Caribbean was not a burden, but a gift.[6] In London in January 1981, on the eve of a succession of angry inner-city rebellions, he told an audience: 'The first thing I want you to get out of your mind is that you are not visitors here ... you belong here. You are living here, part of English society.' As he went on to explain, this was not to cancel a diasporic identity with the conventional formulas of a national culture. He was, rather, connecting the given realities of location with the radicalism of the historic experience of the black Atlantic, imagining an indigenous black population propelling England into a future that otherwise would have remained unimaginable. The theme underlying the lecture suggests that it is only the black presence that allows the formerly imperial nation fully to see itself, and thereby (in his terms) to realize its own modernity. In its own way, this is a classic Hegelian formulation elegantly turned inside out – the slave finally settling accounts with the master, forced by a profane history to do his job for him and imagine a better future for humanity at large.[7]

Perhaps the choreographed elegance of this view is too abstract, too distracted from the raw chaos in which quite contrary pressures intervene. Even so, it carries a certain truth. And it allows us to place Stuart Hall's lifelong engagements with the imperatives of English civilization in a deeper history. I find myself, sometimes unexpectedly, looping back to this West Indian moment of the fifties and sixties, *seeing* a postcolonialism happening – as a historical process – and seeing too the transformation in the symbolic and cognitive forms of England, a history racked by the full theatre of repressions and traumas, amnesia and displacements. And sometimes, confronted by these extraordinary developments, I enter into conversation with an imaginary Stuart Hall, quizzing him with unbecoming zeal about *what it was like*. His eyes flash with humour, the gentle laugh rolls and seems almost – in this virtual scenario – to touch me: but wisdom keeps its own counsel, and history evades once more (as ultimately it must) the questioner from the present. Such are the tantalizing engagements of historical enquiry. Patently, this is a mute dialogue with its own fair share of projections. But I can use this more formal occasion, not exactly to pursue my own private reveries, but to continue a public conversation. I can do this, at one remove, by looking back at C.L.R. James. There is an episode which for long has intrigued me. It may appear at first

sight, perhaps, to be tangential to the themes I've outlined here. But
I doubt that it is.

When the English cricket season drew to its close in the late summer
of 1938, James set off for the USA, intending to return to Britain in
time for the opening of the next season. He had political work to do
for his section of the Fourth International, to which he was then
dedicated. He went as a political militant, planning from the outset (it
would seem) to pay a visit to Trotsky, who was living out his multiple
exile in Coyoacán. Maybe he made the trip to recover from a love affair
that had run aground; maybe his British comrades had sent him in
order to 'straighten him out', to rid him of heresies that, in the 1990s,
pass the eye of the innocent reader unnoticed; or maybe both motives
were at work.[8] By April 1939 he was in Los Angeles, *en route* to
Coyoacán, and billed to speak in a black church on 'The Negro
Question'. There he sighted for the first time a young white woman,
Constance Webb, eighteen years old, an aspiring model, poet, actress
and dancer, and already married. Perhaps Webb, in a red coat, asked a
question from the floor; or perhaps James visited the apartment of
some comrades after the meeting, and she was awoken, and when
getting up she put on a red dressing gown. Memories differ. Yet it is
clear he fell for her. He travelled on to Coyoacán, talked at length with
the Old Man, and famously disputed with him the political significance
of black self-activity and of sport. On his return, sailing from Veracruz
to New Orleans and cut adrift from the incessant demands of his
political life, he wrote Webb long, seemingly hallucinogenic letters,
funny and lyrical, his own interior reveries.

By December 1939 he was back in New York, the locale in which all
his political commitments were compressed. He had travelled through
the South. And he had, by virtue of his visa having expired, become
that peculiarly modern figure, 'an illegal'. In New York his own political groupuscule existed as a minority faction inside a party that itself
had split from its majority rival: the Johnson–Forest tendency con-
cocted a firebrand, cocksure, high-voltage Marxism which was lived as
much as it was theorized. Through it, James made common cause with
Raya Dunayevskaya and Grace Lee, two extraordinary women who –
respectively – took on the labour of recasting economic thought and
philosophy. There were, maybe, some seventy comrades in all,
throughout the US. (A while later they made contact with Cornelius
Castoriadis in Paris, a contact which, when James returned to England,
required various day trips to Boulogne to effect a rendezvous; but in
the forties they found him a little ultra-leftist.) This tiny group determined to anticipate the intellectual life that socialist civilization would

bring. It was a political duty to see Robeson's *Othello* on Broadway, and it was assumed afterwards that discussion would be informed and energetic.

In April 1940 James met briefly with Webb on a quick political excursion to Los Angeles. Her previous husband was no longer around, and she was with a man, Eddie Keller, whom James believed to be 'a dismal failure'. A few months later he received a letter and the change of name alerted him to the fact that the two had married. James replied:

> But, my dear Constance, this noble Bolshevik whom a million Nazis could not demoralize (that's the way I feel at any rate) is quite often very sick and tired at all the difficulties the revolution places in the way of one's private life. Sometimes I feel like a motherless child a long way from home.[9]

He wrote a short letter on 21 August after hearing of the death of Trotsky, and then (on 1 October) a note explaining that he was about to go into hospital for an operation. At this point the correspondence stopped for three years.

In August 1943 he writes to her again. He describes his illness of late 1940, and the moment in 1942 when he collapsed in the street from a perforated ulcer. He insists: 'I have at last got hold of Marxism'.[10] And he goes on to tell of the fact that, as a result of his illness combined with his loss of Webb, he started going to the movies. As he put this subsequently: 'I have discovered why I went to the movies so often the last two or three years. Somewhere, somehow I found them some substitute for you. I would like to see what goes on in a man's mind really'.[11] And through the letters we can see him enjoying the modest pleasures of modern life – getting an early supper of meatballs, for example, to catch the 6.15 showing of Rita Hayworth in *Cover Girl*. 'And me?' he asked in reopening their correspondence:

> I am much the same. I have aged a little – grayer in the temples, a little thinner, not much, a little more serious, a few lines in my face, but since I have come here they have almost disappeared; my hands are more nervous than before, but I am much the same, quieter externally, more explosive inside; and very very sure of what I am doing politically – of myself as a person, doubtful and more than a little worried as to my future. You see. There it is.[12]

The correspondence picked up again. Webb's reply is lost: but it prompted James to write:

> Your letter was a whirlwind, a complete body-blow.[13]

It seems as if she had complained to him about the confinement and disappointments of her life. But things didn't work out as James had hoped. She divorced Keller only to become engaged to Jack Gilford, a minor Hollywood star, fellow-traveller, and future Oscar nominee (for his part in *Catch-22*). This relationship lasted a year or so. In May 1944, she broke with Gilford, moved to New York, and spent that spring and summer acting in *The Seagull* in Connecticut – playing, presumably, the part of Nina. Through all this time James's frustrations intensified. On his forty-fourth birthday he wrote to her, compiling a full roster of his rivals, listing their vices and virtues, but drawing the line at her dalliance with a West Point cadet. Shortly after, he destroyed all her letters and photos.

In 1946, seven lean and lonely years after his first overtures to her, a new intimacy emerged between them, sparked, it seems, by Webb's decision to write an essay on Richard Wright. James subsequently arranged a mail-order divorce from his wife Juanita, who had remained in Trinidad when he had first sailed to Europe. ('She lives in the West Indies, is a stenographer, and is not interested in the World Revolution.'[14]) He and Webb married. In her words:

> Nello and I were married by a justice of the peace in New Jersey with two bigoted policemen as witnesses. They almost dared us to kiss after the ceremony and became red in the face with anger when we did so. Neither of us really wanted to exhibit our personal feelings, simply wanted to get away as quickly as possible. But neither could we allow such blatant and rampant bigotry to go unnoticed. In some fear and trembling we embraced, brushed our mouths together quickly, and hurried out of sight. Our fear was real, not imagined. As far away as Greenwich Village, a most bohemian liberal area, black and white couples were being attacked and beaten, often dragged from restaurants. And New Jersey was notorious for its hatred of blacks, particularly when they coupled with whites.[15]

Matrimony did little to still the turbulence of their relationship. In the autumn of 1947 a further massive crisis occurred, evident in a flurry of Western Union telegrams, which culminated in Constance's departure and James's incoherent and chaotic notes alluding to the collapse. Dunayevskaya and Lee appear to have figured in the break-up, mutual passions and anxieties encoded in the appropriate formulas of the Bolshevik cadre. A further reconciliation in the following year heralded the possibility of a shared future. The mail-order divorce from Juanita failed to convince the US authorities. In August 1948 James decamped to Reno in order to accomplish in Nevada what he had failed to secure by mail from Mexico. On the journey from Veracruz he had found himself suspended from the everyday imperatives of the political activist: in the Nevada desert something similar occurred, the biblical echoes in James's prose again alluding to its mythic dimensions. Removed from the glitz of New York, the clarity of the light was pronounced: it was as if the air itself had thinned. He took a job as a labourer at Pyramid Lake Ranch. After the physical labour, in the afternoons and evenings, his intellectual work was ferocious. He translated Daniel Guérin's history of the French Revolution. He immersed himself in Racine and classical French tragedy. He drafted ten thousand words a day of his *Notes on Dialectics*, designed as a discussion document for the militants of the Johnson–Forest tendency, and dispatched to the cells of Marxist workers in Detroit. He wrote like a man possessed. And on his trips to Reno he systematically played the machines, a true obsessive.

The divorce from Juanita was finalized. He and Constance married again. Their son was born. Early in 1952 she left him for the last time. James wrote to his friend Freddie Paine: 'You thought it would be easy to get her back. Freddie that will be the most difficult thing in the world. But that is what I want. We shall see.'[16] Illness took over his body. The FBI closed in. In 1953 James was arrested, interned, and deported, back to England.

Such, in sum, comprised the contours of their relationship – its bare bones, its breaks and reconciliations. It is, one might suppose, remarkable less for its dramas than for its ordinariness. But James's letters reveal an interior which can barely be glimpsed from the public writings. Not only do the letters to Webb throw into relief his own crisis: they cut back and forth between his own subjective turbulence, on the one hand, and, on the other, the crisis in his capacity to imagine an appropriate politics. Or, to be more accurate about this, in his own mind these were one and the same thing, a conviction that makes him simultaneously compelling and unnerving.

Writing was James's forte. The correspondence was peculiarly his terrain. In July 1944, when both he and Webb were living in New York, his letters comprised some thirty thousand words. From the Gulf of Mexico in 1939 he declared to her: 'Write him 3 pages and he writes back 23'.[17] Another letter opens: 'This is going to be a long letter. It will last a few days, I think.' One of the early letters of July 1944 announces: 'I shall order a quire of paper or a ream. I don't know which but the larger one. I shall also order meals for a month or two. There shall be relays of post-men at this end and yours. And after a period of training I shall begin to write. God! How I shall write.'[18] He adopted the guise of father, uncle, teacher, master. The imperative dominates his side of the correspondence, from the second sentence of his very first letter. She was to be his protégée, as he imagined Grace and Raya to have been, and as – at different moments – were 'Bill' and 'Francis' (Eric Williams and Nkrumah). The boundaries between peremptory instruction and self-irony were not always easy to disentangle. Writing from this position of purported authority, he was in the habit of splitting Constance his correspondent into two fantasized figures: Monica (the virgin, after Leonardo), and – strikingly unimaginative – Frosty.

Yet he was also conscious of how he was positioning himself, at least at moments. He saw himself also as a split being – split between revolutionary politics and the intimacies of the interior life; between Europe and America; between black and white. Often he depicted his own subjective life as one representative of an older historical forma-tion, in contrast to Webb, whom he increasingly believed to be repre-sentative of a feminized future. At many poignant instances he became aware not only of his own vulnerabilities but also of his lack of a voice – for all his unrivalled public charisma – that could articulate his inner self. He knew well enough his capacity to project his desires onto her: in one of his very first letters he had confided: 'You know the tricks one's desires play on us.'[19]

These ambivalences were accentuated by his projections of Webb as a social being, and suggest too how he imagined history to work. For all his firebrand Marxism, and notwithstanding the fact that he lived on the front line of the emergent Cold War, James loved the United States. He loved hamburgers and milk shakes and Cokes and subways and the movies. He was, like many visitors to the USA, entranced by the possibilities of living modern life at its sharpest tempo. And this potentiality he projected through the image of Monica, the idealized projection of an emancipated future. Time and again he returned to this connection. She – Constance/Monica – became in his mind the eroticized fusion of both the futuristic possibilities of an Americanized mass culture *and* the social or historic possibilities represented by the socialist breakthrough of 1917, the genetic carrier of a new universalism.

'But you have become for me a symbol', he wrote in August 1944. 'Does this add to your burdens? Take it in your stride.'[20] 'You are to me an ambassador of American civilization – and you don't know it.'[21] This was, for James, explicitly a feminized civilization. There is much on shopping, women's clothes and fashion. He has his line on how Ginger Rogers looks in a cocktail dress. Like any moviegoer, he knows the female stars. He fantasizes about shopping for clothes for Con-stance, with a palpable narcissism slipping through the confines of his prose. But also, this being James, he determined to integrate this figure with that of the – unconscious – inheritor of the historical advances of 1917. A letter of July 1944 shows this movement.

You and your particular style I have admired from the very first moment I saw you. You are young and gay and American, without the English or continental desire to 'waltz', but ready to 'cut a rug' instead. I love it. Nowhere in the whole world could anything like you appear but in America of the post-war, and I am pretty certain you are a product of the West.

He goes on:

I belong to the twentieth century. I have a comprehensive view of life. I become more and more interested in all aspects of life, as in our modern society all aspects of life become more closely interrelated. I can only completely love someone on whom and with whom I can exercise all my powers, and that means someone who is such that she continuously stimulates me by her own manifold gifts and responses to life.... Now ... you were born and grew up after the Russian Revolution. Do you know what this means? The mental world in which you grew up as a child was the widest and freest the world has ever known. The greatest group of men the bourgeois world has ever known were Ricardo, Goethe, Shelley, Beethoven, Hegel and that group. They lived in a world which had been illuminated by the French Revolution. Think of all the things you have studied and read and talked about from early, what you were doing, at 15 for instance. But, unlike Europeans, you did it without fear, without perpetual anxiety, even without hunger, i.e., without these things being a major and permanent part of the society around you.[22]

The world-spirit – humanity conscious of itself, of history – converges with everyday life and mass culture, and takes living form in Constance Webb.

James consciously attempted to refashion his own self too, integrating what manifestly remained unintegrated, and to invent for himself an inner voice that would be an extension of his public and political voice. Critical in this – and representing an important moment in twentieth-century Marxism – was his attempt to imagine a communism that would derive, not from sacrifice and the incessant disciplining of the self (in the cause of History), but from the expansion of subjectivity, the expansion of the self. There is even the occasional suggestion that James's defences against Freud might be lifted. ('L.T. [Trotsky] was always reading Freud. It is a pity we do not know what his ideas were. I suppose he dared not write them down.'[23]) The quest for this new self went hand in hand with his quest for Webb, the two inextricably fused in his own imagination. Characteristically, James tried to write himself out of the crisis. This is what happened at Reno, in his rethinking of Hegel and in his *Notes on Dialectics*. On 7 October 1947 he wrote to Webb:

This is the man who loves you. I took up the dialectic five years ago. I knew a lot of things before and I was able to master it. I know a lot of things about loving you. I am only just beginning to apply them. I feel all sorts of new powers, freedoms, etc., surging in me. You released so many of my constrictions. What are you going to do? I am bursting all over with love for you. Who, who can give you anything like the love I have – any of those third-rate men? They haven't as much in all of them as I have in my little-finger. I'll make you feel like a queen of a tournament every hour of the day. We will *live*. This is our new world – where there is no distinction between political and personal any more. I would wash the dishes and sweep the floor so as to have you always with me, literally that. 50%. I want it that way. You make me twice as strong, my work will be easy, yours too – both of us sharing everything and making love every second of the day.[24]

From the ranch in Nevada, while he was writing on the dialectic, he declared:

And all the time, consciously, sometimes unconsciously, I am thinking of you. Page after page on the dialectic. . . . I am working on two planes – it and us. . . . But I feel it all one place – when I go to Reno and play the machine. I seem to have no control. But I am getting that in hand at last.[25]

But this proved an impossible route. James wrote himself into a metaphysical corner. By attempting to effect this reconciliation of opposites through Hegel, he dissolved the concrete realities of *his* everyday into the abstractions of a teleological history. Every aspect of modern life was to fall under his scrutiny. Raya would do the work on economics, Grace on philosophy; Constance was to be recruited to take on the aesthetic, and urged to *terrorize* T.S. Eliot and the *Partisan Review*. James himself would weave it all together, as the master builder.

I had something on my mind. It expressed itself as a problem I have to solve. What exactly was the relation of Kant and his synthetic logic . . . to his age? For days it is on my mind and I cannot forget it. *It is the last link in the chain.* I'll get it, but it's *tough*.[26]

His ferocious intellectual labours in the desert in Nevada were evidence as much of him spinning out of control as of fruitful reflection. He was losing the plot – as much as he was losing Webb – and the consequences can be seen in his *Notes on Dialectics*.

James becomes interesting again when he begins to retreat from, or unlearn, this desperate version of a high Hegelianism. The single work he completed on American civilization was his study of Melville – *Mariners, Renegades and Castaways* – written while he was interned. In it is both a work of allegory – history becomes reduced to allegory – and a work of repression, in which the broken insights of the forties appear, but are pressed into the service of the overarching allegorical requirements of the book's narrative. Clearly, in Ahab lie the 'demons' (James's word) of James's own inner conflicts: for it was Ahab, James insisted, who 'lived entirely in abstractions'.[27]

And yet he was always conscious of his own predicament. Fredric Warburg, his publisher in Britain, believed that 'Excess, perhaps, was James' crime, an excess of words whose relevance to the contemporary tragedy was less than he supposed.'[28] Maybe so. But James was absolutely convinced that tragedy was what history was about, and that the millions of individual destinies of the twentieth century were given shape by the tragic dramas of history. Tragedy, for James, constituted the highest form of human expression, both in historic actuality and in its imaginative representations. 'Tragedy shows the will of man at its most indomitable scope . . .'[29] Oedipus, Lear, Ahab . . . and Toussaint L'Ouverture. The inner voice he sought was the tragic voice, one that could speak in fullest recognition of the universal task of human self-realization and its historical impediments. At times, James could position himself in the vanguard of this self-conscious history, even in his most intimate moments.

> When I think of some air-force officer kissing you it seems to me a sacrilege and a waste. It has taken me years of hard work and life and experience in many countries and in a great intellectual and social tradition to appreciate you and to love you as you should be loved, to love you as you need to be loved, as you must be loved if you are to be what you have in you to be.[30]

On other occasions, though, the tragic hero became a more remote and sadder figure:

> And the last seven years I believe I have been the loneliest man in the world; our ideas and plans and perspectives are so big, our work, our concrete sphere is so small. It is a terrible, a breaking strain upon the personality. We shall share it.[31]

In this recounting of James's letters to Constance Webb there have been many maybes, perhapses and 'it seems'. It is necessarily tentative. The story comprises no more than a cameo, speaking for itself. Or – perhaps – this is precisely what it cannot do: speak for itself. There are too many silences. More certain is the fact that James returned to England in 1953, and threw himself into that West Indian moment of independence and federation, improvising day by day how the essentials of a postcolonial politics might be imagined. Reading *Beyond A Boundary*, or the lectures, essays and interviews of the subsequent period, in which white England was confronted and a new politics cohered, the compacted crises of Reno – psychic, philosophical, political – remain invisible on the surface of the texts. But this is not to suppose that they weren't formative.

After he had died in 1989, Channel 4 in Britain broadcast a discussion about his life, to which Stuart Hall contributed. When asked to sum up (in some forty seconds) James's achievements, Hall chose to emphasize his world-historical aspect: 'He is one of the few world-historical figures I have ever been privileged to meet.' When Hall and I talked about James for *History Workshop Journal* I asked him about this. I can still hear the rhythms and cadences of his reply. 'The things that he was pulled to are indeed the moments that anybody who's interested in the history of modernity would at some point in their lives have read and studied. It's not that he was an actor in all these spheres. You could say, however, that if your curriculum was to know about the things which James knew about, you would come out of that process knowing about the world, understanding the modern world. You would have taken, eaten, broken bread with the dramas . . . that have made the modern world. So what do you call someone like that other than world-historical . . . '[32]

James's burial in Trinidad was testament to him as hero, the Odyssean hero returned. In its early moments the funeral was a public event, with many speeches and much processing. And yet it caught, too, the ambivalence. He was finally carried down the main street in Tunapuna by a relaxed cortège comprised of representatives of the Oil Workers' Union, who sported sparkling white gloves and nifty sweatshirts. By this stage of events, there was neither a band nor further formalities. The dust from the road rose silently into the air. And, interrupting the usual transactions of the day, curious faces looked out at the scene from the hairdresser's and the roti stalls.

Notes

1. Stuart Hall, 'The Formation of a Diasporic Intellectual', in David Morley and Kuan-Hsing Chen, eds., *Stuart Hall: Critical Dialogues*, London: Routledge, 1996, p. 492.

2. Mary Chamberlain, *Narratives of Exile and Return*, London: Macmillan, 1997.

3. Hall, 'Formation of a Diasporic Intellectual', p. 489.

4. Hall, 'Formation of a Diasporic Intellectual', p. 488.

5. Stuart Hall, 'Old and New Identities, Old and New Ethnicities', in Anthony D. King ed., *Culture, Globalization and the World-System*, London: Macmillan, 1991, p. 18; and see too Stuart Hall, 'What Is This "Black" in Black Popular Culture?', in *Stuart Hall: Critical Dialogues*.

6. Stuart Hall, 'Breaking Bread with History: C.L.R. James and *The Black Jacobins*', *History Workshop Journal*, 46, 1998, p. 24.

7. C.L.R. James, *80th Birthday Lectures*, London, Race Today, 1981, p. 48. I am drawing here from my own 'Black Metropolis, White England' in Mica Nava and Alan O'Shea, eds., *Modern Times: Reflections on a Century of English Modernity*, London, Routledge, 1996.

8. For an overall discussion, see Scott McLemee and Paul Le Blanc, eds., *C.L.R. James and Revolutionary Marxism: Selected Writings of C.L.R. James, 1939–1949*, New Jersey, Humanities Press, 1994.

9. C.L.R. James, *Special Delivery: The Letters of C.L.R. James to Constance Webb, 1939–1948*, Oxford, Blackwell, 1996, p. 66.

10. *Special Delivery*, p. 71.

11. *Special Delivery*, p. 276.

12. *Special Delivery*, p. 71.

13. *Special Delivery*, p. 71.

14. Selwyn R. Cudjoe, '"As Ever Darling, All My Love, Nello": The Love Letters of C.L.R. James', in Selwyn R. Cudjoe and William E. Cain, eds., *C.L.R. James: His Intellectual Legacies*, Amherst, University of Massachusetts Press, 1995, p. 232.

15. Cudjoe, 'The Love Letters', p. 232.

16. Cudjoe, 'The Love Letters', p. 238.

17. *Special Delivery*, p. 46.

18. *Special Delivery*, pp. 228 and 141.

19. *Special Delivery*, p. 55.

20. *Special Delivery*, p. 174.

21. *Special Delivery*, p. 183.

22. *Special Delivery*, pp. 132–3.

23. *Special Delivery*, p. 271.

24. *Special Delivery*, p. 298.

25. *Special Delivery*, p. 359.

26. Cudjoe, 'The Love Letters', p. 234.

27. C.L.R. James, *Mariners, Renegades and Castaways: The Story of Herman Melville and the World We Live In*, Detroit, Bewick, 1978, p. 9.

28. Cudjoe, 'The Love Letters', p. 219.

29. James, *Mariners, Renegades and Castaways*, p. 70.

30. *Special Delivery*, p. 256.

31. *Special Delivery*, p. 352.

32. Hall, 'Breaking Bread with History', p. 30.

25

The Permanence of Pluralism

David Scott

Puor piipl fed-op
If wi ongri agen yu a go si wi nyyn
Bounty Killer, 'Any Time', 1998

There is scarcely a postcolonial society today that is not in fundamental crisis. The specific features of this crisis are, of course, very varied. Too many cultures and too many histories are involved for it to be otherwise. There are crises of personal and collective security emanating from forms of violence (ethnic, party-political, criminal); there are crises of governance as a consequence of loss of legitimacy on the part of the state; there are crises of civility arising from the dissolution of the structures of the bourgeois public sphere; there are crises of economic survival that are the result of the ravages of structural adjustment programmes, and so on. But what these crises share – in places as distant and distinct from each other as, say, Sri Lanka and Jamaica – is the pervasive sense of a breakdown not merely in a few discrete areas of development policy or constitutional arrangement or political organization, but of the modern nation-state project as a whole. What is in crisis, in other words, is not simply the coherence or otherwise of rival ideological positions, but the conceptual and institutional bases themselves upon which the secular–modern project of building 'new nations' was undertaken and sustained.

To use an iconic shorthand, it is the Bandung project *as such* that is now in crisis.[1] It is no longer clear that the *horizon* of Bandung (whether in its liberal or radical forms) can – or indeed *ought* to – continue to frame the ways in which we think critically about the present, reconstruct the past, and imagine possible futures. For this reason the *demand* in the cognitive–political present cannot be formulated in the old languages of emancipation. It is no longer clear where such emancipation is supposed to lead us. Clichés about freedom and democracy sound hollow precisely because what is at stake in the contemporary crisis in the postcolonial world is the very horizon of hopes embodied in the secular concepts and institutions of political modernity itself. This is why thinking through the current impasse cannot simply be a matter of choosing from among available options. This would be to assume that the questions in relation to which these options emerged as options *as such* are themselves stable and unchanging. And it is *this* that can no longer be taken for granted. The form of the contemporary problem, in other words, is not whether to choose better answers, but whether the *questions* that defined the anti-colonial and nationalist projects ought to continue to define our postcolonial present. Theorizing the present demands a kind of investigation that makes the register of these constitutive questions visible.

Stuart Hall's mode of intellectual practice is, in many ways, an exemplification of just such a practice of theorizing. For one way of describing a 'conjuncture' (one of the crucial categories of his thought) is precisely as a contingent historical moment defined by the *reorganization* of an existing configuration of questions and answers, the reorganization of an existing cognitive–political problem-space. A conjuncture is the outcome of an historical interruption and *reconfiguration* of an always-already-configured field of argument and its determinate discursive positions. For Hall, therefore, to grasp a particular conjuncture it cannot be enough to enquire whether a new answer (a new proposition) can be arrived at; one must also seek to understand whether in fact a new *question* has been posed. It will be evident, then, that a conjuncture is not merely a category in a social–historical reconstruction; it is a category in a *strategic intervention*. For what is important in the theorization of any conjuncture is not only whether it is possible to identify the question to which the proposition addresses itself as an answer, but whether that question *continues* to be a question worth having answers to.[2] This is the sense in which Stuart Hall is, preeminently, a theorist of the present.

The Present as a New Conjuncture

Mid-morning on Wednesday, 23 September 1998, Donald Phipps, popularly known as 'Zeeks', was arrested and taken into police custody at Kingston's Central Police Station. He had been wanted for questioning in connection with alleged cases of attempted murder, wounding with intent, and possession of an illegal firearm. As news of Zeeks's arrest spread (revved up by rumours that in the process he had been shot by the police) outraged citizens blocked off streets in the heart of downtown Kingston with tyres, old cars, refrigerators, and whatever else they could lay their hands on, and set them afire. Over 1,000 angry, placard-bearing protesters converged on the walled police station where Zeeks was being held, shouting 'Justice for Zeeks!' and demanding his immediate release. Some of the hastily prepared placards bore ominous threats: 'No Zeeks, no peace!'; 'If no Zeeks, no school, no bus, and no store open!' In others there was a note of desperation: 'No Zeeks, no business for us'; 'Without Zeeks no life in the west.' Store owners and business people were urged to close their establishments and send their employees home, and a general advisory against travelling into the city was issued. The police in the meantime were hurriedly being reinforced by truckloads of heavily armed soldiers; but it was obvious to everyone that the security forces had lost control of the city. The pre-eminent sign of this was that police yielded to the people's demand to *see* their Zeeks, who was then brought out onto a balcony from which he addressed his supporters, appealing to them for calm. The rioting and protesting continued for two days, leaving at least one person dead from gunshot wounds, several people injured, and the commercial life of the old city crippled.

Needless to say, Jamaica's governing elite was thrown into a state of utter panic. There was a sense both of indignation and of horror. As one newspaper editorialized, the 'violence and mob rule' were an indication of the 'impotence' of the security forces and the 'general lack of leadership in the country'. The newspaper urged the government to act quickly and decisively before it was too late, before 'we slip into greater anarchy and societal decay'.[3] That the so-called lawless had taken over the streets of the capital city, had even disabled and destroyed an armoured car, was one thing; but that the state had been so brazenly obliged to surrender its authority to the will of an ungovernable crowd was, as the editor went on, 'chillingly frightening'. Indeed, it was an omen. It was one more sign that a whole order of politics and society that this elite had been the principal architects of was coming rapidly, calamitously, to an end.

Zeeks is what is known in Jamaican political parlance as an 'area leader', a euphemism that basically means that he is formally recognized by the political parties as someone responsible for the mobilization of votes at election time, and the distribution of work (when there is work to be had). On the streets, however, Zeeks is known as a 'don' or, more colloquially and affectionately, a 'dads'.[4] He looks after people in his community; he is their provider, their benefactor, their protector, the keeper of the peace, the dispenser of justice. Zeeks is the don of the community of Matthews Lane (Matches Lane, in Jamaican creole). Matches Lane is part of the warp and woof of what Carl Stone called the 'clientelistic' structure of modern Jamaican politics.[5] Situated in the West Kingston electoral constituency controlled by the opposition party, the Jamaica Labour Party (JLP), Matthews Lane is a small enclave of traditional support for the party in power, the People's National Party (PNP). Most of this constituency is controlled by 'enforcers' from a community called Tivoli Gardens, largely the post-independence invention of the leader of the opposition, Edward Seaga, who is also the member of parliament for the constituency. Tivoli Gardens and Matthews Lane have been carrying on a 'war' for many years, but recently, and independently of the political parties, the two area dons, Zeeks and his Tivoli counterpart, arrived at a peace agreement. As a result, a certain order has prevailed in these communities.

This sidestepping of the apparatus of party-political patronage is a comparatively new – and to my mind a decisive – development. As the same editorial went on insightfully:

> The community dons are a complex derivative of a political culture that spawn[s] political enclaves, the protected garrisons, to be defended by the 'leader' and his 'soldiers' to the benefit of this or that party. As [a] reward, the dons receive the spoils to be shared among the people of the community. . . . But in recent years the capacity of the state to manage the pork barrel has been diminished. At the same time a stagnant economy has been unable to provide jobs for a largely under-skilled work force, deepening the dependence of these communities on the area dons. . . . Critically too, unable to flex any economic muscle, our political leadership has not demonstrated the capacity to exert any moral authority to challenge the ascendancy of the dons.

In consequence, the dons have grown increasingly independent of the political parties. In fact, many people felt that Zeeks's arrest was precipitated by the state's desire to break the alliance between Tivoli Gardens and Matthews Lane, and thereby to regain the initiative in the bid for control of West Kingston.

I think that the 'Zeeks affair' (as it is now referred to in the local public sphere) is one index of the crisis of the Jamaican postcolonial present. I think it is a profound crisis. In my view, what this event points to is not merely a temporary collapse of moral consensus in the social and political order, but more fundamentally the collapse of the old secular–modernist *grounds* on which it was assumed such consensus could be secured and sustained. What I mean by this is that what makes contemporary Jamaica so seemingly unstable and volatile is not only the fact that the 'lawless' are in the streets burning tyres and blocking roads, but that their protest and their demands are not intelligible any longer within the established vocabulary of politics. Indeed, what alarms the governing elite is precisely that their protest and their

demands have *no* recognizable politics (or no *recognizable* politics).
Zeeks's supporters were not, for instance, demanding anything from
their parliamentary representative; they were not seeking to replace the
political party in power; they were certainly not attempting to overthrow
the government. They simply wanted back their 'dads', who, so far as
they were concerned, had been illegitimately taken from them by the
police. These are people – black, poor, and urban – who have felt not
only *dis*empowered and *dis*connected from the political process of the
postcolonial state, but also systematically *dis*regarded and *dis*respected
by the governing elite. For them, new nationhood has been, to paraphrase Kamau Brathwaite, one long 'age of dis'.[6]

Another way of saying what I'm saying here, perhaps, is to say that
the ghost of M.G. Smith is haunting the landscape of the Jamaican
political–modern. For Smith, it may be recalled, was deeply sceptical
that societies such as the former slave plantation societies of the
colonial and postcolonial Caribbean – plural societies, as he called
them, following J.S. Furnivall – could be assumed to rest on consensus,
on a structure of common, internally generated values. He would,
perhaps, have nodded his head knowingly at the chaos in Kingston
over Zeeks, at the symptoms of what Furnivall would have called the
'feebleness of social will' in contemporary Jamaica. In this chapter, I
want to revisit some aspects of the debate about the plural society
theory of M.G. Smith (a debate in which Stuart Hall has himself had a
share).[7] I want to return to this debate in what I have suggested is a
new conjuncture, a new present, in postcolonial Jamaica, one characterized above all by the collapse of the moral and conceptual grounds
of social and political consensus. The plural society debate has been
(together with the 'creole society' debate, to which it is connected, and
the 'plantation society' debate) one of the defining debates in Caribbean studies in the postcolonial period. It is that debate that one has
had to pass through in the fashioning of an understanding of the
intersection of culture and power in the Caribbean. Needless to say,
there has been a good deal of contentious discussion about Smith's
theory. By and large, this discussion has turned on the *aptness* of the
model, on the extent to which it does or does not adequately capture
the complex realities of class, culture, race, and ethnicity in these
former slave societies. From the early doubts of Lloyd Braithwaite and
Raymond Smith to the more recent ones of Diane Austin-Broos there
is a large and very important archive of scholarly work devoted to the
criticism, extension, and revision of the theory of plural societies.[8]

This is not what interests me here, however. I am not concerned to
speak in favour or against the plural society thesis as such. I am not
interested in judging whether – or to what extent – it can be said,

looking back, that M.G. Smith got the Caribbean right or wrong. The preoccupation with retrospective judgements of this kind presupposes that we, standing where we are, inhabit the same conjuncture, the same cognitive–political context of options or space of questions, as Smith did, standing where he stood. I have a strong doubt about this presupposition, and therefore I have a different preoccupation.

I want to *historicize* Smith's theory of plural societies; I want to *locate* his theoretical project in relation to the cultural–political conjuncture in which it was produced in Jamaica in the 1950s. I want to read Smith in this way because what interests me primarily is the way in which *difference* has gotten written into – or out of – the Bandung project of the national–modern. Central to the modernizing ethos of the Bandung project was a certain rationalization of the domain of the political. To put it more concretely, it has been an intrinsic part of the modernist enterprise of building national economies and national states to seek progressively to integrate the social and cultural formations around a single standardized order: a single conception of the national good, and a single portrait of the national citizen–subject.[9] This has entailed the secular idea that *difference* (religious, ethnic, cultural) is at best a distraction, and at worse a hindrance to the progressive, improving objectives of nation-state building. Difference, on this view, is essentially to be overcome (assimilated, regulated, marginalized, eradicated), rather than embraced and worked with as part of what politics is. But does this conception of the relation between difference and the political continue to be an intellectually and politically sustainable one? This is the *general* register of my concern. M.G. Smith's theory of pluralism is essentially a modernist theory about the political management of difference in the colonial and postcolonial Caribbean. My *specific* question is whether the demand that constituted the conjuncture in which his theory of difference was formulated continues to be a demand with a purchase on the conjuncture that constitutes our own cultural–political present. My suspicion, to run ahead of myself somewhat, is that it is not. My suspicion is that our present – the present, so to speak, *after* Zeeks – constitutes a new conjuncture in which the demand might usefully be reformulated as a demand to embrace the *permanence* of pluralism.

Locating Plural Society Theory

The problem of the historical location of M.G. Smith's plural society theory has not gone entirely unexamined. In 1980 Don Robotham published a polemic against Smith.[10] At the time a prominent member of the leading Marxist party in Jamaica, the Worker's Party of Jamaica (WPJ), Robotham sought to carry out a kind of ideology critique on Smith's theory. He believed that Smith, who had returned to Jamaica in September 1952 after an absence of more than a decade, developed his theory in direct response to the crisis of the Jamaican nationalist movement. Smith, as is well known, was a close friend of the Manley family.[11] Specifically, Robotham sought to demonstrate the middle-class character of Smith's theory, and, more centrally, the relation between the political fortunes of the middle class and the theory's historical trajectory. Pluralism, he argued, is the 'false-consciousness' of the nationalist middle class, and plural society theory

> is nothing but a scientific abstraction derived from the ideological conscious-
> ness of the Jamaican anti-colonial middle class of the period. The whole
> course of the development of this theory thus reflects closely the ups and
> downs of the socio-political development of this class during that critical
> decade which preceded Jamaican independence.[12]

While I won't be concerned to locate plural society theory in Smith's supposed class motives or in the facts of his biography, I think that Robotham points us in an important direction.[13] In my view, the problem-space in which Smith developed his thesis about the plural society can be thought along two interconnected analytical axes. One of these, to be sure, is the *politico-ideological* context of the crisis of the nationalist movement in Jamaica in the 1950s, as Robotham suggests; the other is the *conceptual* context of Parsonian sociology. In large measure, these contexts of argument (as one might call them, in Quentin Skinner's terms) together constituted the discursive space in which Smith thought and wrote in the 1950s, the space in which the generative questions about moral consensus and its political implications were constructed and deliberated.

Smith's conceptual problem-space was defined by the prevailing influence of Parsonian assumptions in sociology and anthropology concerning the nature of social order and the bases and modes of social integration. (It will be remembered that Talcott Parsons's *The Social System*, as well as the volume edited by Parsons and Edward Shils, *Toward a General Theory of Action*, were both published in 1951.) Among social theorists influenced by Parsons's theory of action, there was a general methodological presumption in favour of an underlying inter-nally generated set of common values. Societies were, *necessarily*, con-sensual normative systems, and the only question for the Parsonian was the identification of these constitutive values and norms. (This view, of course, has an older lineage, in Durkheim, and to a somewhat less extent, in Weber.) Smith doubted the validity of this assumption, at least where societies founded in conquest, slavery, and colonial domination were concerned. For it seemed to him to imply the willing submission of *all* members of a society, and in consequence to leave untheorized (indeed *untheorizable*) the whole dimension of power, force, coercion. This is why the work of scholar and colonial civil servant J.S. Furnivall attracted him. In his 1948 book *Colonial Policy and Practice*, Furnivall had suggested a distinction between societies that derive their integration from normative consensus (Parsonian societies, so to speak), and societies that depended for their order on regulation by force. These latter societies were, importantly, colonial societies, 'tropical dependencies' in Furnivall's vocabulary, that had been 'brought within the modern world' by the 'contact between East and West'. In these societies, as Furnivall famously put it, people

> mix but do not combine. Each group holds by its own religion, its own culture and language, its own ideas and ways. As individuals they meet, but only in the market-place, in buying and selling. There is a plural society, with different sections of the community living side by side, but separately, within the same political unit.[14]

Here, for Smith, was a conceptual language with which to intervene in and problematize the normative Parsonian space. His conceptual field was defined by the question of whether colonial Caribbean society was a Parsonian society, or a plural one. And the conceptual demand he is obliged to respond to, therefore, is the demand to demonstrate that there are other bases than normative consensus upon which the Caribbean social formation is held together.

The *politico-ideological* problem-space to which Smith returned in September 1952 was unquestionably defined by the crisis of the Jamaican nationalist movement. Robotham is right to point us in this direction. The political party leading that movement, the PNP, was – and continued up until recently to be – the voice of the nationalist brown middle class. Its founding leader, N.W. Manley, was very much an embodiment of the ethos of this class (or class section). The party had been founded (in the wake of labour riots in 1938) in the radical–democratic vision of an egalitarian alliance between the brown middle class (which was demanding self-government) and the black working classes (which were demanding better working conditions). Up until the end of the 1940s the strong Marxist Left in the party had sought, in difficult circumstances, to sustain this vision. However the party had failed to win either of the two elections since adult suffrage in 1944. Thus in March 1952, under pressure internally (from the Right within the party) and externally (from the growing context of the Cold War) the party expelled its communist wing – the famous 4Hs – and began to turn sharply away from its socialist commitments to unambiguously elitist ones.[15] It now abandoned the ideal of overcoming the old antipathy between the browns and blacks. The grain of the historical detail (the internal party reorganization, the emergence of Michael Manley's leadership, the increasing state repression of Rastafari, and so on) need not detain us here. What is necessary to appreciate is that the fundamental political and ideological question thrown up by this crisis was how now to imagine the community of the emerging nation? What would be the relationship between the black and brown sections of the population in the new order? With the collapse of the Left–democratic project, in other words, what would be the normative basis of an integrated postcolonial society? What would be the grounds of consensus?

The discursive context in relation to which Smith's plural society theory was developed in the decade between his return to Jamaica and independence ten years later, in August 1962, was therefore framed by a conceptual demand to interrupt Parsonian assumptions about social order, and a politico-ideological demand to think through the widening breach between the two social/cultural sections of the emerging nation. Smith published four major statements of the theory of plural societies in this period. The earliest statement is formulated in the essay 'Some Aspects of Social Structure in the British Caribbean about 1820', written while carrying out fieldwork in Carriacou in late 1952 and early 1953, and published in 1953.[16] Using contemporary accounts of social conditions in St Vincent and Jamaica, Smith's concern is to describe the main social categories into which the population was divided in around 1820, from top to bottom: Whites, Free Coloureds and Free Blacks, and Slaves. He finds that a principle of 'status' defines the maintenance of a hierarchical structure in which each of these categories of persons is culturally differentiated from the other in the sense that they adhere to different institutions. As he put it, they differed from one another 'in their religious observances and concepts, their legal and political institutions, education, kinship and mating patterns, family organization, property rights, land tenure and use, division of labor, language, occupations and technology, community organization and associations, markets, value-systems, recreation and folklore'. In effect, he goes on:

> the population of a British West Indian colony at this period was culturally pluralistic – that is to say, it contained sections which practiced different forms of the same institutions. Thus the population constituted a plural

society, that is, a society divided into sections, each of which practiced different cultures.[17]

A central theme in the essay, however, is the extent to which the various categories of persons into which the society was differentiated adopted the values and practices of the dominant group, the extent, in other words, of acculturation. Smith is least ambiguous where the 'Coloured' section of the population (whether slave or free) is concerned. Their Eurocentric desire is virtually what constitutes them. Where the slaves are concerned Smith remarks that though there is evidence of 'partial imitation of the whites', and practices that mark 'the different stages of acculturation to white standards', the limitations to this were 'so severe' that the tendency to an inclusive society was 'stronger than the tendency to adopt white institutions and standards, thus inhibiting acculturation'. This is the central conceptual problem for Smith: the structural 'inhibiting' of the process of acculturation in the Caribbean. Conceptually, in other words, the problem of acculturation operates as a kind of background in relation to which the problem of pluralism itself emerges. To put it another way, it was as though the question animating Smith – the question governing the appearance of other questions – was whether acculturation in Jamaica had been a success or a failure. Of course, this question was itself provoked by an initial doubt, by the suspicion not only of failure, but of *systemic* failure. The conceptual project of the theory was to explore this, and to work out the logic of the failure. In this sense, therefore, it is not the problem of pluralism that gives rise to the problem of acculturation; it is the *failure* of acculturation that produces the structural *effect* of pluralism. Only later does pluralism itself – now understood as an almost self-standing characteristic of the social/cultural formation – become the *generative* centrepiece of the theory.

This idea of the centrality of acculturation is crucial to Robotham's politico-ideological argument because – rightly, in my view – he thinks of acculturation as defining the ethos of the Jamaican brown middle class. The story of the formation of this class (or class section) is, needless to say, far too complex a story to enter into here in any detail.[18] However it is enough for my purposes to note that this middle class has historically been constituted around the moral ideal of social and cultural improvement: the cultivation of a certain kind of taste, the display of good manners, civility, respectability, decency, facility with the English language, and so on. This middle class has felt a keen sense of its entitlement to national leadership. It has felt that it alone embodied the historical destiny of the nation. It has believed, therefore, that it alone had the capacity and the duty to educate the black masses for their eventual self-government. This has been its acculturationist project. At the same time this moral and political desire to embody the nation in itself has historically been marked by a crippling paradox: antagonistic though it was to the colonial regime that kept it outside of power, its cultural aspirations were nevertheless pro-British, Eurocentric; critical though it was of the racism of the colonial order, it was alienated from the subaltern classes by an almost existential horror of blackness. And therefore, while it felt its historic task was to seek a gradual but progressive convergence on a cultural–political consensus defined by the hegemony of the norms of 'brownness' it harboured a deep suspicion of the practical impossibility of any such consensus.

It is the faltering faith in that historic task of drawing the social/cultural sections together on the ground of the hegemony of its values that Robotham detects in subsequent formulations of Smith's plural society theory. Certainly by the fourth major statement, 'The Plural Framework of Jamaican Society', published in 1961 on the eve of independence, the theme of acculturation is virtually absent.[19] Rather than a description emphasizing the *process* by which acculturation is inhibited or blocked there is a focus on the composite plural *structure* itself and the mode of its regulation and maintenance. The optic, in other words, has shifted. In this essay Smith defines Jamaican society as divided into three 'institutional systems' or 'cultural sections' externally held together by the instrumentalities of the market and the state. As he puts it in summary fashion: 'The integration of these three sections has never been high; and for cohesion Jamaica has depended mainly on those forms of social control implicit in the economic system and explicit in government.'[20]

It is not hard to agree with Robotham, then, that there was a discernible shift of emphasis in M.G. Smith's theory. Nor is it hard to agree that this shift, in turn, can be mapped onto a movement from optimism to pessimism on the part of the section of the middle class leading the anti-colonial nationalist movement in Jamaica. The story of the plural society theory, in this view, is rightly the story of a 'disillusioned nationalism'. By the end of the 1950s and the beginning of the 1960s, as its ability to imagine a cohesive – that is, acculturated – national community dimmed, the theory increasingly pictured Jamaican society as a structure of rigidly separate social sections held together precariously by the external forces of the market and the state. The generative question that defined the conjuncture in which Smith's views took shape was defined by a dilemma that may be summarized as follows: without the lubricant of acculturation to establish a ground of common values and so cement the social/cultural sections, how could one imagine the community of the emerging nation? It is this crisis of consensus, reflected in the tension between acculturation and pluralism, that M.G. Smith tried – to my mind, brilliantly – to theorize. In the end, for Smith, the new nation could be little more than a hierarchical juxtaposition of these sections, unevenly mediated by the market, and precariously, and often oppressively, regulated by the state.

The Permanence of Pluralism

Robotham's story is not only a story about the correspondence between the theory of pluralism and the ambitions of the nationalist middle class. It is more precisely a normative story about the betrayal of the Left by the liberals in the anti-colonial movement, and thus the betrayal of the promise of radical social and political transformation by reformists. As such it is a chapter in the larger story of the betrayal of socialism by liberalism. For Robotham, this is the *real* betrayal of M.G. Smith's plural society theory.

But standing where *we* are, on *this* side of the global collapse of the Bandung and socialist projects, is it so self-evident that the cultural and moral ethos of the Jamaican revolutionary Left (in whose name Robotham was speaking) was really fundamentally different from that of the liberals (like M.G. Smith) they criticized – at least on this terrain of acculturation/pluralism? This is an important question not only because in the social origins of its leading members Robotham's Marxist Left was as brown and middle-class as its liberal opponents (sometimes more incongruously so), but more significantly because in its constitutive rationality his Marxism-Leninism and their liberalism shared conceptually more than they cared to realize.[21] They both shared the progressivisms and rationalisms of the Enlightenment project. They shared, therefore, the assumption of the cultural backwardness of Zeeks and his supporters, their need of cultural and moral improvement. And similarly they shared the corollary view that what those demonstrators outside Central Police Station in September 1998 needed most of all was the *direction* of a rational political leadership that would interpret and channel their will in the interest of the nation. In effect, therefore, in their vision of a postcolonial order they shared the cultural–political desire to *overcome* pluralism rather than embrace – and think through – it.[22]

It seems to me, then, that from the point of view of the postcolonial present there is a more important story to be told than the story of the *ideological* rivalry between the Left and the liberals in the Jamaican nationalist movement. This would be a story in which the Left and the liberals constitute not the irreconcilable polarities that they appear to be in Robotham's betrayal narrative, but rather competing ideological moments in what is in fact a *common* secular–modernization project. If in the Left's betrayal narrative the imagined community of the nation is pictured as an embattled space of class interests, class struggle, class conflict, and class complicities, in the story of the making (and unmaking) of the secular–modernization project what is at stake is the *rationality* through which the construction of the moral and political order of the postcolonial state was imagined and pursued. The Left and the liberals shared the *ground* of this rationality.

Between the publication of M.G. Smith's formative essays on the plural society, in the 1950s and 1960s, and the present, significant changes have taken place in Jamaican society, culture, and politics. These transformations, still more or less inchoate, still more or less fluid, appear to be reorganizing not only the (sociological) relations between dominant and subaltern classes, but also the cultural–political *rationality* through which relations of dominance/subordination are constituted as such. I am not interested here in itemizing these changes so much as in sketching in brief outline a story about the *dissolution* of the nationalist modernization project, and the social and political eclipse of the brown middle class that drove that project. The value of this story for our present conjuncture, I think, is that it cuts across Robotham's ideology distinctions (between Left and Right, liberals and Marxists, progressives and conservatives) that seem no longer to have a critical purchase on the cognitive–political space of the postcolonial Jamaica we inhabit.

The aspirations of the acculturationist brown middle class had been defeated in 1962, so that the first decade of Jamaican independence was governed by a liberal national–modernist logic in which the plural sections were held together (precariously so in the middle and late 1960s) by the coercive power of the state administered by Alexander Bustamante's Jamaica Labour Party. M.G. Smith cast a long shadow over the 1960s. The 1970s mark at once a break and a revival. With the coming to power of the PNP, led by Michael Manley, in 1972, the promise of a brown-middle-class-inspired undertaking in acculturationist social transformation was re-opened. This was possible because for the first time the enlightened nationalist middle class was in a position to define the direction of the Jamaican postcolonial state. The PNP victory effectively reactivated the acculturationist project of the 1940s that had been suspended with the expulsion of the Left in 1952. (Parenthetically, it should also be remembered that this is the moment when Kamau Brathwaite's 'creole society' model emerges to challenge Smith.[23]) It reopened the possibility, therefore, of an alliance between the enlightened brown middle class and the black subaltern classes. A sanctioned space now emerged, for instance, for a certain public affirmation of Africa and black consciousness and, in general, for the cultural expressions of the popular. At the same time, however, the Left (both the 'democratic' socialists and the 'scientific' socialists), while not seeking to supplant the values of the popular in the coercive way that the liberal nationalists sought to do in the 1960s, nevertheless constituted the project of the political domain as the progressive integration of the social and cultural formations around a single conception of the national good and a single conception of the citizen–subject. A larger sense of social justice, and a broader egalitarianism to be sure, but what the Left shared very much with the nationalists and the liberals was the sure idea of a single *direction* to be taken and a single *destination* to be progressively arrived at.

In contemporary Jamaica, by contrast, it is precisely this optimism of the liberal–nationalists and the socialists that has faded.[24] In contemporary Jamaica their ethical–political languages of progressive social transformation and acculturationist cultural consensus have become enfeebled, not to say, irrelevant. What is happening in contemporary Jamaica is that the ordering rationality of the project of the nationalist modern is dissolving. The meta-values that underpinned this rationality (civility, welfarism, cultivation, fairness, and so on) no longer hold in the old ways. Their hegemony has been fractured. To put this another way, the meta-values of 'brownness' (normative values of the Left no less than of the liberals) are losing their authorizing and adjudicating force. And this is happening, I think, from two directions simultaneously.

From one direction, the brown middle class that conceived and drove the anti-colonial nationalist movement is in social and political eclipse. A new black middle class has begun to assert itself in the public culture. One of the domains in which the difference between these sections of the middle class makes itself apparent is in relation to 'culture', and to 'Africa' especially (or rather to 'Africa' *as* 'culture'). The brown middle class, as I have suggested, has been a class of high-culture aspirations constituted around a cautious respectability, good taste, a discriminating care for breeding, and an almost anxious concern for the grammar of proper speech. On the whole, the new black middle class does not share this sensibility. It is less concerned with the virtues of taste or the nationalist ideal of a cultural consensus, and more with markets and money. Unlike the brown middle class, however, it is at home with blackness; it celebrates blackness. At the same time, this is a blackness, notably, no longer connected to any recognizable emancipatory politics. It is a blackness, therefore which, while much more visible in the public culture and much less socially and existentially complicated to inhabit than in the 1970s, is very much the blackness of the consumer. For the liberal and Left brown middle classes of the 1970s blackness was part of an abstract principle of social change. For the black middle class of the 1990s, by contrast, blackness is part of an individual (even individualistic) identity politics, part of an embodied identity whose marginalization is to be overcome by the politics of the new PNP of P.J. Patterson, or the new consumer egalitarianism of the liberalized market.

From another direction, there has been a change in the relation of the popular classes to the dominant ones. This has at least two aspects. The first has to do with the greater degree of autonomy of the popular classes from the apparatuses and institutions of the postcolonial state. Interestingly, this is a result not of direct political resistance, but rather of the increasing failure of the postcolonial state to provide elementary opportunities for people to make a living, and elementary forms of social welfare. As a consequence people have had to invent ways of circumventing the state ('hustling' and 'juggling', in the idiom of the street) in order to survive the harsh economic realities of contemporary Jamaica. The second has to do with the increasing degree of cynicism with which the popular classes treat official authority. There is an increasing (and increasingly demonstrated) distrust of the party politi-cal system, for instance, and of the police force and judiciary. In contemporary Jamaica, no one seriously believes that the political system is any more than what the late Carl Stone said it is, namely a system of patronage and clientelism, and today a rather unyielding one at that.

The contrast that I am drawing here might be summarized in the following way. In the register of *ideology*, there is a discontinuity between the 1960s and 1970s: between liberalism and socialism. In the register of *rationality*, however, there really is none: both imagine a progressive convergence on a consensualist ideal. In the register of *ideology* there is little to give between the 1960s and the 1990s: the latter years see the hegemony of a new liberalism resembling that of the former in many respects. In the register of *rationality*, however, there is a significant gap. In the 1960s and 1970s, the great explosion of the popular occurred in the context of a nation-state project that was confident of its direction and its destination; however misguidedly, and however arrogantly, it *knew* where it was going and how it was getting there. In the present, by contrast, brown-middle-class values no longer hegemon-ize the social, and the middle-class state no longer has the resources to impose (at least in a continuous and systematic way) its discipline and its privilege. In other words, what is striking about the form of social division that marks contemporary Jamaica is that, unlike the social division of the 1960s, this division is characterized neither by the ready assumption of the *moral* authority by the middle class, nor by the middle class's ability to bring the *political* force of the state it manages to bear on securing, cultivating, and reproducing its values.

Theorizing the Political after Zeeks

This, of course, is precisely the moment of Zeeks. The so-called Zeeks affair marks, I believe, a point-of-no-return in the gradual unravelling of the foundations of Jamaica's political modernity. In the remainder of this chapter I want to try (admittedly in a tentative and preliminary way) to draw out some of the implications of what I have been saying for the theorization of the political in contemporary Jamaica. What can it mean to theorize the political *after* Zeeks? What hitherto-dominant assumptions (about the state, for instance, about order, about community, about the modalities of decision-making, about the nature of sovereignty and self-government, about the claims of justice) have now to be rethought? What new critical concepts are necessary to this enterprise? And, in particular, what new understandings of consensus and conflict, of identity and difference, have to be forged so as to make sense of the new demands being made in and on the political order in Jamaica? It seems to me that if Zeeks and his supporters are not simply to congeal into otherness, that is, are not to be reduced either to the quasi-anthropology of social pathology (to the 'culture of violence' discourse that has such wide purchase among opinion-makers in the Jamaican public sphere), or to the more straightforward disciplinary instrumentalities of law and order (as the police and the Minister of Security would like), then a considered and searching engagement with these questions is crucial.

Obviously I can do no more here than sketch, but I would like to suggest some directions our conceptual reorganization might take. We need, first of all, a revised concept of difference. One of the virtues of M.G. Smith's theory of plural societies, I think, is the relative autonomy he accords the social and cultural sections. But we need a way of seeing these 'sections' not as desiderata to be managed by the state or progressively overcome on the way to One Culture (a 'national' one, say), but as modes of flourishing with their own irreducible idioms, and their own historically constituted rationalities and vernacular practices. If we understand difference in this way we shall give up the quaint assumption that Zeeks and his supporters are either alienated from or gravitating towards some privileged set of values.

Such a reconceived conception of difference will entail, of course, a reconsidered understanding of community and of consensus. We need a concept of community in which conflict, dispute, argument, contestation – in short, agonism – are seen as constitutive rather than dispensable to a common life. To do so we shall have to give up the Parsonian idea that community needs a single unifying structure of values, as well as the Lockean idea that it needs a background social contract, to secure and guarantee order. Rather we shall need a concept of community that hangs more on provisional decisions, contingent reasons, practical knowledges. In this conception, we shall also have to give up the idea that consensus can be underwritten by a universalist and rationalist moral-politics of improvement in which the indigestible and unassimilable identities Zeeks and his supporters embody are to be re-educated for middle-class civility. Consensus has now to be seen not as a final destination, a distant horizon, but as one moment in a larger relation permanently open to contestation, open to the moment when difference contests sites of normalized identity and demands a rearrangement of the terms, and perhaps even the very *idiom*, of consensus.

Finally we need a conception of politics and of the domain of the political that comports with these revised conceptions of difference, community, and consensus. Obviously the clientelistic conception that sees the political as a franchise of the state, and politics as how one goes about contesting access to it, is irrelevant to the new demands in contemporary Jamaica. If our presumption is that historically constituted difference is ineradicable and indeed central to human flourishing, and if consensus is a provisional and contingent relation of identity and difference, then we need a conception in which politics is envisaged more as the strategic practice of arriving at *settlements*, and in which the domain of the political is understood precisely as that public domain where settlements are negotiated. Moreover, the idea that politics can be thought of along an ideological continuum – from Left to Right, from progressive to conservative, from Robotham to Smith, and so on – will not help us gain much of a purchase on what Zeeks and his supporters are up to. Theirs is not a demand for a renewal of the old politics of emancipation. It is no longer clear where emancipation might lead them. Zeeks's supporters are not going to be folded neatly into the familiar plot of the liberationist story. And therefore the challenge is to fashion an approach that is open to the idea that (however repellent they may appear) new conceptions of political association and political expression are emerging.

Together what these concepts aim at accomplishing is a displacement of the secular–rationalist frameworks for understanding the relation

between culture and politics. It seems to me that this kind of conceptual revision may help us open up some cognitive space for a more
productive discussion of the political present in contemporary Jamaica.

To sum up, I agree with Robotham that pluralism has been the
anthropological theory of the brown nationalist middle class. I agree
also that there was a decipherable shift in the *accent* of M.G. Smith's
formulations between the early 1950s and the early 1960s: a shift from
an accent on acculturation to one on pluralism. I am very sympathetic
to the view, moreover, that this shift can be mapped *across registers* onto
a shift in the cultural–political aspirations of this class: a shift from an
early hope that the black popular classes would embrace the acculturation process, to an eventual despair that they did – or *would* – not. The
story of the PNP between its founding and independence can indeed
be told in precisely these terms. It is certainly one way, for instance, of
reading the touching nostalgia of Rachel Manley's memoir, *Drumblair*.[25]
But I think that what is more important to see, from the vantage of the
dead end of our postcolonial present, is that Robotham's Marxist
rationalism and Smith's liberal rationalism are in fact cut from the
same modernist cloth. Robotham's Marxism–Leninism embodied a
desire, very much like Smith's anthropological liberalism, to predesign
a future for Zeeks and his supporters on the basis of the unilateral
sovereignty of (brown-middle-class) reason. In effect, they embodied
competing versions of the same civilizing, secular-modernization
mission in which the black popular classes would be guided tutorially
stage by stage in the project of self-determination and social transformation. It is this project, in my view, that has now played itself out in
Jamaica (indeed, it has played itself out elsewhere as well). And if this
is so, if the ideal of the progressive convergence on a rational consensus
is as implausible now as it is impractical, then the challenge of finding
more adequate ways to accommodate contestation and the constitutive
differences that make us up – and to embody them politically – is
difficult to avoid. It is the demand of the present. To think critically in
the contemporary postcolonial world, as Stuart Hall would urge us to
do, it is important to face up to the moral–political impasse we inhabit.
The 'Zeeks affair' obliges us to enlarge our understanding of politics
and the political, and therefore our understanding of what it might
mean to live together in difference.

Notes

Earlier versions of this chapter were read at York University, the University of the West Indies, Princeton University, Columbia University, and the University of Virginia. I am grateful to these institutions for hosting me and to those who offered their comments. I am especially grateful to Talal Asad, Charles Carnegie, Robert Hill, and Raymond Smith for their criticisms and suggestions.

1. I have sought to sketch out some aspects of this in my book *Refashioning Futures: Criticism after Postcoloniality* (Princeton: Princeton University Press, 1999).

2. It should be obvious that I am reading Stuart Hall through R.G. Collingwood's concept of a 'question/answer' complex. See his *An Autobiography* (Oxford: Oxford University Press, 1939).

3. Editorial, 'The State must not Surrender to Mob Rule', *Observer*, 25 September 1998.

4. Outside the courthouse – the infamous Gun Court – where he was charged some days later, women wore T-shirts saying 'Zeeks, Father of the Inner City'.

5. Carl Stone, *Democracy and Clientelism in Jamaica* (New Brunswick, NJ: Transaction Books, 1980).

6. Kamau Brathwaite, 'A Short History of Dis: Or Middle Passages Today', in his *Trench Town Rock* (Providence, RI: Lost Roads Publishers, 1994), p. 73.

7. See Stuart Hall, 'Pluralism, Race and Class in Caribbean Society', in *Race and Class in Post-colonial Society: A Study of Ethnic Group Relations in the English-speaking Caribbean, Bolivia, Chile and Mexico* (Paris: UNESCO, 1977).

8. See Lloyd Braithwaite, 'The Present Status of the Social Sciences in the British Caribbean', in Vera Rubin, ed., *Caribbean Studies: A Symposium* (Kingston: Institute of Social and Economic Research, 1957); R.T. Smith, 'Review of "Social and Cultural Pluralism in the Caribbean"', *American Anthropologist*, 63 (1961): 155–7; and Diane Austin-Broos, 'Culture and Ideology in the English-speaking Caribbean: A View from Jamaica', *American Ethnologist*, 10 (1983): 223–40.

9. For one useful discussion of the failure of the great improving project of the modern state in its various forms, see James C. Scott, *Seeing Like a State: How Certain Schemes to Improve the Human Condition Have Failed* (New Haven: Yale University Press, 1998).

10. Don Robotham, 'Pluralism as an Ideology', *Social and Economic Studies*, 29(1) (1980): 69–89. It is important to note that this essay was originally written while he was a graduate student in anthropology at the University of Chicago in the late 1960s. It was circulating at the University of the West Indies, Mona, in manuscript copy in the late 1970s where, as an undergraduate, I first read it.

11. For biographical details see Douglas Hall, *A Man Divided: Michael Garfield Smith, Jamaican Poet and Anthropologist, 1921–1993* (Kingston: The Press, University of the West Indies, 1997).

12. Robotham, 'Pluralism as an Ideology', p. 69.

13. As is well known, much of Stuart Hall's work in the 1970s and early 1980s was devoted to criticizing the kind of ideology critique articulated here by

Robotham. Among many possible examples, see 'The Question of Ideology: Marxism without Guarantees', in Betty Matthews, ed., *Marx, A Hundred Years On* (London: Lawrence & Wishart, 1983).

14. See J.S. Furnivall, *Colonial Policy and Practice* (Cambridge: Cambridge University Press, 1948), p. 304. It is notable that Furnivall's is the vocabulary of the rationalization of colonial management on the very eve of decolonization. It expresses the anxiety that without the colonial power that has brought and holds the union of people together, there is a danger of the 'whole society relapsing into anarchy' (p. 307).

15. The 4Hs were Richard Hart, Frank and Ken Hill, and Arthur Henry. For some discussion of this period see Trevor Munroe, *The Politics of Constitutional Decolonization, Jamaica 1944–1962* (Kingston: Institute of Social and Economic Research, 1972), and *The Marxist 'Left' in Jamaica, 1940–1950*, Working Paper No. 15 (Kingston: Institute of Social and Economic Research, 1977).

16. M.G. Smith, 'Some Aspects of Social Structure in the British Caribbean about 1820', originally published in *Social and Economic Studies*, 1(4) (1953): 55–79. Reprinted in *The Plural Society in the British West Indies* (Berkeley: University of California Press, 1965), pp. 92–115. All citations from Smith's essays are taken from the latter volume.

17. Smith, ibid., p. 112.

18. There is indeed a history to be written here that would explore the *mentalité* of this class, the fashioning of its moral and cultural sensibilities, and the connection between these and its politics. The best *social* history so far of its early formation is Gad Heuman's *Between Black and White: Race, Politics, and the Free Coloureds in Jamaica, 1792–1865* (Westport, CT: Greenwood Press, 1981).

19. M.G. Smith, 'The Plural Framework of Jamaican Society', originally published in *British Journal of Sociology*, 12 (3) (1961): 249–62. Reprinted in *The Plural Society in the British West Indies*, pp. 162–75.

20. Ibid., p. 175.

21. In recent post-Marxist years, Robotham's views have grown to look more like those he earlier chastised Smith for holding. See the standard brown-middle-class appeal he makes for decency and welfarist selflessness in his Grace Foundation Lecture, *Vision and Voluntarism: Reviving Voluntarism in Jamaica* (Kingston: Grace Kennedy Foundation, 1998). Curious, it seems, are the ways of brownness.

22. See Scott's very interesting discussion of Lenin and the revolutionary party in *Seeing Like a State*, Chapter 5.

23. Kamau Brathwaite's *The Development of Creole Society in Jamaica, 1770–1820* was published by Oxford University Press in 1971.

24. I elaborate this further in 'Fanonian Futures?', in my *Refashioning Futures*.

25. I am thinking especially of the figure of the ageing, slightly decrepit N.W. Manley, forlorn, living the failure of his nationalist dream. See Rachel Manley, *Drumblair: Memories of a Jamaican Childhood* (Kingston: Ian Randle, 1996), especially the last two chapters.

26

Exoticism and Death as a Modern Taboo:
Gangsta Rap and the Search for Intensity

Ove Sernhede

The word 'exoticism' began to appear in dictionaries during the final decades of the nineteenth century. Meyer's conversational dictionary of 1875 contained maybe the word's first appearance; the dictionary used the term 'exoteromani' to designate the 'Schwärmerei für Fremdes' ('enthusiasm for aliens') that developed in the metropolises of Europe at the time (Bitterli 1987). This exoticism was primarily related to the increasing interest of the bourgeoisie in places and peoples from other continents. Fascination with the wild and the primitive became a spice of life and came to have many piquant expressions. Europe was invaded by phenomena such as the Buffalo Bill Wild West Show with North American 'Indians' 'live and in the flesh' and the Fisk Jubilee Singers, with former slaves who sang Negro spirituals. Europe was also visited by entire tribes from 'darkest Africa' who danced and drummed half-naked so that the cultivated European could feel the heat and the damp from his own, inner primeval forest.

The roots of modern exoticism may, as Stuart Hall's discussion on 'The West and the Rest' suggests, be found in the era of the discovery of the New World (Hall 1992). The discovery forced Europe to reflect over what it means to be civilized and European. Interest in the original inhabitants of the newly discovered continent, the 'Indian' or 'savage' as he was called by the philosophers of the day, revealed Europeans' deep underlying ambivalence about their own civilization, whose 'advances' were predicated upon social organization and interpersonal relationships rife with conflict – far from the primitive people's 'carefree and ingenuous lives'. The Enlightenment philosophers' discussions of the 'noble savage' laid bare the new and more flexible identities of the modern epoch. The industrialization and all-encompassing modernization of Europe in the 1800s placed the human being, in the words of Max Weber, in an 'iron cage'. Disciplines such as sociology and psychology, which simply problematized the predicament of modern man, emerged. A longing to escape 'civilization and its discontents' became the basis for a burgeoning fascination with foreign cultures.

The first decades of the twentieth century saw the emergence of cubism and jazz. Both have vital parts of their root systems embedded in cultures south of the Sahara. It is also with these cultural manifestations that Africa and 'the Negro' came into the focus of exoticism. Neither the North American nor the South American native cultures came to be part of any lasting cultural amalgamation with European culture. Black culture, especially the African American, on the other hand, was a significant source of inspiration throughout the twentieth century within arts such as poetry, literature, dance and, naturally, music. The 1920s became so characterized by jazz that the decade is known as 'the Jazz Age'. In Paris, which was the hotbed of escape from bourgeois moralism via primitivism and exoticism in the years between the two world wars, clever theatrical promoters cottoned on to the great interest of the public in everything that had to do with Africans and African Americans. The North American dance show *La Revue nègre*, starring Josephine Baker, became the big event that everyone talked about in Paris immediately upon its première in 1925. Reams were written in the press about the show, which was seen as 'a manifestation of the spirit of modern times'. Through semi-pornographic dance numbers such as 'Dance of the Savages' the inner eye of the audience was transported to a foreign world full of mysteries, a world that was oppressed and thus easily sexually accessible. The passion of the times for the Negro occasionally took reverse racist expression as well. The renowned art dealer Paul Guillaume was incensed over the racist criticism of *La Revue nègre* by the conservative culture reporters. 'We who believe that we have a soul must blush over the poverty of our spiritual lives when faced with the superiority of the blacks. . . . Intelligence in modern man must be black', claimed Guillaume (Rose 1989 p. 53).

The 1920s was the first decade of modern mass culture, and the expanding popular culture was revolutionized by the cinema, radio and the phonograph record. It was with this development that exoticism and primitivism found their way into youth culture, primarily via African American music and dance. The songs of praise of Mezz Mezzrow and the first jazz fanatics to the black man and his culture, the wishes of the Beat Generation and Kerouac (1976) to be 'negro' because 'the best the white world had given . . . had not enough ecstasy, not enough life, joy, kicks, darkness, music not enough night'; the worship of black roots by English 1960s rock and the punk infatuation with black culture in England – all of these examples show how white people projected their own needs and desires on to various forms of black culture. Therewith, they are also examples of exoticism and primitivism. In his ironic and self-critical song 'I Wanna Be Black', Lou Reed comments upon his own male-dominated rock generation's passion for African American culture.

> I wanna be black, I wanna be a panther / Have a girlfriend named Samantha / Have a stable full of foxy little whores / I don't want to be a fucked up middle class college student anymore / I wanna be black / I wanna be like Malcolm X / And cast a hex / Over John Kennedy's grave and have a big prick too I just wanna be black. ('I wanna be black', from *Street Hassle*, Arista 1978)

Lou Reed's lyrics are still relevant. The wish to 'be black' among today's young white males also carries deeply embedded stereotypical notions about black life and masculinity. Behind this wish lies alienation from and criticism of one's own culture. But the fascination with African American culture simultaneously gathers power in deep-seated Western stereotypes; we have much to gain by ridding ourselves of them.

Certainly, the exotization of Native American Indians, Gypsies and Asiatic cultural patterns have left traces in, for example, rock lyrics during various periods. But the youth culture's prototype of the 'noble savage' is the black American, a former slave (Pattison 1987). From the wishes to be black of Mezz Mezzrow to the hip-hop wiggers of today, one can trace the echoes from Rousseau and Guillaume. Beliefs about the African American and his culture as being freer, more sensual and more exciting are not hard to find in white youth culture. These stereotypical notions are to be regarded as expressions of Western exoticism and primitivism and they are still at work. But if we turn to contemporary African American ghetto culture and rap music, this classic exoticizing and primitivism-worshipping belief system must be filled out with additional aspects.

White Negroes, Black Albinos

In 1957, Norman Mailer published his controversial essay 'The White Negro'. Mailer showed that the hipsters and 'the beat generation' that shocked middle-class America with its boundary-crossing hunt for kicks, took their role models from black ghetto culture. The black man as pimp, small-time hustler or jazz musician was made into an ideal by Mailer – 'the existential hero' – precisely because he said yes to every possible pleasure with no guilt or anxiety (see Mailer 1961). Black intellectuals, such as James Baldwin (1963), directed strong criticism at Mailer and said that he reinforced stereotypical notions about black masculinity. Mailer's 'black macho' was a fantasy figure created by white middle-class needs.

Today, more than forty years after Mailer's essay was first published, the 'white negro' syndrome is more current than ever before. The psychopath mentality and the proximity to uninhibited expression of emotion that Mailer in his Reichian–existentialist-influenced youth once thought he could see in the black man, and found attractive, was primarily about the relationship to pleasure, lust and sexuality. The fascination that today's rap artists have for young white men, however, has to an equal degree to do with the relationship of contemporary black ghetto culture and rap to violence, physical strength and death – to being bad, hard and cool.

One aspect of gangsta rap's ability to attract especially young white, middle-class men might have to do with modern society and its relation to violence and death. Many scholars have pointed to the consequences of the disappearance from the cultural patterns of the dominant culture of the traditional forms of ritualized relations to death. French historian Philippe Ariès (1975/1978, p. 204), who has studied traditions and beliefs about death in Western civilization, says that 'a great deal of today's signs of maladaptation may be grounded in the repression of death from social reality'. Death is not a part of life today. Not so long ago the corpse of a newly dead person was put on show in his or her home and everyone who knew him would come to pay repects to the dead. Today death has been made invisible and is found essentially only in hospitals. It seems as if death in highly advanced industrial society, with its hysterical cult of youth and virility, has assumed the role of sexuality as the most taboo of all subjects. We live our lives as if we were immortal; death today is almost a narcissistic infringement. There is today a fear of death that makes us afraid to think about or maybe makes us obsessed with thoughts of death. A dead body fills us with disgust. Death has become obscene. Still, and this is the paradox, the only thing we can be sure about in this modern insecure, risk society is that our life has an end, but we live in a culture that denies and fears this fact – the most basic fact of all.

The situation, at least for middle-class youth, is similar with respect to violence. We all know that violence exists, that it is ultimately the ability of the powers-that-be to use violence that holds the social order together. We see violence in the media every day, but most of us have no real contact with it, and we certainly don't need to use it to put food on the table. Violence is present but still foreign, fearsome but simultaneously alluring. Anyhow, we all need to relate to death and violence. Now that death has been removed from our daily lives, and secularization has made the old rituals that once gave death a meaningful place in our life-world obsolete, death – and violence – has found a flood of representations in popular culture. In various ways our contemporary need to treat, symbolize and 'work through' our relation to death – and violence – is revolving around a lot of prominent themes in movies, music and novels. However, death and violence are a part of daily life in the ghetto in a different way. It is this reality that is romanticized in the pistol-waving branches of rap music that romanticize violence. Here, as in the Satanism-impregnated segments of rock, in the violently oriented communities of video, there is production of ritual patterns and symbolic codes that respond to the need of today's youth to work through their relation to death and violence. Youth culture can be characterized, analysed and understood in many different ways. But, in this context, one feature stands out. It started when the Rolling Stones did 'Sympathy for the Devil', but since then rock music and youth culture have become more and more interested in and occupied with death, violence, brutality, evil, etc. In the 1950s Elvis was not allowed to show his shaking hips on television, and youth culture shocked the society by breaking taboos around sexuality. Today, when the Department of Health is informing kids in school how to have safe anal sex, little remains of the old taboos around sexuality. New taboos are created, and modern man's occupation with death in various forms can be related to our culture's tendency to place taboos upon violence and death. And of course, one aspect of youth culture is, and always has been, the breaking of taboos.

Just as traditional sexual morality was an instrument of discipline, so fear of death is today. The man who dares to live life by looking death in the eye, he who communes daily with death and sees his own finiteness – that person will also crave life! Looked at from this aspect, death is dangerous to the prevailing social order, and nowhere is death more brutal and more dangerous than when borne by the Great Black Revenger. The moral panic about the fascination with the depictions of the violence of ghetto culture thus touches upon an unconscious fear of death's subversive potentialities. It is a fascination that cannot be understood without being related to race-stereotypical beliefs about the black man as monster or 'the wild beast', a representation of a constantly threatening primeval power unleashed upon culture and civilization.

Gangsta rap's depictions of the oppression of white society and of black resistance, as well as its staging of black masculinity through the exposure of well-trained bodies, guns and sexist jargon, has a widespread attraction. I live in Gothenburg – the second city of Sweden – an industrial town with half a million inhabitants. In Gothenburg there are many immigrant rap groups out in the suburbs as well as all-white, inner-city and middle-class rappers.[1] This chapter focuses on the latter: one feature of these groups is their identification with contemporary African American ghetto culture. Some of them refer to themselves as 'black albinos' and their lyrics are full of examples of how they use the black ghetto-culture mythology as a lens through which they see their own reality. Markedly often these young men cultivate a fascination with the black boxer Mike Tyson, a convicted and imprisoned rapist, white society's emblem for brutality, primeval power and uninhibited sexuality. Tyson, who has become something of a cult figure on the inner-city rap scene, grew up in the ghetto and, like so many of the leading rap artists, has experienced life as a 'street kid'. On one group's CD cover the members deliver a tribute to Tyson: 'Last a shoot out for the man Michael Gerard Tyson, the no. 1 all time great who was locked up in a cage for something they couldn't prove.' Another Gothenburg group, launched in the press with the epithet 'unbeatably brutal', have taken their name from the black boxer and call themselves Mike Tajson ('taja' is a slang word for masturbation). When the three band members, being interviewed for a monthly magazine, were asked why they took their name from the world's most famous rapist, they answered: 'Because Mike Tyson has a big black hard one and we have little white wimpy ones.'

Beyond music, other branches of the culture industry have shown interest in African American culture during recent years. A number of audience-drawing films, such as *New Jack City*, *Menace II Society* and *Blood In, Blood Out* were successful in Swedish cinemas. Several literary works that reflect life in the ghetto have also aroused considerable attention. Swedish publishers have realized their commercial potential and have released translations with admirable speed. Jess Mowry's *Way Past Cool* and Kody Scott's *Monster* are two current examples of this 'responsiveness to the needs of the market'. *Way Past Cool* is a predictable and weakly inflammatory youth novel. Mowry is a white 35-year-old who states on the book jacket that he has lived in the ghetto. His romanticizing of the gang community, the blood-dripping scenes of violence and the tiresome pistol-waving probably inspired the rapid translation by the Swedish publisher. I suspect there was a hope that the book's ghetto romance could make it a best seller among trendy young men.

The autobiographical *Monster* has been talked about more in Sweden. Even if the book is not a literary delight, the text breathes authenticity and genuineness. There is no doubt that the author was really involved in what he writes about. The constant presence of death and the many depictions of violence are not effects or gratuitous additions designed to make the story attractive. They are a part of daily reality for many young blacks in South Central Los Angeles. Interesting in the context is how Scott consciously plays with our cultural beliefs about monsters. In psychoanalytically orientated research it has been pointed out that the monsters of fairy tales and popular culture are a representation of the return of the repressed (Bettelheim 1975; Cohen 1992). The monster is both nature and culture. Because it is a union of human and animal, the monster can in a single shape join sides and aspects that the culture has forced the individual to split off and discard. The monster thus becomes, in its primitive, polymorphous perversity, an expression for an archaic longing for absolute pleasure and satisfaction, which is naturally a threat against established reason, the given social order and the dominant culture. In this sense, the monster constitutes one aspect of an unarticulated and unconscious resistance to the reality principle that forces us to refrain from our deepest lusts, desires and fantasies. This is one side of the coin, but the hybrid nature of the monster means that it also carries connotations of fantasies of being torn apart, devoured and annihilated. The monster thus becomes also an ideal personification of the negative stereotypes of racism. When Kody Scott chose to entitle his book *Monster*, it was not a random choice, but rather a highly conscious decision in which he subtly plays with both positive and negative stereotypes as well as the charges created by connotations of unbridled pleasure and bottomless fear. Scott's asocial and amoral story of a black ghetto monster is (not least for its white readers) a titillating tall tale about 'the return of the repressed'. Neither *Monster* nor *Way Past Cool* will be remembered for its literary qualities, but the capacity to fascinate the youngsters I've been interviewing makes them interesting as signs of the times.

Popular Culture, the Body and the Search for Intensity

It is not only in the culture and entertainment industries that black men (and women) have in an increasingly striking way become desirable identification objects for white people. Soft drinks, sport shoes, razors, jeans and much else are marketed today in ad campaigns featuring blacks in starring roles. There is in today's popular culture as a whole a remarkable preoccupation with not only the Black but the Foreign in general. Television series with stars of non-European origin, World Music and 'ethnic influences' in fashion, the clothing manufacturer Benetton's marketing strategies, and the launch of black fashion models such as Naomi Campbell are a few examples which perhaps allow us to talk about new manifestations of exoticism and primitivism. Segments of the modern world of commodities are working hard to create a belief that difference, with respect to ethnicity and race, no longer rests upon the supremacy of Western culture. The Other does not assume the position of a stigmatized or browbeaten object in the same way it once did. To avoid conflict with large groups of non-European origin, the racial and cultural stereotypes of the 1920s and 1930s are no longer marketable. However, it is nevertheless apparent that display of the foreign, the emphasis on difference, is still a spice with which movie producers, ad makers and others excite and create tension in their consumers. The underlying fantasies and traditional taboos that previously surrounded the relationship to the Other are hidden only imperfectly. To anyone who has studied MTV's music videos, it must seem obvious that contemporary culture is presenting open desire for the Other in a completely new way. The foreign is constantly presented as more erotic, sensual and natural. Doubtless, the intent of these images is to highlight intensity, ardour and directness. This is also a prominent element of the fascination with African American culture that we can trace in the craze for primitivism on the part of youth and popular culture during the twentieth century. Primitivism is to a great extent about the expression of the physical and the search for intensity.

The German sociologist and philosopher Thomas Ziehe (1991) also believes that there is a search for intensity or potentiality to be found in contemporary human endeavours to oppose the emptiness characteristic of the late modern world, that is, attempts to charge oneself and create tension in various ways.[2] English sociologists Stanley Cohen and Laurie Taylor (1992) employ a similar metaphor when they discuss the 'escape attempts' of the modern man, his attempts to break out of the grey, prison-like everyday through chasing experiences, news and sensations. The preoccupation with the search for exciting and excessive experiences that we can see today in youth and popular culture, as well as in advertising, and which gains an incisive expression in gangsta rap, reveals a hunt for excitement, passion, pleasure and kicks.

A central element in the search for intensity is about overcoming modern man's alienated relationship to his own body. The notion of opposing modernity via a search for 'origins', 'nature' and 'authenticity' has been expressed in various concepts of 'going back to the body'. Thus, for example, the Italian sociologist Alberto Melucci says that 'The body appears as a secret domain, to which only the individual holds the key, and to which he or she can return to seek a self-definition unfettered by the rules and expectations of society' (Melucci 1989).

In popular culture versions, primitivism has charged the black body with a combination of pleasure and strength that makes it an ideal projection screen for unconscious fantasies. Being black has been made synonymous for whites with having optimal access to one's own physical pleasure. The critic bell hooks (1992) discusses these aspects and uses the British slang expression 'eating the other' to elucidate the bodily and oral (cannibalistic) nature of this desire. The black body's connotations of slavery, pain, orgiastic voluptuousness and death are partially rooted in constantly active stereotypes according to which blacks are closer to their origins and basic instincts than whites; these are beliefs that our reflective and enlightened contemporary world has illuminated and deleted from public debate, but they are nevertheless at work under the surface. They make up one aspect of the unconscious force field that has been a part of the complex weave of the culture for centuries. The hunt for intensity and bodily pleasure preoccupies the modern human being, consciously or unconsciously, in a number of different ways. Taking bell hooks as a point of departure, I believe that it is the Western individual's reflexive relationship to personal pleasure, the constant hunt and striving for 'total pleasure' (Foucault 1977), that has led 'the white west to sustain a romantic fantasy of the "primitive" and the concrete search for a real primitive paradise' (hooks 1992, p. 27). Regardless of whether this paradise is a 'black continent' or a black body.

The black urban ghetto has become a stage for a modern mythology and heroic saga where life swings between omnipotence and obliteration. Herein is also found an intensity in fearlessness before death and the awareness that every new day may be the last. Ice Cube raps: 'Today was a good day, no one I know in South Central L. A. got killed.' The fascination of young, white middle-class males with contemporary ghetto culture may perhaps rightly be seen as a statement that life is too regulated, empty and void of excitement. These males find themselves in the company of Mezz Mezzrow, Jack Kerouac and others who have sought excitement and intensity in black culture. The difference is that today's craze for black culture does not revolve solely around notions of drugs, ecstatic music and unbounded black sexuality; rather, it revolves to an equally great extent around the ghetto life's proximity to brutality, violence and death – the other side of primitivism's passionate search for intensity and kicks.

A macabre example of this is the black rap artist Ice T's *Home Invasion*, one of his top-selling records. The picture on the cover shows black men breaking into a white middle-class home, killing the father and raping the mother. In the middle of the picture, the son of the house sits unconcerned with headphones on, listening to cassettes of black rappers like Ice Cube and Public Enemy. A piece of African jewellery in rasta colours – green, yellow, black and red – hangs round his neck. The book he is reading, the *Autobiography of Malcolm X*, lies open at his feet. Ice T concludes his cover notes with 'The injection of black rage into America's white youth is the last stage of preparation for the revolution.' He further develops the theme on the CD's title track. According to Ice T, American society is on the way to losing its sons in the 'home invasion' that he and other black rappers have staged.

A paradoxical situation has arisen. While segments of the culture and consumer goods industries have an interest in de-stereotyping our images of the Other and working for ethnic equality, segments of contemporary ghetto culture are tending towards doing the opposite. This culture is partially developing its power of attraction through taking advantage of and using the ambivalence between fear and attraction that has long constituted the Western man's relationship to the foreign. Gangsta rap not least is playing upon classical stereotypes with its stylized overtones of sex and violence.

Racism and Sexuality

In the case of the human being in modern industrial society, the classic exoticization of the Other may be seen as a representation of the longing to 'take off' from a culture dominated by alienation and instrumental reason. Through romanticizing foreign places and people, which in some respects are imagined as standing closer to nature – the body – contact is established with a more primeval essence which becomes the Western culture's opposite – its Other. Here are found the genuineness, sensualism, light-heartedness, spontaneity, et cetera, that modern society denies or makes dysfunctional. This type of positive stereotype, which we have all come into contact with, for example in beliefs that blacks are more sensual, rhythmic or musical than whites, converts a stigmatized position to something worth striving to achieve. These stereotypes are certainly not as repulsive as racism's negative stereotypes – though equally stereotypical. The romanticized notions and devoted praises of exoticism are commented upon by Frantz Fanon (1967, p. 10): 'The man who adores the Negro is as sick as the man who abominates him.' Exoticism, as much as racism, is an objectification of the Other. However, compared to racism, exoticism is a rather innocent phenomenon that, as Rose (1989) points out, places the Other on a pedestal or in a museum rather than in an extermination camp. Racism excludes the Other from the social community because he represents a threat to the culture as well as to the identity of the individual. Racism could, as Stuart Hall (1993) has shown, be seen as the denial of the anxiety-inducing possibility that the Other could be a part of ourselves. Racist stereotypes represent the longing for security which, it is imagined, can be created through the drawing of an absolute boundary between us and the Other. In the exoticism that adopts the Other via an identification without reflection, there is a comparable unwillingness to engage oneself in the identity work of modern man. This kind of exoticism also represents a way to avoid the engagement with a multifaceted reality. The most extreme forms of exoticism may, through their projections and idealized notions of the Other, be seen as a flight from painful but necessary aspects of the individuation process. This, of course, is most conspicuous in adolescents.

The 'savage', doubly exposed by Enlightenment philosophers as both 'noble' and 'feared barbarian', became not only the Other – an antithesis and mirror that European culture needed in order to develop its own identity as civilized and superior – but also a representation for Otherness – the banished and unconscious sides of the human being which modern culture did not let through or allow, primarily sexuality and aggression. Stuart Hall (1992, p. 314) speaks of the 'savage' as a personification of modern man's forgotten, repressed and denied 'dark' sides, 'the reverse image of enlightenment and modernity'.

Gangsta rap's controversial exposure of the black man as monster and amoral hedonist thus is based upon stereotypes of long standing. The Enlightenment philosophers, during intense discussions on the characteristics and qualities of various races, had already consigned physical expressivity to the black race and intellectual work to whites. Via this type of classification and categorization, Western racism made the Other into a subordinate being of inferior worth. Support for the notion of black people's bestiality and inferiority was also frequently culled from the scientific disciplines of the day, biology and medicine not least prominently. Appearance was commonly taken as a pretext for 'scientific' observations and analyses that claimed that the African was closer to the ape than to the white man.

That the black man in this way became the primary and most frightening negative stereotype in European culture is probably also a result in part of the history of that culture. In Judaeo-Christian civilization, black has long been the colour of evil. The devil is black, sin is black, and we speak generally about black shadows or black clouds as metaphorical expressions for various types of threats. In our culture, a person with evil intentions has a black soul. White has represented the good, the innocent, the promise of a bright future. According to Frantz

Fanon (1967, p. 188), our culture has made the black man into a symbol of evil. 'In Europe, the Black man is the symbol of Evil . . . he is the bad side of the human character.' The African seen as expression of the dark side of humanity was something of an unreliable beast, from which civilization must protect itself. The 'primitive people's' allegedly inadequate social order and inferior culture, combined with 'bad racial qualities', formed the basis for the fear harboured by the white man that nature's unbridled forces would run amok and disavow the advances of civilization (Pieterse 1992; Baudet 1965). Stereotypical beliefs about the Other were also cultivated in countries that did not have their own colonies. For example, Swedish schoolchildren in the first decades of the twentieth century read in their textbooks that 'negroes are bloodthirsty and prefer not to work, although they are quite strong.'[3]

The duality according to which the black man was seen as a symbol for the darker sides of human nature, but was simultaneously endowed with traits such as spontaneity and physicality, has its most palpable expression in the ambivalence that 'whites' have developed in relationship to sexuality. In Europe and the USA, the black man has first and foremost been associated with activities that, at least in times past, sexually repressed Western society forced its members to restrain. The American sociologist Calvin C. Hernton (1969, p. 100) says that the white man 'sexually wants to be a negro. He wants to enjoy the unbounded sexual behaviour that he imagines negroes enjoy.' In line with this, Frantz Fanon claims that 'the negro symbolizes the biological':

> The white man is convinced that the negro is a beast; if it is not the length of his penis then it is the sexual potency that impresses him. Face to face with this man who is 'different from himself' he needs to defend himself. In other words, to personify the Other. The Other will become the mainstay of his preoccupations and his desires. (Fanon 1967, p. 170)

Important aspects of Western dominance over other cultures, and of Western racism, are based upon processes in which split-off parts of the psyche are projected out into the surrounding world. This also applies to the dominant white attitudes towards blacks. Blacks, in the white conceptual world, are a representation of that which society and culture have pushed aside, made taboo, and designated as dangerous, threatening and forbidden. But these split-off parts of the white psyche, where sexuality is pivotal, are simultaneously the elements or dimensions that make life exciting, rich and vivid. Thus, these projections will come to form the basis of a primarily unconscious envy: blacks have

access to something whites are missing. That which is split off and
projected upon blacks becomes the object of a desire that must be
attacked and destroyed. With its sexually ritualized overtones, lynching
is the cruellest example of this envy.[4] Envy is an ambivalent complex of
emotions; there is a craving to possess certain of the desired attributes
of the Other at the same time that the Other must be destroyed
because he represents something perceived as lacking in oneself.

The lynchings that took place were of black men accused of having
had sexual relations with a white woman. But merely having spoken to,
whistled at, or tried to approach a white woman was sometimes
considered sufficient grounds. The Swedish scholar Gunnar Myrdal,
who saw racism as the 'American Dilemma', was an early proponent of
the theory that white racial oppression had a very strong sexual
component (Myrdal 1962). When a black man was lynched, a common
occurrence in the southern US during the latter part of the nineteenth
century and the first half of the twentieth, he was nearly always
subjected to ritual castration. According to Myrdal, this is evidence that
there was a close connection between lynching and a repressive sexual
morality. The Dutch anthropologist Jan Nederveen Pieterse (1992,
p. 177) has also made a connecthetion between lynchings in the US
South and a certain form of male sexuality: 'Repressed sexuality, white
male domination and violence are so closely interwoven here that they
merge with one another.'

Exoticism: Ambivalence and Desire

It seems as if the force field between attraction and repulsion is based
in an ambivalence towards that which the culture considers threatening, unclean and taboo. Thus, the relationship to one's own body also
becomes critical. Intensive, unbounded experiences in which self-
control temporarily ceases to function, in which the individual 'leaves'
his social and cultural attributes, become a critical marker for that
which is 'otherness' and how this otherness is constituted. It seems as if
there is a connection between, on the one hand, the need to assimilate
and control one's own sexuality and aggression and, on the other hand,
the wish to control the Other's destructiveness and sexuality.[5] The
complexity of white racism as well as of exoticism and primitivism
cannot be understood unless consideration is given to the frustration
and ambivalence developed by white culture with respect to the aspects
of itself it has been forced to repress.

The fascination of white male youth with the former slave culture's
contemporary manifestations is complex (Sernhede 1994, 1995). The

ability of popular culture to romanticize ghetto life as a cool, 'on the edge' life (with the intensity provided by proximity to death) is an important aspect of its power to fascinate. Through identification with the images of popular culture, the search of white youth for intensity, passion, sensuality, pleasure and physicality is ascribed to blacks, and thus the stereotypical beliefs of popular culture come to say more about those who hold them than they do about blacks.

The Other, as a representation for the repressed, thus encompasses both distancing and attraction. Based on this line of thought, the modern form of primitivism, the identification with the Other and the desire for the Other cultivated in contemporary youth culture may be seen as an expression for a wish to come into contact with the foreign in order to demonstrate a distancing from the order that suffocates and prevents contact with experiences of 'total pleasure'. Primitivism and exoticism seek to establish relationships to the sides of the self forbidden by the culture; one wishes to be touched by the untamed intensity and passion from which the culture protects us. This kind of exoticism is founded upon racial and cultural stereotypes that have turned the conceptual world of ordinary racism inside out. White youth who are fascinated by Monster and who identify with the black, uninhibited hedonist Mike Tyson express an unattainable mirage deeply embedded in our culture: the possibility of being allowed to release the total pleasure where lust and death meet. From Mike Tyson and Monster, sexuality and aggression – the polarities of the repressed (and, as we have seen also, of primitivism) – radiate in a titillating 'identification game'. What is rejected or by definition placed outside culture displays many aspects typical of the times. The prerequisite of these identifications is the insecure identity of modern man. The feature of this 'identification game' is the way it is buoyed by stereotypes rooted in ambivalence towards one's own culture – which has been the dilemma of modern Western man for centuries.

However, notions of the Other as a representation of innocence and goodness, and notions of the Other as brutality and threat, have equally little to do with reality. We fear or idealize the Other not because he is evil or good but rather because he, through being different, is charged with beliefs that correspond to deeply embedded unconscious needs. Exoticism also gains its power and dynamics, as Stuart Hall (1989) points out about racism, 'from the mythical and psychological energies invested in culture'. Even though exoticism, as well as racism, for this reason cannot be responded to only with information and rational arguments, I do believe that there is a lot of work for cultural studies practitioners to do in this field of research.

Notes

1. For information about the ethnically mixed suburban youth and hip-hop see Sernhede (1998).

2. It is also possible to discern in the history of modern youth culture expressions of those 'culturally new-seeking movements' that according to Thomas Ziehe (1991) characterize the attempt to manage uncertainty in late modern society. Ziehe talks about subjectivization, ontologization and potentiation. I understand potentiation as the dominant element in the contemporary relationship of white youth to black culture. See also my discussion of subjectivization and ontologization in the relationships of young men to blues and reggae, in Sernhede (1995).

3. The quotation is from a Swedish geography textbook dated 1913, *Jordens länder och folk* (Countries and Peoples of the World) published by Almquist.

4. For a more detailed discussion of the psychoanalytical dimensions of white racism, see Kovel (1970). See also Kristeva (1982, 1991) on the repellent and taboo as 'abject' and our fear of the Other as alienation from repressed and undesirable aspects of ourselves, which are projected onto groups or individuals who are excluded from the social community.

5. 'The white man's burden thus becomes his sexuality and its control, and it is this which is transferred into the need to control the sexuality of the Other' (Gilman 1992, p. 194).

References

Ariès, Philippe (1975/1978): *Essais sur l'histoire de la mort en Occident du moyen âge à nos jours*. Paris: Seuil.

Baldwin, James (1963) *The Fire Next Time*. New York: Dail Press.

Baudet, Henri (1965) *Paradise on Earth*. New Haven/London: Yale University Press.

Bettelheim, Bruno (1975) *The Uses of Enchantment: The Meaning and Importance of Fairy Tales*. New York: Random House.

Bitterli, Urs (1987) 'Die exotische Insel', in Thomas Koebner and Gerhart Pickerodt, (eds.) *Die andere Welt. Studien zum Exotismus*. Frankfurt am Main: Athenäum.

Cohen, Phil (1992) ' "Its racism that dunnit": Hidden Narratives in Theories of Racism', in James Donald and Ali Rattansi (eds.) *Race, Culture and Difference*. London: Sage.

Cohen, Stanley and Laurie Taylor (1992) *Escape Attempts: The Theory and Practice of Resistance of Everyday Life*. 2nd edn. London: Routledge.

Fanon, Frantz (1967) *Black Skin, White Masks*. London: Pluto Press. First published (in French) in 1952.

Foucault, Michel (1977) *Language, Counter-memory and Practice: Selected Essays and Interviews*. New York: Cornell University Press.

Gilman, Sander L. (1992) 'Black Bodies, White Bodies: Towards an Iconography of Female Sexuality in Late Nineteenth-century Art, Medicine and Literature', in James Donald and Ali Rattansi (eds.) *'Race', Culture and Difference*. London: Sage.

Hall, Stuart (1992) 'The West and the Rest: Discourse and Power', in Stuart Hall and Braun Giben (eds.) *Formations of Modernity*, Cambridge: Polity Press.

Hall, Stuart (1993) 'Rasismen som diskurs', *Häften för kritiska studier*, No. 3. Originally published in *Das Argument*, No. 6, 1989.

Hernton, Calvin C. (1969) *Sex and Racism*. St Albans: Paladin.

hooks, bell (1992) 'Eating of the Other', in *Black Looks, Race and Representation*. London: Turnaround.

Kerouac, Jack (1976) *On the Road*. London: Penguin. First published in 1957.

Kovel, Joel (1970) *White Racism, a Psychohistory*. New York: Random House.

Kristeva, Julia (1982) *Powers of Horror: An Essay on Abjection*. New York: Columbia University Press.

Kristeva, Julia (1991) *Strangers to Ourselves*. New York: Columbia University Press.

Mailer, Norman (1961) 'The White Negro', in *Advertisements for Myself*. New York: André Deutsch Ltd. Article originally published in 1957.

Melucci, Alberto (1989) *Nomads of the Present*. London: Radius.

Myrdal, Gunnar (1962) *An American Dilemma: The Negro Problem and Modern Democracy*. New York: Harper & Row. First published 1944.

Pattison, Robert (1987) *The Triumph of Vulgarity*. New York/Oxford: Oxford University Press.

Pieterse, Jan Nederveen (1992) *White on Black: Images of Africa and Blacks in Western Popular Culture*. London: Yale University Press.

Rose, Phyllis (1989) *Jazz Cleopatra: Josephine Baker in Her Times*. New York: St Martin's Press.

Sernhede, Ove (1994) 'Youth and Black Culture as Otherness: Identity, Resistance and Ethnicity', *Migration* 3/4.

Sernhede, Ove (1995) 'Black Music and White Adolescence: Oedipal Rivalry, Absent Fathers and Masculinity', in Aleksandra Åhlund and Raul Granquist (eds.) *Negotiating Identities*. Amsterdam: Radoopi.

Sernhede, Ove (1998) 'Waiting for Mandela', *Soundings*, No. 8.

Ziehe, Thomas (1991) *Zeitvergleiche: Jugend in kulturellen Modernisierungen*. Munich: Juventa.

27

Against the Punitive Wind:
Stuart Hall, the State and the Lessons
of the Great Moving Right Show

Joe Sim

> Theorists and practical men alike have generally agreed that the primary purpose of the state is to maintain order. It is highly desirable that order should be upheld under law and that law should respect rights. But unless the state has the will and the capacity to ensure order, not only bad but eventually good people will flout its authority.
>
> Thatcher 1995, p. 542

> New Labour's . . . mission is to move forward from where Margaret Thatcher left off, rather than dismantle every single thing she did.
>
> Mandelson and Liddle, cited in Gray 1998, p. 5

In a conversation with Stuart Hall in the aftermath of John Major's ascension to the leadership of the Conservative Party, we pondered on the significance of his victory for British politics in general and the state in particular. Stuart was very clear about the meaning of Major's victory: the Thatcherites would remain deeply embedded in the institutions of power while their authoritarian and repressive presence would still be felt in the forthcoming years at different levels of political and civil society. The 'iron times' would continue. This chapter focuses on a major but recently neglected aspect of Hall's work, namely the role of the state in the reproduction of these 'iron times' in the 1980s and 1990s.

Moving Right along with the Strong State

Make no mistake about it: under this regime, the market is to be Free; the people are to be disciplined.

Hall 1980a, p. 5

This short sentence taken from Hall's 1979 Cobden Trust Human Rights Day Lecture perfectly crystallizes his analysis of the corrosive impact of the New Right and the changing configuration of state power at Margaret Thatcher's triumphalist moment. These themes were to pervade a series of key articles and books that appeared in the late 1970s and early 1980s. In particular, Poulantzas's concept of 'authoritarian statism' provided Hall with a rich theoretical seam to mine in his analysis of state power.

The importance of 'authoritarian statism', he wrote, was that it 'represented a new combination of coercion/consent tilted towards the coercive end of the spectrum, while maintaining the outer forms of democratic class rule intact' (Hall 1988, p. 152). However, the concept was 'weak in two major respects'. First, Poulantzas misread the fact that the New Right conceptualized the role of the state as more limited and truncated, and as a bloc was therefore *both* anti-statist *and* state centralist in its field of operations. Second, Poulantzas neglected 'the ways in which popular consent can be so constructed, by a historical bloc seeking hegemony, as to harness to its support popular discontents, neutralise the opposing forces, disaggregate the opposition and really incorporate some strategic elements of popular opinion into its own hegemonic project'. Hence the concept of authoritarian populism: 'a movement towards a dominative and "authoritarian" form of democratic class politics – paradoxically rooted in the 'transformism' (Gramsci's term) of populist discontents' (Hall 1998, pp. 152–3).

Within the Conservative Party the interventionist and unrelenting discipline that the Thatcherite bloc yearned for, imposed through the institutions of law and order and hegemonically cemented by populist campaigns around crime and immorality, became clear and unambiguous in the immediate aftermath of the 1979 election. Writing in 1980, Hall captured this dialectic moment:

The themes of crime and social delinquency, articulated through the discourses of popular morality, touch the direct experience, the anxieties and uncertainties of ordinary people. This has led to a dovetailing of the 'cry for discipline' from below into the call for an enforced restoration of social order 'from above'. This articulation forms the bridge, between the real material sources of popular discontent, and their representation, through specific ideological forces and campaigns, as the general need for a 'disciplined society'. It has, as its principal effect, the awakening of popular support for a restoration of order through imposition: the basis of a populist 'Law and Order' campaign. This, in turn, has given a wide legitimacy to the tilt of the balance within the operations of the state towards the 'coercive' pole, whilst preserving its popular legitimacy. (Hall 1980b, pp. 172–3)

Into the Law and Order Decade

> The Devil is still with us, recording his successes in the crime figures and in all of the other maladies of this society in spite of its material comfort . . . upholding the law is one area where we would wish the state to be stronger than it is.
> Margaret Thatcher, cited in McFadyean and Renn 1984, p. 70

From the moment it came to power, Thatcher's government began the process of strengthening the state's capacity for serious and prolonged intervention into the social body through a huge material and numerical increase in law-and-order 'services' and in the enactment of a draconian array of Acts, Orders and Bills. A number of these developments originated in the continuing war in the North of Ireland, where the strategy of intervening with extreme prejudice had been honed in the imperialist arenas of Malaysia, Singapore and Hong Kong (Hillyard 1987). Others emerged from the searing critique of the post-1945 corporatist settlement articulated by the organic intellectuals who populated the think-tanks of Conservative Party Central Office and in the influence exerted by different pressure groups, through formal and informal networks, who were vociferous in condemning those labelled as responsible for the social and moral malaise afflicting the social order and by extension the society's political destiny.

In coming together, these different strands both legitimized and resulted in an intensification and extension of the power of the state to regulate and discipline the lives and experiences of increasing numbers of individuals in the UK. At the same time, Hall's elaboration of Poulantzas's original thesis with respect to the construction of popular consent for this authoritarian project can be seen in the positioning of particular groups as the 'enemy within'. Their presence provided an unrelenting symbolic reminder for the New Right that the nation was in decline and that the activities and behaviour of these groups if not disciplined and controlled would lead to the collapse of moral and social order.

This line of thought was pivotal to the analysis of the mugging panic that Hall and his co-writers developed in the 1970s. What is important is that successive Conservative governments (and, as I shall illustrate below, Blair's New Labour) continued to identify a range of individuals and groups as symbolic of, and responsible for, the decline in the moral and political state of the nation. As a state institution operating in the realm of civil society, the mass media were (and are) central to the process of demonization in particular and the attempt to construct, however contingent and contradictory, a Thatcherite consensus in general.

From the mid-1970s, the Thatcherites were clear that the mobilization of a cadre of organic intellectuals to fight the 'battle of ideas', as Sir Keith Joseph put it, was the key to constructing a hegemonic consensus around crime and punishment. Joseph, working through the Centre for Policy Studies, aimed to 'get at the fairly small number of people who influence the thinking of a nation'. This was done through targeting and then wining and dining 'people in powerful or influential walks of life: eating our way to victory.' (Halcrow 1989, pp. 66–108). For Thatcher, Joseph's influence was crucial:

> It was Keith who really began to turn the intellectual tide against socialism. He got our fundamental intellectual message across, to students, professors, journalists, the 'intelligentsia' generally ... if Keith hadn't been doing all that work with the intellectuals, all the rest of our work would probably never have resulted in success. (Thatcher 1989, p. 97)

The 'battle of ideas' was taken into the heart of the mass media. Again Joseph was the key figure. Reflecting on his role in the strategy of synchronization, Thatcher pointed out that he had made 'faith in what could be done ... into something that intelligent people were willing to share. And their acceptance spread the message through the press and other media to everybody' (ibid.). His task was facilitated by the appointment of former TV producer Gordon Reece to Thatcher's full-time staff. This appointment was designed to allow the Conservatives to focus not only on their traditional supporters via *The Times* and the *Daily* and *Sunday Telegraph* but also on the middle-England readers of the *Daily Mail* and the *Daily Express*. However the 'real revolution' lay in targeting the *Sun* and the *News of the World*. Both newspapers 'were crucial in communicating Conservative values to non-Conservative voters'. Whatever other demands were placed on Thatcher as Leader of the Opposition, 'when Gordon said we must have lunch with such-and-such an editor that was the priority' (Thatcher 1995, p. 294).

As a member of Mrs Thatcher's first cabinet, Sir Ian Gilmour observed the unfolding of the Conservatives' relationship with the *Sun*.

The key to the relationship was Rupert Murdoch, who was 'as far right as Mrs Thatcher' and regarded the cabinet 'wets' as 'hypocrites and "pissing liberals"' (Gilmour 1993, p. 44).

Despite these developments Thatcher was impatient with the pace of change and with the unreconstituted ideologies of many of those around the cabinet table. The second devastating Conservative victory in the general election of June 1983 provided her with the perfect opportunity in her remorseless pursuit of a government based on those who were 'one of us'. When she reshuffled the cabinet the day after the election her vision was undimmed: 'there was a revolution still to be made, and too few revolutionaries. The appointment of the first Cabinet in the new Parliament ... seemed like a chance to recruit some'(Thatcher 1993, p. 306). Her supporters – those who were ideologically and spiritually 'one of us' – were moved into key offices of the state: Nigel Lawson was installed as Chancellor, Geoffrey Howe as Foreign Secretary, Cecil Parkinson as Trade and Industry Secretary and Norman Tebbit as Employment Secretary.

The other significant promotion went to Leon Brittan, who replaced William Whitelaw as Home Secretary. Historically, Whitelaw has been constructed as a liberal within a cabinet of New Right authoritarians. And yet he did not stand outside or above the intensification and extension in the power of the state that came with Thatcher's first election victory. Despite his 'wet' credentials and his 'social distaste' for Mrs Thatcher, 'professionally, he bound himself completely to her' (Young 1989, p. 235).

Brittan wasted little time in building on Whitelaw's legacy. He was 'the prime example, after Parkinson, of a complete Thatcher creation ... [he] looked like the right sort of Home Secretary for an administration intended to mark the rise to power of Mrs Thatcher's friends' (Young 1989, p. 335). From the outset his intentions were clear: 'On taking office I decided that we needed a strategy which would enable us to pursue our priorities and objectives in a deliberate and coherent way' (cited in Sim 1987, p. 206). Money continued to be poured into the police and prisons, and new legislation extended police powers, particularly in the area of public order, while the centralization and militarization of the police force reinforced their autonomy and lack of accountability (Scraton 1985). This was supplemented by the biggest prison-building programme in the twentieth century. Additionally, the remit of the security services was extended as the definition of subversion became more elastic, while legislation that severely curtailed the right to picket and protest during industrial disputes effectively emasculated the trade union movement as a political force. The moment of the 'coercive state' (Hillyard and Percy-Smith 1988) had arrived and was seen in the ruthless suppression and occupation of the mining communities during the year-long coal dispute and in the incapacitating brutality exercised by the police against political demonstrators and peace campaigners in 1984 and 1985.

However, as Hall has consistently reminded us, a hegemonic project is never complete; it is fought over, disputed and sometimes can be lost. In the case of law and order the attempt by the Thatcherite bloc to achieve hegemony remained incomplete. A series of interlocking events throughout the 1980s raised profound questions both about the capacity of the state to deliver and about the Tories' capabilities of constructing the reinvigorated nation the New Right had promised. These events included: major inner-city disturbances; the unceasing rise in the official crime rate; the low clear-up rate for conventional crimes; several high-profile legal cases which threw doubt on the safety of the convictions of those imprisoned for crimes involving political violence as well as of those involved in 'ordinary crimes'; and the continuing ideological challenge posed by pressure groups such as Inquest who highlighted the sometimes devastating impact of coercive state practices in relation to deaths in custody.

This combined failure meant that 'the Thatcher government needed to reform its crime control policy in such a way that would restore their credibility without alienating the coalition of support they had constructed during the late-1970s' (Benyon and Edwards, 1997 p. 11). From the late 1980s the community became central to the strategy pursued by the Tories. This concept, with its deep hegemonic appeal across the social classes to a mystical present and mythical past, 'was employed by the Conservatives to emphasise the responsibility of private citizens for personal and public safety' (Benyon and Edwards 1997, p. 12). In practice this meant that:

> The Conservatives managed to integrate the community based approach into their ideological framework whilst retaining a commitment to 'hard' policing and retributive penal regimes. This flexible blend of neo-liberal and neo-conservative ideas was characteristic of the free economy–strong state doctrine of the Thatcher Governments. (ibid.)

This development and the emergence of privatized law-and-order 'services' did not curtail the augmentation of state power. Propelled forward by the moral panic surrounding juvenile crime in the early 1990s and led by Michael Howard, 'the government's approach to law and order appeared to veer sharply back in the direction of "authoritarian populism"' (ibid., p. 21). By 1995 the Conservatives had passed seventeen major Acts since 1981 that had strengthened the capacity of the state for disciplined and retributive intervention into the social body. This record stood in sharp contrast to the Tories' attitude to crimes committed by the powerful.

Crime, the Powerful and the Anti-statist Strategy

For Hall, the interventionist and centralizing tendencies inherent in Thatcherism were dialectically related to an anti-statist strategy:

> an 'anti-statist' strategy . . . is not one which refuses to operate through the state; it is one which conceives a more limited state role, and which advances through the attempt, ideologically, to *represent itself* as anti-statist, for the purpose of popular mobilization. (Hall 1988, p. 152; emphasis in the original)

Under the Conservatives this had particular relevance for the policing of the powerful. If the powerless continued to be the 'proper objects of power' (Fiske 1993, p. 235) through the retributive interventionism of the strong state, then for other more powerful groups the eighteen years of Conservative rule meant that their activities remained relatively invisible, comparatively unregulated and effectively decriminalized. The deregulatory discourses that underpinned the politics of the free market had a precipitous impact on those agencies responsible for ensuring that the powerful, both organizationally and individually, were subject to some degree of regulation, however contingent and fragmentary under bourgeois legal arrangements.

Deregulating the regulators

The criminal activities of the powerful and their regulation have been a central concern for critical social theorists since Marx's excoriating critique of capitalist business practices in the nineteenth century (Marx 1977, p. 274). As with the strong state thesis, it is important to recognize that many of the tendencies for noninterventionism and nonpunishment have a history that precedes the emergence of the New Right in the mid-1970s. At the same time it is clear that the commitment of successive Conservative administrations to a political economy of deregulation seriously intensified these historical tendencies. Consequently, in contrast to the huge increase in funding and personnel for those involved in dealing with conventional crimes, there were equally significant cutbacks in the policing and regulation of the activities of the powerful.

The decline in occupational safety was directly linked to the first Thatcher government's commitment 'to removing the "burdens" of social regulation from business' (Pearce and Tombs, 1998 p. 149). As such:

> the Health and Safety Executive was subject to funding cuts during the first two-thirds of the 1980s, accompanied by enormous increases in its workload. The result was that there emerged a state of *de facto* deregulation in the UK. (ibid. pp. 149–50; emphasis in the original)

This had severe consequences. Between 1981 and 1985, 739 workers were killed on building sites. According to the Health and Safety Executive (HSE), 517, or 70 per cent, of these lives could have been saved if minimum safety standards had been observed. The HSE pointed out that 'bad habits, sloppy practices and poor management and organisation seem endemic' (Scraton *et al.* 1991, p. 158). Deaths in the construction industry increased by 42 per cent during this period, while the number of fatal and serious accidents increased by 27 per cent in engineering, 54 per cent in textiles, 32 per cent in food, drink and tobacco, 16 per cent in vehicles, 47 per cent in furniture, and 43 per cent in general metals and goods. At the same time, the number of factory inspectors in the field declined by 19 per cent (*Observer*, 22 August 1989).

In other areas also the process of deregulation underpinned by nonprosecution had a clear impact. Between 1979 and 1988 the number of wage inspectors was halved. In 1987, 4,443 establishments were found to be underpaying their workers. There were nine prosecutions. Overall, between 1979 and 1991, 100,000 companies were caught underpaying their workers. Sixty-seven, or 0.067 per cent, were prosecuted (*Independent*, 25 June 1991). (This in a country with the weakest legal protection for workers in Western Europe). In 1987, the cost of defrauding social security was £500 million and resulted in 14,000 prosecutions, while the cost of income tax evasion was £5,000 million resulting in nine prosecutions (Scraton *et al.* p. 158).

Mrs Thatcher's prime ministerial demise in November 1990 and her replacement by the publicly more acceptable John Major did nothing to lessen the intensity of the interventionist/rolling-back strategy. Major's articulation of an Edwardian 'imaginary community', of an England at ease with itself, in which warm beer was imbibed during cricket-dominated, halcyon summer days and evenings and 'old maids' cycled to church on misty summer mornings, was no less powerful than Thatcher's articulation of Victorian values in providing ideological justification for this strategy. In the field of law, regulation and policing, too, the parallels were striking. In July 1994 the Criminal Justice and Public Order Act passed through Parliament. Not only did the Act criminalize the activities of peaceful protesters, travellers and squatters but it made obstructing a bulldozer while on a peaceful protest a criminal offence punishable by three months' imprisonment and/or a £2,500 fine. A similar punishment awaited those who failed to leave land on which they were protesting and who the police reasonably believed were *about* to commit aggravated trespass.

In sharp contrast it was reported in October 1993 that Iain Smedley, a member of the Institute of Directors Policy Unit, had been seconded to the Department of Trade and Industry to advise on deregulation. His secondment came on the back of a survey by the institute which found that 42 per cent of company directors felt that government regulation and red tape restricted business expansion. In January 1994 the Deregulation and Contracting Out Bill was launched. It was

> designed to remove 450 pieces of legislation and regulations governing, amongst other things, employment protection and the powers of local authorities to enforce regulations covering hygiene and building and construction work ... Health and safety legislation is also targeted in the Bill and, although plans for the sweeping deregulation of this legislation are unlikely to be forthcoming in the short term, the danger in the long term is that the government might eventually seek to water down statutory 'codes of practice' which are seen to be almost as regulatory as the law itself. (*Guardian*, 21 May 1994, cited in Ryan and Sim 1995, pp. 112–13)

This point proved to be prophetic. Between April 1996 and April 1997 the numbers killed at work rose by almost 20 per cent, to 302. Serious accidents rose in every industrial sector while the overall figure increased by two-thirds, to 28,040. The Trades Union Congress blamed 'the 'climate of deregulation' as a key factor in the deteriorating safety record and called for tougher laws to prosecute negligent employers, as well as an end to cuts in the HSE budget' (*Guardian*, 29 July 1997). In November 1996 it was announced that government spending on health and safety at work was to be slashed by more than 12 per cent in real terms. By the end of 1997 there had been a drop in the rate of investigations into workplace accidents to the point where more than 95 per cent of injuries the HSE classified as major, including cases in which the victims suffered amputations, were blinded, poisoned or gassed, had not been investigated (*Guardian*, 12 November 1997).

Income tax evasion and fraud provide a further illustration of this process. In the two decades up to 1996, the accountants Deloitte and Touche estimated that £2 million million had been lost through tax evasion in the UK; meanwhile, the policing of economic crimes by the powerful has been hived-off 'into a self-regulatory labyrinth of "disciplinary tribunals": effectively private courts. Nor do these courts try only "regulatory" offences. They increasingly hear theft charges.' Therefore 'behaviour which would be criminal to any ordinary person, if committed outside of the City environment, is being allowed to be called something else and increasingly dealt with in a different, quasi-civil, regulatory manner' (Elliott and Atkinson 1998, pp. 99–101).

The eighteen years of Conservative rule that ended with Labour's election victory in May 1997 left behind a state whose capacity for intervention and nonintervention in the febrile arena of law and order (despite being subjected to the new managerialism of efficiency, effectiveness and economy) was formidable. By the time of the election, the Conservative Party had generated its own gravediggers. Internal strife, sleaze and extramarital relationships led to a crisis point – the valorization of a traditional bourgeois morality juxtaposed against the morals of the ill-disciplined and permissive detritus could only succeed hegemonically if the male members of the government kept their collective mouths shut and their individual zips up. At the same time the party's claim to be the guardian of law and order was crumbling in the face of damning crime statistics, criminal justice inefficiency, and an ideological onslaught from Labour which under Tony Blair and then Jack Straw had moved to embrace a new realism on crime and punishment. Inevitably this led to the manifesto claim that 'Labour is the party of law and order in Britain today'(Labour Party 1997, p. 23).

The Great Moving Labour Show: Fear and Loathing on the Campaign Trail

> We haven't opposed a criminal justice measure since 1988.
> Jack Straw January 1997, cited in Anderson and Mann 1997, p. 269

It would be sociologically reductionist, politically naïve and contrary to Hall's project to analyse Labour in power as simply a continuation of the Thatcher and Major governments. In the area of law and order the government has developed positions that previous Conservative administrations had either never espoused or to which they were vehemently opposed. The incorporation of the European Convention on Human Rights into UK law; the establishment of the inquiry into the racist murder of Stephen Lawrence; the proposals to change police disciplinary hearings; the references to domestic and racial violence in their flagship Crime and Disorder Act (CDA) and the shift away from the discourse of 'Prison works' to a strategy of prevention, intervention and welfare all appear to signify that there is indeed (to paraphrase Michael Portillo) clear red water between Labour and their retributive prede-cessors. However, Labour's perception about the causes of crime remains deeply embedded within the narrowly defined discourses of family and community, while its response remains deeply reliant on building on the authoritarian legacy of two decades of Conservative rule.

Labour's journey from a party with an apparently nebulous and confused position on crime and punishment to one whose unequivocal message was as central to the creation of its modernist image as the rejected, antediluvian Clause Four has been well documented in the soundbite 'tough on crime and tough on the causes of crime'. The hold of Tony Blair and Jack Straw on the home affairs brief has meant for some 'a substantial retreat from traditional socialist thinking on crime [which] has been accompanied by a continuation of the populist punitive discourse of previous Conservative governments' (Brownlee 1998, p. 333). The party's policy has fuelled 'expectations among the public that crime can be controlled effectively by a policy of deterrence through punishment'; meanwhile, the party has continued to look for explanations within traditional discourses through reproducing 'the culture of blaming pathological individuals and dysfunctional families . . . a tactic which merely serves to reinforce the punitive expectations of the general public' (ibid. p. 334). Central to Labour's strategy is the reassertion of the community. The Crime and Disorder Act:

> will empower communities through the anti-social behaviour order and local partnerships to tackle crime and disorder. Community empowerment and cohesion is central to the task ahead, and the different stakeholders in society need to work in partnership at a local level to deal with crime and disorder. (Labour Party 1998, p. 3)

As noted above, the idea of community was an important discourse in the Conservatives' law-and-order strategy in the late 1980s. By the mid-1990s, Labour leaders, under the influence of the American communi-tarian philosopher Amitâi Etzioni, sought to reinforce and intensify the role of the community as a bulwark against crime and disorder. As Joan Smith has pointed out, the importance of communitarian arguments lay in the fact that they offered a 'theoretical legitimation for the New Right perspectives on social welfare but dressing them in the language of family and community responsibility, and increasingly of 'law and order' (Smith 1997, p. 184). There are four immediate problems with Labour's strategy.

First, appeals to community are based on the false assumption that more community equals less crime and ignore the fact that the collective values of a community may serve to sustain and stimulate criminality rather than deter it. Furthermore:

the most dangerous aspect of appeals to 'community' in the prevention of crime lies where ideals confront social reality. In Britain the idea of 'community' collides with a social and geographical map which is becoming ever more fragmented, economically divided and socially stretched. (Crawford 1998, pp. 15–21)

Second, like the Conservatives before them, Labour in the 1990s retains an ideological commitment to identifying a range of groups – contemporary folk devils – who are regarded as central to the recurring crisis in the social and political order. Young people and single-parent women along with 'the homeless, scroungers, drug takers, illegal immigrants and the conventional criminal have been elided into one apocalyptic vision of chaos and breakdown, an unmanageable detritus out of control' (Ryan and Sim 1995, p. 124). The 'vocabulary of punitive motives' held by the powerful (Melossi 1993, pp. 273–4) which has been reinforced by a 'populist punitiveness' from below (Sparks 1996, p. 9) means that Labour is linked to the Conservatives by a moral umbilical cord based on a restricted understanding of, and response to, the problems of a society that is deeply divided along the fault lines of social class, gender, 'race', age and sexuality. Allied to this is the ongoing targeting by state servants of those who have been at the centre of their authoritarian gaze for nearly three decades. In July 1998 – a full year after Labour's election victory – black people were eight times more likely than whites to be stopped and searched by the police and five times more likely to be arrested (Statewatch 1998, p. 18).

In the Crime and Disorder Act young people and drug takers such as marijuana and ecstasy users are particularly targeted. In public debate the two are usually elided. In practice this means that discussions about crime and the undeniable impact that crimes like burglary have on the powerless become not just the starting point but also the finishing point for the Labour Party and its political representatives. Consequently, the social harm generated against the young through crime and abuse, the devastating impact of drugs such as alcohol and tobacco on this group and others, and the more general social harm generated by the activities of the powerful remain at best marginal and at worst ignored. In the consultation document on crime and justice sent to all local groups in 1998, there are constant references to the young and the drug taker. In contrast one line is devoted to white-

collar crime which in a seven-line paragraph is (wrongly) elided with
international crime and terrorism (Labour Party 1998, p. 7). (This is
one line more than the issue received in the Labour Party's 1997
election manifesto, when it was completely ignored).

Third, while Labour articulates the need for different and new
responses to crime, these responses are built around the very particular
and narrow definitions of what constitutes social harm discussed above.
Consequently the withdrawal of the state from the policing of powerful
individuals and institutions referred to earlier, which underpinned the
Thatcher/Major deregulation anti-statist axis, has received little or no
attention in the party's debates. Interventions into the devastation
wrought by international capital in the workplace therefore remain
vague and unfocused if they exist at all, while the often-desperate
struggle for funding experienced by institutions such as rape crisis
centres and hostels for sheltering the domestically abused has altered
little since the Conservatives were in power.

Fourth, the state in the late 1990s has not only retained the coercive,
militarized capabilities identified by Hall in the late 1970s but importantly is being augmented by the emergence of a private security
network and prison system which 'do not necessarily parallel and run
alongside of the 'old' forms of state power but are dialectically interrelated with them'(Ryan and Sim 1998, p. 199). Thus:

> The state left in place by Margaret Thatcher may present itself as a limited
> one; but it is a state of considerable power. For even where state functions
> are now privatized, it is still the state which sets the boundary links between
> the public and the private. (Coates 1991, p. 158)

In thinking about these developments Anderson and Mann make
the point that anti-social and criminal behaviour undoubtedly exist
among the poor. However, the danger with Labour's position is that it
'will mean a massive increase in the powers of the state at the expense
of the basic freedoms of some of the most vulnerable people in our
society'. Labour's desire to construct a hegemony around crime and
disorder through the targeting of 'winos, squeegee merchants, aggress-
ive beggars', anti-social families and single parents means that 'there is
a strong element of playing up to middle-class fears and prejudices
about the poor in Labour's whole approach . . . [it] has come perilously
close to identifying the central problem of society as the need to
contain and control the underclass' (Anderson and Mann 1997,
p. 269).

More generally, it could be argued that while the state under Labour
will play a very important role in the reconstruction of the society,

crucially it is a reconstruction that is itself rooted in what Hall has called 'regressive modernisation'. The Labour Party and its organic intellectuals seek to construct themselves as leading players in the globalized world order, but theirs is a vision that is built on a 'regressive version of the past' (Hall 1988, p. 2). As Mick Ryan has pointed out, Labour is 'managing its own brand of "authoritarian populism" . . . it seems to me that its approach has more to do with acknowledging loss and re-engaging the public's voice' (Ryan 1998, p. 13). Ryan's point concerning loss is well illustrated in the idealistic conceptualization of a past epoch in which the community operated as a force for social stability.

In a consultation paper published in 1998, the document's anonymous authors argued that:

> In the past large factories and pit villages provided their own stable social conditions. In particular they helped to foster the transition from adolescence to adulthood. Economic deregulation has led to the breakdown of these community ties. As communities have disintegrated all too often levels of crime and disorder have increased. (Labour Party 1998, p. 6)

While its election manifesto recognized the changing role of women, the Labour Party is ideologically shackled to the imagined community of a working-class past which, as a number of feminist scholars have noted, far from reducing crime was criminogenic for many (though not all) women, and their children, in terms of sexual exploitation and violence. Labour's modernization strategy in relation to crime control, legitimated by the political accommodation inherent in the 'philosophy' of the 'third way', not only leaves it facing in two directions at once but also leaves the authoritarianism at the heart of the Conservatives' interventionist and non-interventionist strategy relatively untouched and indeed ripe for further development.

Conclusion

It is now two decades since the publication of *Policing the Crisis*. That book and Hall's subsequent work counselled against an analysis of the state built on a homogenized, reductionist and instrumentalist understanding of the role of its institutions and its servants. His work demanded and still demands a personal and political consciousness that recognizes that moments and conjunctures lead to possibilities. The politics of closure is not an option. It is therefore both ideologically and politically possible to realize that the moment of the authoritarian

state has not yet passed (despite the postmodernist attempt to airbrush
it out of academic debate) but that the present conjuncture remains
open to the politics of Gramsci's 'good sense'. As Hall argued at the
end of *The Hard Road to Renewal* (1988), this means making and
winning majorities not through the negative contestation of ideas but
through developing a positive perspective on a range of social issues
and concerns. This should lead to thinking about the role of state
institutions in terms that are expansive, responsive and regulative
rather than curtailing, prescriptive and centralizing. This remains a
formidable task, as such a strategy can only be developed if those on
the Left 'take command of the agenda itself, rather than be dragged
along in the slipstream of the Adam Smith Institute' (Hall 1988,
p. 279). Whether New Labour is capable of recognizing, let alone
developing, such a proactive, educative strategy remains a moot,
though desperately important, point more than a decade after Hall
came to this conclusion. Stepping from the long shadow of a state
which for all of its contingencies and contradictions remains ideologically committed to, and materially interventionist in defence of, an
unequal social order requires New Labour to possess vision, commitment and courage. The party and its often supine organic intellectuals
could do worse than examine and learn from Stuart Hall's work, for it
contains these qualities in abundance.

References

Anderson, P. and Mann, N. (1997) *Safety First: The Making of New Labour*,
    London: Granta.
Benyon, J. and Edwards, A. (1997) 'Understanding Less, Condemning More?:
    Conservative Law and Order 1979–1997'. Paper presented to the Annual PSA
    Conference, University of Ulster, 8–10 April.
Brownlee, I. (1998) 'New Labour – New Penology? Punitive Rhetoric and the
    Limits of Managerialism in Criminal Justice Policy', *Journal of Law and Society*
    25(3), September, pp. 313–35.
Coates, D. (1991) *Running the Country*, London: Hodder & Stoughton.
Crawford, A. (1998) 'Community Safety and the Quest for Security: Holding
    Back the Dynamics of Exclusion'. Paper presented to the conference on 'New
    Directions in Criminal Justice – Labour's Crime Policy Examined'. University
    of Hull, July.
Elliott, L. and Atkinson, D. (1998) *The Age of Insecurity*, London: Verso.
Fiske, J. (1993) *Power Plays, Power Works*, London: Verso.
Gilmour, I. (1993) *Dancing with Dogma: Britain Under Thatcherism*, London:
    Pocket Books.
Gray, A. (1998) 'New Labour – New Labour Discipline', *Capital and Class* 65,
    Summer, pp. 1–8.

Halcrow, M. (1989) *Keith Joseph: A Single Mind*, Basingstoke: Macmillan.

Hall, S. (1980a) *Drifting into a Law and Order Society*, London: Cobden Trust.

Hall, S. (1980b) 'Popular Democratic vs. Authoritarian Populism: Two Ways of "Taking Democracy Seriously"', in Hunt, A., ed., *Marxism and Democracy*, London: Lawrence & Wishart.

Hall, S. (1988) *The Hard Road to Renewal*, London: Verso.

Hillyard, P. (1987) 'The Normalisation of Special Powers: From Northern Ireland to Britain', in Scraton, P. ed., *Law, Order and the Authoritarian State*, Milton Keynes: Open University Press.

Hillyard, P. and Percy-Smith, J. (1988) *The Coercive State*, London: Fontana.

Labour Party (1997) *New Labour Because Britain Deserves Better*, London: Labour Party.

Labour Party (1998) *Local Policy Forum 1998 Crime and Justice Consultation Paper*, London: Labour Party.

Marx, K. (1977) *Capital*, Volume 1, London: Lawrence & Wishart.

McFadyean, M. and Renn, M. (1984) *Thatcher's Reign*, London: Chatto & Windus.

Melossi, D. (1993) 'Gazette of Morality and Social Whip: Punishment, Hegemony and the Case of the USA 1970–1992', *Social and Legal Studies* 2(3), September, pp. 259–79.

Pearce, F. and Tombs, S. (1998) *Toxic Capitalism: Corporate Crime and the Chemical Industry*, Aldershot: Dartmouth.

Ryan, M. (1998) 'Penal Policy Making Towards the Millennium. Elites and Populists: New Labour and the New Criminology'. Unpublished paper.

Ryan, M. and Sim, J. (1995) 'The Penal System in England and Wales: Round Up the Usual Suspects', in Ruggiero, V., Ryan, M. and Sim, J. eds., *Western European Penal Systems: A Critical Anatomy*, London: Sage, pp. 93–127.

Ryan, M. and Sim, J. (1998) 'Power, Punishment and Prisons in England and Wales 1975–1996', in Weiss, R. and South, N., eds., *Comparing Prison Systems*, Amsterdam: Gordon and Breach.

Scraton, P. (1985) *The State of the Police*, London: Pluto.

Scraton, P., Sim, J. and Skidmore, P. (1991) *Prisons Under Protest*, Milton Keynes: Open University Press.

Sim, J. (1987) 'Working for the Clampdown: Prisons and Politics in England and Wales', in Scraton, P., ed., *Law, Order and The Authoritarian State*, Milton Keynes: Open University Press.

Smith, J. (1997) 'The Ideology of "Family and Community": New Labour Abandons the Welfare State', in Panitch, L. ed., *Socialist Register 1997*, London: Merlin Press.

Sparks, R. (1996) 'Penal Politics and Politics Proper: The New "Austerity" and Contemporary English Political Culture'. Paper presented to the Law and Society Association Conference, University of Strathclyde, Glasgow, July.

Statewatch (1998) 'UK! Stop and Search and Arrest and Racism', *Statewatch* 8, (3–4), May–August, pp. 16–19.

Thatcher, M. (1993) *Margaret Thatcher: The Downing Street Years*, London: HarperCollins.

Thatcher, M. (1995) *The Path to Power*, London: HarperCollins.

Young, H. (1989) *One of Us*, Basingstoke: Macmillan.

Acknowledgements

Many thanks are due to the following for their help in the preparation of this paper: Annette Ballinger, Roy Coleman, Gillian Hall, Paddy Hillyard, Barbara Hudson, Jason Powell, Marion Price, Mick Ryan, Steve Tombs and Dave Whyte.

28

Thinking Cultural Questions in
'Pure' Literary Terms[1]

Gayatri Chakravorty Spivak

This is a reading of Jamaica Kincaid's *Lucy*, based on the conviction that rhetorically sensitive approaches to literature enhance rather than detract from the political.[2] Indeed, in order 'to give an account, within a materialist theory, of how social ideas arise', it is possible to call upon the resources of a rhetorically sensitive reading of literature.[3] If *Lucy* is read without that sensitivity, it is a story about a situation, not a subject. If read in its literariness, however, it erases the migrant-as-victim into the unmarked ethical agent. There is a homology between that erasure and the classic Marxist transcription of the worker from victim to 'agent of production'. I read *Lucy*, paying attention to it as a paratactic event, as resisting 'the preferred reading',[4] the reading in black and white, the reading of the story as race–class–gender predicament of the migrant situation. This is not a popular position, but I have long drawn comfort from Hall's fighting words, which describe

> fundamental agreements . . . bind[ing] . . . opposing positions into a complex unity, . . . effect[ing] its systematic *inclusions* (for example, those 'definitions of the situation' which regularly . . . 'have access' to the structuring of any controversial topic) and *exclusions* (for example, those groups, interpretations, positions, aspects of the reality of the system which are regularly 'ruled out of court' as 'extremist', 'irrational', 'meaningless', 'utopian', 'impractical', etc.). (CM 346)

Playing in such a 'structured ideological field', in the academic workplace in the United States, the 'cultural studies' style of work in literature is today encouraged to remain narcissistic, question-begging, ridden with plot summary and stereotypes, citing sensational detail without method, a quick-fix institutionalization of heroic beginnings in Birmingham. ('I don't know what to say about American cultural studies. I am completely dumbfounded by it.'[5]) I find myself insisting on restoring rhetorical reading practices because I believe, in an irrational, utopian, and impractical way, that such reading can be an ethical motor that undermines the ideological field. If to be born human is to be born angled towards an other and others, then to account for this the human being presupposes the quite-other. Such presuppositions can battle bodies-without-organs like 'the nation'. This is the bottom line of being-human as being-in-the-ethical-relation. By definition, we cannot – no self can – reach the quite-other. Thus the ethical situation can only be figured in the ethical experience of the impossible. And literature, as a play of figures, can give us imaginative access to the experience.[6]

In today's United States, the ethical is inscribed into the phrase 'human rights'. Class struggle has given way to the impatient triumph-alism of human rights expressed as politico-economic blackmail leading to military intervention; or to 'the suppression of the savage' as in non-governmental organization (NGO) 'gender training', which swiftly suppresses primitive gendering in order to create the individual.[7]

I agree with Hall's prescient formulation that

> the various discourses ... of individual 'rights and duties', of 'free agents', of the 'rights of man' and of 'representative democracy' – in short, the whole enormously complex sphere of legal, political, economic and philo-sophical discourses which compose the dense ideological complex of a modern capitalist society, all stem from or are rooted in the same premises upon which the market and the ideas of a 'market society' and of 'market rationality' are founded. . . . It is also crucial that 'ideology' is now under-stood not as what is hidden and concealed, but precisely as what is most open, apparent, manifest – what 'takes place on the surface and in view of all men'. What is hidden, repressed, or inflected out of sight, are its real foundations. This is the source or site of its *unconsciousness*. (CM 324, 325)

It is this site of *unconsciousness* that a literary reading may open up. This is not a recommendation for the psychoanalytic investigation of litera-ture or society. 'Unconsciousness' is a textual figure, not the uncon-scious. 'It is ... in this general sense that Althusser speaks of ideology as "that new form of specific unconsciousness called 'consciousness'"' (CM 326). We can use another formulation here, and say that the text makes available 'the hinterland of migrancy', in a rhetorical rather than a polemical frame.[8]

It is not that *Lucy*, or any novel, is a text for imitation. It is just that if we constitute ourselves as the implied reader of the novel, we move from rights as problem-solving (the opening page of the novel) to responsibility as the ability to love (the end). If the first step of socialism is to claim rights, the second step is to acknowledge responsibility: 'A training in literary reading is not a sphere where a socialism [as rights/responsibility], a socialist culture – already fully formed – might be simply 'expressed'. But [the literary classroom] is one place where socialist ethics might be remotely constituted. That is why ['literature'] matters. Otherwise, to tell you the truth, I don't give a damn about it.'[9]

Events described in narrative fiction never really happened. If we want to read narrative fiction in a specifically 'literary' way, we have to admit that what happens on its pages is language or prose. Roman Jakobson, one of the leading linguists of the twentieth century, made the point that the specifically 'poetic' or 'literary' function of language is in play or at work where what matters is the message itself, not what the message says. Common sense tells us that Jakobson must be correct. Although we often treat narrative literature as if it is gossip about nonexistent people, or something the author is trying to tell us directly, in doing so we go against the specific nature of literature. The things described in narrative fiction did not really happen. And if the author were addressing you directly, he or she would find out who you were and write the message clearly in expository prose, perhaps using some examples, but certainly not simply 'tell a story'!

What happens in literature *as* literature is the peculiarity of its language. I don't know all the literatures of the world. But the phenomenon that what happens in literature *as* literature is the peculiarity of its language applies to the literatures I can move around in: English, Bengali, French, German, Sanskrit, Hindi, Greek, Latin, Spanish, Italian – all Indo-European. It is of literature written in English that I mostly write, even more often of literature produced in the United States – 'American Literature', as it is called. There I am confident that my bit of common sense will apply: What happens in literature *as* literature is the peculiarity or singularity of its language. If 'the same story' is told again in other words, it ignores the fictive or literary quality of fiction.

With this simple conviction in hand, I will read Jamaica Kincaid's *Lucy*. What mainly happens in this novel is, I believe, parataxis.

According to the *Oxford Companion to the English Language*, 'parataxis' means '[p]unctuating two or more sentences as if they were one. Placing together phrases, clauses, and sentences, often without conjunctions, often with *and, but, so* and with minimal or no use of subordination.'[10] Etymologically, it means 'placing side by side'. It is borrowed from the name of a military formation. 'Parataxis' is a fine old Greek word which has described this particular characteristic of linguistic practice for a thousand years or more.

I would even like to propose that, with this literary characteristic of placing side by side without conjunctions, *Lucy* resists and alters any reading that would categorize it only by its subject matter – a story about a migrant governess, and therefore an instantiation of received ideas about hybridity and diaspora. There is such massive immigration into the United States that many books of so-called literary criticism do produce such categorization. Yet I think it may be said that, if we paid attention to the singularity of the language happening in examples of narrative fiction, we would often find that that piece of work resists categorization by general remarks that we could make by considering simply its story line.

By looking at the singularity of language happening on the page, we do not ignore the story line. Language cannot happen without content. It is just that focusing on the singularity of the language allows us to notice that the literariness of literature makes the language itself part of the content. (This happens in life too, but we take it for granted. I would give you examples, if I weren't eager to get to parataxis, get to *Lucy*.)

Parataxis is to place side by side without conjunctions. The poet and critic Bob Perelman makes large claims for parataxis. But he also quotes an impatient critic who sees only its negative value: ' "It is the product of a generation raised in front of a television: an endless succession of depthless images and empty sounds, each canceling the previous one." '[11] Perelman knows, however, that the power of language can only operate on the reader reading. And readers are made, not born. You have to learn to read. If the critic and teacher is able to produce readers who can receive the power of language, the power of parataxis (the power in language to withhold its own power of making connections) need not perish. That is why reading is taught, today institutionally, in the past culturally, in the family. Thus I want not just to describe the novel, but to move step by step into a reading of the singularity of its language.

The title is simply the first name of the central character. As you take the first step into the story, therefore, you realize that the putting together of the 'I' that inhabits the name may be what it is 'about', as you may with any text that names itself in this way. In order to see if it is so, and then, after taking note that indeed it may be so – '[I]t was my first day', the book begins – you try to see how it is that the book goes about it. And you notice that the sentences seem mostly to be simply placed side by side: 'It was all wrong. The sun was shining but the air was cold' (5) is a pretty typical example.

But you notice something more. That the absence of connection that is the mark of a paratactic style infects the story line as well. The singularity of the language – an overwhelming sense of parataxis (and how the relatively more connected passages negotiate it) – becomes a formal description – a homology for what the language describes. Because the Jakobsonian 'poetic' or literary function takes over, we recognize it as a novel. This is partly what Roland Barthes taught us thirty-three years ago, in his powerful essay 'Introduction to the Structural Analysis of Narratives': 'It is therefore legitimate to posit a "secondary" relation between sentence and discourse – a relation which will be referred to as homological, in order to respect the purely formal nature of the correspondence.' Bits of narrative relate to each other to make a chain of meaning that is like a sentence laid out as a relief map.[12] In this novel the sentences and, seemingly, the narrative, are arranged paratactically.

Let us look at a few passages.

> When they were gone away, I studied my books, and at night I went to school. I was unhappy. I looked at a map. An ocean stood between me and the place I came from, but would it have made a difference if it had been a teacup of water? I could not go back. (9–10)

This is an example of paratactic writing from the opening section, 'Poor Visitor', in which Lucy arrives in the US as an *au pair*. Here is her description of parataxis on a higher level of homology: a description of 'a famous building, an important street, a park, a bridge when built was thought to be a spectacle' (3). These are places that are ranged one after the other, just like sentences in parataxis: '[T]hese places were points of happiness to me ... I would imagine myself entering and leaving them, and ... entering and leaving over and over again – [they] would see me through a bad feeling I did not have a name for' (3). Entering and leaving over and over again to see one through a bad feeling without a name is the paratactic affective structure, the minimum with which the text sets out to establish the subject. We could think of this as the rhetorical representation of a withdrawal from affective connectives, whether before or after the diasporic cut, but prior to questions of hybridity.

'Now that I saw these places, they looked ordinary, dirty, worn down by so many people entering and leaving them in real life, and it occurred to me that I could not be the only person in the world for whom they were a fixture of fantasy' (4). It occurred to me that I could not be the only person in the world living in affective parataxis: this is the minimal resource with which the subject sets out. (By 'subject' I always mean the capital 'I' that is the figure of the speaker or focalizer in the novel, neither subject matter nor character.[13])

It is in the third section, 'The Tongue', that homological parataxis becomes the theme of the text. 'Tongue' is a metonym for language itself. (Metonym is as ancient a name as parataxis. It means 'change of name'. According to the *Oxford English Dictionary*, it is 'a figure of speech which constitutes in substituting for the name of a thing the name of something closely related'.) Language or a tongue is that with which we communicate. But in this section, the tongue is a metonym for (the failure of) sexual contact. 'Sucking tongue' (43), in a marvellous appropriation of adolescent language, is shown to be without affective content even when accompanied by all the appropriate physical signs of affect: 'For a long time I had understood that a sigh and shudder was an appropriate response to a tongue passing along the side of your neck' (49).

We could pass this off as an accurate description of the sexual instincts of adolescent libido, but it is the power of repeated parataxis, entering and leaving experiences with licking and shuddering, that relates more to the fact that this is narrative *fiction* we are reading. Here, for example, is a description of Mariah, Lucy's mistress, and her husband Lewis:

> After Lewis licked Mariah's neck and she leaned against him and sighed and shuddered at the same time, they both stood there, as if stuck together. . . . But to look at them, they seemed as if they couldn't be more apart if they were on separate planets. (48–49)

And Lewis's loss of love for Mariah is discovered by the subject in the following way: 'I saw Lewis standing behind Dinah, his arms around her shoulders, and he was licking her neck over and over again, and how she liked it' (79).

Yet the 'I' of *Lucy* does not grow into 'something real' as she enters and leaves transactions with the tongue.

There is Hugh, her holiday love affair, where the reader senses some advance in loving. Yet her leavetaking from him has the classic paratactic connective. It is the singularity of the language rather than some hint of plotline that establishes the narrative cue. First, there is a sentence about her girlfriend Peggy, with whom she has very little in common. They had been disappointed in a boy they meet on an evening out in the city. That is what the subject recalls, without a connective, as she says goodbye to Hugh:

> We [Peggy and I] were so disappointed that we went back to my room . . . and kissed each other until we were exhausted and fell asleep. Her tongue was narrow and pointed and soft. And that was how I said goodbye to Hugh, my arms and legs wrapped tightly around him, my tongue in his mouth, thinking of all the people I had held in this way. (83)

'And that was how'. Not a logical connective, at all.

No. This is not a matter of an adolescent sexual initiation where the subject connects without connecting. This, to repeat, is parataxis as dominant narrative figure running reading, where the absence of conjunction is felt as absence, if we read for singularity of language, respecting literature as fiction. Kissing Peggy can have no useful affective correspondence with kissing Hugh on the story line.

In the next section we move to other body parts. If we are tracking prose happening, it is as if the subject is unable to enter whole persons. When Lucy meets Paul, the reader again feels that a progress has been made in the skill of loving. And yet, if we pick up the prose signals, we encounter a body part – Paul's hands – and an aggressively paratactic presentation of a memory: 'Paul's hands, as they moved about the tank, looked strange also; the flesh looked like bone, and as if it had been placed in a solution that had leached all the life away. And I remembered this' (102).

This is followed by a most peculiar and lengthy memory of Lucy's disappointment that she was not sexually abused as a child. The sequence ends with the admission that she did not know what the genial abuser's hands were like: 'But his hands – what did they look like? I did not know, and I never would know. And so it was' – surely the reader is meant to notice that this is altogether hopeless as a connective – '[a]nd so it was that hands, moving about in the fish tank – reminded me of some other hands lost forever in a warm sea' (109).

The last section of the book is called 'Lucy', and here this structure – of spatio-temporal progress measured paratactically – is particularly pronounced. 'It was my first day' – the first line of the entire novel and a personal statement without anchor that soon marks a false hope – has changed to the austere and unassailable correctness of '[I]t was January again', but the parataxis is thicker. 'The world was thin and pale and cold again', the sentence continues. 'I was making a new beginning again' (133). Certainly this chapter opening has an ironic relationship to the book opening. But my point is that this is not achieved by a resolution of parataxis – but rather, with the insistence on 'again', by its thickening.

One may say that for 'Lucy' the chapter, *Lucy* the book is a 'past', the subject's brief metropolitan history. It is therefore interesting that the chapter is insistent, in its figuration, not upon the seamlessness of the past and the present, nor upon their discontinuity, but upon their paratactic relationship. They are arranged side by side. Suddenly, the past happens as past. 'I had begun to see the past like this: there is a line; you can draw it yourself, or sometimes it gets drawn for you; either way, there it is, your past, a collection of people you used to be and things you used to do' (137). Even the passage about spatio-temporal parataxis is given in parataxis. It is an abyssal homology. A paragraph follows where 'I used to be' is repeated like an incantation. And then there is an announcement of the final movement of the novel, still relentlessly paratactic, describing the departure from the country of origin: 'My leaving began on the night I heard my father had died' (138).

The only way that this thickening of parataxis is interrupted is by the use of the word 'remind'. It is time now to speak of Lucy's Mother. *Lucy* cannot inhabit the proper name 'Lucy' because the subject resists what it perceives as an indistinguishability from the Mother: 'My past was my mother', the book says in the next to the last section, entitled 'Cold Heart'.

> I could hear her voice, and she spoke to me not in English or the French patois that she sometimes spoke, or in any language that needed help from the tongue; she spoke to me in language anyone female could understand. And I was undeniably that – female. Oh, it was a laugh, for I had spent so much time saying I did not want to be like my mother that I missed the whole story: I was not like my mother – I was my mother. (90)

It is when she speaks of her mother that she signals beyond language: 'not a language that needed help from the tongue'; and, earlier, 'I had come to feel that my mother's love for me was designed solely to make me into an echo of her; and I didn't know why, but I felt that I would rather be dead than become just an echo of someone. *That was not a figure of speech*' (36; emphasis mine). This emphatic assertion of an unwanted continuity is also prior to hybridity or diaspora.

It is Mariah, with her sincere but historically contaminated desire to establish a multiculturalist feminist bond, who helps Lucy, however unwittingly, to come to a resolution of this problem that a figure of speech – like parataxis – cannot control. If we are reading the book as literature, this is the only real problem that the text can declare. 'The times that I loved Mariah it was because she reminded me of my mother. The times that I did not love Mariah it was because she reminded me of my mother' (58). This is the failed invitation to assimilate: benevolent multiculturalism inviting to dominant hybridity through 'gender training'. The subject grasps this in terms of the only model of continuity available to it: the good and bad mother.

> Mariah left the room and came back with a large book and opened it to the first chapter. She gave it to me. I read the first sentence. 'Woman? Very simple, say the fanciers of simple formulas: she is a womb, an ovary; she is a

female – this word is sufficient to define her.' I had to stop. Mariah had completely misinterpreted my situation. My life could not really be explained by this thick book that made my hands hurt as I tried to keep it open. (132)

This is the very end of the next to the last section. It is after this that we will graduate to the last section, named 'Lucy', where a canny reader will hope for a fulfilment of the project of a book whose title is a first name. What is it that Mariah's book teaches the subject? That simply rejecting the explanation of woman as mother will not explain Lucy's life as woman. The section has one more sentence, which simply refers to the sentence in Mariah's book as 'that'.

My life was at once something more simple and more complicated than that: for ten of my twenty years, half of my life, I had been mourning the end of a love affair, perhaps the only true love in my whole life I would ever know. (132)

This mysterious passage, describing a past that is bigger than the book, can be explained by her story about her mother, also given in this section: 'I was not an only child, but it was almost as if I were ashamed of this, because I had never told anyone, *not even Mariah*. I was an only child until I was nine years old.' The love affair mentioned in the previous passage had ended when she was ten.

... and then in the space of five years my mother had three male children; each time a new child was born, my mother and father announced to each other with great seriousness that the new child would go to university in England and study to become a doctor or lawyer or someone who would occupy an important and influential position in society. . . . [W]henever I saw her eyes fill up with tears at the thought of how proud she would be at some deed her sons had accomplished, I felt a sword go through my heart, for there was no accompanying scenario in which she saw me, *her only identical offspring*, in a remotely similar situation. . . . As I was telling Mariah all these things . . . I suddenly had to stop speaking; . . . my tongue [mark this important metonym] had collapsed in my throat. (130; emphasis mine)

This is no cliché of so-called 'diasporic' experience, for what is envied is the brothers' brighter diasporic future; nor is it a simple rage of black against white. If one wants to reduce *this* to a formula, one might say: the solution to our Mothers' cultural gendering in the country of origin is not Eurocentric economic migration felt as diaspora. Further, the quick 'gender training', now offered by big NGOs like Oxfam, training women to be women, the newest twist of global feminism, however good-hearted, is no solution. 'Mariah wanted to rescue me' (130). The problem is not solved by rage against Mariah.

The telling of this story to her contradicts the book's paratactic vision of 'the past', fulfils the text's dramatic irony, making it bigger than the narrator. To see how the resolution of this problem exceeds the book, we must digress.

It is well known that the word 'diaspora' means something like 'scattered abroad', from *dia* plus *speirein* (to sow). Moses predicted that the Jews would be dispersed if they did not obey the Ten Command-ments, although '[i]t is particularly to be noted that deportation to a foreign land . . . is not the *sole* prospect which the author holds out before his people, it is but one beside many other afflictions, most of which are to fall upon Israel in its own land'.[14] Diaspora is one of the punishments a people suffers if it disobeys the law. In Deuteronomy, the book of the Old Testament where the curses are uttered, they are balanced against the rewards (indistinguishable at this stage from blessings) that are earned if the people obey. Deuteronomy was among the first books of the Bible to be translated into Greek, which gives us the word 'diaspora.'

> The Pentateuch [the first five books of the Bible] was translated into Greek in Egypt before the middle of the third century BC. . . . The evidence shows that it was prompted by the need of Jews in Egypt for a version of the Scripture in the Greek language (then more familiar to them than Hebrew or even Aramaic) either for public use in the synagogue or for private reading and study.[15]

Diaspora is thus full of affect. The word is given wide currency among migrant groups today for the sake of the affect. But the connection with responsibility and reparation – we are here because we are guilty, by some unspecified guilt against the law – is now gone or legitimized by reversal: we are here because you are guilty. *Lucy* questions this easy reversal. We cannot evaluate diaspora from this text.

The narrative (rather than merely linguistic) style of *Lucy* delivers a devastating judgement upon herself and brings back the ancient dias-poric thematic of responsibility and reparation. For her, 'diaspora' or 'migration' is a way of using parataxis, a severing of connection as a solution – rather than the source – of a problem. We receive the shock of that displacement in the very beginning of the novel: 'Oh, I had imagined that with my one swift act – leaving home and coming to this new place – I could leave behind me, as if it were an old garment never to be worn again, my sad thoughts, my sad feelings, and my discontent with life in general as it presented itself to me' (6–7).

This does not mean that the themes that we have come to expect in novels of underclass female migration ('diaspora', in the Euro-US today) are absent in *Lucy*. Some of the analysis and descriptions of

Mariah do indeed fit those expectations. Indeed, here again we encounter distinctions in hybridity, a comment on the desire to claim hybridity:

> 'I was looking forward to telling you that I have Indian blood [Mariah tells her, for example]. . . . But now . . . I feel you will take it the wrong way.' . . . Wrong way? Right way? What could she mean? . . . My grandmother is a Carib Indian. . . . My grandmother is alive; the Indians she came from are all dead. . . . In fact, one of the museums to which Mariah had taken me devoted a whole section to people, all dead, who were more or less related to my grandmother. (40)

'[H]er novel *Lucy* runs a rich white urban family through the shredder of a young black au pair's rage,' a critic writes.[16] Yet to reduce the novel to just that race–class subplot is to miss not only that the subject here dismisses all museumization of cultures of origin but also the displacing power of parataxis.

Lucy is not able to love Mariah, *as she is not able to love anyone, as she is not able to love her mother.* In *Lucy*, Lucy is not defined simply by the binary opposition of 'rich white' and 'black au pair', by, as it were, Hegel's famous lordship and bondage dialectic, where what 'the bondsman does is really the action of the lord'.[17] In the beginning, love itself is disparaged because Mariah can love.

Before we consider how the paratactic rhetoric of the novel works to question the self-indulgences of contemporary diasporism, let us consider the subject's inability to establish a connection with her proper name through the history of its other holders – John Milton's Lucifer and William Wordsworth's Lucy – her inability, in other words, to inhabit colonial hybridity in comfort.

Kincaid's early education had been 'anglophile'. Could she have known that, like most of the English Romantics, Wordsworth undertook to rewrite Milton? I cannot know, and in the end perhaps it does not matter, or matters differently, as I will suggest at the close of the chapter, in a feminist way, a woman's way. But first the names themselves.

Her naming as Lucifer comes after her love affair with her mother has ended.

> [U]nder her breath she [my mother] said, 'I named you after Satan himself. Lucy, short for Lucifer. What a botheration from the moment you were conceived.' I not only heard it quite clearly when she said it but I heard the words *before they came out of her mouth*. (152; emphasis mine)

Again, beyond language. Lucy resents her mother but accepts this name. 'I did not grow to like the name Lucy – I would have much preferred to be called Lucifer outright – but whenever I saw my name I always reached out to give it a strong embrace' (153).

Percy Shelley had suggested that, unbeknownst to the author, Milton's Satan, the light-carrying unbending rebel, is the hero of *Paradise Lost*:

> Nothing can exceed the energy and magnificence of the character of Satan as expressed in *Paradise Lost*. . . . Milton's Devil as a moral being is so far superior to his God as one who perseveres in some purpose which he has conceived to be excellent in spite of adversity and torture, is to one who in the cold security of undoubted triumph inflicts the most horrible revenge upon his enemy.[18]

A plot summary reading of *Lucy* may take on such a reading. But this praise of individualism is not enough for a mother–daughter relationship severed by economic migration in search, precisely, of possessive individualism. Before the book ends, the subject will claim Lucifer in a less transparent way, as she tastes the moral dilemma of diasporic guilt, when metropolitan multiculturalist judgement is accepted and transformed:

> Mariah said that I was feeling guilty. Guilty! I had always thought that was a judgment passed on you by others, and so it was new to me that it could be a judgment you pass on yourself. Guilty! But I did not feel like a murderer; I felt like Lucifer, doomed to build wrong upon wrong. (139)

Notice once again Mariah's crucial role. The subject is now able to state the text's end, in the broadest possible sense: 'The Lucy was the only part of my name I cared to hold on to' (149), although the logic of the story would give this the lie.

In terms of the story, her naming by her mother may have happened before her reading of Wordsworth's 'The Daffodils', and certainly before the visit organized by Mariah to show her the flowers that she had only read about but never seen. In textual time, however, this realization of what had been the epistemic violation of an earlier form of colonialism – memorizing Wordsworth in school – comes before. This scene of violation or makeover is what produces colonial hybridity. The general style of the passage continues to be paratactic. If we are reading only for 'what the plot called for' (6), the exchange between characters as 'real' people can be read as expected: determined by received ideas of race and class, and by gendering as understood by a cultural difference imagined by an author who knows the dominant pretty well: 'It wasn't her fault. It wasn't my fault. But nothing could change the fact that where she saw beautiful flowers I saw sorrow and bitterness'

(30). But we must remember that what is being undermined by Mariah is not some authentic cultural experience of origin or identity, but the memory inscribed by a colonial poetry lesson upon a Caribbean island. That memory can be fitted into a thoroughly historically organized narrative, the story of colonial occupation. Yet, if we have been following the homologies of a general parataxis along various levels, we can even read that historical narrative itself as two 'sentences' describing the same space, once as 'pre-colonial', and again as 'colonial', one after the other, one over the other, the other under the one, with no connection but violation, the type case of colonial hybridity. Nothing to celebrate, but a kind of intimacy with the other none the less, an enabling violation, the imaginative sedimentation of the civilizing mission. On this level of homology, it may be said that Lucy wants to save that parataxis from the too-quick ministrations of the metropolitan multiculturalist.

Jamaica Kincaid glosses this in her own case:

> And I thought how I had crossed a line; but at whose expense? I cannot begin to look, because what if it is someone I know? I have joined the conquering class: who else could afford this garden – a garden in which I grow things that it would be much cheaper to buy at the store? My feet are (so to speak) in two worlds, I was thinking as I looked farther into the garden and saw, beyond the pumpkin patch, a fox. . . . In the place I am from, I would have been a picture of shame. . . . In the place where I am from, I would not have allowed a man with the same description as such a woman to kiss me.[19]

Kincaid is talking about entering the imperial class by having a garden in the United States. She is crossing not the colour line but a class line. She is not talking specifically about race, but about empire. In the essay from which this passage is quoted, the talk is of Mexico and the Aztecs, of the British Empire, of the hybridization of plants, of the prejudice in an Oxford reference book on gardening. It is a gloss on entering the class of 'Mariah' as Kincaid's work becomes a textbook read by immigrant schoolgirls in the schoolrooms of the new metropolis, the United States, the postcolonial superpower. In the case of the old colonialism, which famously had wanted to breed 'a class English in everything but blood', Lucy had bridged the gap of parataxis with duplicity, the technique of the colonial subject in the 'past' of the book.[20]

Perhaps such daytime duplicities are exploded by dreams. After the first day that begins the new life – the book we hold in our hands – Lucy attempts to use the marks of her failure to conceal the failure of connection. She tells her dream of the night before, precisely to these

new colonizers. All subjects made over by old colonialisms negotiate
these alliances in the new metropolis. It is hard to put neat plus and
minus signs – like 'black' and 'white'. This is the postcolonial predicament. This is what Kincaid's text plays out, *as literature.* The subject
gives us a clue. At the end of the first section, she tells her dream to
both husband and wife, her masters, and Lewis simply makes fun of
her in the name of Freud. Uncomprehending, the subject ends the
first section with these words: 'I had meant by telling them my dream
that I had taken them in, because only people who were very important
to me had ever shown up in my dreams. I did not know if they
understood that' (15). After this begins a section entitled simply
'Mariah', where a real bond is established, to be half-rejected because
the mother must be half-mourned. And before that half-rejection can
be signalled at the end of the book, one realization is given in a
curiously flat paragraph that seems to escape parataxis:

> I had realized that the origin of my presence on the island – my ancestral
> history – was the result of a foul deed; but that was not what made me, at
> fourteen or so, stand up in school choir practice and say that I did not wish
> to sing 'Rule, Britannia!' ... I disliked the descendants of the Britons for
> being unbeautiful, for not cooking well, for wearing ugly clothes, for not
> liking to really dance.... If only we had been ruled by the French.... I
> understand the situation better now; I understand that my pen pal [from a
> French island] and I were in the same boat. (135–6)

If this is postcolonial solidarity, hard enough to achieve, alas, in the
autobiographical passage there is the unease of diaspora. Kincaid
worries that she has entered the conquering class at the expense of
someone she knows, that her own people would be profoundly
ashamed of her access to class privilege. The novel will play this out
differently at its end.

Will Wordsworth, if I read him as a metonym for the imaginative
riches of the colonizing tradition, offer Lucy an answer?

(Metonym, let us recall, means 'change of name'. The *Oxford Companion to the English Language* says it is 'a figure of speech which
designates something by the name of something associated with it'.
Figures of speech do not obey the handbooks exactly. You learn how
to recognize these figures by family resemblance, as it were. We
substitute the name 'Wordsworth' for the name 'colonial imagination',
then. The former is something more than an example of the latter,
since Kincaid is not writing us directly. Because he figures in a novel, I
read 'Wordsworth' here as a figure. But a figure cannot be stripped of
content. It says something by the very logic that allows us to recognize
it as a figure – a logic that rests not only on the history of the language

but upon 'empirical' history. The British took part of the West Indies. Wordsworth was taught to West Indian schoolgirls. That figures in our story. Our cue is daffodils. But Wordsworth had a famous Lucy. Some say his Lucy poems are his best work. And our story wants to fill that proper name with being. What was Wordsworth's Lucy like? Perhaps this can be called 'intertextuality'.[21])

Wordsworth's Lucy had little being of her own, existing on the page only to inspire the poet. By the end of the Lucy sequence, death in infancy had emptied her name of all human and individual significance. One may say that, in the world of literature, where singularity of language is all that happens and remains, Lucy had died in order that the 'I' of the poem might know what Karl Marx called species-life, and Hegel the innocence of not-doing (*Nicht-tun*): 'Nature is the human being's *body without organs*, that is to say nature in so far as it is not the human body.'[22] Wordsworth's Lucy is immortal because Nature is her great body without organs, neither hearing nor seeing:

> No motion has she now, no force;
> She neither hears nor sees.
> Rolled round in earth's diurnal course,
> With rocks, and stones, and trees.

The subject of *Lucy* wants to be able to act in her proper name. The paratactic relationship with nature marks an even more intimate break than the suture of the pre-colonial and colonial worlds. It is a relationship – a relationship without relationship, Nature my body without organs is before and after I am proper to myself, although always there. It is pre- and post-propriation. 'My' birth and death are events within it. That relationship is before and after the gift of time, if there is any, that allows us to be proper to ourselves.

Thus the Wordsworthian line leads only to a redoubled parataxis for the subject of *Lucy*. It leads not only to the parataxis between the mind-sets of the colonizer and the colonized, but also to that between species-life and species-being – being-nature and being-human. This last parataxis is also the parataxis between genders if you like, since Wordsworth, like most men of two hundred years ago and many men now, used women to develop a sense of self, and *his* Lucy may be a splendid example of that. The name misfires there as well. We have already seen the paratactic failures of connection between the subject of *Lucy* and men in sexualized gender roles.

As 'Jamaica Kincaid', the author of *Lucy*, without any noticeable 'feminist' declaration, wants to claim responsibility for the human part in nature. At the end of the passage I have already quoted, we saw her looking at a fox. Let us pick up where we left off:

> That night, lying in my bed, I heard from beyond the hedge where he had emerged sounds of incredible agony; he must have found his prey; but the fox is in nature. . . . *I am not in nature*. . . . To me, the world is cracked, unwhole, not pure, accidental; and the idea of moments of joy for no reason is *very strange* (emphasis mine).

It is the distinction between being-in-nature and being-in-culture that allows Kincaid the diasporic responsibility of the Eurocentric economic migrant, a displaced line of the unreasonable ethical guilt of the Jew in diaspora as outlined in Deuteronomy. For the responsible diasporic, that is the strangeness of felt joy when I may have entered the conquering class at the expense of people whom I might know. It is that uncertainty of the 'might' – 'what if' in the Kincaid passage – that is the secret of this responsibility. It is noticeable that Kincaid, again with no flags raised, takes the gender-active part also when she invokes the place left behind: 'I would not have allowed a man with the same description as such a woman to kiss me.'

Following the singularity of its language, reading *Lucy* as a piece of literature, we may glimpse a critique of a politically correct and self-indulgent bit of contemporary diasporism – a real playing out of colonial and diasporic hybridity, where diaspora is a class line, even if not perceptible from the metropolis. *Lucy* is a book of arrested passage.

We can follow this singularity page by page, sentence by sentence, word by resonant word, and our enjoyment of *Lucy* as literature will be enhanced. Here let us move to the very last sentence of the novel, which will show us that the subject will accede to her name somewhere outside of this text, this story. And in that accession, 'Wordsworth' and 'Mariah' will be revised, as well as the too-quick readings that reduce all diasporic narrative to victimage and/or resistance.

Let me explain the idea of something taking place outside the text. This cannot be 'true', of course. Yet, if what happens in the literary text is the singularity of its language and that singularity is in its figuration, that figuration can point to the depth of the content by signalling that the content cannot be contained by the text as recepta-cle. To note this is not to say that the text has failed. It is to say that the text has succeeded in signalling beyond itself. It is high praise for the book, not dispraise.

It is through the logic embedded in figuration that the text points. As we know, metaphor is the chief of figures. *Lucy* ends with a metaphoric sequence that signals beyond itself.[23]

The subject of *Lucy* wants to be the subject loving, not merely the object of love. This may be represented by the sequence that closes the text. The opening of the notebook – a beautiful notebook that Mariah has given her as an expression of real solidarity, in response to the subject's remark that 'my life stretched ahead of me like a book of blank pages' (163) – may be the beginning of a new text, a text that will do what *Lucy* has only tried: to speak the subject in its own name. We had nothing but the first name – parcelled out between Milton and Wordsworth – in the first try. This new text will be specifically hers. The subject writes her full name: Lucy Josephine Potter. ('Jamaica Kincaid' happened to have a three-tiered name as well: Elaine Potter Richardson.)

As she focuses upon her name, her inability to love 'someone so much that I would die from it' (164) overwhelms her. The tears come as a surprise, not motivated by the subject who wants to be herself. Yet they are not an example of affective parataxis. Unlike her own descriptions of sex, feeling is here securely tied to gesture – the shame brings the tears. Her name is washed away until there is nothing but a blur. The text that will live in this new (note)book cannot be an access to the self, but rather an access to others, through a self-annihilating love. 'Wordsworth' had not been able to name the other as a self. But that other text towards which *Lucy* travels beyond its own pages will correct that error by turning the name of the self into not a blank but a productive blur.

Perhaps. That book, not being in language, has no guarantee. Characterologically, if one thinks of Lucy as a 'real' person, there is also no guarantee in that contrary temperament. She 'is' more like Milton's Lucifer. The text tugs in the other direction. The virtue of Jamaica Kincaid's book is this push-and-pull between 'Lucy' and *Lucy*. For any promise of a step beyond is also a reminder that the text is staged as not performing that step. Once again, this is not dispraise, but praise of the text's organization, which it would perhaps be better to call 'formalization'.

This may, in the end, be the singularity of this text, a singularity it shares with *A Question of Power*, a novel by the Southern African writer Bessie Head. The migrant woman of colour is not allowed to be the unmarked subject of loving. It is the benevolent master who is allowed to love the victim. When a novel that seems an obvious example of black diasporic writing inhabits a theme of unmarked loving, we cannot read it. In that other book, the love for Mariah, which cannot emerge because of the criticism of her inherited and therefore chosen way of life, will take shape for a reader, as much as her love for her mother, which cannot emerge out of hatred. Perhaps. Perhaps. For that is not a book, but simply a part of the task of reading this one. The book swings between symptom and critique.[24]

In an interview with Jamaica Kincaid, Leslie Garis quotes Henry Louis Gates Jr:

> [S]he never feels the necessity of claiming the existence of a black world or a female sensibility. She assumes them both.... [W]e can get beyond the large theme of racism and get to deeper themes of how black people love and cry and live and die.[25]

Gates is right, of course. I should like to add a rider. Not just black people, but people. This is not to write off black specificity by claiming history-transcending universality for great art. It is to question why white specificity is unmarked as 'white', whereas black specificity cannot choose to be so. When a novel that seems an obvious example of black diasporic writing inhabits a theme of unmarked loving, we cannot read it:

> It seemed almost incidental that he was African. So vast had his inner perceptions grown over the years that he preferred an identification with mankind to an identification with a particular environment. And yet, as an African, he seemed to have made one of the most perfect statements: 'I am just anyone'.[26]

This passage is the opening of *A Question of Power*. If we work at the weave of desire in it, we will get to what I find in *Lucy*: a longing for unmarked humanity, without denying black specificity; an access to the subjectship of loving, 'perhaps ... the whole universe ... that was another perfect statement, to him – love was freedom of heart,' writes Bessie Head.

I should like to repeat here something I said in an interview a few months ago: cultural studies is a study of teleopoesis (imaginative interruptions in structures of the past), which is the domain of the metropolitan minority claiming a history that makes the metropolis possible. It's not the domain of what is called postcolonial criticism, which is to reclaim a history that was allowed to stagnate – on the way to an unmarked modernity. Chinua Achebe is the noblest model of this, and the moment of that innocent reclaiming is now past.

'Unmarked modernity' is the synchronic statement entailed by an 'unmarked being-in-time', where 'cultural' identity seems 'natural' and pre-comprehended. One can then be the subject of loving rather than, at best, an object of benevolence. *Lucy*'s longing points to what *may* be an impossible book, but also may not. Perhaps. The difference between a blank – an absence – and a blur – something there to remake.

We who are from subordinated cultures must accept the new as agents as we mourn the past with appropriate rites as subjects – a necessary but impossible task of cultural translation, bigger than any individual narrator. It is the singularity of the language of the novel that led me into this reading; yet even this can have no adequate justification, for it may be that the textuality of my stereotype of myself led me to this reading. The power of fiction is that it is unverifiable. To learn to read fiction is to work with this power.

The moment for postcolonial longing may be past. And Perelman writes: '[I]n the seventies, . . . faith in the rebirth of modernist ambition and of the cultural centrality of poetry was easier to maintain. Today parataxis can seem symptomatic of late capitalism.'[27] When was the postcolonial, indeed?

Toni Morrison's *Beloved* stages not parataxis, but hypotaxis – a style some say is the exact opposite of parataxis – in which many sinuous clauses modify and intermodify each other as the long sentences move dreamlike. And yet, just as *Lucy* finally uses parataxis to point to a connectedness outside the covers, perhaps, so does *Beloved* use hypotaxis, a style of passing on and into the next sentence, to pronounce, in the end, '[T]his is not a story to pass on.' Sethe, as daughter and mother, caught between slavery and citizenship, can only half-mourn.[28] Is this because women, by historical definition, not essence, relate differently or obliquely to the history of language, especially public language – published literature – which is also singular and unverifiable? (The matrilineality of slavery is no exception to this.) If you take another famous American pair – Hemingway, fiercely paratactic, perhaps most so in *The Old Man and the Sea*; and Faulkner, text sinking under the weight of hypotactic sentences signalling a history that has gone awry by its very weight, – you will not find such rhetorical irony. I do not offer these as conclusions, but questions. The only way to consider them is to read these texts in the singularity of their languaging. Otherwise, to tell you the truth, I don't give a damn about it.

Lucy shows a resistance to multicultural hybridization by falling on colonial hybridization, the subjectivity of the colonial subject. 'The notion that only the multi-cultural cities of the First World are "diaspora-ised" is a fantasy which can only be sustained by those who have never lived in the hybridised spaces of a Third World, so-called "colonial", city.'[29] I would now like to take a step beyond the novel, and conclude by introducing a problematic that the discussion of diaspora and the Third World can take on board.

After the gradual dismantling of the big colonies and the New Immigration (after 1947 and 1965), and the dubious end of the Cold War (1989), a certain ideologeme has been cooking itself in the Euro–US sated socius: that the migrant has no history and not enough class to make a difference. Over the years, my greatest debt to Stuart Hall has been his discussion of ideology. Hall's tracking of ideology helps me to pursue this ideologeme.

In 1981, Stuart Hall wrote: 'the more or less continuous struggle over the culture of working people, the labouring classes and the poor ... must be the starting point for any study ... of the transformations of ... popular culture' (DP 227).

The stability of the factory floor disappeared overseas with post-fordism, international subcontracting, and the progressive feminization of labour. The predominance of finance capital and the 'spectralization of the rural' in globalization today occludes the question of organized labour.[30] Willy-nilly, the removal of the place of origin of the migrant from the history of the present (although sometimes secure in the consolidation of a glorious past) – Etienne Balibar and Martin Bernal, let us say – reflects this seeming disappearance of the internationally differentiated question of class, so that even the new transnationalist radical, focused on the migrant as an effectively historyless object of intellectual and political activism, works to conserve a strengthened metropolis, culturally destabilized, but economically not displaced from its exploitative position, as the migrant is inserted into the circuit of hegemony. Here is 'a very severe fracture, a deep rupture – especially in popular culture in the postwar period. . . . [n]ot only a matter of a change in cultural relations between the classes, but of the changed relationship between the people and the concentration and expansion of the new cultural apparatuses themselves' (DP 230). I feel that a rhetorical reading of *Lucy* can be expanded into 'the criticism to which such an ideological complex is subjected by the first representatives of the new historical phase' (Gramsci, cited in DP 237).

The paradox of this emergent ideological formation is precisely that, within the metropolis, it produces the simulacrum of liberating the masses from 'their subordinate place'. But the world is larger than the metropolis. We might therefore complicate the privileging of hybridity in the diaspora with the question of colonial hybridization in the interest of a looser and more global definition of class. Otherwise, and by a quite different kind of generalization,

in the sphere of the state and juridico-political ideology, the *political* classes and class relations are represented as individual subjects (citizens, the voter, the sovereign individual in the eyes of the law and the representative system, [the migrant, the minority], etc.): and these individual political legal subjects are then 'bound together' as members of the *nation*, united by the 'social contract', and by their common and mutual general interest. (CM 337)

I have emphasized the word 'political' because the argument here is not only economic. This gives us the possibility of expanding the class argument into a consideration of the migrant as Janus-faced in the history of the present, especially when a second-, third-, or many-generation hyphenated metropolitan hybrid is called upon to fulfil a demographic political or economic agenda in the interest of the metropolis; play Madeleine Albright to the bombing of the Balkans.

Notes

1. The title of this chapter is a quotation from Stuart Hall, 'The Formation of A Diasporic Intellectual', in David Morley and Kuan-Hsing Chen, eds., *Stuart Hall: Critical Dialogue in Cultural Studies* (London: Routledge, 1996), p. 498. My thanks to Jean Franco and Deborah White for critical readings, and Bill Michael for research assistance.

2. Jamaica Kincaid, *Lucy* (New York: Plume, 1991); hereafter cited in the text by parenthetical page references only.

3. Stuart Hall, 'The Problem of Ideology – Marxism without Guarantees', in *Journal of Communication Inquiry* 10(2) (1986), p. 29. Hereafter cited in the text as PI, with page references following.

4. Stuart Hall, 'Culture, the Media and "the Ideological Effect"', in J. Curran *et al.*, eds., *Mass Communication and Society*, (London: Edward Arnold 1977), p. 344. Hereafter cited in the text as CM, with page references following.

5. Stuart Hall, 'Cultural Studies and its Theoretical Legacies', in Morley and Chen, *Stuart Hall*, p. 273.

6. This passage, on ethics and literature is from 'A Moral Dilemma', in Spivak, *Red Thread* (Cambridge: Harvard University Press, forthcoming).

7. I have discussed this in 'Feminism Without Frontiers' (in preparation for *Interventions*) with reference to Sarah Cummings *et al.* eds., *Gender Training: The Source Book* (Amsterdam: Royal Tropical Institute, 1998).

8. Stuart Hall, 'The Hinterland of Science: Ideology and the "Sociology of Knowledge",' in *On Ideology* (London: Hutchinson, 1977), pp. 9–32, discusses the same kind of relationship that I am suggesting between the literary and the geopolitical 'scientific' implications of metropolitan multiculturalism.

9. Stuart Hall, 'Notes on Deconstructing "The Popular"', in Raphael Samuel, ed., *People's History and Socialist Theory* (London: Routledge, 1981), p. 239, wording altered. Hereafter cited in the text as DP, with page reference following.

10. Tom McArthur, ed., *Oxford Companion to the English Language* (New York: Oxford University Press, 1992), p. 750.

11. Eliot Weinberger, 'A Note on *Montemara*, America and the World', *Sulfur*, No. 20: 197 (Fall 1987), cited in Bob Perelman, *Language Writing and Literary History* (Princeton: Princeton University Press, 1996), p. 62.

12. Roland Barthes, 'Introduction to the Structural Analysis of Narratives', in his *Image–Music–Text*, translated by Stephen Heath (New York: Hill & Wang, 1977), p. 84. The passage quoted is from the first part of the essay and mired in binary oppositions. The word 'legitimate' gives a hint of this. By the end of the essay, Barthes is much wilder, moving from homology to definitions that want not 'to strain the phylogenetic hypothesis!' (p. 124). Thus my invocation of paratactic contamination of the story line is not altogether out of the Barthesian line.

13. For 'focalization', and the distinction between 'story' and 'text' that I will invoke below, see Shlomith Rimmon-Keenan, *Narrative Fiction: Contemporary Poetics* (New York: Methuen, 1983), chapters 2–6.

14. S.R. Driver, *A Critical and Exegetical Commentary on Deuteronomy* (Edinburgh: T. and T. Clark, 3d edn, 1978), p. 304.

15. F.G. Kenyon, *The Text of the Greek Bible* (London: Duckworth, 3d edn, 1975), p. 14.

16. Diane Simmons, *Jamaica Kincaid* (New York: Twayne, 1994), p. 1.

17. Georg Wilhelm Friedrich Hegel, *The Phenomenology of Spirit*, translated by A.V. Miller (Oxford: Clarendon, 1977), p. 116. In Hegel the bondsman sublates 'its own being-for-self' – Miller unaccountably translates this as 'sets aside', not even the more conservative 'supersedes', 'overcomes', or yet 'transcends' – 'and in so doing itself does what the other does to it'. If I followed this through I might be accused of betraying Kincaid's Antiguan specificity.

18. Percy Bysshe Shelley, 'A Defence of Poetry', in Bruce R. McElderry Jr., ed., *Shelley's Critical Prose* (Lincoln, NB: University of Nebraska Press, 1967), p. 24.

19. Jamaica Kincaid, 'Flowers of Evil', *New Yorker* (5 October 1992), pp. 159, 158.

20. Thomas Babington Macaulay, 'Minute on Indian Education', in *Macaulay: Poetry and Prose*, edited by G.M. Young (Cambridge, MA: Harvard University Press, 1967), pp. 723–4.

21. Michael Riffaterre, *Text Production*, translated by Terese Lyons (New York: Columbia University Press), 1983.

22. Karl Marx, 'Economic and Philosophical Manuscripts', in his *Early Writings*, translated by Rodney Livingstone and Gregor Benton (New York: Vintage, 1975), p. 328; translation modified. The Hegelian passage is to be found in Hegel, *Phenomenology*, p. 488.

23. It may be worth recalling that Barthes assigns the metaphoric to 'sapiential discourse' (Barthes, 'Structural Analysis', p. 84).

24. Perelman, *Marginalization*, pp. 61, 69.

25. Leslie Garis, 'Through West Indian Eyes', *New York Times Magazine* (7 October 1990), p. 80.

26. Bessie Head, *A Question of Power* (New York: Pantheon, 1973), p. 11.

27. Perelman, *Marginalization*, p. 62.

28. Toni Morrison, *Beloved* (New York: Plume, 1987), p. 275.

29. Stuart Hall, 'When Was "the Post-colonial?": Thinking at the Limit', in

Iain Chambers and Lidia Curti, eds. *The Post-colonial Question: Common Skies, Divided Horizons* (London: Routledge, 1996), p. 250.

30. By 'spectralization of the rural' I mean that biopiracy, genetic engineering, chemical fertilizers and other globalizing phenomena engage the rural directly in the circuit of a disembodied hi-tech electronified capitalism, bypassing industry. It is interesting to note that the IMF concentrated only on energy and agriculture, not on industry at all, in order to restructure the Russian economy to integrate it into the global system. The entire question of IMF-sponsored reform is brilliantly discussed in Boris Kagarlitsky, *The Mirage of Modernization*, translated by Renfrey Clarke (New York: Monthly Review, 1995) and Roger Burbach *et al.*, *Globalization and Its Discontents: The Rise of Postmodern Socialisms* (London: Pluto Press, 1997).

29

Studies in a Post-colonial Body

Gilane Tawadros

This text was written following my first visit to South Africa on the occasion of the Second Johannesburg Biennial. A major international art roadshow made little sense in this racially segregated and economically divided country. It seemed to underline the futility of contemporary art in a context where there were so many other pressing social, political and economic issues. This impression was reinforced when I returned to London and the inquiry began into the brutal racially motivated murder of Stephen Lawrence in south-east London. The question of the place of contemporary art in relation to wider socio-economic and cultural issues was the subject of a number of lengthy conversations I had with Stuart Hall. In the course of these conversations, Stuart rearticulated a position which, for me, has been one of the most important aspects of his work: namely, the understanding that acts of racism and racial violence are not isolated incidents or individual acts, removed from the cultural fabric of our lives. Stuart has consistently argued that notions of cultural value, belonging and worth are defined and fixed by the decisions we make about what is or is not our culture. This text is an attempt to articulate the place of contemporary artworks in the context of extreme political violence where our notions of value, belonging and worth are at their most fragile.

The clinical studies that make up the last section of Frantz Fanon's *The Wretched of the Earth* are the most painful and difficult passsages for me in Fanon's writings, making explicit as they do the physical and psychological violence of colonialism whose wounds are still visible in our societies. The most powerful artworks do not offer any easy answers or solutions to this violence. They pose questions that force us to confront some of the uncomfortable things that we might prefer to forget. One of the most important aspects of Stuart's writings for me is the way that they make explicit the contingency of the personal to the political, the cultural to the social and the past to the present. They reflect his profound understanding of the essential role of the artist and intellectual: to ask the most difficult questions, but not necessarily to answer them.

I

In the Maquis, when I heard that she'd been raped by the French, I first of all felt angry with the swine. Then I said, 'Oh, well, there's not much harm done; she wasn't killed. She can start her life over again.' And then a few weeks later I came to realize that they'd raped her because they were looking for me. In fact, it was to punish her for keeping silence that she'd been violated . . . This woman had saved my life and had protected the organization. It was because of me that she had been dishonoured. And yet she didn't say to me: 'Look at all I've had to bear for you.' On the contrary, she said: 'Forget about me; begin your life over again, for I have been dishonoured . . .' So I decided to take her back; but I didn't know at all how I'd behave when I saw her. And often, while I was looking at the photo of my daughter, I used to think that she too was dishonoured, like as if everything that had to do with my wife was rotten. If they'd tortured her or knocked out all her teeth or broken an arm I wouldn't have minded. But that thing – how can you forget a thing like that? And why did she have to tell me about it all?[1]

II

The stitches are rough and clumsily sewn. The hand of a hurried or amateur seamstress, or of someone who is unaccustomed to stitching skin. The coarse black thread darts in and out of the outer seam, pointing haphazardly in different directions. It has the appearance of human skin but it is only animal fibre. It looks like a mouth sewn shut. The niches cut out of the wall used to house family souvenirs: framed photographs, mementoes of different journeys and moments, sometimes cut flowers. The shoes look out of place there but no one can recollect how they came to be incarcerated behind the screens of animal skin. There are some boxes stacked on the floor below. They too are made of animal skin but they are empty. There is nothing left to store in the boxes. The women have disappeared. Their clothes have gone with them. Only the shoes remain. Worn and moulded to fit the shape of the women's individual feet, they are useless keepsakes; more useless than photographs, which at least capture the semblance of an individual. But they cannot be discarded until we can be sure that they have died.

III

The sites that the photographs document are themselves banal and barely worth recording for posterity. In most cases, the objects that once were situated there have been removed. They record that removal, so perhaps they could be described as photographs of absence: the holes in the brickwork where the nails had been hammered in and the empty plinths where the statues had stood. It's curious how quickly people forget and how easily they remember once their memory has been jogged. The recollections begin characteristically with an account of what the person remembers of the site and what once stood there. Then they begin to recount what they felt about the object and what it represented. Some of them go on to talk about the old country and you get the sense that they are ambivalent about this new, reunified nation. Recent developments in what used to be the Eastern quarter are not just replacing the earlier buildings but erasing their memory. A field of cranes is harvesting a new city. Soon there will be no empty spaces. No one will remember that they had once been occupied and then vacated. Sweet oblivion.

IV

I left the town where I had been a student to join the Maquis. After some months, I had news of my people. I learnt that my mother had been killed point-blank by a French soldier, and two of my sisters had been taken to the soldiers' quarters. Up to now, I have no news of what happened to them. I was terribly shaken by the death of my mother. Since my father had died some years before, I was the only man in the family, and my sole ambition has always been to manage to do something to make life easier for my mother and my sisters. One day we went to an estate belonging to settlers, where the agent, who was an active colonist, had already killed two Algerian civilians. We came to his house, at night, but he wasn't there. Only his wife was at home. When she saw us she started to cry and implored us not to kill her: 'I know you've come for my husband,' she said, 'but he isn't here. I've told him again and again not to have anything to do with politics.' We decided to wait for her husband. But as far as I was concerned, when I looked at that woman I thought of my mother. She was sitting in an armchair and her thoughts seemed to be elsewhere. I wondered why we didn't kill her; then all of a sudden she noticed I was looking at her. She flung herself upon me screaming, 'Please don't kill me . . . I have children.' A moment after she was dead; I'd killed her with my knife.[2]

V

She has made a virtue of filling in the blank spaces. They are not monuments in the grand sense but solid shadows of everyday things. They do not commemorate individuals or historic events but moments in space and time. The space beneath the bed where you rummaged as a child in search of your mother's secrets. *Remember, remember the fifth of November.* Do you remember the time we hid behind the cupboard in our parents' room? It was fun for a while but then you started to feel really claustrophobic and wanted to come out. I held you there for a while but you started screaming so I let you go. Memories in physical form. But they are opaque memories cast in dark rubber and murky wax. Why is it that I only seem to recall the insignificant episodes? Maybe it is better to forget after all. We'll never know the whole truth about what happened anyway. What did Stalin say? The death of one man is a tragedy, the death of millions is a statistic.

VI

We weren't a bit cross with him. Every Thursday we used to go and play with catapults together, on the hill above the village. He was a good friend of ours. He usen't to go to school any more because he wanted to be a mason like his father. One day we decided to kill him, because the Europeans want to kill all the Arabs. We can't kill big people. But we could kill ones like him, because he was the same age as us. We didn't know how to kill him. We wanted to throw him into a ditch, but he'd only have been hurt. So we got the knife at home and we killed him.

But why did you pick on him?

Because he used to play with us. Another boy wouldn't have gone up the hill with us.

And yet you were pals?

Well then, why do they want to kill us? His father is in the militia and he said we ought to have our throats cut.

But he didn't say anything to you?

Him? No.

You know he is dead now.

Yes.

What does being dead mean?

When it's all finished, you go to heaven.

Was it you that killed him?

Yes.

Does having killed somebody worry you?
No, since they want to kill us, so . . .
Do you mind being in prison?
No.[3]

VII

It was Deleuze who spoke about 'a zone of indiscernibility' in relation
to his paintings. I've often imagined that he was referring to the
physical and psychic spaces that are created within the frame of the
canvas. They are ambiguous spaces where the distinction between the
human and the animal becomes collapsed, where the internal body
convulses into the external body. Humanity twisted in upon itself and
spilling, excreting. The agony and the ecstacy. The Soviet film-maker
understood about that. The old woman with her broken spectacles and
blood streaming down her bespectacled face. The young mother who
loses grip of her child's pram which cascades down the steps at Odessa.
The baby screaming. The screaming mother. What do you make of his
Popes, then? The revenge of a lapsed Irish Catholic, perhaps? The
painter has disrobed the Pope, divesting him of his vested interests.
Trapped like a caged animal. Pope Innocent X. But there's nothing
innocent about him. He's laughing now. A ribbed carcass of meat
decorates each side of his throne. The power and the glory.

VIII

*Sometimes we almost wanted to tell them that if they had a bit of consideration
for us they'd speak out without forcing us to spend hours tearing information
word by word out of them. But you might as well talk to the wall. To all the
questions we asked they'd only say 'I don't know.' Even when we asked them
what their name was. If we asked them where they lived, they'd say 'I don't
know.' So of course, we have to go through with it. But they scream too much.
At the beginning that made me laugh. But afterwards I was a bit shaken.
Nowadays as soon as I hear someone shouting I can tell you at exactly what
stage of the questioning we've got to. The chap who's had two blows of the fist
and a belt of the baton behind his ear has a certain way of speaking of shouting
and of saying he's innocent. After he's been left two hours strung up by the
wrists he has another kind of voice. After the bath, still another. And so on. But
above all it's after the electricity that it becomes really too much. You'd say that
the chap was going to die any minute. Of course there are some that don't
scream; those are the tough ones. But they think they're going to be killed right*

away. But we're not interested in killing them. What we want is information.[4]

IX

At that particular time of day, the light streamed into the space through the long, thin aperture. From a distance it could almost have been an abstract painting filling the frame of the window. The wooden tables were simply made and each one marked a stage in the process. Artist or artisan? The labour of the artist and the artistic endeavour of the labourer have mingled in this quiet space, defined by the light. The artwork, the product of this labour, is missing. Only the residue of the process remains as if that in itself is enough. Don't ask me what he was making. Anyway, haven't you missed the point? No end justifies the means. And it's not the answer that counts but the question. *And the women come and go talking of Michelangelo.* It reminded me of one of the tombs I had visited where the wall paintings had been left incomplete. The artist had begun to sketch the outlines of his drawings on the wall but his work had evidently been interrupted. I imagined that perhaps the dead man had died prematurely.

Notes

1. Frantz Fanon, 'Colonial War and Mental Disorders', *The Wretched of the Earth*, London: Penguin Books, 1971, p. 207.
2. Ibid., p. 211.
3. Ibid., pp. 217–18.
4. Ibid., p. 213.

30

Modernity and Difference

Charles Taylor

One set of issues has been very underexamined in contemporary scholarship. These issues have to do with how we understand the rise of modernity, its relation to the predecessor 'traditional' cultures, and the scope for difference within this. Some crucial questions here have been, as it were, kept off our screens by the hold of too narrow – one might say, too monistic – theories in this area.

I'd like to lay out, in programmatic fashion, some ways that these questions can be approached. I am conscious in doing this of approaching the concerns that have animated much of Stuart Hall's work over several decades. Stuart has constantly sought to open new ways of talking about contemporary realities, which are difficult to bring in focus through the languages dominant in our recognized university disciplines. I should like here to follow a little way in his footsteps.

My remarks will centre around two related themes, which can be captured in the phrases 'multiple modernities' and 'social imaginary', respectively.

'Multiple Modernities'

Two ways of understanding the rise of modernity seem to be at large in our culture. They are in effect two different 'takes' on what makes our contemporary society different from its forebears. In one take, we can look on the difference between present-day society and, say, that of medieval Europe as analogous to the difference between medieval Europe and China or India. In other words, we can think of the difference as one between civilizations, each with its own culture.

Or, alternatively, we can see the change from earlier centuries to today as involving something like 'development', as the demise of a 'traditional' society and the rise of the 'modern'. And in this perspective, which seems to be the dominant one, things look rather different.

I want to call the first kind of understanding a 'cultural' one, and the second 'acultural'. In using these terms, I'm leaning on a use of the word 'culture' that is analogous to the sense it often has in anthropology. I am evoking the picture of a plurality of human cultures, each of which has a language and a set of practices which define specific understandings of personhood, social relations, states of mind/soul, goods and bads, virtues and vices, and the like. These languages are often mutually untranslatable.

With this model in mind, a 'cultural' theory of modernity is one that characterizes the transformations that have issued in the modern West mainly in terms of the rise of a new culture. The contemporary Atlantic world is seen as a culture (or group of closely related cultures) among others, with its own specific understandings, for example, of person, nature, the good, to be contrasted to all others, including its own predecessor civilization (with which it obviously also has a lot in common).

By contrast, an 'acultural' theory is one that describes these transformations in terms of some culture-neutral operation. By this I mean an operation that is not defined in terms of the specific cultures it carries us from and to, but rather is seen as of a type that any traditional culture could undergo.

An example of an acultural type of theory, indeed a paradigm case, would be one that conceives of modernity as the growth of reason, defined in various ways: for example, as the growth of scientific consciousness, or the development of a secular outlook, or the rise of instrumental rationality, or an ever-clearer distinction between fact-finding and evaluation. Or else modernity might be accounted for in terms of social as well as intellectual changes: the transformations, including the intellectual ones, are seen as coming about as a result of increased mobility, concentration of populations, industrialization, or the like. In all these cases, modernity is conceived as a set of transformations which any and every culture can go through – and which all will probably be forced to undergo.

These changes are not defined by their end point in a specific constellation of understandings of, say, person, society, good; they are rather described as a type of transformation to which any culture could in principle serve as 'input'. For instance, any culture could suffer the impact of growing scientific consciousness; any religion could undergo 'secularization'; any set of ultimate ends could be challenged by a growth of instrumental thinking; any metaphysic could be dislocated by the split between fact and value.

It should be evident that the dominant theories of modernity over the last two centuries have been of the acultural sort. One might argue that this is wrong for a host of reasons. But what I want to bring out here is that these dominant theories tend to prejudge the case against diversity, and too easily predict a future of greater and greater uniformity across cultures.

Acultural theories tend to describe the transition to modernity in terms of a loss of traditional beliefs and allegiances. This may be seen as coming about as a result of institutional changes: for example, mobility and urbanization erode the beliefs and reference points of static rural society. Or the loss may be supposed to arise from the increasing operation of modern scientific reason. The change may be positively valued – or it may be judged a disaster by those for whom the traditional reference points were valuable, and scientific reason was too narrow. But all these theories concur in describing the process: old views and loyalties are eroded. Old horizons are washed away, in Nietzsche's image. The sea of faith recedes, following Matthew Arnold. This stanza from his 'Dover Beach' captures this perspective:

> The Sea of Faith
> Was once, too, at the full, and round earth's shore
> Lay like the folds of a bright girdle furled.
> But now I only hear
> Its melancholy, long, withdrawing roar,
> Retreating, to the breath
> Of the night-wind, down the vast edges drear
> And naked shingles of the world.[1]

Now the view that modernity arises through the dissipation of certain unsupported religious and metaphysical beliefs seems to imply that the paths of different civilizations are bound to converge. As they lose their traditional illusions, they will come together on the 'rationally grounded' outlook that has resisted the challenge of change. The march of modernity will end up making all cultures look the same. This means, of course, that we expect they will end up looking like us.

This idea of 'modernity' (in the singular) as a point of convergence is very much imbued with the logic of the acultural theory. 'Development' occurs in 'traditional' societies through 'modernization'. For this concept of the 'traditional', what matters is not the specific features of earlier societies, which are very different from each other. What is crucial is just that by holding people within a sacred horizon, a fixed community, and unchallengeable custom, traditional societies impede development. Over against the blazing light of modern reason, all traditional societies look alike in their immobile night.

What they hold us back from is 'development', conceived as the unfolding of our potentiality to grasp our real predicament and apply instrumental reason to it. The instrumental individual of secular outlook is always already there, ready to emerge when the traditional impediments fall away.

'Development' occurs through 'modernization', which designates the ensemble of those culture-neutral processes, both in outlook (individuation, rise of instrumental reason), and in institutions and practices (industrialization, urbanization, mass literacy, the introduction of markets and bureaucratic states) that carry us through the transition.

This viewpoint projects a future in which we all emerge together into a single, homogeneous world culture. In our 'traditional' societies, we were very different from each other. But once these earlier horizons have been lost, we shall all be the same.

A cultural theory opens up a rather different gamut of prospects. If the transition to modernity is like the rise of a new culture, analogous to the conversion of the Roman Empire to Christianity, or of Indonesia to Islam after the fourteenth century, then as in all such cases, the starting point will leave its impress on the end product. So Christianity was deeply marked by Greek philosophy, and Indonesian Islam is rather unlike the religion of the rest of the Islamic world. In a parallel fashion, transitions to what we might recognize as modernity, taking place in different civilizations, will produce different results, reflecting the civilizations' divergent starting points. Their understandings of the person, social relations, states of mind, goods and bads, virtues and vices, sacred and profane, are likely to be distinct. The future of our world will be one in which all societies will undergo change, in institutions and outlook, and some of these changes may be parallel. But it will not converge, because new differences will emerge from the old.

Thus, instead of speaking of 'modernity' in the singular, we should better speak of 'multiple modernities'.

Now the belief in modernity as convergence is not just the fruit of an acultural theory. Just as the account of the transition to modernity as our 'coming to see' certain things contains a partial truth, so there is undoubtedly *some* convergence involved in the triumphal march of modernity. A viable theory of alternative modernities has to be able to relate both the pull to sameness and the forces making for difference.

From one point of view, modernity is like a wave, flowing over and engulfing one traditional culture after another. If we understand by modernity, *inter alia*, the changes discussed above that carry the transition – namely, the emergence of a market-industrial economy, of a bureaucratically organized state, of modes of popular rule – then its progress is, indeed, wavelike. The first two changes, if not the third, are in a sense irresistible. Whoever fails to take them on, or some good functional equivalent, will fall so far behind in the power stakes as to be taken over, and forced to undergo these changes anyway. It was a stark appreciation of these power relations that impelled Japanese elites in the Meiji era, for instance, to undertake pre-emptive modernization. The fate of other Asian societies that had not managed to do so was an eloquent plea for this policy. There are good reasons in the relations of force for the onward march of modernity so defined.

But modernity as lived from the inside, as it were, is something different. The institutional changes just described always shake up and alter traditional culture. They did this in the original development in the West, and they have done this elsewhere. But outside those cases where the original culture is destroyed, and the people either die or are forcibly assimilated – and European colonialism has a number of such cases to its discredit – a successful transition involves a people finding resources in their traditional culture that, modified and transposed, will enable them to take on the new practices. In this sense, modernity is not a single wave. It would be better, as I have just suggested, to speak of multiple modernities, as the cultures that emerge in the world to carry the institutional changes turn out to differ in important ways from each other. Thus a Japanese modernity, an Indian modernity, various modulations of Islamic modernity will probably enter alongside the gamut of Western societies, which are also far from being totally uniform.

Seen in this perspective, we can see that modernity – the wave – can be felt as a threat to a traditional culture. It will remain an external threat to those deeply committed against change. But there is another reaction, among those who want to take on some version of the institutional changes. Unlike the conservatives, they don't want to refuse these innovations. They want of course to avoid the fate of those aboriginal people who have simply been engulfed and made over by the external power. What they are looking for is a creative adaptation, drawing on the cultural resources of their tradition, which would enable them to take on the new practices successfully. In short they want to do what has already been done in the West. But they see, or sense, that that cannot consist in copying the West's adaptations. The creative adaptation using traditional resources has by definition to be different from culture to culture. Just taking over Western modernity couldn't be the answer. Or, otherwise put, this answer comes too close to engulfment. They have to invent their own modernity.

There is thus a 'call to difference' felt by 'modernizing' elites which corresponds to something objective in their situation. This is of course part of the background to nationalism.

Now just wanting a creative adaptation doesn't ensure that one brings it off. And some of the formulae proposed look with hindsight pretty much non-starters; as for instance the idea put forward by the government of Ching China after the Opium War, which can be roughly rendered: we'll take their technology and keep our culture. There are moments where the 'modernizers' begin to look indistinguishable from the conservative enemies of change.

This kind of resistance results in what Rajeev Bhargava has called 'patchwork' solutions, which attempt to tack the new power-conferring practices onto an unchanged way of life.[2] But these institutions and practices almost always require new disciplines, new understandings of agency, new forms of sociability. We have only to think of what is required to participate as an entrepreneur in a modern market economy, or the kind of 'rationalized' co-ordination required by a modern bureaucracy, to see that this is so. The really creative adaptation is one that can modify our existing culture so as to make, for example, successful entrepreneurship and bureaucratic organization henceforth part of our repertory. This generally cannot be brought about without profound changes in our earlier way of life.

The point of the 'multiple modernities' thesis is that these adaptations don't have to and generally won't be identical across civilizations. Something is indeed converging here, while other things diverge. It might be tempting to say: the institutions and practices converge, while the cultures find new forms of differentiation. But that can only be a first approximation. Because in fact the institutional forms will also frequently be different.

Take the example just mentioned of entrepreneurship. This is a condition of successful participation in a market economy, itself a condition of economic growth, and hence welfare and/or power. But it is clear that the entrepreneurial cultures of Japan, Chinese societies, the Indian merchant castes and groups differ from each other and from those of the West. Indeed, business cultures differ even between the societies of the Atlantic region, as Francis Fukuyama has persuasively argued.[3] But with the cultures also go differences in form: in size of firm, basis of trust within it, its modes of procedure, et cetera. These forms-and-cultures will be more or less successful in different circumstances, and they may thus keep tabs on each other, and even try to borrow; but this doesn't mean that they can or will converge.

We have to remember that what is required by the 'wave' of modernity is that one should come up not with identical institutions but with functionally equivalent ones. The 'bottom line' is, for example, competing successfully in the international market. More than one kind of firm and business culture can enable this; as will more than one way of

relating the state to the private sector – differences to which the
mindless neo-liberalism fashionable today is blind. A given society will,
indeed must, adopt the mode for which it has the cultural resources.
That is the essence of creative adaptation.

The cultures of entrepreneurship provide, of course, only one
example. There is also important research to be done on the place and
use of media in society; on the ways the functions of the North Atlantic
'welfare state' are assumed or not by different kinds of community:
family, clan, caste, et cetera.; on the very different political cultures of
representative democracies: For instance, in India there is a strong
attachment of masses of people to the forms of parliamentary democracy, but the way these are 'imagined' by Indian voters obviously differs
from North Atlantic models; and yet remarkably little work has been
done on the shape of this social imaginary. Again, modern societies
obviously differ greatly in the place they have for religion, and this is
so even between states that are alike in espousing some variant of
'secularism'. What exists under this label in India, for instance, is
completely different from its counterpart in France or the USA. And
there are many more such areas begging for further study.

If this perspective of divergence in convergence is right, then we can
see how exclusive reliance on an acultural theory unfits us for what is
perhaps the most important task of social sciences in our day: understanding the full gamut of alternative modernities that are in the
making in different parts of the world. It locks us into an ethnocentric
prison, condemned to project our own forms onto everyone else, and
blissfully unaware of what we are doing.

The 'Social Imaginary'

The term 'social imaginary' has already arisen in the above discussion,
and inevitably so, because any attempt to define the different cultures
of modernity cannot be satisfied just with marking differences in
explicit theory and in institutions. Indeed, these may not be very great.
What matters, and what helps determine the repertory of practices that
a given population has at its disposal, is how the society with its
institutions and practices is imagined by those who live in and by these.

It is important to distinguish the social imaginary from social theory.
There are a number of crucial differences between the two. I speak of
'imaginary', first, because I'm talking about the way ordinary people
'imagine' their social surroundings, and this is often not expressed in
theoretical terms: it is carried in images, stories, legends, et cetera. But
it is also the case, second, that theory is often the possession of small

minority, whereas what is interesting in a social imaginary is that it is
shared by large groups of people, if not the whole society. That leads
to a third difference: the social imaginary is that common understanding which makes possible common practices, and widely shared sense
of legitimacy.

The social imaginary sometimes evolves in the same direction as
theory, but often considerably after it. Thus the modern notion of a
social order based on the mutual benefit of equal participants is
elaborated first in theories of the State of Nature and contract in the
seventeenth century (for example, Grotius and Locke). But something
similar only enters the social imaginary, and hence action, of significant
groups in the following century. We see this, for instance with the
developing idea of the public sphere in the eighteenth century. The
dispersed publications and small-group or local exchanges come to be
construed as one big debate, from which the 'public opinion' of a
whole society emerges. This is the first time that such a meta-topical,
continuing space is conceived of as grounded in nothing other than
common action in secular time, that is, without the kind of action-
transcendent grounding in higher time that kingdoms, Churches, long-
established legal systems enjoyed.[4]

After, and partly on the basis of the public sphere, the modern
theory of legitimacy mutates into a social imaginary that makes popular
sovereignty the main, and later the only possible, basis of legitimacy.
We can see how older ideas of legitimacy are colonized, as it were, with
the new understandings of order, and then transformed, in certain
cases, without a clear break.

The United States is a case in point. The reigning notions of legitimacy
in Britain and America, the ones that fired the English Civil War, for
instance, as well as the beginnings of the Colonies' rebellion, were
basically backward-looking. They turned around the idea of an 'ancient
constitution', an order based on law holding 'since time out of mind', in
which Parliament had its rightful place beside the King. This was typical
of premodern understandings of order, which referred back to a 'time
of origins' (Eliade's phrase), which was not in ordinary time.

This earlier justification emerges from the American Revolution
transformed into a full-fledged foundation in popular sovereignty,
whereby the US constitution is put in the mouth of 'We, the people'.
The transition is the easier, because what was understood as the
traditional law gave an important place to elected assemblies and their
consent to taxation. All that was needed was (a) to shift the balance in
these so as to make elections the only source of legitimate power, and
(b) to reconceive what was taking place in these elections as an
expression of a popular will to refound the state.

Now what has to take place for this change to come off is a transformed social imaginary, in which the idea of foundation is taken out
of the mythical early time, and seen as something that people can do
today. In other words, it becomes something that can be brought
about by collective action in contemporary, purely secular time. This
happened sometime in the eighteenth century, but really more
towards its end than its beginning. Elites propounded *theories* of founding action beforehand, but these had not adequately sunk into the
general social imaginary for them to be acted on. So that 1688, radical
departure as it may seem to us in retrospect, was presented as an act
of continuity, of return to a pre-existent legality. (We are fooled by a
change in semantics. The 'Glorious Revolution' had the original sense
of a return to the original position; not the modern sense of a innovative turn-over. Of course, it helped by its *Wirkungsgeschichte* to alter
the sense.)

This fit between theory and social imaginary is crucial to any outcome. Popular sovereignty could be invoked in the American case,
because it had a generally agreed institutional meaning. All colonists
agreed that the way to found a new constitution was through some
kind of assembly, perhaps slightly larger than the normal one, such as
in Massachusetts in 1779. The force of the old representative institutions helped to 'interpret' in practical terms the new concept of
popular sovereignty.

The case of the French Revolution was quite different, with fateful
effects. The impossibility remarked by all historians of 'bringing the
Revolution to an end'[5] came partly from this, that any particular
expression of popular sovereignty could be challenged by some other,
with substantial support. Thus the members of the Convention were
eventually purged in 1793 under threat of the activists from the Paris
sections, and that in the name of the 'people'. The immediate consequences are too horrible and too well known to need repetition.

Similarly, there may be a gap between the theory and social imaginary of political elites, and those of the less educated classes, or those of
people in rural areas. This again is something that has been well
documented for France during most of the nineteenth century, in
spite of the confident remarks of republican leaders about the nation
'one and indivisible'.[6] The transformation wrought by the Third
Republic was to make this vision of France real for the first time. We
can only understand this change as a transformation of the social
imaginary.

So, looking at the modern social imaginary has obvious relevance
and interest for the history of the last few centuries. But it is not just
relevant to the past. One of the most important features of modern

society is precisely that it has developed a new range of social imaginaries, which underlie its peculiar understandings of legitimation, most specially popular sovereignty. These are at the heart of modern political life, and the problems it suffers from.

Here something that arose in the discussion of multiple modernities becomes relevant. Once one sees modern cultures in the plural, one can see that the differences do not only lie between 'civilizations'. Even different North Atlantic societies diverge in significant ways. I referred to this above in connection with entrepreneurial cultures. But it is also evident in the social imaginaries underpinning popular sovereignty. The work of Pierre Rosanvallon, tracing the advent of universal suffrage in France, illustrates this very tellingly.[7]

Modern society invents or imagines a new collective agency that it requires: the 'people', sometimes also called in France and America in the eighteenth century the 'nation'. This collective agency must have a certain kind of unity if it is to function as it is supposed to. How are we to understand this unity?

One of the most common modes has been what we call 'nationalism', that is, the understanding of the people's unity as grounded in a pre-existing oneness as a nation, defined by language, culture or history. Modern nationalism is still something that baffles us. Some authors have understood that it requires a certain form of social imaginary.[8] But not all seem to understand the importance of this.

We need to understand better the important features of this kind of social imaginary, the more so in that theories of nationalism tend to be rather thin. We have to understand the ways in which it incorporates typically modern understandings of time, of space, of history – for instance, the typical narrativity of the growth of potential culture or consciousness into actualization, which involves a very different temporality from the pre-modern modes.

We also have to understand how this social imaginary can be imposed by elites on very different kinds of popular imaginaries, producing a wide range of compromise forms, which are very different from each other. People still often speak as though 'nationalism' were a single phenomenon, perhaps with less or more virulent forms, but in essence the same from Scotland to the Respublika Srbska; and this seems very wrong.

And not only nationalism, but the modern phenomena, and problems, of civil society, of the public sphere, of the conditions of mutual trust, of secular regimes, of multiculturalism, all need to be re-examined in this light. In addition, there is the entire phenomenon of 'development', that is, the evolution of societies under the impress of others, more 'advanced', who borrow, adapt, create new and hybrid forms. We are still looking for a language to understand this, to bridge differences, make comparative studies.

I have been trying to suggest in this chapter some directions in which we might look for the languages we need. I hope they will prove fruitful.

Notes

1. Matthew Arnold, 'Dover Beach', ll. 21–8.

2. Oral communication by Rajeev Bhargava to the 'Alternative Modernities' seminar, held by the Centre for Transcultural Studies, Delhi, December 1997.

3. See Francis Fukuyama, *Trust: The Social Virtue and the Creation of Prosperity*, New York: Free Press, 1996.

4. I have discussed this in 'Modernity and the Rise of the Public Sphere', in *The Tanner Lectures on Human Values*, Vol. 14, 1993, Salt Lake City: Utah University Press, pp. 203–60.

5. François Furet, *La Révolution française*, Paris, 1988.

6. This gap has been admirably traced by Eugen Weber, *Peasants into Frenchmen*, London: Chatto, 1977.

7. See Pierre Rosanvallon, *Le Sacre du citoyen*, Paris: Gallimard.

8. See especially Benedict Anderson, *Imagined Communities*, London: Verso, 1991, to which these reflections obviously owe a great deal.

31

Reading Stuart Hall in Southern Africa

Keyan G. Tomaselli

Narrating the Crisis[1] was the title of a book on the South African news media under apartheid (Tomaselli *et al.* 1987). The source of this title is obviously a play on the Birmingham Centre for Contemporary Cultural Studies's (BCCCS) landmark study, *Policing the Crisis*, edited by Stuart Hall *et al.* (1978).

Narrating the Crisis had followed the inauguration of *Critical Arts: A Journal for Media Studies* in 1980, where a group of anti-apartheid South African scholars sought to develop theories pertinent to a critique of South African media, drama and literature. None had then heard of BCCCS, let alone Stuart Hall. It was coincidentally through the Witwatersrand University History Workshop in 1981, around which radical historians, sociologists, literary and anthropological scholars coalesced, that its editors learned from some British scholars of BCCCS and *Policing the Crisis*. Some of us involved with *Critical Arts* had independently of BCCCS forged similar – if much less theorized, and inconsistent and fragmentary – approaches in our own studies. My discussion below will derive from the *Critical Arts* experience between 1980 and 1998.[2]

In 1985, the University of Natal, Durban, established the Contemporary Cultural Studies Unit (CCSU). The stimulus for this initiative was the 16 June 1976 Soweto student uprising. A faculty–student committee realized that resistance in South Africa was failing, partly because two crucial sites of mobilization were absent domestically: media and culture. These sites had been so effectively colonized in the service of apartheid that even liberal anthropologists were wary of teaching 'cultural anthropology'. CCSU's mandate was to work with anti-apartheid organisations (see Tomaselli 1988; NeSmith 1988). Stuart Hall and Richard Johnson had been consulted by the committee on using the Birmingham model.

It was most fitting, then, that Stuart Hall was able to participate in a conference organized in Durban by our renamed Centre for Cultural and Media Studies (CCMS), in January 1997. Hall (1997) engagingly summed up the week's deliberations. The conference marked a new articulation of our programmes, which now also included issues of identity in relation to media and democracy in Southern Africa.[3] The defeat of apartheid in the early 1990s had made this meeting possible.

Contours of South African Cultural Studies

The trajectories of differing positions within broader debates that might be called cultural studies, and the ways in which they travelled to, within, and between opposed historical blocs within South Africa, has been discussed elsewhere (Muller and Tomaselli 1998). Contemporary cultural studies (CCS) under apartheid followed contours familiar from the British debates between the culturalists as articulated by E.P. Thompson on the one hand, and CCS piloted by Hall and Johnson on the other. In South Africa, labour sociologists, oral historians and union activists pressed forward on the culturalist route. Conversely, media and some performance scholars preferred the Birmingham synthesis of culturalism and humanist structuralism. The work of Hall (1980a), and his protégés (Johnson 1979), together with Antonio Gramsci (1971) and Armand Mattelart (among them Mattelart and Siegelaub 1979, 1983),[4] played key roles in the development of the media strategies.

In comparison with their counterparts elsewhere, cultural theorists of both the CCS and culturalist tendencies in South Africa stood in a unique relation to history as the second millennium approached. Unlike Europe, South Africa had not yet experienced or lost a golden age. If anything, South Africa after 1990[5] had passed through the threshold of an age still to be won. Not all cultural theorists had lost their innocence, however. Neither had the still struggling masses. While expectations were perhaps unrealistically high, their respective relations to critique was still one of a hoped-for empowerment rather than a nostalgic resignation to new, but a not so different set of power-brokers.

A persistent optimism about the role of intellectuals remained somewhat unsoured in comparison to the experience of centuries of deceit which had so powerfully driven the cynical visions of Michel Foucault, Louis Althusser, Jean Baudrillard and others. A praxis-based cultural studies in South Africa had always been aligned with an ascendent political trajectory. But this practice, in victory after 1990, was simultaneously tempered by the excesses of the postmodern, postindustrial, and post-Cold War era into which South Africa re-emerged after decades of isolation via boycotts and sanctions. The structural cards dealt the new Government of National Unity required the adoption of solutions already put in place by an information-ordered globalizing world in which capital now reigned supreme. One strand of South African cultural and media studies as indicated in *Critical Arts* both engaged and critiqued these emergent assumptions and practices, increasingly within an African context. Others sought their conceptual nirvanas in Western post-structuralist orientations that appropriated Hall directly from the metropole (Cooper and Steyn 1996).

The genuflection to the metropole for theory did not necessarily indicate a lack of historical imagination amongst South African scholars. What it did mean, however, was that the scholastics, orientated towards the past and aware of the pitfalls of history and naïve optimism, tended to drift into political inactivity. Others made their mark in parliamentary and governmental structures, while the ones most cynically reported on in the media simply got onto the lucrative 'gravy train' when it stopped long enough in the parliamentary station to switch governments.

Contours of Struggle, Discourses of Liberation

Apartheid had entered its last decade at the beginning of the 1980s. Lines of tension crossed all classes and groups within the social formation as a whole. The state itself was racked with conflict, internal dissension, contrary political positions, and an unwinnable war in Angola. The influence of the militarist 'securocrats' waned in the face of those within the government who preferred to jettison apartheid in favour of a negotiated settlement in which a relative white Afrikaner privilege could be protected. Academic practices at the anti-apartheid English-language universities during this period also reflected the political and ideological schisms of the society as a whole. Particular tendencies, whether on the left, centre, or the right wings, themselves struggled over assumptions, theories, and ideologies. In this war of ideas, left-wing academics fought more with the liberals than they did with apartheid supporters. The paradox in South Africa has always been that liberalism has been in opposition.

Many centre-to-left academics worked within the Mass Democratic Movement (MDM) and the allied labour unions. One particular labour tendency had coalesced around historical materialist correspondence theorists. This 'workerist' position developed an analysis based on absolute knowledge of the reality of objective, 'out-there', concretely referrable objects, independent of textual contamination. The brutality of real conditions had a concrete impact on real people, they argued, irrespective of how they made sense of it. The mobilizing role of language and representation was not a major dimension in the work of this tendency. This position derived from the framework offered by E.P. Thompson (1965) and, as mentioned earlier, found its articulation mainly via the Witwatersrand History Workshop, and the Junction Avenue Theatre Company. This strand of 'culturalism' was hostile to structuralist theory and formalist semiology. Structuralism was argued to suppress human agency and the authenticity of the experience of the oppressed classes (Sitas 1984).

The workerists accused CCS scholars of intellectualizing and reifying popular experience. The conflict between culturalism and CCS centred on the semiotic studies of popular anti-apartheid theatre. CCS theorists of popular theatre had applied a historical materialist semiotics reconstituted from C.S. Peirce, and later Volosinov (1973), to the study of performance genres found in the work of black consciousness, labour and community theatre practitioners (Steadman 1988; Tomaselli and Muller 1987). This approach was, however, quite different to the Saussurean-based structuralist semiology, which had so incensed the workerists.

The confrontation between the culturalists and CCS constituencies was triggered by two articles that semiotized a workers' strike, the role-playing exercise used by the union lawyer to re-create the incident for presentation in court, and its final mutation into a worker play (Tomaselli 1981a; 1981b). Some labour theatre activists felt that semiotics was an untimely and inappropriate intellectual imposition which disempowered the strategic significance of their cultural work within the union movement (Sitas 1984). They argued that structuralist analysis objectified people who were already dehumanized under apartheid – and that this had seriously negative effects on how cultural work was viewed within the labour movement itself.

This largely unpublished culturalist critique endured in the face of the CCS counter-argument. CCS – which was extended into media studies – argued that popularizing semiotics provided a critical weapon against both apartheid practices and dominant social constructions of reality. CCS contended that it was necessary to contest dominant forms of representation to enhance the cultural work of the labour movement. These scholars began to argue for ideology as a *level of analysis*. Ideology was understood to have no direct relationship to the truth or falsity of prevailing ideas. They asserted that it is possible that even objectively established 'knowledge' could have an ideological function. Following Hall, it was argued that ideological dimensions are not true or false: their effectiveness is judged in terms of their ability to identify the structural positions of those who promulgate ideas, while at the same time providing a sense of dynamism in smoothing over the contradictions that exist within a particular social formation.

The cultural theorists who had coalesced around *Critical Arts* largely agreed that structuralist semiology was guilty of determinist and dehumanizing tendencies. But it was only somewhat later that the actual differences between structuralist semiology and pragmatist Peircean semiotics were elaborated upon in an attempt to bridge this gap (Shepperson and Tomaselli 1998). By that time, apartheid was being dismantled. The cultural studies mesh of historical materialism and semiotics had tried to explain and interpret enactments of class experiences in an affirmative way not possible in semiology. At the root of the difference between the two positions were the issues of language and interpretation: CCS and culturalism were unable to talk to each other constructively because of their epistemological divergences: the one examined the metonymic relationship between role-playing representations (theatre) and actual events (strikes), while the other denied the metonymic dimension and made clear distinctions between 'working' and 'leisure' lives, the 'stage' and the 'audience'.

A third tendency, which existed in parallel with, rather than intersecting, the above debates, was structuralism, found in Screen Theory applications. Screen Theory is based largely on the work of the late Christian Metz, which reads Saussure's formalism through Lacanian psychoanalysis and Louis Althusser's (1971) theory of ideology. The assumption of this theory is that the text 'positions' ahistorical and unlocated viewers into 'reading' films in terms of a Metzian 'narrative inscription' (see, for example, Higgins 1991, 1993). For John Higgins (1991: 112), the question is 'how film for the analyst becomes the object of knowledge distinct from film as the object of commonsense understanding'.

Higgins attacked Michael Chapman's (1991: 86) CCS emphasis, which called for dialectically derived 'useful insights about the relation of "texts" to social reality'. This is the old text-versus-context argument (Hall 1980c) where texts are argued to provide their own rules for interpretation, irrespective of the context of exhibition or the differing ways that interpretive communities make sense of these texts.

Chapman argues for multi-accentuated analysis involving context – he is less concerned with the text than with the social, cultural and political conditions within which texts are interpreted. Like the waspish debates over labour theatre discussed above, this testy interchange occurred within left-wing theoretical discourses. But in this instance it was over questions of representation. Where Higgins (1991: 111) accuses Chapman of reducing film to an example of bourgeois ideology,

Chapman was calling for recognition of the experience brought to the viewing of films by South African schoolchildren – something of the culturalist position.

Text-bound readings, however, gloss over the production circuit which includes distribution, exchange and consumption, recirculation, repackaging and reception, rearticulation of meanings, and so on. Texts always speak to and for an envisaged constellation of subjects – a specific 'type' of readership/viewership. There is no guarantee that the response of the reader/viewer will coincide with the intention of the individual author – or its semiological form as determined by the researcher. In short, criticism exists not merely 'for the sake of litera-ture', but for the sake of knowledge. To understand how that know-ledge is acquired, *Critical Arts* argued the necessity of examining the contexts of both reader/viewer and writer/director, as well as the relationship between media, ideology, and economy. Ideology reveals conclusions but not necessarily the mechanisms for arriving at those conclusions. Knowledge helps us penetrate into the mechanisms that produce conclusions out of 'premises'. As Hall's (1980c) encoding/decoding article suggested, the author (or protagonist) or work-as-object are decoded within 'fields of significations', and experienced in conjunctures of social, historical, political and economic conditions, which structure both the author's and readers' 'realities'.

A sustained reflection in *Critical Arts* especially on the finally sterile polarization of the culturalist–CCS arc led to the beginnings of a serious reconsideration of the appropriate role of cultural theorists in the context of mass political movements and struggles during the latter part of the 1980s when such movements had assumed centre-stage in resistance. This reconsideration attempted to position critique in a way that did justice to theory and history on the one hand, and political strategy on the other, without subordinating one to the other. These academic–community/union links represented a concrete attempt at praxis, in what was self-consciously understood as not the end of the road but just the next moment in the debate and the struggle.

The Right

The response from conservatives and right-wing academics during the 1980s to the intra-left squabbles was one of bemusement and incompre-hension. During the earlier Althusserian/Poulantzian moment – the mid-1970s to early 1980s – they had detected the lack of an affirmative dimension in Marxism, and lack of theory and political strategy in culturalism. What possible use could CCS, a 'negative' approach, and culturalism, an 'unscientific' set of descriptions, have in normative research designed to order and govern society? These approaches additionally lacked problem-solving dimensions: quantitative methods and substantiating empirical evidence were ignored; further, questions of policy and strategy were not even addressed. At the end of the day, both CCS and culturalism were considered by these detractors to be a curious distraction in the broader scheme of things. Marxism as method was tolerated; but Marxism as a political philosophy (communism) was demonized as the 'enemy' – to be fought with everything at hand, including the academy. It was not surprising, then, that while all three volumes of Marx's *Capital* could be legitimately bought and taught, it was Lenin's works and, ironically, Althusser's *Lenin and Other Essays*,[6] which were banned. Since media theory tended to operate in the realm of philosophy, at least in its First World manifestations, this approach, while considered 'political', was not thought of as 'communication studies', or necessarily threatening to the security of the state while it remained in the obtuse language of social theorists, located on a few English-speaking campuses.

Gramsci's writings came to South Africa rather later than had Althusser and Poulantzas, and not really via Hall at all. Belinda Bozzoli's (1981) application of Gramsci in understanding relations between the class and the state, and how organic intellectuals provided ways for the ruling class to embed itself within the social formation during times of stress, was pivotal to his subsequent adoption in South African media studies.

Almost coterminously with Bozzoli, the apartheid state tumbled to Gramsci in the Steyn Commission of Inquiry into the Mass Media (see Republic of South Africa 1981). It is not clear how this discovery came about, but the commissioners found in Gramsci a very useful conceptual framework to explain revolution to themselves, especially where black journalists – described as the 'shock troops' of the revolution – were concerned. The commissioners had partly blamed the growing crisis of hegemony on the libertarian English-language and black consciousness presses. By curtailing these media, the commission hoped to remove the 'hard, tangible and exploitative images' that exposed the structural contradictions of apartheid to the world. The Internal Security Act (1981) outlawed any 'doctrine, ideology or scheme' based on the works of Lenin, Engels, Marx or Mao Tse-tung, *or any other recognized theorist or exponent of these tenets.* Where previously the theorists had been listed, now they could include publications, academics, and activists working to overthrow apartheid, irrespective of whether collective ownership was an issue or not.

This kind of back-handed reactionary appropriation of Gramsci for purposes opposed to his own objectives, added a new and chilling dimension to the state's appreciation of the potential effect of an application of Gramscian strategies in South Africa. These intellectuals of apartheid found evidence of their worst fears within Gramsci's Marxism – an *affirmative* dimension that could underwrite a Marxist analysis in actual anti-apartheid struggle. The earlier negative and culturally sterile structuralist critique offered by Marxism of capitalism in general, now read via Gramsci, was a serious intellectual threat, supported by a growing strategy of popular resistance, spreading across the country as a whole from the early 1980s on. The co-operative relations that had developed between the radicalizing English-language universities, and the University of Western Cape, and the unions and the United Democratic Front (UDF), provided the ground on which theory and practice interlinked via sustained working-class-led struggle.

The UDF, established in 1983, offered a means of engaging hegemony, and possibilities of a trans-class mobilization via counter-ideology. A key strategy was the popular mobilization of both cultural expression and popular media as sites of grassroots democratic mobilization.

The Steyn Commission had predicted the intensification of struggle now that an affirmative theoretical dimension via Gramsci had been identified by the left. Barely seven years after the formation of the UDF, at end of the decade, the apartheid government was gasping its last. Though *Prison Notebooks* was never banned, very severe restrictions on the media between 1986 and 2 February 1990 attempted to curtail information on the depth of the crisis facing the state and capital.

Cultural studies, by the late 1980s, paradoxically, also gave to the state's propaganda intellectuals a more sophisticated discursive arsenal. Its propaganda become multi-accentuated, and tried to speak to a variety of constituencies simultaneously. This was marked by attempts to co-opt both the discourses of the Left and Western liberalism in terms of separately inflected messages designed to convince both interpretive communities that political reform was real. The state failed completely, partly because its ideologues did not ultimately understand neo-Marxist analysis, especially with regard to language, media and representation – the very areas that had been analysed by Hall and the BCCCS in other contexts.

The Bosses Have Changed: Cultural Studies Tamed

The partial shift in South Africa from resistance to policy studies after 1990 does not mean that a hard-won critical edge is being necessarily vitiated. Romantic notions of democracy and of the benignness of the current political terrain dominated by the ANC were not taken for granted by all CCS scholars. The romantic idealist political assumptions espoused by students from disadvantaged communities is seriously cautioned by other postcolonial experiences. These students have yet to understand that the new class of apparatchiks may well fall into temptation and embourgeoisement as did the one they have replaced. This brings into play the urgent need for a sophisticated discussion on issues of ethnicity, identity, postcoloniality and so on. On this occasion, Stuart Hall's more recent work has been again most useful. Indeed, his participation at the Durban conference offered key insights into conundrums facing the sometimes essentialist perspectives of some CCS scholars drawn from Southern Africa (Hall 1997). As Ruth Teer-Tomaselli (1997: x) commented on the significance of Hall's presentation:

> Students of cultural studies in the period of post-modernism have turned their collective backs on Althusserian-type structuralism. Yet cultural identity remains largely about the recognition of whom we are, with whom we associate ourselves and our aspirations, with whom we empathise, to whom we say 'yes'. As Stuart Hall puts it . . . we are a culmination of personal and social histories: 'those different ways in which at different historical moments people have addressed us, have called us and the recognition this implies. Yes, that is me'. That is a moment of identity, of identification.

Teer-Tomaselli concludes that the irony here is that the term 'interpellation', which in our postmodern, poststructuralist world has no purpose, is here in Hall's later work nevertheless reinvented as a mechanism in identity-creation. This consistency of theoretical appropriation and integration is the strength of Hall's lifetime of work: it draws on intensive and extensive readings of the history of philosophy and theory, and is simultaneously a culmination and conceptual extension and updating of this reading.

The participants in the Durban conference all owed their original derivations to Birmingham, and Hall in particular, in one way or another.[7] However, the Southern African applications have also taken on new indigenized dimensions, in relation to the identities, fractured or unified, that the participating academics brought with them: essentialized African, poststructuralist double-consciousness, modernist, travelling academic, as well as English, South African, Norwegian, Zimbabwean, and so on. Some have superseded Hall's (1980c) seminal encoding/decoding model in their discussions. These new voices incorporate interpretive frameworks that depart from Hall in line with utterly different interpretations, based in the spiritual cosmologies of Third and Fourth World peoples.[8] Their encoding structures derive from orality-based ontologies which are less inclined to make hard distinctions between object and subject, waking and dreaming, and so on (Ong 1982).

Conclusion

Critical Arts's approach to cultural studies has progressed both in parallel with, and through, intersections of the general field as led by Stuart Hall. It was through media analysis that cultural studies was first discovered by the journal, though briefly preceded by a materialist/culturalist semiotic of popular performance. An early Althusserianism was later engaged by a Gramscian agency, returning to Hall when issues of identity were introduced into the mix, made possible by the end of apartheid. Where British cultural studies was initially integrated with European articulations, South African media studies of the 1980s borrowed from South American, African and Soviet examples. After 1990, South Africans engaged issues of representation, symbolic forms, and identity in relation to questions of reception and interpretation as well. For those who visit shopping malls, engage with soap operas, and find pleasure in situation comedies, and who aspire in terms of advertising messages, identity becomes a complex hypermediated practice of consumption in the post-apartheid period. In understanding the intersection between power and consumption, the realization that power is always uneven (Teer-Tomaselli 1997: xv) cautions the celebration of the popular and postmodernism via conspicuous consumption.

Whilst the impact of Hall's work globally has been astonishing, from media studies to accountancy, there is always the danger in our corporatizing academic practices of Hall himself being 'consumed', his writings used for quotable quotes, for opportunistic conceptual legitimation, with his ideas being taken as given, rather than being constantly tested, engaged and applied. The man's work is far too important for us to allow this to occur.

Notes

1. *Narrating the Crisis* was titled *The Press in South Africa* in the UK and US editions.
2. This chapter draws heavily on *Retrospective* (Tomaselli *et al.* 1983) and Tomaselli, Muller and Shepperson (1996).
3. The Identities, Democracy, Culture and Communication in Southern Africa Conference was held in Durban in January 1997 under the auspices of

the journal *Media, Culture and Society* and CCMS, University of Natal. Papers from this meeting were published in *Critical Arts* (1997) and *Media, Culture and Society* (1997), amongst other titles, and in Waldahl (1998).

4. Both of the anthologies of Mattelart and Siegelaub, and other works by Mattelart, sold hundreds, and *Rethinking Culture* (Tomaselli 1988), sold thousands of copies during the mid to late 1980s. Like the BCCCS stencilled papers series, the individual chapters that later made up *Rethinking Culture* were drawn from individually issued monographs, and were sold separately. Some 10,000 of these were sold between 1985 and 1988. Purchasers were students, activists, community organizers and organizations. CCSU had become both publisher and a distributor to ensure that these works reached beyond the academy into popular anti-apartheid social movements.

5. It was in February 1990 that the apartheid government unbanned the liberation movements and released Nelson Mandela. South Africa's first democratic elections were held in April 1994.

6. Presumably because 'Lenin' was in the title of Althusser's book. Where Althusser was 'negative' and philosophical, Lenin was positively associated with concrete *strategy*, revolution and the success of communism. His works were therefore considered a danger to the state.

7. Delegates came from the UK, Zimbabwe and Norway. Stuart and Catherine Hall came from the UK with various members of the board of *Media, Culture and Society* – Paddy Scannell, Philip Schlesinger, Colin Sparks, and Anna Reading, amongst others. Staff from the University of Zimbabwe's Diploma in Media Studies were also participants. The diploma course was established in co-operation with the Department of Media and Communication, University of Oslo, which owes much of its own orientation to British cultural studies, especially that offered by Graham Murdock (Murdock 1991; Ronning and Lundby 1991).

8. The term 'Fourth World' refers to the political and social space occupied by indigenous populations that have been marginalized as a result of colonization. Communities in the Fourth World are usually described (or identify themselves) as First Peoples.

References

Althusser, L. *For Marx*. (1971) London: Allen Lane.
Bozzoli, B. (1981) *Capital and Ideology in South Africa, 1890–1993: The Political Nature of a Ruling Class*. London: Routledge & Kegan Paul.
Chapman, M. (1991) 'Running on Empty: Film Studies in South Africa', in Prinsloo, J. and Criticos, C. (eds.) *Media Matters in South Africa*. Durban: Media Resource Centre, University of Natal, 83–6.
Cooper, B. and Steyn, A. (1996) *Transgressing Boundaries: New Directions for the Study of Culture in Africa*. Cape Town: University of Cape Town Press.
Gramsci, A. (1971) *Prison Notebooks*. London: Lawrence and Wishart.
Hall, S. (1997) 'Random Thoughts Provoked by the Conference "Identities, Democracy, Culture and Communication in Southern Africa"', *Critical Arts*, 11(1/2), 1–16.

Hall, S. (1986) 'Gramsci's Relevance for the Study of Race & Ethnicity', *Journal of Communication Inquiry*, 10(2), 5–27.

Hall, S. (1980a) 'Cultural Studies and the Centre: Some Problematics and Problems', in Hall, S., Hobson, D., Low, A. and Willis, P. (eds.) *Culture, Media, Language*. London: Hutchinson, 15–47.

Hall, S. (1980b) 'Encoding/Decoding', in Hall, S., Hobson, D. Low, A. and Willis, P. (eds.) *Culture, Media, Language*. London: Hutchinson, 128–38.

Hall, S. (1980c) 'Recent Developments in Theories of Language and Ideology: A Critical Note', in Hall S., Hobson, D., Low, A. and Willis, P. (eds.) *Culture, Media, Language*. London: Hutchinson, 157–62.

Hall, S. *et al.* (1978) *Policing the Crisis: 'Mugging', the State and Law and Order*. London: Lawrence & Wishart.

Higgins, J. (1991) 'Critical Cinema and the Reality of Reflection'. In Prinsloo, J. and Criticos, C. (eds.) *Media Matters in South Africa*. Durban: Media Resource Centre, University of Natal, 110–22.

Higgins, J. (1992) 'Documentary Realism and Film Pleasure: Two Moments from Euzhan Palcy's *A Dry White Season*', *Literator*, 13(1), 93–100.

Johnson, R. (1979) 'Three Problematics: Elements of a Theory of Working Class Culture', in Clarke, J., Critcher, C. and Johnson, R. (eds.) *Working Class Culture: Studies in History and Theory*. London: Hutchinson.

Mattelart, A. and Siegelaub, S. (eds.) (1979) *Communication and Class Struggle: Liberation, Socialism*. New York: International General.

Mattelart, A. and Siegelaub, S. (eds.) (1983) *Communication and Class Struggle: Capitalism, Imperialism*. New York: International General.

Muller, J. and Tomaselli, K.G. (1998) 'Becoming Appropriately Modern: A Genealogy of Cultural Studies in South Africa 1948–1989', in Denzin, N. (ed.) *Cultural Studies: A Research Volume*. Stamford, CT: JAI Press, 53–74.

Murdock, G. (1991) 'Communications: Modernity and the Human Sciences', in Ronning, H. and Lundby, K. (eds.) *Media and Communication: Readings in Methodology, History and Culture*. Oslo: Norwegian University Press, 53–66.

NeSmith, G. (ed.) (1988) 'Cultural Studies in South Africa'. Theme issue, *Journal of Communication Inquiry*, 12(1), 1–44.

Ong, W. (1982) *Orality and Literacy: Technologizing the Word*. London: Methuen.

Republic of South Africa (1981) *Report of the Steyn Commission of Inquiry into the Mass Media*. Pretoria: Government Printer.

Ronning, H. and Lundby, K. (eds.) (1991) *Media and Communication: Readings in Methodology, History and Culture*. Oslo: Norwegian University Press.

Shepperson, A. and Tomaselli, K.G. (1998) 'Die Folgen der Apartheid und Überwindung durch Zeichenanalyse: Semiotik in Südafrika', *Zeitschrift für Semiotik*, 20(1/2), 161–73.

Sitas, A. (1984) 'Culture and Production: The Contradictions of Working Class Theatre in South Africa', *Africa Perspective*, 1(2), 84–111.

Steadman, I. (1988) 'Popular Culture and Performance', in Tomaselli, K.G. (ed.) *Rethinking Culture*. Bellville: Anthropos, 112–34.

Teer-Tomaselli, R.E. (1997) 'Shifting Spaces: Popular Culture and National Identity', *Critical Arts*, 11(5), i–xv.

Thompson, E.P. (1965) *The Making of the English Working Class*. London: Penguin.

Tomaselli, K.G. (1981a) From the Laser to the Candle: Ilanga Le So Phonela Abasebanzi', *South African Labour Bulletin*, 6(6), 64–70.

Tomaselli, K.G. (1981b) 'The Semiotics of Alternative Performance in South Africa', *Critical Arts*, 2(1), 14–33.

Tomaselli, K.G. (1988) *Rethinking Culture*. Bellville: Anthropos.

Tomaselli, K.G. and Muller, J. (1987) 'Class, Race and Oppression: Metaphor and Metonymy in Black South African Theatre', *Critical Arts*, 4(3), 40–59.

Tomaselli, K.G., Steadman, I., Gardner, S. *et al.* (1983) *Retrospective*. Critical Arts Monograph No 1. Durban. Http:\\www.und.ac.za/und/ccms

Tomaselli, K.G., Tomaselli, R.E. and Muller, J (eds.) (1987) *Narrating the Crisis: Hegemony and the South African Press*. Bellville: Anthropos. Published in the UK as *The Press in South Africa*. London: James Currey.

Tomaselli, K.G., Muller, J. and Shepperson, A. (1996) 'Negotiations, Transitions and Uncertainty Principles: Critical Arts in the Worlds of the Post', *Critical Arts*, 10(2), i–xxiii.

Volosinov, V.I. (1973) *Marxism and the Philosophy of Language*. New York: Seminar Press.

Waldahl, R. (ed.) (1998) *Perspectives on Media, Culture and Democracy*. Report Series No. 33, Oslo: University of Oslo.

32

Blood Borders:
Being Indian and Belonging

Gail Guthrie Valaskakis

Jack Forbes (1987: 121) writes, about being Indian, 'I really resent white people trying to dissect us and tell us what makes a person a Native American.'

> How much Indian blood do you have?
> What tribe are you?
> Oh, I never heard
> of that one.

In an article entitled 'Native by Nature?' Rick Harp (1994: 46) writes, about being tribal:

> How might I exist indeed? For me, a self-identifying Plains Cree – whose passport reads 'Canadian', whose first and (currently) only language is English, whose mother is Native and whose father is not, whose entire life has been spent in urban environments, and whose education has been wholly obtained from non-Native institutions – the question is as immediate and urgent as it is profound.

For as long as I can remember, blood borders and these conflicts of identification and recognition that spiral around them have been part of being Indian, and traversing these borders has been a daily ritual in the discourse of Native collective and individual experience. In Indian country, membership matters; and it is ensnared in a cluster of rules and exceptions, ancestries and endorsements. For Indians, blood and belonging are a maze of policies and practices that is inevitably political, and irrevocably personal. In my case, my father is a tribal member of the reservation where I was raised; my mother is non-Indian; my brother is a tribal member, and I am not enrolled.

But if the contradictions and anomalies of Indian blood borders are

personally difficult and socially divisive, they are also politically important. In Indian country today, tribal membership may be a double-
edged sword, but it penetrates to the core of Indian resistance and
empowerment in current battles over the politics of difference, identity
and sovereignty. Like so many issues that involve Indians, membership
is entangled in ageless struggles over power and control, over history
and heritage, over acculturation and autonomy. Ricocheting through
time and space, Indian membership policies are colonial codes that cut
across and construct Native identity and reality. In the cultural and
political struggles of today, these codes that determine who is an Indian
also define the tribal borders of Indian nations within nation-states and
test the boundaries of Indian self-determination.

That identity and difference related to race, gender or nation are
culturally constructed and historically constituted is widely recognized
in the literature on cultural studies, feminism, history and interpretive
anthropology (Said 1978; S. Hall 1993; Carter 1998; Geertz 1973). For
Indians, this work creates an opening to understand colonial experience, nationalist discourse and identity politics as epistemological and
representational knots. In the words of Rick Harp (1994: 47), 'Colonialism isn't just about the forcible acquisition of control over land and
resources, it is also – perhaps even more so – about a particular way of
knowing and relating to reality.' Like the Orientalist images of Said's
(1978) Middle Eastern analysis, North Americans' representations of
themselves and of Indians are grounded in ways of knowing and
experiencing Otherness. The politicized images of Indianness that
emerge and recede over time are woven into policies – colonial and
current – that not only identify Indians, but construct Indian identity.
The Native contest over membership, over who is an Indian, what
signifies Indianness and what being Indian means is articulated to the
long struggle of Indian nations to represent and empower themselves.
This struggle over domination and resistance is expressed in the voices
and practices of the subjective communities that express competing
claims to common culture.

As Stuart Hall (1993: 356) writes, national cultures are systems of
representations, social collectivities held together in circulating images of
seeming similarity. Like the cultural formations of the nation-states in
which they live, Indian nations reconstruct their historical hybridity as
'the primordial unity of "one people"' in narratives that 'project the
ruptures and conquests, which are their real history, backward in an
apparently seamless and unbroken continuity towards pure, mythic
time'. The sense of a unified 'oneness' of Indian tribes (or even
individual bands) that emerges in their narratives and images of tribal
heritage confronts a pan-Indian sense of 'oneness', with appropriated

representations that can reinforce, transform or threaten tribal traditions. At the same time, both tribalism and pan-Indianism encircle a
sense of 'difference' that forges their relationship to the nation-states
in which they have always been an anomalous presence. As Catherine
Hall's (1993) historical analysis of English identity suggests, the placement of Indians in Canada and the United States is rooted in representations articulated to shifting boundaries that distinguish Indians from
Others. These mutable boundaries that both define the nature of
'imagined communities' of belonging and exclude those who do not
belong (and may even threaten the imagined unity), construct and
defend the cultural basis of communal groups (Paul Gilroy, cited in C.
Hall 1993: 357). But the process of building, fortifying and expanding
cultural unity is jagged-edged and unstable. As colonialist policies and
practices illustrate, there is always a tension between ideological
positions that exclude and contain the outsider and those that forcibly
remake the Other into an insider. At the same time, outsiders construct
their own cultural boundaries, positions and collective subjectivities in
a politicized process that situates their respective expressions of
resistance.

For Indians, the relationship between 'sameness', 'difference' and
national formations has always been a particularly precarious proposition. Like other peoples of colour, Indians are positioned outside
the perimeters of dominant continental cultures, and their reality is
framed within ideological perspectives of inferiority and exclusion. At
the same time, their unique placement as indigenous peoples means
that the exclusion of Indians is an inevitable intrusion upon the
'commonness' of cultural representations in North American nation-
states. How can Canada or the United States construct a cultural basis
for collective unity that excludes the original inhabitants and owners of
the land? The nation-building projects of North America have always
involved eliminating, absorbing or containing Indians. And the imagined communities of Canada and the United States, which have represented Indians as different, inferior and dispensable, have produced
not only military operations to eliminate, confine or restrain Indians,
but institutional and legal policies to enforce their acculturation. These
policies reflect the long-held assumption that 'If Indians were an alien
race because they had a different religion, language, social organization
and political status than other Americans, they could be absorbed only
if they became the same as other Americans' (Harmon 1990: 101). But
recasting and absorbing Indians has not been easy.

Indians have countered the North American project to dominate,
change and absorb them with assertions of the very features that disrupt
and and even threaten the imagined commonness of the dominant

cultures of Canada and the United States: their distinct, aboriginal status and culture. Indian resistance is sometimes confrontational, but more often it is transformational, expressed in the emergent images and lateral movements of cultural persistence. Like the folk hero Coyote, the Trickster in Native narratives, who takes on many forms but always survives, Indians manoeuvre through systems of bureaucratic entanglements, claiming the discourse that excludes them. Native North Americans have always proclaimed the extent and nature of their *difference* in their struggles with nation-states over land and sovereignty, culture and self-determination. From this position of declared distinction, Indians erect borders between themselves and Others that are actively perforated, but discursively impermeable. Indians express their indigenous status in North America, a position that cuts across the imagined unity of its nation-states and defines who Indians are in relation to who they are not. Indians are not newcomers or immigrants, not Euro-Americans or Euro-Canadians, and they do not perceive themselves as part of the ethnic or multicultural mix of North America.

But these borders between Indians and Others built in aboriginality are also constructed in representational boundaries of imagined Indian unity – appropriated and created; but cutting across the imagined unity of Indians, there are borders that Indians have erected among themselves. Indian solidarity is spliced with blood borders that spiral between tribes and within communities. This perplex of Indian bloodism is prolonged and layered, and it encircles issues of cultural or local identity and tribal membership that are as unrelenting as they are immediate. Today, the Indian struggle to construct, represent and regulate their communities – and their expressions of pan-Indianism – as blood-related unities is articulated to tensions that are both historical and current.

The heritage of Indian nations and communities, like the nation-states in which they are located, is not rooted in tribal or racial purity. Even before colonial expansion pressed Indian tribes into war with their neighbours and even before government-ordered relocation created shared reservations of cohabiting tribes, Indians absorbed other Indians. Native adoption, assimilation and intermarriage created societies that were tribally hydrid. Since the marriage of Pocahontas in the first American colony of Jamestown, Virginia, in the 1600s, Indian nations have not only fought with but married, captured and claimed non-Indians. Thirty years ago, Stuart Levine (and Lurie 1970: 11) wrote about being Indian:

Real 'Indian-ness', by the way, is not necessarily measured on racial lines. There are tribesmen on reservations who number among themselves virtually no one who is a 'full-blooded' Indian. Different tribes require different degrees of 'blood' for membership; some have no such requirements at all, and among the millions of Indians living in the general population, the proportion of 'blood' runs anywhere from four-fourths to infinitesimal.

Today, the historical hybridity of Indian tribes is increasing, and it is expressed in seemingly contradictory constructions of 'one' Indian people and many, individual, blood-unified Indian nations. Paul Chaat Smith (1994: 38) writes, 'What made us one people is the common legacy of colonialism and diaspora,' a perspective that resonates with the rhetoric of pan-Indianism that has been a political force since the 1960s and 1970s. But like the representational basis of Indian membership, this legacy of 'commoness' is discursive, and it is wrapped in representations that collapse the diverse historical experiences of physical, cultural and legal dislocation into the vague expressions of Indian collective memory. Among Indians, the pain of the past circulates outside reservations in images of common Indian experience, transformed, lived and imagined; and these narratives of memory and myth are reconstructed in the discourse inside Indian communities which is articulated to cultural, economic and political strategies of 'survivance' (Vizenor 1994).

In Canada today, Indians negotiate the issue of blood quotas in the backdraft of revisions to the government's complex membership policy and the forward force of sovereignty and self-determination, land and resources, all of which relate to land claims, administrative autonomy and treaty rights. In the United States, Indians struggle with similar issues of land and treaties, sovereignty and self-determination, interwoven with the pressures of gaming profits – real or potential – that press tribes to define and refine their membership. These struggles extend to the increasing numbers of urban Indians for whom reservations remain 'home', a cultural construct that they return to easily and often; and the spread of young Indians, removed or reclaimed, for whom the reservation has never been home. At the same time, on both sides of the border, Indians recognize the fragility – and the importance – of traditional culture, an insight that has not only redeemed Indian blood, but placed value on the experience and knowledge of elders, whose age often resonates with bloodlines.

The current contest of blood and borders is further complicated by what Rayna Green (1988) names 'The Tribe Called Wannabe', those who, inspired by romanticism, spirituality, alienation or conviction, reconstitute themselves as Indians. The most common claim may be that of a rediscovered Cherokee great-grandmother, but history is full of examples, of bloodless, self-designated, Indians-in-disguise like the

Englishman Archie Belany, who became Grey Owl, and Sylvester Long, who transformed himself into Chief Buffalo Child Long Lance. These personifications of white imagination and Native customs confuse the marks of Indian identification for Others and challenge the meaning of Indianness for Indians themselves. John Tootoosis (in Ruffo 1996: 128) wrote about Grey Owl in 1936:

> An Indian can tell who's Indian.
> Grey Owl can't sing or dance,
> But he's doing good
> and when we meet
> I call him brother.

But as David Foster (1997: 13A) writes about Indians in the United States, 'Never mind the New Age pretenders who claim kinship to a Cherokee princess they saw in a dream. More nettlesome for the nation's five hundred and fifty-four federally recognized tribes is what to do with their own sons and daughters.' Foster notes that the number of people who identity themselves as Indian on US census records has nearly tripled since 1970, but Indian bloodlines are thinning. 'One federal study estimated that the percentage of Indians who are full-bloods – sixty percent in 1980 – will fall to thirty-four percent in 2000 and to three-tenths of one percent in 2080' (Foster 1997: 14A). Indians manoeuvre through a minefield of tribal membership that reflects both the perplexities of self-designation and the problems of uncoupling blood and belonging. But if the borders between Indians and Others today are fraught with fantastic and real conjectures of identity, culture and economics, Indian bloodism has deeper roots in the imagined nations of North America.

In the latter half of the nineteenth century, Indian blood and belonging became absorbed in 'the heyday of dubious assumptions about race, based on a cluster of biological or historical speculations' (Carter 1998: 11). These assumption not only collapsed race, culture and character, but mapped their fusion in gradations of oppositional Otherness: Christian and pagan, savage and civilized. The evolutionary theories and racially based notions that emerged at the turn of the twentieth century to qualify, and classify, Indians reflect concepts of purity and authenticity that are entrenched in the legal systems of the United States and Canada, where they not only frame Indian political and territorial dependence, but define Indians themselves.

References

Carter, Sarah (1998) *Capturing Women*. Montreal and Kingston: McGill-Queens University Press.

Forbes, Jack (1987) 'Shouting Back to the Geese', in Brian Swann and Arnold Krupat, eds., *I Tell You Now: Autobiographical Essays by Native American Writers*. Lincoln, NB: University of Nebraska Press, pp. 111–26.

Foster, David (1997) 'Intermarriage Clouds Claims of Indian Ancestry', Associated Press and *Milwaukee Journal Sentinel*. 27 February, pp. 13A-n14A.

Geertz, Clifford (1973) *The Interpretation of Culture*. New York: Basic Books.

Green, Rayna (1988) 'The Tribe Called Wannabe: Playing Indian in America and Europe', *Folklore*, Vol. 99, No. 1, pp. 30–55.

Hall, Catherine (1993) 'From Greenland's Icy Mountains . . . to Africa's Golden Sand: Ethnicity, Race and Nation in Mid-Nineteenth-Century England', *Gender and History*, Vol. 5, No. 2, pp. 213–25.

Hall, Stuart (1993) 'Culture, Community, Nation', *Cultural Studies*, Vol. 7, No. 3, October, pp. 349–63.

Harmon, Alexandra (1990) 'When Is an Indian Not an Indian? "Friends of the Indian" and the Problems of Indian Identity', *Journal of Ethnic Studies*, Vol. 18, No. 2, Summer. pp. 95–117.

Harp, Rick (1994) 'Native by Nature?', in Elenor M. Godway and Geraldine Finn, eds., *Who is this 'We'?* Montreal: Black Rose Books, pp. 45–55.

Levine, Stuart and Nancy O. Lurie, eds. (1970) *The American Indian Today*. Baltimore: Pelican.

Ruffo, Armand Garnet (1996) *Grey Owl: The Mystery of Archie Belaney*. Regina, Saskatchewan: Coteau Books.

Said, Edward W (1978) *Orientalism*. New York: Vintage.

Smith, Paul Chaat (1994) 'Home of the Brave', *C Magazine*, Summer, pp. 32–42.

Strong, Pauline Turner and Barrik Van Winkle (1996) ' "Indian Blood": Reflections on the Reckoning and Refiguring of Native North American Identity', *Cultural Anthropology* 11 (4): 547–76.

Vizenor, Gerald (1994) *Manifest Manners: Postindian Warriors of Survivance*. Hanover and London: Wesleyan University Press.

33

The Cultural Politics of the Mass-mediated Emperor System in Japan[1]

Shunya Yoshimi

From the cultural studies perspective, in any analysis of the historical relationship between modernity, power and the media in modern Japan, the emperor system is an almost inescapable topic. This inevitability may be due to the fact that cultural studies has often addressed the cultural politics of both national integration and the myths of nationhood. In the age of television-dominated media and mass consumerism, I believe the relationship between the English monarchy and the ideology of 'Englishness' still proves to be an interesting theme for cultural studies in the UK, especially after the death of Princess Diana. As for Japan, the modern emperor system was reinvented in the mid-nineteenth century under the influence of Europe and continues to penetrate into the everyday consciousness of the Japanese people.

As Takashi Fujitani and Kouji Taki have demonstrated in their respective books, the body of the emperor was the very centre on which the power to consolidate the formation of modern 'Japanese' culture was based (Fujitani 1996; Taki 1988; Yoshimi 1995). Furthermore, the focus on the modern emperor system by the cultural critics in Japan may also be driven by one ever-enduring theme of cultural studies research: the power relationship between the media and the audience. Informed by the perspectives offered by cultural studies, I believe that all forms of media are articulated through the cultural formations of power. By this I do not mean that the media are simply manipulated by the so-called culture industry, but rather that the media can only exist socially because they are dependent upon cultural formations of power from the beginning.

In this chapter, I would like to analyse the intrinsic relationship between the media and cultural formations of power by addressing the modern emperor system in Japan. I will reconsider the modern emperor system as a system of hegemonic media communication in which the image of the nation has been encoded/decoded through various modern information technologies. Moreover, I want to explore new approaches to analysing the modern emperor system, which not only was the foundational source of national sentiment in modern Japan, but has continued to frame the national identity of the Japanese since World War Two. To this end, I will first outline how the historical development of the media system from the nineteenth century became inseparable from the construction of the emperor system itself, and in some respects became the enabling structure of the modern emperor system in Japan.

The Modern Emperor System as a Media Construction

In modern Japan, the telegraphic network formed the basic contours of the first nationwide media system. When Commodore Perry and Tokugawa government officials met in Yokohama in 1854, the significance of telegraphic technology was demonstrated for the first time in Japan. While the Japanese provided an exhibition of sumo wrestling to the Americans, the Americans displayed a small-scale model railway and a telegraphic instrument to the Japanese. Regarding this exchange, Perry wrote the following in his report on the 'expedition' to the China Seas and Japan:

> The Americans turned with pride to the exhibition of the telegraph and the railroad. It was a happy contrast, which a higher civilization presented, to the disgusting display on the part of the Japanese officials. In place of a show of brute animal force, there was a triumphant revelation, to a partially enlightened people, of the success of science and enterprise. (Perry 1856)

Here Perry forcefully describes the unequal relationship framed between 'Japan' as an object of an imperialistic gaze and the 'West' as a subject parading the latest technology. At that time, railways and telegraphs were not simply means of transportation and communication; rather, they were politically mediated objects that made it possible for Europe and America to be represented as the 'civilized Self', and those on the other side of the ocean as the 'uncivilized Other'. Accordingly, the Japanese people constituted the audience for whom the West displayed its technological superiority.

Just as these new information technologies were being used as politically mediated objects to assert the dominance of the West, so the dichotomy 'civilized/uncivilized' continued to frame the dynamic between the centre (the new Meiji nation-state based in Tokyo) and the periphery (rural areas of Japan) as these new technologies were systematically introduced throughout Japan. In the early Meiji period (1870–1890), the telegraphic network was mediated by the power relationships of centre to periphery and emperor to subjects; as the network developed, it expanded and reproduced these relationships. Yokohama and Tokyo were connected by telegraph in 1869, and the Tokyo–Nagasaki route and the Tokyo–Aomori route were created in 1873 and 1874 respectively, completing a mainline route that traversed the island chain just a few years after the Meiji Restoration (1868). Then, as if to sanction this development, the emperor embarked upon several official tours beginning in 1876. In the Japanese rural periphery that the emperor officially visited, telegraph lines were constructed under great pressure just prior to his tour. For example, the Akita–Hirosaki route was completed for the occasion of the Tohoku–Hokkaido imperial tour of 1881. Construction of these telegraph routes often had to be rushed: 'for the purpose of the Northern Tour, the acceleration of aerial wiring was ordered'. These telegraphic routes were called the 'Imperial Tour Lines' (*Gojunko-sen*), and the Bureau of Communications wrote:

> The fact that so many places are part of the Imperial Tour Lines has made it possible for the entire nation's major areas to be connected in just over ten years. The Emperor embarked on an Imperial tour of all the areas in the nation from 1877 to 1880 to inspect the new conditions of the people. On that occasion, the Emperor oversaw construction in those places that did not formerly have telegraphic facilities on the route. . . . Because the Imperial Tour Lines required rapid installation, surveying construction proceeded continuously, and it was not uncommon for timber to be put in place all day and all night. (Tokai Denki Tsushin-kyoku 1962)

The people in the periphery (the Japanese countryside) responded aggressively to the political symbolism of this telegraphic technology. When the construction of a nationwide telegraphic network began in earnest in the early 1870s, curious rumours surrounding the telegraph erupted, and people in every region attempted to obstruct the construction of the network. In April 1872, concerning one of these rumours a newspaper reported:

> Recently, the preparations for telegraph lines in the vicinity of Aki (Hiroshima) and Nagato (Yamaguchi) prefectures have given rise to a number of evil accounts. It is said that the practice of sending messages by wire must be 'Christian', and, moreover, that the blood of unmarried girls is used to coat the wires, and that virgins are apprehended in the order of the number on the eaves of their houses. (*Shinbun Zasshi*, April 1872)

In addition, the newspaper reported that these types of rumours continued to circulate to the point where 'there are some women who dye their teeth and slouch their shoulders, as well as those who attempt in vain to damage the telegraphs, poles, and wires'. The report goes on to say that 'in every area, wires have been cut off by people hurling stones and throwing various objects at the lines, and damaging ceramic parts attached to the poles, brackets, covers, etc.'. These incidents were not at all the blind acts of deeply superstitious people frightened by the strangeness of modern science. Rather, people began to read the introduction of new technologies, such as the telegraphic network and railway, as essentially political intrusions into the periphery. Soon thereafter, the 'technological politics' of the centre was opposed by the people through often imaginative forms of oral communication and violence which were informed by their collective memory.

Such clashes between the Japanese people and the hegemonic, administrative operations of the modern state can be linked to other popular reactions against media forms of the early Meiji period. One such example is the reaction to the various plans undertaken in the 1870s and 1880s to spread the national symbols to all regions of the nation. Among these, the attempt to distribute nationally the talisman (*ofuda*) and calendar (*koyomi*) of Ise Shrine is an early example.[2] In 1871, the Meiji government issued an official order to prohibit certain activities of Ise Shrine priests, including the distribution of talismans and calendars to rural believers. Thereafter, the method of distribution changed: talismans were printed by the Central Shrine Agency and distributed to 7 million households across the nation through the regional bureaus of the agency. The talismans that were nationally printed and distributed by the Meiji government were received by the people as different objects from those talismans that had once been distributed directly to the people by priests travelling on foot from the low-level shrines in Ise. The former talismans distributed by priests were read by the people as being more directly linked to the hearts and minds of the people.

The abrupt and new way of distributing talismans contributed to the already growing lack of faith in the new Meiji government, and many ominous rumours, such as the following, were rampant: 'There are cases when out of nowhere the name of a deity on an amulet turned into a butterfly, and everyone in the family became ill and eventually died'; '[The distribution] will haunt us with a disaster that will bring forth a fire of purification.' In Shizuoka Prefecture, a massive number of talismans were released into the Abe River, exemplifying the observation of 'various groundless acts committed by ignorant people in fear, such as sealing (the talismans) away or throwing them into water or fire' (Yasumaru 1988). These popular responses to the state project provide insights into the political meanings of modern media. The Meiji government usurped the previous right of Ise Shrine priests to manage the talismans in order to use the talisman as a form of media to shift the consciousness of the people to the national centre. Specifically, the Meiji government used the media of the talisman precisely because the talisman directly referenced the enshrined deity of the Ise Shrine, Amaterasu Omikami (the Sun Goddess), who in some national myths was the 'origin' of the Japanese Imperial Household. The talisman received by the people, however, was a sign that could limitlessly and metaphorically stimulate the collective memory of the people. As such, the talismans were a symbolic medium that multiplied the interaction of various levels of popular meanings at the deepest level of consciousness for the Japanese people.

Soon thereafter, a new media form, which would eliminate the popular associations made in connection with the talisman and would better focus the consciousness of the people on the nation, was being invented on the basis of photographic technology. This media was the *goshin'ei*, the Emperor's portrait, which was displayed in elementary and middle schools all over the country from the late 1880s.[3] As Koji Taki and Takashi Fujitani have outlined in detail in their books, the visual relationship whereby the people see the emperor and, at the same time, are seen by the emperor was first established with the regional tours that the Meiji emperor frequently made in the 1870s and 1880s (Fujitani 1996; Taki 1988). The *goshin'ei*, however, was a media strategy that endlessly reproduced on a national level the visual relationship between the emperor and the people, independent of the physical presence of the emperor's body.

The *goshin'ei* was not a simple photographic portrait of the emperor: it was nationally produced and distributed as a form of media that would replace symbolically the presence that the physical body of the emperor had occupied in the regional tours. It is no coincidence that just as elementary and middle schools were required to display the imperial gift of the *goshin'ei*, the emperor's regional tours, which had once been undertaken with such zeal, suddenly ended. The connection between these events is clearly demonstrated by the use of the term '*gohatsuren*' (imperial departure) when the portrait was sent to each school from Tokyo, and the term '*gochakuren*' (imperial arrival) when the portrait reached the schools. In the 1890s, the Imperial Rescript on Education was distributed to each school and the regulations for school holiday ceremonies were nationally established. The *goshin'ei*, Imperial Rescript, and holiday ceremonies became the standard set for the performances that transformed schools into a stage for the gazing relationship of the nation. (Yoshimi 1994).

The relationship between the media and the modern emperor system continued as the media developed further in modern Japan. The construction of the radio broadcast network in the late 1920s mirrored the construction of the telegraphic network in the 1870s. In line with the contemporary radio mania in the United States, from 1922 radio grew in popularity among amateur radio operators in Japan. Many magazines directed at radio fans were published, and one group of amateurs established their own radio company. The selling of commercial broadcasting companies and transceivers, as Westinghouse had done in the US, was being planned in Japan. Subsequently, in 1924, private enterprises in Tokyo, Osaka, and Nagoya established three broadcasting stations in these cities.[4] In the following year, however, based on the powerful intervention of the Bureau of Communications, these stations were combined into NHK, which would become the foundation of the first national broadcasting network. After its inauguration, NHK's efforts were directed toward the 1928 accession ceremony of the Showa emperor. Just before the ceremony, the nationwide radio broadcasting network was completed, and listeners across Japan were informed in detail about the emperor's passage from Tokyo to Kyoto, the accession ceremony held at the Imperial Palace in Kyoto, and the course of the emperor's return to Tokyo. NHK's policy was to 'align as best as possible the accession ceremony with programming for women and children, and to broadcast continuously the memorial speech associated with the ceremony'.

From the 1930s, the radio network became the most powerful medium, mobilizing the consciousness of the people towards war. Unsurprisingly the emperor's body was located at the centre of the war effort. However, in contrast to the voices of Hitler and Roosevelt, the emperor's voice was never formally broadcast over the air waves until his announcment of Japan's defeat in World War Two. The emperor's body was thought to be certifiable only through the voice not being used to an audience, and thus it was a considerable problem when the emperor's voice was unintentionally picked up by a microphone during the live broadcast of a military parade in December 1928. Thereafter, NHK directed greater attention to avoiding recording the emperor's voice, cutting the transmission from microphones just before the emperor spoke at ceremonies. (Takeyama 1989). The emperor's body was represented by the radio as silence.

All of this does not mean that the modern emperor system strengthened its control over the nation's territories by externally applying media technologies such as the telegraph, radio, and photography.

Rather, we should think of the modern emperor system itself as a discursive system of power, which was significantly mediated by these technologies. The modern emperor system is itself a media system in which the various interpretive practices by the Japanese people on the topic of the appearance or disappearance of the emperor define and bind together the national space of modern Japan. The emperor system does not exist in some essential form outside of the nationwide media system. Furthermore, the nationwide media system in modern Japan could not exist if it were not organized around the emperor's body.

David Cannadine has shown how the manners and symbolism of the British royal family, which are today considered to be 'traditional', were mostly 'invented' between the ascension of Queen Victoria to the title Empress of India in 1877 and the outbreak of World War One (Cannadine 1983). Changes in the media at that time, such as popular national daily newspapers and photographic printing, also greatly influenced the structuration of this new British monarchy. The significance of Cannadine's argument is relevant to the modern emperor system in Japan. From the appearance of the Meiji emperor's body to the space of the imperial capital of Tokyo where the manners of the imperial household were maintained, the 'tradition' of the emperor system in Japan was to a considerable degree a modern invention.

The Royal Wedding and the Reform of the Emperor System

The modern Japanese emperor system does not exist in some essential form as a deep cultural code of 'Japanese culture'. I believe that the modern emperor system was constructed as a discursive and interpretive system which was mediated by the nationwide organization of various forms of media, such as photography, telegraph, radio, textbooks, songs, newspapers and magazines. It is important to consider how such a mass-mediated emperor system was reconstructed as the hegemonic organization of discourse and media in Japan in the era following World War Two. The photograph of the Showa emperor meeting with General MacArthur, which was immediately published in the newspapers on 29 September 1945, is very suggestive. In this widely distributed photograph, the Showa emperor played the role of an inferior assistant to the overbearing masculinity of General MacArthur.[5] Between 1946 and 1947 the Showa emperor made numerous trips throughout Japan, a postwar evocation of the earlier tours made by the Meiji emperor. Images of these tours were captured on newsreels which made a great impression on the Japanese people.

What was more epochal to the postwar emperor system than these tours, however, was the marriage of the crown prince in April 1959. At this time, television and weekly magazines were becoming the dominant media forms. The marriage of the crown prince and Michiko Shoda, the daughter of the president of Nisshin Foods Inc., occurred at the very time when the desires of Japanese people were being tied to the television screen, and the ceremony was historically significant as an event that advanced the structural transition of the modern emperor system.

Regarding the 'fever' surrounding the royal wedding, Keiichi Matsushita initiated an argument worthy of investigation. He stated that the 'boom' surrounding the crown princess occurred because the postwar emperor structure is fundamentally different from the prewar emperor system:

> The emperor system, which continues to be resurrected, of course is not the system of absolute monarchy, nor is it the system of limited monarchy. The current emperor system, changing into a system of mass monarchy, has absorbed new energy from the call of the 'mass'.

Matsushita described the postwar Japanese emperor system as having undergone a structural transition into a 'mass monarchy'. The point that bears emphasis is that the emperor system, which once regarded the emperor as a 'living god' and as the pinnacle of all things, was transformed into a system that views all members of the imperial household as media 'stars'. This transition was clearly articulated in popular references to the crown princess and the marriage parade. According to Matsushita (1959):

> People do not go to the Crown Prince's parade to worship the 'living god'. Now, people just go to see the stars the media focus on. The media actively made him and her into stars. In particular, one can see a frenzied exposure of the Crown Princess: her hobbies, habits, and handwriting, the size of her hips (91.4 cm) and chest (82.6 cm), and the fact that she has frizzy hair were suddenly brought to light. These things were done to raise the star value of the Crown Princess.

To take an example, the magazine *Myojo* included a star calendar of the Crown Princess in one issue, and sponsored a contest to 'find women who look like Michiko Shoda'. Here, we see an obvious case of the 'consciousness of "I too am Michiko"'. The photograph of the crown princess, unlike the *goshin'ei* of the past, was a *buromaido* (wallet-size star photo) of the day.

Matsushita further pointed to the fact that the coverage of the royal wedding was framed by two symbols: *heimin* (commoner) and *ren'ai* (love match). According to Matsushita, '*Heimin* is a term that derives its meaning during the bourgeois revolution when the aristocratic class was opposed to the commoners, but today class divisions among commoners are more important.' Of course, Michiko Shoda was no ordinary *heimin*: to be exact, she was the daughter of a typical Japanese capitalist. Despite these realities, the *heimin* quality of the crown princess was repeatedly emphasized by the mass media. As for the crown prince's choice, the perspective of *ren'ai* was stressed even though the pairing was conceived by imperial household masterminds. The new 'royal family' was said to be more popular and full of love.[6]

It was clear that the model of this new family was 'American' family life. According to Matsushita, this image of the ideal 'home' became the core symbol of the postwar mass emperor system. The most salient point here is his argument that the birth of the mass emperor system, in which people envy the image of the imperial household as their model for future consumption, actually resulted from the collapse of the former absolute, prewar emperor system. 'The terms of the mass emperor system in Japan are the renunciation of the emperor as divinity that accompanied defeat in war, the establishment of the new constitution, and the sudden emergence of the mass society which had been suppressed by the former emperor system.' That is, the collapse of the hierarchical authority that had supported the pre-war emperor system immediately revealed conditions of a mass society to the country. Yet, this 'new' mass society also generated a hierarchical value system, in which the imperial household was envied as a family of stars and became the model of the ideal 'home' precisely became the imperial household was envied by the populace. It could be said too that the postwar imperial household also created its own means of escaping obsolescence by becoming the central focus of the new national values.

A similar reading can be made from a number of photographs that were published in newspapers and magazines during that time. One of these depicts the crown prince and princess riding in a horse-drawn carriage and the crowd that greets them with an ovation. Interestingly, many in the crowd are looking down on the couple from the second floors of stores along the roadside. From the Daimyo and Shogun of medieval Japan to the Meiji emperor, historical evidence of crowds greeting the elite can be found time and time again, but it is rare indeed to see depictions of crowds greeting from above the symbols of authority.[7] Moreover, the position of the camera that took this shot was higher than that of the crowd that greeted the royal couple. In this photograph the imperial family completely lost its privileged position as the centre that overlooks the people of the nation from above, and was relegated to the passive position of being a photographed object. At the same time, the privileged standpoint of viewing the nation's people looking at the royal family was taken by a massive number of camera crews mobilized by the media. Another photograph is even more symbolic. In this picture, mannequins of tennis players modelled after the crown prince and princess are located to the side of a department store escalator, and shoppers riding the escalator look down on them. The symbol of the *Goseikon* (royal wedding) is completely positioned here as a model of mass consumption.

The 'fever' that erupted over the royal wedding in 1958 and 1959 helped to drive the explosive expansion of television. The number of televisions registered in Japan passed 1 million in April 1958, increased dramatically after the engagement was announced at the end of that year, and exceeded 3 million in October 1959. In turn, the relay broadcast of the marriage parade, the highlight of a series of 'fevers', was driven by the competition among three stations (NHK, NTV, and KRT [now TBS]). Each station placed around forty TV cameras along the parade route. Relay broadcast vans which connected the TV cameras with the studio were used. Each station sent approximately ten outside relay broadcast vans to strategic places. In the sky, four television station helicopters battled for coverage. The cameras pursued the passing horse-drawn carriage by paralleling it, and tried to take close-up photographs of the expressions of the crown prince and princess.

This close-up was the most sought-after image. Each television company invested a great deal of effort in shooting close-ups of the cheerful expressions of the couple. NTV, for example, distributed its cameras and based its entire coverage on the slogan 'The Close-up Couple'. Special rails for the cameras to move on were laid, Western sounds were used in the background to emphasize the sound of the hoofs of the horses drawing the carriage, and special sound effects were used to add to the cheers of the spectators. Furthermore, each broadcasting station devised a plan to shoot the procession from a bird's-eye view by placing a camera on top of a tall crane.

Akira Takahashi and others conducted a study of the connection between the television coverage and the popular response to the marriage parade. They pointed out that the television coverage clearly surpassed the actual experience along the roadside and exerted a powerful influence on viewers. Their research showed that while the sightseers of the parade along the roadside came in contact with the 'real thing', they could see it for only a few minutes. In contrast, 'the site as it is reconstructed' on television showed close-ups of the hero and heroine with the motion of the frenzied crowd, and gave the audiences an impression of going beyond the momentary contact of sightseeing. In addition, Takahashi *et al.* mentioned that the audio coverage, by building a bridge from one screen to another, instantly projected the entire structure and mood of the parade. They reviewed the effects of television viewing with regard to this kind of roadside experience, and made approximately 600 households, whose residents lived along the route of the marriage parade, into the objects of a sample study. According to this study, the number of households where even just one family member went out to view the parade amounted to no more than 17 per cent of the total, despite the fact that these households were adjacent to the parade route. The majority 'gave up the chance bestowed by geographical proximity, and turned to the site as it is reconstructed'. When viewers gave a reason for this choice, they did not refer to the negative reason of the crowding along the roadside; rather, they stated that the whole picture could be seen over television while only part could be seen along the roadside. They thought that more than what is 'seen by the eye' could be understood by watching television because of the presence of announcers and commentators. Takahashi *et al.* suggested that the dramatization of the royal wedding by the media translated into a victory of the mass-mediated experience over the desires of the people for direct experience (Takahashi *et al.* 1959).

The above study shows that for many Japanese people, the marriage ceremony of the crown prince was a television experience that they individually received in their homes as a festive portrait edited for their consumption. In fact, the number of people who watched the parade on television is estimated to have reached nearly 15 million, whereas the number of people who actually went to the parade did not exceed 500,000. The marriage of the crown prince, as an event that symbolized the birth of the postwar mass emperor system, was constructed primarily on television screens.

The relationship between the royal wedding in postwar Japan and the media had a forerunner in the media event of Queen Elizabeth's coronation in 1953. With regard to the reception of coronations in British society, a number of essays have been written, from a variety of perspectives. Here, I would like to address the points made by David Chaney, who takes three events as representative national ceremonies held in Britain from 1946 to 1953: the triumphal return march from World War Two (1946), the National Ceremony of the British Empire (1951), and Queen Elizabeth's coronation (1953). He explores changes in the BBC's coverage of these ceremonies. He sees many inconsistencies in how the media focused on the first two of these ceremonies. In contrast, for the coronation ceremony, which was held under the auspices of the Conservative government, its staging and the remote coverage by broadcast stations were unified performances organized within a single medium (Chaney 1983). Several years later, parts of this method of staging coronation ceremonies were introduced to Japan. In fact, the Japanese crown prince had attended Queen Elizabeth's coronation. His visit to Britain and Queen Elizabeth's coronation were covered extensively by the Japanese mass media, and the interests of the media began to shift from the emperor to the crown prince.

The Royal Family in Women's Weekly Magazines

Television was not the only form of media that was expanding at the time of the royal wedding. Weekly magazines, a form of media that is key to mass consumer culture in contemporary Japan, went through an explosive development from the late 1950s to the early 1960s. Certainly, some weekly magazines published by large-scale newspaper companies, like *Shukan Asahi* and *Sandei Mainichi*, had existed since the 1920s, but these publications were primarily in a newspaper style, containing news and editorials. In 1956, however, a new type of weekly magazine targeting *sarariiman* (salaried male employees), 'OL' (female office employees, also known as 'office ladies'), and boys and girls began to be published by large-scale publishing companies. Some examples were *Shukan Shincho* (the Shinchosha publishing company), *Shukan Bunshun* (Bungei shunjusha), *Shukan Gendai* (Kodansha), *Shukan Josei* (Kawade shobo), *Josei Jishin* (Kobunsha), *Josei Sebun* (Shogakukan), *Shonen Sandei* (Shogakukan), and *Shonen Magajin* (Kodansha) et cetera. In 1959, the number of weekly magazines published was greater than the number of monthly magazines, putting the former at the forefront of contemporary Japanese magazine media.[8] These weekly magazines differed greatly from the previous styles of newspaper coverage and weekly magazine editorials. They vaguely referenced actual events, establishing on a national scale a system of representation wherein the narrative telling of events was the centre of emphasis.

The rise of weekly magazines did not occur simultaneously with the popular expansion of television. With both television and weekly magazines, which developed in a parallel fashion from the late 1950s through the 1960s, we can see similar textual structures which were shaped by the nationwide consumption of popular images. An example that demonstrated this point particularly clearly was the *waido sho* ('wide show') programme; these programmes later constituted the majority of Japanese television programmes. Takahiko Asada shows the efforts to promote the 'wide show' in the early 1960s, and gives the example of

NET's *Terebi Shukanshi* ('Television Weekly Magazine', Thursday, 10 p.m.) which aired for one year from April 1961. This programme began with the following question: 'What kind of programme will come about once the appeal of weekly magazines is transferred to the television screen?' As a result, the programme, for the most part, integrated a variety of magazine-like elements, including cover stories, comics, and columns. Before long, following this precedent, NET's *Kijima Norio Moningu Sho* ('Morning Show', Monday–Friday), designed by Takahiko Asada among others, began in April 1964. Here, again, a television version of weekly magazine journalism was the background concept of the programme. Since each broadcast was planned to start at 9 a.m., Asada and his colleagues targeted women viewers, and chose topics they would be interested in. In this way, the show gained a large number of viewers in its first year and became a great success. Programmes similar to the show appeared one after another, and they still remain the dominant style of daytime television programme (Asada 1987).

Among the weekly magazines that suddenly appeared in the late 1950s, women's weekly magazines such as *Shukan Josei, Josei Jishin,* and *Josei Sebun,* were especially similar in quality to the 'wide show'. Monthly women's magazines published from the Taisho period, like *Shufu no Tomo* and *Fujin Koron,* were primarily targeted at middle-class households and offered cultural education and practical knowledge to housewives. But the weekly women's magazines of the late 1950s and later targeted the growing number of 'office ladies' in the centre of cities, and played the role of deeply internalizing the gaze of male desire into the self-consciousness of women living during that period of high economic growth. Weekly women's magazines became the dominant form of women's magazines in the 1960s by publishing on a great variety of topics, such as beauty, fashion, ways of finding boyfriends, marriage techniques, news of the royal family, and gossip about people who turn to crime and scandals. According to the 1990 ABC Association Public Report, the sales of women's weekly magazines even surpassed sales of the main men's weekly magazines.[9] Articles that dealt directly with the imperial household, and especially the crown princess, appeared in every issue of these women's weekly magazines as 'occasional news' items. How did the weekly magazine media discuss the crown prince's family? What kinds of images of the royal family were displayed in the magazines? In order to examine these issues, I want to consider the ways in which the royal family was mentioned in *Josei Jishin* from the magazine's inauguration in December 1958 until 1975.

The first characteristics, which can be seen instantly in the articles

devoted to the royal family, are the focus on the crown princess's
fashion and her catalogue-like display. In the 'Special Memorial Issue
of the Royal Marriage' (17 April 1959), the various clothes that Michiko
Shoda wore just before the wedding are shown in photographs.
Descriptions like the following were appended: 'She's wearing a dark-
blue, tailored suit and white blouse – a neat, casual design. The suit is
made of medium-quality worsted, and the material used is double-wide
at 2.4 metres.' In an article entitled 'Michiko's Jewel-covered Case', we
are shown 'Michiko's accessory collection' of pearls. Such articles that
presented the crown princess as a model at the forefront of the fashion
world made up the central core of articles on the royal family until the
early 1960s. No space was wasted: photographs of the crown princess in
both dresses and Japanese clothing were lined up on both sides of the
page, along with short descriptions similar to those found in fashion
magazine articles, and details of the crown princess's hairstyles. In the
3 January 1963 issue, the prices of the clothing and personal accessories
worn by the crown princess were displayed, and readers were recommended to acquire the same kind of fashions by adjusting their
budgets.

When her first child, Hironomiya, was born in 1960, the focus of the
articles shifted to the relationship between 'mother' Michiko and her
child. As a result, only secondary interest was directed at the 'father',
the crown prince. From the 1960s to the early 1970s, the coverage of
the royal family in *Josei Jishin* centred on various *kateiteki* ('homey')
presentations of Princess Michiko, Hironomiya, Ayanomiya, Norino-
miya, and so on. An early example was the photo series entitled 'My
Afternoon with Mommy' of 24 August 1960, which pictures from an
angle Michiko pushing the baby carriage; reminiscent of the previously
discussed fashion articles, the caption reads, 'During a Karuizawa
afternoon, Michiko wears a cup-sleeved one-piece dress. It is made of
top-quality cotton. This is resort wear accentuated by a cloth belt and
bow. By not leaving out the accessories, this summer resort wear looks
smart.' At first, Hironomiya is added as just one of the items in the
sections on fashion and the royal family. Before long, though, the
magazine's focus shifts more directly to the mother–child relationship,
as the following article titles indicate: 'Such a Cute Prince', 'His Small
Hand Holding a Large Stone', and 'His Smile Returned.'

The vision of the royal family portrayed by the media was based on
the snapshot, and not the portrait photograph. The most typical
example of this can be discerned in a series of mother–child photographs. In his study, Kashiwagi Hiroshi focuses on a photograph of the
crown princess, sitting with her daughter at a table in a garden, which
appeared in the issue of 7 November 1970. The table set 'appears to be

Early American', and a Snoopy doll is sitting in an empty chair. Through the photograph display, 'the image of a family practising the American way of life' is projected. With the appearance of photographs showing the crown prince's family as the model of an American family, the media's view of the royal family completed the transition from representing the emperor in portrait photographs to representing him in snapshots. In the case of portrait photography, where the camera and subject face each other, not only is the subject objectified by the camera, but the subject also views the camera. Moreover, portrait photography provides the occasion for the subject to view the people who are looking at the photograph. In the *goshin'ei*, the emperor in the photograph had viewed the countless people of the nation who lined up before him. In snapshots, however, such as those of the royal family, the subject is in the end only the object that is viewed. Images, having become part of everyday experience, are the objects of possible consumption. As Kashiwagi (1990) points out, this is the world of advertising photography.

It is particularly significant that the image of the crown prince's family as a possible object of consumption was constructed through the gendering of Princess Michiko. Yasuko Muramatsu has analysed the coverage of the royal family in 1990 when the Heisei emperor's ascension ceremony and the wedding ceremony of the second son, Ayanomiya, were held. She pointed out that the amount of exposure of the female members of the royal family far exceeded the coverage of the male members. Her explanation was that 'women are definitely phenomena that are gazed at, and thus can be said to be objects of consumption' (Muramatsu 1991). If we return to the series of royal family articles in *Josei Jishin*, the readers' popularity questionnaire 'You Picked Them: Japan's 50 "VIP" Women' published on 1 May 1971 shows the crown princess directly as an object that is looked at and consumed. According to this article, the crown princess received an overwhelming 40 per cent of the votes (4,033 out of 10,926). It goes without saying that these results reflect only the conservative readership of *Josei Jishin*. Nevertheless, this vote clearly showed how the weekly women's magazines skilfully structured the image of women in the Royal Family as objects to be looked at, and how they conformed that image to the consciousness of female readers.

Given the fact that the relationship between the family of the crown prince and the post-1945 popular consciousness has continued, several scholars have elaborated on the theory of the mass emperor system since the work of Matsushita. For example, Teruko Inoue, elaborating on Matsushita's conclusions, argues that the coverage of the crown prince's family since the late 1950s offers a model for the proliferation of 'my home-ism' during the period of high economic growth. The story from the meeting of the prince and Michiko to their engagement, marriage, and child–bearing was read in practice as the ideal form of the love match that became the norm in the postwar period. According to Inoue, 'The scandals surrounding the divorces and affairs of the TV stars that crowded the weekly magazines were a deviation from the so-called "love match" family. If these scandals reinforced the ideology of the love family from a negative standpoint, the mass media coverage of the crown prince's wedding and the birth of their son performed the function of reinforcing that ideology from a so-called positive stand-point' (Inoue 1980). The activities of the post-1945 royal family, including its female members, were monitored twenty-four hours a day by the media (like *The Truman Show*), and even their private interests and family life were positioned as objects of media information. Displayed through the media, the female members modelled images of fashion, childcare, education, and lifestyles.

The Over-determined Discourses on the Emperor

In this chapter, I first addressed the modern emperor system as a discursive and interpretive system that was initially mediated by the nationally structured media of portrait photography, telegraphs and radio. Then, I investigated the nature of the transition that occurred when the focus of these media structures shifted in the period after World War Two from the emperor as a 'living god' to the family of the crown prince as seen object. There is a clear break between the prewar emperor system, in which the emperor possessed the privileged gazing position, and the postwar mass emperor system, in which families sitting in front of TV sets consume images of the royal family. However, if we investigate the sites where these discourses and interpretations interact, it becomes clear that what actually exists is not a singular emperor system, nor two distinct emperor systems neatly separated by the year 1945. Rather, we have a complex, over-determined, mass-mediated emperor system marked by the mutual overlapping and compounding of all these elements. The elements of this emperor system have often contradictory meanings in multi-layered contexts. A focus on the different ways in which the 'prewar' and 'postwar' modern emperor systems interact suggests to me that the relationship between the two systems is indicative of a process of complicated change and continuity and is not a clean, simple break in the history of the modern emperor system.

The trend to show the imperial family as the model of the modern

Japanese family was also evident in the prewar period. Michio Nakajima points out that on the occasion of the Taisho emperor's death, 'the overflowing humanity' of the members of the emperor's family, who worried about the emperor's condition and tended to him, was consciously reported through the mass media. Morever, moments of intimacy in the imperial family, with the empress and crown prince serving their husband and father respectively, can easily be found in the newspapers. At the same time, the 'family' image of emotional exchange between parents and children, and among siblings, began to be pushed in the everyday consciousness of the people. In this image, the children surround the parents (the emperor and the empress) who constitute the symbolic centre. During this period, the Japanese state elite, who had felt the crisis that came with the global collapse of monarchies following World War One, began to reform the image of the imperial household as a model for the 'homes' of the 'common people'. According to Nakajima, 'The Taisho Emperor's illness was a splendid chance to propagandize that the imperial family, the nucleus of national unity and membership, was not cold and formal. Rather, sharing intimacy as in the typical home of the nation's people, it was warm and rich in parent–child and sibling love' (Nakajima 1990).

Furthermore, during the period of worsening health of the Showa emperor in the late 1980s, the mass media in Japan were overcome by anxiety and the people were urged to a series of exercises in 'self-restraint'.[10] Significantly, though, the nervous anxiety did not signify an emotional rebirth of the prewar emperor system. In the interview survey I conducted with some other researchers near the Imperial Palace just after the emperor's death, we noticed a striking difference between the views of the mourners who were over fifty and the opinions of those under thirty. The former group came to mourn as a means to affirm for themselves their experiences of World War Two and its aftermath. For the latter group, the act of entering the Imperial Palace was recognized as an experience that diverged from the television image. One young person said, 'I'm interested because of the television coverage, but for some reason I came to the memorial anyway.' Another said, 'This type of huge event happens only once in a lifetime, so I came as a tourist.' They both spoke of the emperor as a 'nice grandfather', and they stated that this impression 'came from television and weekly magazines'. The post-1945 mass-mediated emperor system had structured the crown prince's family as an object to be viewed and consumed, and, before long, this system also came to integrate the emperor into the discourse of the objectified crown prince's family, extensively diluting the intensity of the meanings that surrounded the emperor's body. Nevertheless, this group action of public mourning does show a continuity with the prewar emperor system of public attendance in Imperial Palace Square.

The image of the royal family as a model of home life consequently became another complex interpretive code layered upon the mass-mediated emperor system. On the one hand, this code commodified the gender of the crown princess by focusing on her fashion and child-care/education. On the other hand, it also restructured the social identity of the Showa emperor as a grandfather from the perspective of the royal family's grandchildren. Moreover, the origin of this representation goes back to the 1920s when the advent of a mass consumer society became global. It is critical that we understand the context in which these different codes were articulated and how these codes interacted with the media in different historical periods and with different media audiences. In fact, even the *goshin'ei*, the most central medium for the prewar emperor system, did not function as a singular code of the modern nation. With the popularization of techniques of photographic reproduction from the time of the Russo–Japanese War, the portrait photograph of the Meiji emperor was hung on the walls of village homes, and played the role of a semi-magical tutelary spirit that supported modern Japanese nationalism from below. Nevertheless, the meaning of this representation of the emperor shifted according to whether it was hung in classrooms or rural homes, or was concealed by an individual.

Furthermore, the same image in the same place could produce multiple, contradictory meanings over time. As Peter Stallybrass and Allon White have argued, it is possible to grasp the symbol 'pig' as 'a site of competing, conflicting and contradictory definitions'. They emphasize that, in different domains of discourse, 'pigs' can be constructed according to different grids or sets of society which are often brought into conflict with each other. Since the discourses articulate the symbolic and metaphorical resources of different classes and groups whose anchorage points occupy distinct and different sites and locations, they coexist in uneven and often incompatible ways (Stallybrass and White 1986). This discussion on the symbol 'pig' is applicable to the symbol 'emperor' found in the process of structuring the modern Japanese nation. Within the post-1945 popular emperor system, the social functions borne by various symbols of consumer society related to the crown princess and royal family become clear when symbols associated with 'emperor' are understood in the context of the layered power dynamics of the meanings they hold.

Notes

1. Originally this chapter was presented at the 1996 conference 'Dialogue with Cultural Studies' which took place at the Institute of Socio-Information and Communication Studies at Tokyo University. At this conference, Stuart Hall, David Morley, Angela McRobbie, Charlotte Brunsdon, Ali Rattansi, and Colin Sparks came to Japan and led very exciting discussions with cultural studies scholars in the Japanese and Asian contexts. We organized five intensive workshops: Nation and Postcolonialism; Body, Space and Capitalism; Media, Gender and Sexuality; Media, Technology and Audience; Internationalization of Cultural Studies. My paper was presented in the workshop on Media, Technology and Audience. All papers, discussions and comments from this seminal conference were published in Japanese in the spring of 1999. I would like to thank Jason Creigh and Sandra Collins for their invaluable help in translating this essay.

2. The talisman and the calendar of Ise Shrine (situated in Mie Prefecture) were the most sacred and popular media in ordinary people's religious life in eighteenth- and early-nineteenth-century Japan. Ise Shrine was the pre-eminent religious centre of pilgrimage of the day. This was the time of the enthusiastic pilgrimage movement named Okagemairi, when several million people suddenly within a year made a pilgrimage to the shrine from all over the country. Secular power could not prohibit such pilgrimages. And as the talisman of Ise Shrine was believed to have sacred power, a great many people danced in the streets very enthusiastically when someone scattered the talismans at the end of the Tokugawa regime. After the Meiji Restoration in 1868, the Meiji government elite shrewdly used this popular religious centre as a symbol of national integration. They reorganized the shrine system and placed Ise Shrine, which was then reconnected with the myth of the imperial household – at the top of the nationwide hierarchy of shrines.

3. In the strict sense, this portrait was not the photograph of the actual emperor himself. An Italian painter drew an idealistic portrait of the Meiji emperor according to the conventions of Western realism, and the government made many photographs of this painting. Many differences exist between the portrait photograph of the Meiji emperor and the *goshin'ei* painted by the Western painter.

4. In 1924, only these three broadcasting stations were officially permitted by the state. The great Kanto earthquake in 1923 had had a great impact on the government elite's concept of radio broadcasting. After the experience of earthquake, the elite understood the political and administrative functions of radio and began to control the radio waves more thoroughly.

5. In this photograph we can read the continuity of the power formation from the prewar emperor system to postwar US hegemony. After World War Two, the Japanese imperial household lost its 'transcendental' position toward the nation and came to hold its place by maintaining the image of US superiority. The US army of occupation also very shrewdly used the mass-mediated image of the emperor in postwar Japan in order to accomplish the goals of the occupation.

6. Usually, the family of the emperor should be translated as 'imperial family'. But as the English royal family has been the definite model for the family of the Japanese emperor, I dare to translate them as 'royal family' here.

7. Despite the famous argument put forth by Foucault on the relation between power and the gaze, Japanese power in the Tokugawa period did not want to be seen directly by the people. The people of the day were prohibited from seeing the Daimyo and the Shogun directly, even when these feudal lords made their processions in the streets. Moreover, each inferior person could not see his direct superior among the samurai class. Thus, power during the Tokugawa period was constructed not through gazing, but through the prohibition of gazing. It was this system that Meiji government elite tried to change. When the Meiji emperor made his tours, the government ordered officials in each local region to force people to look up at the emperor directly. But people were not allowed to look at the emperor from above, because the emperor should be able to look over the nation from the centripetal point. The emperor was not only the object of gazing, but also the key subject of disciplinal gazing of the modern state.

8. The importance of the weekly mass magazine in the popular consciousness can be easily seen when you get on a train in Japan. Many advertisements hang from the ceiling, most of them advertisements for weekly magazines. The influential consumer culture of the weekly magazine developed especially from the 1960s. The Japanese comic culture which has influenced the world has been a byproduct of the culture.

9. The sales of the three main women's weekly magazines, *Josei Jishin* (950,000), *Josei Sebun* (940,000), and *Shukan Josei* (630,000) clearly surpass those of the main men's weekly magazines: *Shukan Posuto* (700,000), *Shukan Bunshun* (630,000), *Shukan Gendai* (610,000), and *Shukan Shincho* (590,000). This contrasts to the sales of representative women's magazines (such as *Shufu no Tomo* or *Fujin Kurabu*) in the period before World War Two.

10. This 'self-restraint' was an almost unanimous behaviour presented by people, communities, towns and companies just before the death of the Showa emperor. Festivals which usually took place widely in the autumn were cancelled in order to refrain from having any festive occasions during the emperor's illness. In a word, people had already gone into mourning before the death of the emperor. The people's response to the death of the Showa emperor has been stimulatingly documented by Norma Field (Field 1991).

References

Asada, Takahiko (1987) *Waido Sho no Genten*, Shinsensha.

Cannadine, David (1983) 'The Context, Performance and Meaning of Ritual: The British Monarchy and the "Invention of Traditon", c. 1820–1977', in Hobsbawm, Eric and Ranger, Terence, *The Invention of Tradition*, Cambridge University Press.

Chaney, David (1983) 'A Symbolic Mirror of Ourselves: Civic Ritual in Mass Society', *Media, Culture and Society*, Vol. 15, No. 2, pp. 119–35.

Dayan, Daniel and Katz, Elihu (1992) *Media Events*, Harvard University Press.

Field, Norma (1991) *In the Realm of a Dying Emperor*, Pantheon Books.

Fujitani, Takashi (1996) *Splendid Monarchy*, University of California Press.

Inoue, Teruko (1980) 'Maihomu-shugi: sono Sinboru toshiteno Koushitu', in Inoue, *Joseigaku to sono Shuhen*, Keiso Shobo, pp. 36–52.

Kashiwagi, Hiroshi (1990) 'Tenno no Imeji omegutte', in Kashiwagi *et al.*, *Joho Shihai*, Kisekisha, pp. 46–53.

Matsushita, Keiichi (1959) 'Taishu Tennousei-ron', *Chuo Koron*, April, pp. 30–47.

Muramatsu, Yasuko (1991) '90 Nendai no Tenno-sei to Senzen tono Renzoku-sei: Kokumin tono Renzokusei no Mondaiten', *Shinbungaku Hyoron*, No. 40, pp. 193–211.

Nakajima, Michio (1990) *Tenno no Daigawari to Kokumin*, Aoki Shoten.

Perry, M.C. (1856) *Narrative of Expedition of an American Squadron to the China Seas and Japan*. New edition published by AMS Press, 1967.

Stallybrass, Peter and White, Allon (1986) *The Politics and Poetics of Transgression*, Methuen.

Taki, Koji (1988) *Tenno no Shouzo*, Iwanami Shoten.

Takahashi, Akira *et al.* (1959) 'Terebi to Kodokuna Gunshu', *Hoso to Senden*, June, pp. 3–13.

Takeyama, Akiko (1989) *Gykuon Hoso*, Banseisha.

Tokai Denki Tsushin-kyoku, ed. (1962) *Tokai no Denshin Denwa*, Denki Tsushin Kyokai Nagoya-shibu.

Yasumaru, Yoshio (1988) 'Kindai Tenkanki niokeru Shukyo to Kokka', in Yasumaru and Miyaji, Masato, eds., *Shukyo to Kokka: Kindai Nihon Shiso Taikei 5*, Iwanami Shoten.

Yoshimi, Shunya (1994) 'Undokai no Shiso: Meiji Nihon to Shukusai Bunka', *Shiso*, No. 845, pp. 137–62.

Yoshimi, Shunya (1995) 'Les Rituels politiques du Japon moderne: Tournées impériales et stratégies dans le Japon de Meiji', *Annales*, Vol. 50, No. 2, March–April, pp. 341–71.

Yoshimi, Shunya *et al.* (1992) 'Tenno no Shi to Kicho suru Hitobito', in Kurihara, Akira *et al.*, eds., *Kiroku Tenno no Shi*, Chikuma Shobo, pp. 47–135.

34

How Do We Look? Unfixing the Singular Black (Female) Subject

Lola Young

Subjects that matter

> The fact is 'black' has never been just there ... it has always been
> an unstable identity, psychically, culturally and politically ...
> something constructed, told, spoken, not simply found.
>
> Hall 1987; 45

The disruption of the term 'black' marked by Stuart Hall's interrogation of marginality and the postmodern subject has produced some productive meditations on the possibilities of organizing under a sign that is inherently unstable and fragmented. But the destabilizing of 'black' within a paradigm constructed around the cultural politics of identity by a number of black intellectuals has been accompanied by the continued development of conservative black racial politics which tends to espouse a more essentialized, less fluid vision of what it means to be black. This conservatism apparently makes it possible to identify some of us as not really being black at all: for example, a black individual who has sexual or close social relationships with white people, or a 'light-skinned' black person, or a black person who uses chemicals to straighten her – or, more rarely, his – hair, may be accused of being some sort of 'race traitor'.

These competing constructions of black identity may be seen in struggle in a number of representations that refer to the physical appearance of black people. Drawing on material contained in, and suggested by, letters and features in *Pride* (a magazine for black British women), and comments made by respondents in the research of Amina Mama, and Debbie Weekes, I argue that such representations constitute a site of conflict and ambivalence for black diaspora people, particularly women. My focus is on women because they hold a key symbolic position as actual or potential reproducers/bearers of the 'race'; they demarcate the boundaries of racial/national groups; they are deemed responsible for preserving and handing down culture through being primarily responsible for child-rearing (McClintock 1993: 62). Notions of beauty and sexual attraction are intimately linked to these gendered functions, and turn on women's symbolic representativeness and their attractiveness to men.

These issues are also of consequence because they strike at the heart of how black people perceive difference *within* black communities – difference articulated as a range of conceptions about skin colour, hair texture and other phenotypical signifiers of blackness. These markers of racial identity are assigned meaningfulness and incorporated into essentialist beliefs about what black people are, and should be, and so tell us something about racialized identification within black communities. But this is not just about a narrative of 'race': if we examine what black people say or write about skin, hair and beauty, and black identity, it becomes clear that it is also necessary to address how gender, sexuality and class are implicated in racialized constructions of what constitutes 'good-looking' for black people. Thus although currently the most common assessment of phenomena such as 'colourism' or 'shadism' and associated practices within black communities is that they are the manifestation of an internalized, colonial-induced racial self-hatred, the aims of this chapter are to use Stuart Hall's remarks on black subjectivity – written in 1988 in the context of a discussion of black British film – as a stimulus to thinking about the multiple ways in which blackness is looked upon by black people, and to suggest that it is necessary to develop more complex analytical models.

Colour/Class/Nation

> The end of the essential black subject ... entails a recognition that the central issues of race always appear historically in articulation, in a formation with other categories and divisions and are constantly crossed and recrossed by the categories of class, of gender and ethnicity.
>
> (Hall 1988: 28)

With regard to debates about the fixity of the black racialized subject, and the extent to which colonial and racist oppression determines our experiences, comments made by interviewees, and the images and texts in black-focused magazines are significant for the inherently contradictory nature of the positions articulated; but incongruity and ambivalence are frequently denied, since they indicate the impossibility of claiming a singular black identity and experience.

Before discussing some specific examples, I want briefly to raise an important aspect of the discursive regimes operating around the black subject. In summary, the ways of thinking about the psychological damage done to black peoples' self-esteem are informed by psychological experiments performed in the USA over the last fifty or so years (Tucker 1994; Mama 1995; Morawski 1997). Mama argues that the literature and research on the black psyche is inadequate in several respects, and her critical review of previous studies of black psychopathology demonstrates that researchers have frequently made their observations on the assumption that there is a unitary black psyche upon which racism has a singular set of effects (Mama 1995: 43). For Mama, then:

> Racial oppression . . . is inadequately conceptualised as monolithic, total and homogeneous in its effects. The nuances and intricate sets of social etiquette and behaviour, of betrayal and collusion, of inversion and resistance that constitute racism as a social process are barely touched upon. (Mama 1995, 48)

Given the masculinist bias of much that has been written about 'race' and racism in the past, it is hardly surprising that the subject in question is implicitly male.

In this section, I will discuss both academic and popular material relating to hair, skin colour and beauty, and attempt to think through the ways in which class, gender, sexuality and nation are embedded in popular discourses on black women's bodies.[1] In order to broaden out the discussion from an exclusively British context, I will refer to *Tribute* – a publication aimed at middle-class black South Africans – and the reporting of remarks made by black South Africans on the subject of black women models and the feminine ideal.[2]

Before I tackle these aspects of social experience, I want to raise some points about the status of colour in black communities. First it needs to be said that this subject is one which many black people have difficulty discussing. On the one hand there is an acknowledgement that debilitating beliefs in the superiority of lighter-skinned black peoples are still prevalent, and that such beliefs feed into a dislike of those considered to be 'too light to be black' on the grounds that they – especially black women, it seems – have an unfair advantage socially, economically and sexually. On the other hand, there are a number of black people who, in opposition to such beliefs, which they perceive as being perpetuated by white colonial racism, declare that to be dark black and wear 'natural' hairstyles is to be really black/African.

The experience of one of Mama's respondents is instructive in this respect: she gives the following account of an encounter between a black nationalist, Rastafarian woman, Claudette, and Mona:

> she [Claudette] said 'why do you straighten your hair?' So I [Mona] said 'I don't straighten my hair. It's um . . . very fine.' Anyway, I immediately got paranoid (laughs). I immediately thought – Oh shit, here we go again – I'm accused of straightening it – it's the way it stands. I immediately felt my blackness was being challenged. That happens quite often, particularly with people who I initially feel, um, whose consciousness level is quite high. (Mama, 1995: 135)

The repeated questioning of her hairstyle led Mona to plait extensions into her hair in order to disguise it and to make her look 'natural', thus supposedly conforming to an Afrocentric ideal. The question of appearance is clearly central here, since Mona, in spite of having thought of herself as an 'aware black woman', is now in the position of adding extensions to her own, unprocessed hair: extensions which would be made either from someone else's hair – probably a woman of Asian descent – or from synthetic material. Indicated here is a hierarchy of acceptably black hairstyles, with relaxed or straightened hair being the demon which must be laid to rest, characterized as it is as representing abject self-hatred.

As Mama points out, Claudette seems to need to assert her own sense of what it means to be a black woman by monitoring others who appear not to conform to her ideological norm. Contradiction and irony are both embedded in this narrative of authenticity and identity: as Weekes (1997) and Mercer (1994) have suggested, there exists a desire to eschew what is seen as Western binary thinking, and yet this version of the Afrocentric ideal needs to have its oppositional Other in order to make sense. Thus, Mercer argues that

> The patterns and practices of aesthetic stylization developed by black cultures in the West may be seen as modalities of cultural struggle *inscribed* in a critical engagement with the dominant white culture and at the same time *expressive* of a neo-African approach to the pleasures of beauty at the level of everyday life. (Mercer 1994: 114)

But the extent to which the critical engagement posited here can produce radical alternatives is delimited by what amounts to an inversion of the paradigm rather than a rejection of it altogether. In Mama's example, then, Mona serves as an example of someone to be castigated who functions as a measure of Claudette's own commitment to black struggles. Mama argues:

> Behind this process lie specific, stereotypical prescriptions of what an authentic black or African person should look like. This is somewhat ironic given the facts. A large proportion of the population of Caribbean descent, from whom most of the black people in Britain are descended, are racially mixed, and as those who have visited or come from the continent will be aware, Africans cover a whole spectrum of shades and appearances, most of which do not fit into the 'Negro' type featuring in imperialist anthropology and racist mythology. (Mama 1995: 136)

Underpinning judgements such as those of Claudette concerning the physical appearance of black people are certain historical notions which are important to note in the context of the remarks made by various black South Africans to which reference is made later in this chapter.

There is a marked reluctance to discuss these issues, especially those relating to colourism, and particularly in public forums as this is perceived as 'washing dirty laundry in public'. In addition, there are those who declare that colourism in contemporary black British communities has diminished significantly (see, for example, Weekes 1997; James 1993). However the extent to which colourism has been undermined is questionable. Recent academic research, articles and letters in popular black magazines and newspapers, and the experiences of friends and relatives, suggest that this pernicious practice is still with us.

Winston James gives the standard explanation of colour differentiation as arising from the privileged status accorded light-skinned black people in slave societies (James 1993: 234). James identifies a 'viciously self-immolating' impulse to lessen the gap between privileged whites and disenfranchised blacks through the attempt to 'breed out' the black by marrying 'light'. James's analysis notes how class then became bound up with notions of colour-indexed social, material and cultural inferiority and superiority, arguing that 'the *forced coincidence* of colour and class in Caribbean societies ... has lasted to the present day' (James 1993: 234–5).

Where James's emphasis is on an historical account of the class relations enmeshed in colourism, Debbie Weekes's account of young black women's perceptions and observations about physical appearance and attraction privileges the words of the young female respondents without submitting them to a class-based analysis: indeed, she avoids looking beyond a rather oversimplified application of the term 'strategic essentialism' to explain the interviewees' essentialist perceptions of colour difference (Weekes 1997). Weekes does acknowledge that heterosexual attraction and desire have an important part to play in perceptions of physical attraction, a point to which I will return.

Weekes's study is focused on skin colour, and it attempts to account for and to rationalize the meaning of skin differentiation amongst a small group of young black British women. She argues that the adoption of a sensibility that views 'broad noses and dark skin' as a desirable norm for considering black to be beautiful is both an empowering and a strategic move. Weekes locates this empowerment as producing a redefinition of what it means to be black and female. However, the redefinition is predicated on its 'visual and physical distance from whiteness. . . . Through this process, Black individuals who wish to redefine notions of Blackness do so from the position of subject rather than object. Black people who do so wish to redefine themselves in order to exert some control over their lives' (Weekes 1997, 123).

The question arises: how far have the signs of 'race' been redefined? Rather than being reconceptualized in any radical way, they have simply been reinscribed as markers of racial identification and affiliation, and of ontological truth, for embedded in this discourse is the belief that 'broad noses and dark skin' and 'natural' hair indicate a more authentic blackness. By using whiteness as the benchmark, what is claimed by Weekes to be a 'strategic essentialism' serves to reinforce the notion that white women and black women represent polar opposites of the spectrum of femininity. What notion of 'control' are we discussing when Weekes has to concede that it is still white norms and values that remain at the centre of the redefinition of blackness? Weekes is right to argue for the necessity of understanding expressions of biologically essentialist notions 'in the context of Black people's marginal positions in society' but the insistence on such beliefs constituting a *strategic essentialism* is, I believe, misplaced (Weekes 1997: 123). What is characterized by Weekes as 'empowerment' is contingent on a series of denials – of difference, of contradiction, of ambivalence – which produce unresolvable tensions within an essentialist paradigm.

In the North American context, colourism is arguably more openly discussed, though even there it is still something of a taboo subject (see, for example, Russell *et al.* 1993; Funderburg 1994). The study conducted by Russell *et al.* uses a number of sources to emphasize the pervasiveness of colourism and associated ideas about, for example, hair texture and processing. The authors appear to lament the lack of 'racial purity' occasioned by the intermixture of black and white people during slavery, because of the resultant difficulties in defining blackness. Rather than seeing such 'mixture' as undermining absolutist racial categories, they argue that the lack of clarity regarding racialized boundaries has brought about 'a race grouping more social than biological. . . . Were it not for this artificial grouping, part of the legacy of racism, Blacks might not criticize each other so harshly for having skin or hair that does not meet some arbitrary standard' (Russell *et al.*, 1993; 80). The evident desire for racial homogeneity produces the fantasy that uniformity of appearance would render internal conflict obsolete.[3]

Hall has noted how difficult it is to analyse effectively texts, representations and social phenomena across 'race' and class, and this is particularly so in popular media discourses (Hall 1988). Much of the discussion about intra-black colour-based antagonisms in black-themed magazines and media is concerned to emphasize manifestations of 'colourism' within a 'race-bound' paradigm that does not seek to account for, or to analyse, how class, ethnicity, gender or sexuality impact on how colour difference within black communities is perceived.[4] However, although not made explicit, the issues of class and social and economic status are often present in the remarks made by the writers themselves and/or in the reports or respondents' comments. For example, in a *Pride* feature about black women who hate other black women, one interviewee is reported as explaining her dislike of the only other black colleague at her workplace thus:

> 'Because I worked hard on my Mancunian accent, and don't wear tacky *Versace* sunglasses in the office, I felt I was a good example of an aspirational Black woman. Then *she* came in with her round-the-way-girl braids, her big dangly earrings and 10-inch red talons, which set me back two centuries. On top of that, she talks like she just stepped off a plane from Kingston.'
> (Blackwood and Adebola 1997: 22)

The newcomer's style, appearance and accent mark her as lacking the desire for, or means of achieving, upward social mobility; the anxiety is that her 'primitiveness' will taint the self-identified 'good example of an aspirational Black woman' with the stain of backwardness: the construction of the self as autonomous, progressing in isolation from the black masses, is exposed here as a fragile one.

These anxieties resonate with remarks made by Romeo Khumalo – a popular black South African radio and television personality – in reaction to the promotion of Sudanese model Alek Wek. Derogatory comments made about Wek by several black Africans involved in the fashion industry focused on her dark skin and 'negroid' features, and Khumalo is reported as saying, 'I would not be seen dead next to her. . . . She looks more like a peasant than a supermodel.' Accusations were also made by some black fashion editors that Wek's looks conformed to an outmoded view of black femininity 'drawn from colonial literature, depicting them as thickset'. The fashion editor of *Ebony South Africa* is quoted as saying, 'She is just a face imposed on blacks to make them think that here is someone they can identify with.'[5] Within these remarks are embedded not only tenacious ideas about the association of the darkest skin colour with primitiveness, but also the evident desire to be seen as progressive, upwardly socially mobile and to have shed the backwardness that is attributed to black African countries. It seems clear that the burden of representation in this respect falls upon black women, thus implicating notions of gender and nation within an intricate set of interconnected abstractions.

To return to the ways in which class is woven through discourses on black beauty: Janice Cheddie's analysis of the ways in which the fashion world has used black models suggests how discourses on class, 'race' and gender intersected with the prevailing political climate during the rise of the civil rights movement in the USA; Cheddie's analysis foregrounds class as a factor in the fashion and style choices made by African Americans in the 1940s. She argues thus:

> The codes and aesthetics, which developed out of the emerging black middle class [in the USA], were not an attempt to copy the dominant ideas of beauty and attractiveness, but rather an attempt by that class to distance itself from the black 'mass'. The black bourgeois attempted to project, through the image of the black lady, an image of a sophisticated, urbane and civilised black elite, which was differentiated from the black mass by its manners, morals and aesthetics, factors which made the reclamation of black femininity crucial to its agenda. (Cheddie 1994: 38)

The attempt at distancing may be an explanation for the representations of the rising black middle class in South Africa, where images of ideal homes and black brides dressed all in white seem to resonate with bourgeois European aesthetic values and norms. However, Cheddie argues that the strategy of adopting what appear to be the trappings of white middle-class style choices was not entirely reactionary since the aim was to 'challenge, from within the dominant culture, notions of the black woman's sexuality as primitive and exotic' (Cheddie 1994: 38).

The question of black sexuality and heterosexual attraction returns to haunt us here. One of the interviewees in the *Pride* report, described as a 'blue-black babe', categorically states the problem as she sees it:

> From as far back as I can remember, these pale-skinned girls have always been favoured over us. They walk up and down with 'superiority' stamped on their foreheads, thinking that they're all that and can have any man they want – even if they look like dogs. (Blackwood and Adebola 1997: 22)

I noted earlier that Weekes recognized sexuality as a factor to be considered when examining statements made by her respondents; for Mama, heterosexual attraction is the key component in the assessments that black women make about their own and each other's hair and skin colour. Arguably, most men have internalized certain ideas and fantasies about female attractiveness which most women can never hope to achieve. In Western culture, where dominant views about how a woman should look are based on an idealized and pervasive white femininity, it is not surprising that black women and men see such values as the norm or at least as some sort of touchstone. Mama takes this further and claims that

> men of all colours share the dominant racialized notions of female attractiveness which few black women can ever hope to attain. Skin-bleaching and hair-straightening are therefore less about black women wanting to be white than about black women wanting to be attractive, especially to men in a patriarchal world that assumes beauty to be blonde and blue-eyed, and makes it imperative for women to be attractive enough to succeed with men. (Mama 1995: 151)

This claim for the centrality of heterosexual desire is rendered more complex by women's representative function with regard to the community/nation. Sander Gilman has written about the ways in which considerations of female beauty and health are connected to judgements about a woman's fitness to reproduce the 'race', thereby linking sexuality to discourses on the nation (see especially Gilman 1995: 58). In this regard the status of beauty competitions is worthy of brief examination.

The idea that women have a symbolic role in bringing the community or nation together is evidenced in a number of interesting and significant ways. The women who end up representing their nations in international competitions are charged with a special responsibility to uphold a set of idealized values regarding sexual conduct, civic duty, and patriotic sensibilities. The title of 'Miss' followed by a named country implies a certain unity of purpose; the title also connotes both typicality – through its plainness and apparent anonymity – *and* special attributes. Richard Wilk, in his study of beauty competitions in Belize, describes how such competitions may seem as though they are capable of serving

> the state's goals of 'domesticating difference', of channelling potentially dangerous social divisions into the realm of aesthetics and tastes. But they can also fail in getting this message across, and can end up emphasizing and exacerbating the very divisions they are meant to minimize or control. (Wilk 1996: 218)

The inaugural *Face of Africa* competition is a case in point.

Early in 1997, this pan-African beauty event sparked controversy because the winner – a tall thin Nigerian woman, Patricia Onweagba – was deemed by some commentators to be too great a concession to a 'white European look' in terms of her body shape. One of the judges is quoted as saying that the choice had been made consciously as the judges recognized the necessity for 'the girl to make it overseas, not in Africa'.[6] This idea – that one woman may represent and address the nation/community – is implicit in many of the remarks made in regard to 'black beauty'.[7]

Black women play a key role in the construction of a national image that allows them to compete (literally, in international beauty pageants) with women from elsewhere, and it appears that African women, in particular, are required to appear sophisticated, civilized and cultured in order that the nation may bathe in their reflected glory *and* to reflect well on their actual or potential male partners. In this context, Khumalo's allusions to Wek's peasant origins take on the status of a judgement of her inappropriateness as a representative of the (black) (South) African 'race', a judgement related not only to her skin colour but also to her class and consequent lack of convergence with Khumalo's vision of the brave new black South African.[8]

The South African magazine *Tribune* offers another example of how 'woman' is figured as the nation. A full-page, full-colour advertisement for 'Caivil' haircare products shows a young black woman in three-quarters profile, with short, processed hair, smooth, even-toned skin, and eyes directed to meet the reader's gaze, against a backdrop of an expanse of sea and mountains.[9] The sun (setting or rising?) glows softly behind her and on the water. The image is headed 'The Portrait of the Nation'. To which nation this actually refers is not clear, as the landscape could be European, American *or* African: clearly this is a multinational advertisement for the modern black diaspora woman. Combined with a feature on the facing page introduced by the quotation 'It was only when people like Richard and Marina Maponya dared speak out that others started feeling more comfortable about their middle-class values and lifestyles', the impression is given that the socially aspirant black South African is linked to the young woman in the advertisement, who is represented as symbolic of the people's hopes and desires. Thanks to corporate interests in minimizing production costs – by designing an advertisement that could be used virtually anywhere that has a black population – the nation posited will have a universalized 'black diaspora female look' which is indebted to African-American values as much as to white European norms.

It may well be the case that such nationalist longings broadly fit into

Cheddie's theory that black people are seeking to counter the still-evident desire of the Western fashion industry to promote a primitivist narrative around certain black models. In common with Waris Dirie and Iman, Wek's career trajectory is recounted as a narrative of the 'native born in a mud hut', who enters the modern world thanks to exposure to the cultured sophistication of European or North American fashion houses. Inevitably in what we might term these 'grass skirts to riches' romances, the black woman is discovered on the streets of London – or a similarly modern city – by a white male photographer who is then invited by the media to comment on her 'look'.[10]

(Un)fixing the Subject

> What is at issue here is the recognition of the extraordinary diversity of subject positions, social experiences and cultural identities which compose the category 'black'; that is the recognition that 'black' is essentially a politically and culturally *constructed* category, which cannot be grounded in a set of fixed trans-cultural or transcendental racial categories and which therefore has no guarantees in Nature. (Hall 1988: 28)

Certain strands of black radical discourse claim that the darker your skin, the thicker your lips, the curlier your hair, the funkier your walk, the more authentically 'African' you are considered to be, whilst in a parallel black world conventionally supremacist colour-coding identifies dark black skin with ugliness. These contradictory beliefs – and other permutations of the skin/hair/appearance nexus – surface within Britain's black communities and elsewhere amongst black diaspora peoples.

Whether it is argued that critical comments about black women's appearance stem from a desire to secure male approval, or that acts such as hair-straightening, changing skin colour and related cultural practices indicate that black people are 'racial dupes', clinging to class-based colonial racist hierarchies, I feel that we still do not have more than a fragment of the complex physical, social, cultural and economic processes that are involved in making choices (and criticisms) about appearance. Perhaps for some it is possible to exploit a particular look as part of a strategy for gaining access to the world of white privilege, albeit in a limited way. And for some, no doubt, body styling is targeted at the male to whom is abrogated the right to determine what his partner should look like.[11] But there are, in truth, a multiplicity of reasons for doing what we do to our bodies, our skin, our hair, some of which may not be as easily containable in terms like 'black consciousness' or 'natural' or 'coconut' as those who wish to regulate us would like to think. The act of looking for signifiers of political consciousness, racial integrity and authenticity is an attempt to control, to 'master', in order to be able continually to reaffirm the coherence and stability of the self. That the act of looking and assessing in this context is a means of affirming self-worth and delineating the boundaries in order to feel a sense of control and self-determination does not diminish the insidiousness of this kind of essentialism.[12]

Stuart Hall notes how

> Racism, of course, operates by constructing impassable symbolic boundaries between racially constituted categories, and its typically binary system of representation constantly marks and tries to fix and naturalize the difference between belongingness and otherness. (Hall 1988: 28)

This desire for the closure which can never really be secured – whether it is attempted by black or white people – speaks of an anxiety about racialized identities. The very necessity to police and monitor, and to denigrate those who do not conform, indicates the instability of the racial sign 'black' and its refusal to be contained and codified; this seems, in turn, to produce more attempts at closure. If we allow ourselves to become consumed by the idea that to be dark is to be really black, or that it is more desirable to be light-skinned, or that it is somehow detrimental to the idea of black progress for a dark-skinned woman to be valorized by the ever-fickle fashion industry, we are surely missing the point. Our energies should be aimed at the system that constructs and produces us as racialized, gendered, classed and sexualized subjects in such a way that we are constantly placed in a hierachy and presented to each other as natural enemies, forever in competition with each other.

Notes

1. It should be noted that there exists very little rigorous, academic research into, and analysis of, what constitutes beauty for black people in Britain, research that involves black women articulating their own fears, desires and fantasies on the subject.

2. My remarks are also informed by examinations of the following publications: the *Voice* (UK black newspaper), *Ebony* and *Essence* (USA), *Raça* (Brazil) and *Ebony South Africa, Thandi* and *Tribute: Home and Bride* (South Africa). With the exception of the *Voice*, these publications are primarily directed at middle-class and/or socially aspirant black women.

3. However in a number of African countries – I am particularly thinking

of Nigeria, Ethiopia and Rwanda here – there is serious tribal, ethnic and/or religious conflict. It will be argued that such conflicts are still part of the colonial legacy, and as such not produced by Africans. However, this does not invalidate my assertion that it is not only racialized differences that need to be tackled. The question of the continued effects of colonialism, who is to take responsibility for change and how, is another question altogether and cannot be dealt with here.

4. See, for example, *Pride* and *Ebony*. Also, in some of the academic accounts to which I refer, such as Mama (1995) Weekes (1997) and Russell *et al.* (1993), class is notably understated.

5. All quotations are taken from the *Sunday Times*, 1 March 1998. See also the *Daily Telegraph*, 2 March 1998.

6. *Daily Telegraph*, 2 March 1998.

7. Comments made in the letters pages in both *Pride* and the US edition of *Ebony* regarding the skin colour of models used make this clear.

8. Khumalo appeared on the front cover of *Ebony South Africa* (February 1997), described as South Africa's most eligible bachelor, in spite of being photographed with his long-term partner, Lesley-Ann Smith.

9. *Tribute*, February 1997.

10. For a discussion of other examples, see Young (forthcoming).

11. There appears to be virtually no academic research available that considers the hair/style choices of black lesbians in Britain at present, although Akuba Grace Quansah is working on this area for her PhD.

References

Banton, M. (1988) *Racial Consciousness*, London and New York: Longman.

Blackwood, S. and Adebola, Y. (1997) 'Black vs Black: The Women Who Hate Their Own', *Pride*, March, pp. 20–23.

Cheddie, J. (1994) 'Ladies First: Race, Fashion and Black Femininity', in *Versus*, 2, pp. 37–9.

Cohen, C.B. *et al.* (eds.) (1996) *Beauty Queens on the Global Stage: Gender, Contests and Power*, New York and London: Routledge.

duCille, A. (1996) *Skin Trade*, Cambridge, MA, and London: Harvard University Press.

Dyer, R. (1997) *White*, London and New York: Routledge.

Funderburg, L. (1994) *Black, White, Other: Biracial Americans Talk About Race and Identity*, New York: Quill.

Gilman, S.L. (1995) *Health and Illness: Images of Difference*, London: Reaction Books.

Goonatilake, S. (1995) 'The Self Wandering Between Cultural Localization and Globalization', in Pieterse, J.N. and Parekh, B. (eds.) *The Decolonization of Imagination: Culture, Knowledge and Power*, London and New Jersey: Zed Books, pp. 225–39.

Gordon, L. (1996) 'Race, Sex, and Matrices of Desire in an Antiblack World', in Zack, N. (ed.) *Race/Sex: Their Sameness, Difference, and Interplay*, New York and London: Routledge, pp. 117–32.

Hall, S. (1987) 'Minimal Selves', in Apignanesi, L. (ed.) *Identity: The Real Me*, ICA Documents no. 6, London, ICA.

Hall, S. (1988) 'New Ethnicities', in Mercer, K. and Julien, I. (eds.) ICA Document no 7, *Black Film, British Cinema*, London: ICA.

James, W. (1993) 'Migration, Racism and Identity Formation: The Caribbean Experience in Britain', in James, W. and Harris, C. (eds.) *Inside Babylon: The Caribbean Diaspora in Britain*, London, and New York: Verso, pp. 231–87.

Mama, A. (1995) *Beyond the Masks: Race, Gender and Subjectivity*, London and New York: Routledge.

McClintock, A. (1993) 'Family Feuds: Gender, Nationalism and the Family', *Feminist Review* 44, Summer, pp. 61–80.

McGranahan, C. (1996) 'Miss Tibet, or Tibet Misrepresented? The Trope of Woman-as-Nation in the Struggle for Tibet', in Cohen, C.B. *et al.* (eds.) *Beauty Queens on the Global Stage: Gender, Contests and Power*, New York and London: Routledge, pp. 161–84.

Mercer, K. (1994) *Welcome to the Jungle: New Positions in Black Cultural Studies*, London and New York: Routledge.

Morawski, J.G. (1997) 'White Experimenters, White Blood, and Other White Conditions: Locating the Psychologist's Race', in M. Fine *et al.* (eds.) *Off White: Readings on Race, Power and Society*, New York: Routledge, pp. 13–28.

Parker, A. *et al.* (eds.) (1992) *Nationalisms and Sexualities*, London and New York: Routledge.

Russell, K. *et al.* (1993) *The Colour Complex: The Politics of Skin Color Among African Americans*, New York: Anchor Books.

Tucker, W.H. (1994) *The Science and Politics of Racial Research*, Chicago: University of Illinois Press.

van Esterik, P. (1996) 'The Politics of Beauty in Thailand', in Cohen, C.B. *et al.* (eds.) *Beauty Queens on the Global Stage: Gender, Contests and Power*, New York and London: Routledge, pp. 203–16.

Venn, C. (1996) 'History Lessons: Formations of Subjects, (Post)colonialism, and an Other Project', in Schwarz, B. (ed.) *The Expansion of England: Race, Ethnicity and Cultural History*, London and New York: Routledge pp. 32–60.

Weekes, D. (1997) 'Shades of Blackness: Young Black Female Constructions of Beauty', in Mirza, H.S. (ed.) *Black British Feminism: A Reader*, London and New York, Routledge, pp. 113–26.

Wilk, R. (1996) 'Connections and Contradictions: From the Crooked Tree Cashew Queen to Miss World Belize', in Cohen, C.B. *et al.* (eds.) *Beauty Queens on the Global Stage: Gender, Contests and Power*, New York and London: Routledge, pp. 217–32.

Young, L. (1998) 'Racializing Femininity', in Arthurs, J. and Grimshaw, J. (eds.) *Women's Bodies: Discipline and Transgression*, London, Cassell, pp. 67–90.

Notes on Contributors

Ien Ang is Professor of Cultural Studies and Director of the Research Centre in Intercommunal Studies at the University of Western Sydney, Australia.

Michèle Barrett is Professor of Modern Literary and Cultural Theory in the School of English and Drama at Queen Mary and Westfield College, University of London.

Wendy Brown is Professor of Political Science and Women's Studies at the University of California, Berkeley.

Judith Butler is Maxine Elliot Professor of Rhetoric and Comparative Literature at the University of California, Berkeley.

Néstor García Canclini is Professor-investigator at the Universidad Autónoma Metropolitana-Iztapalapa.

Angie Chabram-Dernersesian is Associate Professor of Chicana/o Studies and a member of the Cultural Studies Executive Committee and the Chicana Latina Research Institute at the University of California, Davis.

Iain Chambers is Professor of English Culture in the Faculty of Letters and Philosophy at the Istituto Universitario Orientale, Naples.

John Clarke is Professor of Social Policy at the Open University, UK.

James Clifford is Professor and Director of the History of Consciousness Programme, University of California at Santa Cruz.

Paul du Gay is Senior Lecturer in Sociology at the Open University, UK.

Paul Gilroy is Professor of African-American Studies and Sociology at Yale University.

Henry A. Giroux is the Waterbury Chair Professor of Education at Penn State University in State College, Pennsylvania.

Lawrence Grossberg is Morris Davis Professor of Communication Studies at the University of North Carolina at Chapel Hill, USA.

Glenn Jordan is Senior Lecturer in Cultural Studies at the University of Glamorgan, Wales.

Myung Koo Kang is Professor in the Department of Communications, Seoul National University, Korea.

Gail Lewis is Lecturer in Social Policy at the Open University, UK.

Rolf Lindner is Professor of European Ethnology, Humboldt University, Berlin.

Angela McRobbie is Professor of Communications at Goldsmiths College, University of London.

Doreen Massey is Professor of Geography at the Open University, UK.

Kobena Mercer is Visiting Professor in the African Studies Program at New York University.

David Morley is Professor of Communications in the Department of Media and Communications at Goldsmiths College, University of London.

Sean Nixon is Senior Lecturer in Sociology, University of Essex, UK.

Flemming Røgilds is a poet.

Bill Schwarz is Reader in Communications and Cultural Studies in the Department of Media and Communications at Goldsmiths College, University of London.

David Scott teaches in the Department of Anthropology, Columbia University, New York.

Ove Sernhede is Lecturer at the Unit for Cultural Studies, Gothenburg University.

Joe Sim is Professor of Criminology in the School of Law and Applied Social Studies at Liverpool John Moores University.

Gayatri Chakravorty Spivak is Professor of English and Comparative Literature at Columbia University, New York.

Gilane Tawadros is Director of the Institute of International Visual Arts (inIVA), London.

Charles Taylor teaches Philosophy at McGill University, Montreal.

Keyan G. Tomaselli is Professor in the Department of Cultural and Media Studies, University of Natal, South Africa.

Gail Guthrie Valaskakis is Research Director at the Aboriginal Healing Foundation in Ottawa. She is also University Research Professor Adjunct at Concordia University, Montreal.

Chris Weedon is Reader in Critical and Cultural Theory at Cardiff University.

Shunya Yoshimi is Associate Professor at the Institute of Socio-information and Communication Studies, University of Tokyo.

Lola Young is Professor of Cultural Studies at Middlesex University and Project Director of the National Museum and Archives of Black History and Culture.